The Editor

GORDON MCMULLAN is Professor of English at King's College London and Director of the London Shakespeare Centre. He is a general textual editor of *The Norton Shakespeare*, Third Edition, and a general editor of Arden Early Modern Drama. He is the author of *Shakespeare and the Idea of Late Writing: Authorship in the Proximity of Death* and *The Politics of Unease in the Plays of John Fletcher,* and editor of the Arden Shakespeare edition of *Henry VIII* and the Norton Critical Edition of *1 Henry IV*. He has edited or co-edited several collections of essays, including *Late Style and Its Discontents, Women Making Shakespeare, Reading the Medieval in Early Modern England,* and *In Arden: Editing Shakespeare.*

A NORTON CRITICAL EDITION

William Shakespeare
ROMEO AND JULIET

TEXT OF THE PLAY

SOURCES, CONTEXTS,
AND EARLY REWRITINGS

CRITICISM AND LATER REWRITINGS

Edited by

GORDON McMULLAN
KING'S COLLEGE LONDON

W · W · NORTON & COMPANY · *New York* · *London*

W. W. Norton & Company has been independent since its founding in 1923, when William Warder Norton and Mary D. Herter Norton first published lectures delivered at the People's Institute, the adult education division of New York City's Cooper Union. The firm soon expanded their program beyond the Institute, publishing books by celebrated academics from America and abroad. By midcentury, the two major pillars of Norton's publishing program—trade books and college texts—were firmly established. In the 1950s, the Norton family transferred control of the company to its employees, and today—with a staff of four hundred and a comparable number of trade, college, and professional titles published each year—W. W. Norton & Company stands as the largest and oldest publishing house owned wholly by its employees.

Library of Congress Cataloging-in-Publication Data

Names: Shakespeare, William, 1564–1616, author. | McMullan, Gordon, 1962– editor.
Title: Romeo and Juliet : text of the play, sources, contexts, and early rewritings, criticism and later rewritings / William Shakespeare; Edited by Gordon McMullan.
Description: First edition. | New York : W. W. Norton & Company, 2016. | Series: A Norton critical edition | Includes bibliographical references.
Identifiers: LCCN 2016013759 | ISBN 9780393926262 (pbk.)
Subjects: LCSH: Shakespeare, William, 1564–1616.
   Romeo and Juliet.
Classification: LCC PR2831.A2 M36 2016 | DDC 822.3/3—dc23
LC record available at https://lccn.loc.gov/2016013759

W. W. Norton & Company, Inc., 500 Fifth Avenue, New York, NY 10110 wwnorton.com

W. W. Norton & Company Ltd., 15 Carlisle Street, London W1D 3BS

1 2 3 4 5 6 7 8 9 0

Contents

Illustrations

Introduction

Romeo and Juliet is arguably the best-known play in the Shakespeare canon, better-known even than *Hamlet. Hamlet*, though, is generally considered to be *deep*: very apparently, it has a series of mysteries at its heart—plot, character, psychology, meaning, origins, texts—all of which have, at one point or another in the course of the history of people going to see it in the theater or reading it on the page, been the subject of puzzlement and uncertainty and a great deal of philosophical reflection. Not so *Romeo and Juliet*, which—as we all know—is a straightforward romantic boy-meets-girl story with action, comic elements, and a movingly tragic conclusion. Or so we think. The celebrated literary critic Frank Kermode thought otherwise, however, and I wholeheartedly agree with him, taking his assertion about the play as the moral of this Norton Critical Edition. "*Romeo and Juliet*," he stated, "is not a simple play; to suppose that it is would be the most elementary mistake one could make concerning it." This is an enormously valuable statement about the play, underlining as it does the need for readers and theatergoers to come to *Romeo and Juliet* afresh and to read it not only for its appealing simplicities but also for its wonderfully productive complexities.

Generations of students who have been obliged to read *Romeo and Juliet* in high school—often in their very early teens—have tended not to think of it as a complicated play—as anything but, in fact—but that is because their teachers chose it for them as a first experience of Shakespeare that would not be too daunting: more fun than *Julius Caesar*, less gory than *Macbeth*. And in many ways the play is exactly right for this role: it is fast-moving, funny, engaging, tragic, sentimental, sexy, and colorful; it draws teenage readers and audience members into the story and requires them to relate to one or other of its protagonists, depending on their gender and orientation; and in the second half of the twentieth century it was made into two very fine and engaging movies—by Franco Zeffirelli and by Baz Luhrmann—which continue to enable the new reader of Shakespeare to discover the pleasures of performance. Yet *Romeo and Juliet* is also, I wish to argue, a play that, as you progress through life, repays repeated revisiting, as it begins to dawn on you that the way the younger generation in the play behaves is not so different from the way the older generation behaves and that the two are catastrophically wrapped up with each other. Revisiting is something that does not always happen—all too often the play is omitted from university Shakespeare course schedules precisely because students have already studied it in high school—which is a genuine pity, because *Romeo and Juliet* is a play that rewards critical engagement at so many levels, a play whose richness only begins to become truly apparent as the reader's or theatergoer's knowledge—of history, of genre, of desire, of death—grows and changes and matures. If I have a hope for this Norton Critical Edition, it is that, whatever stage of your education or life you have reached when you first read *Romeo and Juliet*, you will return to it more than once in future years. I believe it will reward you in fascinatingly different ways each time you do so.

The play itself plays powerful games with the generations. The opening scene—pp. 4–12 in this Norton Critical Edition—sets the tone. It begins with young testosterone-driven men conversationally competing with each other to assert their masculinity in terms that would have been familiar to the audience as a negotiation between action and restraint. "I strike quickly, being moved," boasts the Capulet servant Samson, foregrounding his assumed role as Man of Action, to which his sidekick Gregory replies, "But thou art not quickly moved to strike," ironically emphasizing instead Samson's restraint as Man of Temperance. Samson insists, saying, "I will take the wall of any man or maid of Montague's," that is, he will claim higher social status over anyone from the Montague household, whether servant or master, man or woman, by insisting on passing them on the side further away from the dirt that would have built up in the roads in this period; it would be normal for the lower-status person (and Samson is at the bottom of the pile) to move to the street side. "That shows thee a weak slave, for the weakest goes to the wall," retorts Gregory, playing with the proverbial expression "the weak goest to the wall," meaning that he is too weak to stand on his own feet and needs a wall to lean against. His words in turn prod Samson into punning back and boasting of his manliness in two respects—his fighting prowess with men and his sexual prowess with women: "'Tis true," he says, "and therefore women, being the weaker vessels, are ever thrust to the wall; therefore I will push Montague's men from the wall and thrust his maids to the wall" (1.1.18–22). Here, Samson picks up on St. Peter's assertion in a book of the New Testament, First Peter 3:7, that women are "weaker vessels" than men—an expression used over the centuries to support the belief that women are leaky containers for fluids and for babies—claiming that he will shove the men of the Montague household into the mud of the street and push their women up against the wall and rape them. Gregory, apparently a little uncomfortable with the shift from brawling to sex, notes that "[t]he quarrel is between our masters and us their men"—suggesting that family feuds should not involve women—and Samson replies: "When I have fought with the men, I will be civil with the maids—I will cut off their heads" (1.1.26–28)— an escalation of violence through his glossing of "heads" as "maidenheads," that is, hymens. Thus he sets himself up as a sexual tyrant who will rape virgins, and he finishes the conversation with a phallic joke: "Me they shall feel while I am able to stand"—that is, have an erection—"and 'tis known I am a pretty piece of flesh," which Gregory picks up on, as soon as he sees a Montague servant, by punning on penis and sword: "Draw thy tool!" he cries. So fighting and raping seem much the same, conversationally speaking.

So much for the servants of the Montagues and the Capulets; so much for working-class masculinity in the play. But class, atypically in Shakespeare, turns out to have little to do with it, since the moment Tybalt enters, any sense we may have picked up from Benvolio's intervention (whose name ironically means "goodwill" or "wellmeaning") that the aristocrats will be better behaved than their servants is rapidly dismissed. Tybalt is dangerous, inflammable, murderous: "Look upon thy death," he tells Benvolio. (And, later, Romeo turns out the same way, murdering the murderer.) The scene thus escalates socially—and then we find that the older generation are no different from either their servants or the younger members of the two households, that the rhetoric of violent masculinity crosses all status boundaries and marks out the aging Montague and Capulet males as no different behaviorally from their children or staff. "What noise is this?" asks Old Capulet, and then, when he sees what is happening, demands "Give me my long sword," an order that does at least two things—it marks him out comically as both old-fashioned (long swords were medieval, not Renaissance, weapons) and somewhat optimistic about his masculine prowess: his wife caustically suggests his longsword days are over and what he needs is a crutch. At this point Old Montague enters with his sword out, and Old Capulet is furious: "Old Montague is come / And flourishes his blade in spite of me" (1.1.87–88). Not only does this repartee suggest an endless escalation of phallic puns, it also makes clear that the idea parodied in Samson and Gregory's banter—that there might be two negotiable cultural versions of masculinity, the impulsive Man of Action and the restrained Man of Temperance—is naïve in every social respect, since the norm for the men in this play, whatever their status, is to reject manly restraint out of hand and look, at every opportunity, to incite or imagine violence and, specifically, sexual violence.

We encounter Romeo within this context—one that he is wholly unable, despite his best efforts once he has been transformed by meeting and falling in love with Juliet, to escape. Masculinity is negotiated in the play not as something fixed and unchanging but as the product of stereotypes and subject-positions—that is, of stances adopted in respect of the self rather than anything innate. Romeo's identity is initially constructed from conventions of courtly love for the impossible object of desire, something many in his audience would have recognized from the poetry of Petrarch and the English sonneteers (including Shakespeare) who wrote in Petrarch's wake; he then adapts to a version of desire that appears to allow for physical and emotional fulfillment. Romeo's own masculinity is simultaneously established and put into question by his opening obsession with the "fair Rosaline"—"A madness most discreet, / A choking gall, and a preserving sweet" (1.1.203–04). Benvolio's frank argument that all Romeo needs to do is find another beautiful woman to fall for—"Tut, man," he says: "one fire burns out another's burning, / One pain is lessened by another's anguish [. . .]. Take thou some new infection to thy eye, / And the rank poison of the old will die" (1.2.48–49, 52–53)—seems terribly cynical to Romeo at this moment, but this is precisely what happens: once Romeo sees Juliet, he instantly forgets about Rosaline—and we, the audience, never quite forget this. But his language at first is not that of the individual in love but of the stereotyped courtly lover he is playing; it is a *role*, crucially, not an innate identity. Benvolio, adopting the language of Romeo's genre, suggests that he should "compare" Rosaline's "face with some that I shall show, / And will make thee think thy swan a crow" (1.2.93–94), and Romeo, outraged, answers exactly according to the courtly love script:

> When the devout religion of mine eye
> Maintains such falsehood, then turn tears to fire,
> And these, who, often drowned, could never die,
> Transparent heretics, be burnt for liars.
> One fairer than my love? The all-seeing sun
> Ne'er saw her match since first the world begun. (1.2.95–100)

Benvolio's urge to make comparisons is familiar enough to anyone who knows Shakespeare's sonnets—"My mistress' eyes are nothing like the sun," say, or the best-known of all of them, "Shall I compare thee to a summer's day?"—and in *Romeo and Juliet*, Shakespeare seems wilfully to refuse to differentiate between his two vocations: poet and playwright. Here the language of the sonnet—and in particular the language of courtly love as renegotiated for the sonnet form—is made the material of theater.

This is at its most apparent when Romeo and Juliet meet. One of the grand moments in the history of romantic love, the free, untrammelled meeting of the two great dramatic lovers in all the innocence of their youthful, mutual desire, this moment it is, in fact, however, a little more complicated, a little more verbally shaped, than that might make it sound. The lines are some of the most famous in all of Shakespeare's plays:

> ROMEO   If I profane with my unworthiest hand
> This holy shrine, the gentle sin is this:
> My lips, two blushing pilgrims, ready stand
> To smooth that rough touch with a tender kiss.
> JULIET   Good pilgrim, you do wrong your hand too much,
> Which mannerly devotion shows in this;
> For saints have hands that pilgrims' hands do touch,
> And palm to palm is holy palmers' kiss.
> ROMEO   Have not saints lips, and holy palmers too?
> JULIET   Ay, pilgrim, lips that they must use in prayer.
> ROMEO   Oh, then, dear saint, let lips do what hands do;
> They pray; grant thou, lest faith turn to despair.
> JULIET   Saints do not move, though grant for prayers' sake.
> ROMEO   Then move not, while my prayer's effect I take.
> Thus from my lips, by yours, my sin is purged.
> JULIET   Then have my lips the sin that they have took.
> ROMEO   Sin from thy lips? Oh, trespass sweetly urged!
> Give me my sin again.
> JULIET   You kiss by the book. (1.4.208–25)

This is, as you will perhaps have noticed, an extended sonnet. In other words, this conversation—so free, so natural, so much the spontaneous dialogue of two instantly infatuated young people—is in fact circumscribed, rhetorically speaking: for one thing, the language the young sonneteers use depends upon a series of overtly Catholic images—pilgrims, priests, saints, sin—which, while contextually appropriate to the play's setting in early sixteenth-century Verona, would have made uncomfortable listening for at least some of the Protestant members of the audience—a discomfort brought to a head much later when Juliet describes Romeo as "the god of my idolatry" (2.1.156). (Good Christian girls shouldn't treat boys as idols to worship, and any girl who talks naturally of saints and pilgrims might well sound idolatrous to the more vehement kinds of Protestant.) Moreover, the conversation follows the precise rules required for the construction of a sonnet: the alternating rhymes, the Petrarchan form, the various technical requirements. Mercutio has already forewarned us of Romeo's relationship with the sonnet: "Now is he for the numbers that Petrarch flow'd in" (2.3.45–46), he notes dismissively, reminding us that to adopt a genre underlines the fact that others have been there before you.

Gayle Whittier (see pp. 211–28) has valuably shown the extent of the immersion of the play in the sonnet world, mapping Romeo's progress as a trainee sonneteer. First, the fledgling poet offers seven lines toward a sonnet:

> Why, then, O brawling love! O loving hate!
> O anything, of nothing first create!
> O heavy lightness, serious vanity,
> Misshapen chaos of well-seeming forms,
> Feather of lead, bright smoke, cold fire, sick health,
> Still-waking sleep, that is not what it is!
> This love feel I, that feel not love in this. (1.1.186–92)

This is a rather cumbersome effort, but it shows him in training, as it were, so that when he meets Juliet and a superior form of desire envelops him, Romeo has served his apprenticeship and is ready for his masterpiece, which he creates jointly with her. That she likewise has learned to read the world by way of Petrarch is apparent when she says of Romeo, in a kind of negative blazon (that is, the listing of the parts of the beloved's body), "What's Montague? It is nor hand nor foot, / Nor arm nor face, nor any other part / Belonging to a man" (2.1.82–84). So they are both familiar with the Petrarchan mode, which explains the ease with which they create their mutual sonnet—which in turn serves as a verbal demonstration of the natural accomplishment we can imagine in their eventual lovemaking. Even at this moment of supreme mutual expression, though, the rules of patriarchy must be observed: in the creation of the sonnet it is Romeo who leads (as in a dance) and Juliet who follows or "counters"; and, since the poem is in a certain sense a competition, it is a Romeo who is the manly winner, Juliet who submits, graceful and feminine. At the same time, Juliet's coy reference to an "other part / Belonging to a man" suggests that she is more knowing than Romeo might assume.

The sonnet that Romeo and Juliet co-create serves both to reinforce the naturalness of their mutual attraction and to mark out the cultural constructedness of "natural" desire. The poem establishes a relationship between the sexes in which the woman is the holy object of devotion and the man the pilgrim worshipper and so on the one hand defines masculinity and femininity in terms both religiously absolute and debatable (since the audience, whatever their residual attachment to their erstwhile Catholicism, will certainly have felt at least ambivalent about the phrasing) and on the other affirms the dominance of the male over the female; it serves also to lead us steadily toward the social crisis of tragedy, with Mercutio's prior warnings against such relationships as the ominous backdrop. Most painfully of all, the language of the sonnet reappears later at the moment of greatest crisis, when Romeo, holding in his arms what he believes is Juliet's corpse, describes the evidence of his eyes: "Beauty's ensign yet / Is crimson in thy lips and in thy cheeks, / And Death's pale flag is not advanced there" (5.3.94–96). Thinking he is simply using poetic language, he is in fact stating the physiological truth. The sonnet, then, is embedded at key moments both in the plot and in the establishment of the identities of the lovers: it foregrounds both the beauty of the moment and its dependence not on "natural," "spontaneous" mutual desire but on modes of thinking about the sexual other that are shaped verbally in ways that the audience would recognize but would associate with contexts other than theater. And it functions to negotiate the transition from comedy (the drama of desire) to tragedy (the drama of death).

As Dympna Callaghan notes (see pp. 282–304), Shakespeare's main source for *Romeo and Juliet*—Arthur Brooke's *Tragicall History of Romeous and Juliet,* published in 1562 (two years before Shakespeare was born)—has an underlying moral which Shakespeare seems to reject and which is quite different from what we have come to understand as the "meaning" of the play. The "star-cross'd lovers" prologue points us in a certain direction: "star-cross'd lovers" cannot be blamed for what happens to them because it is their destiny; their love is "death-marked" because of their families' longstanding feud, with "ancient grudge" and "parents' rage." It is not their fault in any way. Yet Brooke saw things quite differently. "To this end," he writes, "is this tragicall matter written, to describe unto thee a couple of unfortunate lovers thralling themselves to unhonest desire, neglecting the authority and advice of parents and friends"—that is, the blame, for Brooke, lies fairly and squarely with Romeo and Juliet themselves for "neglecting the authority [. . .] of parents," for "thralling" (that is, enslaving) "themselves to unhonest desire"—in other words, for transgressing social codes, for failing to honor father and mother, for unchastity. Which is not how we have come to view the plot at all. It can be a shock to realize that the story Shakespeare inherited meant something quite different to its first readers than it has come to mean for us.

Callaghan outlines the place *Romeo and Juliet* has had over the last few centuries in the creation and maintenance of what she calls "the ideology of romantic love," that is, in the invention of something that we tend to take entirely for granted—that two people of different sexes meet, fall in love, and become as one in a relationship appointed, as it were, by higher powers. This ideology—despite the everyday evidence of separation, divorce, and domestic violence—continues to operate and is at its most marked, in Western culture, in horrified reactions to the practice of arranged marriage, anathema to most Western Christians or post-Christians but perfectly normal to millions of people in other cultures, and of course it is an arranged marriage that poses the direct threat to the lovers' happiness in *Romeo and Juliet*. But we have to understand that what we understand to be "universal" is often actually "local" in the sense of being culturally or geographically specific, and the argument of Callaghan and the social theorists whose work she invokes is that romantic love should be understood not as a given, as something "natural," as the kind of relationship to which all people everywhere aspire, but rather as a construct, as a cultural phenomenon created in history in certain specific locales—as something, in fact, created somewhere between the Middle Ages and now and perhaps specifically in Shakespeare's time. Certainly *Romeo and Juliet* has become, over time, the absolute embodiment, the tragic paradigm, of romantic love, the story of two young people who fall in love but whose lives are destroyed by the social pressures that refuse to let them achieve their desires. For Callaghan, it is slightly different. *Romeo and Juliet,* she argues,

> was written at the historical moment when the ideologies and institutions of desire—romantic love and the family, which are now for us completely naturalized—were being negotiated. Indeed, the play consolidates a certain formation of desiring subjectivity attendant upon Protestant and especially Puritan ideologies of marriage and the family required by, or at least very conducive to the emergent economic formation of, capitalism. (59; see p. 283)

In other words, what we take for granted now—an ideal of romantic love that presumes that we are heterosexual, that we can exercise choice, and that we are seeking to establish a self-contained family unit—was something that was being created in Shakespeare's day in response both to the Reformation—the turning inward of the external authority of the church—and to the emergence of capitalism as the dominant economic mode of the West: the establishment of markets, privilege for those with capital, and varying levels of choice dependent upon economic status. (If you want to see a contemporary instance of the nexus of romantic love and capitalism, you only have to look at the cover of this Norton Critical Edition, a detail from the graffiti wall at the supposed "Juliet's House" in Verona, which demonstrates graphically the primacy of the Romeo and Juliet story in the global discourse of romantic love: young tourist couples flock to Verona, thereby producing vast income for the city, to visit a building which may be—but probably isn't—the house once lived in by the Capulets and to stand on "Juliet's balcony," which was in fact added to the building centuries later.) Romeo and Juliet's mutual desire marks the consolidation of a mindset that is so natural for us that it is hard to imagine a time prior to its existence—yet the play was written at the very beginning of this way of thinking.

The emergence of this discourse of limited, legitimized desire did not take place without resistance, however, and Shakespeare recognizes this. There is one figure in the play who is not defined in sonnet terms and whose relationship both to the norms established by romantic love and to normative masculinity is deeply ambivalent. This figure—who most markedly both embodies and crosses the boundaries of masculinity in the play and is thus its most troubling figure—is Mercutio. Mercutio arguably represents a homosocial principle that counters the normative heterosexuality of the young lovers. By "homoerotic," I mean the kind of male bonding that creates and sustains patriarchy—not necessarily what we in the early twenty-first century would call *homosexual* behavior, but its social counterpart, the kind of preference displayed by men for men, along with associated forms of misogyny, characteristic of certain team sports or professional associations or fraternities. Mercutio's relationship to Romeo is very much of this kind. He is king of the phallic pun, relentless with his erection jokes: "Prick love for pricking, and you beat love down," he argues; "This drivelling love is like a great natural that runs lolling up and down to hide his bauble in a hole" (1.4.26; 2.3.105–06). In the process, he lets slip his own investment (as one critic has put it) in Romeo's erection. He seems, in fact, to be in the same position but gender-reversed, as several of the young women in Shakespeare's early comedies—Hermia and Helena in *A Midsummer Night's Dream,* for instance—who express their sadness at the loss of friendship that necessarily happens when their childhood girlfriends acquire boyfriends and fiancés. Mercutio mocks Romeo's desire for Rosaline and typically reduces that desire to the purely physical, the exclusively sexual—"I conjure thee," he cries, "by Rosaline's bright eyes, / By her high forehead and her scarlet lip, / By her fine foot, straight leg, and quivering thigh, / And the demesnes that there adjacent lie" (that is, her genitalia) (2.1.17–20). Thus Mercutio, deploying the poetic blazon to objectify the female body, elides any suggestion that actual emotion is involved in desire between men and women, insisting that it is only relations between men that are emotionally fulfilling.

In the process, not surprisingly, he crosses the line repeatedly into misogyny. The best-known instance of this is his Queen Mab speech:

MERCUTIO Oh, then, I see Queen Mab hath been with you.
  She is the fairies' midwife, and she comes
  In shape no bigger than an agate-stone

On the fore-finger of an alderman,
Drawn with a team of little atomies
Athwart men's noses as they lie asleep;
Her wagon-spokes made of long spiders' legs,
The cover of the wings of grasshoppers,
The traces of the smallest spider's web,
The collars of the moonshine's watery beams,
Her whip of cricket's bone, the lash of film,
Her wagoner a small grey-coated gnat,
Not so big as a round little worm
Prick'd from the lazy finger of a maid;
Her chariot is an empty hazel-nut
Made by the joiner squirrel or old grub,
Time out o' mind the fairies' coachmakers.
And in this state she gallops night by night
Through lovers' brains, and then they dream of love;
O'er courtiers' knees, that dream on court'sies straight,
O'er lawyers' fingers, who straight dream on fees,
O'er ladies' lips, who straight on kisses dream,
Which oft the angry Mab with blisters plagues,
Because their breaths with sweetmeats tainted are:
Sometime she gallops o'er a courtier's nose,
And then dreams he of smelling out a suit;
And sometime comes she with a tithe-pig's tail
Tickling a parson's nose as a' lies asleep,
Then dreams, he of another benefice:
Sometime she driveth o'er a soldier's neck,
And then dreams he of cutting foreign throats,
Of breaches, ambuscadoes, Spanish blades,
Of healths five-fathom deep; and then anon
Drums in his ear, at which he starts and wakes,
And being thus frighted swears a prayer or two
And sleeps again. This is that very Mab
That plaits the manes of horses in the night,
And bakes the elflocks in foul sluttish hairs,
Which once untangled, much misfortune bodes:
This is the hag, when maids lie on their backs,
That presses them and learns them first to bear,
Making them women of good carriage:
This is she—
ROMEO   Peace, peace, Mercutio, peace!
Thou talk'st of nothing. (1.4.51–94)

It is a remarkable speech. It defines female sexuality as monstrous,
scary, disruptive. Midwives were a significant source of stress to early
modern men, since they had privileged access to a key moment in a
woman's life from which men were excluded. The many folktales

involving midwives exchanging children at birth, with parents bringing up monsters ("changelings") while the midwives bring up princes
and princesses as peasants or, more simply, destroy the newborn
children, all testify to patriarchal fears and fantasies of the mysteries
of childbirth. Mercutio's language is the language of misogyny: "hag"
and "slut" and, implicitly, "witch." And he offers a mechanistic image
of sex: women are "carriages"; they "bear" (both men and children).
His images are those of nightmares (another negative female image,
the night-mare), and Queen Mab herself is an ambivalent creature,
attractive but perversely powerful. And, in the end, the nightmare
he evokes gets to Romeo, who has his first inkling (even as Mercutio
would pull his friend away from his tragic trajectory) of the tragedy
to come: "my mind misgives," he says.

Mercutio's imaginings are catching. He offers, on the subject of
desire, a different perspective from that of the sonnet writers and
of those, like Romeo and Juliet, who adopt the language of the sonnet to express their emotions. The blazon was a standard element in
sonnet writing and the objectifying of the female body was part and
parcel of the sonneteer's armory, but the overtness of Mercutio's
misogyny is a little different from the courtly love language of the
sonnets, as is his homoerotic expression—though Shakespeare himself wrote sonnets to a young man as well as to women, so the gendering of the object of affection in the sonnet itself is not as straight
as you might expect—in which case Mercutio perhaps does some of
the work within the frame of *Romeo and Juliet* that the "young man"
sonnets do within the frame of Shakespeare's sonnets, both confirming and questioning the available generic categories. Either way,
Mercutio offers a discomfort in the play that can be removed only
by death.

As I hope these brief analyses of the opening scene, of the meeting of the romantic protagonists, and of Mercutio's Queen Mab
speech make clear, *Romeo and Juliet* is, as Frank Kermode points
out, not a "simple play." It is a play that is rich in possibilities for the
critic, opening up a vast space of cultural experience and understanding between then and now and at the same time enabling us
to see the ways in which how we think now, what we take for granted
culturally in the early twenty-first century, are the product of histories that have unfolded between Shakespeare's time and our own. It
is a play that explores youth and old age, masculinity and femininity, love and violence, individuality and sociability, language and the
visual, poetry and theater. Its plot and characterizations underline
for us the interconnectedness of a life led in society, within cultural
norms, within codes of behavior and belief; it marks out the choices
and absences of choice to which we are subject; and it expresses these
things both in exquisite dialogue—as when Romeo and Juliet's first

conversation forms a perfect sonnet—and in disturbing monologue—
as when Mercutio rails against what, for him, is the generative and
thus disruptive role in a world he would prefer to be singly gendered—
and it is the power of this language, above all, that draws us back to
the play again and again. *Romeo and Juliet* has invited reimagining
from the very beginning—the play is, after all, itself a reimagining of
earlier versions of the story—and it continues to inspire writers, critics, theater directors, filmmakers, and all of us to address it afresh
from the perspective of our own moment.

I have chosen so far to draw out threads from *Romeo and Juliet* by
addressing just some aspects of the play's astonishingly rich first act.
I hope, as you read through the entire play, that you will be able
to see for yourself how these threads ramify and interweave as the
plot develops and how, by the end of the play, the tragedy reaches its
conclusion as a direct result of the social, cultural, and rhetorical
tensions these opening scenes have established in the audience's
consciousness. I have already cited a few of the critics whose work
is included later in this Norton Critical Edition, and part of my
intention has been quietly to underline that, for all of the pleasure
and value that comes from approaching the play yourself with your
own set of expectations and experiences and with your own knowledge of the world, there is also real value in seeing how critics have,
across the centuries, understood this wonderful play and drawn
out lines of engagement, which can be very satisfying to pick up
and pursue for yourself. As ever with criticism, you read it not simply to take the critic at his or her word but in order to develop your
own informed understanding and then create your own reading,
enhanced by and building upon the readings of others. That is the
logic of Norton Critical Editions—to provide you with a text that
has stood the test of time and to offer a route through the myriad
ways in which that text has been understood across the centuries
and, in particular, over the last fifty or so years.

    This Norton Critical Edition of *Romeo and Juliet*, then, not only
presents a fresh text of the play itself—of, that is, the Second Quarto
of the play, which is generally agreed to be the most authoritative
early text—but also aims, by way of extracts from sources, critics, and
scriptwriters, to tell a series of stories about the play, beginning
with its origins and ending with its late-twentieth- and early-twenty-
first-century adaptations, and encompassing the responses it has
provoked from the seventeenth century to the present day in Britain, in the United States, and in other parts of the world. The critical story this Norton Critical Edition tells begins before the play
even existed, with extracts from five underlying sources without
which the play could not have come into being: Luigi Da Porto's

"A Tale about Two Noble Lovers," Matteo Bandello's "The Unfortunate Death of Two Most Wretched Lovers," Pierre Boiastuau's "Of
Two Lovers," Arthur Brooke's "Romeus and Juliet," and William
Painter's "The Goodly History of the Love between Rhomeo and
Julietta." As the names of these writers suggest, Shakespeare
acquired the story from English translations (certainly Brooke, perhaps Painter) of a French translation of an Italian version of an
earlier Italian version of a story that arguably goes back as far as
Dante. In other words, Shakespeare dramatizes material from a
Continental prose genre, the novella, and in so doing adapts and
reshapes for the English stage material that would have been fairly
well known to his audiences. This Norton Critical Edition includes
selections from each of these sources focusing on two sections of
the play—the meeting of Romeo and Juliet, and their deaths—so
that you will be able to compare these moments with Shakespeare's
own version.

After the excerpts from the play's sources, you will find two
instances of early adaptation of the play, both from the mid-to-late
seventeenth century—one from Germany, one from England—each
making it clear both how popular the play was and how quickly it
was reworked for particular locations and particular moments. The
German adaptation, the anonymous *Romio und Julieta*, based on
the Second Quarto text that is the base text for this Norton Critical
Edition, faithfully reproduced its language in many places, yet it
also adds new dimensions, not least a comic character, Pickleherring, who is present across the length of the play, conflating Peter
and some of the other comic servants in Shakespeare's play but intro-
ducing an element of the Continental carnivalesque which looks
odd, to say the least, to those of us brought up in the Anglo-American
tradition: the excerpt included here is chosen deliberately to show-
case Pickleherring's role. The English adaptation, Thomas Otway's
The History and Fall of Caius Marius, which dates from 1680, reworks
Romeo and Juliet in overtly political ways, downplaying the romantic
relationship between the protagonists: as you will see from the final
scene, reproduced here, even the deaths of Romeo and Juliet offer a
very different understanding of the contexts for their mutual desire.

The critical selections begin with an essay from Stanley Wells,
whose work on Shakespeare spans more than fifty years, offering
an overview of the range of issues any serious critic needs to address
if he or she is to begin to make sense of *Romeo and Juliet*, many of
which are addressed in fuller ways in the essays that follow. From
there, we take the reader on a critical journey from the eighteenth
century to the present, beginning with the confident assertions of
Johnson, Hazlitt, and Coleridge and the creative reflections of Helena Faucit—one of the most famous actresses of the later nineteenth

century—on the roles she had played. The bulk of the critical selections, however, necessarily dates from the twentieth and twenty-first centuries, addressing issues from genre and imagery (Granville-Barker, Snyder, Whittier) to the language of desire and death (Levenson, Davis) and expressing some of the intensity of critical engagement with the play and the films made of it across this period. Wendy Wall's interest lies in the language of generation in the history of the editing of the texts of the play, while Joseph Porter reflects on Mercutio's troubling eloquence. Callaghan reads the play's negotiations of masculinity in the context of the emerging ideology of romantic love and of the deterministic effect of that ideology on the actions of both men and women, while Sasha Roberts reveals how personal identity is shown in *Romeo and Juliet* to be a negotiation of gender, sexuality, age, social position, and ethnicity that exerts immense pressure both on masculinity and on femininity.

These tensions, social and sexual, and their later manifestations in twentieth-century culture underpin the continued appeal of *Romeo and Juliet* on stage and screen. The final section of this Norton Critical Edition consequently turns to mid- to late twentieth-century remakings of *Romeo and Juliet* in the theatre and on the screen. It is of course impossible in the bounds of a Norton Critical Edition to do justice to the rich history of *Romeo and Juliet* on stage around the world—that would take many volumes by itself—so as a snapshot, we provide two interviews with major Royal Shakespeare Company actors discussing their roles—Niamh Cusack on Juliet and David Tennant on Romeo—each of whom offers fascinating, frank reflections on the challenges and rewards of acting the play's leads. Turning to the cinema, we consider first Zeffirelli's and then Luhrmann's films of the play, along with the highly successful tongue-in-cheek "biographical" film *Shakespeare in Love*. The brief excerpt from the script of Baz Luhrmann and Craig Pearce's *Shakespeare's Romeo + Juliet* demonstrates both the film's relocation of the play to a fantasy version of late twentieth-century southern California as well as the cutting and reordering required to turn Shakespearean drama into Hollywood blockbuster. Critical essays by Courtney Lehmann and Barbara Hodgdon explore the renegotiations of Shakespeare for postmodernity—in particular the postmodern renegotiation of Shakespearean authorship—that these movies perform: as Hodgdon notes of Luhrmann's *Romeo + Juliet*, "it bears watching precisely because it has been watching us." And finally we offer a new essay by Susan Bennett in which she describes a radical theater adaptation of *Romeo and Juliet* set in Iraq and performed as part of the World Shakespeare Festival that accompanied the 2012 London Olympics—an adaptation that graphically demonstrates both the ways in which the play lends itself afresh to new contexts and new global histories and the uncomfortable nexus of capital and ideology within which, in the early twenty-first century, any renegotiation of Shakespeare's work inevitably finds itself.

I am very grateful to a number of people who have made a difference to this Norton Critical Edition: first and foremost, to all of the authors and critics who gave their permission for their materials to be reproduced or excerpted for this edition; to Sally Barnden for providing invaluable and highly efficient research assistance at a crucial stage; to Kareen Seidler for generously offering the as-yet-unpublished text of her translation of *Romio und Julieta*, an excerpt from which appears here; to Susan Bennett for her willingness to rework her essay on *Romeo and Juliet in Baghdad* for this Norton Critical Edition (and to Valerie Traub and Jacqueline Baker for agreeing to let us include it prior to publication of the fuller version); and to my friends and relations for tolerating the apparently endless antisocial weekends of Norton-related work over the last few years. At W. W. Norton, Thea Goodrich was generous with her time and forgiving of delays. I am grateful above all to Carol Bemis, editor of the Norton Critical Editions, for her immense patience in waiting for me to complete this project. Shortly after I began working on it, I was invited to become a general textual editor of another Norton enterprise, *The Norton Shakespeare*, Third Edition, which meant editing *Romeo and Juliet* for both editions as well as overseeing, with my indefatigable fellow general textual editor Suzanne Gossett, the creation of a new text of the complete works, a process which, not surprisingly, slowed down the production of this Norton Critical Edition a very great deal. Carol has been astonishingly understanding and generous in face of such long-term provocation, and I appreciate it more than I can easily say.

A Note on the Text

The history of the text of *Romeo and Juliet* is a complex and fascinating one. As with a number of Shakespeare's plays (most famously *Hamlet*), there is more than one early text with a good degree of authority—a word that editors use to mean that the text in question can be associated with Shakespeare, that derives either from a manuscript in which Shakespeare had a hand or from a performance by Shakespeare's company. There are two early texts of *Romeo and Juliet* that demand attention from editors and critics—the First Quarto (Q1) of 1597 and the Second Quarto (Q2) of 1599—which are different from each other in fascinating ways and which have provoked lengthy discussions of their origins and modes of transmission. A Norton Critical Edition is not the place to go into extended detail about such debates, but Wendy Wall's essay in this volume, which relates the language of family and generation in the play to the ways in which editors discuss the relationship between Q1 and Q2, provides an engaging concise account.

The version of *Romeo and Juliet* most familiar to readers and theatergoers is Q2, "THE MOST EXcellent and lamentable Tragedie, of Romeo and *Iuliet. Newly corrected, augmented, and amended:* As it hath bene sundry times publiquely acted, by the right Honourable the Lord Chamberlaine his Seruants. LONDON Printed by Thomas Creede, for Cuthbert Burby, and are to be sold at his shop neare the Exchange. 1599." This is the source for all seventeenth-century editions of the play, including Q3, Q4, and, most notably, the First Folio of 1623.

Q1—"AN EXCELLENT conceited Tragedie of Romeo and Iuliet, As it hath been often (with great applause) plaid publiquely, by the right Honourable the L. of *Hunsdon* his Seruants. LONDON, Printed by Iohn Danter. 1597"—is different in key respects from its better-known cousin, and for centuries has been included by editors in the group of early Shakespeare quartos for which the early twentieth-century scholar A. W. Pollard coined the term "Bad Quartos." Various theories have been put forward to account for the features of these texts, which are less convincingly printed than the better-known, fuller quartos and are now usually termed "short" quartos to avoid the moral implications of the word "bad." Some consider them Shakespeare's "first drafts"; others "pirated" texts memorially reconstructed by actors who had played in them; others argue that Shakespeare wrote two distinct versions of several of his plays, a consciously "literary" version for publication and a shorter "acting" version.

Q2 is a fuller, more professionally printed, more convincing text. It is a quarter or so longer than Q1, certain passages have no equivalent in Q1, lines attributed to one character in Q1 are spoken by another in Q2, lineation diverges frequently, and there are many differences at the level of the individual word. Certain features of Q2 (e.g., words or lines that appear to have been added in the wrong place, or have been retained despite an attempt at deletion) suggest that it was set from Shakespeare's "foul papers," that is, from a draft of the play in the playwright's own hand, as opposed to a "fair copy," that is, a finished manuscript without insertions, deletions, or other afterthoughts.

Q1 is shorter, more perfunctory, and less well-printed than Q2, yet it intrigues editors, not least because some of its readings have seemed preferable to those of Q2. One section of Q2 (1.2.53–1.3.36) appears to have been set not from Q2's primary manuscript source but from Q1 itself, perhaps because a page or two of the copy manuscript for Q2 had been mislaid. Q1's prologue differs from that in Q2 in instructive ways: for Q2 the mutual hatred of the Montagues and Capulets is "ancient," habitual, a feud lasting generations; Q1, by contrast, suggests that the two families were close ("household friends") until they fell out. Key speeches, such as Mercutio's "Queen Mab" narrative, vary in order and content between Q1 and Q2, suggesting that the two quartos represent different stages of the composition process. Characterization at times differs tangibly between Q1 and Q2. Q1's Nurse is generally less intrusive than Q2's, and she sides more with Juliet than with Juliet's parents; she is also an active figure at a key moment in Q1 but not in Q2. At Q1 Sc. 12/Q2 3.3, Romeo, in despair at the news of his banishment, reaches for a knife to kill himself. In Q2, there is no stage direction: Romeo's suicidal action is implied by the Friar's words beginning, "Hold thy desperate hand." Q1, however, does provide a stage direction, one that records the active intervention of the Nurse. The full Q1 stage direction reads, *"He offers to stab himselfe, and Nurse snatches the dagger away,"* during or after which the Nurse utters a wordless cry ("Ah?") before the Friar says, "Hold, stay thy hand."

This Norton Critical Edition offers an edited text of the more familiar Q2, modernized and made accessible for the twenty-first-century reader. We also include facsimiles of the openings in each of Q1 [G1v–G2r] and Q2 [G4v–H1r] that present the moment of Romeo's attempted suicide so that you can see the differences for yourself and compare them with our edited, modernized text.

Rom: Spakest thou of *Iuliet*, how is it with her?
Doth she not thinke me an olde murderer,
Now I haue stainde the childhood of her ioy,
With bloud remou'd but little from her owne?
Where is she? and how doth she? And what sayes
My conceal'd Lady to our canceld loue?

   Nur: Oh she saith nothing, but weepes and pules,
And now fals on her bed, now on the ground,
And *Tybalt* cryes, and then on *Romeo* calles.

   Rom: As if that name shot from the deadly leuel of a gun
Did murder her, as that names cursed hand
Murderd her kinsman. Ah tell me holy Fryer
In what vile part of this Anatomy
Doth my name lye? Tell me that I may sacke
The hatefull mansion?

        He offers to stab himselfe, and Nurse snatches
                 the dagger away.

   Nur: Ah?
   Fr: Hold, stay thy hand: art thou a man? thy forme
Cryes out thou art, but thy wilde actes denote
The vnresonable furyes of a beast.
Vnseemely woman in a seeming man,
Or ill beseeming beast in seeming both,
Thou hast amaz'd me. By my holy order,
I thought thy disposition better temperd,
Hast thou slaine *Tybalt*? wilt thou slay thy selfe?
And slay thy Lady too, that liues in thee?
Rouse vp thy spirits, thy Lady *Iuliet* liues,
For whose sweet sake thou wert but lately dead:
There art thou happy. *Tybalt* would kill thee,
But thou sluest *Tybalt*, there art thou happy too.
A packe of blessings lights vpon thy backe,
Happines Courts thee in his best array:
But like a misbehaude and sullen wench
Thou frownst vpon thy Fate that smilles on thee.

                               Take

Facsimile of Q1, *Romeo and Juliet* Scene 12. © The British Library Board. Shelfmark C.34.k.55. p. 44, sig. G1v (*left*) and p. 45, sig. G2r (*right*).

Take heede, take heede, for such dye miserable.
Goe get thee to thy loue as was decreed:
Ascend her Chamber Window, hence and comfort her,
But looke thou stay not till the watch be set:
For then thou canst not passe to *Mantua.*
Nurse prouide all things in a readines,
Comfort thy Mistresse, haste the house to bed,
Which heauy sorrow makes them apt vnto.

    Nur: Good Lord what a thing learning is,
I could haue stayde heere all this night
To heare good counsell. Well Sir,
Ile tell my Lady that you will come.
    Rom: Doe so and bidde my sweet prepare to childe,
Farwell good Nurse.

Nurse offers to goe in and turnes againe.

    Nur: Heere is a Ring Sir, that she bad me giue you,
    Rom: How well my comfort is reuiud by this.

Exit Nurse.

    Fr: Soiorne in *Mantua,* Ile finde out your man,
And he shall signifie from time to time:
Euery good hap that doth befall thee heere,
Farwell.
    Rom: But that a ioy, past ioy cryes out on me,
It were a griefe so breefe to part with thee.

*Enter olde Capolet and his Wife, with
County Paris.*

    Cap: Thinges haue fallen out Sir so vnluckily,
That we haue had no time to moue my daughter.

Looke

Fri. Let me diſpute with thee of thy eſtate.

Ro. Thou canſt not ſpeak of that thou doſt not feele,
Wert thou as young as I, *Iuliet* thy loue,
An houre but married, *Tybalt* murdered,
Doting like me, and like me baniſhed,
Then mighteſt thou ſpeake,
Then mightſt thou teare thy hayre,
And fall vpon the ground as I do now,
Taking the meaſure of an vnmade graue.

Enter Nurſe, and knocke.

Fri. Ariſe one knocks, good *Romeo* hide thy ſelfe.

Ro. Not I, vnleſſe the breath of hartſicke grones,
Myſt-like infold me from the ſearch of eyes.

They knocke.

Fri. Hark how they knock (whoſe there) *Romeo* ariſe,
Thou wilt be taken, ſtay a while, ſtand vp.

Slud knock.

Run to my ſtudie by and by, Gods will
What ſimplenes is this? I come, I come.

Knocke.

Who knocks ſo hard? whēce come you? whats your will?

Enter Nurſe.

Nur. Let me come in, and you ſhal know my errant:
I come from Lady *Iuliet.*

Fri. Welcome then.

Nur. O holy Frier, O tell me holy Frier,
Wheres my Ladyes Lord? wheres *Romeo?*

Fri. There on the ground,
With his owne teares made drunke.

Nur. O he is euen in my miſtreſſe caſe,
Iuſt in her caſe, O wofull ſimpathy:
Pitious prediccament, euen ſo lies ſhe,
Blubbring and weeping, weeping and blubbring,
Stand vp, ſtand vp, ſtand and you be a man,
For *Iuliets* ſake, for her ſake riſe and ſtand:
Why ſhould you fall into ſo deepe an O?

Rom. Nurſe.   *Nur.* Ah

Facsimile of Q2, *Romeo and Juliet* 3.3. © The British Library Board.
Shelfmark C.12.g.18. p. 52, sig. G4v (*left*) and p. 53, sig. H1r (*right*).

Nur. Ah fir,ah fir,deaths the end of all.

Ro. Spakeſt thou of *Iuliet?*how is it with her?
Doth not ſhe thinke me an old murtherer,
Now I haue ſtaind the childhood of our ioy,
With bloud remoued,but little from her owne?
Where is ſhe?and how doth ſhe?and what ſayes
My conceald Lady to our canceld loue?

Nur. Oh ſhe ſayes nothing ſir,but weeps and weeps,
And now falls on her bed,and then ſtarts vp,
And *Tybalt* calls,and then on *Romeo* cries,
And then downe falls againe.

Ro. As if that name ſhot from the deadly leuell of a gun,
Did murther her, as that names curſed hand
Murderd her kinſman.Oh tell me Frier,tell me,
In what vile part of this Anatomie
Doth my name lodge?Tell me that I may ſacke
The hateſull manſion.

Fri. Hold thy deſperate hand:
Art thou a man?thy forme cries out thou art:
Thy teares are womaniſh,thy wild acts deuote
The vnreaſonable furie of a beaſt.
Vnſeemely woman in a ſeeming man,
And ilbeſeeming beaſt in ſeeming both,
Thou haſt amaz'd me. By my holy order,
I thought thy diſpoſition better temperd.
Haſt thou ſlaine *Tybalt?* wilt thou ſley thy ſelfe?
And ſley thy Lady,that in thy life lies,
By doing damned hate vpon thy ſelfe?
Why rayleſt thou on thy birth?the heauen and earth?
Since birth,and heauen, and earth all three do meet,
In thee at once,which thou at once wouldſt looſe.
Fie, fie, thou ſhameſt thy ſhape,thy loue,thy wit,
Which like a Vſurer aboundſt in all:
And vſeſt none in that true vſe indeed,
Which ſhould bedecke thy ſhape,thy loue,thy wit:
Thy Noble ſhape is but a forme of waxe,

H

Digreſſing

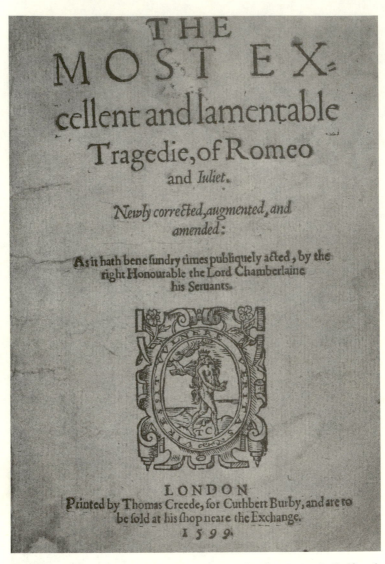

THE
MOST EX=
cellent and lamentable
Tragedie, of Romeo
and *Iuliet.*

Newly corrected, augmented, and
amended:

As it hath bene sundry times publiquely acted, by the
right Honourable the Lord Chamberlaine
his Seruants.

LONDON
Printed by Thomas Creede, for Cuthbert Burby, and are to
be sold at his shop neare the Exchange.
1 5 9 9.

Title page of Q2, *Romeo and Juliet.* © The British Library Board. Shelfmark
C.12.g.18. p. 1, sig. A3r.

The Text of
ROMEO AND JULIET

The Most Lamentable Tragedy of Romeo and Juliet

[THE PERSONS OF THE PLAY

CHORUS

PRINCE Escalus
MERCUTIO, kinsman to the Prince
County PARIS, kinsman to the Prince
Page to Mercutio
PAGE to Paris

CAPULET
CAPULET'S WIFE
JULIET, daughter to Capulet
TYBALT, nephew to Capulet's wife
CAPULET'S COUSIN
NURSE
PETER, servant to Nurse
PETRUCCIO, companion to Tybalt
Page to Tybalt
SAMSON, a Capulet retainer
GREGORY, a Capulet retainer
HEAD SERVINGMAN in the Capulet household
Three SERVINGMEN in the Capulet household

MONTAGUE
MONTAGUE'S WIFE
ROMEO, son to Montague
BENVOLIO, nephew to Montague
BALTHASAR, servant to Romeo
ABRAHAM, a Montague retainer
Servingmen

FRIAR LAURENCE
FRIAR JOHN

3

CHIEF WATCHMAN
WATCHMEN
OFFICER
CITIZENS of Verona
APOTHECARY
Three MUSICIANS
Masquers, Guests, Gentlewomen, Musicians, Servingmen,
   Attendants]

The Prologue

[*Enter* CHORUS.]

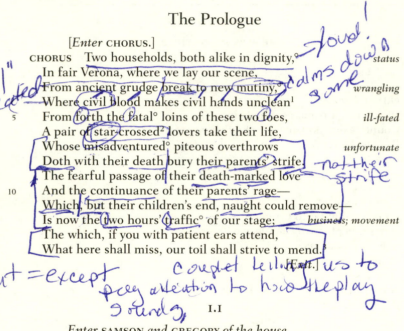

CHORUS   Two households, both alike in dignity,°   *status*
  In fair Verona, where we lay our scene,
  From ancient grudge break to new mutiny,°   *wrangling*
  Where civil blood makes civil hands unclean[1]
5 From forth the fatal° loins of these two foes,   *ill-fated*
  A pair of star-crossed[2] lovers take their life,
  Whose misadventured° piteous overthrows   *unfortunate*
  Doth with their death bury their parents' strife.
  The fearful passage of their death-marked love
10 And the continuance of their parents' rage—
  Which, but their children's end, naught could remove—
  Is now the two hours' traffic° of our stage;   *business; movement*
  The which, if you with patient ears attend,
  What here shall miss, our toil shall strive to mend.[3]

                        [*Exit.*]

1.1

Enter SAMSON *and* GREGORY *of the house
of Capulet, with swords and bucklers.*°   *small round shields*

SAMSON   Gregory, on my word, we'll not carry coals.[1]
GREGORY   No, for then we should be colliers.[2]

The Prologue
1. Where citizens' hands are stained with the blood of their fellow citizens.
2. Thwarted by the adverse influence of the stars appearing at the time of their birth, which controlled their destinies.
3. *What . . . mend:* The actors will try to rectify whatever is missing or ill-told in the Prologue.
1.1 Location: A street or public place in Verona.
1. We'll not suffer humiliation.
2. Professional coal porters, proverbially sneaky.

SAMSON   I mean, an° we be in choler,° we'll draw.°   *if / anger / draw swords*
GREGORY   Ay. While you live, draw your neck
5   out of collar.°   *a noose*
SAMSON   I strike quickly,° being moved.[3]   *vigorously*
GREGORY   But thou art not quickly° moved to   *speedily*
     strike.
SAMSON   A dog of the house of Montague moves me.
10   GREGORY   To move is to stir, and to be valiant
     is to stand;[4] therefore, if thou art moved,
     thou runn'st away.
SAMSON   A dog of that house shall move me to
     stand. I will take the wall of[5] any man or maid
15   of Montague's.
GREGORY   That shows thee a weak slave, for
     the weakest goes to the wall.[6]
SAMSON   'Tis true—and therefore women,
     being the weaker vessels,[7] are ever thrust to
20   the wall;° therefore I will push Montague's   *(sexually) assaulted*
     men from the wall, and thrust his maids to
     the wall.
GREGORY   The quarrel is between our masters
     and us their men.
25   SAMSON   'Tis all one.° I will show myself a tyrant: *the same*
     when I have fought with the men, I will be
     civil with the maids—I will cut off their
     heads.
GREGORY   The heads of the maids?
30   SAMSON   Ay, the heads of the maids—or their
     maidenheads; take it in what sense thou wilt.
GREGORY   They must take it in sense° that   *through sensation*
     feel it.
SAMSON   Me they shall feel while I am able
35   to stand, and 'tis known I am a pretty piece of
     flesh.[8]
GREGORY   'Tis well thou art not fish; if thou
     hadst, thou hadst been Poor John.[9]

---

3. Being roused to anger.
4. Stand firm against assault. Playing, as with "strike" and "stir," on sexual arousal.
5. I will assert superiority over. The sidewalk nearest the wall was cleaner than that nearer
   the street.
6. Proverbial: The weakest are always pushed aside.
7. Paul's description of women in 1 Peter 3:7.
8. An attractive fellow possessed of an impressive member.
9. Dried salted hake, appropriate as a taunt because it is shriveled and cheap. "Neither
   fish nor flesh" was proverbial for an uncategorizable oddity.

Enter [ABRAHAM *and another Servingman*
of the Montagues].

Draw thy tool;¹ here comes of the house of
40 Montagues.

SAMSON My naked weapon is out. Quarrel; I
will back thee.

GREGORY How, turn thy back and run?

SAMSON Fear me not.²

45 GREGORY No, marry,³ I fear thee!

SAMSON Let us take the law of our sides; let
them begin.

GREGORY I will frown as I pass by, and let them
take it as they list.°   like

50 SAMSON Nay, as they dare. I will bite my thumb
at them,⁴ which is disgrace to them if they
bear it.

[*He bites his thumb.*]

ABRAHAM Do you bite your thumb at us, sir?

SAMSON I do bite my thumb, sir.

55 ABRAHAM Do you bite your thumb at us, sir?

SAMSON [*aside to* GREGORY] Is the law of our
side if I say "Ay"?

GREGORY [*aside to* SAMSON] No.

SAMSON —No, sir, I do not bite my thumb at
60 you, sir; but I bite my thumb, sir.

GREGORY Do you quarrel, sir?

ABRAHAM Quarrel, sir? No, sir.

SAMSON But if you do, sir, I am for you;⁵ I serve
as good a man as you.

65 ABRAHAM No better.

SAMSON Well, sir.

Enter BENVOLIO.

GREGORY [*aside to* SAMSON] Say "better." Here
comes one of my master's kinsmen.

SAMSON [*to* ABRAHAM] Yes, better, sir.

70 ABRAHAM You lie.

SAMSON Draw, if you be men. —Gregory,
remember thy washing° blow.   slashing; violent

---

1. Weapon (and continuing the bawdy wordplay).
2. Do not doubt my fortitude; in the next line, Gregory takes it in the modern sense of "Do
   not be afraid of me."
3. By the Virgin Mary, a mild oath with a meaning similar to "indeed."
4. Flick the thumbnail from behind the upper teeth, an insulting gesture.
5. I accept your invitation to fight.

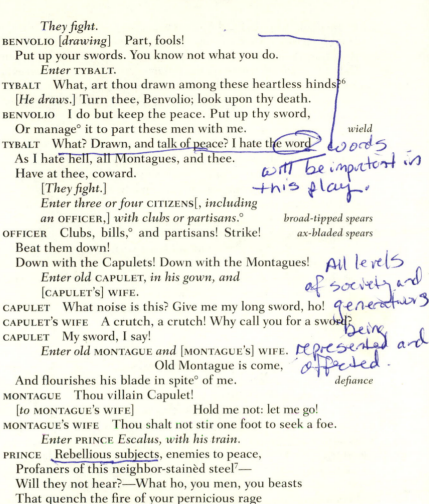

They fight.
BENVOLIO [*drawing*]   Part, fools!
Put up your swords. You know not what you do.
     Enter TYBALT.
75   TYBALT   What, art thou drawn among these heartless hinds?[6]
     [*He draws.*] Turn thee, Benvolio; look upon thy death.
     BENVOLIO   I do but keep the peace. Put up thy sword,
     Or manage° it to part these men with me.   wield
     TYBALT   What? Drawn, and talk of peace? I hate the word   *words*
80   As I hate hell, all Montagues, and thee.   *will be important in*
     Have at thee, coward.   *this play.*
          [*They fight.*]
     Enter three or four CITIZENS[, *including*
     an OFFICER,] *with clubs or partisans.*°   *broad-tipped spears*
     OFFICER   Clubs, bills,° and partisans! Strike!   *ax-bladed spears*
     Beat them down!
     Down with the Capulets! Down with the Montagues!   *All levels*
          Enter old CAPULET, *in his gown, and*   *of society and*
          [CAPULET'S] *WIFE.*   *generations*
85   CAPULET   What noise is this? Give me my long sword, ho!   *being*
     CAPULET'S WIFE   A crutch, a crutch! Why call you for a sword?   *represented and*
     CAPULET   My sword, I say!   *affected.*
          Enter old MONTAGUE *and* [MONTAGUE'S] *WIFE.*
                         Old Montague is come,
     And flourishes his blade in spite° of me.   *defiance*
     MONTAGUE   Thou villain Capulet!
     [*to* MONTAGUE'S WIFE]   Hold me not: let me go!
90   MONTAGUE'S WIFE   Thou shalt not stir one foot to seek a foe.
          Enter PRINCE *Escalus, with his train.*
     PRINCE   Rebellious subjects, enemies to peace,
     Profaners of this neighbor-stainèd steel[7]—
     Will they not hear?—What ho, you men, you beasts
     That quench the fire of your pernicious rage
95   With purple° fountains issuing from your veins!   *crimson*
     On pain of torture, from those bloody hands
     Throw your mistempered[8] weapons to the ground,
     And hear the sentence of your movèd° prince.   *furious*
     Three civil brawls, bred of an airy° word   *unsubstantial*

                    Tybalt Line 79

---

6. These cowardly servants, punning on female deer ("hinds") unprotected by a stag
   ("hart/heart").
7. You who defile weapons with the stains of your neighbors' blood.
8. Badly shaped and hardened, as well as unnecessarily wrathful by disposition.

100 By thee, old Capulet, and Montague,
    Have thrice disturbed the quiet of our streets
    And made Verona's ancient° citizens   *elderly*
    Cast by° their grave-beseeming ornaments⁹   *Cast away*
    To wield old partisans in hands as old,
105 Cankered° with peace, to part your cankered°   *Rusty / malignant*
    hate.
    If ever you disturb our streets again,
    Your lives shall pay the forfeit° of the peace.   *ransom*
    For this time, all the rest depart away!
    —You, Capulet, shall go along with me;
110 —And Montague, come you this afternoon,
    To know our farther pleasure in this case,
    To old Freetown,¹ our common judgment-place.
    Once more, on pain of death, all men depart!

                    Exeunt [all but MONTAGUE,
                 MONTAGUE'S WIFE, *and* BENVOLIO].

    MONTAGUE   Who set this ancient quarrel new abroach?°   *open*
115 Speak, nephew. Were you by when it began?
    BENVOLIO   Here were the servants of your adversary
    And yours, close fighting ere I did approach.
    I drew to part them. In the instant came
    The fiery Tybalt, with his sword prepared,
120 Which, as he breathed° defiance to my ears,   *uttered*
    He swung about his head and cut the winds.
    Who, nothing hurt withal,° hissed him in scorn.   *by that*
    While we were interchanging thrusts and blows
    Came more and more, and fought on part and part²
125 Till the Prince came, who parted either part.
    MONTAGUE'S WIFE   Oh, where is Romeo? Saw you him today?
    Right glad I am he was not at this fray.
    BENVOLIO   Madam, an hour before the worshipped sun
    Peered forth° the golden window of the East,   *out from*
130 A troubled mind drive° me to walk abroad   *drove*
    Where, underneath the grove of sycamore³
    That westward rooteth° from this city side,   *grows out*
    So early walking did I see your son.

---

9. Attire and symbolic staffs appropriate to grave old age. Possibly playing on the old men's proximity to the grave.
1. In the Italian source, the Capulet house is called Villa Franca, which Brooke translates as "Freetown."
2. Fought for one side and the other.
3. Associated with melancholy lovers, who are "sick-amour."

Towards him I made, but he was ware° of me   wary
135 And stole into the covert° of the wood.   covering
I, measuring his affections° by my own,   inclination
Which then most sought where most might not be found,[4]
Being one too many by my weary self,
Pursued my humor,° not pursuing his,[5]
140 And gladly shunned who gladly fled from me.
MONTAGUE   Many a morning hath he there been seen,
With tears augmenting the fresh morning's dew,
Adding to clouds more clouds with his deep sighs;
But all so soon as the all-cheering sun
145 Should in the farthest East begin to draw
The shady curtains from Aurora's[6] bed,
Away from light steals home my heavy° son   melancholy
And private in his chamber pens himself,
Shuts up his windows, locks fair daylight out,
150 And makes himself an artificial night.
Black and portentous° must this humor[7] prove,   ominous (of illness)
Unless good counsel may the cause remove.
BENVOLIO   My noble uncle, do you know the cause?
MONTAGUE   I neither know it nor can learn of him.
155 BENVOLIO   Have you importuned him by any° means?   all
MONTAGUE   Both by myself and many other friends;
But he his own affection's counselor°   confidant
Is to himself—I will not say how true[8]—
But to himself so secret and so close,°   discreet
160 So far from sounding and discovery,°   fathoming and revelation
As is the bud bit with an envious worm°   a spiteful grub (larva)
Ere he can spread his sweet leaves° to the air   petals
Or dedicate his beauty to the same.
Could we but learn from whence his sorrows grow,
165 We would as willingly give cure as know.
        Enter ROMEO.
BENVOLIO   See where he comes. So please you,°   please you = please
step aside;

---

4. *where . . . found*: in a place where I was unlikely to have company.
5. Q1's briefer version of this exchange entails a direct juxtaposition between Romeo and Benvolio, whose melancholy here takes on darker connotations in light of Q1's version of the final scene.
6. Goddess of the dawn in classical legend.
7. "Humors," essential bodily fluids, were considered the basis of human beings' physical and psychological constitution. Too much black bile caused melancholy and a host of illnesses and derangements.
8. Loyal, but also invoking the proverbial wisdom that only one who is "true to him- or herself" can be upstanding in dealing with others.

I'll know his grievance or be much denied.

MONTAGUE   I would° thou wert so happy° by thy   *wish / fortunate*
     stay
To hear true shrift°—Come, madam, let's away.   *confession*
          Exeunt [MONTAGUE *and* MONTAGUE'S WIFE].

BENVOLIO   Good morrow, cousin.

170   ROMEO   Is the day so young?

BENVOLIO   But new° struck nine.   *Only just*

ROMEO   Ay me. Sad hours seem long.
Was that my father that went hence so fast?

BENVOLIO   It was. What sadness lengthens Romeo's hours?

ROMEO   Not having that which, having, makes them short.

175   BENVOLIO   In love?

ROMEO   Out.

BENVOLIO   Of love?

ROMEO   Out of her favor where I am in love.

BENVOLIO   Alas that Love, so gentle in his view,°   *appearance*

180   Should be so tyrannous and rough in proof.°   *experience*

ROMEO   Alas that Love, whose view is muffled still,[9]
Should without eyes see pathways to his will.°   *intention; lust*
Where shall we dine?
          [*He sees signs of the brawl.*]
                    Oh, me! What fray was here?
Yet tell me not, for I have heard it all;

185   Here's much to do with hate, but more with love.
Why, then, O brawling love, O loving hate,
O anything of nothing first created,[1]
O heavy lightness, serious vanity,
Misshapen chaos of well-seeming forms,

190   Feather of lead, bright smoke, cold fire, sick health,
Still-waking° sleep that is not what it is—   *Always awake*
This love feel I, that feel no love in this.
Dost thou not laugh?

BENVOLIO   No, coz,° I rather weep.   *cousin*

ROMEO   Good heart, at what?

BENVOLIO   At thy good heart's oppression.°   *affliction*

195   ROMEO   Why, such is love's transgression.
Griefs of mine own lie heavy in my breast,
Which thou wilt propagate° to have it pressed[2]   *multiply*

---

9. Who cannot see. Cupid was often depicted as blind or blindfolded.
1. Inverting the proverb "Nothing can come of nothing" and also recalling the doctrine
   that God made the world out of nothing. Romeo catalogs the "miraculous" paradoxes of
   love.
2. Burdened; embraced.

With more of thine: this love that thou hast shown
Doth add more grief to too much of mine own.
200 Love is a smoke made with the fume of sighs;
Being purged,° a fire sparkling in lovers' eyes;   *clarified*
Being vexed,° a sea nourished with loving tears.   *stirred up*
What is it else? A madness most discreet,°   *wise*
A choking gall, and a preserving sweet.
Farewell, my coz.
205 BENVOLIO   Soft;° I will go along.   *Wait*
An if° you leave me so, you do me wrong.   *An if = if*
ROMEO Tut, I have lost myself; I am not here.
This is not Romeo: he's some other where.
BENVOLIO Tell me, in sadness,[3] who is that you love?
210 ROMEO What, shall I groan and tell thee?
BENVOLIO Groan? Why, no. But sadly tell me who.
ROMEO A sick man in sadness makes his will:
A word ill urged to one that is so ill.
In sadness, cousin, I do love a woman—
215 BENVOLIO I aimed so near when I supposed you loved.
ROMEO A right good mark,° man!—and she's fair   *target; vulva*
I love.
BENVOLIO A right fair mark, fair coz, is soonest hit.
ROMEO Well, in that hit you miss; she'll not be hit
With Cupid's arrow. She hath Dian's wit,[4]
220 And, in strong proof° of chastity well-armed,° *tested armor / covered*
From Love's weak childish bow she lives uncharmed.
She will not stay° the siege of loving terms,   *undergo*
Nor bide th'encounter of assailing eyes,[5]
Nor ope her lap to saint-seducing gold.[6]
225 Oh, she is rich in beauty; only poor
That, when she dies, with beauty dies her store.°   *wealth*
BENVOLIO Then she hath sworn that she will still°   *always*
live chaste?
ROMEO She hath, and in that sparing° make huge   *refraining; thrift*
waste:
For beauty starved with her severity

---

3. Seriousness, although Romeo plays on the sense "melancholy."
4. The scruples and cleverness of Diana, the classical goddess of hunting and chastity.
5. *th'encounter of assailing eyes*: military metaphors for courtship conventionally used in
   Petrarchan love poetry.
6. To golden gifts that are irresistibly persuasive. Also, in classical legend, Jupiter descended
   upon Danaë as a shower of gold.

230   Cuts beauty off from all posterity.[7]
         She is too fair, too wise, wisely too fair,°   *just*
         To merit bliss° by making me despair.[8]   *heaven's blessing*
         She hath forsworn to love, and in that vow
         Do I live dead that live to tell it now.
235   BENVOLIO   Be ruled by me: forget to think of her.
      ROMEO   Oh, teach me how I should forget to think!
      BENVOLIO   By giving liberty unto thine eyes.
         Examine other beauties.
      ROMEO   'Tis the way
         To call hers, exquisite, in question more.[9]
240   These happy masks that kiss fair ladies' brows,
         Being black, puts us in mind they hide the fair.
         He that is strucken blind cannot forget
         The precious treasure of his eyesight lost.
         Show me a mistress that is passing° fair: *surpassingly*
245   What doth her beauty serve but as a note
         Where I may read who passed that passing fair?
         Farewell. Thou canst not teach me to forget.
      BENVOLIO   I'll pay° that doctrine, or else die in   *impart*
         debt.[1]   *Exeunt.*

                          1.2

         Enter CAPULET, *County*° PARIS, *and* [*a*   *Count*
         SERVINGMAN].
      CAPULET   But Montague is bound° as well as I,   *under oath*
         In penalty alike, and 'tis not hard, I think,
         For men so old as we to keep the peace.
      PARIS   Of honorable reckoning[1] are you both,
5   And pity 'tis you lived at odds so long.
         But now, my lord, what say you to my suit?
      CAPULET   But saying o'er what I have said before:
         My child is yet a stranger in the world;
         She hath not seen the change of fourteen years.
10   Let two more summers wither in their pride
         Ere we may think her ripe to be a bride.

7. *For . . . posterity:* Since she will not have children, her beauty will die with her. *starved:* killed.
8. Despair of salvation, a grave sin.
9. *in question more:* more intensely to mind.
1. Die whatever the cost to me; die still owing you the doctrine of forgetfulness.
1.2 Location: A street or plaza in Verona.
1. Repute, with a play on "accounting."

PARIS   Younger than she are happy mothers made.
CAPULET   And too soon marred are those so early made.
Earth hath swallowed all my hopes but she,[2]
15   She's the hopeful lady of my earth°   body
But woo her, gentle Paris; get her heart—
My will to her consent is but a part—
And, she agreed, within her scope of choice
Lies my consent and fair-according voice.
20   This night I hold an old-accustomed feast
Whereto I have invited many a guest,
Such as I love; and you among the store
One more, most welcome, makes my number more.
At my poor house look to behold this night
25   Earth-treading stars that make dark heaven light.
Such comfort as do lusty young men feel
When well-appareled April on the heel
Of limping winter treads, even such delight,
Among fresh fennel[3] buds, shall you this night
30   Inherit° at my house. Hear all, all see,   Enjoy
And like her most whose merit most shall be;
Which one more view, of many, mine being one,
May stand in number, though in reck'ning none.[4]
Come, go with me. [to SERVINGMAN] Go,
sirrah;° trudge about   (address to an inferior)
35   Through fair Verona; find those persons out
Whose names are written there [giving him
a paper], and to them say
My house and welcome on their pleasure stay.°   wait
                    Exeunt [CAPULET and PARIS].
SERVINGMAN   "Find them out whose names
are written." Here[5] it is written that the
40   shoemaker should meddle with his yard° and   yardstick
the tailor with his last,° the fisher with his   shoe form
pencil° and the painter with his nets. But I am   paintbrush
sent to find those persons whose names are
here writ, and can never find° what names   figure out
45   the writing person hath here writ. I must to
the learned.

---

2. Many editors have conjectured that this and the following line, which are not present in Q1, were deleted by Shakespeare in the process of writing the scene.
3. A plant associated with weddings and brides.
4. *Which . . . none*: Upon another inspection of the many young women, my daughter may make a part of the gorgeous display but be of no account by herself. "One" was proverbially "no number."
5. Editors sometimes change the original punctuation and move "Here" to the end of the previous sentence. In either case, the illiterate Servingman is exasperated.

Enter BENVOLIO *and* ROMEO.

In good time—

BENVOLIO   Tut, man, one fire burns out another's burning;
One pain is lessened by another's anguish;
50   Turn giddy,° and be holp° by backward   *Turn until dizzy / helped*
turning;
One desperate grief cures with another's languish.[6]
Take thou some new infection[7] to thy eye,
And the rank poison of the old will die.
ROMEO   Your plantain leaf[8] is excellent for that.
BENVOLIO   For what, I pray thee?
55   ROMEO   For your broken° shin.   *gashed*
BENVOLIO   Why, Romeo, art thou mad?
ROMEO   Not mad, but bound more than a madman is:
Shut up in prison, kept without my food,
Whipped and tormented, and—
[*to* SERVINGMAN]   Good e'en,°   *evening (afternoon)*
good fellow.
60   SERVINGMAN   God gi° good e'en. I pray, sir, can   *give you*
you read?
ROMEO   Ay—mine own fortune in my misery.[9]
SERVINGMAN   Perhaps you have learned it
without book.[1] But, I pray, can you read any-
thing you see?
65   ROMEO   Ay, if I know the letters and the language.
SERVINGMAN   Ye say honestly. Rest you merry.[2]
ROMEO   Stay, fellow. I can read.
He reads the letter.
"Signor Martino and his wife and daughters;
County Anselm and his beauteous sisters;
70   The lady widow of Vitruvio;
Signor Placentio and his lovely nieces;
Mercutio and his brother Valentine;
Mine uncle Capulet, his wife and daughters;
My fair niece Rosaline; Livia;

---

6. *cures . . . languish*: is displaced by the languishing pain of a new grief.
7. New object of passion, which causes a distortion of sight in the lover.
8. The ordinary plantain leaf, used to dress wounds or bruises and thought to have cura-
tive powers.
9. Romeo takes "read" to mean "understand" or "perceive," as in "to read one's fortune."
1. *without book*: from memory or by ear, as well as through experience rather than
education.
2. A farewell. The Servingman takes Romeo to mean "if only I knew the letters and the
language."

75   Signor Valentio and his cousin Tybalt;
     Lucio and the lively Helena."
     A fair assembly! Whither should they come?
SERVINGMAN   Up.[3]
ROMEO   Whither to supper?
80   SERVINGMAN   To our house.
ROMEO   Whose house?
SERVINGMAN   My master's.
ROMEO   Indeed, I should have asked you that before.
SERVINGMAN   Now I'll tell you without asking.
85   My master is the great rich Capulet, and—if
     you be not of the house of Montagues—I
     pray come and crush° a cup of wine. Rest you   *drink*
     merry.   [*Exit.*]
BENVOLIO   At this same ancient° feast of Capulet's   *traditional*
90   Sups the fair Rosaline, whom thou so loves,
     With all the admired beauties of Verona.
     Go thither, and with unattainted° eye   *unbiased*
     Compare her face with some that I shall show,
     And I will make thee think thy swan a crow.
95   ROMEO   When the devout religion° of mine eye   *pious belief*
     Maintains such falsehood, then turn tears to fire;
     And these° who, often drowned, could never die,   *these eyes*
     Transparent° heretics, be burnt for liars.   *Obvious; self-evident*
     One fairer than my love? The all-seeing sun
100   Ne'er saw her match since first the world begun.
BENVOLIO   Tut, you saw her fair, none else being by,
     Herself poised with° herself in either eye;   *balanced against*
     But in that crystal scales let there be weighed
     Your lady's love against some other maid
105   That I will show you shining at this feast,
     And she shall scant show well that now seems best.
ROMEO   I'll go along no such sight to be shown,
     But to rejoice in splendor of mine own.
                                      [*Exeunt.*]

---

3. "Come up" is an expression of scorn.

1.3

Enter CAPULET'S WIFE *and* NURSE.

CAPULET'S WIFE   Nurse, where's my daughter?
    Call her forth to me.
NURSE   Now, by my maidenhead at twelve year old,[1]
    I bade her come.—What,[2] lamb! What, ladybird!
5   God forbid[3]—where's this girl? What, Juliet!
      Enter JULIET.
JULIET   How now? Who calls?
NURSE   Your mother.
JULIET   Madam, I am here. What is your will?
CAPULET'S WIFE   This is the matter.—Nurse, give
    leave° a while;   *excuse us*
10   We must talk in secret.—Nurse, come back again;
    I have remembered me. Thou's° hear our   *You shall*
    counsel.°   *secrets*
    Thou knowest my daughter's of a pretty age.
NURSE   Faith, I can tell her age unto an hour.
CAPULET'S WIFE   She's not fourteen.
15 NURSE   I'll lay fourteen of my teeth—and yet,
    to my teen° be it spoken, I have but four—   *sorrow*
    she's not fourteen. How long is it now to
    Lammastide?[4]
CAPULET'S WIFE   A fortnight and odd days.
20 NURSE   Even or odd, of all days in the year,
    Come Lammas Eve at night shall she be fourteen.
    Susan[5] and she—God rest all Christian souls—
    Were of an age. Well, Susan is with God;
    She was too good for me. But, as I said,
25   On Lammas Eve at night shall she be fourteen—
    That shall she, marry! I remember it well.
    'Tis since the earthquake now eleven years,
    And she was weaned—I never shall forget it—
    Of all the days of the year upon that day;
30   For I had then laid wormwood[6] to my dug,°   *on my nipple*
    Sitting in the sun under the dovehouse wall—
    My lord and you were then at Mantua—

1.3 Location: Capulet's house.
1. Presumably the latest date that the Nurse could swear by her virginity.
2. An expression of impatience.
3. Either an apology for the promiscuous connotation of "ladybird" or fearing something
   amiss in Juliet's absence.
4. August 1, originally celebrated by the church as a harvest festival.
5. The Nurse evidently suckled Juliet after her own daughter died.
6. A proverbially bitter plant extract.

Nay, I do bear a brain°—but, as I said,   *memory*
When it did taste the wormwood on the nipple
35   Of my dug and felt it bitter, pretty fool°—   *(an endearment)*
To see it tetchy,° and fall out with the dug!   *peevish*
"Shake," quoth the dovehouse;[7] 'twas no need, I trow,
To bid me trudge.°   *remove myself*
And since that time it is eleven years,
40   For then she could stand high-lone°—nay, by   *upright alone*
         th' rood,°   *cross*
She could have run and waddled all about,
For, even the day before, she broke her brow,°   *cut her forehead*
And then my husband—God be with his soul;
'A° was a merry man—took up the child.   *He*
45   "Yea?" quoth he. "Dost thou fall upon thy face?
Thou wilt fall backward when thou hast more wit,°   *knowledge*
Wilt thou not, Jule?" And, by my holidam,°   *Holy Lady*
The pretty wretch left° crying, and said "Ay!"   *stopped*
To see now how a jest shall come about!°   *come true*
50   I warrant, an° I should live a thousand years,   *if*
I never should forget it. "Wilt thou not, Jule?" quoth he,
And, pretty fool, it stinted° and said "Ay!"   *she ceased*

CAPULET'S WIFE   Enough of this. I pray thee, hold thy peace.

NURSE   Yes, madam—yet I cannot choose but laugh
55   To think it should leave crying and say "Ay!"
And yet I warrant° it had upon it° brow   *assure you / its*
A bump as big as a young cock'rel's stone°—   *rooster's testicle*
A perilous knock—and it cried bitterly.
"Yea?" quoth my husband. "Fall'st upon thy face?
60   Thou wilt fall backward when thou comest to age,
Wilt thou not, Jule?" It stinted and said "Ay!"

JULIET   And stint thou too, I pray thee, Nurse, say I.

NURSE   Peace, I have done. God mark° thee to his   *elect*
         grace,
Thou wast the prettiest babe that e'er I nursed;
65   An° I might live to see thee married once,°   *If / one day*
I have my wish.

CAPULET'S WIFE   Marry,° that "marry" is the very   *Truly*
         theme
I came to talk of.—Tell me, daughter Juliet,
How stands your dispositions to be married?

---

7. The dovehouse shook with the earthquake.

70 JULIET It is an hour that I dream not of.
    NURSE "An hour"! Were not I thine only nurse,
        I would say thou hadst sucked wisdom from thy teat.[8]
    CAPULET'S WIFE Well, think of marriage now. Younger
        than you
        Here in Verona, ladies of esteem,
75   Are made already mothers; by my count,
        I was your mother much upon these years
        That you are now a maid. Thus, then, in brief:
        The valiant Paris seeks you for his love.
    NURSE A man, young lady! Lady, such a man
80   As all the world—Why, he's a man of wax![9]
    CAPULET'S WIFE Verona's summer hath not such a flower.
    NURSE Nay, he's a flower, in faith, a very flower!
    CAPULET'S WIFE What say you? Can you love the gentleman?
        This night you shall behold him at our feast;
85   Read o'er the volume of young Paris' face,
        And find delight writ there with beauty's pen;
        Examine every married lineament,[1]
        And see how one° another lends content;[2]   one to
        And what obscured in this fair volume lies
90   Find written in the margin[3] of his eyes.
        This precious book of love, this unbound°   single; unrestrained
            lover,
        To beautify him only lacks a cover.
        The fish lives in the sea, and 'tis much pride
        For fair without the fair within to hide;[4]
95   That book in many's eyes doth share the glory
        That in gold clasps locks in the golden story.[5]
        So shall you share all that he doth possess
        By having him, making yourself no less.
    NURSE No less? Nay, bigger—women grow° by   swell with child
        men!
100 CAPULET'S WIFE Speak briefly: can you like of Paris' love?
    JULIET I'll look° to like, if looking liking move;[6]   expect; examine

---

8. From the teat that nourished you.
9. Model of perfection, as if sculpted rather than born.
1. Harmoniously composed feature; a joined line of flowing handwriting.
2. Meaning; happiness.
3. Glosses to difficult passages of text were set in the margin.
4. *For fair . . . hide:* For a lovely setting (Juliet) to frame and enrich the fair Paris.
5. *That book . . . story:* Many esteem a book's golden binding as highly as the story it contains. The speech thoroughly confuses who is covering whom.
6. If looking can motivate liking.

But no more deep will I endart mine eye[7]
Than your consent gives strength to make it fly.

Enter a SERVINGMAN.

SERVINGMAN Madam, the guests are come;
105 supper served up; you called; my young lady
asked for; the Nurse cursed in the pantry;
and everything in extremity.° *a terrible state* I must hence
to wait;° I beseech you follow straight.° *serve / immediately*

CAPULET'S WIFE We follow thee.

[*Exit* SERVINGMAN.]

—Juliet, the County stays.° *the Count awaits*
110 NURSE Go, girl! Seek happy nights to° happy *at the end of*
days. *Exeunt.*

1.4

Enter ROMEO, MERCUTIO, [*and*] BENVOLIO,
with five or six other Masquers,[1] *torchbearers.*

ROMEO What, shall this speech° be spoke for our *prologue*
excuse,
Or shall we on without apology?

BENVOLIO The date is out of° such prolixity. *past for*
We'll have no Cupid, hoodwinked[2] with a scarf,
5 Bearing a Tartar's painted bow of lath,[3]
Scaring the ladies like a crowkeeper.° *scarecrow*
But let them measure° us by what they will, *judge*
We'll measure° them a measure° and be gone. *apportion / dance*

ROMEO Give me a torch. I am not for this ambling;° *dancing*
10 Being but heavy,° I will bear the light. *melancholy*

MERCUTIO Nay, gentle° Romeo, we must have *noble; softhearted*
you dance.

ROMEO Not I, believe me. You have dancing shoes
With nimble soles; I have a soul of lead
So stakes me to the ground I cannot move.

7. Sink my eye like an arrow into its target; shoot glances that, like Cupid's arrows, inflame his passions.
1.4 Location: Before Capulet's house.
1. Performers or participants in an aristocratic masked entertainment, consisting of dances and sometimes dumb shows and set speeches.
2. Blindfolded and foolish Cupid, a typical costume for the presenter of the masque's theme.
3. Short bow shaped like the upper lip, made of the thin wood used for theatrical properties. Tartars, a dark-skinned, supposedly savage people in Asia Minor, were renowned for their archery.

15 MERCUTIO   You are a lover; borrow Cupid's wings,
And soar with them above a common bound.[4]
ROMEO   I am too sore° empiercèd with his shaft   *deeply*
To soar with his light° feathers, and, so   *cheery; agile; wanton*
  bound,
I cannot bound a pitch[5] above dull woe;
20 Under love's heavy burden do I sink.
MERCUTIO   And to sink in it should you burden love:
Too great oppression for a tender thing.[6]
ROMEO   Is love a tender thing? It is too rough,
Too rude, too boist'rous, and it pricks like thorn.
25 MERCUTIO   If love be rough with you, be rough with love;
Prick° love for pricking, and you beat love   *Stab; sexually penetrate*
  down.[7]
Give me a case[8] to put my visage in—
A visor for a visor[9]—what care I
What curious eye doth quote° deformities?   *notice*
30 Here are the beetle brows° shall blush for me.   *protruding eyebrows*
BENVOLIO   Come, knock and enter—and, no sooner in,
But every man betake him to his legs.°   *to dancing; to flight*
ROMEO   A torch for me. Let wantons light of heart
Tickle the senseless rushes° with their heels,   *floor matting*
35 For I am proverbed with a grandsire° phrase: *an ancient*
I'll be a candleholder and look on.[1]
The game was ne'er so fair, and I am done.[2]
MERCUTIO   Tut, dun's the mouse[3]—the constable's
  own word.°   *phrase*
If thou art dun, we'll draw thee from the mire[4]
40 Or—save your reverence[5]—love wherein thou stickest
Up to the ears. Come; we burn daylight.° Ho!   *waste time*
ROMEO   Nay, that's not so.
MERCUTIO   I mean, sir, in delay
We waste our lights in vain, light lights by day.
Take our good meaning, for our judgment sits

---

4. A normal limit; an average dancer's leap.
5. Height from which a hawk stoops to kill.
6. Suggesting a pudendum.
7. *Prick . . . down*: Playing on the sense "satiate desire by fulfilling it."
8. Literally, "mask," but also slang for the vagina.
9. Mask for an ugly face. Proverbial: "A well-favored visor to hide an ill-favored face."
1. Proverbial: "A good candleholder proves a good gamester. A spectator loses nothing."
2. Proverbial: "When play is best, it is time to leave."
3. Proverbial: "Keep silent and unseen, like a mouse."
4. In the Christmas game "Dun Is in the Mire," players pantomimed drawing a log representing a horse out of a boggy road. Mercutio is suggesting that Romeo is a stick-in-the-mud.
5. An apology for crude language, here used mockingly.

45   Five times in that ere once in our fine wits.[6]

ROMEO   And we mean° well in going to this masque;   *intend*

But 'tis no wit° to go.   *intelligence*

MERCUTIO   Why, may one ask?

ROMEO   I dreamed a dream tonight°   *last night*

MERCUTIO   And so did I.

ROMEO   Well, what was yours?

MERCUTIO   That dreamers often lie.

50   ROMEO   In bed asleep while they do dream things true.

MERCUTIO   Oh, then, I see Queen Mab[7] hath been with you

She is the fairies' midwife, and she comes

In shape no bigger than an agate stone[8]

On the forefinger of an alderman,

55   Drawn with a team of little atomi°   *atoms*

Over men's noses as they lie asleep,

Her wagon-spokes made of long spinners'° legs,   *spiders'*

The cover of the wings of grasshoppers,

Her traces of the smallest spider web,

60   Her collars of the moonshine's wat'ry beams,

Her whip of cricket's bone, the lash of film,°   *spider's-web thread*

Her wagoner° a small gray-coated gnat   *driver*

Not half so big as a round little worm

Pricked from the lazy finger of a maid.[9]

65   Her chariot is an empty hazelnut

Made by the joiner° squirrel or old grub[1]—   *carpenter*

Time out o'mind the fairies' coach-makers—

And in this state° she gallops night by night   *regal finery*

Through lovers' brains, and then they dream of love;

70   On courtiers' knees, that dream on curtsies straight;[2]

O'er lawyers' fingers, who straight dream on fees;

O'er ladies' lips, who straight on kisses dream,

Which oft the angry Mab with blisters plagues

Because their breath with sweetmeats°   *candies*

tainted are.

75   Sometime she gallops o'er a courtier's nose,

---

6. *Take . . . wits*: Understand my intended good meaning using common sense ("judgment"), which is five times as trustworthy as witty ingenuity ("fine wits").
7. Possibly Celtic, but probably Shakespeare's invention. "Queen" suggested "queen," which
meant "whore," and "Mab" was a stereotypical name for prostitutes.
8. A small human figure was often carved on agate stones set in seal rings.
9. According to popular belief, worms generated in idle girls' fingers.
1. Grubs bore holes.
2. Dream of respectful bows immediately.

And then dreams he of smelling out a suit;[3]
And sometime comes she with a tithe-pig's[4] tail,
Tickling a parson's nose as 'a° lies asleep—   *he*
Then he dreams of another benefice;[5]
80 Sometime she driveth o'er a soldier's neck,
And then dreams he of cutting foreign throats,
Of breaches, ambuscadoes, Spanish blades,[6]
Of healths five fathom deep[7]—and then anon°   *soon*
Drums in his ear, at which he starts and wakes
85 And, being thus frighted, swears a prayer or two
And sleeps again. This is that very Mab
That plaits° the manes of horses in the night,   *entangles*
And bakes the elflocks[8] in foul sluttish° hairs   *dirty*
Which, once untangled, much misfortune bodes.
90 This is the hag, when maids lie on their backs,
That presses them,[9] and learns° them first to bear,   *teaches*
Making them women of good carriage.[1]
This is she—
ROMEO   Peace, peace, Mercutio, peace!
Thou talk'st of nothing.°   *imaginings; a vagina*
MERCUTIO   True, I talk of dreams,
95 Which are the children of an idle brain,
Begot of nothing but vain fantasy,°   *empty imagination*
Which is as thin of substance as the air
And more inconstant than the wind, who woos
Even now the frozen bosom of the North
100 And, being angered, puffs away from thence,
Turning his side to the dew-dropping South.
BENVOLIO This wind you talk of blows us from ourselves;
Supper is done, and we shall come too late.
ROMEO I fear too early, for my mind misgives°   *fears*
105 Some consequence yet hanging in the stars
Shall bitterly begin his fearful date°   *period*
With this night's revels and expire° the term   *finish*
Of a despisèd life closed in my breast

---

3. A petition at court, which the courtier could facilitate for a fee.
4. Pig paid as a tithe to the parish for the support of the priest.
5. Pluralism—holding multiple benefices simultaneously—was a common source of corruption in the early modern church.
6. Swords made in Toledo were famous for their quality. *breaches*: burst fortifications. *ambuscadoes*: ambushes.
7. Fantastically deep cups of liquor.
8. And hardens the tangles. According to folk legend, unknotting them would anger the malicious elves.
9. Evil spirits were supposed to be responsible for erotic dreams, taking the form of an illusory sexual partner.
1. Excellent deportment; the capacity for carrying the weight of a lover; childbearing.

By some vile forfeit of untimely death.[2]
110 But He that hath the steerage of my course
Direct my suit—On, lusty gentlemen!
BENVOLIO Strike, drum!
They march about the stage, and SERVINGMEN *come*
forth with napkins. Enter [HEAD SERVINGMAN].
HEAD SERVINGMAN Where's Potpan, that he
helps not to take away? He shift a trencher!°   *wooden plate*
115 He scrape a trencher!
FIRST SERVINGMAN When good manners shall
lie all in one or two men's hands—and they
unwashed too—tis a foul° thing.   *bad; dirty*
HEAD SERVINGMAN Away with the joint-stools![3]
120 Remove the court-cupboard!° Look to the   *sideboard*
plate!°—Good thou, save me a piece of mar-   *silverware*
zipan, and, as thou loves me, let the porter
let in Susan Grindstone and Nell, Anthony,
and Potpan.
125 SECOND SERVINGMAN Ay, boy, ready.
HEAD SERVINGMAN You are looked for and
called for, asked for and sought for, in the
great chamber.
THIRD SERVINGMAN We cannot be here and
130 there too.—Cheerly, boys! Be brisk a while,
and the longer liver take all.[4]
                    Exeunt [SERVINGMEN].
[*Enter* [CAPULET, CAPULET'S WIFE, JULIET,
CAPULET'S COUSIN, PARIS, TYBALT, NURSE, *a*
SERVINGMAN, *Attendants, Tybalt's Page,*
Musicians, and] *all the Guests and Gentlewomen*
to the Masquers.[5]
CAPULET Welcome, gentlemen! Ladies that have their toes
Unplagued with corns will walk a bout° with you.   *dance a turn*
—Ah, my mistresses, which of you all
135 Will now deny to dance? She that makes dainty,°   *coyly demurs*
She I'll swear hath corns. Am I come near ye now?[6]
—Welcome, gentlemen! I have seen the day

2. As fate prematurely foreclosing on a mortgaged life.
3. Stools made by a furniture maker, commonly used for seating at large banquets.
4. Proverbial, meaning "Life is short."
5. Although neither Paris nor Rosaline speaks in this scene, directors have sometimes used
    the ball as an opportunity to develop their presence in the play.
6. Does that strike home?

That I have worn a visor, and could tell
A whispering tale in a fair lady's ear,
140 Such as would please: 'tis gone, 'tis gone, 'tis gone!
You are welcome, gentlemen!—Come, musicians, play.
    Music plays, and they dance.
A hall,[7] a hall! Give room!—And foot it, girls!
[*to Attendants*]   More light, you knaves! And turn
    the tables up,[8]
And quench the fire; the room is grown too hot.
145 —Ah, sirrah, this unlooked-for° sport comes well!   unexpected
—Nay, sit, nay, sit, good cousin° Capulet,   kinsman
For you and I are past our dancing days.
How long is't now since last yourself and I
Were in a masque?
CAPULET'S COUSIN   By'r Lady, thirty years.
150 CAPULET   What, man? 'Tis not so much, 'tis not so much;
'Tis since the nuptial of Lucentio—
Come Pentecost[9] as quickly as it will,
Some five-and-twenty years—and then we masqued.
CAPULET'S COUSIN   'Tis more, 'tis more! His son is elder, sir;
His son is thirty.
155 CAPULET   Will you tell me that?
His son was but a ward[1] two years ago.
ROMEO [*apart to a* SERVINGMAN]   What lady's that which
    doth enrich the hand
Of yonder knight?
SERVINGMAN   I know not, sir.
ROMEO   Oh, she doth teach the torches to burn bright!
160 It seems she hangs upon the cheek of night
As a rich jewel in an Ethiop's ear:[2]
Beauty too rich for use, for earth too dear.[3]
So shows a snowy dove trooping° with crows   flocking
As yonder lady o'er her fellows shows.
165 The measure° done, I'll watch her place of stand[4]   dance
And, touching hers, make blessèd my rude hand.

---

7. Make space in the hall.
8. Dismantle and stack the trestle tables.
9. The seventh Sunday after Easter, a standard reference point in the medieval and Renaissance calendar.
1. Subject to a guardian; a minor.
2. In Romeo's image, a jewel shines brighter against an Ethiopian's proverbially dark skin.
3. Too precious for this world; too valuable to die and be buried in earth.
4. Where Juliet waits between dances.

Did my heart love till now? Forswear it, sight,
For I ne'er saw true beauty till this night.

TYBALT   This, by his voice, should be a Montague.
[*to his Page*]   Fetch me my rapier, boy.
                           [*Exit Tybalt's Page.*]

170   What? Dares the slave
Come hither, covered with an antic face,[5]
To fleer° and scorn at our solemnity?°   *sneer / festivity*
Now, by the stock and honor of my kin,
To strike him dead I hold it not a sin.

175 CAPULET   Why, how now, kinsman? Wherefore storm you so?

TYBALT   Uncle, this is a Montague, our foe,
A villain° that is hither come in spite   *An ill-doer; a slave*
To scorn at our solemnity this night.

CAPULET   Young Romeo, is it?

TYBALT   'Tis he, that villain Romeo.

180 CAPULET   Content° thee, gentle coz. Let him alone.   *Calm*
'A bears him like a portly° gentleman,   *dignified*
And, to say truth, Verona brags of him
To be a virtuous and well-governed° youth;   *sensible*
I would not for the wealth of all this town

185 Here in my house do him disparagement.
Therefore, be patient; take no note of him.
It is my will, the which if thou respect,
Show a fair presence,° and put off these frowns,   *demeanor*
An ill-beseeming semblance° for a feast.   *expression*

190 TYBALT   It fits when such a villain is a guest;
I'll not endure him.

CAPULET   He shall be endured!
What, goodman[6] boy? I say he shall. Go to![7]
Am I the master here or you? Go to!
You'll "not endure him"? God shall mend my soul,

195 You'll make a mutiny° among my guests!   *brawl*
You will set cock-a-hoop![8] You'll be the man!

TYBALT   Why, uncle, 'tis a shame—

CAPULET   Go to, go to;
You are a saucy boy. Is't so, indeed?

---

5. A grotesque mask; a playful mask.
6. Courtesy title applied to a commoner (and thus an insult to the noble Tybalt).
7. An expression of impatience.
8. You will abandon restraint, like a drinker who removes the tap ("cock") from the barrel or like a boastfully crowing rooster.

This trick° may chance to scathe° you. I know   *stupidity / harm*
   what:⁹

200   You must contrary me—marry, 'tis time¹—
   [*A dance ends, and* JULIET *moves to her*
   place of stand, where ROMEO *awaits.*]
   [*to Masquers*] Well said,° my hearts! [*to*   *done*
   TYBALT] You are a princock.° Go.   *cheeky boy*
   Be quiet, or— [*to Attendants*] More light! More
   light, for shame!
   —I'll make you quiet. [*to Masquers*] What, cheerly, my
   hearts!

TYBALT [*aside*]   Patience perforce° with willful   *enforced*
   choler° meeting   *rash anger*
205   Makes my flesh tremble in their different° greeting.   *hostile*
   I will withdraw, but this intrusion shall,
   Now seeming sweet, convert to bitt'rest gall. *Exit.*

ROMEO   If I profane with my unworthiest hand²
   This holy shrine, the gentle sin is this:
210   My lips, two blushing pilgrims,³ did ready stand
   To smooth that rough touch with a tender kiss.

JULIET   Good pilgrim, you do wrong your hand too much,
   Which mannerly° devotion shows in this;   *seemly*
   For saints⁴ have hands that pilgrims' hands do touch,
215   And palm to palm is holy palmers'° kiss.   *pilgrims'*

ROMEO   Have not saints lips, and holy palmers too?

JULIET   Ay, pilgrim, lips that they must use in prayer.

ROMEO   Oh, then, dear saint, let lips do what hands do:
   They pray; grant thou, lest faith turn to despair.

220 JULIET   Saints do not move, though grant for prayer's sake.⁵

ROMEO   Then move not while my prayer's effect I take.
   [*He kisses her.*]
   Thus from my lips, by thine, my sin is purged.

JULIET   Then have my lips the sin that they have took.

---

9. I mean what I say.
1. Time to teach you a lesson; time that you became obedient.
2. Romeo and Juliet's first conversation takes the form of a shared sonnet.
3. John Florio's *World of Words* (1598) translates the Italian word *romeo* as "roamer," "wan-
derer," or "palmer" (pilgrim to the Holy Land).
4. Statues or pictures of saints, which attracted Catholic pilgrims. The Elizabethan Angli-
can Church held that the worship of such images was blasphemy; to an English audience, therefore, Romeo's description of his love could sound like idolatry.
5. Again identifying the saint with her image. As a statue she does not move, but as a saint
in heaven she can intercede with God on behalf of the worshipper.

ROMEO   Sin from my lips? Oh, trespass sweetly urged![6]
    Give me my sin again.°   *back*
    [*He kisses her.*]
225 JULIET   You kiss by th' book.[7]
NURSE   Madam, your mother craves a word with you.
    [JULIET *goes to speak with* CAPULET'S WIFE.]
ROMEO [*to* NURSE]   What is her mother?
NURSE   Marry, bachelor,°   *young man*
    Her mother is the lady of the house,
    And a good lady, and a wise and virtuous.
230 I nursed her daughter that you talked withal.°   *with*
    I tell you, he that can lay hold of her
    Shall have the chinks.°   *plenty of coins*
ROMEO [*aside*]   Is she a Capulet?
    Oh, dear account!° My life is my foe's debt.[8]   *costly reckoning*
BENVOLIO   Away! Begone! The sport is at the best.
235 ROMEO   Ay, so I fear; the more is my unrest.
    [*The Masquers prepare to depart.*]
CAPULET   Nay, gentlemen, prepare not to be gone!
    We have a trifling foolish banquet towards[9]
    [*They whisper in his ear.*]
    Is it e'en so? Why, then I thank you all;
    I thank you, honest gentlemen. Good night!
240 —More torches here! —Come on, then: let's to bed.
    —Ah, sirrah, by my fay,° it waxes late!   *faith*
    I'll to my rest.
        [*Exeunt* CAPULET, CAPULET'S WIFE, *and*
        CAPULET'S COUSIN, *and* SERVINGMAN; *all*
        others move toward the doors, and exeunt;
        JULIET *and* NURSE *remain.*]
JULIET   Come hither, Nurse. What is yond gentleman?
NURSE   The son and heir of old Tiberio.
245 JULIET   What's he that now is going out of door?
NURSE   Marry, that, I think, be young Petruccio.
JULIET   What's he that follows here that would not dance?
NURSE   I know not.
JULIET   Go ask his name.   [*Exit* NURSE.]
        If he be marrièd,

---

6. Sweetly argued that the first kiss was a transgression, and sweetly advocated that the transgression of a second kiss is needed to take away the sin of the first.
7. According to the rules; implies "proficiently," "politely," or "with poetic flatteries."
8. A debt owing to my foe; in the power of my foe.
9. A paltry dessert coming.

250 My grave is like° to be my wedding-bed.   *likely*
    [*Enter* NURSE.]
NURSE   His name is Romeo, and a Montague,
    The only son of your great enemy.
JULIET   My only love sprung from my only hate!
    Too early seen unknown, and known too late!
255 Prodigious° birth of love it is to me   *Monstrous; ominous*
    That I must love a loathèd enemy.
NURSE   What's tis?° What's tis?   *this* (dialect pronunciation)
JULIET   A rhyme I learned even now
    Of one I danced withal.
            One calls within, "Juliet!"
NURSE   Anon,° anon!   *Right away*
    Come, let's away; the strangers all are gone.
                                    Exeunt.

                                2.0
    [*Enter* CHORUS.]
CHORUS   Now old° desire doth in his deathbed lie,   *Romeo's former*
    And young affection gapes° to be his heir;   *longs*
    That fair for which love groaned for and would die,
    With tender Juliet matched,° is now not fair.   *compared*
5   Now Romeo is beloved and loves again,°   *in return; once more*
    Alike bewitchèd by the charm of looks;[1]
    But to his foe supposed° he must complain,[2]   *presumed*
    And she steal love's sweet bait from fearful° hooks.   *fearsome*
    Being held a foe, he may not have access
10 To breathe such vows as lovers use° to swear,   *are accustomed*
    And she as much in love, her means much less
    To meet her new belovèd anywhere.
    But passion lends them power, time means, to meet,
    Temp'ring extremities° with extreme sweet.   *Mitigating dangers*
                                    [*Exit.*]

2.0
1. Appearances; desirous glances.
2. Conventionally, make lovesick speeches.

2.1

Enter ROMEO *alone.*[1]

ROMEO   Can I go forward when my heart is here?
Turn back, dull earth,[2] and find thy center[3] out.
   [*He withdraws.*]
   Enter BENVOLIO *with* MERCUTIO.

BENVOLIO   Romeo! My cousin Romeo! Romeo!

MERCUTIO   He is wise and, on my life, hath stol'n
him° home to bed.   *himself*

5 BENVOLIO   He ran this way, and leapt this orchard wall.
Call, good Mercutio.

MERCUTIO   Nay, I'll conjure,° too.   *summon as a spirit*
Romeo! Humors![4] Madman! Passion! Lover!
Appear thou in the likeness of a sigh;
Speak but one rhyme, and I am satisfied;

10 Cry but "Ay me!", pronounce but "love" and "dove";
Speak to my gossip° Venus one fair word,   *crony*
One nickname for her purblind° son and heir,   *dim-sighted; blind*
Young Abraham Cupid,[5] he that shot so true
When King Cophetua loved the beggar maid.[6]

15 —He heareth not, he stirreth not, he moveth not:
The ape[7] is dead, and I must conjure him.
—I conjure thee by Rosaline's bright eyes,
By her high forehead and her scarlet lip,
By her fine foot, straight leg, and quivering thigh,

20 And the demesnes° that there adjacent lie,   *estates*
That in thy likeness thou appear to us!

BENVOLIO   An if he hear thee, thou wilt anger him.

MERCUTIO   This cannot anger him. 'Twould anger him
To raise a spirit[8] in his mistress' circle

2.1 Location: Outside Capulet's house.

1. The main stage represents the area outside the wall of Capulet's orchard and then the inside of the orchard below the window of Juliet's room. Romeo is imagined to leap over the garden wall when he withdraws at line 2.
2. Romeo's flesh, drawing on two traditional views of the human body: animated dust or clay, and a "microcosm," or little world, which mirrors the order of the universe. Earth was the most sluggish and immobile element.
3. The point in the earth toward which everything falls; or Romeo's heart (metaphorically, Juliet).
4. Pure moods, not mixed together to form an even "temper."
5. Cupid, as Mercutio's nickname suggests, is at once a young boy and a patriarch, the oldest of the gods.
6. The story of a king who falls in love with a beggar and makes her his queen was the subject of a popular ballad.
7. Foolish creature (a disrespectful endearment), or alluding to a magician's trick of "reviving" an ape that had been trained to play dead.
8. A word for "semen"; the entire speech is filled with obscene wordplay.

25   Of some strange° nature, letting it there stand   *other person's*
        Till she had laid it and conjured it down:
        That were some spite. My invocation
        Is fair and honest in his mistress' name;
        I conjure only but to raise up him.

30 BENVOLIO   Come, he hath hid himself among these trees
        To be consorted° with the humorous⁹ night.   *in company*
        Blind is his love, and best befits the dark.

   MERCUTIO   If love be blind, love cannot hit the mark.°   *target; vulva*
        Now will he sit under a medlar¹ tree
35   And wish his mistress were that kind of fruit
        As maids call medlars when they laugh alone.
        —O Romeo, that she were—oh, that she were—
        An open-arse,° thou a popp'rin' pear!²   *medlar*
        Romeo, good night!—I'll to my truckle bed;³
40   This field bed⁴ is too cold for me to sleep.
        Come: shall we go?

   BENVOLIO   Go, then; for 'tis in vain
        To seek him here that means not to be found.
                        Exeunt [BENVOLIO *and* MERCUTIO].
                [ROMEO *comes forward.*]

   ROMEO   He jests at scars that never felt a wound⁵—
        But soft,° what light through yonder window breaks?   *wait; hush*
45   It is the East, and Juliet is the sun.
        Arise, fair sun, and kill the envious moon,⁶
        Who is already sick and pale with grief
        That thou, her maid, art far more fair than she.
        Be not her maid, since she is envious;
50   Her vestal° livery is but sick and green,⁷   *virginal*
        And none but fools do wear it. Cast it off.
                [*Enter* JULIET *above.*]
        It is my lady—oh, it is my love—

---

9. Damp; melancholy.
1. A fruit thought to resemble the female sex organs or the anus, with a play on "meddle"
   in the sense "have sexual intercourse with."
2. A pear from Poperinghe in Flanders, punning on "popper-in" or "pop her in."
3. Small bed, often for a child, that was stored under a larger one.
4. A lying place in the open, and a soldier's portable bed.
5. Rhymes with "found." This line precedes a scene change in most editions, although the
   location remains the same if both the inside and the outside of the orchard are supposed to be visible onstage.
6. Emblem of Diana, goddess of chastity.
7. Unfulfilled sexual desire was thought to cause green sickness (anemia) in adolescent
   girls; also alluding to the moon's pallor.

Oh, that she knew she were!
She speaks, yet she says nothing. What of that?
55 Her eye discourses; I will answer it.
I am too bold; 'tis not to me she speaks.
Two of the fairest stars in all the heaven,
Having some business, do entreat her eyes
To twinkle in their spheres[8] till they return.
60 What if her eyes were there, they in her head?
The brightness of her cheek would shame those stars
As daylight doth a lamp; her eye in heaven
Would through the airy region° stream so bright   *ethereal sky*
That birds would sing and think it were not night.
65 See how she leans her cheek upon her hand—
Oh, that I were a glove upon that hand,
That I might touch that cheek!
JULIET   Ay me!
ROMEO [*aside*]   She speaks.
Oh, speak again, bright angel, for thou art
As glorious to this night, being o'er my head,
70 As is a wingèd messenger° of heaven   *angel*
Unto the white upturnèd[9] wond'ring eyes
Of mortals that fall back to gaze[1] on him
When he bestrides the lazy puffing clouds
And sails upon the bosom of the air.
75 JULIET O Romeo, Romeo, wherefore° art thou Romeo?   *why*
Deny thy father and refuse thy name.
Or, if thou wilt not, be but sworn my love,
And I'll no longer be a Capulet.
ROMEO [*aside*]   Shall I hear more, or shall I speak at this?
80 JULIET 'Tis but thy name that is my enemy;
Thou art thyself, though° not a Montague.
What's "Montague"? It is nor hand, nor foot,
Nor arm, nor face, nor any other part
Belonging to a man. Oh, be some other name!
85 What's in a name? That which we call a rose
By any other word would smell as sweet;
So Romeo would, were he not Romeo called,
Retain that dear perfection which he owes°   *owns*

---

8. In Ptolemaic astronomy, crystalline spheres around the earth that carried the heavenly
   bodies in their rotations.
9. Turned up, revealing the whites at the bottoms.
1. Fall backward in gazing.

Without that title. Romeo, doff° thy name,   *shed*
90   And, for thy name, which is no part of thee,
Take all myself.
ROMEO   I take thee at thy word.[2]
Call me but "love," and I'll be new baptized:[3]
Henceforth I never will be Romeo.
JULIET   What man art thou that, thus bescreened in night,
So stumblest on my counsel?°   *private thoughts*
95   ROMEO   By a name
I know not how to tell thee who I am.
My name, dear saint, is hateful to myself
Because it is an enemy to thee;
Had I it written, I would tear the word.
100   JULIET   My ears have yet not drunk a hundred words
Of thy tongue's uttering, yet I know the sound.
Art thou not Romeo, and a Montague?
ROMEO   Neither, fair maid, if either thee dislike.°   *displeases you*
JULIET   How camest thou hither, tell me—and wherefore?
105   The orchard walls are high and hard to climb,
And the place death, considering who thou art,
If any of my kinsmen find thee here.
ROMEO   With love's light wings did I o'erperch° these   *fly over*
walls,
For stony limits cannot hold love out,
110   And what love can do, that dares love attempt;
Therefore thy kinsmen are no stop° to me.   *obstacle*
JULIET   If they do see thee, they will murder thee.
ROMEO   Alack, there lies more peril in thine eye
Than twenty of their swords. Look thou but sweet,
115   And I am proof against° their enmity.   *impervious to*
JULIET   I would not for the world they saw thee here.
ROMEO   I have night's cloak to hide me from their eyes,
And, but° thou love me, let them find me here: *unless*
My life were better ended by their hate
120   Than death proroguèd,° wanting of° thy love.   *deferred / lacking*
JULIET   By whose direction found'st thou out this place?
ROMEO   By love, that first did prompt me to inquire.
He lent me counsel, and I lent him eyes.
I am no pilot, yet wert thou as far
125   As that vast shore washed with the farthest sea,

2. At face value; as you have asked me to.
3. Given a new name; born into a new persona.

I should adventure° for such merchandise.   *voyage*
JULIET   Thou knowest the mask of night is on my face,
    Else would a maiden blush bepaint my cheek
    For that which thou hast heard me speak tonight.
130   Fain° would I dwell on form°—fain, fain deny   *Gladly / propriety*
    What I have spoke—but farewell, compliment.°   *polite convention*
    Dost thou love me? I know thou wilt say "Ay,"
    And I will take thy word; yet, if thou swear'st,   *— Say it!*
    Thou mayst prove false. At lovers' perjuries   *mean it!.*
135   They say Jove laughs. O gentle Romeo,
    If thou dost love, pronounce° it faithfully,   *utter*
    Or if thou thinkest I am too quickly won,
    I'll frown and be perverse° and say thee nay   *contrary*
    So thou wilt woo—but else° not for the world.   *otherwise*
140   In truth, fair Montague, I am too fond,°   *infatuated*
    And therefore thou mayst think my behavior   *Juliet is 13 years old*
      light.°   *licentious; capricious*
    But trust me, gentleman, I'll prove more true
    Than those that have the coying° to be strange.°   *coyness / distant*
    I should have been more strange, I must confess,
145   But that thou overheard'st, ere I was ware,°   *aware*
    My true-love passion. Therefore pardon me,
    And not° impute this yielding to light love,   *do not*
    Which the dark night hath so discoverèd.°   *revealed*
ROMEO   Lady, by yonder blessèd moon I vow,
150   That tips with silver all these fruit-tree tops—
JULIET   Oh, swear not by the moon, th'inconstant moon
    That monthly changes in her circled orb,°   *orbital sphere*
    Lest that thy love prove likewise variable.
ROMEO   What shall I swear by?
JULIET   Do not swear at all,
155   Or, if thou wilt, swear by thy gracious self,
    Which is the god of my idolatry,[4]
    And I'll believe thee.
ROMEO   If my heart's dear love—
JULIET   Well, do not swear. Although I joy in thee,
    I have no joy of this contract° tonight;   *exchange of vows*
160   It is too rash, too unadvised,° too sudden,   *undeliberated*
    Too like the lightning which doth cease to be

---

4. Not only was loving a man more than God idolatrous, but so was swearing oaths by anything other than God.

Ere one can say, "It lightens." Sweet, good night.
This bud of love by summer's ripening breath
May prove a beauteous flower when next we meet.
Good night, good night; as sweet repose and rest
Come to thy heart as that within my breast.
ROMEO   Oh, wilt thou leave me so unsatisfied?
JULIET   What satisfaction canst thou have tonight?
ROMEO   Th'exchange of thy love's faithful vow for mine.
170   JULIET   I gave thee mine before thou didst request it,
And yet I would it were° to give again.   *were available*
ROMEO   Wouldst thou withdraw it? For what
    purpose, love?
JULIET   But to be frank° and give it thee again;   *generous; honest*
And yet I wish but for the thing I have.
175   My bounty is as boundless as the sea,
My love as deep; the more I give to thee,
The more I have, for both are infinite.
    [NURSE *calls within.*]
I hear some noise within! Dear love, adieu.
—Anon,° good Nurse! —Sweet Montague, be true.   *One moment*
180   Stay but a little. I will come again.   [*Exit* JULIET.]
ROMEO   O blessèd, blessèd night! I am afeared,
Being in night, all this is but a dream,
Too flattering-sweet to be substantial.
    [*Enter* JULIET *above.*]
JULIET   Three words, dear Romeo, and good night indeed.
185   If that thy bent of love be honorable,
Thy purpose marriage, send me word tomorrow,
By one that I'll procure to come to thee,
Where and what time thou wilt perform the rite,
And all my fortunes at thy foot I'll lay,
190   And follow thee, my lord, throughout the world.
NURSE [*within*]   Madam!
JULIET   I come; anon! —But if thou meanest not well,
I do beseech thee—
NURSE [*within*]   Madam!
JULIET   By and by! I come!
—To cease thy strife,° and leave me to my grief.   *striving*
Tomorrow will I send.
195   ROMEO   So thrive my soul.[5]
JULIET   A thousand times good night.   [*Exit.*]
ROMEO   A thousand times the worse to want° thy light.   *lack*

5. On peril of damnation.

Love goes toward love as schoolboys from their books,
But love from love toward school with heavy looks.

Enter JULIET *again.*

200 JULIET Hist,° Romeo, hist!—Oh, for a falconer's   *(falconer's call)*
           voice
        To lure this tercel-gentle[6] back again.
        Bondage[7] is hoarse and may not speak aloud,
        Else would I tear° the cave where Echo[8] lies   *split with cries*
        And make her airy tongue more hoarse than mine
205   With repetition of my "Romeo."
     ROMEO It is my soul that calls upon my name.
        How silver-sweet sound lovers' tongues by night,
        Like softest music to attending ears.
     JULIET Romeo!
     ROMEO   Mine eyas?°   *young hawk*
     JULIET   What o'clock tomorrow
        Shall I send to thee?
210 ROMEO   By the hour of nine.
     JULIET I will not fail. 'Tis twenty year till then.
        I have forgot why I did call thee back.
     ROMEO Let me stand here till thou remember it.
     JULIET I shall forget to have thee still° stand there,   *always*
215   Rememb'ring how I love thy company.
     ROMEO And I'll still stay to have thee still forget,
        Forgetting any other home but this.
     JULIET 'Tis almost morning. I would have thee gone,
        And yet no farther than a wanton's° bird,   *spoiled child's*
220   That lets it hop a little from his hand,
        Like a poor prisoner in his twisted gyves,°   *fetters*
        And with a silken thread plucks it back again,
        So loving-jealous of his liberty.
     ROMEO I would° I were thy bird.   *wish*
     JULIET   Sweet, so would I—
225   Yet I should kill thee with much cherishing.
        Good night, good night. Parting is such sweet sorrow
        That I shall say "good night" till it be morrow.
     ROMEO Sleep dwell upon thine eyes, peace in thy breast;
        Would I were sleep and peace, so sweet to rest.
                              [*Exit* JULIET.]

6. A male peregrine falcon. Literally, a noble ("gentle") hawk.
7. Confinement within her family's home; duty owed her family.
8. In classical legend, a woman who, scorned by Narcissus, wasted away with grief until
   only a voice remained to haunt empty caves.

230 Hence will I to my ghostly° friar's close° cell   *spiritual / small; private*
     His help to crave and my dear hap° to tell.   *fortune*

                              Exit.

                              2.2

     Enter FRIAR LAURENCE *alone, with a basket.*
     FRIAR LAURENCE   The gray°-eyed morn smiles on the   *pale blue*
         frowning night,
     Check'ring the eastern clouds with streaks of light,
     And fleckled° darkness like a drunkard reels   *dappled*
     From forth° day's path and Titan's¹ burning wheels.   *Out of*
5   Now ere the sun advance° his burning eye   *brings up*
     The day to cheer and night's dank dew to dry,
     I must upfill this osier cage° of ours   *willow basket*
     With baleful weeds and precious-juicèd flowers.
     The earth that's nature's mother is her tomb;
10   What is her burying grave, that is her womb,
     And from her womb children of divers° kind   *several; varied*
     We sucking on her natural bosom find:
     Many for many virtues° excellent,   *healthful properties*
     None but for some,² and yet all different.
15   Oh, mickle° is the powerful grace³ that lies   *great*
     In plants, herbs, stones, and their true qualities;
     For naught° so vile that on the earth doth live   *nothing is*
     But to the earth some special good doth give;
     Nor aught so good but, strained° from that fair use,   *twisted*
20   Revolts from true birth, stumbling on abuse.⁴
     Virtue itself turns vice, being misapplied,
     And vice sometime by action dignified.
         Enter ROMEO.
     Within the infant rind of this weak flower
     Poison hath residence and medicine power:
25   For this, being smelled, with that part° cheers   *act*
         each part;°   *bodily member*
     Being tasted, stays all senses with the heart.⁵

2.2 Location: A street in Verona.
1. In Q2, these four lines (2.2.1–4) appear twice, once spoken by Romeo at the end of the
   previous scene and again by Friar Laurence here, a textual redundancy that requires
   editorial intervention. *Titan:* Helios, a classical sun god, was descended from the
   Titans. He traveled across the sky in a chariot.
2. None that is not excellent for some use.
3. *powerful grace:* divine beneficence.
4. Turns from its intended benefits if it happens to be misused.
5. *stays . . . heart:* paralyzes the heart, along with all the senses.

Two such opposèd kings encamp them still°   *always*
.In man as well as herbs—grace and rude will—
And, where the worser is predominant,
30   Full soon the canker° death eats up that plant.   *grub; cancer*
ROMEO   Good morrow, Father.
FRIAR LAURENCE   Benedicite.°   *God bless you (Latin)*
What early tongue so sweet saluteth me?
Young son, it argues a distempered° head   *disturbed*
So soon to bid good morrow to thy bed.
35   Care keeps his watch in every old man's eye,
And, where care lodges, sleep will never lie;
But where unbruisèd° youth with unstuffed°   *fresh / unanxious*
      brain
Doth couch his limbs, there golden sleep doth reign.
Therefore thy earliness doth me assure
40   Thou art uproused with some distemp'rature—
Or, if not so, then here I hit it right:
Our Romeo hath not been in bed tonight.
ROMEO   That last is true; the sweeter rest was mine.
FRIAR LAURENCE   God pardon sin! Wast thou with Rosaline?
45 ROMEO   With Rosaline, my ghostly Father? No,
I have forgot that name and that name's woe.
FRIAR LAURENCE   That's my good son. But where hast
      thou been, then?
ROMEO   I'll tell thee ere thou ask it me again.
I have been feasting with mine enemy,
50   Where on a sudden one hath wounded me
That's by me wounded; both our remedies
Within thy help and holy physic° lies.   *medicine*
I bear no hatred, blessèd man, for, lo,
My intercession° likewise steads° my foe.   *request / benefits*
55 FRIAR LAURENCE   Be plain, good son, and homely°   *direct*
      in thy drift;
Riddling confession finds but riddling shrift.°   *absolution*
ROMEO   Then plainly know my heart's dear love is set
On the fair daughter of rich Capulet.
As mine on hers, so hers is set on mine,
60   And all combined, save what thou must combine
By holy marriage. When, and where, and how
We met, we wooed, and made exchange of vow,
I'll tell thee as we pass; but this I pray,
That thou consent to marry us today.
65 FRIAR LAURENCE   Holy Saint Francis, what a change is here!
Is Rosaline, that thou didst love so dear,

So soon forsaken? Young men's love, then, lies
Not truly in their hearts but in their eyes.
Jesu Maria, what a deal of brine
70   Hath washed thy sallow° cheeks for Rosaline!   *yellowed*
How much salt water thrown away in waste
To season° love that of it doth not taste!   *preserve; flavor*
The sun not yet thy sighs[6] from heaven clears,
Thy old° groans yet ringing in mine ancient ears;   *former*
75   Lo, here upon thy cheek the stain doth sit
Of an old tear that is not washed off yet.
If ere thou wast thyself and these woes thine,
Thou and these woes were all for Rosaline—
And art thou changed? Pronounce this
       sentence,° then: *maxim; verdict*
80   Women may fall when there's no strength in men.
ROMEO   Thou chid'st me oft for loving Rosaline—
FRIAR LAURENCE   For doting, not for loving, pupil mine.
ROMEO   And bad'st me bury love.
FRIAR LAURENCE   Not in a grave
To lay one in, another out to have.
85   ROMEO   I pray thee, chide me not. Her I love now
Doth grace for grace and love for love allow;
The other did not so.
FRIAR LAURENCE   Oh, she knew well
Thy love did read by rote, that could not spell.[7]
But come, young waverer, come, go with me.
90   In one respect I'll thy assistant be,
For this alliance may so happy prove
To turn your households' rancor to pure love.
ROMEO   Oh, let us hence; I stand° on sudden haste.   *depend; insist*
FRIAR LAURENCE   Wisely and slow; they stumble that
       run fast.   *Exeunt.*

                         2.3

              Enter BENVOLIO *and* MERCUTIO.
MERCUTIO   Where the devil should this Romeo
       be? Came he not home tonight?°   *last night*
BENVOLIO   Not to his father's; I spoke with his man.

6. The mist Romeo's exhalations produced.
7. *did read . . . spell*: did recite the memorized phrases of love poetry, without understanding or meaning them.
2.3 Location: Scene continues.

MERCUTIO   Why, that same pale,° hard-hearted   *fair-skinned; frigid*
wench, that Rosaline,
5   Torments him so that he will sure run mad.
BENVOLIO   Tybalt, the kinsman to old Capulet,
Hath sent a letter to his father's house.
MERCUTIO   A challenge, on my life.
BENVOLIO   Romeo will answer° it.   *accept*
10 MERCUTIO   Any man that can write may
answer a letter.
BENVOLIO   Nay, he will answer the letter's
master how he dares, being dared.
MERCUTIO   Alas, poor Romeo, he is already
15   dead—stabbed with a white wench's black
eye, run through the ear with a love song, the
very pin[1] of his heart cleft with the blind bow-
boy's butt-shaft[2]—and is he a man to encounter Tybalt?
20 BENVOLIO   Why, what is Tybalt?
MERCUTIO   More than Prince of Cats.[3] Oh, he's
the courageous captain of compliments!°   *formalities of dueling*
fights as you sing prick-song;[4] keeps time, dis-
tance,[5] and proportion;° he rests his minim   *harmony; form*
25   rests,[6] one, two—and the third in your bosom;
the very butcher of a silk button;[7] a duelist, a
duelist; a gentleman of the very first house, of
the first and second cause[8]—ah, the immortal *passata*, the *punta riversa*, the *hai*![9]
30 BENVOLIO   The what?
MERCUTIO   The pox of° such antic,° lisping,   *on / grotesque*
affecting° fantasies,° these new tuners of   *affected / bizarrely*
                                                mannered men

---

1. Peg in the center of an archery target.
2. Blunt practice arrow, fit for children and hence for Cupid.
3. Called Tybalt or Tibert in medieval stories of Reynard the fox. "Catso," from the Italian
   word for "penis," was also slang for a rogue.
4. Sung from sheet music and thus more precise and invariable than extempore or remembered music.
5. Musical intervals between notes; also, a set space to be kept between combatants.
6. Short musical rests, referring to the brief strategic pauses in a duel.
7. Alluding to the boast of an Italian fencing master in London that he could "hit any
   Englishman with a thrust upon any button."
8. *gentleman . . . cause*: superior practitioner of taking up quarrels as duels. *first house*: the
   best fencing school. *cause*: a reason that according to the etiquette of fencing would
   require an honorable gentleman to seek a duel.
9. Italian fencing terms for, respectively, a lunging sword thrust, backhanded thrust, and
   thrust that reaches through.

accent.[1] "By Jesu, a very good blade, a very
tall° man, a very good whore!" Why,° is not   *valiant / Why, now*
35 this a lamentable thing, grandsire, that we
should be thus afflicted with these strange[2]
flies, these fashionmongers, these
"pardon-me's,"[3] who stand so much on the
new form that they cannot sit at ease on the
40 old bench?[4] Oh, their bones, their bones![5]
   Enter ROMEO.
BENVOLIO   Here comes Romeo! Here comes
Romeo!
MERCUTIO   Without his roe, like a dried herring.[6] O flesh, flesh, how art thou fishified![7]
45 Now is he for the numbers° that Petrarch[8]   *verses*
flowed in; Laura to° his lady was a kitchen   *compared to*
wench—marry, she had a better love to ber-
hyme her—Dido[9] a dowdy, Cleopatra a
gypsy,[1] Helen and Hero[2] hildings° and har-   *hussies*
50 lots, Thisbe[3] a gray-eye° or so. But not to   *blue-eyed*
the purpose.° Signor Romeo, *bonjour*: there's   *of consequence*
a French salutation to your French slop.°   *loose breaches*
You gave us the counterfeit fairly last night.
ROMEO   Good morrow to you both. What
55 counterfeit did I give you?
MERCUTIO   The slip,[4] sir, the slip—can you
not conceive?°   *understand*

---

1. These faddishly novel speakers, such as those importing foreign phrases. A typical
   Renaissance English satire, here seemingly unaffected by the fact that Italian is the
   native tongue of Verona.
2. Newfangled; foreign.
3. *pardon-me's*: the fastidiously mannered, affecting the French *pardonnez-moi*.
4. *who . . . bench*: as if both Mercutio and Benvolio were elderly ("grandsire"), viewing the
   decline of the young. *stand*: insist. *form*: etiquette; fashion; bench.
5. *Oh . . . bones*: Aching on the austere furniture of their predecessors; infected with the
   "bone disease," syphilis.
6. Emaciated, since the roe is removed in curing. This leaves Romeo's name a mournful
   wail, "Me, O." He is also missing his roe deer (female, named Rosaline).
7. Gone pale and limp, turned into a herring. Fish, thought weak and relatively unnour-
   ishing, was the substitute for "flesh" (meat) during fasts.
8. Petrarch's sonnets addressed to Laura were the model for an English love-sonnet craze.
9. The beautiful queen of Carthage who fell in love with Aeneas but was deserted by him
   in Virgil's *Aeneid*.
1. A term of abuse. Gypsies were supposed to have come from Egypt, where Cleopatra was
   queen and lover of Julius Caesar and Mark Antony.
2. Helen's abduction by Paris initiated the Trojan War. Hero was Leander's lover in a tragic
   legend.
3. Beloved of Pyramus in a classical legend that parallels *Romeo and Juliet*. The young lovers, coming from hostile families, die as a result of a missed meeting and misinter-
   preted evidence.
4. Counterfeit coin. To "give the slip" is to steal off.

ROMEO Pardon, good Mercutio. My business
was great, and in such a case as mine, a man
60 may strain° courtesy.   *nearly abandon*

MERCUTIO That's as much as to say such a
case as yours constrains a man to bow in the
hams.[5]

ROMEO Meaning to curtsy?[6]

65 MERCUTIO Thou hast most kindly hit[7] it.

ROMEO A most courteous exposition.

MERCUTIO Nay, I am the very pink° of courtesy.   *nonpareil; carnation*

ROMEO Pink for flower?°   *dianthus; vulva*

MERCUTIO Right.

70 ROMEO Why, then, is my pump° well flowered.[8] *shoe; penis*

MERCUTIO Sure wit! Follow me° this jest now   *Chase; respond to*
till thou hast worn out thy pump, that when
the single° sole of it is worn, the jest may   *thin*
remain after the wearing, solely singular.°   *utterly unique*

75 ROMEO Oh, single-soled° jest, solely° singular *shoddy / only*
for the singleness!°   *foolishness*

MERCUTIO Come between us, good Benvolio;
my wits faints.[9]

ROMEO Switch and spurs,[1] switch and spurs,
80 or I'll cry a match!°   *claim a victory*

MERCUTIO Nay, if our wits run the wild goose
chase,[2] I am done; for thou hast more of the
wild goose° in one of thy wits than I am sure   *folly*
I have in my whole five.° Was I with° you   *(five senses) / even*
85 there for the goose?[3]   *with*

ROMEO Thou wast never with me for anything
when thou wast not there for the goose.

MERCUTIO I will bite thee by the ear[4] for that
jest.

90 ROMEO Nay, good goose, bite not![5]

MERCUTIO Thy wit is very bitter sweeting;°   *apple*
it is a most sharp sauce.°   *mockery*

---

5. Playing on "business" as "sexual intercourse" and "case" as "vagina." Mercutio suggests
   that Romeo is sexually exhausted and cannot stand up straight.
6. Pronounced the same as "courtesy."
7. Most truly guessed it; most truly sexually penetrated it.
8. Pinked, or decoratively perforated.
9. Treating the exchange of wit as a duel.
1. Flog your wits to a full gallop; continue.
2. A cross-country horse race in which the leader chose the course and the rest had to
   follow.
3. Silliness; whore's company.
4. Usually suggesting affectionate nibbling.
5. A proverbial cry for mercy, here used ironically.

Mercutio attempting to make Romeo more masculine

ROMEO   And is it not, then, well served in to a
sweet goose?

95   MERCUTIO   Oh, here's a wit of cheverel° that   *kid leather*
stretches from an inch narrow to an ell
broad!⁶

ROMEO   I stretch it out for that word "broad,"
which, added to the goose, proves thee far
100   and wide a broad goose.⁷

MERCUTIO   Why, is not this better now than
groaning for love? Now art thou sociable; now
art thou Romeo; now art thou what thou art
by art° as well as by nature, for this driveling   *learning*
105   love is like a great natural° that runs lolling up   *idiot*
and down to hide his bauble⁸ in a hole.

BENVOLIO   Stop there! Stop there!

MERCUTIO   Thou desirest me to stop in⁹ my
tale against the hair. ¹

110   BENVOLIO   Thou wouldst else have made thy
tale° large.   *story; penis ("tail")*

MERCUTIO   Oh, thou art deceived! I would
have made it short, for I was come to the
whole depth of my tale, and meant indeed to
115   occupy the argument° no longer.   *topic*

Enter NURSE *and her man*[, PETER].

ROMEO   Here's goodly gear!² A sail! A sail!³

MERCUTIO   Two, two: a shirt° and a smock.°   *man / woman*

NURSE   Peter.

PETER   Anon.°   *At your service*

120   NURSE   My fan, Peter.

MERCUTIO   Good Peter, to hide her face, for
her fan's the fairer face.

NURSE   God ye° good morrow,° gentlemen.   *give you / morning*

MERCUTIO   God ye good e'en,° fair gentlewoman.   *afternoon*

125   NURSE   Is it good e'en?

MERCUTIO   'Tis no less, I tell ye, for the bawdy
hand of the dial is now upon the prick° of   *mark; penis*
noon.

---

6. That spreads itself very thin (an ell was 45 inches).
7. A gross idiot; a licentious fellow; a goose fattened for the table.
8. *that . . . bauble:* who runs to cover up a jester's wand, grotesquely carved at one end;
"bauble" also suggests penis.
9. Cease; stuff in.
1. Against the grain; against the pubic hair.
2. Spoken ironically of Mercutio's witticisms or the Nurse's voluminous appearance.
3. A sailor's cry upon sighting another ship.

NURSE   Out upon you!⁴ What° a man are you?   *What sort of*
130 ROMEO   One, gentlewoman, that God hath
      made himself to mar.⁵
      NURSE   By my troth, it is well said. "For him-
      self to mar." quoth 'a?°—Gentlemen, can any   *he*
      of you tell me where I may find the young
135 Romeo?
      ROMEO   I can tell you, but young Romeo will
      be older when you have found him than he
      was when you sought him. I am the youngest
      of that name, for fault° of a worse.   *lack*
140 NURSE   You say well.
      MERCUTIO   Yea, is the worst well? Very well
      took, i'faith; wisely, wisely.
      NURSE [*to* ROMEO]   If you be he, sir, I desire
      some confidence with you.
145 BENVOLIO   She will indite⁶ him to some supper.
      MERCUTIO   A bawd, a bawd, a bawd! So, ho!⁷
      ROMEO   What hast thou found?°   *spotted; figured out*
      MERCUTIO   No hare,° sir, unless a hare, sir, in   *prostitute*
      a lenten pie⁸ that is something stale and
150 hoar ere it be spent.⁹
          [*He walks by them and sings.*]
          An old hare hoar,
          And an old hare hoar
          Is very good meat in Lent;
          But a hare that is hoar
155   Is too much for a score¹
          When it hoars° ere it be spent.   *turns moldy; whores*
      Romeo, will you come to your father's? We'll
      to dinner thither.
      ROMEO   I will follow you.
160 MERCUTIO   Farewell, ancient lady, farewell.
          [*Sings.*]   Lady, lady, lady!²
                  Exeunt [MERCUTIO *and* BENVOLIO].

4. An expression of indignation.
5. *One . . . mar*: combines two proverbial expressions. "It is his to make or mar" suggests
   that Mercutio has the free will to determine his own character. "He is a man of God's
   making" places the blame for Mercutio's character on God.
6. Deliberately substituted for "invite," to mock the Nurse's erroneous use of "confidence"
   for "conference" in the line above.
7. The cry of a hunter who has spotted his quarry.
8. Meat illicitly eaten during Lent by disguising it in a pie, just as the Nurse's unattrac-
   tiveness hides whatever promiscuity she may practice.
9. Somewhat stale and moldy by the time the last of the rationed luxury is consumed.
1. Is too much to pay for.
2. Refrain to a ballad about a perfectly chaste woman, intended derisively.

NURSE I pray you, sir, what saucy merchant°   *commoner*
was this that was so full of his ropery?°   *knavery*
ROMEO A gentleman, Nurse, that loves to
165   hear himself talk, and will speak more in a
minute than he will stand to° in a month.   *perform*
NURSE An 'a° speak anything against me, I'll   *If he*
take him down° an 'a were lustier[3] than he   *humble him*
is, and twenty such jacks;° and, if I cannot,   *scoundrels*
170   I'll find those that shall. Scurvy knave! I am
none of his flirt-gills;° I am none of his skains   *loose women*
mates.[4] [She *turns to* PETER, *her man.*] And
thou must stand by, too, and suffer every
knave to use me at his pleasure!
175 PETER I saw no man use you at his pleasure;
if I had, my weapon should quickly have been
out. I warrant you, I dare draw as soon as
another man if I see occasion in a good quarrel, and the law on my side.
180 NURSE Now, afore God, I am so vexed that
every part about me quivers. Scurvy knave!
[*to* ROMEO] Pray you, sir, a word; and, as I
told you, my young lady bid me inquire you
out. What she bid me say I will keep to
185   myself; but first let me tell ye, if ye should
lead her in a fool's paradise, as they say, it
were a very gross° kind of behavior, as they   *outrageous*
say, for the gentlewoman is young, and there-
fore if you should deal double° with her, truly   *falsely, forcefully*
190   it were an ill thing to be offered to any gentlewoman, and very weak° dealing.   *poor*
ROMEO Nurse, commend me to thy lady and
mistress. I protest° unto thee—   *swear*
NURSE Good heart—and i'faith I will tell her
195   as much. Lord, Lord, she will be a joyful
woman!
ROMEO What wilt thou tell her, Nurse? Thou
dost not mark° me.   *pay attention to*
NURSE I will tell her, sir, that you do protest[5]—
200   which, as I take it, is a gentlemanlike offer.

3. Stronger; hornier.
4. Knife-wielding rogues.
5. The Nurse takes this as a marriage offer, probably confusing "protest" with "propose."

ROMEO   Bid her devise some means to come to shrift
   this afternoon,
  And there she shall, at Friar Laurence' cell,
  Be shrived[6] and married, [*He offers money.*] Here is
   for thy pains.
NURSE   No, truly, sir, not a penny.
205 ROMEO   Go to—I say you shall.
NURSE   This afternoon, sir? Well, she shall be there.
ROMEO   And stay, good Nurse, behind the abbey wall.
  Within this hour my man shall be with thee
  And bring thee cords made like a tackled stair,°   *a knotted ladder*
210   Which to the high topgallant[7] of my joy
  Must be my convoy° in the secret night.   *means of conveyance*
  Farewell. Be trusty, and I'll quit° thy pains.   *repay*
  Farewell. Commend me to thy mistress.
NURSE   Now God in heaven bless thee! Hark you, sir.
215 ROMEO   What say'st thou, my dear Nurse?
NURSE   Is your man secret?° Did you ne'er hear say,   *discreet*
  "Two may keep counsel, putting one away"?
ROMEO   Warrant thee, my man's as true as steel.
NURSE   Well, sir, my mistress is the sweetest
220   lady. Lord, Lord, when 'twas a little prating
  thing— Oh, there is a nobleman in town,
  one Paris, that would fain lay knife aboard;[8]
  but she, good soul, had as lief° see a toad, a   *gladly*
  very toad, as see him. I anger her sometimes,
225   and tell her that Paris is the properer° man;   *more handsome*
  but, I'll warrant you, when I say so she looks
  as pale as any clout° in the versal° world.   *sheet / entire*
  Doth not "rosemary"[9] and "Romeo" begin
  both with a° letter?   *the same*
230 ROMEO   Ay, Nurse. What of that? Both with
  an "R."
NURSE   Ah, mocker, that's the dog's name![1]
  "R" is for the—no, I know it begins with
  some other letter; and she hath the prettiest
235   sententious[2] of it—of you and rosemary—
  that it would do you good to hear it.

6. Absolved after confession.
7. The highest platform on a mast, from which the topgallant sail was handled.
8. One claimed a place at dinner by laying one's personal knife on the table ("board").
9. A token of remembrance, between lovers and also of the dead.
1. "R"—the sound "arr"—was thought to resemble a dog's snarl.
2. Blunder for "sentences"; sayings.

ROMEO   Commend me to thy lady.
NURSE   Ay, a thousand times. Peter!
PETER   Anon!
240   NURSE   Before,° and apace.°   *Exeunt.*   *Lead / quickly*

2.4

Enter JULIET.

JULIET   The clock struck nine when I did send the Nurse;
     In half an hour she promised to return.
     Perchance she cannot meet him— That's not so.
     Oh, she is lame! Love's heralds should be thoughts
5   Which ten times faster glides than the sun's beams,
     Driving back shadows over louring° hills.   *dark; threatening*
     Therefore do nimble-pinioned° doves draw Love;°   *winged / Venus*
     And therefore hath the wind-swift Cupid wings.
     Now is the sun upon the highmost hill°   *zenith*
10   Of this day's journey, and from nine till twelve
     Is three long hours, yet she is not come.
     Had she affections° and warm youthful blood,   *passions*
     She would be as swift in motion as a ball;
     My words would bandy° her to my sweet love,   *volley (as in tennis)*
15   And his to me.
     But old folks: many feign° as they were dead,   *act*
     Unwieldy, slow, heavy, and pale as lead.
         Enter NURSE [*and* PETER].
     O God, she comes! O honey Nurse, what news?
     Hast thou met with him? Send thy man away.
20   NURSE   Peter, stay° at the gate.   [*Exit* PETER.]   *wait*
JULIET   Now, good sweet Nurse—O Lord, why lookest
     thou sad?
     Though news be sad, yet tell them merrily;
     If good, thou shamest the music of sweet news
     By playing it to me with so sour a face.
25   NURSE   I am a-weary; give me leave° a while   *let me alone*
     Fie, how my bones ache! What a jaunce° have I!   *trotting about*
JULIET   I would thou hadst my bones and I thy news.
     Nay, come; I pray thee, speak. Good, good Nurse, speak.
NURSE   Jesu, what haste! Can you not stay a while?
30   Do you not see that I am out of breath?

2.4 Location: Capulet's orchard.

JULIET   How art thou out of breath when thou hast breath
    To say to me that thou art out of breath?
    The excuse that thou dost make in this delay
    Is longer than the tale thou dost excuse!
35   Is thy news good or bad? Answer to that—
    Say either, and I'll stay° the circumstance.°   *wait for / full details*
    Let me be satisfied: is't good or bad?
NURSE   Well, you have made a simple° choice.   *foolish*
    You know not how to choose a man. Romeo?
40   No, not he. Though his face be better than
    any man's, yet his leg excels all men's; and
    for a hand, and a foot, and a body, though
    they be not to be talked on,° yet they are past   *worth mentioning*
    compare. He is not the flower of courtesy,
45   but I'll warrant him as gentle as a lamb. Go
    thy ways[1] wench; serve God. What, have you
    dined at home?
JULIET   No, no. But all this did I know before.
    What says he of our marriage? What of that?
50 NURSE   Lord, how my head aches! What a head have I!
    It beats as it would fall in twenty pieces.
    My back!—O t' other side—ah, my back, my back![2]
    Beshrew° your heart for sending me about   *Curse (mild oath)*
    To catch my death with jauncing up and down.
55 JULIET   I'faith, I am sorry that thou art not well.
    Sweet, sweet, sweet Nurse, tell me: what says my love?
NURSE   Your love says, like an honest gentleman,
    And a courteous, and a kind, and a handsome,
    And I warrant a virtuous— Where is your mother?
60 JULIET   Where is my mother? Why, she is within.
    Where should she be? How oddly thou repliest:
    "Your love says, like an honest° gentleman,   *honorable*
    'Where is your mother?'"
NURSE   O God's Lady,° dear,   *Mary, Mother of God*
    Are you so hot?° Marry, come up, I trow![3]   *impatient; aroused*
65   Is this the poultice for my aching bones?
    Henceforward do your messages yourself.
JULIET   Here's such a coil!° Come, what says Romeo?   *to-do*
NURSE   Have you got leave to go to shrift today?
JULIET   I have.

---

1. Off you go; do as you will do.
2. Perhaps the Nurse is giving Juliet directions to rub her back.
3. *Marry . . . trow*: an expression of indignant or amused surprise and reproof.

70 NURSE   Then hie° you hence to Friar Laurence' cell;   *hurry*
There stays a husband to make you a wife.
Now comes the wanton° blood up in your cheeks;   *fickle; lustful*
They'll be in scarlet straight° at any news.   *immediately*
Hie you to church. I must another way
75 To fetch a ladder by the which your love
Must climb a bird's nest soon when it is dark.
I am the drudge and toil in your delight,
But you shall bear the burden⁴ soon at night.
Go! I'll to dinner; hie you to the cell.
80 JULIET   Hie to high fortune! Honest Nurse, farewell.

Exeunt.

2.5

Enter FRIAR [LAURENCE] *and* ROMEO.
FRIAR LAURENCE   So smile the heavens upon this holy act
That after-hours with sorrow chide us not.
ROMEO   Amen, amen. But come what sorrow can,
It cannot countervail the exchange of joy
5 That one short minute gives me in her sight.
Do thou but close° our hands with holy words,   *join*
Then love-devouring death do what he dare—
It is enough I may but call her mine.
FRIAR LAURENCE   These violent° delights have   *sudden; intense*
violent ends
10 And in their triumph die, like fire and powder¹
Which, as they kiss, consume. The sweetest honey
Is loathsome in his own deliciousness,
And in the taste confounds the appetite.²
Therefore love moderately: long love doth so;
15 Too swift arrives as tardy as too slow.
Enter JULIET.
Here comes the lady. Oh, so light³ a foot
Will ne'er wear out the everlasting flint;⁴

---

4. Do the work; carry a lover; sing the theme of a duet, alluding to the sounds of
lovemaking.
2.5 Location: Friar Laurence's cell.
1. Gunpowder. *triumph*: victory; celebration.
2. *The sweetest . . . appetite*: from the proverb "Too much honey cloys the stomach."
his: its. *confounds*: overwhelms.
3. Swift; dainty: free of care; sexually open.
4. Will never endure or subdue the hard road of life.

A lover may bestride the gossamers°   *spiders' threads*
That idles in the wanton° summer air   *playful*
20   And yet not fall, so light is vanity.[5]
JULIET   Good even° to my ghostly° confessor.   *evening / spiritual*
FRIAR LAURENCE   Romeo shall thank thee, daughter,
      for us both.
            [ROMEO *kisses her.*]
JULIET   As much to him,[6] else is his thanks too much.
            [JULIET *returns his kiss.*]
ROMEO   Ah, Juliet, if the measure° of thy joy   *measuring vessel*
25   Be heaped like mine, and that thy skill be more
To blazon° it, then sweeten with thy breath°   *describe; trumpet / speech*
This neighbor air, and let rich music tongue
Unfold the imagined° happiness that both   *unexpressed ideas of*
Receive in either by this dear encounter.
30   JULIET   Conceit,° more rich in matter than in words,   *Imagination*
Brags of his substance,[7] not of ornament.°   *rhetoric; form*
They are but beggars that can count their worth,
But my true love is grown to such excess,
I cannot sum up sum of half my wealth.[8]
35   FRIAR LAURENCE   Come; come with me, and we will
      make short work.
For, by your leaves, you shall not stay alone
Till holy church incorporate two in one.[9]
                        [*Exeunt.*]

Knock off the crap talk. Give me something real.

Comedy to tragedy

3.1

Enter MERCUTIO, BENVOLIO, [*Mercutio's Page,*] *and*
[*Montague's*] *Men.*
BENVOLIO   I pray thee, good Mercutio, let's retire.
The day is hot, the Capels abroad,°   *about*
And if we meet we shall not scape a brawl—
For now, these hot days, is the mad blood stirring.

5. Temporary worldly pleasure.
6. An equal amount.
7. Wealth; content.
8. I . . . *wealth*: The amount is too large to be understood precisely.
9. Literally, put two into one body. Marriage mystically united man and woman in "one flesh" (Genesis 2:2).
3.1 Location: A street in Verona.

5 MERCUTIO   Thou art like one of these fellows
that, when he enters the confines of a tavern,
claps me° his sword upon the table and says,   *claps me = claps*
"God send me no need of thee"—and, by the
operation° of the second cup, draws him on   *effect*
10 the drawer[1] when indeed there is no need.

BENVOLIO   Am I like such a fellow?

MERCUTIO   Come, come, thou art as hot a jack°   *rogue*
in thy mood as any in Italy, and as soon
moved° to be moody,° and as soon moody to   *provoked / angry*
15 be° moved.   *at being*

BENVOLIO   And what to?

MERCUTIO   Nay, an there were two such, we
should have none shortly, for one would kill
the other. Thou—why, thou wilt quarrel
20 with a man that hath a hair more or a hair
less in his beard than thou hast. Thou wilt
quarrel with a man for cracking nuts, having
no other reason but because thou hast hazel
eyes. What eye but such an eye would spy
25 out such a quarrel? Thy head is as full of
quarrels as an egg is full of meat,° and yet   *foodstuff*
thy head hath been beaten as addle° as an   *rotten; confused*
egg for quarreling. Thou hast quarreled with
a man for coughing in the street, because he
30 hath wakened thy dog that hath lain asleep
in the sun. Didst thou not fall out with a tailor for wearing his new doublet before Easter?[2] With another for tying his new shoes
with old ribbon? And yet thou wilt tutor me
35 from quarreling!

BENVOLIO   An I were so apt to quarrel as thou
art, any man should buy the fee-simple[3] of
my life for an hour and a quarter.

MERCUTIO   The fee-simple? Oh, simple!°   *foolish*
Enter TYBALT, PETRUCCIO, *and others*
[*of Capulet's Men*].

40 BENVOLIO   By my head, here comes the Capulets.

MERCUTIO   By my heel, I care not.

---

1. Draws his sword on the server.
2. New fashions came out at Easter, after the austere penitence of Lent.
3. Outright possession of land, usually an inherited right; here, the whole value of Benvolio's life.

TYBALT [*to* PETRUCCIO *and Capulets*]   Follow me close,
for I will speak to them.
[*to the Montagues*]   Gentlemen, good e'en. A word
with one of you.

MERCUTIO   And but one word with one of us?
45   Couple it with something; make it a word *word*
and a blow.

TYBALT   You shall find me apt enough to that,
sir, an you will give me occasion.

MERCUTIO   Could you not take some occasion
50   without giving?

TYBALT   Mercutio, thou consortest° with Romeo.   associate

MERCUTIO   "Consort"?° What, dost thou make   Play in a band
us minstrels? An thou make minstrels of us,
look to hear nothing but discords. Here's my
55   fiddlestick;° here's that shall make you dance.   (rapier)
Zounds!° "Consort"!   By God's wounds

BENVOLIO   We talk here in the public haunt° of   gathering place
men.
Either withdraw unto some private place,
Or reason coldly° of your grievances,   dispassionately
60   Or else depart.° Here all eyes gaze on us.   separate

MERCUTIO   Men's eyes were made to look, and
let them gaze. I will not budge for no man's
pleasure, I.

Enter ROMEO.

TYBALT   Well, peace be with you, sir; here comes my man.
65   MERCUTIO   But I'll be hanged, sir, if he wear your livery,[4]
Marry, go before to field, he'll be your follower;°   servant; pursuer
Your worship in that sense may call him "man."

TYBALT   Romeo, the love I bear thee can afford
No better term than this: thou art a villain.°   base commoner; rogue
70   ROMEO   Tybalt, the reason that I have to love thee
Doth much excuse the appertaining rage
To[5] such a greeting. Villain am I none.
Therefore, farewell. I see thou knowest me not.

TYBALT   Boy, this shall not excuse the injuries
75   That thou hast done me; therefore turn and draw.

ROMEO   I do protest I never injuried thee,
But love thee better than thou canst devise

4. Mercutio obnoxiously mistakes Tybalt's "my man" for "personal servant."
5. *Doth . . . To:* Permits me to put aside my otherwise appropriate anger at.

Till thou shalt know the reason of my love.
And so, good Capulet—which name I tender°   *regard; love*
80   As dearly as mine own—be satisfied.

MERCUTIO   Oh, calm, dishonorable, vile submission!
Alla stoccata carries it away![6]
[*He draws.*]
Tybalt, you ratcatcher, will you walk?°   *withdraw to fight*

TYBALT   What wouldst thou have with me?

85   MERCUTIO   Good King of Cats, nothing but
one of your nine lives. That I mean to make
bold withal° and, as you shall use me hereaf-   *be so bold as to take*
ter,[7] dry-beat° the rest of the eight. Will you   *soundly thrash*
pluck your sword out of his pilcher° by the   *leather scabbard*
90   ears? Make haste, lest mine be about your
ears ere it be out.

TYBALT [*drawing*]   I am for you.
[*They fight.*]

ROMEO   Gentle Mercutio, put thy rapier up!

MERCUTIO [*to* TYBALT]   Come, sir, your *passata*!°   *forward thrust*

95   ROMEO   Draw, Benvolio! Beat down their weapons.
Gentlemen, for shame, forbear this outrage.°   *criminal violence*
Tybalt! Mercutio! The Prince expressly hath
Forbid this bandying° in Verona streets.   *strife*
Hold, Tybalt! Good Mercutio—
[TYBALT *under Romeo's arm thrusts* MERCUTIO *in.*]

100   PETRUCCIO   Away, Tybalt!
[*Exeunt* TYBALT, PETRUCCIO,
and Capulet's Men.]

MERCUTIO   I am hurt.
A plague o'both houses! I am sped.°   *finished*
Is he gone and hath nothing?

BENVOLIO   What, art thou hurt?

MERCUTIO   Ay, ay, a scratch, a scratch. Marry, 'tis enough.
Where is my page? —Go, villain, fetch a surgeon.
[*Exit Page.*]

105   ROMEO   Courage, man; the hurt cannot be much.

MERCUTIO   No? 'Tis not so deep as a well, nor
so wide as a church door, but 'tis enough;
'twill serve. Ask for me tomorrow, and you
shall find me a grave man: I am peppered,° I   *done for*
110   warrant, for this world. A plague o'both your

6. The rapier thrust wins the day.
7. And, according to how you subsequently treat me.

houses! Zounds! A dog, a rat, a mouse, a cat,
to scratch a man to death—a braggart, a
rogue, a villain that fights by the book of
arithmetic.[8] Why the devil came you between
115 us? I was hurt under your arm.
ROMEO   I thought all for the best.
MERCUTIO   Help me into some house, Benvolio,
Or I shall faint. A plague o'both your houses!
They have made worms' meat of me;
120 I have it, and soundly, too. Your houses—

                          Exeunt [all but ROMEO].

ROMEO   This gentleman, the Prince's near ally,°   relative
My very° friend, hath got this mortal hurt   true
In my behalf, my reputation stained
With Tybalt's slander—Tybalt, that an hour
125 Hath been my cousin. O sweet Juliet,
Thy beauty hath made me effeminate,
And in my temper[9] softened valor's steel.
         Enter BENVOLIO.
BENVOLIO   O Romeo, Romeo, brave Mercutio is dead.
That gallant spirit hath aspired° the clouds,   ascended to
130 Which too untimely here did scorn the earth.
ROMEO   This day's black fate on more days doth
   depend;°   hang over
This but begins the woe others must end.
         [*Enter* TYBALT.]
BENVOLIO   Here comes the furious Tybalt back again.
ROMEO   He gan° in triumph, and Mercutio slain?   going
135 Away to heaven, respective lenity,°   respectful lenience
And fire and fury be my conduct° now!   guide
—Now, Tybalt, take the "villain" back again
That late thou gavest me, for Mercutio's soul
Is but a little way above our heads,
140 Staying for thine to keep him company;
Either thou, or I, or both, must go with him.
TYBALT   Thou, wretched boy, that didst consort°   accompany
   him here,
Shalt with him hence.
ROMEO   This shall determine that.
         They fight; TYBALT *falls* [*and dies*].

---

8. By the numbers; according to a fencing manual.
9. Emotional makeup, here suggesting the hardened character of a fighting man (*temper:*
to harden steel). It was believed that too much time with or passion for women would
cause a man to become effeminate.

Compressed / fine.

BENVOLIO   Romeo, away; be gone!

145   The citizens are up,° and Tybalt slain.   *up in arms*
       Stand not amazed,° the Prince will doom°   *stupefied / sentence (to)*
          thee death
       If thou art taken. Hence! Be gone! Away!
ROMEO   Oh, I am fortune's fool.°   *dupe*
BENVOLIO   Why dost thou stay?
                                   Exit ROMEO.

          Enter CITIZENS.
CITIZEN   Which way ran he that killed Mercutio?
150   Tybalt, that murderer—which way ran he?
BENVOLIO   There lies that Tybalt.
CITIZEN   Up, sir; go with me.
       I charge thee in the Prince's name obey.
          Enter PRINCE, *old* MONTAGUE,
             CAPULET[, MONTAGUE'S WIFE, CAPULET'S
             WIFE, *and Attendants*].
PRINCE   Where are the vile beginners of this fray?
BENVOLIO   O noble Prince, I can discover° all   *reveal*
155   The unlucky manage° of this fatal brawl.   *handling*
       There lies the man, slain by young Romeo,
       That slew thy kinsman, brave Mercutio.
CAPULET'S WIFE   Tybalt, my cousin! O my brother's child!
       O Prince, O cousin, husband! Oh, the blood is spilled
160   Of my dear kinsman! Prince, as thou art true,
       For blood of ours shed blood of Montague.
       O cousin, cousin!
PRINCE   Benvolio, who began this bloody fray?
BENVOLIO   Tybalt here slain, whom Romeo's hand
          did slay—
165   Romeo that spoke him° fair,° bid him bethink   *to him / courteously*
       How nice° the quarrel was, and urged withal°   *trivial / also*
       Your high displeasure. All this, utterèd
       With gentle breath, calm look, knees humbly bowed,
       Could not take° truce with the unruly spleen°   *arrange / bitter mood*
170   Of Tybalt, deaf to peace, but that he tilts
       With piercing steel at bold Mercutio's breast,
       Who, all as hot, turns deadly point to point,
       And, with a martial scorn, with one hand beats
       Cold death aside,[1] and with the other sends
175   It back to Tybalt, whose dexterity
       Retorts° it. Romeo he cries aloud,   *Returns*

       _____

1. *with . . . aside*: The two would have been fighting either with daggers in or cloaks rolled
   about their second hand to ward off the other's weapon.

"Hold, friends! Friends, part!" and, swifter than
   his tongue,
His agile arm beats down their fatal points,
And twixt them rushes—underneath whose arm
180 An envious° thrust from Tybalt hit the life   A *malicious*
Of stout° Mercutio. And then Tybalt fled—   *courageous*
But by and by comes back to Romeo,
Who had but newly entertained° revenge,   *considered*
And to't they go like lightning, for ere I
185 Could draw to part them was stout Tybalt slain
And, as he fell, did Romeo turn and fly.
This is the truth, or let Benvolio die.
CAPULET'S WIFE   He is a kinsman to the Montague:
Affection makes him false; he speaks not true.
190 Some twenty of them fought in this black strife,
And all those twenty could but kill one life.
I beg for justice—which thou, Prince, must give.
Romeo slew Tybalt; Romeo must not live.
PRINCE   Romeo slew him; he slew Mercutio;
195 Who now the price of his° dear blood doth owe?   *(Mercutio's)*
MONTAGUE   Not Romeo, Prince; he was Mercutio's friend.
His fault° concludes but what the law should end—   *offense*
The life of Tybalt.
PRINCE   And for that offense
Immediately we do exile him hence.
200 I have an interest in your hearts' proceeding;
My blood° for your rude brawls doth lie a-bleeding.   *kinsman*
But I'll amerce° you with so strong a fine   *penalize*
That you shall all repent the loss of mine:
It will be deaf to pleading and excuses.
205 Nor tears nor prayers shall purchase out° abuses;   *compensate for*
Therefore use none. Let Romeo hence in haste;
Else, when he is found, that hour is his last.
Bear hence this body, and attend our will.
Mercy but murders, pardoning those that kill.
                              Exeunt.

3.2

Enter JULIET *alone.*

JULIET Gallop apace,° you fiery-footed steeds,   *quickly*
Towards Phoebus' lodging;[1] such a wagoner°   *charioteer*
As Phaëthon[2] would whip you to the west,
And bring in cloudy night immediately.
5   Spread thy close° curtain, love-performing night,   *covering*
That runaways'[3] eyes may wink,° and Romeo   *close*
Leap to these arms, untalked of and unseen.
Lovers can see to do their amorous rites,
And by their own beauties; or, if love be blind,
10   It best agrees with night. Come, civil° night,   *solemn*
Thou sober-suited matron all in black,
And learn me how to lose a winning match,[4]
Played for a pair of stainless maidenhoods.
Hood my unmanned° blood, bating[5] in my   *untamed; virgin*
    cheeks,
15   With thy black mantle, till strange° love grow bold;   *shy*
Think true love acted simple° modesty.   *mere: innocent*
Come, night; come, Romeo; come, thou day in night,
For thou wilt lie upon the wings of night
Whiter than new snow upon a raven's back.
20   Come, gentle night; come, loving, black-browed night,
Give me my Romeo; and, when I shall die.
Take him and cut him out in little stars,[6]
And he will make the face of heaven so fine
That all the world will be in love with night
25   And pay no worship to the garish sun.
Oh, I have bought the mansion of a love,
But not possessed it; and though I am sold,[7]
Not yet enjoyed. So tedious is this day
As is the night before some festival
30   To an impatient child that hath new robes

3.2 Location: Capulet's house.
1. Under the world to the west, where the sun god Phoebus Apollo was imagined to rest with his fiery chariot at night.
2. The son of Apollo, who rashly attempted to steer his father's chariot across the sky. To save the earth from scorching, Jupiter struck him down with a lightning bolt.
3. Either the runaway horses of the sun or roving and curious vagabonds.
4. Competition. A husband and a marriage ("match") are won by surrendering.
5. Fluttering like a restless falcon before its eyes are covered with a "hood" to calm it.
6. *Take . . . stars:* an imagined transformation, based on those in Ovid's *Metamorphoses,* whereby Romeo also dies and is immortalized. Also, "die" could mean "have an orgasm."
7. *Oh . . . sold:* The image is inverted: first Juliet buys the mansion, and then she becomes the "sold" house.

And may not wear them.
   Enter NURSE *with cords.*
         Oh, here comes my nurse,
And she brings news, and every tongue that speaks
But Romeo's name speaks heavenly eloquence.
Now, Nurse, what news? What, hast thou there
The cords that Romeo bid thee fetch?
35 NURSE   Ay, ay, the cords.
JULIET Ay me, what news? Why dost thou wring thy hands?
NURSE Ah, welladay,° he's dead, he's dead, he's dead!   *alas*
We are undone, lady; we are undone.
Alack the day—he's gone, he's killed, he's dead!
JULIET Can heaven be so envious?°   *spiteful; jealous*
40 NURSE   Romeo can,
Though heaven cannot. O Romeo, Romeo!
Whoever would have thought it? Romeo!
JULIET What devil art thou that dost torment me thus?
This torture should be roared in dismal hell.
45 Hath Romeo slain himself? Say thou but "Ay,"
And that bare vowel "I" shall poison more
Than the death-darting eye of cockatrice,[8]
I am not I if there be such an "Ay,"
Or those eyes shut that makes thee answer "Ay."
50 If he be slain, say "Ay," or, if not, "No."
Brief sounds determine my weal° or woe.   *welfare*
NURSE I saw the wound—I saw it with mine eyes,
God save the mark[9]—here on his manly breast.
A piteous corpse, a bloody, piteous corpse,
55 Pale, pale as ashes, all bedaubed in blood,
All in gore° blood; I swooned at the sight.   *clotted*
JULIET O break, my heart; poor bankrupt, break at once!
To prison,[1] eyes; ne'er look on liberty.
Vile earth,[2] to earth resign; end motion° here; *movement; emotion*
60 And thou and Romeo press[3] one heavy° bier.   *weighty; sad*
NURSE O Tybalt, Tybalt, the best friend I had!
O courteous Tybalt, honest° gentleman,   *honorable*
That ever I should live to see thee dead!

8. A mythical serpent that kills by merely looking.
9. An apology for mentioning something unpleasant, but also emphasizing the fatal "mark" of the rapier.
1. Bankruptcy—to "break" financially—was punishable by imprisonment.
2. The despised body, echoing Ecclesiastes 12:7: "Then shall the dust return to the earth as it was."
3. Burden; embrace.

JULIET   What storm is this that blows so contrary?
65   Is Romeo slaughtered, and is Tybalt dead,
     My dearest cousin and my dearer lord?
     Then, dreadful trumpet, sound the general doom,[4]
     For who is living if those two are gone?
NURSE   Tybalt is gone, and Romeo banishèd;
70   Romeo, that killed him, he is banishèd.
JULIET   O God, did Romeo's hand shed Tybalt's blood?
NURSE   It did, it did, alas the day, it did!
JULIET   O serpent heart, hid with° a flow'ring°   by / lovely; benign
     face!
     Did ever dragon keep° so fair a cave?   guard
75   Beautiful tyrant, fiend angelical,
     Dove-feathered raven, wolvish-ravening lamb,
     Despisèd substance of divinest show,°   appearance
     Just opposite to what thou justly° seem'st,   precisely; rightfully
     A damnèd saint, an honorable villain.
80   O nature, what hadst thou to do[5] in hell
     When thou didst bower[6] the spirit of a fiend
     In mortal paradise of such sweet flesh?
     Was ever book containing such vile matter
     So fairly bound? Oh, that deceit should dwell
     In such a gorgeous palace.
85   NURSE   There's no trust,
     No faith, no honesty in men: all perjured,
     All forsworn, all naught,° all dissemblers.   wicked
     Ah, where's my man? Give me some aqua vitae.°   brandy
     These griefs, these woes, these sorrows, make me old.
     Shame come to Romeo.
90   JULIET   Blistered be thy tongue
     For such a wish! He was not born to shame;
     Upon his brow shame is ashamed to sit,
     For 'tis a throne where honor may be crowned
     Sole monarch of the universal earth.
95   Oh, what a beast was I to chide at him!
NURSE   Will you speak well of him that killed your cousin?
JULIET   Shall I speak ill of him that is my husband?
     Ah, poor my° lord, what tongue shall smooth°   my poor / praise
       thy name
     When I, thy three hours' wife, have mangled it?

4. The Last Judgment announced with angels' trumpets.
5. What were you doing.
6. Lodge or enclose, suggesting a surrounding garden.

100 But wherefore, villain, didst thou kill my cousin?
    That villain cousin would have killed my husband.
    Back, foolish tears, back to your native spring;
    Your tributary[7] drops belong to woe,
    Which you, mistaking, offer up to joy.[8]
105 My husband lives that Tybalt would have slain,
    And Tybalt's dead that would have slain my husband:
    All this is comfort. Wherefore° weep I, then?   *Why*
    Some word there was, worser than Tybalt's death,
    That murdered me; I would forget it fain,°   *gladly*
110 But, oh, it presses to my memory
    Like damnèd guilty deeds to sinners' minds:
    Tybalt is dead and Romeo banishèd.
    That "banishèd"—that one word, "banishèd"—
    Hath slain ten thousand Tybalts. Tybalt's death
115 Was woe enough if it had ended there;
    Or, if sour woe delights in fellowship,
    And needly° will be ranked with[9] other griefs,   *necessarily*
    Why followed not, when she said, "Tybalt's dead,"
    "Thy father" or "Thy mother"—nay, or both—
120 Which modern° lamentation might have   *ordinary*
        moved?°   *produced*
    But with a rearward[1] following "Tybalt's death,"
    "Romeo is banishèd"—to speak that word
    Is father, mother, Tybalt, Romeo, Juliet,
    All slain, all dead. "Romeo is banishèd"—
125 There is no end, no limit, measure, bound,
    In that word's death; no words can that woe sound.°   *utter; fathom*
    —Where is my father and my mother, Nurse?
    NURSE   Weeping and wailing over Tybalt's corpse.
    Will you go to them? I will bring you thither.
130 JULIET   Wash they his wounds with tears? Mine shall be spent,
    When theirs are dry, for Romeo's banishment.
    Take up those cords. Poor ropes, you are beguiled°—   *cheated*
    Both you and I—for Romeo is exiled;
    He made you for a highway to my bed,
135 But I, a maid, die maiden-widowèd.
    Come, cords, come, Nurse; I'll to my wedding bed,
    And death, not Romeo, take my maidenhead.
    NURSE   Hie to your chamber. I'll find Romeo

7. Tribute-paying; in-flowing.
8. Offer up to a joyful (and thus inappropriate) occasion.
9. Will be accompanied by.
1. *rearward*: rearguard action, with a pun on "afterword."

To comfort you; I wot° well where he is.   *know*
140   Hark ye, your Romeo will be here at night.
        I'll to him; he is hid at Laurence' cell.
JULIET   Oh, find him! Give this ring to my true knight,
        And bid him come to take his last farewell.

                                           Exeunt.

3·3

Enter FRIAR [LAURENCE].

FRIAR LAURENCE   Romeo, come forth, come forth, thou
        fearful man.
        Affliction is enamored of thy parts,°   *qualities*
        And thou art wedded to calamity.
             [*Enter* ROMEO.]
ROMEO   Father, what news? What is the Prince's doom?°   *sentence*
5   What sorrow craves acquaintance at my hand
        That I yet know not?
FRIAR LAURENCE   Too familiar
        Is my dear son with such sour company.
        I bring thee tidings of the Prince's doom.
ROMEO   What less than doomsday is the Prince's doom?
10   FRIAR LAURENCE   A gentler judgment vanished° from   *escaped*
        his lips:
        Not body's death, but body's banishment.
ROMEO   Ha? Banishment? Be merciful; say "death,"
        For exile hath more terror in his look,
        Much more than death. Do not say "banishment."
15   FRIAR LAURENCE   Here from Verona art thou banishèd.
        Be patient,° for the world is broad and wide.   *able to endure*
ROMEO   There is no world without° Verona walls   *outside*
        But purgatory, torture, hell itself;
        Hence banishèd is banished from the world,
20   And world's exile is death. Then "banishèd"
        Is death mis-termed: calling death "banishèd,"
        Thou cutt'st my head off with a golden ax,
        And smilest upon the stroke that murders me.
FRIAR LAURENCE   Oh, deadly° sin! Oh, rude   *damnable*
        unthankfulness!
25   Thy fault our law calls death,° but the kind   *a capital offense*
        Prince,

3.3 Location: Friar Laurence's cell.

Taking thy part, hath rushed° aside the law,   *forced*
And turned that black word "death" to "banishment."
This is dear mercy, and thou seest it not.
ROMEO   'Tis torture and not mercy! Heaven is here
30   Where Juliet lives—and every cat and dog
And little mouse, every unworthy thing,
Live here in heaven and may look on her,
But Romeo may not. More validity,°   *health*
More honorable state, more courtship,° lives   *courtly state; wooing*
35   In carrion flies than Romeo. They may seize
On the white wonder of dear Juliet's hand,
And steal immortal blessing from her lips,
Who even in pure and vestal° modesty   *virginal*
Still° blush, as thinking their own kisses[1] sin.   *Always*
40   This may flies do, when I from this must fly—
And sayest thou yet that exile is not death?
But Romeo may not; he is banishèd.
Flies may do this, but I from this must fly:
They are free men, but I am banishèd.
45   Hadst thou no poison mixed no sharp-ground knife,
No sudden mean° of death—though ne'er so   *method*
mean°—   *ignoble*
But "banishèd" to kill me? "Banishèd"?
O Friar, the damnèd use that word in hell;[2]
Howling attends it. How hast thóu the heart,
50   Being a divine, a ghostly confessor,
A sin-absolver, and my friend professed,
To mangle me with that word "banishèd"?
FRIAR LAURENCE   Then, fond° madman, hear   *foolish; infatuated*
me a little speak.
ROMEO   Oh, thou wilt speak again of banishment.
55   FRIAR LAURENCE   I'll give thee armor to keep off that word:
Adversity's sweet milk, philosophy,
To comfort thee, though thou art banishèd.
ROMEO   Yet "banishèd"? Hang up° philosophy!   *Hang up = Hang*
Unless philosophy can make a Juliet,
60   Displant° a town, reverse a prince's doom,   *Uproot*
It helps not, it prevails not. Talk no more.
FRIAR LAURENCE   Oh, then I see that madmen have no ears.
ROMEO   How should they, when that wise men have no eyes?

1. Their touching each other in closing.
2. Because they are banished from heaven.

FRIAR LAURENCE   Let me dispute° with thee of thy   *discuss*
   estate.°   *position*

65 ROMEO   Thou canst not speak of that thou dost not feel.
   Wert thou as young as I, Juliet thy love,
   An hour but° married, Tybalt murderèd,   *Only an hour*
   Doting like me, and like me banishèd,
   Then mightst thou speak; then mightst thou tear thy hair

70   And fall upon the ground, as I do now,
   Taking the measure of an unmade grave.
      NURSE *knocks* [*within*].

FRIAR LAURENCE   Arise! One knocks. Good Romeo,
   hide thyself.

ROMEO   Not I, unless the breath of heartsick groans
   Mistlike enfold me from the search of eyes.
      Knock [*within*].

75 FRIAR LAURENCE   Hark, how they knock! —Who's
   there? —Romeo, arise;
   Thou wilt be taken! —Stay a while! —Stand up!
      [*Loud*] *knock* [*within*].
   Run to my study. —By and by! —God's will,°   *By providence*
   What simpleness° is this? —I come, I come!   *stupidity*
      Knock [*within*].
   Who knocks so hard? Whence come you? What's
   your will?

80 NURSE [*within*][3]   Let me come in, and you shall know
   my errand.
   I come from Lady Juliet.
      Enter NURSE.

FRIAR LAURENCE   Welcome, then.

NURSE   O holy Friar! Oh, tell me, holy Friar,
   Where's my lady's lord? Where's Romeo?

FRIAR LAURENCE   There on the ground, with his
   own tears made drunk.

85 NURSE   Oh, he is even° in my mistress'   *exactly*
   case,°   *condition; vagina*
   Just in her case. Oh, woeful sympathy,
   Piteous predicament! Even so lies she,
   Blubb'ring and weeping, weeping and blubb'ring.
   —Stand up, stand up! Stand an° you be a man!   *if*

90   For Juliet's sake, for her sake, rise and stand.
   Why should you fall into so deep an O?°   *a groaning; a vagina*

ROMEO   Nurse—

---

3. Behind one of the doors at the back of the stage, representing the door of the cell.

NURSE   Ah, sir; ah, sir; death's the end of all.[4]

ROMEO   Spakest thou of Juliet? How is it with her?
Doth not she think me an old° murderer   *a practiced*
95   Now I have stained the childhood of our joy
With blood removed but little from her own?
Where is she? And how doth she? And what says
My concealed lady° to our canceled° love?   *secret wife / invalidated*

NURSE   Oh, she says nothing, sir, but weeps and weeps,
100   And now falls on her bed, and then starts up,
And Tybalt calls, and then on Romeo cries,
And then down falls again.

ROMEO   As if that name,
Shot from the deadly level° of a gun,   *aim*
Did murder her, as that name's cursèd hand
105   Murdered her kinsman. Oh, tell me, Friar, tell me,
In what vile part of this anatomy
Doth my name lodge? Tell me, that I may sack
The hateful mansion.
            [*He offers to stab himself.*][5]

FRIAR LAURENCE   Hold° thy desperate hand!   *Restrain*
Art thou a man? Thy form cries out thou art.
110   Thy tears are womanish; thy wild acts denote
The unreasonable° fury of a beast;   *incapable of reason*
Unseemly° woman in a seeming man,   *Inappropriate; immodest*
And ill-beseeming beast in seeming both[6]—
Thou hast amazed me. By my holy order,
115   I thought thy disposition better tempered.
Hast thou slain Tybalt? Wilt thou slay thyself?
And slay thy lady, that in thy life lives,
By doing damnèd° hate upon thyself?   *sinful*
Why railest thou on thy birth, the heaven, and earth,
120   Since birth,° and heaven,° and earth,° all   *nobility / soul / body*
three, do meet
In thee at once, which thou at once wouldst lose?
Fie, fie! Thou shamest thy shape, thy love, thy wit,
Which like a usurer abound'st in all,
And usest none in that true use indeed
125   Which should bedeck thy shape, thy love, thy wit.[7]

4. A proverbial consolation.
5. In Q1's version of this scene, a stage direction indicates that the Nurse "*snatches the dagger away*" from Romeo.
6. An unnatural beast in seeming both man and unreasoning animal, or both man and woman.
7. *Thou shamest . . . wit*: You abound in looks, love, and intelligence ("wit"), but you do not use them judiciously and are therefore like a usurer who acquires money for its own sake, without putting it to good use.

Thy noble shape is but a form° of wax,   *figure*
Digressing° from the valor of a man;   *If it deviates*
Thy dear love sworn but hollow perjury,
Killing that love which thou hast vowed to cherish;
130 Thy wit, that ornament° to shape and love,   *necessary accessory*
Misshapen° in the conduct° of them both,   *Inept / management*
Like powder in a skill-less soldier's flask,
Is set afire by thine own ignorance,
And thou dismembered with thine own defense.°   *weapon*
135 What, rouse thee, man! Thy Juliet is alive,
For whose dear sake thou wast but lately dead;
There art thou happy. Tybalt would kill thee,
But thou slewest Tybalt; there art thou happy.
The law that threatened death becomes thy friend
140 And turns it to exile; there art thou happy.
A pack of blessings light upon thy back;
Happiness courts thee in her best array;
But, like a mishavèd° and sullen wench,   *misbehaved*
Thou pouts upon thy fortune and thy love.
145 Take heed, take heed, for such die miserable.
Go; get thee to thy love as was decreed;
Ascend her chamber; hence and comfort her.
But look thou stay not till the watch be set,[8]
For then thou canst not pass to Mantua,
150 Where thou shalt live till we can find a time
To blaze° your marriage, reconcile your friends,°   *make public / kin*
Beg pardon of the Prince, and call thee back
With twenty hundred thousand times more joy
Than thou went'st forth in lamentation.
155 —Go before, Nurse. Commend me to thy lady,
And bid her hasten all the house to bed,
Which heavy sorrow makes them apt unto.
Romeo is coming.
NURSE   O Lord, I could have stayed here all the night
160 To hear good counsel. Oh, what learning is!
My lord, I'll tell my lady you will come.
ROMEO   Do so, and bid my sweet prepare to chide.
NURSE   Here, sir: a ring she bid me give you, sir.
Hie you,° make haste, for it grows very late.   [*Exit.*]   *Hurry*
165 ROMEO   How well my comfort° is revived by this.   *happiness*

8. Until the guards take up their positions (at the city gates).

FRIAR LAURENCE   Go hence. Good night—and
     here stands° all your state: *and on this depends*
    Either be gone before the watch be set,
    Or, by the break of day, disguised from hence.
    Sojourn in Mantua. I'll find out your man,
170   And he shall signify from time to time
    Every good hap° to you that chances here.   *event*
    Give me thy hand. 'Tis late, Farewell. Goodnight.
ROMEO   But that a joy past joy calls out on me,
    It were a grief so brief° to part with thee.   *hastily*
175   Farewell.   *Exeunt.*

3·4

Enter old CAPULET, [CAPULET'S] WIFE, *and* PARIS.
CAPULET   Things have fall'n out, sir, so unluckily
    That we have had no time to move° our daughter.   *persuade*
    Look you, she loved her kinsman Tybalt dearly,
    And so did I. Well, we were born to die.
5   'Tis very late; she'll not come down tonight.
    I promise you, but for your company
    I would have been abed an hour ago.
PARIS   These times of woe afford no times to woo.
    —Madam, good night; commend me to your daughter.
10 CAPULET'S WIFE   I will, and know her mind early tomorrow.
    Tonight she's mewed up to¹ her heaviness.°   *sadness*
CAPULET   Sir Paris, I will make a desperate tender°   *reckless offer*
    Of my child's love. I think she will be ruled
    In all respects by me; nay, more, I doubt it not.
15   —Wife, go you to her ere you go to bed,
    Acquaint her here of my son Paris' love,
    And bid her—mark you me?—on Wednesday next—
    But soft, what day is this?
PARIS   Monday, my lord.
CAPULET   Monday? Ha, ha! Well, Wednesday is too soon;
20   O'Thursday let it be; o'Thursday, tell her,
    She shall be married to this noble earl.
    —Will you be ready? Do you like this haste?
    We'll keep° no great ado—a friend or two—   *celebrate with*
    For, hark you, Tybalt being slain so late,°   *recently*

3.4 Location: Capulet's house.
1. Shut in with. The "mews" are hawks' housing.

25   It may be thought we held° him carelessly,°   *regarded / indifferently*
      Being our kinsman, if we revel much.
      Therefore we'll have some half a dozen friends,
      And there an end. But what say you to Thursday?
      PARIS   My lord, I would° that Thursday were tomorrow.   *wish*
30   CAPULET   Well, get you gone; o'Thursday be it, then.
      [*to* CAPULET'S WIFE] Go you to Juliet ere you go to bed.
      Prepare her, wife, against° this wedding day.   *for*
      —Farewell, my lord. —Light to my chamber, ho!
      —Afore me,² it is so very late
35   That we may call it early by and by!
      Goodnight.   *Exeunt.*

3·5

      Enter ROMEO *and* JULIET *aloft.*
      JULIET   Wilt thou be gone? It is not yet near day.
      It was the nightingale, and not the lark,
      That pierced the fearful hollow of thine ear.
      Nightly she sings on yond pom'granate tree.
5   Believe me, love: it was the nightingale.
      ROMEO   It was the lark, the herald of the morn,
      No nightingale. Look, love, what envious° streaks   *spiteful*
      Do lace the severing° clouds in yonder East.   *parting*
      Night's candles are burnt out, and jocund day
10   Stands tiptoe on the misty mountain tops.
      I must be gone and live, or stay and die.
      JULIET   Yond light is not daylight—I know it, I—
      It is some meteor that the sun exhales¹
      To be to thee this night a torchbearer
15   And light thee on thy way to Mantua.
      Therefore stay yet; thou need'st not to be gone.
      ROMEO   Let me be ta'en, let me be put to death;
      I am content, so° thou wilt have it so.   *as long as*
      I'll say yon gray is not the morning's eye—
20   'Tis but the pale reflex° of Cynthia's° brow—   *reflection / the moon's*
      Nor that is not the lark whose notes do beat
      The vaulty heaven so high above our heads.
      I have more care° to stay than will to go.   *desire*
      Come, death, and welcome: Juliet wills it so.

2. *Afore me*: A mild oath.
3.5 Location: The upper acting area represents Juliet's window or balcony. The main stage
represents Capulet's orchard until line 59, then Juliet's bedroom from line 64.
1. Breathes. Meteors were thought to be impure vapors that the sun had drawn up from
the earth and ignited and were usually considered bad omens.

25   How is't, my soul? Let's talk; it is not day.
        JULIET   It is, it is! Hie hence; be gone. Away!
        It is the lark that sings so out of tune,
        Straining° harsh discords and unpleasing   *Distorting: tuning up*
            sharps.[2]
        Some say the lark makes sweet division;°   *variations on a melody*
30   This doth not so, for she divideth us.
        Some say the lark and loathèd toad change eyes;[3]
        Oh, now I would they had changed voices too,
        Since arm from arm that voice doth us affray,°   *frighten*
        Hunting thee hence with hunt's-up[4] to the day.
35   Oh, now be gone! More light and light it grows.
        ROMEO   More light and light, more dark and dark our woes.
                Enter NURSE.
        NURSE   Madam!
        JULIET   Nurse?
        NURSE   Your lady mother is coming to your chamber.
40   The day is broke; be wary; look about.   [*Exit.*]
        JULIET   Then, window, let day in and let life out.
        ROMEO   Farewell, farewell. One kiss, and I'll descend.
                [*He goeth down.*][5]
        JULIET   Art thou gone so, love, lord—ay, husband,
            friend?°   *lover*
        I must hear from thee every day in the hour,
45   For in a minute there are many days—
        Oh, by this count I shall be much in years
        Ere I again behold my Romeo!
        ROMEO   Farewell.
        I will omit no opportunity
50   That may convey my greetings, love, to thee.
        JULIET   Oh, think'st thou we shall ever meet again?
        ROMEO   I doubt it not, and all these woes shall serve
        For sweet discourses° in our times to come.   *conversations*
        JULIET   O God, I have an ill-divining° soul!   *a misfortune-predicting*
55   Methinks I see thee, now thou art so low,
        As one dead in the bottom of a tomb;
        Either my eyesight fails, or thou lookest pale.
        ROMEO   And trust me, love, in my eye so do you;

---

2. Harsh sounds, too-high tones.
3. A folk explanation for the supposed ugliness of the lark's eyes and the beauty of the
   toad's. *change*: exchange.
4. Morning song used to wake the bride after the wedding night.
5. Romeo descends using the ladder of cords mentioned earlier.

Dry sorrow drinks our blood.[6] Adieu, adieu.   *Exit.*

60 JULIET   O Fortune, Fortune, all men call thee fickle;
If thou art fickle, what dost thou with him
That is renowned for faith?° Be fickle, Fortune,   *fidelity*
For then I hope thou wilt not keep him long,
But send him back.
          Enter [CAPULET'S WIFE *below*].
CAPULET'S WIFE   Ho, daughter, are you up?

65 JULIET   Who is't that calls? —It is my lady mother.
Is she not down° so late or up so early?   *in bed*
What unaccustomed cause procures° her hither?   *brings*
          [JULIET *goeth down and enters below.*]
CAPULET'S WIFE   Why, how now, Juliet?
JULIET   Madam, I am not well.
CAPULET'S WIFE   Evermore weeping for your cousin's death?

70   What, wilt thou wash him from his grave with tears?
An if thou couldst, thou couldst not make him live;
Therefore have done. Some grief shows much of love,
But much of grief shows still° some want° of wit.   *always / lack*
JULIET   Yet let me weep for such a feeling° loss.   *profound*
75 CAPULET'S WIFE   So shall you feel° the loss,   *experience; touch*
but not the friend°   *kin*
Which you weep for.
JULIET   Feeling so the loss.
I cannot choose but ever weep the friend.°   *lover*
CAPULET'S WIFE   Well, girl, thou weep'st not so much
for his death
As that the villain lives which slaughtered him.
JULIET   What villain, madam?
80 CAPULET'S WIFE   That same villain Romeo.
JULIET [*aside*] Villain and he be many miles asunder.
—God pardon; I do with all my heart,
And yet no man like° he doth grieve my   *so much as; resembling*
heart.
CAPULET'S WIFE   That is because the traitor murderer lives.
85 JULIET   Ay, madam, from the reach of these my hands.
Would none but I might venge my cousin's death.
CAPULET'S WIFE   We will have vengeance for it, fear thou not.
Then weep no more. I'll send to one in Mantua,

---

6. *Dry . . . blood*: Each sigh supposedly cost the heart a drop of blood. Thus, the lovers are
pale. *Dry*: Thirsty.

                Where that same banished renegade doth live,
90   Shall give him such an unaccustomed dram
                That he shall soon keep Tybalt company;
                And then I hope thou wilt be satisfied.°   *sufficiently avenged*
JULIET   Indeed, I never shall be satisfied
                With Romeo till I behold him—dead—
95   Is my poor heart[7] so for a kinsman vexed.
                Madam, if you could find out but a man
                To bear a poison, I would temper° it   *mix; dilute*
                That Romeo should, upon receipt thereof,
                Soon sleep in quiet. Oh, how my heart abhors
100   To hear him named, and cannot come to him—
                To wreak the love I bore my cousin
                Upon his body that hath slaughtered him.
CAPULET'S WIFE   Find thou the means, and I'll find such a man.
                But now I'll tell thee joyful tidings, girl.
105   JULIET   And joy comes well in such a needy time.
                What are they, beseech your ladyship?
CAPULET'S WIFE   Well, well, thou hast a careful°   *solicitous*
                father, child;
                One who, to put thee from thy heaviness,
                Hath sorted out a sudden° day of joy   *chosen an immediate*
110   That thou expects not, nor I looked not for.
JULIET   Madam, in happy° time. What day is that?   *at a fortunate*
CAPULET'S WIFE   Marry, my child, early next Thursday morn,
                The gallant, young, and noble gentleman,
                The County Paris, at Saint Peter's Church
115   Shall happily make thee there a joyful bride!
JULIET   Now, by Saint Peter's Church—and Peter, too—
                He shall not make me there a joyful bride!
                I wonder° at this haste, that I must wed   *am astonished*
                Ere he that should be husband comes to woo.
120   I pray you tell my lord and father, madam,
                I will not marry yet—and when I do, I swear
                It shall be Romeo, whom you know I hate,
                Rather than Paris. These are news indeed!
CAPULET'S WIFE   Here comes your father; tell him so yourself,
125   And see how he will take it at your hands.
                Enter CAPULET *and* NURSE.

---

7. *till . . . heart:* Juliet allows her mother to understand that she will not be satisfied "till I
behold him dead," while privately meaning that until she beholds him, "dead is my poor
heart."

CAPULET   When the sun sets, the earth doth drizzle°   *weep out*
     dew;
     But for the sunset of my brother's son
     It rains downright.
     How now? A conduit,° girl? What, still in tears?   *fountain*
130   Evermore show'ring? In one little body
     Thou counterfeits a bark,° a sea, a wind—   *represent a ship*
     For still thy eyes, which I may call the sea,
     Do ebb and flow with tears; the bark thy body is,
     Sailing in this salt flood, the winds thy sighs,
135   Who,° raging with thy tears and they with them,   *Which*
     Without a sudden calm will overset
     Thy tempest-tossèd body. —How now, wife,
     Have you delivered to her our decree?

CAPULET'S WIFE   Ay, sir, but she will none,° she gives   *not agree*
     you thanks.
140   I would the fool° were married to her grave.   *peevish child*

CAPULET   Soft! Take me with you;[8] take me with you, wife.
     How? Will she none? Doth she not give us thanks?
     Is she not proud?° Doth she not count her blessed,   *gratified*
     Unworthy as she is, that we have wrought°   *contrived for*
145   So worthy a gentleman to be her bride?°   *bridegroom*

JULIET   Not proud you have, but thankful that you have.
     Proud can I never be of what I hate,
     But thankful even for hate° that is meant   *a hateful thing*
     love.°   *as love*

CAPULET   How, how, how, how? Chopped logic?°   *Mere sophistry*
     What is this?
150   "Proud," and "I thank you," and "I thank you not,"
     And yet "not proud," mistress minion,° you?   *spoiled child*
     Thank me no thankings, nor proud me no prouds,
     But fettle° your fine joints 'gainst° Thursday next   *prepare / for*
     To go with Paris to Saint Peter's Church,
155   Or I will drag thee on a hurdle[9] thither.
     Out,[1] you green-sickness carrion! Out, you baggage,
     You tallow face!

CAPULET'S WIFE   Fie, fie! What, are you mad?

JULIET   Good father, I beseech you on my knees,
160   Hear me with patience but to speak a word.

---

8. Not so fast, let me understand you.
9. A sledge used to draw traitors through the streets to execution.
1. An expression of disgust and impatience.

CAPULET   Hang thee, young baggage, disobedient wretch!
    I tell thee what: get thee to church o'Thursday,
    Or never after look me in the face.
    Speak not; reply not; do not answer me.
165   My fingers itch. —Wife, we scarce thought us blessed
    That God had lent us but this only child,
    But now I see this one is one too much,
    And that we have a curse in having her.
    Out on her, hilding!°   hussy
NURSE   God in heaven bless her!
170   You are to blame, my lord, to rate° her so.   berate
CAPULET   And why, my Lady Wisdom? Hold your tongue,
    Good Prudence. Smatter° with your gossips.° Go!   Chatter / cronies
NURSE   I speak no treason.
CAPULET   Oh, God gi' good e'en!°   (for God's sake)
NURSE   May not one speak?
CAPULET   Peace, you mumbling fool!
175   Utter your gravity° o'er a gossip's bowl,°   wisdom / drinking bowl
    For here we need it not.
CAPULETS WIFE   You are too hot.°   irascible; rash
CAPULET   God's bread,° it makes me mad!   By the communion bread
    Day, night, hour, tide, time, work, play,
    Alone, in company—still my care° hath been   business
180   To have her matched; and, having now provided
    A gentleman of noble parentage,
    Of fair demesnes,° youthful, and nobly lined,°   estates / descended
    Stuffed, as they say, with honorable parts,°   qualities
    Proportioned as one's thought would wish a man,[2]
185   And then to have a wretched, puling fool,
    A whining mammet° in her fortune's tender,[3]   puppet
    To answer, "I'll not wed; I cannot love;
    I am too young; I pray you, pardon me."
    —But, an you will not wed, I'll pardon you:°   excuse you (to leave)
190   Graze where you will, you shall not house with me!
    Look to't; think on't; I do not use° to jest.   make it customary
    Thursday is near. Lay hand on heart;[4] advise.°   consider
    An you be mine, I'll give you to my friend;
    An you be not, hang, beg, starve, die in the streets—
195   For, by my soul, I'll ne'er acknowledge thee,
    Nor what is mine shall never do thee good,

2. Shaped as handsomely as you can imagine.
3. When good fortune is offered her.
4. Ascertain your feelings.

Trust to't. Bethink you; I'll not be forsworn.   *Exit.*
JULIET   Is there no pity sitting in the clouds
    That sees into the bottom of my grief?
200   O sweet my° mother, cast me not away!   *my sweet*
    Delay this marriage for a month, a week—
    Or, if you do not, make the bridal bed
    In that dim monument° where Tybalt lies.   *sepulcher*
CAPULET'S WIFE   Talk not to me, for I'll not speak a word.
205   Do as thou wilt, for I have done with thee.   *Exit.*
JULIET   O God! O Nurse, how shall this be prevented?
    My husband is on earth, my faith° in heaven.   *marriage vows*
    How shall that faith return again to earth
    Unless that husband send it me from heaven
210   By leaving earth?[5] Comfort me; counsel me!
    Alack, alack, that heaven should practice stratagems
    Upon so soft a subject as myself!
    What say'st thou? Hast thou not a word of joy?
    Some comfort, Nurse!
NURSE   Faith, here it is.
215   Romeo is banished, and all the world to nothing[6]
    That he dares ne'er come back to challenge° you;   *claim*
    Or, if he do, it needs must be by stealth.
    Then, since the case so stands as now it doth,
    I think it best you married with the County.
220   Oh, he's a lovely gentleman!
    Romeo's a dishclout° to him. An eagle, madam,   *dishcloth*
    Hath not so green, so quick, so fair an eye
    As Paris hath. Beshrew° my very heart,   *Curse*
    I think you are happy° in this second match,   *lucky*
225   For it excels your first—or, if it did not,
    Your first is dead, or 'twere as good he were
    As living here and you no use of him.
JULIET   Speak'st thou from thy heart?
NURSE   And from my soul, too; else beshrew them both.
230 JULIET   Amen.
NURSE   What?
JULIET   Well, thou hast comforted me marvelous much.
    Go in and tell my lady I am gone,
    Having displeased my father, to Laurence' cell

---

5. *How . . . earth:* How can I swear marriage vows again unless Romeo dies first, thus
releasing me from my vows to him?
6. *all . . . nothing:* it's a sure bet.

235 To make confession and to be absolved.
NURSE Marry, I will, and this is wisely done. [*Exit.*]
JULIET Ancient damnation![7] O most wicked fiend!
  Is it more sin to wish me thus forsworn,
  Or to dispraise my lord with that same tongue
240 Which she hath praised him with, above compare,
  So many thousand times? Go, counselor;
  Thou and my bosom° henceforth shall be   *heart's contents*
    twain.°   *divided*
  I'll to the Friar to know his remedy.
  If all else fail, myself have power to die.   *Exit.*

4.1

Enter FRIAR [LAURENCE] *and County* PARIS.

FRIAR LAURENCE On Thursday, sir? The time is very short. ~~If I~~ *ShALL*
PARIS My father Capulet will have it so,
  And I am nothing slow[1] to slack his haste.
FRIAR LAURENCE You say you do not know the lady's mind?
5 Uneven is the course,[2] I like it not.
PARIS Immoderately she weeps for Tybalt's death,
  And therefore have I little talk of love,
  For Venus smiles not in a house of tears.
  Now, sir, her father counts it dangerous
10 That she do give her sorrow so much sway,
  And in his wisdom hastes our marriage
  To stop the inundation of her tears,
  Which, too much minded° by herself alone,   *brooded over*
  May be put from her by society.°   *company*
15 Now do you know the reason of this haste.
FRIAR LAURENCE [*aside*] I would I knew not why it
    should be slowed.

Enter JULIET.

  —Look, sir, here comes the lady toward my cell.
PARIS Happily met, my lady and my wife.
JULIET That may be, sir, when I may be a wife. *O courtship*
20 PARIS That "may be" must be, love, on Thursday next.
  — double-speak.

---

7. Damnable old woman (with a hint of "original sin").
4.1 Location: Friar Laurence's cell.
1. Not reluctant; not trying to drag behind him.
2. The plan is irregular; this is a tricky road to follow.

The woods

JULIET What must be shall be.

FRIAR LAURENCE   That's a certain text.

PARIS Come you to make confession to this father?

JULIET To answer that, I should confess to you.

PARIS Do not deny to him that you love me.

25 JULIET I will confess to you that I love him.

PARIS So will ye, I am sure, that you love me.

JULIET If I do so, it will be of more price°   *value*
    Being spoke behind your back than to your face.

PARIS Poor soul, thy face is much abused with tears.

30 JULIET The tears have got small victory by that,
    For it was bad enough before their spite.°   *injury*

PARIS Thou wrong'st it more than tears with that report.

JULIET That is no slander, sir, which is a truth;
    And what I spake, I spake it to my face.

35 PARIS Thy face is mine, and thou hast slandered it.

JULIET It may be so, for it is not mine own.³
    —Are you at leisure, holy Father, now,
    Or shall I come to you at evening mass?

FRIAR LAURENCE My leisure serves me, pensive°   *sorrowful*
    daughter, now.

40 —My lord, we must entreat the time alone.

PARIS God shield° I should disturb devotion.   *forbid*
    —Juliet, on Thursday early will I rouse ye;
    Till then, adieu, and keep this holy kiss.   *Exit.*

JULIET Oh, shut the door, and, when thou hast done so,

45 Come weep with me—past hope, past care, past help.

FRIAR LAURENCE O Juliet, I already know thy
      grief;°   *grievous situation*
    It strains me past the compass° of my wits.   *limit*
    I hear thou must—and nothing may prorogue° it— *postpone*
    On Thursday next be married to this County.

50 JULIET Tell me not, Friar, that thou hearest of this
    Unless thou tell me how I may prevent it.
    If in thy wisdom thou canst give no help,
    Do thou but call my resolution wise,
    And with this knife I'll help it presently.°   *immediately*

55 God joined my heart and Romeo's, thou our hands,
    And ere this hand, by thee to Romeo's sealed,

---

3. Because it belongs to Romeo; also because Juliet, in her ambiguous replies, is not showing Paris her true face.

Shall be the label[4] to another deed,
Or my true heart with treacherous revolt
Turn to another, this shall slay them both.
60   Therefore, out of thy long-experienced time,
Give me some present counsel, or behold,
    [*She draws a knife.*]
Twixt my extremes° and me, this bloody knife   *extreme difficulties*
Shall play the umpire, arbitrating that
Which the commission° of thy years and art°   *authority / learning*
65   Could to no issue of true honor bring.
Be not so long to speak; I long to die
If what thou speak'st speak not of remedy.
FRIAR LAURENCE   Hold, daughter! I do spy a kind of hope,
Which craves as desperate° an execution[5]   *reckless*
70   As that is desperate° which we would prevent.   *hopeless*
If, rather than to marry County Paris,
Thou hast the strength of will to slay thyself,
Then is it likely thou wilt undertake
A thing like death to chide away this shame,
75   That cop'st° with death himself to scape   *Who wrestles*
    from it.°   *(shame)*
An if thou darest, I'll give thee remedy.
JULIET   Oh, bid me leap, rather than marry Paris,
From off the battlements of any tower,
Or walk in thievish° ways, or bid me lurk   *thief-infested*
80   Where serpents are; chain me with roaring bears;
Or hide me nightly in a charnel house,°   *burial vault*
O'ercovered quite with dead men's rattling bones,
With reeky° shanks and yellow chapless[6] skulls;   *foully damp*
Or bid me go into a new-made grave,
85   And hide me with a dead man in his shroud—
Things that, to hear them told, have made me tremble—
And I will do it without fear or doubt°   *dread; hesitation*
To live an unstained wife to my sweet love.
FRIAR LAURENCE   Hold, then. Go home; be merry;
    give consent
90   To marry Paris. Wednesday is tomorrow.
Tomorrow night look° that thou lie alone;   *be sure*
Let not the Nurse lie with thee in thy chamber.

---

4. Ribbon attaching a seal to a legal document (deed), and so a pledge confirming another marriage.
5. A performance; a killing.
6. Without lower jaws.

Take thou this vial, being then in bed,
And this distilling° liquor drink thou off,   *permeating*
95   When presently through all thy veins shall run
A cold and drowsy humor°—for no pulse   *bodily fluid*
Shall keep his° native progress but surcease;°   *its / cease*
No warmth, no breath shall testify thou livest;
The roses in thy lips and cheeks shall fade
100 To wanny° ashes; thy eyes' windows° fall   *pale / lids*
Like death when he shuts up the day of life;
Each part, deprived of supple government;°   *control of movement*
Shall stiff and stark and cold appear, like death—
And in this borrowed likeness of shrunk death
105 Thou shalt continue two-and-forty hours,
And then awake as from a pleasant sleep.
Now, when the bridegroom in the morning comes
To rouse thee from thy bed, there art thou dead.
Then, as the manner of our country is,
110 In thy best robes, uncovered on the bier,
Be borne to burial in thy kindred's grave—
Thou shalt be borne to that same ancient vault
Where all the kindred of the Capulets lie.
In the meantime, against° thou shalt awake,   *in preparation for when*
115 Shall Romeo by my letters know our drift;°   *scheme*
And hither shall he come, and he and I
Will watch° thy waking, and that very night   *keep vigil for*
Shall Romeo bear thee hence to Mantua,
And this shall free thee from this present shame,
120 If no inconstant toy° nor womanish fear   *fickle whim*
Abate thy valor in the acting it.
JULIET   Give me, give me—oh, tell not me of fear!
FRIAR LAURENCE   Hold! Get you gone; be strong and
          prosperous
In this resolve. I'll send a friar with speed
125 To Mantua, with my letters° to thy lord.   *letter*
JULIET   Love give me strength, and strength shall help afford.
Farewell, dear Father.   *Exeunt.*

4.2

Enter Father CAPULET, [CAPULET'S WIFE,] NURSE,
and two or three SERVINGMEN.

CAPULET [*to* FIRST SERVINGMAN, *giving him a paper*]   So many
  guests invite as here are writ.
                              [*Exit* FIRST SERVINGMAN.]
  [*to* SECOND SERVINGMAN]   Sirrah, go hire me
  twenty cunning° cooks.   *skillful*
SECOND SERVINGMAN   You shall have none ill,
  sir, for I'll try° if they can lick their   *test*
5   fingers.
CAPULET   How, canst thou try them so?
SECOND SERVINGMAN   Marry, sir, 'tis an ill
  cook that cannot lick his own fingers; therefore he that cannot lick his fingers goes not
10   with me.
CAPULET   Go! Be gone.
  We shall be much unfurnished° for this time.   *unprepared*
                         [*Exit* SECOND SERVINGMAN.]
  —What, is my daughter gone to Friar Laurence?
NURSE   Ay, forsooth.
15   CAPULET   Well, he may chance to do some good on her.
  A peevish, self-willed harlotry it is.[1]
          Enter JULIET.
NURSE   See where she comes from shrift° with   *absolution*
  merry look.
CAPULET   How now, my headstrong, where have you
  been gadding?
JULIET   Where I have learnt me to repent the sin
20   Of disobedient opposition
  To you and your behests, and am enjoined
  By holy Laurence to fall prostrate here
  To beg your pardon.
          [*She kneels down.*]
                         Pardon, I beseech you.
  Henceforward I am ever ruled by you.
25   CAPULET   —Send for the County! Go tell him of this.
  I'll have this knot knit up tomorrow morning.

4.2 Location: Capulet's house.
1. An obstinate, self-willed brat she is.

JULIET   I met the youthful lord at Laurence' cell,
And gave him what becomèd° love I might,   *becoming; suitable*
Not stepping o'er the bounds of modesty.
30   CAPULET   Why, I am glad on't!° This is well. Stand up!   *of it*
This is as't should be. —Let me see the County;
Ay, marry, go, I say, and fetch him hither.
Now, afore God, this reverend holy friar—
All our whole city is much bound to him.
35   JULIET   Nurse, will you go with me into my closet°   *chamber*
To help me sort such needful ornaments
As you think fit to furnish me tomorrow?
CAPULET'S WIFE   No, not till Thursday; there is time enough.
CAPULET   Go, Nurse; go with her. We'll to church tomorrow.
                    Exeunt [JULIET *and* NURSE].
40   CAPULET'S WIFE   We shall be short in our provision:
'Tis now near night.
CAPULET   Tush, I will stir about,
And all things shall be well, I warrant thee, wife.
Go thou to Juliet; help to deck up her.
I'll not to bed tonight. Let me alone;
45   I'll play the housewife for this once. —What ho!
—They are all forth. Well, I will walk myself
To County Paris to prepare up him
Against tomorrow. My heart is wondrous light
Since this same wayward girl is so reclaimed.[2]
                    Exeunt.

                    4·3

                    Enter JULIET *and* NURSE.
JULIET   Ay, those attires are best. But, gentle Nurse,
I pray thee leave me to myself tonight,
For I have need of many orisons°   *prayers*
To move the heavens to smile upon my state,
5   Which, well thou knowest, is cross° and full of sin.   *adverse*
                    Enter [CAPULET'S WIFE].
CAPULET'S WIFE   What, are you busy, ho? Need you my help?
JULIET   No, madam. We have culled such necessaries
As are behooveful° for our state° tomorrow.   *needful / ceremony*
So please° you, let me now be left alone,   *If it pleases*
10   And let the Nurse this night sit up with you,

---

2. Reformed; claimed in marriage.
4.3 Location: Capulet's house.

For I am sure you have your hands full all
In this so sudden business.

CAPULET'S WIFE   Good night.
Get thee to bed and rest, for thou hast need.

JULIET   Farewell.

                Exeunt [CAPULET'S WIFE *and* NURSE].
                God knows when we shall meet again.
15   I have a faint cold fear thrills° through my veins,   *pierces*
     That almost freezes up the heat of life.
     I'll call them back again to comfort me.
     —Nurse!—What should she do here?
     My dismal° scene I needs must act alone.   *calamitous*
20   Come, vial.
     What if this mixture do not work at all?
     Shall I be married, then, tomorrow morning?
     No, no, this shall forbid it. [*She places a knife beside her.*]
        Lie thou there.
     What if it be a poison which the Friar
25   Subtly hath ministered to have me dead,
     Lest in this marriage he should be dishonored
     Because he married me before to Romeo?
     I fear it is—and yet methinks it should not,°   *not be*
     For he hath still° been tried° a holy man.   *always / proved*
30   How, if when I am laid into the tomb,
     I wake before the time that Romeo
     Come to redeem me? There's a fearful point!
     Shall I not then be stifled in the vault,
     To whose foul mouth no healthsome air breathes in,
35   And there die, strangled,° ere my Romeo comes?   *suffocated*
     Or, if I live, is it not very like°   *likely*
     The horrible conceit of death and night,
     Together with the terror of the place,
     As° in a vault, an ancient receptacle   *As it is*
40   Where, for this many hundred years, the bones
     Of all my buried ancestors are packed—
     Where bloody Tybalt, yet but green° in earth,   *newly*
     Lies fest'ring in his shroud—where, as they say,
     At some hours in the night spirits resort—
45   Alack, alack! Is it not like that I,
     So early waking, what with loathsome smells
     And shrieks like mandrakes¹ torn out of the earth

---

1. Plants with forked roots thought to resemble a man. Popular belief held that they uttered
   a death- or madness-producing shriek upon being pulled up.

That living mortals, hearing them, run mad—
Oh, if I wake, shall I not be distraught,
50 Environèd with all these hideous fears,
And madly play with my forefathers' joints,
And pluck the mangled Tybalt from his shroud,
And, in this rage,° with some great kinsman's bone,   *insanity*
As with a club, dash out my desp'rate brains?
55 Oh, look! Methinks I see my cousin's ghost,
Seeking out Romeo that did spit his body
Upon a rapier's point. —Stay, Tybalt, stay!
—Romeo, Romeo, Romeo! Here's drink. I drink to thee.
[*She drinks from the vial and falls upon
her bed within the curtains.*]

4·4

Enter [CAPULET'S WIFE] *and* NURSE.
CAPULET'S WIFE   Hold! Take these keys and fetch
    more spices, Nurse.
NURSE   They call for dates and quinces in the
    pastry.°   *pastry kitchen*
Enter old CAPULET.
CAPULET   Come, stir, stir, stir! The second cock hath crowed;
    The curfew bell[1] hath rung; 'tis three o'clock!
5 Look to the baked meats, good Angelica;[2]
    Spare not for cost.
NURSE   Go, you cotquean,° go!   *old housewife*
    Get you to bed. Faith, you'll be sick tomorrow
    For this night's watching.°   *wakefulness*
CAPULET   No, not a whit. What, I have watched ere now
10 All night for lesser cause, and ne'er been sick!
CAPULET'S WIFE   Ay, you have been a mouse-hunt° in   *skirt chaser*
    your time,
    But I will watch° you from such watching now.   *guard*
                Exeunt [CAPULET'S WIFE] *and* NURSE.
CAPULET   A jealous-hood,[3] jealous-hood!
    Enter three or four [SERVINGMEN] *with
    spits and logs and baskets.*
                        —Now, fellow, what is there?

4·4 Location: Scene continues.
1. Also rung at daybreak.
2. It is unclear whether Capulet refers to his wife or the Nurse.
3. Jealousy; jealous woman.

FIRST SERVINGMAN   Things for the cook, sir, but I know
    not what.
CAPULET   Make haste, make haste!
                            [*Exit* FIRST SERVINGMAN.]
15   —Sirrah, fetch drier logs.
    Call Peter; he will show thee where they are.
SECOND SERVINGMAN   I have a head, sir, that will
    find out logs,[4]
And never trouble Peter for the matter.
                            [*Exit* SECOND SERVINGMAN.]
CAPULET   Mass,° and well said! A merry   *By the mass*
    whoreson,° ha!   *rogue*
20 Thou shalt be loggerhead° Good Father,   *wooden-headed*
    'tis day!
The County will be here with music straight,
For so he said he would.
        Play music [*within*].
                        I hear him near!
Nurse! Wife! What ho! What, Nurse, I say!
        Enter NURSE.
Go waken Juliet; go and trim her up.
25 I'll go and chat with Paris. Hie, make haste,
    Make haste! The bridegroom, he is come already!
    Make haste, I say!
NURSE   Mistress! What, Mistress Juliet! —Fast,°   *Asleep*
    I warrant her, she—
Why, lamb! Why, lady! Fie, you slug-a-bed!
30 Why, love, I say! Madam! Sweetheart! Why, bride!
    What, not a word? You take your pennyworth's°   *bits (of sleep)*
        now;
Sleep for a week—for the next night, I warrant,
The County Paris hath set up his rest[5]
That you shall rest but little, God forgive me.
35 Marry, and amen! —How sound is she asleep!
    I needs must wake her. —Madam, madam, madam!
Ay, let the County take° you in your bed: *catch; sexually possess*
He'll fright you up, i'faith. Will it not be?
        [*She draws back the curtains.*]
What, dressed and in your clothes, and down again?
40 I must needs wake you. Lady, lady, lady!

---

4. I have a good head for finding things, so I can certainly find the logs; my head knows all
   about logs (I am a blockhead).
5. *hath . . . rest*: has resolved (from staking everything in the card game primero), with
   bawdy pun.

Alas, alas! —Help, help! My lady's dead!
Oh, welladay,° that ever I was born!   *alas*
Some aqua vitae, ho! My lord! My lady!
       [*Enter* CAPULET'S WIFE.]
CAPULET'S WIFE   What noise is here?
NURSE   Oh, lamentable day!
CAPULET'S WIFE   What is the matter?
45   NURSE   Look! Look! Oh, heavy day!
CAPULET'S WIFE   O me, O me! —My child, my only life!
    Revive, look up, or I will die with thee!
    —Help, help! Call help!
          Enter [CAPULET].
CAPULET   For shame, bring Juliet forth! Her lord is come.
50   NURSE   She's dead, deceased; she's dead, alack the day!
CAPULET'S WIFE   Alack the day! She's dead, she's dead,
    she's dead!
CAPULET   Ha! Let me see her. Out,° alas, she's cold!   *Woe*
    Her blood is settled,° and her joints are stiff;   *motionless*
    Life and these lips have long been separated.
55   Death lies on her like an untimely frost
    Upon the sweetest flower of all the field.
NURSE   Oh, lamentable day!
CAPULET'S WIFE   Oh, woeful time!
CAPULET   Death, that hath ta'en her hence to make me wail,
    Ties up my tongue and will not let me speak.
          Enter FRIAR [LAURENCE] *and the County* [PARIS].
60   FRIAR LAURENCE   Come, is the bride ready to go to church?
CAPULET   Ready to go, but never to return.
    —O son, the night before thy wedding day
    Hath Death lain with thy wife. There she lies,
    Flower as she was, deflowered by him.
65   Death is my son-in-law; Death is my heir;
    My daughter he hath wedded. I will die
    And leave him all. Life, living,° all is Death's.   *property*
PARIS [*as to* JULIET]   Have I thought,° love, to see   *expected*
    this morning's face,
    And doth it give me such a sight as this?
70   CAPULET'S WIFE   Accursed, unhappy, wretched, hateful day!
    Most miserable hour that e'er time saw
    In lasting labor of his pilgrimage!
    But one, poor one, one poor and loving child,
    But one thing to rejoice and solace in—
75   And cruel death hath catched it from my sight.
NURSE   Oh, woe! Oh, woeful, woeful, woeful day!

Most lamentable day! Most woeful day
That ever, ever I did yet behold!
Oh, day! Oh, day! Oh, day! Oh, hateful day!
80   Never was seen so black a day as this.
Oh, woeful day! Oh, woeful day!
PARIS   Beguiled,° divorcèd, wrongèd, spited,°   *Cheated / injured*
slain!
Most detestable death, by thee beguiled,
By cruel, cruel thee quite overthrown.
85   O love, O life—not life, but love in death.
CAPULET   Despised, distressed, hated, martyred, killed!
Uncomfortable° time, why cam'st thou now   *Comfortless*
To murder, murder our solemnity?°   *festivity*
O child, O child, my soul and not my child,[6]
90   Dead art thou. Alack, my child is dead,
And with my child my joys are burièd.
FRIAR LAURENCE   Peace, ho, for shame! Confusion's°   *Destruction's*
care lives not
In these confusions.° Heaven and yourself   *commotions*
Had part in this fair maid; now heaven hath all,
95   And all the better is it for the maid.
Your part in her you could not keep from death,
But heaven keeps his part in eternal life.
The most you sought was her promotion,°   *social advancement*
For 'twas your heaven° she should be   *highest ambition*
advanced;
100   And weep ye now, seeing she is advanced
Above the clouds, as high as heaven itself?
Oh, in this love you love your child so ill
That you run mad, seeing that she is well.
She's not well married that lives married long,
105   But she's best married that dies married young.
Dry up your tears, and stick your rosemary[7]
On this fair corpse; and, as the custom is,
And in her best array, bear her to church.
For, though some nature° bids us all lament.   *affection*
110   Yet nature's tears are reason's merriment.°   *laughable idiocy*
CAPULET   All things that we ordainèd festival
Turn from their office° to black funeral: *due function*
Our instruments to melancholy bells,

6. *not my child*: because dead and only a corpse.
7. Traditionally, a symbol of remembrance.

	Our wedding cheer° to a sad burial feast,	*fare*
115	Our solemn° hymns to sullen° dirges change;	*ceremonial / mournful*
	Our bridal flowers serve for a buried corpse,	
	And all things change them to the contrary.	

FRIAR LAURENCE   Sir, go you in; and, madam, go with him;
And go, Sir Paris. Everyone prepare
120   To follow this fair corpse unto her grave.
The heavens do lour° upon you for some   *hang threatening*
    ill;°   *offense*
Move° them no more by crossing their high will.   *Anger*

                    Exeunt [all but the NURSE].
        [*Enter three* MUSICIANS.]

FIRST MUSICIAN   Faith, we may put° up our pipes   . *pack*
    and be gone.

NURSE   Honest good fellows—ah, put up, put up!
125   For well you know this is a pitiful case.

FIRST MUSICIAN   Ay, by my troth, the case may be
    amended.[8]   *Exit* [NURSE].
        Enter [PETER].

PETER   Musicians! O musicians! "Heart's
    Ease"!° "Heart's Ease"! Oh, an you will have   *(popular song)*
    me live, play "Heart's Ease"!

130   FIRST MUSICIAN   Why "Heart's Ease"?

PETER   O musicians, because my heart itself
    plays "My heart is full." Oh, play me some
    merry dump° to comfort me.   *sad tune*

MUSICIANS   Not a dump, we! 'Tis no time to play now.

135   PETER   You will not, then?

FIRST MUSICIAN   No.

PETER   I will, then, give it you soundly°   *thoroughly; in sound*

FIRST MUSICIAN   What will you give us?

PETER   No money, on my faith, but the gleek.[9]
140   I will give you the minstrel.[1]

FIRST MUSICIAN   Then will I give you the
    serving-creature.

PETER   Then will I lay the serving-creature's
    dagger on your pate. I will carry° no crotch-   *bear; sing*
145   ets;[2] I'll re you, I'll fa you, do you note° me?   *heed*

8. Things could be better; the instrument case can be repaired.
9. To "give the gleek" was to make a fool of or play a trick on.
1. I will insultingly call you a minstrel.
2. Whimsy; quarter notes.

FIRST MUSICIAN   An you re us and fa us, you
     note° us.   *give notes to*

SECOND MUSICIAN   Pray you, put up your
     dagger, and put out° your wit.   *show; quench*

150 PETER   Then have at you with my wit! I will
     dry-beat° you with an iron° wit, and put up   *thrash / a merciless*
     my iron dagger. Answer[3] me like men.
     [*Sings.*]   When griping griefs the heart doth wound,
               Then music with her silver sound[4]—
155 Why "silver sound"? Why "music with her silver sound"?
     What say you, Simon Catling?[5]

FIRST MUSICIAN   Marry, sir, because silver
     hath a sweet sound.

PETER   Prates!° What say you, Hugh Rebeck?[6]   *Chatter*

160 SECOND MUSICIAN   I say "silver sound," because
     musicians sound for silver.

PETER   Prates, too! What say you, James Soundpost?[7]

THIRD MUSICIAN   Faith, I know not what to say.

PETER   Oh, I cry you mercy!° You are the   *beg your pardon*
165 singer; I will say for you. It is "music with
     her silver sound," because musicians have
     no gold for sounding.[8]
     [*Sings.*]   Then music with her silver sound
               With speedy help doth lend redress.   *Exit.*

170 FIRST MUSICIAN   What a pestilent knave is this same!

SECOND MUSICIAN   Hang him, jack! Come,
     we'll in here, tarry for the mourners, and
     stay° dinner.   *Exeunt.*   *await*

5.1

Enter ROMEO.

ROMEO   If I may trust the flattering° truth of sleep,   *encouraging*
     My dreams presage some joyful news at hand.
     My bosom's lord sits lightly in his throne,[1]
     And all this day an unaccustomed spirit

---

3. Defy; respond to.
4. Lines from the song "In Commendation of Music," by Richard Edwardes, printed in *The Paradise of Dainty Devices* (1576).
5. *Catling*: catgut used for stringed instruments.
6. *Rebeck*: three-stringed instrument.
7. *Soundpost*: supporting peg fixed between the sounding board and back of a stringed instrument.
8. Musicians are given no gold for playing; they are poor and have no gold to jingle.
5.1 Location: A street in Mantua.
1. Love rules in the heart; the heart is at ease in the chest.

5   Lifts me above the ground with cheerful thoughts.
       I dreamt my lady came and found me dead—
       Strange dream that gives a dead man leave to think—
       And breathed such life with kisses in° my lips   into
       That I revived and was an emperor.
10   Ah me, how sweet is love itself possessed°   enjoyed in reality
       When but love's shadows° are so rich in joy!   dreams; images
              Enter [BALTHASAR,] Romeo's man.[2]
       News from Verona! How now, Balthasar?
       Dost thou not bring me letters from the Friar?
       How doth my lady? Is my father well?
15   How doth my lady Juliet? That I ask again,
       For nothing can be ill if she be well.
       BALTHASAR   Then she is well, and nothing can be ill.
       Her body sleeps in Capels' monument,
       And her immortal part with angels lives.
20   I saw her laid low in her kindred's vault,
       And presently° took post[3] to tell it you.   immediately
       Oh, pardon me for bringing these ill news,
       Since you did leave it for my office,° sir.   duty
       ROMEO   Is it e'en so? Then I deny° you, stars!   repudiate
25   —Thou knowest my lodging. Get me ink and paper,
       And hire post-horses; I will hence tonight.
       BALTHASAR   I do beseech you, sir, have patience:
       Your looks are pale and wild, and do import°   signify
       Some misadventure.
       ROMEO   Tush, thou art deceived.
30   Leave me, and do the thing I bid thee do.
       Hast thou no letters to me from the Friar?
       BALTHASAR   No, my good lord.
       ROMEO   No matter. Get thee gone,
       And hire those horses. I'll be with thee straight.
                                 Exit [BALTHASAR].
       Well, Juliet, I will lie with thee tonight.
35   Let's see for means. O mischief, thou art swift
       To enter in the thoughts of desperate men.
       I do remember an apothecary,
       And hereabouts 'a dwells, which late I noted,
       In tattered weeds,° with overwhelming°   clothes /overhanging
         brows,

---

2. In Q1, the stage direction indicates that Romeo's man is "booted," as if he has just dismounted.
3. Set out on post-horses.

40	Culling of simples.° Meager were his looks;	*herbs*
	Sharp misery had worn him to the bones;	
	And in his needy° shop a tortoise hung,	*poor*
	An alligator stuffed, and other skins	
	Of ill-shaped fishes; and, about his shelves,	
45	A beggarly account° of empty boxes,	*sparse collection*
	Green earthen pots, bladders, and musty seeds,	
	Remnants of packthread,° and old cakes of roses[4]	*twine*
	Were thinly scattered to make up a show.	
	Noting this penury, to myself I said,	
50	"An if a man did need a poison now,	
	Whose sale is present death[5] in Mantua,	
	Here lives a caitiff° wretch would sell it him."	*pitiful*
	Oh, this same thought did but forerun my need,	
	And this same needy man must sell it me.	
55	As I remember, this should be the house.	
	Being holiday, the beggar's shop is shut.	
	—What ho, Apothecary!	

[*Enter* APOTHECARY.]

APOTHECARY   Who calls so loud?

ROMEO   Come hither, man. I see that thou art poor.
    Hold, there is forty ducats.[6] Let me have

60	A dram of poison, such soon-speeding gear[7]	
	As will disperse itself through all the veins	
	That the life-weary taker may fall dead,	
	And that the trunk° may be discharged of breath	*body*
	As violently as hasty powder fired	
65	Doth hurry from the fatal cannon's womb.	

APOTHECARY   Such mortal drugs I have, but Mantua's law
    Is death to any he° that utters° them.   *man / offers to sell*

ROMEO   Art thou so bare° and full of wretchedness,   *destitute*
    And fearest to die? Famine is in thy cheeks;

70	Need and oppression starveth in thy eyes;
	Contempt and beggary hangs upon thy back.
	The world is not thy friend, nor the world's law;
	The world affords° no law to make thee rich;
	Then be not poor, but break it, and take this.
75	APOTHECARY My poverty, but not my will, consents.
	ROMEO I pay thy poverty and not thy will.

[handwritten margin notes: "Romeo is unsympathetic to the apothecary" and "will but not consent"]

---

4. Rose petals pressed into cake form and used as a sachet.
5. Punishable by immediate death.
6. Various gold coins used at times in much of Europe, and Shakespeare's usual currency
   for plays not set in England.
7. Quick-working stuff; quick-killing stuff.

APOTHECARY   Put this in any liquid thing you will,
And drink it off; and if you had the strength
Of twenty men, it would dispatch you straight.°   *immediately*
80 ROMEO   There is thy gold—worse poison to men's souls,
Doing more murder in this loathsome world
Than these poor compounds that thou mayst not sell.
I sell thee poison; thou hast sold me none.
Farewell. Buy food, and get thyself in flesh.°   *grow fatter*
              [*Exit* APOTHECARY.]
85 Come, cordial° and not poison, go with me   *restorative*
To Juliet's grave, for there must I use thee.   *Exit.*

5.2

Enter FRIAR JOHN.
FRIAR JOHN   Holy Franciscan Friar! Brother, ho!
              Enter FRIAR LAURENCE.
FRIAR LAURENCE   This same should be the voice of Friar John.
—Welcome from Mantua! What says Romeo?
Or, if his mind° be writ, give me his letter.   *thoughts*
5 FRIAR JOHN   Going to find a barefoot brother out,
One of our order, to associate me,[1]
Here in this city visiting the sick,
And finding him, the searchers[2] of the town,
Suspecting that we both were in a house
10 Where the infectious pestilence did reign,
Sealed up the doors and would not let us forth,
So that my speed to Mantua there was stayed.°   *stopped*
FRIAR LAURENCE   Who bare my letter, then, to Romeo?
FRIAR JOHN   I could not send it—here it is again—
15 Nor get a messenger to bring it thee,
So fearful were they of infection.°   *contagion*
FRIAR LAURENCE   Unhappy fortune! By my brotherhood,
The letter was not nice° but full of charge,°   *trivial / importance*
Of dear import,° and the neglecting it   *serious consequence*
20 May do much danger. Friar John, go hence,
Get me an iron crow,° and bring it straight   *crowbar*
Unto my cell.

5.2 Location: Friar Laurence's cell.
1. Franciscan friars (barefoot because the order is sworn to poverty) traveled only in pairs. *associate*: accompany.
2. Health officers appointed to examine corpses and identify houses infected with the plague.

FRIAR JOHN   Brother, I'll go and bring it thee.
                                                    Exit.
FRIAR LAURENCE   Now must I to the monument alone.
        Within this three hours will fair Juliet wake;
25   She will beshrew° me much that Romeo   *curse*
        Hath had no notice of these accidents,°   *events*
        But I will write again to Mantua
        And keep her at my cell till Romeo come.
        Poor living corpse, closed in a dead man's tomb!   *Exit.*

5.3

        Enter PARIS *and his* PAGE.
PARIS   Give me thy torch, boy—hence, and stand
            aloof°—   *stay apart*
        Yet put it out, for I would not be seen.
        Under yond young trees lay thee all along,°   *stretched out*
        Holding thy ear close to the hollow ground;
5   So shall no foot upon the churchyard tread,
        Being° loose, unfirm with digging up of graves,   *The ground being*
        But thou shalt hear it. Whistle then to me
        As signal that thou hearest something approach.
        Give me those flowers. Do as I bid thee. Go.
10 PAGE [*aside*]   I am almost afraid to stand alone
        Here in the churchyard, yet I will adventure.°   *risk it*
            [*He retires.*]
    PARIS [*as to* JULIET]   Sweet flower, with flowers thy
            bridal bed I strew—
        Oh, woe, thy canopy° is dust and stones—   *covering; bed hangings*
        Which with sweet° water nightly I will dew,   *perfumed*
15   Or, wanting that, with tears distilled by moans.
        The obsequies° that I for thee will keep°   *funeral rites / perform*
        Nightly shall be to strew thy grave and weep.
            [PAGE *whistles.*]
        The boy gives warning something doth approach.
        What cursèd foot wanders this way tonight
20   To cross° my obsequies and true love's rite?   *thwart*
            Enter ROMEO *and* [BALTHASAR].
        What? With a torch? Muffle me, night, a while.
            [*He retires.*]

5.3 Location: The Capulet mausoleum.

ROMEO   Give me that mattock° and the   *pickax*
    wrenching iron.
    Hold; take this letter; early in the morning
    See thou deliver it to my lord and father.
25   Give me the light. Upon thy life, I charge thee,
    Whate'er thou hearest or seest, stand all aloof,
    And do not interrupt me in my course.
    Why I descend into this bed of death
    Is partly to behold my lady's face,
30   But chiefly to take thence from her dead finger
    A precious ring, a ring that I must use
    In dear° employment. Therefore, hence; be   *important; tender*
    gone.
    But if thou, jealous° dost return to pry   *suspicious*
    In what I farther shall intend to do,
35   By heaven, I will tear thee joint by joint
    And strew this hungry churchyard with thy limbs!
    The time and my intents are savage-wild,
    More fierce and more inexorable far
    Than empty° tigers or the roaring sea.   *hungry*
40 BALTHASAR   I will be gone, sir, and not trouble ye.
  ROMEO   So shalt thou show me friendship. Take thou that.
      [*He gives* BALTHASAR *money.*]
    Live, and be prosperous; and farewell, good fellow.
  BALTHASAR [*aside*]   For all this same, I'll hide me here about.
    His looks I fear, and his intents I doubt.°   *suspect*
      [*He retires.*]
      [ROMEO *opens the tomb.*]
45 ROMEO   Thou detestable maw, thou womb¹ of death,
    Gorged with the dearest morsel of the earth,
    Thus I enforce thy rotten jaws to open,
    And, in despite,° I'll cram thee with more food.   *defiant ill will*
  PARIS [*apart*]   This is that banished, haughty Montague
50   That murdered my love's cousin, with which grief
    It is supposèd the fair creature died,
    And here is come to do some villainous shame
    To the dead bodies. I will apprehend him.
      [*He steps forward.*]
    —Stop thy unhallowed° toil, vile Montague!   *unholy*
55   Can vengeance be pursued further than death?
    Condemnèd villain, I do apprehend thee.

---

1. Belly; also playing on the birthplace of Romeo's death.

Obey and go with me, for thou must die.
ROMEO   I must indeed, and therefore came I hither.
Good gentle youth, tempt not a desp'rate° man;   *despairing; violent*
60   Fly hence and leave me. Think upon these gone;
Let them affright thee. I beseech thee, youth,
Put not another sin upon my head
By urging me to fury. Oh, be gone!
By heaven, I love thee better than myself,
65   For I come hither armed against myself.
Stay not; be gone. Live, and hereafter say
A madman's mercy bid thee run away.
PARIS   I do defy thy conjuration,°   *entreaty*
And apprehend thee for a felon here.
70   ROMEO   Wilt thou provoke me? Then have at thee, boy!
[*They fight.*]
PAGE   O Lord, they fight! I will go call the watch.
[*Exit.*]

PARIS   Oh, I am slain! If thou be merciful,
Open the tomb; lay me with Juliet.
[*He dies.*]
ROMEO   In faith, I will. —Let me peruse this face.
75   Mercutio's kinsman, noble County Paris!
What said my man when my betossèd° soul   *storm-tossed*
Did not attend° him as we rode? I think   *listen to*
He told me Paris should have married Juliet.
Said he not so? Or did I dream it so?
80   Or am I mad, hearing him talk of Juliet,
To think it was so? —Oh, give me thy hand,
One writ with me in sour misfortune's book.
I'll bury thee in a triumphant° grave,
A grave—oh, no, a lantern,° slaughtered youth,   *magnificent lighthouse*
85   For here lies Juliet, and her beauty makes
This vault a feasting presence[2] full of light.
Death, lie thou there, by a dead man interred.
How oft when men are at the point of death
Have they been merry, which their keepers° call   *sick nurses; jailers*
90   A light'ning before death? Oh, how may I
Call this a light'ning? —O my love, my wife,
Death that hath sucked the honey of thy breath
Hath had no power yet upon thy beauty.

2. Festive royal chamber for receiving guests.

Thou art not conquered:° beauty's   *overpowered; seduced*
   ensign° yet   *flag*
95 Is crimson in thy lips and in thy cheeks,
And death's pale flag is not advancèd there.
—Tybalt, liest thou there in thy bloody sheet?
Oh, what more favor can I do to thee
Than with that hand that cut thy youth in twain
100 To sunder his° that was thine enemy?   *the youth of him*
Forgive me, cousin. —Ah, dear Juliet,
Why art thou yet so fair? Shall I believe
That unsubstantial° death is amorous,   *immaterial*
And that the lean abhorrèd monster keeps
105 Thee here in dark to be his paramour?
For fear of that I still will stay with thee,
And never from this pallet of dim night
Depart again. Here, here will I remain
With worms that are thy chambermaids; oh, here
110 Will I set up my everlasting rest,[3]
And shake the yoke of inauspicious stars
From this world-wearied flesh. Eyes, look your last;
Arms, take your last embrace; and lips—O you,
The doors of breath—seal with a righteous kiss
115 A dateless bargain° to engrossing[4] death.   *An eternal contract*
Come, bitter conduct,° come, unsavory guide,   *conductor; leader*
Thou desperate pilot, now at once run on
The dashing rocks thy seasick, weary bark!
Here's to my love. [*He drinks.*] O true apothecary,
120 Thy drugs are quick.° Thus, with a kiss, I die.   *fast; vigorous*
   [*He falls and dies.*]
   Enter FRIAR [LAURENCE] *with lantern,*
   crow, and spade.

FRIAR LAURENCE Saint Francis be my speed!° How   *help*
  oft tonight
Have my old feet stumbled at graves!—Who's there?
   [BALTHASAR *steps forward.*]
BALTHASAR Here's one, a friend, and one that knows
  you well.
FRIAR Bliss be upon you! Tell me, good my friend,
125 What torch is yond that vainly lends his light
To grubs and eyeless skulls? As I discern,
It burneth in the Capels' monument.

---

3. Make my final determination.
4. Buying up in large quantities to monopolize; writing a legal document.

BALTHASAR   It doth so, holy sir, and there's my master,
    One that you love.
FRIAR LAURENCE   Who is it?
BALTHASAR   Romeo.
FRIAR LAURENCE   How long hath he been there?
130 BALTHASAR   Full half an hour.
FRIAR LAURENCE   Go with me to the vault.
BALTHASAR   I dare not, sir.
    My master knows not but I am gone hence,
    And fearfully° did menace me with death   *fearsomely*
    If I did stay to look on his intents.
135 FRIAR LAURENCE   Stay, then. I'll go alone. Fear comes
    upon me.
    Oh, much I fear some ill unthrifty° thing.   *unfortunate*
BALTHASAR   As I did sleep under this young tree here,
    I dreamt my master and another fought,
    And that my master slew him.
        [FRIAR LAURENCE *moves toward the vault.*]
FRIAR LAURENCE   Romeo!
140 Alack, alack, what blood is this which stains
    The stony entrance of this sepulcher?
    What mean these masterless and gory swords
    To lie discolored by this place of peace?
    Romeo! Oh, pale! Who else? What, Paris too?
145 And steeped in blood? Ah, what an unkind°   *an unnatural; a cruel*
    hour
    Is guilty of this lamentable chance!°   *event*
        [JULIET *rises.*]
    The lady stirs!
JULIET   O comfortable° Friar, where is my lord?   *solace-giving*
    I do remember well where I should be,
150 And there I am. Where is my Romeo?
FRIAR LAURENCE   I hear some noise. —Lady, come
    from that nest
    Of death, contagion, and unnatural sleep.
    A greater power than we can contradict
    Hath thwarted our intents. Come. Come away!
155 Thy husband in thy bosom there lies dead,
    And Paris, too. Come—I'll dispose of thee
    Among a sisterhood of holy nuns.
    Stay not to question, for the watch is coming.
    Come! Go, good Juliet! I dare no longer stay.
160 JULIET   Go, get thee hence, for I will not away.
                                Exit [FRIAR LAURENCE].
    What's here? A cup closed in my true love's hand?

Poison I see hath been his timeless° end.   *untimely; lasting*
O churl,° drunk all, and left no friendly drop   *miser*
To help me after? I will kiss thy lips:
165   Haply° some poison yet doth hang on them   *Perhaps*
To make me die with a restorative.⁵
Thy lips are warm!
          Enter [PAGE *and* WATCHMEN].
CHIEF WATCHMAN   Lead, boy. Which way?
JULIET   Yea, noise? Then I'll be brief.
          [*She takes Romeo's dagger.*]
                                        O happy° dagger,   *fortunate*
170   This is thy sheath; there rust and let me die.
          [*She stabs herself and falls.*]
PAGE   This is the place—there, where the torch doth
    burn.
CHIEF WATCHMAN   The ground is bloody. Search about
    the churchyard.
Go, some of you; whoe'er you find, attach.°   *arrest*
          [*Exeunt some of the watch.*]
Pitiful sight! Here lies the County, slain,
175   And Juliet, bleeding, warm, and newly dead,
Who here hath lain this two days burièd.
Go tell the Prince! Run to the Capulets;
Raise up the Montagues! Some others, search.
          [*Exeunt others of the watch.*]
We see the ground° whereon these woes do lie,   *earth*
180   But the true ground° of all these piteous woes   *cause*
We cannot without circumstance° descry.   *a fuller account*
          Enter [SECOND WATCHMAN *with*]
          Romeo's man [BALTHASAR].
SECOND WATCHMAN   Here's Romeo's man; we found
    him in the churchyard.
CHIEF WATCHMAN   Hold him in safety° till the Prince   *securely*
    come hither.
          Enter [THIRD WATCHMAN *with* FRIAR LAURENCE].
THIRD WATCHMAN   Here is a friar that trembles, sighs,
    and weeps.
185   We took this mattock and this spade from him
As he was coming from this churchyard's side.⁶
CHIEF WATCHMAN   A great suspicion! Stay° the Friar, too.   *Hold*
          Enter the PRINCE [*with Attendants*].

---

5. Both the kiss, which is healing, and the poison, which restores them to each other.
6. This side of the churchyard.

PRINCE   What misadventure is so early up
         That calls our person from our morning rest?
              Enter [CAPULET *and* CAPULET'S WIFE].
190 CAPULET   What should it be that is so shrieked abroad?
     CAPULET'S WIFE   Oh, the people in the street cry "Romeo,"
         Some "Juliet," and some "Paris," and all run
         With open° outcry toward our monument!   *public; open-mouthed*
     PRINCE   What fear is this which startles° in your ears?   *bursts out*
195 CHIEF WATCHMAN   Sovereign, here lies the County
              Paris slain,
         And Romeo dead, and Juliet—dead before—
         Warm, and new killed.
     PRINCE   Search, seek, and know how this foul murder
              comes.
     CHIEF WATCHMAN   Here is a friar, and slaughtered
              Romeo's man,
200   With instruments upon them fit to open
         These dead men's tombs.
     CAPULET   O Heavens! O wife, look how our daughter bleeds!
         This dagger hath mista'en, for lo, his house°   *scabbard*
         Is empty on the back of Montague,
205   And it mis-sheathèd in my daughter's bosom.
     CAPULET'S WIFE   O me, this sight of death is as a bell
         That warns° my old age to a sepulcher.   *summons*
              Enter MONTAGUE [*with Attendants*].
     PRINCE   Come, Montague, for thou art early up
         To see thy son and heir now early down.
210 MONTAGUE   Alas, my liege, my wife is dead tonight;
         Grief of my son's exile hath stopped her breath.
         What further woe conspires against mine age?
     PRINCE   Look, and thou shalt see.
     MONTAGUE [*as to* ROMEO]   O thou untaught! What
              manners is in this,
215   To press before° thy father to a grave?   *To shove ahead of*
     PRINCE   Seal up the mouth of outrage[7] for a while,
         Till we can clear these ambiguities
         And know their spring, their head, their true descent;
         And then will I be general of your woes
220   And lead you even to death. Meantime, forbear,
         And let mischance be slave to° patience.   *overruled by*
         Bring forth the parties of suspicion.

---

7. Of impassioned exclamation.

FRIAR LAURENCE   I am the greatest,° able to do least,   *most suspect*
    Yet most suspected as the time and place
225   Doth make against me of this direful murder.
    And here I stand both to impeach and purge,
    Myself condemnèd and myself excused.[8]
PRINCE   Then say at once what thou dost know in this.
FRIAR   I will be brief, for my short date° of breath   *duration*
230   Is not so long as is a tedious tale.
    Romeo, there dead, was husband to that Juliet,
    And she, there dead—that's Romeo's faithful wife.
    I married them, and their stol'n marriage day
    Was Tybalt's doomsday, whose untimely death
235   Banished the new-made bridegroom from this city—
    For whom, and not for Tybalt, Juliet pined.
    —You, to remove that siege of grief from her,
    Betrothed and would have married her perforce°   *forcibly*
    To County Paris. Then comes she to me,
240   And, with wild looks, bid me devise some mean°   *method*
    To rid her from this second marriage,
    Or in my cell there would she kill herself.
    Then gave I her—so tutored by my art[9]—
    A sleeping potion, which so took effect
245   As I intended, for it wrought on her
    The form° of death. Meantime I writ to Romeo   *appearance*
    That he should hither come as this° dire night   *as this = this*
    To help to take her from her borrowed grave,
    Being the time the potion's force should cease.
250   But he which bore my letter, Friar John,
    Was stayed by accident, and yesternight
    Returned my letter back. Then, all alone,
    At the prefixèd° hour of her waking,   *prearranged*
    Came I to take her from her kindred's vault,
255   Meaning to keep her closely° at my cell   *secretly*
    Till I conveniently° could send to Romeo.   *befittingly*
    But when I came, some minute ere the time
    Of her awakening, here untimely lay
    The noble Paris and true Romeo, dead.
260   She wakes, and I entreated her come forth
    And bear this work of heaven with patience;
    But then a noise did scare me from the tomb,
    And she, too desperate, would not go with me,

8. *to impeach . . . excused*: to accuse myself of what I am guilty of and clear myself of what I am not.
9. As I knew through my medical study to do.

But, as it seems, did violence on herself.
265 All this I know—and to the marriage
     Her Nurse is privy; and, if aught in this
     Miscarried by my fault, let my old life
     Be sacrificed some hour before his° time   its
     Unto the rigor of severest law.
270 PRINCE We still° have known thee for a holy man.   always
     —Where's Romeo's man? What can he say to this?
     BALTHASAR I brought my master news of Juliet's death,
     And then in post° he came from Mantua   haste
     To this same place, to this same monument.
275 This letter he early bid me give his father,
     And threatened me with death, going in the vault,
     If I departed not and left him there.
     PRINCE Give me the letter; I will look on it.
     Where is the County's page that raised the watch?
280 —Sirrah, what made° your master in this place?   did
     PAGE He came with flowers to strew his lady's grave,
     And bid me stand aloof, and so I did.
     Anon° comes one with light to ope the tomb,   Soon
     And by and by my master drew on him,
285 And then I ran away to call the watch.
     PRINCE This letter doth make good the Friar's words—
     Their course of love, the tidings of her death.
     And here he writes that he did buy a poison
     Of a poor 'pothecary, and therewithal
290 Came to this vault to die and lie with Juliet.
     Where be these enemies? —Capulet, Montague:
     See what a scourge is laid upon your hate,
     That heaven finds means to kill your joys°   happiness; children
         with love,
     And I, for winking at° your discords, too   closing my eyes to
295 Have lost a brace of kinsmen. All are punished.
     CAPULET O brother Montague, give me thy hand.
     This is my daughter's jointure,° for no more   marriage portion
     Can I demand.
     MONTAGUE   But I can give thee more;
     For I will ray° her statue in pure gold,   array (i.e., gild)
300 That whiles Verona by that name is known
     There shall no figure at such rate be set[1]
     As that of true and faithful Juliet.
     CAPULET As rich shall Romeo's by his lady's lie,
     Poor sacrifices of our enmity.

---

1. No figure shall be so valued; no figure shall be erected at such a price.

305   PRINCE   A glooming° peace this morning with   *frowning; dark*
       it brings;
       The sun for sorrow will not show his head.
       Go hence to have more talk of these sad things—
       Some shall be pardoned, and some punishèd—
       For never was a story of more woe
310   Than this of Juliet and her Romeo.   [*Exeunt.*]

Unnatural ending - young die before old.

Textual Variants

Edd   editorial tradition
F   First Folio (1623)
F2   Second Folio (1632)
Q1   First Quarto (1597)
Q2   Second Quarto (1599)

Q3   Third Quarto (reprint of Q2, 1609)
Q4   Fourth Quarto (reprint of Q3, 1622)
SD   stage direction
SP   speech prefix

Prologue
0 SD [Edd]
14 SD [Edd]

1.1 [Edd]
0 SD [Edd] *Enter . . . with Swords and Bucklers, of the house of Capulet.*
9+ Montague [Edd] *Mountague*
31 in [Q1] not in Q2
38 SD ABRAHAM . . . *Servingman* [Edd] *two other serving men*
38 SD *of the Montagues* [Q1]
52 SD [Edd]
53 SP+ [Edd] *Abram.*
56 SD [Edd]
58 SD [Edd]
67 SD [Edd]
69 SD [Edd]
73 SD [Edd]
76 SD [Edd]
81 SD1 [Q1]
81 SD2 *including an* OFFICER [Edd]
86 SP+ [Edd] *Wife.*
86 crutch [Edd] crowch
89 SD [Edd]
90 SP+ [Edd] M. *Wife. 2.*
113 SD *all . . .* BENVOLIO [Edd]
157 his [Q3] is
169 SD MONTAGUE . . . WIFE [Edd]
183 SD [Edd]
189 well-seeming [Q4] welseeing

1.2 [Edd]
0 SD *a* SERVINGMAN [Edd] *the Clowne*

34 SD [Edd]
36 SD [Edd]
37 SD CAPULET *and* PARIS [Edd]
48 one [Q1] on
59 SD [Edd]
88 SD [Edd]
108 SD [Edd]

1.3 [Edd]
53 SP, 67 SP, 73 SP, 81 SP, 83 SP, 100 SP [Edd] *Old La.*
103 it [Q1] not in Q2
109 SP [Edd] *Mo.*
109 SD [Edd]

1.4 [Edd]
21 SP [Edd] *Horatio.*
29 quote [Edd] cote
37 done [Q1] dum
40 your [F] you
43 light lights [Edd] lights lights
55 atomi [Q1] ottamie
60 collars [Edd] collors
61 film [F2] Philome
64 maid [Q1] man
88 elflocks [Q1] Elklocks
112 SD HEAD SERVINGMAN [Edd] Romeo
113 SP+ [Edd] *Ser*
121–22 marzipan [Edd] March-pane
131 SD1 SERVINGMEN [Edd]
131 SD2 CAPULET . . . and [Edd]
132 SP+ [Edd] 1. *Capu.*
133 a bout [Edd] about
143 SD [Edd]
149, 154 [Edd] 2. *Capu.*

157 SD [Edd]
170 SD1, SD2 [Edd]
200 SD [Edd]
201 SD1, SD2 [Edd]
202 SD [Edd]
203 SD [Edd]
204 SD [Edd]
221 SD [Edd]
225 SD [Edd]
226 SD [Edd]
227 SD [Edd]
232 SD [Edd]
235 SD [This edn]
237 SD [Q1]
242 SD *Exeunt* [Q1]
242 SD CAPULET . . . *remain* [Edd]
249 SD [Edd]
250 SD [Edd]

2.0 [Edd]
0 SD [Edd]
4 matched [Q3] match
14 SD [Edd]

2.1 [Edd]
2 SD1 [Edd]
6 SP [Q1] not in Q2
7 Romeo [Q1] *Mer. Romeo*
10 pronounce [Q1] prouaunt
10 dove [Q1] day
12 heir [Q1] her
38 open-arse [Edd] open, or
42 SD1 BENVOLIO *and* MERCUTIO [Q4]
42 SD2 [Edd]
51 SD [Edd]
58 do [Q1] to
67 SD [Edd]
79 SD [Edd]
83 nor . . . part [Q1] not in Q2
83–84 ³nor . . . / . . . name [Edd] ô be some other name / Belonging to a man.
87 were [Q1] wene
125 washed [Q1] washeth
143 the [Edd] not in Q2
152 circled [Q1] circle
177 SD [F]
180 SD [Edd]
183 SD [Edd]
191 SP, 193 SP1 [Edd] not in Q2
191, 193 SD [Edd]

191, 193 Madam! [Edd] in margin
192 SP, 193 SP2 [Edd] not in Q2
196 SD [F1]
204 mine [Q1] not in Q2
209 Mine eyas [This edn] My Neece
228 SP [Q1] *Iu.*
229 Would [Q1, reading "I would"] *Ro.* Would
229 rest. [Q1] rest / The grey eyde morne smiles on the frowning night, / Checkring the Easterne Clouds with streaks of light, / And darknesse fleckted like a drunkard reeles, / From forth daies pathway, made by *Tytans* wheeles.
229 SD [Edd]

2.2 [Edd]
1 SP+ [Edd] *Fri.*
2 Check'ring [Q2 after 230] Checking

2.3 [Edd]
20 SP [Q1] *Ro.*
38 "pardon-me's" [Q1 (pardonmees)] pardons mees
115 SD PETER [Edd]
143 SD [Edd]
150 SD [Q1]
161 SD1 [Edd]
161 SD2 MERCUTIO *and* BENVOLIO [Q1]
172 SD [Q1]
182 SD [Edd]
203 SD [Edd]
232 dog's name [Q3] dog, name

2.4 [Edd]
11 three [Q3] there
15 And [Q4] *M.* And
17 SD *and* PETER [Edd]
20 SD [Edd]

2.5 [Edd]
22 SD [Edd]
23 SD [Edd]
37 SD [Q1]

3.1 [Edd]
0 SD *Mercutio's Page* [Edd]
0 SD *Montague's* [Edd]
39 SD *of . . . Men* [Edd]
42 SD [Edd]

43 SD [Edd]
82 SD [Edd]
92 SD1, SD2 [Edd]
94 SD [Edd]
99 SD [Q1]
100 SP [Edd] not in Q2
100 SD [Edd]
104 SD [Edd]
120 SD *all but* ROMEO [Edd]
132 SD [Q1]
136 and [Q3] end
143 SD *and dies* [Edd]
152 SD MONTAGUE'S WIFE . . .
  Attendants [Edd] *their wives,
  and all*
178 agile [Q1] aged
196 SP MONTAGUE [Q4] *Capu.*

3.2 [Edd]
1 SP [Q1]
45, 48, 49, 50 "Ay" [Edd] I
47 darting [Q3] arting
49 shut [Edd] shot
60 one [Q4] on
60 bier [Edd] beare
72 SP NURSE It [Q1] It
73 SP [Q1] *Nur.*
74 Did [F2] *Iu.* Did
76 Dove-feathered [Edd] Rauenous
  doue-featherd
79 damnèd [Q4] dimme

3.3 [Edd]
0 SD [Q1] *Enter Frier and* Romeo
3 SD [Q1]
62 madmen [Q1] mad man
71 SD NURSE *knocks* [Q1] *Enter
  Nurse, and knocke*
71 SD *within* [Edd]
74 SD *within* [Edd] *They knocke*
76 SD *Loud* [Edd] *Slud*
76 SD *within* [Edd]
78 SD *within* [Edd]
80 SD [Edd]
108 SD [Edd, drawing on Q1]
110 denote [Q1] deuote
117 lives [Q1] lies
144 pouts upon [Q4] puts up
164 SD [Q1]
168 disguised [Q3] disguise

3.4 [Edd]
10 SP [Edd] *La.*
13 be [Q3] me

23 We'll [Q1 (Wee'le)] Well,
31 SD [Edd]

3.5 [Edd]
13 exhales [Q3] exhale,
19 the [Q1] the the
36 SD [Edd] *Enter Madame and
  Nurse.*
40 SD [Edd]
42 SD [Q1]
54 SP [Q4] *Ro.*
64 SD CAPULET'S WIFE [Edd]
  Mother
64 SD *below* [Edd]
**64 SP, 68 SP1, 69 SP, 75 SP,
  78 SP, 80 SP2, 84 SP, 87 SP**
  [Edd] *La.*
67 SD JULIET . . . *down* [Q1]
67 SD *and . . . below* [Edd]
81 SD [Edd]
103 SP, 203 SP [Edd] *Mo.*
107, 112, 124 SP [Edd] *M.*
139 SP, 158 SP [Edd] *La.*
161 SP, 171 SP, 177 SP [Edd] *Fa.*
173 CAPULET Oh, [Q1] Father, ô
174 SP1 [Q4] not in Q2
174 SP2 [Edd] *Fa.*
176 SP [Edd] *Wi.*
182 lined [Edd] liand
236 SD [Q4]

4.1 [Edd]
16 SD [Edd]
61 SD [Edd]
72 slay [Q1] stay
83 chapless [Q1] chapels
85 shroud [Q4] not in Q2
98 breath [Q1] breast
100 To wanny [Edd] too many
110 In [Q3] Is
112 shalt [Q3] shall
116 and he [Q3] an he
117 waking [Q3] walking

4.2 [Edd]
0 SD CAPULET'S WIFE [Edd]
  Mother
1 SD1, SD2 [Edd]
2 SD [Edd]
12 SD [Edd]
23 SD [Q1]
38, 40 SP [Edd] *Mo.*
39, 41 SP [Edd] *Fa.*
39 SD JULIET *and* NURSE [Edd]

4.3 [Edd]

5 SD [Edd] *Mother*
6 SP, 12 SP [Edd] *Mo.*
14 SD CAPULET'S . . . NURSE [Edd]
23 SD [Edd]
49 wake [Q4] walke
58 SD *She falls upon her bed within the curtains* [Q1]
58 SD *drinks from the vial and* [Edd]

4.4 [Edd]

0 SD CAPULET'S WIFE [Edd] *Lady of the house*
1 SP, 11 SP [Edd] *La.*
12 SD CAPULET'S WIFE [Edd] *Lady*
13 SD SERVINGMEN [Q1]
14 SP [Edd] *Fel.*
15 SD [Edd]
17 SP [Edd] *Fel.*
18 SD [Q1]
20 Thou [Edd] Twou
22 SD *within* [Edd]
38 SD [Edd]
43 SD [Q1]
44 SP1, 45 SP1, 46 SP, 57 SP2, 70 SP [Edd] *Mo.*
48 SD CAPULET [Edd] *Father*
49, 52, 58, 61, 111 SP [Edd] *Fa.*
51 SP [Edd] *M.*
68 SD [This edn]
86 SP [Edd] *Fat.*
122 SD1 *all* . . . NURSE [Q1] *manet*
122 SD2 [Q1]
122 SD2 *three* [Edd]
123 SP [Edd] *Musi.*
126 SP [Edd] *Fid.*
126 by my [Q1] my my
126 SD1 NURSE [Edd] *omnes*
126 SD2 PETER [Q4] *Will Kenip*
130 SP [Edd] *Fidler.*
134 SP [Edd] *Minstrels*
136 SP, 138 SP, 141 SP, 146 SP [Edd] *Minst.*
148 SP [Edd] *Minstrel.*
150 PETER Then . . . with I [Q4] Then . . . wit. / *Peter.* I
153 SD [Edd]
168 SD [Edd]
170 SP [Edd] *Min.*

5.1 [Edd]

3 lord [Q1] L.
11 SD BALTHASAR [Q1]
17 SP+ [Q1] *Man.*
24 e'en [Edd] in

33 SD BALTHASAR [Q1]
57 SD [Q1]
58 SP [Q1] *Kom.*
66 SP, 75 SP, 77 SP [Q1] *Poti.*
76 pay [Q1] pray
84 SD [Edd]

5.2 [Edd]

0 SD [Q1] *Enter Frier* John *to Frier* Lawrence.

5.3 [Edd]

10 SD [Edd]
11 SD [Edd]
12 SD [This edn]
17 SD [Edd] *Whistle Boy*
21 SD1 BALTHASAR [Q+] Peter
21 SD2 [Edd]
40 SP, 43 SP [Q1] *Pet.*
41 SD [Edd]
43 SD [Edd]
44 SD1 [Edd]
44 SD2 [Q1]
49 SD [Edd]
53 SD [Edd]
68 conjuration [Q1 (conjurations)] commiration
70 SD [Q1]
71 SP [Q1 (*Boy:*)] not in Q2 (line italicized and set as SD)
73 SD [Edd]
102 Shall [Edd] I will beleeue, / Shall
108 again. [Q4] againe, come, lye thou in my arme, / Heer's to thy health, where ere thou tumblest in. / O true Appothecarie! / Thy drugs are quicke. Thus with a kisse I die. / Depart againe,
119 SD [Edd]
120 SD1 *falls* [Q1]
120 SD1 *and dies* [Edd]
122 SD [Edd]
123 SP+ [Q4] *Man.*
139 SD [Edd]
146 SD [Q1]
160 SD FRIAR LAURENCE [Edd]
167 SD PAGE *and* WATCHMEN [Edd] *Boy and Watch*
168 SP, 172 SP [Edd] *Watch.*
169 SD [Edd]
170 SD [Q1]
171 SP [Q4] *Watch boy.*
173 SD [Edd]
178 SD [Edd]

181 SD SECOND WATCHMAN with [Q1 (*Enter one with*)]
181 SD BALTHASAR [Edd]
182 SP [Edd] *Watch.*
183 SD [Edd] *Enter Frier, and another Watchman.*
187 too [F] too too
187 SD *with Attendants* [Q1 (*with others*)]
189 SD CAPULET *and* CAPULET'S WIFE [Q4] *Capels*

190 shrieked [Edd] shrike
195 SP [Edd] *Watch.*
199 SP [Edd] *Wat.*
199 slaughtered [Q4] Slaughter
201 tombs [Q4] Tombes. *Enter Capulet and his wife*
207 SD *with Attendants* [Edd]
209 early [Q3] earling
214 SD [This edn]
281 SP [Edd] *Boy.*
310 SD [F]

SOURCES, CONTEXTS, AND EARLY REWRITINGS

LUIGI DA PORTO

A Tale about Two Noble Lovers (ca. 1530)[†]

* * *

This youth remained apart from the others at the party, all alone and unsure of himself, and rarely did he join in the dancing or conversation, as one who, drawn to that house by Love, now felt very uneasy there. This grieved the maiden greatly, because she had heard that he was most charming and fun-loving. Once midnight had passed and the festivities were drawing to a close, there began the dance of the torch or hat, however we may wish to call it, still used to bring festivities to an end. In this dance, in which men and women form a circle and change partners at will, no woman chose the young man who, by chance, found himself next to the already enamoured maiden. On her other side was a young nobleman, known as Marcuccio the Cross-Eyed, whose hands were habitually very cold, in July no less than in January. Thus when Romeo Montecchi—for this was the young man's name—arrived on the woman's left and, as is done in this dance, took her fair hand in his, the maid said to him almost immediately, perhaps eager to hear him speak: "Praised be your arrival here at my side, Messer Romeo."

The youth, who had already noticed her glances, replied in amazement at her words: "What do you mean, praised be my arrival?" And she answered: "Yes, praised be your arrival at my side, because you at least will keep my left hand warm while Marcuccio freezes my right one." Romeo, somewhat emboldened, continued: "If I warm your hand with mine, you set my heart on fire with your beautiful eyes." After a fleeting smile the woman spoke further to him, taking care not to be seen with him or heard speaking to him: "I swear to you Romeo, on my faith, that no woman present appears as beautiful to my eyes as you do." To which the youth replied, already aflame: "Whatever I may be, should it not displease your beauty, I shall be its faithful servant." Having left the festivities shortly afterwards, Romeo returned to his own home where, after giving thought to the cruelty of his former love, who granted him scant reward for his considerable suffering, he resolved to devote himself wholly to her, should she so wish, even though she belonged to the enemy faction.

† From Luigi Da Porto, "A Tale about Two Noble Lovers," trans. Nicole Prunster, in *Romeo and Juliet Before Shakespeare: Four Tales of Star-Crossed Lovers* (Toronto: Centre for Reformation and Renaissance Studies, 2000), pp. 30–32, 42–46. Reprinted by permission of the publisher.

On the other hand the maiden, thinking of little else but him, after much sighing deemed that she would ever be happy if she could have him as her husband. But because of the feud between the two families, she greatly feared that there was little hope of achieving such a happy outcome. Thus living ever prey to two opposing thoughts, she repeated to herself: "Oh fool that I am, for what vain hope am I allowing myself to be led into this strange labyrinth? I shall be alone there, unable to find my way out at will, since Romeo Montecchi loves me not. As there is a feud between his family and mine, he cannot be seeking other than my dishonour. And even supposing he wanted me as his wife, my father would never consent to give me to him." Changing then her way of thinking, she said: "Who knows, in order to consolidate the peace between these two families that are already sick and tired of feuding, perhaps it could still come about that I have him the way I want!" And dwelling on this thought, she began granting him now and then the courtesy of her gaze.

With both lovers thus equally aflame and bearing the dear name and image of the other engraved in their hearts, they began to look lovingly upon one another, sometimes in church or at some window, with the result that their well-being depended upon seeing one another. He above all was so enflamed by her charming ways that he passed almost the entire night alone in front of her house, at great risk to his life. Sometimes he climbed up on the balcony outside her bedroom window where, without her or anyone else knowing, he would sit and listen to her beautiful voice; at other times he would lie in the street.

As Love would have it, one night when the moon was shining more brightly than usual it happened that, while Romeo was climbing onto this balcony, the maiden came to open the window, either by chance or because she had heard him the other evenings; and leaning out, she saw him. Believing that not she but someone else had opened the balcony window, Romeo made as if to flee into the shadow of some wall. Having realised who it was and calling him by name, she said to him: "What are you doing here all alone at this hour?" And he, having by this time recognised her, replied: "That which Love wills." "And if you were to be caught," said the woman, "could you not easily lose your life?" "My lady," replied Romeo, "it is true that I could easily lose my life, and I surely shall one night, if you do not help me. But since I am as near to death everywhere else as I am here, I am striving to die as close as I can to your person, with which I yearn to live forever, should you and heaven so please."

To this the maiden replied: "I shall never be to blame if you do not live honestly with me. If only it no longer depended on you or on the enmity I see dividing your family and mine!" The youth replied: "You can be assured that it is not possible to long for something more than I constantly long for you! Thus if it should please you to be mine as I wish to be yours, I shall do so willingly, nor shall I fear that another will ever take you from me." After saying this and arranging to speak to each other at greater leisure some other night, they both departed.

Having subsequently returned various times to talk to her, one evening when it was snowing heavily the youth met her again at the longed for place and said to her: "Ah, why do you make me suffer like this? Do you feel no pity for me, that every night in weather like this I wait for you here in this street?" To this the woman replied: "Certainly I pity you, but what do you want me to do, if not beg you to go away?" The young man replied: "I would ask that you let me come into your room, where we would be able to converse in greater comfort." The fair maiden then replied, almost in anger: "Romeo, I love you as much as one can rightfully love anyone, and I grant you more than befits my virtue. This I do won over by love and your high worth. But if you think that by courting me for a long time or by any other means to enjoy my love in any way other than as my beloved, then banish this thought, because it will avail you nothing. And to spare you the danger in which I see you place your life every night by coming to these parts, I declare that, if you should see fit to accept me as your wife, I am willing to give myself wholly to you and to accompany you unhesitatingly wherever it pleases you to go." "This is my sole desire," said the youth, "let it be done now." "Let it be done," replied the woman, "but let it then be repeated in the presence of my confessor, Frate Lorenzo of the Order of St Francis, if you wish me to give myself wholly and happily to you." "Oh," Romeo said to her, "so it is Frate Lorenzo from Reggio who knows your heart's every secret?" "Yes," she replied, "and to satisfy me let him be witness to all we do." And having arranged their affairs carefully, they took leave of one another.

*   *   *

[T]he evening following the day of his wife's burial he entered Verona unrecognised. After waiting for nightfall and hearing nothing but silence all around, he headed towards the Church of the Friars Minor where the crypt was. This church was in the Citadel in which these friars used to live at that time and although they thereafter left it (I know not why) to go and reside in the St Zeno area, now known as St Bernardino, still this church was named after St Francis. Near the outer side of the church walls there were then standing certain stone tombs such as we often see outside churches. One of these, in which the beautiful maid lay, was the old burial place of all the Capelletti.

Having approached it at what must have been around four o'clock and being the man of great strength that he was, Romeo succeeded in raising the cover of the tomb. After propping it up with some pieces of wood that he had brought with him so that it could not close unintentionally, he went into the tomb and closed it behind him. The unfortunate youth had brought with him a dark lantern to enable him to behold his wife. Once enclosed in the crypt, he immediately took the lantern out and opened it. Amongst bones and the remains of many bodies he saw his beautiful Giulietta lying there as if dead. Thus he immediately began to lament, shedding copious tears: "Eyes, how dazzling you were to mine while it so pleased heaven! Oh, mouth, so sweetly kissed by mine a thousand times! Oh, beautiful breast, who harboured so joyfully my heart! How is it I now find you blind, dumb, and cold? How is it that I can see, speak, or live without you? Oh, my poor wife! Where have you been led by Love, who wills that so small a space should snuff out and enclose two wretched lovers? Alas! Other than this was I promised by that same hope and desire that first enflamed me with love for you. Oh, my cursed life, what sustains you?"

Thus speaking Romeo kissed her eyes, mouth and breast, lamenting through ever more copious tears. "Oh, walls above me, why do you not bring my life to an end more quickly by falling on me? But since death is within the reach of everyone, how base it is to desire it and yet not seize it!" Thus after taking out the phial containing the deadly poison that he had in his sleeve, he continued: "I know not what fate leads me to die on top of these enemies of mine whom I have slain and in their tomb, but since, oh my soul, it is fitting that we thus die near our lady, let us die forthwith." And having poured the lethal water into his mouth, he swallowed it all. Then taking the beloved maiden into his arms he said, embracing her tightly: "Oh, beautiful body, final object of all my desires, should any feeling remain in you now that your soul has departed or should your soul behold my cruel death, I pray that it not mind if at least I die in secret and full of woe as I was not able to live openly and happily with you." And clasping her tightly he awaited death.

The hour had already arrived when the maiden's warmth was supposed to have counteracted the cold and potent effect of the powder and she was to have awakened. Thus it was that, held tightly and shaken by Romeo, she awoke in his arms and, with her feelings restored, she uttered a deep sigh and the following words: "Alas, where am I? Who is holding me? Wretch that I am, who is kissing me?" And believing Frate Lorenzo responsible, she cried: "Is this how you show your loyalty to Romeo, friar? Is this how you intend leading me to safety?" Romeo was dumbfounded on hearing the woman and realising that she was alive; perhaps recalling Pygmalion, he said: "Don't you recognise me, oh, my sweet wife? Can you not see that I am your wretched husband who has stolen back alone from Mantua to die at your side?"

On seeing herself in the crypt and feeling herself in the arms of someone who claimed to be Romeo, Giulietta was almost beside herself. After pushing him away from herself somewhat and examining his face, she kissed him countless times and said: "What folly made you place your life in danger by coming in here? Was it not enough for you to have learned from my letters how I, with Frate Lorenzo's help, was to feign death, and that soon I would be with you again?" Then realising his great error the wretched youth began to lament: "Oh, my most accursed fate! Oh, unfortunate Romeo, infinitely more sorrowful than all other lovers! Those letters of yours never reached me." He then explained to her how Pietro had told him of her apparent death as though it were real; wherefore, believing her dead, he had taken the poison here at her side so as to keep her company. Since this poison was lethal, he could already feel its deadly effects in all his limbs.

On hearing this, the ill-fated maiden was so overcome by grief that she knew not what to do besides tearing her beautiful hair and beating her innocent breast. Kissing again and again the already recumbent Romeo, she shed abundant tears over him and, having turned paler than ashes, she said all atremble: "Thus, my lord, because of me you must die here before me? And heaven will allow me to go on living, if only for a short time, after you are dead? Woe is me! If at least I could give you my life and die alone!" To which the youth replied weakly: "If my faithfulness and love were ever dear to you, my living hope, I beg you that life not displease you after I am gone, if for no other reason than you may at least think of him who, afire because of your beauty, is dying before your beautiful eyes," To this the woman replied: "If you die because of my apparent death, what ought I do if you really die? I regret only that I have no way of dying before you do and because I go on living, I am abhorrent to myself. But it is my fervent hope that, just as I was the cause of your death, so, before long, shall I be its companion." And after labouring to utter these words, she fell senseless. Once she had regained consciousness, with her lovely mouth she then set pitifully about capturing the last breath of her cherished lover who was rapidly approaching his end.

In the meantime Frate Lorenzo, who had learned how and when the maiden had drunk the powder and been buried as though dead, knowing that it was time the effects of the said powder began wearing off, came to the crypt with a trusted companion about an hour before daybreak. Arriving there and hearing her weeping and wailing, he peered between the lid and the crypt and saw a light inside. Greatly amazed, he concluded that the maiden had somehow taken the light in there with her and that, after awaking, she was lamenting and weeping thus out of fear of some dead body or perhaps of remaining shut in that place for ever. With the help of his companion he promptly opened the tomb and saw Giulietta who, dishevelled and grief-stricken, had sat up and gathered her near-dead lover into her lap. Addressing her, he said: "So, my daughter, you feared that I would leave you to die in here?" Hearing the friar and weeping twice as much, she answered: "On the contrary, I fear you may take me out alive. Ah, for pity's sake, close the tomb up again and begone so that I may die. Or else hand me a knife so that by wounding myself in the breast I may put an end to my grief. Oh, father, father, how well you sent the letter! How well shall I be wed! How well you will lead me to Romeo! Behold him here already dead in my lap." And telling him all that had happened, she showed him Romeo.

On hearing these things, Frate Lorenzo appeared stunned and gazing at the youth who was about to pass from this life into the next, spoke thus: "Oh, Romeo, what dire misfortune has taken you from me? Say something to me, look at me a moment! Oh, Romeo, see your beloved Giulietta who begs you to look at her! Why don't you at least answer her in whose lovely lap you are lying?" At the dear name of his wife Romeo raised briefly eyes made dim and heavy by approaching death and, after seeing her, closed them again. Shortly thereafter, with death coursing through his writhing limbs, he gave a short sigh and died.

Once the wretched lover had died in the way I have described to you, following much weeping the friar said to the maid as day was already drawing near: "And you, Giulietta, what will you do?" She promptly replied: "I shall die in here." "What? My daughter," he said, "don't say this. Come on out, for even though I do not know what to do with you, you can always shut yourself away in some holy convent, ever praying to God on your own behalf as well as that of your dead husband, if he has need of it." To which the woman replied: "Father, I ask nothing else of you but this favour which, for the love that you bore his happy memory"—and she indicated Romeo—"you will willingly do for me: and this is that you never make known our death, so that our bodies may remain together for ever in this tomb. And if by chance our death should become known, I beg you in the name of this same love to entreat our unfortunate fathers on both our behalves that it not displease them to leave in the same tomb those whom Love burned in the same fire and led to the same death."

Having turned to the reclining body of Romeo, whose head she had placed on a pillow that had been left in the crypt with her, and having closed his eyes completely Giulietta said while bathing his cold face with tears: "What am I supposed to do, my lord, now that you are no longer alive? What else is left for me where you are concerned, except to join you in death? Nothing else to be sure, in order that death may not separate me from you, as only it was able to do." Having spoken thus, she focused her mind on her great misfortune;

recalling the loss of her dear lover and resolving to live no longer, she drew in her breath, held it for some time, then letting it out with a great cry she fell lifeless on the dead body of Romeo.

* * *

MATTEO BANDELLO

The Unfortunate Death of Two Most Wretched Lovers (1554)[†]

* * *

It happened one day, as has already been said, that Romeo went in costume to the Capelletti party and although there was little friendship between them, they did not insult one another. After Romeo had been there some time with a mask covering his face, he removed it and withdrew to sit in a corner from where he could easily see everyone in the room which, lit as it was by many torches, was as bright as if it had been day. Everyone was looking at Romeo, particularly the women, and all were amazed that he should dally so openly in that house. Nevertheless, because Romeo was not only very handsome but a well-mannered and courteous young man as well, he was loved by most people. His enemies did not give as much thought to him as they would have done had he been older. Romeo set himself up there as judge of the beauty of the women present at the party, and praised in varying degrees this woman and that according to the desire they aroused in him.

He was keeping himself thus entertained without dancing when an indescribably lovely maiden whom he did not know caught his attention. The sight of her gave him immeasurable pleasure and he deemed her to be the most beautiful and charming young woman he had ever seen. It seemed to Romeo that the more intently he gazed at her, the more her beauty and charms increased. Thus he began to look upon her most amorously, unable to take his eyes off her. Since looking at her aroused such unaccustomed joy in him, he resolved to make every effort to gain her favour and love. Thus it was that the love he bore the other woman, vanquished by the new love, gave way to such flames as only death thereafter would extinguish.

Once Romeo had entered this alluring labyrinth, lacking the courage to find out who the young woman was, he feasted his eyes on

† From Matteo Bandello, "The Unfortunate Death of Two Most Wretched Lovers," trans. Nicole Prunster, in *Romeo and Juliet Before Shakespeare: Four Tales of Star-Crossed Lovers* (Toronto: Centre for Reformation Studies, 2000), pp. 53–56, 79–84. Reprinted by permission of the publisher.

the captivating sight of her and, giving his close attention to all she did, he drank love's sweet poison, awed by her every attribute and gesture. As I have already said, he was sitting in a corner in front of which all passed when they were dancing. Giulietta—for this was the name of the maiden that Romeo liked so much—was the daughter of the owner of the house whose party it was. Although she did not yet know Romeo, still he seemed to her the most handsome and charming youth that one could encounter. She found wondrous satisfaction in looking, and stealing every now and then sweet and furtive glances at him, she felt I know not what sweetness in her heart that overwhelmed her with joyful and extreme pleasure. The maiden longed for Romeo to begin dancing so that she could see him better and hear him speak, seeming as it did to her that the sweetness of his speech must equal that from his eyes which she appeared to enjoy so immeasurably while she went on looking at him. But he remained seated all by himself, and showed no inclination to dance.

He was wholly intent upon gazing in admiration at the beautiful young maid and she had no other thought but to look at him. They were looking at one another in such a way that, with their eyes at times meeting and their ardent glances uniting, they readily realised that their gazes were amorous. Thus every time their eyes met, both filled the air with amorous sighs and it appeared that, for the time being, they desired nothing more than to be able to disclose their newly kindled flame by talking to one another.

With both of them now lost in this fond contemplation, the dancing festivities came to an end and the dance of the torch began, which others call the dance of the hat. While this amusement was underway, Romeo, who was invited to join the dance by a woman, joined in and did what was expected of him. Having given the torch to a woman, he went close to Giulietta as the rules of the dance demanded and took her by the hand, to the boundless pleasure of both concerned. Giulietta had ended up between Romeo and someone known as Marcuccio the Cross-Eyed, a very pleasant courtier generally well regarded for his capacity for light-hearted witticisms and pleasantries. Hence he always had some anecdote at the ready to make the company laugh, and he would amuse himself most willingly without causing offence to anyone. In all weather and seasons, his hands were always much colder and frozen than the coldest alpine ice, and although he stayed by the fire warming them at length, nevertheless they remained icy cold.

As Giulietta—who had Romeo on her left and Marcuccio on her right—felt her beloved take her hand, she turned slightly towards him, perhaps eager to hear him speak, and said with a happy expression and trembling voice: "Blessed be your arrival at my side!"; and thus saying, she squeezed his hand lovingly. The astute youth, who was nobody's fool, answered her thus while gently squeezing her hand: "My lady, what does this blessing of yours mean?"; and looking at her beseechingly, he hung on her answer, sighing. Laughing sweetly, she then answered: "Do not be amazed, kind young sir, if I bless your coming here, for Messer Marcuccio has for some time been freezing me all over with the chill of his cold hand and you mercifully warm me with your soft hand." To this Romeo immediately added: "My lady, it means a great deal to me that I am able to do you some service, and I yearn for nothing else in the world other than to be able to serve you. Hence I shall consider myself blessed whenever you deign to command me as you would your humblest servant. I can truly say that if my hand warms you, with the fire of your beautiful eyes you make me burn all over, ensuring that if you deny me help so that I can withstand such a fire, it will not be long before you see me burn up and turn to ashes."

No sooner was he able to finish saying these last words than the game of the torch came to an end. Thus Giulietta, who was burning with love, had no time to give him any answer other than to say, sighing and squeezing his hand: "Alas, what can I say to you if not that I belong far more to you than I do to myself?" Since everyone was leaving, Romeo waited to see in which direction the young maid would head; but it was not long before he knew beyond any doubt that she was the daughter of the master of the house, and he also sought verification of this by inquiring of a well-wisher of his about many women. This aggrieved him greatly, believing as he did that to achieve the desired outcome of this love of his would be a difficult and dangerous enterprise. But the wound was already open and love's poison had gone deep.

On the other hand Giulietta, eager to know the identity of the youth in whose power she already felt herself wholly to be, after summoning her old wet-nurse entered a room, went to a window lit up by many torches blazing in the street, and began asking her who so-and-so was wearing such-and-such an outfit, who was this one and that other carrying a sword. She also inquired of her the identity of the handsome youth holding the mask in his hand. The kindly old woman, who knew almost everybody, named first one and then the other, and knowing Romeo very well, told Giulietta who he was. On hearing the Montecchi name the maiden was stunned, despairing of ever being able to have Romeo as her husband because of the hostile rivalry between their two families; nonetheless she allowed no sign of her despair to show.

* * *

After weeping at length, he gave voice to a flood of words that would have moved the most hardened hearts in the world to pity.

Having decided at last that he no longer wished to live, he took out
the small phial that he had brought, emptied the poisoned water that
it contained into his mouth, and swallowed it in a single draught.
Once he had done this, he called Pietro who was waiting in a corner of the cemetery and told him to come up onto the tomb. When
he had done so and was leaning at the edge of the tomb, Romeo
spoke to him thus: "Here you see, oh, Pietro! my wife. You already
know something of the love which I bore her and still bear her. I am
well aware that I could as much live without her as a body can live
without a soul, thus I brought with me the envenomed water which,
as you know, kills a man in less than an hour. I drank it gladly and
willingly in order to die here next to the woman I so loved in life.
This I do so that I may at least be buried with her once I am dead if
I am not permitted to be with her while I am alive. You can see the
phial wherein was the water which, if you remember, we were given
in Mantua by that man from Spoleto who kept asps and other serpents. May God in his mercy and infinite goodness forgive me, for
I have not killed myself to offend him but so as not to remain alive
without my dear wife. And if you see my eyes wet with tears, do
not think that I am weeping out of self-pity because I am dying so
young; rather my weeping is caused by the profound grief that I
feel for the death of her who was worthy of living a more happy and
peaceful life. You are to give this letter to my father to whom I have
written telling him what I want him to do after my death regarding
both this tomb and my servants in Mantua. I have seen to it that you,
who have served me faithfully, will have no need to go on serving
others. I am certain that my father will carry out all that I ask of him
in my letter. Off with you now! I can feel death close at hand because
I am aware that the poison in the deadly water is already paralysing
my limbs. Close up the tomb and let me die next to my wife."

Pietro was so grief-stricken by what Romeo had said that he thought
his heart would break within him from the boundless sorrow that he
felt. His outpouring of words to his master was wasted for no longer
could anything counteract the poisonous water which had by this
time spread throughout his entire body. Having taken Giulietta in his
arms and kissing her constantly, Romeo awaited his unavoidable end,
now close at hand, all the while telling Pietro to close the tomb.

Giulietta, in whom the powder had already run its course, awoke
precisely at that time. Feeling herself kissed, she suspected that it was
the friar who, after coming to take her from the tomb to his room,
was holding her in his arms and, spurred on by lust, was kissing her.
She said: "Ah, Father Lorenzo, is this the trust that Romeo had in
you? Move away!" And rousing herself to escape from his arms, she
opened her eyes and saw she was in Romeo's arms, for she recognised
him easily even though he was dressed as a German. "Alas, you are

here, my life?" she said, "Where is Frate Lorenzo? Why do you not take me out of this tomb? Let us away, for the love of God!"

When Romeo saw Giulietta open her eyes and heard her speak, thereby realising that she was not dead but alive, he was overwhelmed simultaneously with happiness and grief of unbelievable and incalculable magnitude. Weeping and holding his beloved wife tightly against his chest, he said: "Ah, life of my life and heart of my body, what man alive ever felt as much joy as I do at this moment? I was convinced that you were dead and now I am holding you in my arms, alive and well! But what suffering ever equalled mine, what most heartfelt sorrow compares to my grief, since I feel that I have reached the end of my wretched days and my life is fading when more than ever it behooves me to live! For if I go on living another half-hour, this is all the time I have left in this life. What one person ever experienced simultaneously more extreme happiness and boundless grief than I clearly feel? I am more happy than words can describe, overflowing with joy and contentment, since I suddenly see you alive, my sweet wife, whom I believed dead and for whom I have wept so bitterly. Truly, my most loving wife, it is only right that in this case I rejoice with you. Yet I suffer incalculable grief and sorrow without equal when I think that very soon I shall be allowed no longer to see, hear and remain with you, enjoying your most sweet company that I so longed for. It is indeed true that the joy of seeing you alive greatly exceeds the grief besetting me as the time draws near when I must leave you. And I pray the Lord our God that the years by which he is shortening my unhappy youth, he add to yours. May he grant you a long life and a happier destiny than mine, for I feel that my life is already coming to an end."

Giulietta, who had already raised herself up somewhat, said to Romeo on hearing what he was saying: "What is the meaning of these words, my lord, that you are now uttering? Is this the comfort you wish to give me? Have you come here from Mantua to give me news of this kind? What is the matter with you?" The unfortunate Romeo then told her about the poison he had drunk. "Alas! Alas!" said Giulietta. "What is this I hear? What are you telling me? Woe is me! From what I hear then, Frate Lorenzo did not write to you about the plan that he and I had devised together. And yet he promised me he would write telling you everything!" Thus overwhelmed with the most bitter grief, weeping, crying out, sighing and becoming almost beside herself with anguish, she related in detail what she and the friar had planned so that she would not be compelled to wed the husband her father wished her to have.

When Romeo heard this, sorrow infinitely increased his woes. While Giulietta was wildly bewailing their misfortune and invoking heaven and the stars together with all the most merciless elements,

Romeo saw there the body of Tebaldo whom he had killed in the fight several months earlier, as you have already heard. Having recognised him, he turned towards him and said: "Tebaldo, wherever you may be, you must know that I was not trying to harm you but rather I entered the fray to check it, and I advised you to make your men withdraw because I would make mine lay down their arms. But full as you were of fury and age-old hatred, you did not heed my words; instead you fell upon me with a treacherous heart in order to harm me. Forced as I was by you and having lost my patience, I refused to fall back so much as an inch and as I defended myself your ill-luck so had it that I killed you. I now ask your forgiveness for the offence I did you, the more so since I had already become your relative by taking your cousin as my wife. If you desire revenge from me, you have obtained it. And what greater revenge could you wish for than knowing that he who killed you should have poisoned himself in your presence and is voluntarily dying in front of you, to end up buried next to you? If in life we waged war, in death we will have no quarrel within our shared tomb."

On hearing the husband's piteous talk and his wife's weeping, Pietro was dumbstruck, not knowing if what he was seeing and hearing was true or if in fact he was dreaming; nor did he know what to say or do, so stunned was he. Wretched Giulietta, the most sorrowful of women since her sorrow knew no end, addressed Romeo: "Since it did not please God that we live together, may it at least please him that I be buried here with you. But come now what may, you can be sure that I will never leave here without you." After taking her again in his arms, Romeo began to plead lovingly with her to take heart and to think about living, because he would depart comforted by the certainty that she was still alive; and he dwelt at some length on this matter. He felt himself gradually losing consciousness, his vision was almost completely blurred and he was so lacking in physical strength that he could no longer sit up. Thus giving way he collapsed, and looking his wife pitifully in the face, said: "Alas, my life, I am dying."

For whatever reason, Frate Lorenzo had not wished to take Giulietta to his room the night she was buried. Seeing that Romeo did not turn up, the following night accompanied by a trusted friar of his he then went armed with tools to open the tomb, arriving just as Romeo collapsed. Noticing the open tomb and recognising Pietro, he said: "Good health to you! Where is Romeo?" Hearing the friar's voice and recognising him, Giulietta said raising her head: "May God forgive you! You did a fine job of sending the letter to Romeo!" "I did send it," replied the friar, "Friar Anselmo, whom you know, took it. Why do you say this?" Weeping bitterly, Giulietta answered: "Come on up and you will see." The friar climbed up and seeing Romeo lying almost lifeless, said: "Romeo, my son, what is the matter?" Romeo opened his weary eyes, recognised him and said softly that he entrusted Giulietta to him, that he no longer needed either help or counsel, and that, having repented his sins, he asked for God's and the friar's forgiveness for them. The ill-fated lover was barely able to utter these last words and lightly beat his breast before his strength drained away and, after closing his eyes, he died.

I do not have the heart to show how grievous, agonizing and almost unbearable this was to his disconsolate wife, but let those who love truly, imagine how it would be to find themselves part of such a horrible spectacle. Lamenting wretchedly and to no purpose, she wept for him at length; then calling his beloved name over and over in vain, overcome with anguish she fell unconscious over her husband's body and remained senseless for some time. The friar and Pietro, both extremely grief-stricken, managed to revive her, whereupon she wrung her hands and weeping without restraint, she shed as many tears as any woman ever did.

Giulietta then said, kissing the dead body: "Ah, sweetest haven of all my thoughts and of all the pleasure I have ever known, my beloved and only lord, how bitter now has your sweetness become to me! You have run your course while you are still in the bloom of your lovely and fair youth, for you did not cherish life which is so highly valued by everyone else. You chose to die when others most delight in living, and you have arrived at the destination which everybody must reach sooner or later. My lord, you came to finish your days in the lap of the woman whom you loved above all else and by whom you are loved as by no other, and you have come to bury yourself of your own free will there where you believed her to be dead and buried. Never did you think that I would weep these most bitter and heartfelt tears for you. Never would you have believed that you would not find me on going to the other world. I am convinced that on not finding me there you returned here to see if I am following you. Do I not sense that your spirit, wandering around in here, is leaving and is already amazed, or rather, is grieved that I should be delaying so? My lord, I can see you, I can hear you, I recognise you and know that the only thing you are waiting for is for me to come with you. Do not fear, my lord, doubt not that I wish to remain here without your company, for life without you would be much more arduous and more agonizing still than any imaginable way of dying, because without you I would not be alive, and even if it seemed to others that I was, living thus for me would be like a slow and painful death. Thus can you be assured, my dear lord, that very soon I shall come and be with you for ever. And in what company more trusted and dear to me can I depart this wretched life of suffering, than by coming after you and following in your footsteps? Absolutely none, as far as I believe."

Close at hand and overcome with boundless pity, the friar and
Pietro were weeping as they did their utmost to comfort her, but all
in vain. Frate Lorenzo said to her: "My daughter, what is done cannot be undone. If Romeo could be brought back to life with tears,
we would all dissolve into tears to help him; but nothing can be done.
Take comfort and think about living, and if you do not wish to return
home, I shall see to putting you in a very devout convent where you
will be able to pray for the soul of your Romeo while serving God."
She adamantly refused to listen to him, but persevering in her dire
resolve, she lamented not being able to restore Romeo's life by offering her own, and she determined to die. Having then drawn her
spirits together within herself, without uttering a word she died with
Romeo in her lap.

*   *   *

PIERRE BOAISTUAU

Of Two Lovers (1559)[†]

*   *   *

The Capellet family (as we have pointed out at the beginning of
this tale) was on bad terms with the Montesches, which was why
the latter were not at the banquet, with the exception of the young
Rhomeo Montesche who arrived masked after supper, accompanied
by several other young noblemen. After they had remained for some
time with their faces covered by their masks, they removed them.
Somewhat uncomfortable, Rhomeo withdrew to a corner of the hall,
but because of the brightness of the torches that had been lit, he was
immediately noticed by everyone, especially the women, for besides
the innate beauty with which nature had endowed him, they admired
even more his confidence and the fact of his having dared to enter
with such familiarity the house of those who had little reason to wish
him well. Nevertheless the Capellets, hiding their hatred either out
of consideration for those present or respect for his age, harmed him
neither with deeds nor words. For this reason he was able to gaze
openly and at leisure on the women, which he managed to do with
such good grace that there was no woman who did not derive pleasure from his presence.

After he had passed judgement on the excellence of each woman
in turn according as fancy led him, he espied amongst the others one

---

[†] From Pierre Boaistuau, "Of Two Lovers," trans. Nicole Prunster, in *Romeo and Juliet Before
Shakespeare: Four Tales of Star-Crossed Lovers* (Toronto: Centre for Reformation and
Renaissance Studies, 2000), pp. 88–92, 116–19. Reprinted by permission of the publisher.

extremely beautiful young girl who, although he had never seen her before, appealed to him more than all others. To her he gave pride of place in his heart for unsurpassable beauty. While he was regaling her ceaselessly with piteous looks, the love which he used to bear his first young lady was vanquished by this new fire, which then grew and strengthened to such an extent that death alone could ever extinguish it, as you will understand from one of the most unusual tales that mortal man could imagine.

Thus feeling himself buffeted by this new storm, the young Rhomeo did not know how to react; but so dumbfounded and shaken was he by these new flames that he almost did not know himself, with the result that he lacked the boldness to enquire who she was, devoting all his attention to feasting his eyes on the sight of her, and by this means he admitted love's sweet poison, by which he was at last so affected that a cruel death brought his days to an end. The woman for whom Rhomeo suffered such an unusual passion was named Julliette and was the daughter of Capellet, master of the house in which this gathering was being held. As her eyes wandered here and there, she noticed by chance Rhomeo who seemed to her the most handsome nobleman she had ever looked upon freely. Then love, which was lying in ambush and had never before besieged the tender heart of this young maid, touched her so deeply that whatever resistance she was able to make, she was powerless to resist its strength. From that moment she began to scorn all the splendours of the party and felt no pleasure in her heart except when she had cast a furtive glance at Rhomeo or received one from him. After they had satisfied their impassioned hearts with countless loving looks which more often than not met and became one, the burning rays issuing from them were ample witness to the beginning of their love.

Once love had made this breach in the lovers' hearts, just as they were both seeking some way of talking to one another, Fortune offered them a ready occasion, for a gentleman from the gathering took Julliette by the hand to have her take part in the dance of the torch, which she was able to perform so well and with such grace that for that day it was she who won the prize of honour out of all the young girls in Verona. Rhomeo, having foreseen the place where she would withdraw from the dance, came forward and conducted matters so judiciously that on his way back he was able to be beside her. At the end of the dance Julliette returned to the same spot where she had been at the beginning and ended up seated between Rhomeo and another youth called Marcucio, a courtier much loved by everyone who, because of his witticisms and fine ways was warmly received at all gatherings. Marcucio, as bold amongst virgins as a lion is amongst lambs, seized Julliette's hand forthwith. In winter and summer alike he habitually had hands as cold as a piece of mountain ice, even when he was near the fire. Rhomeo, who was on Julliette's left, seeing that Marcucio was holding her right hand, took Julliette's other hand so as not to fail in his duty and, clasping it tightly for a while, felt so overwhelmed by this new favour that he was dumb-struck, incapable of replying. But Julliette, who realised from the change in his colour that this shortcoming was due to uncontrol-lable love, turned towards him eager to hear him speak. In a voice trembling with both virginal shyness and modesty she said to him: "Blessed be the moment of your arrival at my side"; then, though intending to go on, love so sealed her lips that she was unable to fin-ish what she had started out to say.

At this the youth, beside himself with joy and gladness, asked her with a sigh the reason for this fortunate blessing. A little more self-assured, Julliette answered him, smiling and glancing compassion-ately at him: "My lord, be not amazed if I bless your coming, because for a long time Lord Marcucio's icy hand has completely frozen my own, and you have warmed it for me with your charm." To this Rho-meo promptly replied: "My lady, if heaven has so favoured me that I have done you some agreeable service by turning up here by chance, I deem it put to good use, wishing as I do for no greater good to crown all the joys that I ask in this world than to serve, obey, and honour you wherever my life may lead me, as you will see beyond all doubt when-ever it pleases you to put it to the test. Moreover, if you derived some warmth from the touch of my hand, well may I assure you that flames are dead compared with the bright sparks and blazing fire issuing from your beautiful eyes. So thoroughly has this fire taken hold of all my senses that, if you do not favour me by sending your heavenly graces to my assistance, I await only the moment when I shall be wholly consumed and reduced to ashes."

Scarcely had he finished these last words than the game of the torch came to an end, so Julliette, all aflame with love, clasping his hand tightly, was unable to make any other reply than to whisper to him: "My dear friend, I know not what more certain evidence you want of my love save my assurance that I belong no less to you than you do to yourself, being as I am ready and willing to obey you in all things honourable. I beg that you be content with this for the pres-ent and that you await some other more favourable occasion when we will be able to speak more privately of our affairs." Hearing his friends urging him to leave and not knowing how he could see again her who held his life and death in her hands, Rhomeo took it upon himself to ask a friend who she was. His friend replied that she was the daughter of Capellet, master of the house in which the banquet had just taken place. Indignant beyond measure that Fortune had directed him to such a dangerous place, Rhomeo deemed that it was all but impossible to bring his undertaking to an end.

For her part Julliette, eager to know who the young man was who had flattered her so courteously that evening causing the new wound she how felt in her heart, called an aged lady-in-waiting on whose milk she had been suckled and raised and said to her, leaning forward: "Mother, who are those two youths going out first with two torches in front of them?" To this the dame replied by indicating their family allegiances. Then she questioned her again: "Who is that youth holding a mask and wearing a damask cloak?" "That is Rhomeo Montesche, son of the capital enemy of your father and his allies," she replied. But just the mention of the name Montesche left the maiden completely confused and in deep despair of ever being able to have her beloved Rhomeo as her husband, given the long-standing feud between her family and his. She was nonetheless able (for the time being) to hide her worry and disappointment so well that the dame was not aware of it, but urged her to retire to her room to lie down. Julliette obeyed, but while she was lying in bed and trying to rest as usual, a great storm of confused thoughts began to engulf and buffet her in such a way that she could not even close her eyes. As she tossed this way and that, many fantastic thoughts ran through her mind, making her first resolve to abandon this love affair completely, then to go ahead with it.

Thus the maiden was troubled by two contradictory thoughts, one of which directed her to pursue her resolve while the other laid before her the grave danger towards which she was unwisely rushing. After having wandered at length in love's labyrinth, she was no closer to making up her mind but cried incessantly and reproached herself, saying: "Ah, wretched and unfortunate creature that I am! What causes this unfamiliar tribulation in my soul, which allows me no respite? Woe is me! How do I know if this youth loves me as he says? Could it be that under the cloak of his honeyed words he wants to deprive me of my honour in order to take revenge on my relatives, who have offended his? Would he thus make me the talking piece of all Verona because of my everlasting shame?" Then straight afterwards she dismissed her initial suspicions, saying: "How could it ever be possible that disloyalty and betrayal lurk beneath such beauty and unmatched sweetness? If it is true that the face faithfully conveys our thoughts, I can be sure that he loves me, for I have seen him change colour so often when he was talking to me, so carried away and beside himself that I ought not wish for any other surer sign of this love of his which I hope will accompany me right up to the last breath I take; providing he marries me, that is, for perhaps this new alliance will bring about lasting peace and love between his family and mine." With this fixed thought in mind, her expression changed to joy whenever she noticed Rhomeo pass by her door, and she watched him out of the corner of her eye until she lost sight of him.

＊ ＊ ＊

When the tomb was open, Rhomeo went down two steps holding
the candle in his hand and glimpsed with piteous eyes the body of
her who was his reason for living. Then having bathed her with his
tears and kissed her ardently, holding her in his arms, unable to tear
his eyes away from her, he placed his fearful hands on Julliette's cold
breast. After he had searched various parts of her body in vain for
signs of life, he took the poison out of its box and, having swallowed
a large amount of it, he exclaimed: "Oh, Julliette, of whom the world
was unworthy, what more pleasing death could my heart choose than
to die near you? What more glorious burial than to be enclosed in
your tomb? What better or more worthy epitaph could be conse-
crated to memory than this shared and piteous sacrifice of our lives?"
And while he was striving to resume his mourning with increased
intensity, his heart began trembling due to the virulence of the poison which was gradually taking it over.

Looking here and there, near the body of Julliette Rhomeo espied
that of Thibault not yet completely decomposed and, addressing him
as though he were alive, said: "Cousin Thibault, wherever you may be
I cry out to you now for mercy for the offence I caused you in taking
your life, and if you wish to be avenged on me, what greater or more
cruel satisfaction could you hereafter hope for than to see him who
has harmed you poisoned by his own hand and buried beside you?"
Then having finished what he had to say and feeling his life gradually
ebbing away, getting to his knees he murmured weakly: "Lord God,
who to redeem me came down from your father's bosom and became
flesh in the womb of the Virgin, I beg you to have pity on this poor
afflicted soul, for well I know that this body is no longer but earth."
Then gripped by a desperate pain, he fell onto Julliette's body with
such force that his heart, weakened by excessive anguish and no longer able to withstand this last, cruel strain, lost all its natural feeling
and functions. Thus his soul immediately departed his body and he
was left sprawled out and lifeless.

Friar Laurens, who knew for exactly how long his powder would
work, set out from the Church of St Francis, amazed that he had had
no reply to the letter he had sent Rhomeo by means of his companion, Friar Anselme; and he was considering opening the tomb with
his own tools so as to provide air for Julliette who was about to wake
up. Drawing near the place, he caught a glimpse of the light inside
which filled him with terror, until Pierre, who was nearby, reassured
him that the person within was Rhomeo who had been weeping and
wailing incessantly for half an hour. They then entered the vault and
finding Rhomeo lifeless, gave themselves over to such sorrow as only
those who have truly loved can understand.

Whilst they were thus lamenting, Julliette, noticing the brightness in the tomb as she came out of her trance, did not know if it was a dream or an apparition appearing before her eyes. As she recovered consciousness she recognised Friar Laurens and said to him: "Father, I beg you in God's name, assure me of your promise, for I am completely bewildered." And then speaking openly because he feared being discovered for having tarried there too long, Friar Laurens gave her a precise account of how he had sent Friar Anselme off to Mantua to find Rhomeo, from whom he had had no reply; and how despite everything, he had found Rhomeo dead in the vault. He then showed her Rhomeo's body lying next to hers, begging her, moreover, to bear with patience the misfortune that had occurred and adding that, if it so pleased her, he would take her to some secret nunnery where with time she would be able to ease her sorrow and put her soul at rest.

But the moment Julliette cast her eye on Rhomeo's dead body, she was gripped by such a violent outpouring of tears that, unable to endure the violence of her grief, she gasped uncontrollably, her mouth on his. Then by flinging herself on his body and embracing him tightly, it seemed that with her sighing and sobbing she would restore him to life and revive him. And after having kissed him over and over again, she cried out: "Ah, sweet haven of my thoughts and of all the pleasure that ever I enjoyed! Was your heart truly so steadfast that you chose to be buried here in the arms of your perfect lover? And for my sake you chose to finish your life's course in the bloom of youth when living was supposed to be most dear and delightful to you? How was this tender body able to hold out against the frenzied struggle when death made its appearance? How could your tender and delicate years willingly permit you to shut yourself up in this loathsome, foul place wherein henceforth you will serve as food for worms unworthy of you? Alas! Alas! What need did I have for my sorrows to be renewed, when time and my long patience were supposed to put an end to them once and for all? Ah, poor, wretched creature that I am! While thinking to find a remedy for my love, I have sharpened the knife which has made the cruel wound whose mortal injury I now suffer. Ah, blessed and fortunate tomb, for in centuries to come you will serve as witness to the most perfect union of the two most fortunate lovers who ever existed! To you I bequeath the last sighs and outpouring of her who has been more cruelly subjected than any other to sorrow and death."

Just as she was about to resume her lamentation, Pierre warned Friar Laurens that he could hear a noise near the Citadel, and intimidated by it they moved promptly away, afraid of being caught. Realising she was alone with no one to stop her, Julliette then took Rhomeo in her arms once more and kissed him with such feeling that she appeared more overcome by love than by death. Having drawn

out the dagger that Rhomeo had girded at his side, she stabbed herself with it several times through the heart, murmuring in a weak
and piteous voice: "Ah, death, who are the end of my misfortune and
beginning of my happiness, I welcome you! Fling now your darts
fearlessly at me and think not to prolong my life any further lest my
spirit toil in finding my Rhomeo's amongst so many dead. And you,
my dear lord and faithful husband Rhomeo, if you are still able to
hear me, receive her whom you loved so faithfully and who was
responsible for your violent death! I willingly offer you my soul so that
no one but you may enjoy the love that you had so deservedly won,
and so that our spirits, on emerging from this light, may live together
for all eternity in the place of everlasting immortality." And having
finished what she had to say, she gave up the ghost.

*   *   *

ARTHUR BROOKE

Romeus and Juliet (1562)[†]

The Argument

*   *   *

At length he saw a maid, right fair, of perfect shape,
Which Theseus or Paris would have chosen to their rape.
Whom erst he never saw; of all she pleased him most;
Within himself he said to her, Thou justly may'st thee boast
200 Of perfect shape's renown, and beauty's sounding praise,
Whose like ne hath, ne shall be seen, ne liveth in our days.
And whilst he fixed on her his partial piercèd eye,
His former love, for which of late he ready was to die,
Is now as quite forgot, as it had never been:
205 The proverb saith, 'Unminded oft are they that are unseen.'
And as out of a plank a nail a nail doth drive,
So novel love out of the mind the ancient love doth rive.
This sudden kindlèd fire in time is wox so great,
That only death and both their bloods might quench the
fiery heat.
210 When Romeus saw himself in this new tempest tossed,

---

† From *Brooke's* Romeus and Juliet, *Being the Original of Shakespeare's* Romeo and Juliet,
ed. J. J. Munroe (London: Chatto and Windus, 1908), pp. 8–13, 97–103.

Where both was hope of pleasant port, and danger
    to be lost,
He doubtful, scarcely knew what countenance to keep;
In Lethe's flood his wonted flames were quenched and
    drenchèd deep.
Yea, he forgets himself, ne is the wretch so bold
215 To ask her name, that without force hath him in bondage
    fold.
Ne how t' unloose his bonds doth the poor fool devise,
But only seeketh by her sight to feed his hungry eyes:
Through them he swalloweth down love's sweet
    impoisoned bait.
How surely are the wareless wrapt by those that lie in wait!
220 So is the poison spread throughout his bones and veins,
That in a while, alas, the while, it hasteth deadly pains.
Whilst Juliet, for so this gentle damsel hight,
From side to side on every one did cast about her sight:
At last her floating eyes were anchored fast on him,
225 Who for her sake did banish health and freedom from
    each limb.
He in her sight did seem to pass the rest as far
As Phœbus' shining beams do pass the brightness of a star.
In wait lay warlike Love with golden bow and shaft,
And to his ear with steady hand the bowstring up he raft.
230 Till now she had escaped his sharp inflaming dart,
Till now he listed not assault her young and tender heart.
His whetted arrow loosed, so touched her to the quick,
That through the eye it strake the heart, and there the head
    did stick.
It booted not to strive, for why, she wanted strength;
235 The weaker aye unto the strong of force must yield, at
    length.
The pomps now of the feast her heart 'gins to despise;
And only joyeth when her eyne meet with her lover's eyes.
When their new smitten hearts had fed on loving gleams,
Whilst, passing to and fro their eyes, y-mingled were their
    beams.
240 Each of these lovers 'gan by other's looks to know,
That friendship in their breast had root, and both would
    have it grow.
When thus in both their hearts had Cupid made his breach,
And each of them had sought the mean to end the war by
    speech,
Dame Fortune did assent their purpose to advance,

245 With torch in hand a comely knight did fetch her forth to
            dance;
    She quit herself so well, and with so trim a grace,
    That she the chief praise won that night from all
            Verona race.
    The whilst our Romeus a place had warely won,
    Nigh to the seat where she must sit, the dance once being
            done.
250 Fair Juliet turnèd to her chair with pleasant cheer,
    And glad she was her Romeus approachèd was so near.
    At th' one side of her chair her lover Romeo,
    And on the other side there sat one called Mercutio;
    A courtier that each where was highly had in price,
255 For he was courteous of his speech, and pleasant of device.
    Even as a lion would among the lambs be bold,
    Such was among the bashful maids Mercutio to behold.
    With friendly gripe he seized fair Juliet's snowish hand:
    A gift he had that Nature gave him in his swathing band,
260 That frozen mountain ice was never half so cold,
    As were his hands, though ne'er so near the fire he did
            them hold.
    As soon as had the knight the virgin's right hand raught,
    Within his trembling hand her left hath loving Romeus
            caught.
    For he wist well himself for her abode most pain,
265 And well he wist she loved him best, unless she list to
            feign.
    Then she with tender hand his tender palm hath
            pressed;
    What joy, trow you, was graffèd so in Romeus' cloven breast?
    The sudden sweet delight hath stoppèd quite his tongue,
    Ne can he claim of her his right, ne crave redress of wrong.
270 But she espied straightway, by changing of his hue
    From pale to red, from red to pale, and so from pale anew,
    That veh'ment love was cause, why so his tongue did stay,
    And so much more she longed to hear what Love could
            teach him say.
    When she had longèd long, and he long held his peace,
275 And her desire of hearing him, by silence did increase,
    At last, with trembling voice and shamefast cheer, the maid
    Unto her Romeus turned herself, and thus to him she said:
    'O blessed be the time of thy arrival here:'
    But ere she could speak forth the rest, to her Love
            drew so near,
280 And so within her mouth, her tongue he gluèd fast,

That no one word could 'scape her more than what
    already passed.
In great contented ease the young man straight is rapt:
'What chance,' quoth he, 'un'ware to me, O lady mine,
    is hapt,
That gives you worthy cause my coming here to bliss?'
285 Fair Juliet was come again unto herself by this:
First ruthfully she looked, then said with smiling cheer:
'Marvel no whit, my heart's delight, my only knight and fere,
Mercutio's icy hand had all-to frozen mine,
And of thy goodness thou again hast warmèd it with thine.'
290 Whereto with stayèd brow, 'gan Romeus to reply:
'If so the gods have granted me such favour from the sky,
That by my being here some service I have done
That pleaseth you, I am as glad, as I a realm had won.
O well-bestowèd time, that hath the happy hire,
295 Which I would wish, if I might have, my wishèd heart's
    desire.
For I of God would crave, as price of pains forepast,
To serve, obey, and honour you, so long as life shall last;
As proof shall teach you plain, if that you like to try
His faultless truth, that nill for aught unto his lady lie.
300 But if my touchèd hand have warmèd yours some deal,
Assure yourself the heat is cold, which in your hand you
    feel,
Compared to such quick sparks and glowing furious glead,
As from your beauty's pleasant eyne, Love causèd to
    proceed;
Which have so set on fire each feeling part of mine,
305 That lo, my mind doth melt away, my outward parts do pine.
And but you help, all whole, to ashes shall I turn;
Wherefore, alas, have ruth on him, whom you do force
    to burn.'
   Even with his ended tale, the torches' dance had end,
And Juliet of force must part from her new chosen friend.
310 His hand she claspèd hard, and all her parts did shake,
When leisureless with whisp'ring voice thus did she
    answer make:
You are no more your own, dear friend, than I am yours,
My honour savèd, prest t' obey your will, while life endures.
Lo, here the lucky lot that seld true lovers find,
315 Each takes away the other's heart, and leaves the own behind.
A happy life is love, if God grant from above,
That heart with heart by even weight do make exchange of
    love.

But Romeus gone from her, his heart for care is cold;
He hath forgot to ask her name that hath his heart in hold.
320 With forgèd careless cheer, of one he seeks to know,
Both how she hight, and whence she came, that him
     enchanted so.
So hath he learned her name, and know'th she is no
     geast,
Her father was a Capulet, and master of the feast.
Thus hath his foe in choice to give him life or death,
325 That scarcely can his woeful breast keep in the lively
     breath.
Wherefore with piteous plaint fierce Fortune doth he blame,
That in his ruth and wretched plight doth seek her laughing
     game.
And he reproveth Love, chief cause of his unrest,
Who ease and freedom hath exiled out of his youthful breast.

❅   ❅   ❅

330 And then our Romeus (the vault-stone set upright),
Descended down, and in his hand he bare the candle
     light.
And then with piteous eye the body of his wife
He 'gan behold, who surely was the organ of his life;
For whom unhappy now he is, but erst was blissed,
335 He watered her with tears, and then a hundred times her
     kissed;
And in his folded arms full straitly he her plight,
But no way could his greedy eyes be fillèd with her sight:
His fearful hands he laid upon her stomach cold,
And them on divers parts beside the woeful wight did
     hold.
340 But when he could not find the signs of life he sought,
Out of his cursèd box he drew the poison that he bought;
Whereof he greedily devoured the greater part,
And then he cried, with deadly sigh fetched from his
     mourning heart:
'O Juliet, of whom the world unworthy was,
345 From which, for world's unworthiness thy worthy ghost
     did pass,
What death more pleasant could my heart wish to abide
Than that which here it suff' reth now, so near thy
     friendly side?
Or else so glorious tomb how could my youth have
     craved,
As in one self-same vault with thee haply to be ingraved?
350 What epitaph more worth, or half so excellent,

To consecrate my memory, could any man invent,
As this our mutual and our piteous sacrifice
Of life, set light for love?'
                        But while he talketh in this wise,
And thought as yet awhile his dolours to enforce,
355 His tender heart began to faint, pressed with the
        venom's force;
Which little and little 'gan to overcome his heart,
And whilst his busy eyne he threw about to every part,
He saw, hard by the corse of sleeping Juliet,
Bold Tybalt's carcase dead, which was not all consumèd yet;
360 To whom, as having life, in this sort speaketh he:
  'Ah, cousin dear, Tybalt, whereso thy restless sprite
        now be,
With stretchèd hands to thee for mercy now I cry,
For that before thy kindly hour I forcèd thee to die.
But if with quenchèd life not quenchèd be thine ire,
365 But with revenging lust as yet thy heart be set on fire,
What more amends, or cruel wreak desirest thou
To see on me, than this which here is showed forth to thee
        now?
Who reft by force of arms from thee thy living breath,
The same with his own hand, thou seest, doth poison
        himself to death.
370 And for he causèd thee in tomb too soon to lie,
Too soon also, younger than thou, himself he layeth by.'
  These said, when he 'gan feel the poison's force prevail,
And little and little mastered life for aye began to fail,
Kneeling upon his knees, he said with voice full low,—
375 'Lord Christ, that so to ransom me descendedst long ago
Out of thy Father's bosom, and in the Virgin's womb
Didst put on flesh, oh, let my plaint out of this hollow tomb,
Pierce through the air, and grant my suit may favour find;
Take pity on my sinful and my poor afflicted mind!
380 For well enough I know, this body is but clay,
Nought but a mass of sin, too frail, and subject to decay.'
Then pressed with extreme grief he threw with so great force
His overpressèd parts upon his lady's wailèd corse,
That now his weakened heart, weakened with torments past,
385 Unable to abide this pang, the sharpest and the last,
Remainèd quite deprived of sense and kindly strength,
And so the long imprisoned soul hath freedom won at
        length.
Ah cruel death, too soon, too soon was this divorce,
'Twixt youthful Romeus' heavenly sprite, and his fair earthy
        corse!

390   The friar that knew what time the powder had been
           taken,
       Knew eke the very instant when the sleeper should
           awaken;
       But wondering that he could no kind of answer hear
       Of letters which to Romeus his fellow friar did bear,
       Out of Saint Francis' church himself alone did fare,
395   And for the opening of the tomb meet instruments he bare.
       Approaching nigh the place and seeing there the light,
       Great horror felt he in his heart, by strange and sudden
           sight;
       Till Peter, Romeus' man, his coward heart made bold,
       When of his master's being there the certain news he told:
400   'There hath he been,' quoth he, 'this half hour at the
           least,
       And in this time, I dare well say, his plaint hath still
           increast.'
       Then both they entered in, where they, alas, did find
       The breathless corpse of Romeus, forsaken of the mind:
       Where they have made such moan, as they may best
           conceive,
405   That have with perfect friendship loved, whose friend
           fierce death did reave.
           But whilst with piteous plaint they Romeus' fate
               beweep,
       An hour too late fair Juliet awakèd out of sleep;
       And much amazed to see in tomb so great a light,
       She wist not if she saw a dream, or sprite that walked
           by night.
410   But coming to herself she knew them, and said thus:
           'What, friar Laurence, is it you ? Where is my Romeus?'
       And then the ancient friar, that greatly stood in fear,
       Lest, if they lingered over long they should be taken there,
       In few plain words the whole that was betid, he told,
       And with his finger showed his corpse out-stretchèd,
           stiff, and cold;
415   And then persuaded her with patience to abide
       This sudden great mischance, and saith, that he will soon
           provide
       In some religious house for her a quiet place,
       Where she may spend the rest of life, and where in time,
           percase,
       She may with wisdom's mean measure her mourning breast,
420   And unto her tormented soul call back exilèd rest.
       But lo, as soon as she had cast her ruthful eye

On Romeus' face, that pale and wan fast by her side
    did lie,
Straightway she did unstop the conduits of her tears,
And out they gush;—with cruel hand she tare her golden
    hairs.
425 But when she neither could her swelling sorrow 'suage
Ne yet her tender heart abide her sickness' furious rage,
Fall'n on his corpse she lay, long panting on his face,
And then with all her force and strength the dead corpse
    did embrace.
As though with sighs, with sobs, with force, and busy pain
430 She would him raise, and him restore from death to life
    again:
A thousand times she kissed his mouth, as cold as stone,
And it unkissed again as oft; then 'gan she thus to moan:
 'Ah, pleasant prop of all my thoughts, ah, only ground
Of all the sweet delights that yet in all my life I found,
435 Did such assurèd trust within thy heart repose,
That in this place and at this time, thy churchyard thou hast
    chose
Betwixt the arms of me, thy perfect-loving make?
And thus by means of me to end thy life, and for my sake?
Even in the flow'ring of thy youth, when unto thee
440 Thy life most dear, as to the most, and pleasant ought to be,
How could this tender corpse withstand the cruel fight
Of furious Death, that wonts to fray the stoutest with
    his sight?
How could thy dainty youth agree with willing heart,
In this so foul-infected place to dwell, where now thou art?
445 Where spiteful Fortune hath appointed thee to be
The dainty food of greedy worms, unworthy, sure, of thee.
Alas, alas, alas, what needed now anew
My wonted sorrows, doubled twice, again thus to renew?
Which both the time and eke my patient long abode
450 Should now at length have quenchèd quite, and under foot
    have trode?
Ah, wretch and caitive that I am, even when I thought
To find my painful passion's salve, I missed the thing
    I sought;
And to my mortal harm the fatal knife I ground,
That gave to me so deep, so wide, so cruel deadly wound!
455 Ah thou, most fortunate and most unhappy tomb!
For thou shalt bear, from age to age, witness in time to
    come
Of the most perfect league betwixt a pair of lovers,

That were the most unfortunate and fortunate of others,
Receive the latter sigh, receive the latter pang,
460 Of the most cruel of cruel slaves that wrath and death
          aye wrang.'
     And when our Juliet would continue still her moan,
The friar and the servant fled, and left her there alone;
For they a sudden noise fast by the place did hear,
And lest they might be taken there, greatly they stood
          in fear.
465 When Juliet saw herself left in the vault alone,
That freely she might work her will, for let or stay was none,
Then once for all she took the cause of all her harms,
The body dead of Romeus, and clasped it in her arms;
Then she with earnest kiss sufficiently did prove,
470 That more than by the fear of death, she was attaint by love;
And then past deadly fear, for life ne had she care,
With hasty hand she did draw out the dagger that he ware.
'O welcome Death,' quoth she, 'end of unhappiness,
That also art beginning of assurèd happiness,
475 Fear not to dart me now, thy stripe no longer stay,
Prolong no longer now my life, I hate this long delay;
For straight my parting sprite, out of this carcase fled,
At ease shall find my Romeus' sprite among so many dead.
And thou my loving lord, Romeus, my trusty fere,
480 If knowledge yet do rest in thee, if thou these words
          dost hear,
Receive thou her, whom thou didst love so lawfully,
That caused, alas, thy violent death, although
          unwillingly;
And therefore willingly offers to thee her ghost,
To th'end that no wight else but thou might have just cause
          to boast
485 Th'enjoying of my love, which aye I have reserved
Free from the rest, bound unto thee, that hast it well
          deserved;
That so our parted sprites from light that we see here,
In place of endless light and bliss may ever live y-fere.'
     These said, her ruthless hand through-girt her valiant
          heart:
490 Ah, ladies, help with tears to wail the lady's deadly smart!
She groans, she stretcheth out her limbs, she shuts her eyes,
And from her corpse the sprite doth fly;—what should
          I say?—she dies.

*   *   *

WILLIAM PAINTER

The Goodly History of the True and Constant Love between Rhomeo and Julietta (1567)[†]

*   *   *

The family of the Capellets (as we have declared in the beginninge of thys hystory) was at variance with the Montesches, which was the cause that none of that family repaired to that banket, but onelye the yong gentleman Rhomeo, who came in a maske after supper with certain other yong gentlemen: and after they had remained a certayne space with their visards on, at length they did put of the same, and Rhomeo very shamefast, withdrew himself into a corner of the hall: but by reason of the light of the torches which burned very bright, he was by and by knowen and loked upon of the whole company, but specially of the ladies, for besides his native beauty wherewyth nature had adorned him, they marvelled at his audacity how hee durst presume to enter so secretly into the house of that famyllye which had litle cause to do him any good. Notwithstanding, the Capellets dissembling their mallice, either for the honor of the company, or else for respect of his age, did not misuse him eyther in worde or deede: by meanes whereof wyth free liberty he behelde and viewed the ladies at hys pleasure, which hee dyd so well, and wyth grace so good, as there was none but did very well lyke the presence of his person: and after hee had particularly given judgement uppon the excellency of each one, according to his affection, hee sawe one gentlewoman amonges the reste of surpassinge beautye who (althoughe hee had never seene hir tofore) pleased him above the rest, and attributed unto hir in heart the chyefest place for all perfection in beautye: and feastyng hir incessantlye with piteous lookes, the love whych hee bare to his first gentlewoman, was overcomen with this newe fire, that tooke sutch norishement and vigor in his hart, as he was not able never to quench the same but by death onely : as you may understande by one of the strangest discourses, that ever any mortall man devised. The yong Rhomeo then felyng himselfe thus tossed wyth thys newe tempest, could not tell what countenaunce to use, but was so surprised and chaunged with these last flames, as he had almost forgotten himselfe in sutch wise as he had not audacity to enquyre what shee was, and wholly bente

† From William Painter, "The Goodly History of the True and Constant Love between Rhomeo and Julietta" in *Shakespeare's Library*, vol. II, ed. J. P. Collier (London: Thomas Rodd, 1850), pp. 92–96, 124–27.

himself to feede hys eyes with hir sighte, wherewyth hee moystened the sweete amorous venome, which dyd so empoyson him, as hee ended hys dayes with a kinde of most cruell death. The gentlewoman that dydde put Rhomeo to sutch payne, was called Julietta, and was the daughter of Capellet, the mayster of the house wher that assembly was, who as hir eyes did rolle and wander too and fro, by chaunce espied Rhomeo, which unto hir seemed to be the goodliest personage that ever shee sawe: and love (which lay in wayte never untill that time,) assayling the tender heart of that yong gentlewoman, touched hir so at the quicke, as for any resistance she coulde make, was not able to defende his forces, and then began to set at naught the royalties of the feast, and felt no pleasure in hir heart, but when she had a glimpse by throwing or receiving some sight or looke of Rhomeo. And after they had contented eche others troubled heart with millions of amorous lookes which oftentimes interchangeably encountred and met together, the burning beames gave sufficient testimony of loves privy onsettes.

Love having made the heartes breache of those two lovers, as they two sought meanes to speake together, fortune offered them a very meete and apt occasion. A certayne lord of that troupe and companye tooke Julietta by the hande to daunce, wherein shee behaved hir selfe so well, and wyth so excellent grace, as shee wanne that daye the prise of honour from all the damosels of Verona. Rhomeo, havynge foreseene the place whereunto shee mynded to retire, approched the same, and so dyscretelye used the matter, as hee founde the meanes at hir returne to sit beside hir: Julietta when the daunce was finished, returned to the very place where she was set before, and was placed betwene Rhomeo and an other gentleman called Mercutio, which was a courtlyke gentleman, very well be loved of all men, and by reason of his pleasaunt and curteous behavior was in every company wel intertayned. Mercutio that was of audacity among maydens, as a lyon is among lambes, seazed incontynently upon the hande of Julietta, whose hands wontedly were so cold both in wynter and sommer as the mountayne yce, although the fire's heat did warm the same. Rhomeo whych sat uppon the left side of Julietta, seynge that Mercutio held hir by the right hand, toke hir by the other that he myght not be deceived of his purpose, and strayning the same a little, he felt himself so prest wyth that newe favor, as he remayned mute, not able to aunswer: but she perceyvyng by his chaunge of color, that the fault proceded of the vehemence of love, desyryng to speake unto hym, turned hir selfe towards hym, and wyth tremblyng voyce joyned with virginal shamefastnesse, intermedled with a certayn bashfulnesse, sayd to hym: "Blessed be the howre of your neare approche:" but mynding to procede in further talke, love had so closed up hir mouth, as she was not able to end hir tale.

Wherunto the yong gentleman all ravished with joy and contenta-
tion, sighing, asked hir what was the cause of that ryght fortunate
blessing: Julietta, somwhat more emboldened with pytyful loke and
smyling countenance, said unto him: "Syr, do not marvell yf I do
blesse your comminge hither, bicause sir Mercutio a good tyme wyth
frosty hand hath wholly frosen mine, and you of your curtesy have
warmed the same agayne." Wherunto immediatly Rhomeo replyed:
"Madame, if the heavens have ben so favorable to employe me to do
you some agreable service, being repaired hither by chance amongs
other gentlemen, I esteeme the same well bestowed, craving no
greater benefite for satisfaction of all my contentations received in
this world, than to serve obey and honor you as long as my lyfe doth
last, as experience shall yeld more ample proofe when it shall please
you to geve further assaye : moreover, if you have received any heat by
touche of my hand, you may be well assured that those flames be dead
in respect of the lyvely sparkes and violent fire which sorteth from
your fayre eyes, which fire hath so fiercely inflamed all the most sensible parts of my body, as if I be not succored by the favoure of your
good graces, I do attend the time to be consumed to dust." Scarse had
he made an ende of those last words, but the daunce of the torche
was at an end: whereby Julietta, which wholly burnt in love, straightly
claspyng her hand with hys, had no leysure to make other aunswer,
but softly thus to say: "My deare frend, I know not what other assured
wytnesse you desire of love, but that I let you understand that you be
no more your own, than I am yours, beyng ready and dysposed to
obey you so farre as honour shal permyt, beseechyng you for the
present tyme to content your selfe wyth thys aunswere, untyll some
other season meeter to communicate more secretly of our affaires."
Rhomeo seeing himselfe pressed to part of the company, and for that
hee knew not by what meanes he myght see hir agayne that was hys
life and death, demaunded of one of his friends what shee was, who
made aunswer that she was the daughter of Capellet, the lord of the
house, and mayster of that dayes feast (who wroth beyonde measure
that fortune had sent him to so daungerous a place, thought it impossible to bring to end his enterprise begon.) Julietta covetous on the
other side, to know what yong gentleman he was which had so curte-
ously intertayned hir that nyght, and of whome shee felt the new
wound in hir heart, called an olde gentlewoman of honor which had
nurssed hir and brought hir up, unto whom she sayd leaning upon
hir shoulder: "Mother, what two yong gentlemen be they which first
goe forth with the two torches before them." Unto whome the old
gentlewoman told the name of the houses wherof they came. Then
she asked hir againe, what young gentleman that was which holdeth
the visarde in his hand, wyth the damaske cloke about hym. "It is"
(quod she) "Romeo Montesche, the sonne of youre father's capytall

enimye and deadly foe to all your kinne." But the mayden at the onely
name of Montesche was altogyther amazed, despayrynge for ever to
attayne to husband hir great affectyoned fryend Rhomeo, for the
auncyent hatreds between those two families.

*   *   *

And when they had opened the vaulte, Rhomeo descended downe
two steppes, holdyng the candel in his hand and began to behold
wyth pityfull eye, the body of hir, which was the organ of his eyes,
and kyst it tenderly, holdyng it harde betwen his armes, and not able
to satisfie him selfe with hir sight, put hys fearefull handes uppon the
colde stomacke of Julietta. And after he had touched her in many
places, and not able to feele anye certayne judgemente of lyfe, he
drewe the poyson out of hys boxe, and swallowyng downe a great
quantytye of the same, cryed out: "O Julietta, of whome the worlde
was unworthye, what death is it possyble my hearte coulde choose
oute more agreeable than that whych yt suffereth harde by thee?
what grave more gloryous, than to bee buried in thy tombo? what
more woorthy or excellent epytaphe can bee vowed for memorye,
than the mutuall and pytyfull sacryfice of our lyves?" And thinkinge
to renue his sorrowe, his hearte began to frette through the vyolence
of the poyson, which by lyttle and lyttle assailed the same, and lookyng
about hym, espyed the bodye of the lorde Thibault, lying nexte unto
Julietta, whych as yet was not al together putrified, and speakyng to
the bodye as though it hadde bene alyve, sayde: "In what place so
ever thou arte (O cousyn Thibault) I most heartely do crye the mercy
for the offence whych I have done by depryving of thy lyfe: and yf thy
ghost doe whyshe and crye out for vengeaunce vppon mee, what
greater or more cruell satysfaction canste thou desyre to have, or
henceforth hope for, than to see him whych murdered thee, to bee
empoysoned with his owne handes, and buryed by thy side?" Then
endynge hys talk, felyng by lyttle and lyttle that his lyfe began to
fayle, falling prostrate uppon his knees, wyth feeble voyce hee softely
sayd: "O my Lord God, which to redeeme me didest discend from the
bosom of thy father, and tookest humane fleshe in the wombe of the
vyrgine, I acknowledge and confesse, that this body of myne is nothing else but earth and dust." Then seazed uppon wyth desperate
sorrow, he fell downe uppon the body of Julietta with sutch vehemence, as the heart faint and attenuated with too great torments, not
able to beare so hard a vyolence, was abandoned of all his sense and
naturall powers, in sutch sorte as the siege of hys soule fayled him
at that instant, and his members stretched forthe, remayned stiffe
and colde. Fryer Laurence whych knew the certayne tyme of the
pouders operation, marvelled that he had no answere of the letter
which he sent to Rhomeo by his fellowe fryer Anselme, departed

from S. Frauncis and with instruments for the purpose, determined to open the grave to let in aire to Julietta, whych was ready to wake: and approchyng the place, hee espied a lyght within, which made him afraide untyll that Pietro whych was hard by, had certytied hym that Rhomeo was with in, and had not ceased there to lamente and complayne the space of halfe an houre: and when they two were entred the grave and finding Rhomeo without lyfe, made sutch sorrowe as they can well conceyve whych love their dear fryende wyth lyke perfection. And as they were making theyr complaints, Julietta rising out of hir traunce, and beholding light within the toumbe, uncertayne wheather it were a dreame or fantasie that appeared before his eyes, comming agayne to hir selfe, knew frier Laurence, unto whom she sayd: "Father, I pray thee in the name of God to perfourme thy promise, for I am almost deade." And then frier Laurence concealing nothing from hir, (bycause he feared to be taken through his too long abode in that place) faythfully rehearsed unto hir, how he had sent frier Anselme to Rhomeo at Mantua, from whom as yet hee had receyved no aunswere. Notwithstanding he found Rhomeo dead in the grave, whose body he poyncted unto, lyinge hard by hir, praying hir sith it was so, paciently to beare that sodayne misfortune, and that if it pleased hir, he would convey hir into some monastery of women where she might in time moderate hir sorrow, and give rest unto hir minde. Julietta had no sooner cast eye uppon the deade corps of Rhomeo, but began to breake the fountayne pipes of gushing teares, which ran forth in sutch aboundance, as not able to support the furor of hir griefe, she breathed without ceasing upon his mouth, and then throwen hir selfe uppon his body, and embracing it very hard, seemed that by force of sighes and sobs, she would have revived, and brought him againe to ilfe, and after she had kissed and rekissed hym a million of times, she cried out: "Ah the sweete rest of my cares, and the onely port of all my pleasures and pastimes, hadst thou so sure a hearte to choose thy churchyarde this in place betwene the armes of thy perfect lover, and to ende the course of thy life for my sake in the floure of thy youth when lyfe to thee should have bene most deare and delectable? how had this tender body power to resist the furious cumbat of death, very death it selfe here present? how coulde thy tender and delicate youth willingly permit that thou shouldest approch into this filthy and infected place, where from henceforth thou shalt be the pasture of worms unworthy of thee? Alas, alas, by what meanes shall I now renue my playnts, which time and long pacience ought to have buried and clearely quenched? Ah I, miserable and caitife wretch, thinking to finde remedy for my griefs, have sharpned the knife that hath gieven me this cruell blow, whereof I receive the cause of mortall wound. Ah, happy and fortunate grave which shalt serve in world to come for witnesse of the most perfect

aliaunce that ever was betwene two most infortunate lovers, receyve
now the last sobbing sighes, and intertaynment of the most cruell of
all the cruell subjects of ire and death." And as she thought to continue hir complaynts, Pietro advertised Frier Laurence that he heard
a noyse besides the citadell, wherewyth being afrayd, they speadily
departed, fearing to be taken: and then Julietta seeing hir selfe alone,
and in full liberty, tooke agayne Rhomeo betweene hir armes, kissing
him with sutch affection, as she seemed to be more attaynted with
love than death, and drawing out the dagger which Rhomeo ware by
his side, she pricked hir selfe with many blowes against the heart,
sayinge with feeble and pitiful voice: Ah death the end of sorrow, and
beginning of felicity, thou art most hartely welcome: feare not at this
time to sharpen thy dart: give no longer delay of life, for feare that my
sprite travayle not to finde Rhomeo's ghost amongs sutch number of
carion corpses: and thou my deare lord and loyall husband Rhomeo,
if there rest in thee any knowledge, receyve hir whom thou hast so
faythfully loved, the onely cause of thy violent death, which frank-
ley offreth up hir soule that none but thou shalt joy the love whereof
thou hast made so lawfull conquest, and that our soules passing
from this light, may eternally, live together in the place of everlasting joy." And when she had ended those wordes shee yelded up hir
ghost. * * *

KAREEN SEIDLER

Romio und Julieta: A Case Study of an Early German Shakespeare Adaptation[†]

A mischievous saying claims that the three German national poets
are Goethe, Schiller and Shakespeare. It is commonly assumed that
the last of these three only became known in Germany in the mid-
eighteenth century, when Wieland began translating his plays. Yet
although Shakespeare's *name* was not present on the German stage
beforehand, his *plays* certainly were. In fact, from the 1580s onwards,
English actors travelled to and performed on the Continent. Their
repertoire consisted of English plays, Shakespeare's among them. In
the course of the seventeenth century, these plays were not only
translated but also adapted for the needs of the German *Wander-*
bühne (literally, 'wandering stage'), and therefore travelled a long way
from their originals. The texts that originated with these 'English

† From *Shakespeare Jahrbuch* 147 (2011): 135–41. Reprinted by permission of Kareen
Seidler.

comedians' currently have a low status in scholarly opinion, even lower than that of the so-called 'bad' quartos. Yet in the last few decades the "good news about the 'bad' quartos" has been propagated.[1] These developments throw new light on the German texts of the seventeenth century and make desirable a renewed analysis of these versions [which] * * * provide new insights into the Shakespearean texts and early modern English staging conditions and practices.

* * * The first record of English comedians on the Continent dates from 1585, when "certain unnamed English" played in the town-hall at Elsinore.[2] In the late sixteenth and early seventeenth centuries the German territories were a patchwork of different countries, where the earliest recorded performance of English comedians took place in Leipzig in 1585.[3] From the 1590s onwards, English strolling players are recorded in various cities and also, occasionally, at courts. Although they first performed in their mother tongue, the English comedians were extremely popular with Germans of different social standings who "not vnderstanding a worde they sayde" nevertheless "flocked wonderfully to see theire gesture and Action".[4] The actors' professionalism and their naturalistic acting and miming seem to have constituted a novelty for these audiences. They were also skilled acrobats and musicians and thus "all-round entertainers".[5] The English players have even been credited with founding the German professional theater.[6]

Around the turn of the century, the English comedians started performing in German.[7] Gradually, German actors joined the companies and, after the Thirty Years' War, the companies that called themselves "English comedians" only used this name for publicity, since they mainly consisted of Germans. Towards the end of the seventeenth century, German strolling players wholly took over. The

1. Stephen Urkowitz, "Good news about 'bad' quartos", in *"Bad" Shakespeare: Revaluations of the Shakespeare Canon*, ed. by Maurice Charney (Rutherford, N. J.: Fairleigh Dickinson University Press, 1988), 189–206. See also, for instance, Lukas Erne, *Shakespeare as Literary Dramatist* (Cambridge: Cambridge University Press, 2003); and Kathleen O. Irace, *Reforming the "Bad" Quartos: Performance and Provenance of Six Shakespearean First Editions* (Newark, Del.: University of Delaware Press, 1994).
2. At this performance "the press of folk was such that the wall broke down" (E. K. Chambers, *The Elizabethan Stage*, Vol. 2 [Oxford: Clarendon Press, 1923], 272).
3. Carl Grabau, "Englische Komödianten in Deutschland", *Jahrbuch der Deutschen Shakespeare Gesellshaft* 45 (1909), 311–312.
4. A contemporary account by Fynes Moryson (Charles Hughes [ed.], *Shakespeare's Europe: Unpublished Chapters of Fynes Moryson's Itinerary: Being a Survey of the Condition of Europe at the end of the 16th Century* [London: Sherratt & Hughes, 1903], 304).
5. George W. Brandt/Wiebe Hogendoorn, *Theatre in Europe: A Documentary History: German and Dutch Theatre, 1600–1684* (Cambridge: Cambridge University Press, 1993), 46.
6. Ralf Haekel, *Die Englischen Komödianten in Deutschland* (Heidelberg: Universitätsverlag Winter, 2004), 9.
7. Ernest Brennecke, in collaboration with Henry Brennecke, *Shakespeare in Germany 1590–1700* (Chicago: University of Chicago Press, 1964), 5. The clown was the first to perform in German, usually between acts (Helmul G. Asper, *Hanswurst: Studien zum Lustigmacher auf der Berufsschauspielerbühne in Deutschland im 17. und 18. Jahrhundert* [Emsdetten: Lechte, 1980], 25–26).

English comedians performed in all kinds of venues—town squares, tennis courts, fencing schools, inns, ball-rooms of castles, but also in a few purpose-built theaters.[8] They thus had to quickly adapt to different spaces and audiences: the plays in their repertoire would also be adapted as required.

The earliest surviving version of the Shakespearean *Wanderbühne* adaptations was printed in the 1620 collection, *Engelische Comedien und Tragedien*, namely a German *Titus Andronicus*. * * * Most famously * * * there is *Der Bestrafte Brudermord oder Prinz Hamlet aus Dännemark*, based on *Hamlet* and known in English as *Fratricide Punished*. Because it was first regarded as a possible source for Shakespeare's *Hamlet*, or even as a translation of the lost *Ur-Hamlet*, *Der Bestrafte Brudermord* has received intensive scholarly attention. In comparison, *Romio und Julieta* has been neglected. Der *Bestrafte Brudermord mord* has been published three times in German, and there are no fewer than six English translations. It was also repeatedly performed in the last century, both in English and in German. *Romio und Julieta*, by contrast, has received only two German editions, and been translated into English only once.[9]* * *

When analyzing the plays performed by the English comedians, literary critics are still quick to condemn them, because they are intent on setting *Romio and Julieta* and its peers side by side with their Shakespearean originals. More useful is the approach by Adolf Scherl who believes that *Romio and Julieta*

> ought not to be read as a literary alternative to the famous Shakespeare play. [. . .] It is a text which serves a purpose, serving the theatre, based not on the literary qualities of the text but rather on the effectiveness of the stage action.[1]

8. Brandt/Hogendoorn (1993), 25.
9. German publications of *Der Bestrafte Brudermord*: Rudolph Genée, *Geschichte der Shakespear'schen Dramen in Deutschland* (Leipzig: Wilhelm Englemann, 1870); Albert Cohn, *Shakespeare in Germany in the Sixteenth and Seventeenth Centuries* (New York: Haskell House, 1971 [1865]); Wilhelm Creizenach, *Die Schauspiele der Englischen Komödianten* (Berlin: W. Spemann, 1889). English translations of *Der Bestrafte Brudermord*: Georgina Archer in Cohn (1865); R.G. Latham, *Two Dissertations on the Hamlet of Saxo Grammaticus and of Shakespear* (London: Williams and Norgate, 1872); Horace Howard Furness (ed.), *Hamlet*, A New Variorum Edition of Shakespeare, Vol. 2 (New York: Dover Publications, 1963 [1877]) Appleton Morgan, *Hamlet and the Ur-Hamlet: The Text of the Second Quarto of 1604; with a Conjectural Text of the Alleged Kyd Hamlet Preceding It* (New York: The Shakespeare Society of New York, 1908); Brennecke (1964); Geoffrey Bullough, *Narrative and Dramatic Sources of Shakespeare*. Vol. 7 (London: Routledge, 1973). Performances of *Der Bestrafte Brudermord*: for instance, Oxford Playhouse, directed by William Poel (1924); Birmingham Repertory Theatre, directed by Bernard Hepton (1958/1959); Stuttgarter Theater im Depot, directed by Stephan Barbarino (1989); Theatralia, directed by Daniel Steinbach (2007). German publications of *Romio and Julieta*: Eduard Devrient, *Geschichte der Deutschen Schauspielkunst*, Vol. 2 (Leipzig: Weber, 1848); Cohn (1865). English translation of *Romio and Julieta*: Lothar Bucher in Cohn (1865).
1. Adolf Scherl, "Romeo a Julie z Jižnich Čech," *Divadelini revenue* (2001) 12, 69–70, here 69. Thanks to Pavel Drábek who drew my attention to this article and kindly translated it for me.

Like the other German Shakespeare adaptations of the seventeenth century, *Romio and Julieta* is a theatrical document and must be treated as such.

* * *

How exactly this text (and other early German Shakespeare adaptations) came into being is difficult to establish. Yet a narrative similar to the following might be constructed: When the English players travelled to the Continent, they brought with them English plays (Shakespeare's among them), in print, in manuscript, in their memories or in a combination of several of these. They continuously adapted the plays to the needs of the *Wanderbühne*, changing tone, plot and structure as they saw fit. And about ninety years after Shakespeare first wrote *Romeo and Juliet,* someone wrote down the text that has come down to us.

* * *

The German adaptation contains a number of structural changes, additions and omissions. Among the omissions are most of Shakespeare's monologues and set pieces, the scene in Mantua, and the brawl at the beginning. In fact, *Romio and Julieta* strikingly starts with a reconciliation between Mundige (Shakespeare's Montague) and Capolet, orchestrated by the Prince. Yet the feud is never wholly dispelled, and the initial truce does not prevent any of the deaths. Max Wolff believes that the inconsistency concerning the feud is due to two different sources which the "author" was struggling to combine.[2] Nevertheless, the feud and the resulting generation conflict remain subdued in comparison to Shakespeare's texts—for example, the feud is not mentioned at the end of the play.

As for additions, some examples are 1.2, where Julieta is introduced, and 3.8, where Romio visits the Father (Shakespeare's Friar) to obtain his consent to marry Julieta (during their first meeting, after the 'balcony scene', he does not mention marriage). Some Shakespearean passages are also transposed: for instance, Romio laments Julieta's chastity and not Rosallina's (Shakespeare's Rosaline) in a passage (3.6) which is textually close to Shakespeare. As for structural changes, a notable example is that Julieta is only told that she must marry Paris *after* she has fallen in love with Romio (even though Paris is present on-stage before).

Another major change is Picklhäring, the clown,[3] who is an important character in *Romio and Julieta*. In fact, he can be said to embody

---

2. "Verfasser" (Max Woolff, "Die Tragödie von Romio und Julieta", *Jahrbuch der Deutschen Shakespeare Gesellschaft* 47 [1911], 92–105, here 99). In fact, the play is probably the product of a collaboration (Scherl [2001], 69).

3. I use the term 'clown' in its early modern, Shakespearean sense.

a whole set of changes to the play and its plot. Picklhäring's role not only incorporates that of Peter and those of the other servants, but he even steals some of the Nurse's scenes. Giorgio Melchiori believes that all of the comic roles in the Shakespearean play were played by one actor (namely, Will Kemp).[4] In *Romio and Julieta* the conflation of comic roles is taken one step further, creating the fully-fledged Picklhäring, an irreverent presence throughout the play. In fact, he enjoyed independent fame: not only did "Picklhäring" become a synonym for the clown,[5] but he also features in numerous plays and even has the title role of several interludes.[6]

* * *

From Romio und Julieta (ca. 1680)[†]

IV.iv

Enter JULIETA *and* NURSE.

JULIETA Come, dearest Nurse, and tell me what tumult was this in the house of my father? Has there been an accident? For you know, women's freedom is poor in *Italia*. They are shut in like prisoners. Oh, irksome desire!

NURSE Yes, of course there was a row, though not at your 5
father's house but in the open street. Oh, I wish I knew nothing about it.

JULIETA Has any misfortune or harm befallen our house or friends?

NURSE O woe, O calamity, O Romio, Romio! 10

JULIETA How? What do you say of Romio?

Enter PICKLEHERRING.

PICKLEHERRING O misery, O distress, O pity, O misfortune! What can be worse in the world than torn trousers and

---

4. Giorgio Melchiori. "Peter, Balthasar, and Shakespeare's Art of Doubling", *The Modern Language Review* 78 (1983), 777–792, here 782.

5. This is confirmed by *Romio and Julieta*'s manuscript which does not use italics for Picklhäring's name as it does with the names of other characters.

6. Uwe-K. Ketelsen (ed.), *Komödien des Barock* (Reinbek bei Hamburg: Rowohlt [1970]), 16. 37. The clown was often played by the *Prinzipal*, the leader of the company (Willi Flemming [ed.], *Das Schauspiel der Wanderbühne* [Leipzig: Reclam, 1931], 20), probably because he was such a central figure.

† From *Romio und Julieta*, trans. and ed. Kareen Seidler. The German text on which this translation is based is the extant manuscript of *Romio und Julieta* (Austrian National Library, Vienna, Cod. 13148). The manuscript is undated and has no title page. It has been dated to the second half of the seventeenth century (see e.g., Rudolph Genée, *Geschichte der Shakespear'schen Dramen in Deutschland* [Leipzig: Wilhelm Engelmann, 1870]). Adolf Scherl proposed that the manuscript was composed in 1688 (Adolf Scherl, "Romeo a Julie z jiznich Cech," *Divadelni revue* 12 [2001]: 69–114). Reprinted by permission of Kareen Seidler.

nothing to eat? I am running around like a hound and am
looking for Julieta. Oh, who knows in what hole or corner   15
she is hiding and bawling her eyes out because of the great
bad luck that happened to Romio, I won't run any further
to search for her. I am so tired from running and searching
that I cannot move a tooth in my mouth. But look, there is
our nurse. Ho, Nurse, what are you doing here? Where is   20
Miss Julieta? I bring precious news for her.

NURSE   Be quiet, fool. Open thy calf's eyes. Art thou blind?
Dost thou not see Miss Julieta here?

JULIETA   Heaven preserve me from misfortune! What dost
thou bring, Pickleherring?   25

PICKLEHERRING   Wait, let me first recover my breath.

JULIETA   Is my father or my mother unwell?

PICKLEHERRING   Damn it! It is a thousand times worse.

JULIETA   O Pickleherring, don't keep me in suspense any
longer. Is there any misfortune? Then tell me at once.   30

PICKLEHERRING   No misfortune except that he is as dead as
a stockfish.

NURSE   Yes, Miss Julieta, that is just the thing I did not want
to say. O Romio, Romio!

JULIETA   O heaven preserve me! Is Romio dead?   35

PICKLEHERRING   If the Nurse says that, then she lies like a
beaten witch. I am the man who knows better.

JULIETA   O dear Pickleherring, then say what thou knowest.

PICKLEHERRING   That is why I came here, so I will tell you:
Mercutiusis dead; Tipold has died because Romio has   40
stabbed him to death, so he fled and no one knows where
to find him.

JULIETA   Then my life is no longer worth living. O cruel,
merciless heaven! Ah, miserable me, so full of affliction!
Shall I at last sacrifice myself to death, too?   45

PICKLEHERRING   Rather go home and lie down in bed; that is
he healthier than dying.

NURSE   O good Tipold, how miserably wast thou killed!

JULIETA   What, Tipold? If only Romio were to be found!

PICKLEHERRING   It is true, Miss Julieta, Romio did stab   50
Tipold, but the, Duke has banished him from Verona never
to return as long as he lives.

JULIETA   Ah, all too miserable Julieta! If Romio is banished,
then the light of my life is extinguished, too; and I will also
banish myself from this world.   55

NURSE   Oh, Romio be cursed! One cannot trust anyone.
Who should have thought him so false?

PICKLEHERRING   O thou old feather duster! If thou wert lying
on a pyre I myself would set fire to it and joyfully watch thee
burn.   60

JULIETA   What, Nurse, dost thou curse the one whom my
heart loves?

NURSE   What, Miss Julieta, will you love him who murdered
your cousin?

JULIETA   How Should I hate him who loves my life? Ah, no, I   65
would rather die myself.

NURSE   O Julieta, leave the perjured Romio, and take Count
Paris for your husband.

PICKLEHERRING   No, Julieta, I will give you better advice:
take them both if you like them; then take me for your   70
bridegroom.

JULIETA   Be quiet, Pickleherring. This is no time for joking,
nor is it Christian to take two or three husbands.

PICKLEHERRING   Why not? The Turkish Emperor has so
many wives, they cannot all be counted. And why should I   75
or you not be permitted to take three, four, five, six, seven,
eight, nine, ten wives or husbands? I should not have far to
go if I should seek some in the city of Kallschin, Budweiß,
Gopplitz, Freÿstatt, Lintz or here who desire (or even have)
more than one wife, and wives who desire (or have) more   80
than one husband.

JULIETA   Well, then, I will do it and follow thy advice. Go
with my nurse, Pickleherring, and tell my father and
mother that I love Count Paris.

NURSE   I am glad of it; I will go at once and suggest this to   85
your mother.

PICKLEHERRING   Back, old woman! It would be a bad custom
if an ambassador followed at the back and an old woman
went up front.

                                                              Exit NURSE.

JULIETA   Cursed Nurse, thou who dissuadest me from loving   90
my husband! O my dearest Romio, this shall never happen.
But O Romio, why didst thou murder my cousin? Yet thou
wast in thy right, as he wanted to murder thee, my husband. Yet, Romio, thy banishment pains me, my heart is
bleeding, and it goes to my very heart. Well, then, I will   95
think of ways and means to come to him and take a painful
leave of him.—Come here, Pickleherring. I know thou art
faithful and discreet. Therefore listen to what I say. Here:
receive some ducats and try to find Romio, who can still be
found in Verona, and come with me to my chamber; I will   100
dispatch thee with a letter to him.

PICKLEHERRING   Yes, Yes, you speak well, Miss Julieta.
Though my feet are so tired that I could not mount a donkey, for the sake of the ducats I will run all over Verona as
if I were mad until I have found Romio, and then receive   105
some more ducats from you.

Exeunt JULIETA *and* PICKLEHERRING.

IV.v

Enter FATHER *and* ROMIO.

FATHER   Please, dearest son Romio, be content for once, and
do not allow sadness to get the better of you. For it is still a
most merciful judgment the Duke has pronounced.

ROMIO   O Father, is it life or death? If it is death, I will suffer   110
appropriately.

FATHER   No, my dear child, the word death has been turned
into a most merciful banishment.

ROMIO   Ah, banishment is much worse than death. O cruel
heaven! Am I now to part and leave Julieta and be   115
deprived of her lovely presence? Ah, more than pains of
death!

FATHER   Please, my son, hear me.

ROMIO   O Father, what shall I hear? You will only say "banishment" again.   120

PICKLEHERRING *knocks within.*

PICKLEHERRING   Hello! Is everything closed up? Nobody at
home? Open the door!

FATHER   My child, follow me and hide thyself: the watch
might come and arrest thee.

ROMIO   I don't want to; I would rather drown here in my own   125
tears.

FATHER   O heavens, what madness possesses his senses!

PICKLEHERRING   What the plague! Will I have to wait much
longer? Open, or I will become mad and foolish.

FATHER   Romio, hide yourself. The watch is present.   130

ROMIO   I don't want to and I cannot.

FATHER   Then you are rushing yourself into harm. Who is there?

PICKLEHERRING   The deuce, open the door! I have been
standing until the nails nearly froze off my feet. I have got
a message to deliver, Father, and come from Julieta.   135

FATHER   O joyful messenger, come in!

Enter PICKLEHERRING.

PICKLEHERRING   *Avos gratias, bonus dies, Domine Pater.*

FATHER   Many thanks, Pickleherring. From where hast thou
come?

PICKLEHERRING From the street, from our house, and I 140
wanted to ask the Patribus to tell me where Romio is.

FATHER There he lies and has almost suffocated in sadness
and in his own tears.

PICKLEHERRING Those are fool's pranks. Sir Romio, get up; I
come from Julieta. 145

ROMIO Ah, who pronounces the lovely name Julieta? O
Pickleherring, does she not curse me because I have
stabbed her cousin Tipold?

PICKLEHERRING No, she hasn't told me anything of the kind.
I believe even if you had hanged him, strangled him, bro- 150
ken him on the wheel, spitted him, or even put him on the
donkey, she would not ask about it. But she has commanded
me to look for you and, when I have found you, to say she
asks you to come to her tonight because you are banished,
to say *vale* and farewell to you. 155

ROMIO Ah, is it possible, and should I believe that Julieta
alone is full of gentleness and mercy?

PICKLEHERRING Of course it is possible. And to show that it
is true, Julieta sends you through her ambassador in my person this ring as well as this letter. And I think if you would 160
not go to her, she would call you a rogue to your face.

ROMIO O letter, O ring, be welcome! Thee, my ring, will I
wear adoringly on my finger till pale death cut the thread of
my life and end it. Therefore go, Pickleherring; inform my
Julieta that when night puts on her black mourning dress, I 165
shall obediently appear and take my last farewell. Here,
Pickleherring, for thy trouble receive these few doubloons
as thy beer money.

PICKLEHERRING I thank you, Sir Romio, for these few; if it
were more, it would be even better. 170

Exit PICKLEHERRING.

FATHER Please, Sir Romio, go and take leave of your beloved,
but with such caution that by the break of day you may still
leave the town.

ROMIO Honoured Father, before the morning star retires
and gives way to the world's great light and announces the 175
day, I will go from hence. But my confidence, Father,
stands with you alone—that you report to me in writing in
Mantua how things are with you and my Julieta at all times.

FATHER Have no worry, my son. When you sojourn in Mantua, you shall always receive letters. 180

ROMIO Well, then I yield to the fate of my unlucky star.
Although I travel from here banished, my heart I leave with
Julieta.

Exit ROMIO.

FATHER   May heaven and all heavenly powers give him good
luck on his journey, and bless him with such good luck that   185
he may soon see Verona with joy. In the meantime I will
pray to heaven early and late for his well-being.

Exit FATHER.

THOMAS OTWAY

From The History and Fall of Caius Marius (1680)[†]

SCENE *a Church-yard.*

Enter MARIUS JUNIOR.

MAR. JUN.   As I have wander'd musing to and fro,
Still am I brought to this unlucky place,   250
As I had business with the horrid Dead:
Though could I trust the flattery of Sleep,
My Dreams presage some joyfull news at hand.
My Bosome's Lord sits lightly on his Throne,
And all this day an unaccustom'd Spirit   255
Lifts me above the ground with chearfull thoughts.
I dream'd *Lavinia* came and found me dead,
And breath'd such Life with Kisses on my Lips,
That I reviv'd, and was an Emperour.
       Enter CATULUS.
    CATUL.   My Lord already here?
       MAR. JUN.   My trusty *Catulus*,   260
What News from my *Lavinia*? speak, and bless me.
    CATUL.   She's very well. . . .
       MAR. JUN.   Then nothing can be ill.
Something thou seem'st to know that's terrible.
Out with it boldly, man, What canst thou say
Of my *Lavinia*?
    CATUL.   But one sad word, She's dead.   265
Here in her Kindreds Vault I've seen her laid,
And have bin searching you to tell the News.
    MAR. JUN.   Dead? is it so ? then I deny you, Stars.
Go, hasten quickly, get me Ink and Paper.
'Tis done: I'll hence to night.   270

---

† From Thomas Otway, *The History and Fall of Caius Marius*, Act V in *The Works of Thomas
Otway: Plays, Poems, and Love-Letters*, vol. 1, ed. J. C. Ghosh (Oxford: Clarendon Press,
1932), pp. 511–19. Reprinted by permission of Oxford University Press.

Hast thou no Letters to me from the Priest?
    CATUL.   No, my good Lord.
    MAR. JUN.   No matter, get thee gone. . . .
                        [*Ex.* CATULUS.
       LAVINIA! yet I'll ly with thee to night;
But, for the means. Oh Mischief! thou art swift
To catch the straggling Thoughts of Desp'rate men.   275
I do remember an Apothecary,
That dwelt about this Rendezvous of Death:
Meager and very rufull were his Looks;
Sharp Misery had worn him to the Bones;
And in his needy Shop a Tortoise hung,   280
An Allegator stufft, and other Skins
Of ill-shap'd Fishes: and about his Shelves
A beggarly account of empty Boxes,
Green earthen Pots, Bladders, and musty Seeds,
Remnants of Packthread, and old Cakes of Roses,   285
Were thinly scatter'd, to make up a Show.
Oh for a Poison now! his Need will sell it,
Though it be present Death by *Roman* Law.
As I remember this should be the House.
His Shop is shut: with Beggars all are Holydays.   290
Holla! Apothecary; hoa!
    Enter Apothecary.
    APOTH.   Who's there?
    MAR. JUN.   Come hither, man. I see thou 'rt very poor;
Thou mayst doe any thing: here's fifty *Drachma's,*
Get me a Draught of that will soonest free
A Wretch from all his Cares: thou understand'st me.   295
    APOTH.   Such mortal Drugs I have; but *Roman* Law
Speaks Death to any he that utters 'em.
    MAR. JUN.   Art thou so base and full of Wretchedness,
Yet fear'st to dy? Famine is in thy Cheeks,
Need and Oppression stareth in thy Eyes,   300
Contempt and Beggary hang on thy Back;
The World is not thy Friend, nor the World's Law;
The World affords no Law to make thee rich:
Then be not poor, but break it, and take this.
    APOTH.   My Poverty, but not my Will consents. . . .   305
              [*Goes in, fetches a Vial of Poison.*
Take this and drink it off, the Work is done.
    MAR. JUN.   There is thy Gold, worse Poison to mens Souls,
Doing more Murthers in this loathsome world
Then these poor Compounds thou 'rt forbid to sell.
I sell thee Poison, thou hast sold me none.   310

Farewell . . . buy Food . . . and get thy self in flesh.
Now for the Monument of the *Metelli*. . . .   [*Exit.*
{*Scene draws off, and shews
the Temple and Monument.*

Re-enters.
It should be here: the door is open too.
Th' insatiate mouth of Fate gapes wide for more.
Enter Priest, and Boy with a Mattock and Iron Crow.
PRIEST. Give me the Mattock and the wrenching Iron:
Now take this Letter, with what haste thou canst
Find out young *Marius*, and deliver it.   [*Ex. Boy.*   316
Now must I to the Monument alone.
What Wretch is he that's entring into th' Tomb?
Some Villain come to rob and spoil the Dead.
Whoe're thou art, stop thy unhallowed purpose.   320
MAR. JUN.   Whoe're thou art, I warn thee to be gone,
And do not interrupt my horrid purpose.
For else, by Heav'n, I'll tear thee joint by joint,
And strew this hungry Church-yard with thy Lims.
My Mind and its Intents are savage wild,   325
More fierce and more inexorable far
Then empty Tigers or the roaring Sea.
PRIEST.   Then as a sacrilegious Slave I charge thee,
Obey and go with me, or thou must dy.
MAR. JUN.   I know I must, and therefore I came hither.   330
Good Reverence, do not tempt a desp'rate man.
By Heav'n, I love thee better then my self:
For I against my self come hither arm'd.
Stay not, be gone . . . . Live, and hereafter say,
A Mad-man's Mercy gave thee honest Counsell.   335
PRIEST.   I do defy thy Mercy and thy Counsell,
And here will seize thee as a Thief and Robber.
MAR. JUN.   Wilt thou provoke me? then here, take thy
Wages.   [*Kills him.*
PRIEST.   I'm kill'd. Oh *Marius!* now too late I know thee.
Thou'st slain the onely man could doe thee good.
Lavinia. . . . oh! . . .   [*Dies.*
MAR. JUN.   Let me peruse this Face.   341
It is the honest Priest that joyn'd our hands,
In a Disguize conceal'd. Give me thy Hand,
Since in ill Fate's black Roll with me thou'rt writ,
I'll bury thee in a triumphant Grave.   345
Thou detestable Maw, thou Womb of Death,
Gorg'd with the dearest Morsel of the Earth,

Thus will I force thy rotten Jaws to   [*Pulls down the*
     open, . . .   *side of the Tomb.*
And spite of thee yet cram thee with more Food.
Oh gorgeous Palace! oh my Love! my Wife!   350
Death has had yet no pow'r upon thy Beauty;
That is not conquer'd. Beauty's Ensign yet
Is Crimson in thy Lips and in thy Cheeks;
And the pale Flag is not advanc'd yet there.
Why art thou still so fair? shall I believe   355
That the lean Monster Death is amorous,
And keeps thee here in Darkness for his Paramour?
For fear of that, I'll stay with thee for ever.
Come, bitter Conduct, thou unsavoury Guide:
Here's to my Love. . . . .   [*Drinks the Poison.*
                  And now Eyes look your last.   360
Arms take your last Embrace, whilst on these Lips
I fix the Seal of an eternall Contract. . . .
She breaths and stirs. . . . .   [Lavinia *wakes.*
    Lavin. IN THE TOMB.   Where am I? bless me, Heav'n!
'Tis very cold; and yet here's something warm.   365
    MAR. JUN.   She lives, and we shall both be made immortall.
Speak, my *Lavinia*, speak some heav'nly news,
And tell me how the Gods design to treat us.
    LAVIN.   Oh! I have slept a long Ten thousand years.
What have they done with me? I'll not be us'd thus;   370
I'll not wed *Sylla. Marius* is my Husband.
Is he not, Sir? Methinks you're very like him.
Be good as he is, and protect me.
    MAR. JUN.   Hah!
Wilt thou not own me? am I then but like him?
Much, much indeed I'm chang'd from what I was;   375
And ne'r shall be my self, if thou art lost.
    LAVIN.   The Gods have heard my Vows; it is my *Marius.*
Once more they have restor'd him to my Eyes.
Hadst thou not come, sure I had slept for ever.
But there's a soveraign Charm in thy Embraces,   380
That might doe Wonders, and revive the Dead.
    MAR. JUN.   Ill Fate no more, *Lavinia*, now shall part us,
Nor cruel Parents, nor oppressing Laws.
Did not Heav'n's Pow'rs all wonder at our Loves?
And when thou toldst the tale of thy Disasters,   385
Was there not Sadness and a Gloom amongst 'em?
I know there was: and they in pity sent thee,
Thus to redeem me from this vale of Torments,
And bear me with thee to those Hills of Joys.

This World's gross air grows burthensome already.   390
I'm all a God: such heav'nly Joys transport me,
That mortal Sense grows sick and faints with lasting.
                                              [*Dies.*
    LAVIN.   Oh! to recount my Happiness to thee,
To open all the Treasure of my Soul,
And shew thee how 'tis fill'd, would waste more time   395
Then so impatient Love as mine can spare.
He's gone; he's dead; breathless: alas! my *Marius.*
A Vial too: here, here has bin his Bane.
Oh Churl! drink all? not leave one friendly Drop
For poor *Lavinia?* Yet I'll drain thy Lips.   400
Perhaps some welcom Poison may hang there,
To help me to o'retake thee on thy Journy.
Clammy and damp as Earth. Hah! stains of Bloud?
And a man murther'd? 'Tis th'unhappy *Flamen.*
Who fix their Joys on any thing that's Mortall,   405
Let 'em behold my Portion, and despair.
What shall I doe? how will the Gods dispose me?
Oh! I could rend these Walls with Lamentation,
Tear up the Dead from their corrupted Graves,
And dawb the face of Earth with her own Bowels.   410
      Enter Marius senior, *and Guards driving in* Metellus.
    MAR. SEN.   Pursue the Slave; let not his Gods protect him.
    LAVIN.   More Mischiefs? hah! my Father?
    METELL.   Oh! I am slain.
                       [*Falls down and dies.*
    LAVIN.   And murther'd too. When will my Woes have end?
Come, cruel Tyrant.
    MAR. SEN.   Sure I have known that Face.
  LAVIN. And canst thou think of any one good Turn   415
That I have done thee, and not kill me for't?
    MAR. SEN.   Art thou not call'd *Lavinia?*
    LAVIN.   Once I was:
But by my Woes may now be better known.
    MAR. SEN.   I cannot see thy Face. . . . .
    LAVIN.   You must, and hear me.
By this, you must: nay, I will hold you fast. . . .   420
              [*Seizes his Sword.*
    MAR. SEN.   What wouldst thou say? where's all my Rage gone
now?
    LAVIN.   I am *Lavinia,* born of Noble race.
My blooming Beauty conquer'd many Hearts,
But prov'd the greatest Torment of my own: 424
Though my Vows prosper'd, and my Love was answer'd

By *Marius*, the noblest, goodliest Youth
That Man e're envy'd at, or Virgin sigh'd for.
He was the Son of an unhappy Parent,
And banish'd with him when our Joys were young;
Scarce a night old.

    MAR. SEN.   I do remember't well,   430
And thou art She, that Wonder of thy kind,
That couldst be true to exil'd Misery,
And to and fro through barren Desarts range,
To find th'unhappy Wretch thy Soul was fond of.

    LAVIN.   Do you remember't well?

    MAR. SEN.   In every point.   435

    LAVIN.   You then were gentle, took me in your Arms,
Embrac'd me, blest me, us'd me like a Father.
And sure I was not thankless for the Bounty.

    MAR. SEN.   No; thou wert next the Gods my onely Comfort.
When I lay fainting on the dry parcht Earth,   440
Beneath the scorching heat of burning Noon,
Hungry and dry, no Food nor Friend to chear me:
Then Thou, as by the Gods some Angel sent,
Cam'st by, and in Compassion didst relieve me.   444

    LAVIN.   Did I all this?

    MAR. SEN.   Thou didst, thou sav'dst my Life.
Else I had sunk beneath the weight of Want,
And bin a Prey to my remorseless Foes.

    LAVIN.   And see how well I am at last rewarded.
All could not balance for the short-term'd Life
Of one Old man: You have my Father butcher'd,   450
The onely Comfort I had left on Earth.
The Gods have taken too my Husband from me.
See where he lies, your and my onely Joy.
This Sword yet reeking with my Father's Gore,
Plunge it into my Breast: plunge, plunge it thus.   455
And now let Rage, Distraction and Despair
Seize all Mankind, till they grow mad as I am.
                   [*Stabs her self with his Sword.*

    MAR. SEN.   Nay, now thou hast outdone me much in Cruelty.
Be Nature's Light extinguisht; let the Sun
Withdraw his Beams, and put the world in Darkness,   460
Whilst here I howl away my Life in Sorrows.
Oh! let me bury Me and all my Sins
Here with this good Old man. Thus let me kiss
Thy pale sunk Cheeks, embalm thee with my Tears.
My Son, how cam'st thou by this wretched End?   465
We might have all bin Friends, and in one House

Enjoy'd the Blessings of eternal Peace.
But oh! my cruel Nature has undone me.
                    Enter Messenger.
   MESS.   My Lord, I bring you most disastrous News.
Sylla's return'd: his Army's on their march   470
From *Capua*, and to morrow will reach *Rome.*
At which the Rabble are in new Rebellion,
And your *Sulpitius* mortally is wounded.
     Enter SULPITIUS *(led in by two of the Guards) and* GRANIUS.
   MAR. SEN.   Oh! then I'm ruin'd from this very moment.
Has my good Genius left me? Hope forsakes me.   475
The Name of *Sylla's* banefull to my Fortune.
Be warn'd by me, ye Great ones, how y' embroil
Your Country's Peace, and dip your Hands in Slaughter.
Ambition is a Lust that's never quencht,
Grows more inflam'd and madder by Enjoyment.   480
Bear me away, and lay me on my Bed,
A hopelesse Vessel bound for the dark Land
Of loathsome Death, and loaded deep with Sorrows.
                        [He is led off.
   SULPIT.   A Curse on all Repentance! how I hate it!
I'd rather hear a Dog howl then a Man whine.   485
   GRAN.   You're wounded, Sir: I hope it is not much.
   SULPIT.   No; 'tis not so deep as a Well, nor so wide as a
Church-door. But 'tis enough; 'twill serve; I am pepper'd I
warrant, I warrant for this world. A Pox on all Mad-men
hereafter. If I get a Monument, let this be my Epitaph:

> Sulpitius *lies here, that troublesome Slave,*   491
> *That sent many honester men to the Grave,*
> *And dy'd like a Fool when h' had liv'd like a Knave.*
>   *[Ex. omnes.*

      FINIS.

CRITICISM AND LATER REWRITINGS

STANLEY WELLS

The Challenges of *Romeo and Juliet*†

The story of Romeo and Juliet—one of the great myths of the Western world—first appeared fully formed in an Italian version of 1530, and since then has had a vigorous afterlife, not all of it deriving from Shakespeare. It has been frequently reincarnated and recollected in a multitude of forms and media—prose narratives, verse narratives, drama, opera, orchestral and choral music, ballet, film, television and painting among them. Besides being presented seriously it has been parodied and burlesqued; there are several full-scale nineteenth-century travesties of Shakespeare's play, and its balcony scene in particular has often formed the basis for comic sketches. Romeo is a type name for an ardent lover, and Juliet's 'Romeo, Romeo, wherefore art thou Romeo?' is often jokily declaimed even by people who have never read or seen the play.

Already when, around 1594, Shakespeare decided to base a play on the story, he was able to consult more than one version. He worked closely from *The Tragical History of Romeus and Juliet*, by Arthur Brooke (who, like the hero and heroine of the story, himself died young), first published in 1562 and reprinted in 1587. Brooke had used a moralistic French adaptation, by Pierre Boaistuau, of a story by the Italian Matteo Bandello, and Shakespeare probably also read William Painter's translation of Boaistuau in his *Palace of Pleasure*, of 1567.

Brooke's style is, to say the best, uninspired, but he provided Shakespeare with both a well laid-out story and much valuable detail. Brooke treated the events as historical, ending his poem with the statement that

> The bodies dead removed from vault where they did die
> In stately tomb on pillars great of marble raise they high.
> On every side above were set and eke beneath
> Great store of cunning epitaphs in honour of their death.
> And even at this day the tomb is to be seen,
> So that among the monuments that in Verona been
> There is no monument more worthy of the sight
> Than is the tomb of Juliet, and Romeus her knight.

These lines clearly influenced the end of Shakespeare's play, in which the effect of the lovers' deaths is to some extent alleviated by the consequent reconciliation of their feuding families; and the

† From *Shakespeare Survey* 49 (1996): 1–14. Copyright © 1996 Cambridge University Press. Reprinted by permission of Cambridge University Press.

alleged historicity of the tale continues to be of value to the Veronese tourist industry.

For most people at the present time Shakespeare's play embodies the classic version of the story. But, although it is widely read and frequently performed, it has itself undergone adaptation, sometimes slight, sometimes substantial, in ways that are implicitly critical of the original. The play's ending has proved especially subject to alteration. In a lost version by James Howard performed shortly after the restoration of the monarchy in 1660, the tragedy was endowed with a happy ending. * * * The result was that (as the prompter Downes wrote) 'when the tragedy was revived again 'twas played alternately, tragical one day and tragi-comical another for several days altogether'.[1] Not long after this, in 1680, Thomas Otway wrote a new play, *Caius Marius*, borrowing much of Shakespeare's dialogue. Apparently Otway was dissatisfied with Shakespeare's conclusion, in which Romeo dies before Juliet recovers from the sleeping potion given to her by the Friar. Otway, clearly—and perhaps rightly—thinking that Shakespeare had missed a good opportunity for an affecting passage of dialogue, conceived the notion of causing his heroine to wake before her lover expired, and gave them a touching duologue. When Theophilus Cibber came to adapt Shakespeare's play, in 1744, he incorporated passages from Otway, including the death scene, with only minor changes, and around the same time David Garrick, in a version that follows Shakespeare's text more closely, nevertheless seized upon Otway's basic idea, while writing a new duologue for the lovers in which they go successively mad. This was accepted into the theatrical tradition, and although the American Charlotte Cushman (playing Romeo) returned to Shakespeare in the mid-nineteenth century, Garrick's version appears not to have been completely abandoned until Henry Irving put on the play in 1882.

Garrick's death scene is easily guyed: 'Bless me! how cold it is!' says Juliet on waking, and later, 'And did I wake for this!'; yet Francis Gentleman, writing in 1770, praised it highly: 'no play ever received greater advantage from alteration than this tragedy, especially in the last act; bringing Juliet to life before Romeo dies, is undoubtedly a change of infinite merit. The whole dying scene does Mr Garrick great credit.'[2] In its day, and for long afterwards, it must have been highly actable—and it gave the performer of Romeo a stronger death scene than Shakespeare had provided. Bernard Shaw, writing in 1894, described his first experience of the play, 'in which

1. John Downes, *Rocius Anglicanus* (London, 1708; Facsimile Reprint, Augustan Reprint Society no. 134, Los Angeles, 1969), sig. c3v.
2. Cited in G. C. D. Odell, *Shakespeare from Betterton to Irving*, 2 vols. (New York, 1920), 1.347.

Romeo, instead of dying forthwith when he took the poison, was interrupted by Juliet, who sat up and made him carry her down to the footlights, where she complained of being very cold, and had to be warmed by a love scene, in the middle of which Romeo, who had forgotten all about the poison, was taken ill and died'.[3] No modern director would be likely to interpolate Garrick's words into Shakespeare's text, but in more than one production the terrible irony of the situation has been pointed by Juliet's showing signs of life as Romeo dies which are visible to the audience though not to him.[4]

In the twentieth century English-speaking productions have at least taken Shakespeare's original text as their point of departure, though the dénouement was radically altered in one of Stratford's more iconoclastic versions, the one directed by Michael Bogdanov in 1986. This modern-dress production came to be known as the *Alfa-Romeo and Juliet* because of the presence on stage during part of the action of a bright red sports car. Characteristically of this director, it had a strong political slant which manifested itself especially in his handling of the ending. Academic critics have suggested that when Montague and Capulet say that they will 'raise the lovers' statues in pure gold' they are revealing false, materialistic values.[5] Bogdanov translated this suggestion into theatrical terms. His text came to a halt with Juliet's death; the dead lovers were covered with golden cloths and then, during a brief blackout, they sprang to attention and stood as their own statues; the final episode became a wordless media event, as reporters and photographers flooded the scene, the survivors posed in attitudes suggestive rather of a desire to have their photographs published in *Hello!* magazine than of either true grief or reconciliation, and the Prince spoke part of the prologue—omitted at the start—transposed to the past tense.

* * *

[T]wentieth-century productions, at least since John Gielgud's of 1935, in which he and Laurence Olivier successively played Romeo and Mercutio, and which also had Peggy Ashcroft as Juliet and Edith Evans as the Nurse, have tended to play fuller and purer texts than those of earlier ages; * * * [yet] some of the most

3. From an article called 'The Religion of the Pianoforte' (*The Fortnightly Review*, February 1894), reprinted in part in *Shaw on Shakespeare*, edited by Edwin Wilson (London, 1962), p. 246.
4. See for example Peter Holding, *Romeo and Juliet: Text and Performance* (London, 1992), pp. 61–2 for a description of the scene in a 1976 Stratford production directed by Trevor Nunn and Barry Kyle. In Adrian Noble's 1995 Stratford production, too, Juliet showed signs of life before Romeo died.
5. For example, Marjorie Garber, '*Romeo and Juliet*: Patterns and Paradigms', in *The Shakespeare Plays: A Study Guide* (San Diego, 1979), pp. 50–63; reprinted in '*Romeo and Juliet*': Critical Essays, edited by John F. Andrews (New York and London, 1993), pp. 119–31; p. 131.

theatrically exciting productions, including those of Peter Brook at Stratford in 1947 and Franco Zeffirelli at the Old Vic in 1960, have cut and otherwise altered the text extensively, presenting their vision of it in terms of the theatre of their time rather than offering text-centred performances. Indeed, both the directors I have named explicitly rejected engagement with the text's literary values; Brook declared that 'To come to the theatre merely to listen to the words was the last decadence', and Zeffirelli is reported to have 'said repeatedly that he had no use for [the play's] verse'.[6] And even directors who have been less radical in their treatment of the text than Brook and Bogdanov have made extensive cuts. Later I shall try to identify some of the main areas that have presented problems, and to suggest some reasons why they have done so.

The modern director's task is complicated by the fact that, since Shakespeare wrote, the story of the fated lovers has attracted many other creative artists, some of whom have drawn exclusively on Shakespeare, some on other versions of the tale, and others who have mixed the traditions. There is no reason, for instance, to suppose that Tchaikovsky went beyond Shakespeare for his immensely popular fantasy overture of 1869 (later revised), or Prokofiev and his choreographers for their ballet, first performed in 1938; on the other hand, Bellini's opera *I Capuleti ed i Montecchi* (1830) appears to owe nothing to Shakespeare (though its double death scene bears a suspicious resemblance to Garrick's), and the librettists of the only other successful opera based on the story, Gounod's *Roméo Juliette* (1867), incorporated Garrick's tomb scene into their work, as does Berlioz (wordlessly) in his dramatic symphony of 1839.

The existence and popularity of symphonic, operatic, balletic, filmic, and other offshoots is relevant to the performance history of the play itself because they create images that superimpose themselves on the Shakespearian text, forming expectations in the imaginations of the play's interpreters and audiences which subtly affect our response to efforts to translate that text into performance. In the wonderful *scène d'amour* in Berlioz's work, long-breathed phrases accompanied by rhythmical pulsations speak eloquently of passionate yearning in a manner that would not lead listeners to expect the humour that also lies latent in Shakespeare's dialogue; and Berlioz's musical depiction of the gradual dispersal of the masquers into the night, apparently strumming their guitars and humming snatches of half-remembered song, is not only theatrical as well as musical in its effect but appeared to be reflected, whether consciously or not, in one of the more sensitively directed episodes of Michael Bogdanov's

6. Jill L. Levenson, *'Romeo and Juliet': Shakespeare in Performance* (Manchester, 1987), pp. 66 and 97.

production with the dying away of the sounds of motor bikes as revellers left the Capulets' ball. In a different way, the long tradition of scenically spectacular productions, aided and abetted by the popularity of Zeffirelli's film (discussed in later essays in this volume), with its beautiful Tuscan settings, may lead theatregoers to expect visual splendours.

Also relevant to modern theatrical interpretations is the play's complex literary background. Although the often incandescent quality of its verse is responsible for much of the admiration that the play has evoked, at the same time its self-conscious literariness has repeatedly been implicitly or explicitly criticized as detrimental to its theatrical effectiveness. 'It is a dramatic poem rather than a drama', wrote Henry Irving, 'and I mean to treat it from that point of view.'[7] For all that, he omitted a lot of its poetry while succeeding, according to Henry James, only in making 'this enchanting poem' 'dull . . . mortally slow' and 'tame' by 'smothering' it 'in its accessories'.[8] The history of critical and theatrical reactions to the play demonstrates the fact that Shakespeare worked in a far more literary mode than has been fashionable in the theatre of later ages, and that its literariness has often been regarded as a theatrical handicap.

In a memorable tribute, T. J. B. Spencer wrote that 'Nothing in European drama had hitherto achieved the organisation of so much human experience when Shakespeare, at the age of about thirty, undertook the story of Juliet and Romeo.'[9] The manner in which the play organizes experience is highly self-conscious and deeply indebted to a variety of literary traditions. Many devices of parallelism and repetition create an almost architectural sense of structure. This structure is defined by the appearances of the Prince of Verona. Some productions bring him on to speak the Prologue, appropriately enough since his three appearances within the action have something of a choric function. We first see him in his own right as he enters to exercise his authority at the height of the brawl between the followers of Montague and Capulet in the opening scene; he makes one formal though impassioned speech, and his departure marks a turning point from the public to the private action of the play as Benvolio, after recapitulating what has happened in lines that are usually abbreviated, describes the symptoms of Romeo's lovesickness for Rosaline. The Prince's second appearance comes at the climax of the play's second violent episode, culminating in the killing of Tybalt

7. Cited in Alan Hughes, *Henry Irving, Shakespearean* (Cambridge, 1981), p. 160.
8. Henry James, in an article, 'London Plays', originally published in the *Atlantic Monthly*, August, 1882, and reprinted in *The Scenic Art*, edited by Allan Wade (London, 1949). pp. 162–7; p. 164.
9. T. J. B. Spencer, ed., *Romeo and Juliet,* New Penguin Shakespeare (Harmondsworth, 1967), p. 7.

and Mercutio, which provokes him to another display of authority as he banishes Romeo, the principal turning point of the action; and he reappears in the final scene to preside over the investigation into the lovers' deaths and to apportion responsibility. His are the closing lines which round off the play, returning it to the condition of myth:

> For never was a story of more woe
> Than this of Juliet and her Romeo.

The formality evident in the appearances of the Prince recurs in many other aspects of the play's design. Shakespeare is still sometimes regarded as an inspired improviser, and perhaps in some plays he was, but it is impossible not to feel that before he started to write the dialogue of this play he worked out a ground plan as carefully as if he had been designing an intricate building. One could point, for example, to the parallels in function between Mercutio and the Nurse, both of whom are almost entirely of Shakespeare's creation: he a companion and foil to Romeo, she to Juliet, he consciously mocking Romeo's romanticism with high-spirited, bawdy cynicism, she no less earthy but less aware of the sexual implications of much of what she says, each of them involuntarily failing their companion in their greatest need, he through his accidental death which turns the play from a romantic comedy into a tragedy, she because of the limitations in her understanding of the depths of Juliet's love which leave Juliet to face her fate alone. There are parallels too in the design of scenes: the Capulets' bustling preparations for the ball (1.5) are echoed in those for Juliet's marriage to Paris (4.4); and each of the play's three love duets—one in the evening, at the ball, the second at night, in the garden and on its overlooking balcony, the third at dawn, as the lovers, now married, prepare to part—is interrupted by calls from the Nurse.

These features of the play's structure create an impression of highly patterned formality; they may be regarded as dramatic strengths; and in any case a director can scarcely avoid them without rewriting the play, but there are others that have often suffered under the blue pencil. For example, at a number of points characters recapitulate action that has already been enacted before us. In the opening scene, Benvolio spends ten lines satirically describing Tybalt's intervention in the fray between the servants of the Montagues and Capulets; later, after the fight in which both Mercutio and Tybalt are killed, Benvolio again recapitulates what has happened, this time in twenty-three lines of verse; and in the closing scene the Friar, notoriously, after claiming 'I will be brief', recapitulates the full story of the lovers in one of the longest speeches of a play that is not short of long speeches. 'It is much to be lamented' wrote Johnson, 'that the poet did not conclude the dialogue with the action, and avoid a narrative of events which the audience already knew.'[1]

This technique of recapitulation can be, and has been, defended; for example, Bertrand Evans remarks that, 'far from being a repetitious exercise best deleted on the stage, the Friar's speech is an indispensable part of the total experience of the tragedy; not to be present when some key participants learn how their acts resulted in the pile of bodies in the Capulet tomb—Romeo's, Juliet's, Tybalt's, Paris's—would be to miss too much'.[2] Certainly these speeches constitute a challenge that should be accepted by directors concerned to present the text in its integrity; for the actors, I take it, the challenge is to seek out a psychological subtext that will help them to deliver the lines not merely as a summary of what has gone before but as utterances emanating naturally and spontaneously from the characters as they have conceived it. Performers of Benvolio can portray his summaries of the action as the reactions of a well-meaning but puzzled man desperately attempting to make sense of what has happened; the Friar's long speech has been played in more than one production less as a judicial apportioning of blame (which it unequivocally is in Berlioz, where the role of the Friar encompasses some of the functions of Shakespeare's Prince) than as the frightened reactions of a man who fears he has betrayed his responsibility; the reactions of the other onstage characters as he reveals the secrets, previously unknown to them, of the marriage and the potion are no less important than his own state of mind as he speaks. Nevertheless the speech has been implicitly criticized by directors concerned to streamline the action; Peter Brook and Michael Bogdanov omitted it altogether,[3] and all twelve of the Stratford productions since Brook's have shortened it, some considerably.

The deliberation of the play's structure is of a piece with its self-conscious, even ostentatious literariness and intellectualism. 'Now is he for the numbers that Petrarch flowed in. Laura, to his lady, was a kitchen wench', says Mercutio of Romeo whom he believes to be still in love with the 'pale, hard hearted wench' Rosaline, as if to draw attention to Shakespeare's indebtedness to the Petrarchan tradition, well established in England at the time he was writing, of the besotted lover sighing in vain for an unresponsive beloved—a

---

1. *Johnson on Shakespeare*, edited by Arthur Sherbo, The Yale Edition of the Works of Samuel Johnson (New Haven, 1968), vol. 8, p. 976.
2. Bertrand Evans, *Shakespeare's Tragic Practice* (Oxford, 1979), p. 51.
3. Judging by the prompt book held in the Shakespeare Centre, Stratford-upon-Avon, Brook originally omitted all the text after Juliet's death (like Bogdanov after him) except for the addition of 'Brother Montague give me thy hand' from Capulet and the Prince's concluding six lines spoken by the Chorus, but restored some of the omitted dialogue, including part of the Friar's long speech, in later performances.

situation that he was to dramatize directly in the figures of Sil-
vius and Phoebe in *As You Like It* and that is also related to that
of the chaste young man with no interest in ensuring his own
posterity who is addressed in the first seventeen of Shakespeare's
sonnets. The explicit reference to a major literary influence on
the play—also omitted in most modern performances—is a counterpart to the appearance on stage of a volume of Ovid in *Titus
Andronicus*.

The literary form most strongly associated with Petrarchism was
the sonnet. The Argument to Brooke's poem is in sonnet form, and
Romeo and Juliet, written during the ten or so years when the amatory sonnet cycle was enjoying a vogue greater than ever before or
since, makes direct use of the complete form in the Prologue, in the
rarely performed Chorus to Act 2, and, famously, in the shared sonnet spoken between the lovers on their first meeting. At a number
of other points, too, such as the speech by the Prince that ends the
play, Shakespeare uses the six-line rhyming unit ending in a couplet that forms the final part of the sonnet form as used by Shakespeare and which is also the stanza form of his narrative poem *Venus
and Adonis*, of 1593. Other well established literary conventions, less
obvious to the modern playgoer, that influence the play include the
epithalamium, reflected in Juliet's great speech beginning 'Gallop
apace, you fiery-footed steeds', and the dawn-parting, or 'alba'—one
of the most universal of poetic themes—which provides the basic
structure for the entire scene of dawn-parting between Romeo and
Juliet.[4]

The play's creative use of conventions of lyric poetry is responsible
for much of its enduring popularity as perhaps the greatest of all
expressions of romantic love; it is complemented and to some extent
counterbalanced by an intellectualism manifesting itself especially
in complex wordplay that has stood the passage of time less well and
has often been censured (and, in recent times, defended) by literary
critics as well as being subjected to the more practical criticism of
being excised from acting texts. David Garrick, in the Advertisement
to his 1748 adaptation, states his 'design . . . to clear the original
as much as possible from the jingle and quibble which were always
thought the great objections to reviving it'. 'Jingle' refers to Shakespeare's extensive use of rhyme, regarded by neoclassical critics
as indecorous in tragedy; Garrick's modifications—which included
reducing the sonnet form of the lovers' declaration to two quatrains—
reduced the play's range of poetic style.

4. The theme is studied in its multiple international manifestations in *Eros: An Enquiry
into the Theme of Lovers' Meetings and Partings at Dawn in Poetry*, edited by Arthur T.
Hatto (London, The Hague, Paris, 1965); the section on English, by T. J. B. Spencer,
includes discussion of Shakespeare's use of the motif.

'Quibble' is, if anything, even more integral than rhyme to the effect of the play as Shakespeare wrote it. Wordplay extends from the bawdy of the servants' comic opening dialogue, through the self-conscious jesting of Mercutio and the often involuntary *double entendres* of the Nurse, up to passages of quibbling wordplay spoken in wholly serious, even tragic circumstances by Romeo and Juliet themselves. Modern performers and audiences have been educated into an easier acceptance of wordplay than Garrick, partly as a result of its serious use in post-Freudian literature, above all by James Joyce (whose 'stream of consciousness' technique is anticipated by the Nurse), and also by studies encouraging an historical awareness of its prevalence in uncomic writings by Shakespeare and his contemporaries, such as John Donne. Even so, cuts made in acting versions of the present day suggest that the quibble is still more easily regarded as an ingredient of comedy than as a vehicle of tragic effect. This springs, perhaps, from too limited a notion both of what Shakespeare may encompass within the portmanteau definition of tragedy, and of the language appropriate to the form—if, indeed, it can properly be called a form. It has often been observed that for much of its considerable length *Romeo and Juliet*—especially if, as in Bogdanov's production, the Prologue is omitted—comes closer to our expectations of romantic comedy than of such a tragedy as the one that immediately precedes it in Shakespeare's output, *Titus Andronicus*, to which *Romeo and Juliet* might be regarded as a deliberately contrasting companion piece. If directors are to realize this script in its full richness they need to free themselves of the conventional connotations of tragedy and to play each episode in its own terms. And if audiences are to meet Shakespeare on his own terms they must find room in their responses not only for the direct if poetically heightened expression of heartfelt emotion that has caused the balcony scene to be valued as perhaps the most eloquent of all depictions of romantic love, but also for the contrived artificiality with which Shakespeare endows even the lovers' language at some of the most impassioned points of the play's action. This is not only a 'most excellent and lamentable tragedy', as the title page of the 1599 quarto puts it, it is also, in the terms of the title page of the 'bad' quarto of 1597, 'an excellent conceited tragedy'—which I suppose might be paraphrased as a tragedy notable for the ingenuity of its verbal expression. Under the surface of the play's poetry lies a complicated network of rhetorical figures * * * that are rarely recognized by even the more erudite among the play's modern readers. This poses great problems for the actors, as Bernard Shaw recognized when he wrote 'It should never be forgotten in judging an attempt to play Romeo and Juliet that the parts are made almost impossible except to actors of positive genius, skilled to the last degree in metrical declamation,

by the way in which the poetry, magnificent as it is, is interlarded
by the miserable rhetoric and silly lyrical conceits which were the
foible of the Elizabethans.'[5] The conceit with which Juliet imagines
her and her lover's fate after death, with its hidden wordplay on the
sexual sense of 'die', is as extreme as anything in metaphysical poetry:

> when I shall die
> [or 'he shall die', according to the unauthoritative
>   fourth quarto and some later editors]
> Take him and cut him out in little stars,
> And he will make the face of heaven so fine
> That all the world will be in love with night
> And pay no worship to the garish sun. (3.2.21–5)

Even more difficult, I take it, are the play's several extended passages of dialogue in which characters are required, on the basis of
misunderstanding or of false information, to act out emotions that,
as the audience knows, the true situation does not justify. One such
passage comes just after the lines I have quoted. Juliet's Nurse enters
with the cords designed to make a rope ladder to give Romeo access
to Juliet at night. 'Wringing her hands', as the bad quarto's direction and the good quarto's dialogue tell us, she bemoans Tybalt's
death, of which Juliet has not heard, but in such a way that Juliet
thinks Romeo, not Tybalt, is dead. In a sense the episode is an
extended piece of wordplay on the pronoun 'he':

> Ah, welladay! He's dead, he's dead, he's dead!
> We are undone, lady, we are undone.
> Alack the day, he's gone, he's killed, he's dead!
>   (3.2.37–9)

So says the Nurse, speaking of Tybalt, but Juliet takes her to refer
to Romeo, and even when the Nurse speaks directly of Romeo—

> O Romeo, Romeo,
> Who ever would have thought it Romeo?
>   (3.2.41–2)

Juliet takes her to mean that Romeo is the victim, not the killer. The
misunderstanding continues through a long episode in which Juliet
again resorts to complex wordplay:

> Hath Romeo slain himself? Say thou but 'Ay',
> And that bare vowel 'I' shall poison more
> Than the death-darting eye of cockatrice.
> I am not I if there be such an 'Ay',

---

5. From a review of Forbes-Robertson's production, *The Saturday Review*, 28 September
   1895; reprinted in *Shaw on Shakespeare*, pp. 168–74; p. 173.

> Or those eyes shut that makes thee answer 'Ay'.
> If he be slain, say 'Ay'; or if not, 'No'.
> Brief sounds determine of my weal or woe.
>   (3.2.45–51)

Not until the Nurse resorts to plain statement is the misunderstanding clarified:

> Tybalt is gone and Romeo banishèd.
> Romeo that killed him—he is banishèd.
>   (3.2.69–70)

And even then Juliet launches into a highly mannered lament, full of the oxymorons that are a conspicuous feature of this play's style. This scene has regularly been abbreviated in post-war Stratford productions, every one of which has omitted or shortened the wordplay on 'I', and most of which have abbreviated the oxymorons.

The artifice both of situation and of style in this scene is bound to have a distancing effect; it displays wit on the part of both Shakespeare and Juliet, yet for Juliet the situation is tragic. She needs to speak her lines with a high degree of intellectual control which may seem at odds with the spontaneous expression of deeply felt emotion. But perhaps this is the point: M. M. Mahood regards the puns on 'I' as 'one of Shakespeare's first attempts to reveal a profound disturbance of mind by the use of quibbles'[6] and Jill Levenson too regards Juliet's withdrawal from emotional expression as psychologically plausible: 'Juliet's prothalamium quickly shrinks to mere word-play and sound effects as she glimpses calamity in the Nurse's report, the swift reduction implying that absolute grief has arrested Juliet's imagination.'[7] Those are, I think, subjectively interpretative rather than objectively descriptive comments, but they suggest ways in which the performer may face the need to hold emotion in suspense, as it were, so that we appreciate the paradox of the situation while retaining sympathy with Juliet's plight.

Juliet faces a rather similar situation a little later, when her mother mistakes her grief at Romeo's banishment for mourning for her cousin Tybalt's death combined with anger at his killer, Romeo. She dissembles her true feelings in a series of quibbles and paradoxes:

> Indeed, I never shall be satisfied
> With Romeo till I behold him, dead,
> Is my poor heart so for a kinsman vexed.
> Madam, if you could find out but a man
> To bear a poison, I would temper it

---

6. M. M. Mahood, *Shakespeare's Wordplay* (London, 1968), p. 70.
7. Levenson, *Romeo and Juliet*, p. 7.

That Romeo should, upon receipt thereof,
Soon sleep in quiet. O, how my heart abhors
To hear him named and cannot come to him
To wreak the love I bore my cousin
Upon his body that hath slaughtered him!
                                   (3.5.93–102)

Johnson comments that 'Juliet's equivocations are rather too artful
for a mind disturbed by the loss of a new lover',[8] and they are shortened or cut in the promptbooks of all the productions I have mentioned except one;[9] but perhaps the cleverness of style here is more
encompassable than that in the previous scene as an expression
of Juliet's bewilderment as she tries to respond to her mother's
misplaced sympathy without actually perjuring herself; perhaps,
indeed, it should teach us that wit is not incompatible with tragic
effect.

The play's most notorious instance of discrepancy between what
characters can be expected to be feeling and the manner in which
it is expressed is the scene of mourning following the discovery of
Juliet's supposedly dead body. The keening starts with the Nurse's
words 'O lamentable day!', and is taken up successively by Lady Capulet, Paris, and Old Capulet in a formalized liturgy of grief whose
repetitions culminate in the Nurse's

O woe! O woeful, woeful, woeful day!
Most lamentable day! Most woeful day
That ever, ever, I did yet behold!
O day, O day, O day, O hateful day,
Never was seen so black a day as this!
O woeful day, O woeful day!   (4.4.80–5)

These lines take us into the world of Pyramus and Thisbe; indeed,
one of the reasons for the hypothesis that A Midsummer Night's
Dream dates from later than Romeo and Juliet (about which I am
doubtful) is the suggestion that Bottom's expressions of grief over
the corpse of Thisbe burlesque the Nurse's over Juliet. But it is all too
easy for the lines to burlesque themselves. The classic objections to
the passage were put by Coleridge:

As the audience knows that Juliet is not dead, this scene is, perhaps, excusable. But it is a strong warning to minor dramatists
not to introduce at one time many separate characters agitated
by one and the same circumstance. It is difficult to understand
what effect, whether that of pity or of laughter, Shakespeare

8. Johnson on Shakespeare, vol. 8, p. 951.
9. David Leveaux's, in 1991.

meant to produce;—the occasion and the characteristic speeches are so little in harmony![1]

Over a century later Granville-Barker remarked that 'even faithful Shakespeareans have little good to say of that competition in mourning between Paris and Capulet, Lady Capulet and the Nurse. It has been branded as deliberate burlesque.' He attempts a defence, but admits that 'The passage does jar a little.'[2] Most attempts to justify the scene have proposed that the blatant artificiality of the mourners' expressions of grief represents a deliberate distancing effect, forcing the audience to recall that Juliet is not actually dead even though these people believe her to be so. These defences tend to seem half-hearted and lame.[3] Scholarship came to the aid of criticism when Charles Lower, observing that the passage is particularly inadequately reported in the first quarto, proposed that this is because the lines were delivered simultaneously in the performance on which that text is putatively based: in other words, that the speeches were intended to convey a generalized impression of mourning, not be listened to in their own right.[4] The Oxford editors, while not accepting that this was Shakespeare's original intention as represented in the 'good' quarto, nevertheless (in keeping with their aim of representing the plays so far as possible as they were acted) print the direction '*Paris, Capulet and his Wife, and the Nurse all at once wring their hands and cry out together.*' Whether this represents Shakespeare's own solution of a problem with which he had presented himself, or merely an evasion of it, we can't tell. The scene of mourning, and the episode with the Musicians that follows, have often been omitted and, I think, always abbreviated, even in recent times. Nevertheless, at least one director had anticipated the editors: Peter Holding records that in Terry Hands's 1973 Stratford production this episode, so far from being ridiculous, was

> Perhaps the most affecting . . . successive speakers picked up the tone of lament from their predecessor, overlapping with some of the final phrases and then developing the cry with appropriate personal embellishments. The emotion of the lament was sincere but kept at a certain distance, while allowing the audience simultaneously to enjoy the fact that of course Juliet was still alive.[5]

---

1. Quoted from *The Romantics on Shakespeare*, ed. Jonathan Bate (Harmondsworth, 1992), p. 519.
2. Harley Granville-Barker, *Prefaces to Shakespeare*, Second Series (London, 1930), p. 26.
3. See, for example, Evans, *Shakespeare's Tragic Practice*, pp. 42–3.
4. Charles Lower, '*Romeo and Juliet*, iv.v: A Stage Direction and Purposeful Comedy', *Shakespeare Studies* 8 (1975), 177–94.
5. Holding, *Romeo and Juliet*, p. 56. Richard David also praises this device as 'a brilliant solution and one that was genuinely faithful to Shakespeare's intention': Richard David, *Shakespeare in the Theatre* (Cambridge, 1978), p. 113.

The scene was handled in similar fashion in Adrian Noble's production.

Holding's comment reminds us that these texts, for all their undoubted literary quality, are, fundamentally, scripts for performance, and that at too many points we simply lack information about how their author intended them to be realized on the stage. A successful surmounting in any given production of problems that have previously seemed acute may vindicate Shakespeare's judgement, but equally may simply demonstrate the ingenuity of the interpreter. All criticism must be provisional.

Although there are uncertainties about tone in various passages of the play, perhaps its greatest glory is the wide range of its literary style in both prose and verse, encompassing the vivid, frequently obscene colloquialisms of the servants in the opening scene and elsewhere, the more elegant witticisms of the young blades, the fantasticalities of Mercutio, the controlled inconsequentialities of the Nurse, the humane sententiousness of the Friar, the dignified passion of the Prince, the lyricism of the lovers and also the increasing intensity of their utterance as tragedy overcomes them. Even as one attempts to characterize the play's stylistic range one is conscious of the inadequacy of the attempt to do so within a brief compass, but it may at least be worth insisting that the play is not simply, as the novelist George Moore described it, 'no more than a love-song in dialogue'.[6] No play that Shakespeare—or anyone else—had written up to this date deploys so wide a range of literary expressiveness, and very few later plays do so, either. And it is partly as a result of this stylistic diversity and richness that the play offers so wide a range of opportunities to actors. Performers of minor roles such as Samson and Gregory, Peter, and even the Apothecary—who speaks only seven lines, though he is also picturesquely described by Romeo in lines that provide a challenge to the make-up department—can create a strong impression within a short space. On the other hand, some of the more important characters may seem, at least on the printed page, to lack individuality—by which I suppose I mean that their speeches seem more important for what is said than for who says them. Obviously this is true of the two speeches given to the anonymous Chorus, in which the authorial voice is most apparent. Johnson regarded the second chorus as pointless: 'The use of this chorus is not easily discovered, it conduces nothing to the progress of the play, but relates what is already known, or what the next scene will show; and relates it without adding the improvement of any

---

6. *Confessions of a Young Man* (1888); edited by Susan Dick (Montreal and London, 1972), p. 143; Moore was responding to Irving's spectacular production, which made him long for 'a simple stage, a few simple indications, and the simple recitation of that story of the sacrifice of the two white souls for the reconciliation of two great families'.

moral sentiment',[7] and it has almost always been omitted in performance. The obvious functionality of the speeches of the Prince puts them in a similar category, which no doubt is why some directors have had him speak the opening Chorus while, conversely, Peter Brook gave his closing lines to the actor who had spoken the Chorus (who also played Benvolio). The prince is an authority figure who quells the opening brawl with passionate indignation, exiles Romeo for killing Tybalt, and takes command in the final scene; but we know nothing about him personally except that he is a kinsman of both Mercutio and Paris, and feels some responsibility for their deaths:

> And I, for winking at your discords, too
> Have lost a brace of kinsmen.   (5.3.293–4)

It is just enough to create a sense of personal involvement, and his response—We still have known thee for a holy man'—to the Friar's offer of himself as a sacrifice can be moving, but does not invite detailed characterization. Paris is a relatively undercharacterized role, hard to bring to life, and Benvolio—who is more interesting as satirized by Mercutio (3.1.5–33) than in his own right—vanishes without trace soon afterwards. Tybalt is potentially more interesting—in Bogdanov's production he was having an intralineal affair with Lady Capulet—in spite of Shaw's view that 'Tybalt's is such an unmercifully bad part that one can hardly demand anything from its representation except that he should brush his hair when he comes to his uncle's ball (a condition which he invariably repudiates) and that he should be so consummate a swordsman as to make it safe for Romeo to fall upon him with absolute abandonment . . .'.[8] If these roles constitute challenges to their performers, it is in remaining content with being cast as lay figures: 'don't do something, just stand there'. The composition of the play requires relative colourlessness from some of its constituent parts.

In other roles the challenge lies mainly in suggesting that the lines of the play have not been just learned by the actor, but spring spontaneously from the character he is playing. Friar Laurence has some characteristics in common with the Prince in the relative impersonality of his many sententious, generalizing remarks, but he has a longer role, plays a crucial part in the play's action, and is far more personally involved with a number of the characters. Though the role is not an obvious gift to an actor, it offers opportunities for suggesting a warmly human, compassionate, and even vulnerable man beneath the clerical garb, as Robert Demeger showed

---

7. *Johnson on Shakespeare*, vol. 2, p. 944.
8. *Shaw on Shakespeare*, p. 171.

in the Bogdanov production when, looking exhausted after his efforts to rouse Romeo out of his almost suicidal depression, he watched Romeo go off and then, sighing with relief, produced a cigarette from beneath his scapular and took a quick drag on it. And in Adrian Noble's 1995 production Julian Glover virtually stole the show as a Friar who kept a chemistry set on a bench in his cell and, as Michael Billington wrote, "work[ed] up Juliet's death potion from old chemistry books to her fascination".[9]

If the challenge to the actor in the role of the Friar is to seek out a humanizing subtext, with other roles the problem lies rather in discrepancies of behaviour or of style which the actor may leave unresolved but, at least if he has been trained in the school of Stanislavski, may otherwise seek to reconcile into some semblance of psychological consistency. For much of the action Capulet seems an amiable old buffer genuinely fond of his daughter; when we first see him he expresses the fear that she is too young to be married and declares

> But woo her, gentle Paris, get her heart;
> My will to her consent is but a part,
> And, she agreed, within her scope of choice
> Lies my consent and fair-according voice.
>   (1.2.14–17)

Yet when it comes to the point he reacts with uncontrolled violence to Juliet's prayers that she be not forced into a marriage which we know would be bigamous, in a display of angry indignation that culminates in threats of physical violence.

> An you be mine, I'll give you to my friend.
> An you be not, hang, beg, starve, die in the streets,
> For, by my soul, I'll ne'er acknowledge thee,
> Nor what is mine shall never do thee good.
>   (3.5.191–4)

Is Shakespeare simply careless of consistency, providing his actor here with a strong set piece, regardless of what has come before? Or is he expecting his actor to lead up to this passage by making what he can of earlier signs of tetchiness in Capulet, as for instance in his harsh words to Tybalt at the dance (1.5.75–87), or even by suggesting, as Bogdanov did, that Capulet is more concerned that his daughter should advance his family's social status than achieve personal happiness? Perhaps modern audiences are more conscious of inconsistency of characterization than those of Shakespeare's time; although I found Bogdanov's capitalist monster a caricature, I was also disturbed by the absence of transition in the Adrian Noble production.

9. *Guardian*, 7 April 1995.

If Capulet's rage is a concerted set piece such as might form the basis for an impressive bass aria in an opera by Handel or Rossini, Mercutio's Queen Mab speech is a solo set piece that actually forms the basis of a tenor aria in Berlioz's dramatic symphony; in fact his scherzetto is Mercutio's only verbal contribution to the work, and— along with the Friar's impressive concluding exordium—the only part of it to use words at all close to Shakespeare's; Berlioz apparently regarded the speech as so important, or at least so appealing, that he also composed an orchestral scherzo, 'Queen Mab, the spirit of dreams', which opens Part 4. Within the play it complicates the role of Mercutio in a way that may help to account for the fascination that it has held for actors, audiences, and readers. Mercutio's role—like Shylock's, which also encompasses elements so diverse that they have sometimes been held to be incompatible—has been accused of having taken on a life of its own that endangers the dramatic balance; indeed, according to Dryden Shakespeare 'said himself that he was forced to kill him in the third act, to prevent being killed by him'.[1] This is nonsense, I think; Shakespeare developed the role from a hint in his sources as a foil to Romeo and a counterpart to the Nurse, and Mercutio's death is an essential element in the plot. But the Queen Mab speech has been regarded as a charming excrescence, a piece of self-indulgence on Shakespeare's part that is difficult to integrate into both the play and the role—to Granville-Barker, 'as much and as little to be dramatically justified as a song in an opera is';[2] and more recently Edward Pearlman has proposed that Shakespeare interpolated the speech after completing his first version of the play, remarking that 'without the Queen Mab speech, Mercutio is consistent and coherent; once the speech is added, his character is incoherent on the page and must be reinvented by the collaboration of performer and audience or by the ingenuity and faith of stage-literate readers.'[3] It has also, of course, been defended.[4] Richard David wrote that 'its main purpose . . . is to create a gossamer sense of uneasy mystery so that Romeo's supernatural forebodings do not fall on altogether unprepared ground'.[5] That may be true in terms of the play but probably would not be of much use to an actor trying to reconcile its fancifulness with Mercutio's mocking obscenity elsewhere. But audiences rarely feel it as a problem—or even actors, because for all the accusations of irrelevance this speech generally survives the blue pencil. Mercutio's wordplay, bawdy as it is, marks him as a clever man, and

1. John Dryden, *'Of Dramatic Poesy' and other Essays*, ed. George Watson, Everyman's Library, 2 vols. (London, 1962), vol. 1, p. 180.
2. Granville-Barker, *Prefaces to Shakespeare*, p. 7.
3. E. Pearlman, 'Shakespeare at Work: *Romeo and Juliet*' *English Literary Renaissance*, 24.2 (Spring 1994), pp. 315–42; p. 336.
4. Pearlman summarizes arguments for the speech's relevance in his footnote 20.
5. David, *Shakespeare in the Theatre*, p. 115.

there is a cerebral quality to Queen Mab that is in line with this. In any case the speech is moving into obscenity in its closing lines, when Mercutio's fancy seems in danger of getting out of hand and Romeo halts him in his tracks as if to save him from his over-heated imaginings, provoking Mercutio to deny their validity:

> I talk of dreams,
> Which are the children of an idle brain,
> Begot of nothing but vain fantasy,
> Which is as thin of substance as the air,
> And more inconstant than the wind . . .
> (1.4.96–100)

in terms that demonstrate the very 'fantasy' that he is denigrating. The role seems to me to be one of fascinating complexity rather than of irreconcilable discrepancies; but it certainly faces the actor with challenges in the handling of verse. In recent times it has become complicated by psychological interpretations of subtext proposing that the evident homosociality of the young men verges on, or even merges into, homosexuality. In Terry Hands's Swan Theatre production of 1989 the actor conveyed in both gesture and body language an intense but undirected sexuality that motivated the bawdy; a sense of male bonding not quite amounting to direct homosexuality was conveyed in one of the character's bawdiest passages (2.1), full of fantasies about Romeo's sexuality, in which he leapt on Benvolio's back and groped his crotch as if impelled to mock the absent Romeo by the pressure of repressed impulses within himself. Later he kissed Romeo on the lips, heartily if not lingeringly.

Perhaps the most complete character in the play as written is that of the Nurse, one of Shakespeare's few (if unknowing) gifts to actresses who are no longer able to play young women. The main danger here, in my experience, is sentimentalization. I remember a production at Stratford by John Barton and Karolos Koun in 1965 in which the role was sensitively played by a deeply sympathetic actress, Elizabeth Spriggs, but in which she made what seemed to me to be the mistake of suggesting that the Nurse's attempts to reconcile Juliet to the thought of marrying Paris went against the grain, as if she was doing her duty by the parents while identifying with the desires of the daughter. It was interesting but implausible.

The roles of which I have spoken so far are all ones that can be played by what are known as character actors. Romeo and Juliet themselves come firmly into the category of romantic lead, with all the challenges and problems that the term implies. For one thing, there is the matter of age. Juliet is emphatically and repeatedly stated to be not yet fourteen. This may not have caused difficulties when the role was played by a highly trained boy; now that women have taken over, it is often said that actors with the experience to encompass the technical difficulties of the part will inevitably be too old to look it. But recent directors seem to have more difficulty in casting plausible Romeos than Juliets. His exact age is not given, but too many actors, Ian McKellen among them, in 1976, when he was, I believe, thirty-five,—and, I should say, Kenneth Branagh in the sound recording—try too hard to look and/or sound younger than their years. Henry James wrote that 'it is with Romeo as with Juliet; by the time an actor has acquired the assurance necessary for playing the part, he has lost his youth and his slimness'.[6] Though the role is a passionate one it is not heroic, which may explain why it has appealed to women. By all accounts the most successful Romeo of the nineteenth century was Charlotte Cushman, playing to the Juliet of her sister Susan. Admittedly the text was tailored to emphasize the role. And I think this is a crucial pointer to the principal challenges offered by the title roles. *Romeo and Juliet* does not accord such prominence to its tragic lovers as Shakespeare's other double tragedy, *Antony and Cleopatra* does to its, especially at its end. Even more to the point, Romeo and Juliet are not as vividly characterized as the later pair, or, still more importantly, as other roles in the same play, notably Mercutio and the Nurse. Though I spoke of these characters as foils to the lovers, there are times when the actors playing the lovers may feel that it is they who are acting as foils to the supposedly subsidiary characters: Peter Holding remarks that 'Productions have occasionally been dominated by Mercutio or the Nurse.'[7] This no doubt helps to explain why actors go to some pains to find comic touches in the lovers' verse: in the balcony scene, for instance, Peggy Ashcroft got a laugh on 'I have forgot why I did call thee back,'[8] and in Bogdanov's production there was comedy in the lovers' self-absorption, their wonder at each other—'She speaks', said Romeo, as if it was a remarkable achievement for Juliet to have acquired the skill at such an early age. This is entirely legitimate, but theatrical changes that have been made at the end of the play, and indeed some critical reactions to it, betray a dissatisfaction with the original script that seems designed to make it conform to expectations that may derive from conceptions of tragedy other than those that were in Shakespeare's mind as he wrote. Garrick, we have seen, expanded the lovers' death scene; Peter Brook, like most directors, severely shortened the last scene; in some performances he even went so far (like Gounod's librettist) as to omit the reconciliation of the houses.[9]

6. First published in 'Notes from Paris, 1876', in the *New York Tribune*, 5 February 1876; reprinted in *the Scenic Art*, pp. 51–4; p. 54.
7. Holding, *Romeo and Juliet*, p. 44.
8. Levenson, *Romeo and Juliet*, p. 53.
9. Ibid., p. 67.

In part the alterations to the last scene result from practical considerations of staging; it is notoriously difficult to work out exactly how it would have been played in the theatres of Shakespeare's time. Perhaps Shakespeare was not in this play a complete master of practical stagecraft. Perhaps too some of what I have, somewhat neutrally, described as challenges to be faced might more properly be regarded as weaknesses that have to be overcome. I don't want to imply that *Romeo and Juliet* is in every respect a perfect specimen of dramatic craftsmanship. But I find it interesting that many of the criticisms and alterations to which the play has been subjected over the centuries bring it closer in line with expectations of romantic tragedy, perhaps derived in part from Shakespeare's own practice in later plays; they do not face up to the challenge of interpreting the text as written. They suggest, in short, that perhaps the play's greatest challenge is to our notions of genre. The script can be interpreted in all its richness and diversity only if we abandon the idea that because it is called a tragedy it must centre on the fate of individuals, and accept its emphasis on the multifarious society in which these individuals have their being.

SAMUEL JOHNSON

[On *Romeo and Juliet*]†

＊ ＊ ＊

This play is one of the most pleasing of our author's performances. The scenes are busy and various, the incidents numerous and important, the catastrophe irresistibly affecting and the process of the action carried on with such probability, at least with such congruity to popular opinions, as tragedy requires.

Here is one of the few attempts of Shakespeare to exhibit the conversation of gentlemen, to represent the airy sprightliness of juvenile elegance. Mr Dryden mentions a tradition, which might easily reach his time, of a declaration made by Shakespeare that 'he was obliged to kill Mercutio in the third act, lest he should have been killed by him'. Yet he thinks him 'no such formidable person but that he might have lived through the play and died in his bed', without danger to a poet. Dryden well knew, had he been in quest of truth, that in a pointed sentence more regard is commonly had to the words than the thought and that it is very seldom to be rigorously understood. Mercutio's wit, gaiety and courage will always procure him friends that wish him a longer life; but his death is not precipitated, he has lived out the time allotted him in the construction of the play; nor do I doubt the ability of Shakespeare to have continued his existence, though some of his sallies are perhaps out of the reach of Dryden, whose genius was not very fertile of merriment, nor ductile to humour, but acute, argumentative, comprehensive and sublime.

The Nurse is one of the characters in which the author delighted: he has with great subtlety of distinction drawn her at once loquacious and secret, obsequious and insolent, trusty and dishonest.

† From Samuel Johnson, "Preface to Shakespeare" (1765), in *Samuel Johnson on Shakespeare*, ed. H. R. Woudhuysen (London: Penguin, 1989), pp. 237–38. Copyright © H. Woudhuysen, 1989. Reprinted by permission of Penguin Books Ltd.

His comic scenes are happily wrought, but his pathetic strains are always polluted with some unexpected depravations. His persons, however distressed, 'have a conceit left them in their misery, a miserable conceit'.

WILLIAM HAZLITT

From Characters of Shakespear's Plays[†]

Romeo and Juliet is the only tragedy which Shakespear has written entirely on a love-story. It is supposed to have been his first play, and it deserves to stand in that proud rank. There is the buoyant spirit of youth in every line, in the rapturous intoxication of hope; and in the bitterness of despair. It has been said of *Romeo and Juliet* by a great critic, that "whatever is most intoxicating in the odour of a southern spring, languishing in the song of the nightingale, or voluptuous in the first opening of the rose, is to be found in this poem." The description is true; and yet it does not answer to our idea of the play. For if it has the sweetness of the rose, it has its freshness too; if it has the languor of the nightingale's song, it has also its giddy transport; if it has the softness of a southern spring, it is as glowing and as bright. There is nothing of a sickly and sentimental cast. Romeo and Juliet are in love, but they are not love-sick. Every thing speaks the very soul of pleasure, the high and healthy pulse of the passions: the heart beats, the blood circulates and mantles throughout. Their courtship is not an insipid interchange of sentiments lip-deep, learnt at secondhand from poems and plays,—made up of beauties of the most shadowy kind, of "fancies wan that hang the pensive head," of evanescent smiles and sighs that breathe not, of delicacy that shrinks from the touch and feebleness that scarce supports itself, an elaborate vacuity of thought, and an artificial dearth of sense, spirit, truth, and nature! It is the reverse of all this. It is Shakespear all over, and Shakespear when he was young.

We have heard it objected to *Romeo and Juliet*, that it is founded on an idle passion between a boy and a girl, who have scarcely seen and can have but little sympathy or rational esteem for one another, who have had no experience of the good or ills of life, and whose raptures or despair must be therefore equally groundless and fantastical. Whoever objects to the youth of the parties in this play as

† From *Characters of Shakespear's Plays* (London: C. H. Reynell, 1817; repr. New York: Wiley and Putnam, 1845), pp. 91–94, 98–100.

"too unripe and crude" to pluck the sweets of love, and wishes to see a first-love carried on into a good old age, and the passions taken at the rebound, when their force is spent, may find all this done in the *Stranger* and in other German plays, where they do things by contraries, and transpose nature to inspire sentiment and create philosophy. Shakespear proceeded in a more strait-forward, and, we think, effectual way. He did not endeavour to extract beauty from wrinkles, or the wild throb of passion from the last expiring sigh of indifference. He did not "gather grapes of thorns nor figs of thistles." It was not his way. But he has given a picture of human life, such as it is in the order of nature. He has founded the passion of the two lovers not on the pleasures they had experienced, but on all the pleasures they had *not* experienced. All that was to come of life was theirs. At that untried source of promised happiness they slaked their thirst, and the first eager draught made them drunk with love and joy. They were in full possession of their senses and their affections. Their hopes were of air, their desires of fire. Youth is the season of love, because the heart is then first melted in tenderness from the touch of novelty, and kindled to rapture, for it knows no end of its enjoyments or its wishes. Desire has no limit but itself. Passion, the love and expectation of pleasure, is infinite, extravagant, inexhaustible, till experience comes to check and kill it. Juliet exclaims on her first interview with Romeo—

> "My bounty is as boundless as the sea,
> My love as deep."

And why should it not? What was to hinder the thrilling tide of pleasure, which had just gushed from her heart from flowing on without stint or measure, but experience which she was yet without? What was to abate the transport of the first sweet sense of pleasure, which her heart and her senses had just tasted, but indifference which she was yet a stranger to? What was there to check the ardour of hope, of faith, of constancy, just rising in her breast, but disappointment which she had not yet felt? As are the desires and the hopes of youthful passion, such is the keenness of its disappointments, and their baleful effect. Such is the transition in this play from the highest bliss to the lowest despair, from the nuptial couch to an untimely grave. The only evil that even in apprehension befalls the two lovers is the loss of the greatest possible felicity; yet this loss is fatal to both, for they had rather part with life than bear the thought of surviving all that had made life dear to them. In all this, Shakespear has but followed nature, which existed in his time, as well as now. The modern philosophy, which reduces the whole theory of the mind to habitual impressions, and leaves the natural impulses of passion and imagination out of the account, had not then been discovered; or if it had, would have been little calculated for the uses of poetry.

It is the inadequacy of the same false system of philosophy to account for the strength of our earliest attachments, which has led Mr. Wordsworth to indulge in the mystical visions of Platonism in his Ode on the Progress of Life. He has very admirably described the vividness of our impressions in youth and childhoods and how "they fade by degrees into the light of common day," and he ascribes the change to the supposition of a pre-existent state, as if our early thoughts were nearer heaven, reflections of former trails of glory, shadows of our past being. This is idle. It is not from the knowledge of the past that the first impressions of things derive their gloss and splendour, but from our ignorance of the future, which fills the void to come with the warmth of our desires, with our gayest hopes, and brightest fancies. It is the obscurity spread before it that colours the prospect of life with hope, as it is the cloud which reflects the rainbow. There is no occasion to resort to any mystical union and transmission of feeling through different states of being to account for the romantic enthusiasm of youth; nor to plant the root of hope in the grave, nor to derive it from the skies. Its root is in the heart of man: it lifts its head above the stars. Desire and imagination are inmates of the human breast. The heaven "that lies about us in our infancy" is only a new world, of which we know nothing but what we wish it to be, and believe all that we wish. In youth and boyhood, the world we live in is the world of desire, and of fancy: it is experience that brings us down to the world of reality. What is it that in youth sheds a dewy light round the evening star? That makes the daisy look so bright? That perfumes the hyacinth? That embalms the first kiss of love? It is the delight of novelty, and the seeing no end to the pleasure that we fondly believe is still in store for us. The heart revels in the luxury of its own thoughts, and is unable to sustain the weight of hope and love that presses upon it.—The effects of the passion of love alone might have dissipated Mr. Wordsworth's theory, if he means any thing more by it than an ingenious and poetical allegory. *That* at least is not a link in the chain let down from other worlds; "the purple light of love" is not a dim reflection of the smiles of celestial bliss. It does not appear till the middle of life, and then seems like "another morn risen on mid-day." In this respect the soul comes into the world "in utter nakedness." Love waits for the ripening of the youthful blood. The sense of pleasure precedes the love of pleasure, but with the sense of pleasure, as soon as it is felt, come thronging infinite desires and hopes of pleasure, and love is mature as soon as born. It withers and it dies almost as soon!

*   *   *

Romeo is Hamlet in love. There is the same rich exuberance of passion and sentiment in the one, that there is of thought and sentiment in the other. Both are absent and self-involved, both live out of themselves in a world of imagination. Hamlet is abstracted from every thing; Romeo is abstracted from every thing but his love, and lost in it. His "frail thoughts dally with faint surmise," and are fashioned out of the suggestions of hope, "the flatteries of sleep." He is himself only in his Juliet; she is his only reality, his heart's true home and idol. The rest of the world is to him a passing dream. How finely is this character portrayed where he recollects himself on seeing Paris slain at the tomb of Juliet!

> "What said my man when my betossed soul
> Did not attend him as we rode? I think
> He told me Paris should have married Juliet."

And again, just before he hears the sudden tidings of her death—

> "If I may trust the flattery of sleep,
> My dreams presage some joyful news at hand;
> My bosom's lord sits lightly on his throne,
> And all this day an unaccustom'd spirit
> Lifts me above the ground with cheerful thoughts.
> I dreamt my lady came and found me dead,
> (Strange dream! that gives a dead man leave to think)
> And breath'd such life with kisses on my lips,
> That I reviv'd and was an emperour.
> Ah me! how sweet is love itself possess'd,
> When but love's shadows are so rich in joy!"

Romeo's passion for Juliet is not a first love: it succeeds and drives out his passion for another mistress, Rosaline, as the sun hides the stars. This is perhaps an artifice (not absolutely necessary) to give us a higher opinion of the lady, while the first absolute surrender of her heart to him enhances the richness of the prize. The commencement, progress, and ending of his second passion are however complete in themselves, not injured, if they are not bettered by the first. The outline of the play is taken from an Italian novel; but the dramatic arrangement of the different scenes between the lovers, the more than dramatic interest in the progress of the story, the development of the characters with time and circumstances, just according to the degree and kind of interest excited, are not inferior to the expression of passion and nature. It has been ingeniously remarked among other proofs of skill in the contrivance of the fable, that the improbability of the main incident in the piece, the administering of the sleeping-potion, is softened and obviated from the beginning by the introduction of the Friar on his first appearance culling simples and descanting on their virtues. Of the passionate scenes in this tragedy, that between the Friar and Romeo when he is told of his sentence of banishment, that between Juliet and the Nurse when she hears of it, and of the death of her cousin Tybalt (which bear no proportion in her mind, when passion after the first shock of surprise throws its weight into the scale of her affections) and the last scene at the tomb, are among the most natural and overpowering. In all of these it is not merely the force of any one passion that is given, but the slightest and most unlooked-for transitions from one to another, the mingling currents of every different feeling rising up and prevailing in turn, swayed by the master-mind of the poet, as the waves undulate beneath the gliding storm. * * *

SAMUEL TAYLOR COLERIDGE

[On *Romeo and Juliet*]†

The Seventh Lecture

* * *

I will now * * * proceed to "Romeo and Juliet," not because it is the earliest, or among the earliest of Shakspeare's works of that kind, but because in it are to be found specimens, in degree, of all the excellences which he afterwards displayed in his more perfect dramas, but differing from them in being less forcibly evidenced, and less happily combined: all the parts are more or less present, but they are not united with the same harmony.

There are, however, in "Romeo and Juliet" passages where the poet's whole excellence is evinced, so that nothing superior to them can be met with in the productions of his after years. The main distinction between this play and others is, as I said, that the parts are less happily combined, or to borrow a phrase from the painter, the whole work is less in keeping. Grand portions are produced: we have limbs of giant growth; but the production, as a whole, in which each part gives delight for itself, and the whole, consisting of these delightful parts, communicates the highest intellectual pleasure and satisfaction, is the result of the application of judgment and taste. These are not to be attained but by painful study, and to the sacrifice of the stronger pleasures derived from the dazzling light which a man of

† From Samuel Taylor Coleridge, "The Seventh Lecture" (1819) in *Coleridge's Essays and Lectures on Shakespeare & Some Other Old Poets and Dramatists*, ed. Ernest Rhys (London: J. M. Dent, 1907), pp. 419–24, 432–33.

genius throws over every circumstance, and where we are chiefly struck by vivid and distinct images. Taste is an attainment after a poet has been disciplined by experience, and has added to genius that talent by which he knows what part of his genius he can make acceptable, and intelligible to the portion of mankind for which he writes.

In my mind it would be a hopeless symptom, as regards genius, if I found a young man with anything like perfect taste. In the earlier works of Shakspeare we have a profusion of double epithets, and sometimes even the coarsest terms are employed, if they convey a more vivid image; but by degrees the associations are connected with the image they are designed to impress, and the poet descends from the ideal into the real world so far as to conjoin both—to give a sphere of active operations to the ideal, and to elevate and refine the real.

In "Romeo and Juliet" the principal characters may be divided into two classes: in one class passion—the passion of love—is drawn and drawn truly, as well as beautifully; but the persons are not individualised farther than as the actor appears on the stage. It is a very just description and development of love, without giving, if I may so express myself, the philosophical history of it—without shewing how the man became acted upon by that particular passion, but leading it through all the incidents of the drama, and rendering it predominant.

Tybalt is, in himself, a commonplace personage. And here allow me to remark upon a great distinction between Shakspeare, and all who have written in imitation of him. I know no character in his plays (unless indeed Pistol be an exception) which can be called the mere portrait of an individual: while the reader feels all the satisfaction arising from individuality, yet that very individual is a sort of class character, and this circumstance renders Shakspeare the poet of all ages.

Tybalt is a man abandoned to his passions—with all the pride of family, only because he thought it belonged to him as a member of that family, and valuing himself highly, simply because he does not care for death. This indifference to death is perhaps more common than any other feeling: men are apt to flatter themselves extravagantly, merely because they possess a quality which it is a disgrace not to have, but which a wise man never puts forward, but when it is necessary.

Jeremy Taylor in one part of his voluminous works, speaking of a great man, says that he was naturally a coward, as indeed most men are, knowing the value of life, but the power of his reason enabled him, when required, to conduct himself with uniform courage and hardihood. The good bishop, perhaps, had in his mind a story, told by one of the ancients, of a Philosopher and a Coxcomb, on board the same ship during a storm: the Coxcomb reviled the Philosopher for betraying marks of fear: "Why are you so frightened? I am not afraid of being drowned: I do not care a farthing for my life."—"You are perfectly right," said the Philosopher, "for your life is not worth a farthing."

Shakspeare never takes pains to make his characters win your esteem, but leaves it to the general command of the passions, and to poetic justice. It is most beautiful to observe, in "Romeo and Juliet," that the characters principally engaged in the incidents are preserved innocent from all that could lower them in our opinion, while the rest of the personages, deserving little interest in themselves, derive it from being instrumental in those situations in which the more important personages develope their thoughts and passions.

Look at Capulet—a worthy, noble-minded old man of high rank, with all the impatience that is likely to accompany it. It is delightful to see all the sensibilities of our nature so exquisitely called forth; as if the poet had the hundred arms of the polypus, and had thrown them out in all directions to catch the predominant feeling. We may see in Capulet the manner in which anger seizes hold of everything that comes in its way, in order to express itself, as in the lines where he reproves Tybalt for his fierceness of behaviour, which led him to wish to insult a Montague, and disturb the merriment.—

> "Go to, go to;
> You are a saucy boy. Is't so, indeed?
> This trick may chance to scath you;—I know what.
> You must contrary me! marry, 'tis time.—
> Well said, my hearts!—You are a princox: go:
> Be quiet or—More light, more light!—For shame!
> I'll make you quiet.—What! cheerly, my hearts!"
>   Act I, Scene 5.

The line "This trick may chance to scath you;—I know what," was an allusion to the legacy Tybalt might expect; and then, seeing the lights burn dimly, Capulet turns his anger against the servants. Thus we see that no one passion is so predominant, but that it includes all the parts of the character, and the reader never has a mere abstract of a passion, as of wrath or ambition, but the whole man is presented to him—the one predominant passion acting, if I may so say, as the leader of the band to the rest.

It could not be expected that the poet should introduce such a character as Hamlet into every play; but even in those personages, which are subordinate to a hero so eminently philosophical, the passion is at least rendered instructive, and induces the reader to look with a keener eye, and a finer judgment into human nature.

Shakspeare has this advantage over all other dramatists—that he has availed himself of his psychological genius to develope all the minutiae of the human heart: shewing us the thing that, to common observers, he seems solely intent upon, he makes visible what we should not otherwise have seen: just as, after looking at distant objects through a telescope, when we behold them subsequently with the naked eye, we see them with greater distinctness, and in more detail, than we should otherwise have done.

Mercutio is one of our poet's truly Shakspearean characters; for throughout his plays, but especially in those of the highest order, it is plain that the personages were drawn rather from meditation than from observation, or to speak correctly, more from observation, the child of meditation. It is comparatively easy for a man to go about the world, as if with a pocket-book in his hand, carefully noting down what he sees and hears: by practice he acquires considerable facility in representing what he has observed, himself frequently unconscious of its worth, or its bearings. This is entirely different from the observation of a mind, which, having formed a theory and a system upon its own nature, remarks all things that are examples of its tmth, confirming it in that truth, and, above all, enabling it to convey the truths of philosophy, as mere effects derived from, what we may call, the outward watchings of life.

Hence it is that Shakspeare's favourite characters are full of such lively intellect. Mercutio is a man possessing all the elements of a poet: the whole world was, as it were, subject to his law of association. Whenever he wishes to impress anything, all things become his servants for the purpose: all things tell the same tale, and sound in unison. This faculty, moreover, is combined with the manners and feelings of a perfect gentleman, himself utterly unconscious of his powers. By his loss it was contrived that the whole catastrophe of the tragedy should be brought about: it endears him to Romeo, and gives to the death of Mercutio an importance which it could not otherwise have acquired.

I say this in answer to an observation, I think by Dryden (to which indeed Dr. Johnson has fully replied), that Shakspeare having carried the part of Mercutio as far as he could, till his genius was exhausted, had killed him in the third Act, to get him out of the way. What shallow nonsense! As I have remarked, upon the death of Mercutio the whole catastrophe depends; it is produced by it. The scene in which it occurs serves to show how indifference to any subject but one, and aversion to activity on the part of Romeo, may be overcome and roused to the most resolute and determined conduct. Had not Mercutio been rendered so amiable and so interesting, we could not have felt so strongly the necessity for Romeo's interference, connecting it immediately, and passionately, with the future fortunes of the lover and his mistress.

The Nurse in "Romeo and Juliet" has sometimes been compared to a portrait by Gerard Dow, in which every hair was so exquisitely painted, that it would bear the test of the microscope. Now, I appeal confidently to my hearers whether the closest observation of the manners of one or two old nurses would have enabled Shakspeare to draw this character of admirable generalisation? Surely not. Let any man conjure up in his mind all the qualities and peculiarities that can possibly belong to a nurse, and he will find them in Shakspeare's picture of the old woman: nothing is omitted. This effect is not produced by mere observation. The great prerogative of genius (and Shakspeare felt and availed himself of it) is now to swell itself to the dignity of a god, and now to subdue and keep dormant some part of that lofty nature, and to descend even to the lowest character—to become everything, in fact, but the vicious.

Thus, in the Nurse you have all the garrulity of old-age, and all its fondness; for the affection of old-age is one of the greatest consolations of humanity. I have often thought what a melancholy world this would be without children, and what an inhuman world without the aged.

*　*　*

Love is not, like hunger, a mere selfish appetite: it is an associative quality. The hungry savage is nothing but an animal, thinking only of the satisfaction of his stomach: what is the first effect of love, but to associate the feeling with every object in nature? the trees whisper, the roses exhale their perfumes, the nightingales sing, nay the very skies smile in unison with the feeling of true and pure love. It gives to every object in nature a power of the heart, without which it would indeed be spiritless.

Shakspeare has described this passion in various states and stages, beginning, as was most natural, with love in the young. Does he open his play by making Romeo and Juliet in love at first sight—at the first glimpse, as any ordinary thinker would do? Certainly not: he knew what he was about, and how he was to accomplish what he was about: he was to develope the whole passion, and he commences with the first elements—that sense of imperfection, that yearning to combine itself with something lovely. Romeo became enamoured of the idea he had formed in his own mind, and then, as it were, christened the first real being of the contrary sex as endowed with the perfections he desired. He appears to be in love with Rosaline; but, in truth, he is in love only with his own idea. He felt that necessity of being beloved which no noble mind can be without. Then our poet, our poet who so well knew human nature, introduces Romeo to Juliet, and makes it not only a violent, but a permanent love—a point for which Shakspeare has been ridiculed by the ignorant and unthinking. Romeo is first represented in a state most susceptible of love, and then, seeing Juliet, he took and retained the infection.

This brings me to observe upon a characteristic of Shakspeare, which belongs to a man of profound thought and high genius. It has been too much the custom, when anything that happened in his dramas could not easily be explained by the few words the poet has employed, to pass it idly over, and to say that it is beyond our reach, and beyond the power of philosophy—a sort of terra incognita for discoverers—a great ocean to be hereafter explored. Others have treated such passages as hints and glimpses of something now nonexistent, as the sacred fragments of an ancient and ruined temple all the portions of which are beautiful, although their particular relation to each other is unknown. Shakspeare knew the human mind, and its most minute and intimate workings, and he never introduces a word, or a thought, in vain or out of place: if we do not understand him, it is our own fault or the fault of copyists and typographers; but study, and the possession of some small stock of the knowledge by which he worked, will enable us often to detect and explain his meaning. He never wrote at random, or hit upon points of character and conduct by chance; and the smallest fragment of his mind not unfrequently gives a clue to a most perfect, regular, and consistent whole.

*   *   *

HELENA FAUCIT

From On Some of Shakespeare's Female Characters[†]

*   *   *

My early girlhood's first step upon the stage was made as Juliet. To the last days of my artist life I never acted the character without finding fresh cause to marvel at the genius which created this child-woman, raised by love to heroism of the highest type.

*   *   *

In my first trials at Richmond I had ardour and self-forgetfulness enough; but I was too young, too near the age of Shakespeare's Juliet, considering the tardier development of an English girl, to understand so strong and deep a nature. * * * Hitherto I had only known the outward form of the poet's exquisite creation, and could not reach the deeper meaning that lies beneath it; indeed, I never should have

† From Helena Faucit, Lady Martin, *On Some of Shakespeare's Female Characters*, 5th ed. (London and Edinburgh: Blackwood, 1893), pp. 85, 107, 108, 110, 113, 119, 147, 153–55.

reached it, had I not subsequently been allowed to see the real Shakespeare instead of the imperfect copy, adapted and condensed for the stage, in which I originally knew the play. * * *

With the complete play in my hands, I could not fail to see that the key-note was struck in the Prologue, where the whole purpose of the poet is told within the compass of a sonnet. It speaks of the bitter feuds of "two households" for whose rivalry lives were being sacrificed, and for whose "ancient grudge" the followers of both were continually breaking into "new mutiny." To teach a lesson to the reckless leaders of those brawls, "bred of an airy word," it was necessary that each should suffer in his tenderest point, each lose his dearest hope, his only child—

> "Whose misadventured piteous overthrows
> Do, with their death, bury their parents' strife."

Nor was the lesson to be read to them alone, but to those "rebellious subjects" also, those "enemies of peace," who helped by their violent partisanship to disturb the quiet and security of Verona's streets.

As if to emphasise the purpose shown in the Prologue, almost the last words in the play are those spoken by the Prince of Verona, whose kinsmen Mercutio and Paris had both fallen victims to, a purely hereditary animosity!—

> "Capulet! Montague!
> See what a scourge is laid upon your hate,
> That Heaven finds means to kill your joys with love!
> And I, for winking at your discords too,
> Have lost a brace of kinsmen:—all are punished."

With these passages before me, I started on my study of the play from a fresh point. Romeo and Juliet were no common lovers, In their persons they must be pure, beautiful, generous, devoted, and in every way meet, like the spotless Iphigenia, to be offered up a worthy sacrifice to the gods as an expiation for the past, a healing and propitiation for the future; and in such wise that the remembrance of their death should make impossible any after-enmity—each party alike sharing in the woful penalty.

* * *

Shakespeare, we see, has taken the greatest pains to show the kind of love-sickness into which Romeo has been thrown by the charms of the fair but icy Rosaline, who chose to be "forsworn to love"— that vague yearning of the fancy, that idle listlessness which finds vent in "sighing like furnace," and writing sonnets to his "mistress' eyebrow," and is as unlike the love which is soon to absorb his whole soul "as moonlight is to sunlight, or as water is to wine." Much of it

is but "according to the fashion of the time." Not only Romeo's habits, his very language undergoes a change from the moment he sees
Juliet. It is no longer the fancy but the heart that speaks.

* * *

Poor Juliet! With a father who loves her in a wilful, passionate way,
with the understanding that when he has set his mind upon a thing
her will shall always bend to his; with a mother who, if she love her
daughter, entirely fails to understand her nature, or to feel for her
in a matter where even hard mothers are tender; and having for her
only other friends, her foster-mother,—a coarse-minded, weakly
indulgent, silly woman—over whom, since her infancy, she has ruled
supreme, coaxing and tyrannising by turns,—not one of them having,
as we are brought to see, an idea of marriage beyond the good
worldly match thought necessary for the rich heiress of the Capulets!
Amid such surroundings has bloomed into early girlhood this creature, with a rich imagination full of romance, and with a boundless
capacity for self-devotion.

* * *

Women are deeply in debt to Shakespeare for all the lovely noble
things he has put into his women's hearts and mouths, but surely
for nothing more than for the words in which Juliet's reply is
couched. Only one who knew of what a true woman is capable, in
frankness, in courage, and self-surrender when her heart is possessed by a noble love, could have touched with such delicacy, such
infinite charm of mingled reserve and artless frankness, the avowal
of so fervent yet so modest a love, the secret of which had been so
strangely stolen from her. As the whole scene is the noblest paean
to Love ever written, so is what Juliet now says supreme in subtlety
of feeling and expression, where all is beautiful. Watch all the fluc-
tuations of emotion which pervade it and you will understand what
a task is laid upon the actress to interpret them, not in voice and
tone only, important as these are, but also in manner and in action.
The generous frankness of the giving, the timid drawing back,
fearful of having given too much unsought; the perplexity of the
whole, all summed up in that sweet entreaty for pardon with which
it closes.

* * *

'The fifth act of this play has always impressed me as being wonderfully beautiful,—simple, human, and grand as the finest of the Greek
plays; much finer, indeed—for the ancients know nothing of the
passion of love in its purity, its earnestness, its devotedness, its self-
sacrifice. It needed Christianity to teach us this, and a Shakespeare

in the drama to illustrate it. The Greek dramatists, as a rule, preserved the unities of time, place, and action. Shakespeare put them
aside for higher purposes. His genius could not be so trammelled.
Human lives and human minds he took to work upon, and made all
outside matter subservient to his great end. Time, place, action,
were his instruments, and he made them submit to him. He looked
to the "beyond beyond," where no time is, and would not subject
himself to mere days and hours, which at the best come and go
unheeded, some flying, others dragging their weary length along.

*   *   *

Thus is the "fearful passage of their death-mark'd love" complete.
Had Shakespeare only wished to show true love constant and triumphant throught persistent evil fortune, he might have ended here.
But, as I said in the outset, his purpose, I believe, was far wider and
deeper, and is plainly shown in the elaborate close which he has
written to the scene.

The play opens in the thronged streets of Verona,—perhaps in its
picturesque and stirring marketplace,—where, upon a casual meeting, the hot blood of the retainers of the Montagues and Capulets,
made hotter by the blazing noonday sun, breaks out into a bloody
brawl, in to the midst of which, when at its height, the heads of both
the houses rush with a passion little suited to their years, and are
reduced to order only by the intervention of their Prince. It closes
in the chill midnight, in a churchyard. The actors in the first scene
are all present except the kind Lady Montague, who has died of grief
that very night for her son's exile; and there, locked in each other's
arms in death, lie these two fair young creatures done to death by
reason "of their parents' rage."

Too late—too late for their happiness on earth—do these parents
learn the lesson of amity and brotherly love over the dumbly eloquent
bodies of their immolated children. But they do, with striken hearts,
learn it, and try vainly to make expiation. All future generations may
also learn it there, for never could the lesson be more emphatically
taught. * * *

There is in this play no scope for surmise, no possible misunderstanding of the chief characters or of the poet's purpose, such as
there are in *Hamlet* and *Macbeth*. The chill mists and vapours of
the North seem to shroud these plays in an atmosphere of mystery,
uncertainty, and gloom. But here all is distinct and luminous as the
vivid sunshine, or the clear, tender moonlight of the South. You have
but to throw your mind back into the history of the time, and to let
your heart warm and your imagination kindle with the hot blood and
quick-flashing fancies of the Italian temperament, and the whole tale
of love and woe stands fully revealed before you. Still, to judge Juliet

rightly, we must have clear ideas of Romeo, of her parents, and of all the circumstances that determined her conduct. What I have written, therefore, has been written with this object. Would I might think that in my art I was in some measure able to express what my imagination had conceived of Juliet in her brief hours of exquisite happiness and exquisite suffering!

Twentieth- and Twenty-First-Century Responses

HARLEY GRANVILLE-BARKER

Romeo and Juliet[†]

Romeo and Juliet is lyric tragedy, and this must be the key to its interpreting. It seems to have been Shakespeare's first unquestionable success, proof positive of his unique quality. If marred by one or two clumsy turns, its stagecraft is simple and sufficient; and the command of dramatic effect is masterly already. It is immature work still, but it is not crude. The writing shows us a Shakespeare skilled in devices that he is soon to reject or adapt to new purpose. This, which to the critic is one of the most interesting things about the play, is a stumbling block to its acting. But the passion and poignant beauty of it all, when we surrender ourselves to them, make such reservations of small enough account.

＊　＊　＊

Shakespeare takes Brooke's tale, and at once doubles its dramatic value by turning its months to days.

> These violent delights have violent ends. . . .

and a sense of swiftness belongs to them, too. A Hamlet may wait and wait for his revenge; but it accords with this love and its tragedy that four days should see its birth, consummation and end. Incidentally we can here see the "Double Time"—which has so exercised the ingenuity of commentators, who will credit him with their own— slipping naturally and easily into existence. He makes dramatic use of time when he needs to.

---

† From *Prefaces to Shakespeare*, vol. 2 (London: B. T. Batsford, 1930; reprint, Princeton, NJ: Princeton University Press, 1947), pp. 300, 302–306, 312–15. Reprinted by permission of the Society of Authors as the Literary Representative of the Estate of Harley Granville-Barker.

CAPULET   But soft, what day is this?
PARIS   Monday, my lord.
CAPULET   Monday! Ha! ha! Well, Wednesday is too soon;
           O' Thursday let it be:—o' Thursday, tell her,
           She shall be married to this noble earl. . . .

This sense of the marriage looming but three days ahead is dramatically important; later to intensify it, he even lessens the interval by a day. But (his mind reverting now and then to Brooke's story as he read it, possibly before he saw that he must weave it closer) he will carelessly drop in phrases that are quite contradictory when we examine them. But what audience will examine them as they flash by?

> I anger her sometimes [says the Nurse to Romeo], and tell
> her that Paris is the properer man. . . .

(when neither Paris nor Romeo has been in the field for four and twenty hours).

> Is it more sin to wish me thus forsworn,
> Or to dispraise my lord with that same tongue
> Which she hath praised him with above compare
> So many thousand times?

(when, all allowance made for Juliet's exaggeration, the Nurse has not had twice twenty-four hours in which to praise or dispraise). But notice that this suggestion of the casual slackness of normal life conveniently loosens the tension of the tragedy a little. There is, indeed, less of carelessness than a sort of instinctive artistry about it; and the method is a natural by-product of the freedom of Shakespeare's theater.

But he marshals his main action to very definite purpose. He begins it, not with the star-crossed lovers (though a prologue warns us of them), but with a clash of the two houses; and there is far more significance in this than lies in the fighting. The servants, not the masters, start the quarrel. If Tybalt is a firebrand, Benvolio is a peacemaker; and though Montague and Capulet themselves are drawn in, they have the grace to be a little ashamed after. The hate is cankered; it is an ancient quarrel set new abroach; and even the tetchy Capulet owns that it should not be so hard for men of their age to keep the peace. If it were not for the servants, then, who fight because they always have fought, and the Tybalts, who will quarrel about nothing sooner than not quarrel at all, it is a feud ripe for settling; everyone is weary of it; and no one more weary, more impatient with it than Romeo;

> O me! What fray was here?
> Yet tell me not—for I have heard it all. . . .

We are not launching, then, into a tragedy of fated disaster, but—for a more poignant if less highly heroic theme—of opportunity muddled away and marred by ill-luck. As a man of affairs, poor Friar Laurence proved deplorable; but he had imagination. Nothing was likelier than that the Montagues and Capulets, waking one morning to find Romeo and Juliet married, would have been only too thankful for the excuse to stop killing each other.

> And the continuance of their parents' rage,
> Which, but their children's end, nought could remove . . .

says the Prologue. Nought in such a world as this, surmises the young Shakespeare; in a world where

> I thought all for the best.

avails a hero little; for on the heels of it comes

> O, I am fortune's fool!

Having stated his theme, he develops it, as his habit already is (and was to remain; the method so obviously suits the continuities of the Elizabethan stage), by episodes of immediate contrast in character and treatment. Thus, after the bracing rattle of the fight and the clarion of the Prince's judgment, we have our first sight of Romeo, fantastic, rueful, self-absorbed. His coming is preluded by a long passage of word-music; and, that its relevance may be plain, the verse slips into the tune of it at the first mention of his name. Benvolio's brisk story of the quarrel, dashed with irony, is finishing—

> While we were interchanging thrusts and blows,
> Came more and more, and fought on part and part,
> Till the Prince came, who parted either part.

—when Lady Montague interposes with

> O, where is Romeo? Saw you him to-day?
> Right glad am I he was not at this fray.

and promptly, like a change from wood-wind, brass and tympani to an andante on the strings, comes Benvolio's

> Madam, an hour before the worshipped sun
> Peered forth the golden window of the east . . .

Montague echoes him; and to the wooing smoothness of

> But he, his own affections' counsellor,
> Is to himself—I will not say how true—
> But to himself so secret and so close,
> So far from sounding and discovery,

> As is the bud bit with an envious worm,
> Ere he can spread his sweet leaves to the air,
> Or dedicate his beauty to the sun.
> Could we but learn from whence his sorrows grow,
> We would as willingly give cure as know.

Romeo appears; moody, oblivious of them all three. It is a piece of technique that belongs both to Shakespeare's stage in its simplicity and to the play's own lyrical cast.

Then (for contrasts of character and subject), close upon Romeo's mordant thought-play and word-play with Benvolio come Capulet and Paris, the sugary old tyrant and the man of wax, matchmaking—and such a good match for Juliet as it is to be! Close upon this comes Benvolio's wager that he'll show Romeo at the feast beauties to put Rosaline in the shade; and upon that, our first sight of Juliet, when she is bid take a liking to Paris at the feast if she can.

The scene of the procession of the Maskers to Capulet's house (with Romeo a spoil-sport as befits his mood) is unduly lengthened by the bravura of the Queen Mab speech, which is as much and as little to be dramatically justified as a song in an opera is. But Shakespeare makes it serve to quicken the temper of the action to a pitch against which—as against the dance, too, and Tybalt's rage— Romeo's first encounter with Juliet will show with a quiet beauty all its own. Did he wonder for a moment how to make this stand out from everything else in the play? They share the speaking of a sonnet between them, and it is a charming device.

One must picture them there. The dance is over, the guests and the Maskers are in a little chattering, receding crowd, and the two find themselves alone. Juliet would be for joining the others; but Romeo, his mask doffed, moves towards her, as a pilgrim towards a shrine.

> If I profane with my unworthiest hand . . .

It is hard to see what better first encounter could have been devised. To have lit mutual passion in them at once would have been commonplace; the cheapest of love tragedies might begin like that. But there is something sacramental in this ceremony, something shy and grave and sweet; it is a marriage made already. And she is such a child; touched to earnestness by his trembling earnestness, but breaking into fun at last (her defense when the granted kiss lights passion in him) as the last quatrain's meter breaks for its ending into

> You kiss by the book.

The tragedy to come will be deepened when we remember the innocence of its beginning.

* * *

It is, of course, in the end a tragedy of mischance. Shakespeare was bound by his story, was doubtless content to be; and how make it otherwise? Nevertheless, we discern his deeper dramatic sense, which was to shape the maturer tragedies, already in revolt. Accidents make good incidents, but tragedy determined by them has no significance. So he sets out, we see, in the shaping of his characters, to give all likelihood to the outcome. It is by pure ill-luck that Friar John's speed to Mantua is stayed while Balthasar reaches Romeo with the news of Juliet's death; but it is Romeo's headlong recklessness that leaves Friar Laurence no time to retrieve the mistake. It is, by a more subtle turn, Juliet's overacted repentance of her "disobedient opposition," which prompts the delighted Capulet to

> have this knot knit up to-morrow morning.

And this difference of a day proves also to be the difference between life and death.

Before ever the play begins, the chorus foretells its ending. The star-crossed lovers must, we are warned,

> with their death bury their parents' strife.

But Shakespeare is not content with the plain theme of an innocent happiness foredoomed. He makes good dramatic use of it. Our memory of the Prologue, echoing through the first scenes of happy encounter, lends them a poignancy which makes their beauties doubly beautiful. The sacrament of the marriage, with Romeo's invocation—

> Do thou but close our hands with holy words,
> Then love-devouring death do what he dare,
> It is enough I may but call her mine.

—read into it, stands as symbol of the sacrifice that all love and happiness must make to death. But character also is fate; it is, at any rate, the more dramatic part of it, and the life of Shakespeare's art is to lie in the manifesting of this. These two lovers, then, must in themselves be prone to disaster. They are never so freed from the accidents of their story as his later touch would probably have made them. But by the time he has brought them to their full dramatic stature we cannot—accidents or no—imagine a happy ending, or a Romeo and Juliet married and settled as anything but a burlesque.

So, the turning point of Mercutio's death and Tybalt's and Romeo's banishing being past, Shakespeare brings all his powers to bear upon the molding of the two figures to inevitable tragedy; and the producer of the play must note with care how the thing is done. To begin with, over a succession of scenes—in all but one of which either

Romeo or Juliet is concerned—there is no relaxing of tension, vehemence or speed; for every flagging moment in them there is some fresh spur, they reinforce each other too, the common practice of contrast between scene and scene is more or less foregone. And the play's declamatory method is heightened, now into rhapsody, now into a veritable dervish-whirling of words.

Shakespeare's practical ability—while he still hesitates to discard it—to turn verbal conventions to lively account is shown to the full in the scene between Juliet and the Nurse, with which this stretch of the action begins—his success, also his failure. The passage in which Juliet's bewildered dread finds expression in a cascade of puns is almost invariably cut on the modern stage, and one may sympathize with the actress who shirks it. But it is, in fact, wordplay perfectly adapted to dramatic use; and to the Elizabethans puns were not necessarily comic things.

> Hath Romeo slain himself? Say thou but "I,"
> And that bare vowel "I" shall poison more
> Than the death-dealing eye of cockatrice:
> I am not I, if there be such an "I,"
> Or those eyes shut that make thee answer "I."
> If he be slain, say "I"; or if not, no:
> Brief sounds determine of my weal or woe.

Shut our minds to its present absurdity (but it is no more absurd than any other bygone fashion), allow for the rhetorical method, and consider the emotional effect of the word-music alone—what a vivid expression of the girl's agonized mind it makes, this intoxicated confusion of words and meanings! The whole scene is written in terms of conventional rhetoric. We pass from play upon words to play upon phrase, paradox, antithesis.

> O serpent heart, hid with a flowering face!
> Did ever dragon keep so fair a cave?
> Beautiful tyrant; fiend angelical!
> Dove-feathered raven! wolfish ravening lamb!
> Despised substance of divinest show!
> Just opposite to what thou justly seem'st;
> A damned saint, an honourable villain! . . .

The boy-Juliet was here evidently expected to give a display of virtuosity comparable to the singing of a *scena* in a mid-nineteenth century opera. That there was no danger of the audience finding it ridiculous we may judge by Shakespeare's letting the Nurse burlesque the outcry with her

> There's no trust,
> No faith, no honesty in men; all perjured,
> All forsworn, all naught, all dissemblers!

For it is always a daring thing to sandwich farce with tragedy; and though Shakespeare was fond of doing it, obviously he would not if the tragedy itself were trembling on the edge of farce.

The weakness of the expedient shows later, when, after bringing us from rhetoric to pure drama with the Nurse's

> Will you speak well of him that killed your cousin?

and Juliet's flashing answer,

> Shall I speak ill of him that is my husband?

—one of those master touches that clarify and consummate a whole situation—Shakespeare must needs take us back to another screed of the sort which now shows meretricious by comparison. For a finish, though, we have the fine simplicity, set in formality, of

> JULIET Where is my father and my mother, Nurse?
> NURSE   Weeping and wailing over Tybalt's corse:
>   Will you go to them? I will bring you thither.
> JULIET Wash they his wounds with tears! Mine shall be
>   spent,
>   When theirs are dry, for Romeo's banishment.
>   Take up those cords. Poor ropes, you are beguiled,
>   Both you and I, for Romeo is exiled.
>   He made you for a highway to my bed,
>   But I, a maid, die maiden-widowed.

By one means and another, he has now given us a new and a passionate and desperate Juliet, more fitted to her tragic end.

In the scene that follows, we have desperate Romeo in place of desperate Juliet, with the Friar to lift it to dignity at the finish and to push the story a short step forward. The maturer Shakespeare would not, perhaps, have coupled such similar scenes so closely; but both likeness and repetition serve his present purpose.

To appraise the value of the next effect he makes we must again visualize the Elizabethan stage. Below

> *Enter Capulet, Lady Capulet and Paris.*

With Tybalt hardly buried, Juliet weeping for him, it has been no time for urging Paris' suit.

> 'Tis very late [says Capulet], she'll not come down to-night:
> I promise you, but for your company,
> I should have been a-bed an hour ago.

Paris takes his leave, asks Lady Capulet to commend him to her daughter. She answers him:

> I will, and know her mind early to-morrow;
> To-night she's mewed up to her heaviness.

But *we* know that, at this very moment, Romeo and Juliet, bride and bridegroom, are in each other's arms.

* * *

SUSAN SNYDER

Romeo and Juliet: Comedy into Tragedy[†]

Romeo and Juliet is different from Shakespeare's other tragedies in that it becomes, rather than is, tragic. Other tragedies have reversals, but in *Romeo and Juliet* the reversal is so radical as to constitute a change of genre: the action and the characters begin in familiar comic patterns, and are then transformed—or discarded— to compose the pattern of tragedy.

Comedy and tragedy, being opposed ways of apprehending the real world, project their own opposing worlds. The tragic world is governed by inevitability, and its highest value is personal integrity. In the comic world 'evitability' is assumed; instead of heroic or obstinate adherence to a single course, comedy endorses opportunistic shifts and realistic accommodations as means to an end of new social health. The differing laws of comedy and tragedy point to opposed concepts of law itself. Law in the comic world is extrinsic, imposed on society *en masse*. Its source there is usually human, so that law may either be stretched ingeniously to suit the characters' ends, or flouted, or even annulled by benevolent rulers. Portia plays tricks with the letter and spirit of Venetian law to save Antonio. The Dukes in *The Comedy of Errors* and *A Midsummer Night's Dream*, when the objects are family reunions and happily paired lovers, simply brush aside legal obstacles. Even deep-rooted social laws, like the obedience owed to parents by their children, are constantly overturned. But in the tragic world law is inherent: imposed by the individual's own nature, it may direct him to a conflict with the larger patterns of law inherent in his universe. The large pattern may be divine, as it generally is in Greek tragedy, or it may be natural and social, as in *Macbeth* and *King Lear*. Tragic law cannot be altered; it does no good to tell destruction to stop breeding destruction, or to tell gods or human individuals to stop being themselves.

In these opposed worlds our sense of time and its value also differs. The action of comedy may be quickly paced, but we know that it is moving towards a conclusion of 'all the time in the world'. The

† From *Essays in Criticism* 20 (1970): 391–402. Reprinted by permission of Oxford University Press.

events of tragedy, on the other hand, acquire urgency in their uniqueness and their irrevocability: they will never happen again, and one
by one they move the hero closer to the end of his own time in death.
In comedy short-term urgencies are played against a dominant
expansiveness, while in tragedy a sense that time is limited and
precious grows with our perception of an inevitable outcome.

In its inexorable movement and the gulf it fixes between the central
figure and the others, tragedy has been compared to ritual sacrifice. The protagonist is both hero and victim, separated from the
ordinary, all-important in his own being, but destined for destruction. That is the point of the ritual. Comedy is organized like a game.
The ascendancy goes to the clever ones who can take advantage of
sudden openings, plot strategies, and adapt flexibly to an unexpected
move. But luck and instinct win games as well as skill, and comedy
takes account of the erratic laws of chance that bring a Dogberry
out on top of a Don John and, more basically, of the instinctive
attunement to underlying pattern that crowns lovers, however
unaware and inflexible, with final success.

Romeo and Juliet, young and in love and defiant of obstacles, are
attuned to the basic movement of the comic game toward social
regeneration. But they are not successful: the game turns into a sacrifice, and the favoured lovers become its marked victims. This
shift is illuminated by a study of the play's two worlds and some secondary characters who help to define them.

If we divide the play at Mercutio's death, the death that generates all
those that follow, it becomes apparent that the play's movement up
to this point is essentially comic. With the usual intrigues and go-
betweens, the lovers overcome obstacles in a move toward marriage.
This personal action is set in a broader social context, so that the marriage promises not only private satisfaction but renewed social unity:

> For this alliance may so happy prove
> To turn your households' rancour to pure love.[1]

The state that requires this cure is set out in the first scene. The
Verona of the Montague-Capulet feud is like the typical starting
point of the kind of comedy described by Northrop Frye: 'a society
controlled by habit, ritual bondage, arbitrary law and the older
characters.[2] Even the scene's formal balletic structure, a series of
matched representatives of the warring families entering on cue,
conveys the inflexibility of this society, the arbitrary division that
limits freedom of action.

---

1. II. iii. 91–92. All Shakespeare references are to *The Complete Works*, ed. G. L. Kittredge
   (Boston, 1936).
2. *Anatomy of Criticism* (Princeton, 1957), p. 169. Although the younger generation participates in the feud, they have not created it; it is a legacy from the past.

The feud itself seems more a matter of mechanical reflex than of deeply felt hatred. As H. B. Charlton has noted, its presentation here has a comic aspect.[3] The 'parents' rage' that sounds so ominous in the Prologue becomes in representation an irascible humour: two old men claw at one another only to be dragged back by their wives and scolded by their Prince. Charlton found the play flawed by this failure to plant the seeds of tragedy, but the treatment of the feud makes good sense if Shakespeare is playing on *comic* expectations.

Other aspects of this initial world of *Romeo and Juliet* suggests comedy. Its characters are the minor aristocracy and servants familiar in comedies, concerned not with wars and the fate of kingdoms but with arranging marriages and managing the kitchen. More important, it is a world of possibilities, with Capulet's feast represented to the young men as a field of choice. 'Hear all, all see', says Capulet to Paris, 'And like her most whose merit most shall be' (I, ii, 30–31). 'Go thither', Benvolio tells Romeo, 'and with unattainted eye / Compare her face with some that I shall show . . . [4] and Rosaline will be forgotten for some more approachable beauty. Romeo rejects the words, of course, but in action he soon displays a classic comic adaptability, switching from the impossible love to the possible just as Proteus, Demetrius, Phoebe, and Olivia do in their respective comedies.

Violence and disaster are not absent, of course, but they are unrealized threats. The feast yields a kind of comio emblem when Tybalt's potential violence is rendered harmless by Capulet's festive accommodation.

> Therefore be patient, take no note of him.
> It is my will; the which if thou respect,
> Show a fair presence and put off these frowns,
> An ill-beseeming semblance for a feast.
>
> (I. v. 73–76)

This overruling of Tybalt is significant, for Tybalt is a recognizably tragic character, the only one in this part of the play. He alone takes the feud seriously: It is his inner law, the propeller of his fiery nature. He speaks habitually in the tragic rhetoric of honour and death:

> What, dares the slave
> Come hither, cover'd with an antic face,
> To fleer and scorn at our solemnity?
> Now by the stock and honour of my kin,
> To strike him dead I hold it not a sin.
>
> (I. v. 57–61)

---

3. *Shakespearian Tragedy* (Cambridge, 1948), pp. 56–57.
4. I. ii. 89–90.

Tybalt's single set of absolutes cuts him off from a whole rhetorical range available to the other young men of the play: lyric love, witty fooling, friendly conversation. Ironically, his imperatives come to dominate the play's world only when he himself departs from it. While he is alive, Tybalt is an alien.

In a similar manner, the passing fears of calamity voiced by Romeo, Juliet, and Friar Laurence are not allowed to dominate this atmosphere. If the love of Romeo and Juliet is already imaged as a flash of light swallowed by darkness (an image invoking inexorable natural law), it is also expressed as a sea venture, which suggests luck and skill set against natural hazards, chance seized joyously as an opportunity for action. 'Direct my sail', Romeo tells his captain Fortune;[5] but soon he feels himself in command:

> I am no pilot; yet, wert thou as far
> As that vast shore wash'd with the farthest sea,
> I would adventure for such merchandise.
> (II. ii. 82–84)

The spirit is Bassanio's as he adventures for Portia, a Jason voyaging in quest of the Golden Fleece.[6] Romeo is ready for difficulties with a traditional lovers' stratagem, one that Shakespeare had used before in *Two Gentlemen of Verona:* a rope ladder 'which to the high topgallant of my joy / Must be my convoy in the secret night' (II. iv. 201–202).

But before the ladder can be used, Mercutio's death intervenes to transform this world of exhilarating venture. Mercutio has been almost the incarnation of comic atmosphere. He is the best of game-players, endlessly inventive, full of quick moves and counter-moves. Speech for him is a constant play on multiple possibilities: puns abound because two or three meanings are more fun than one, and Queen Mab brings dreams not only to lovers like Romeo but to courtiers, lawyers, parsons, soldiers, maids. These have nothing to do with the case at hand—Romeo's premonition— but Mercutio is not bound by events. They are merely points of departure for his expansive wit. In Mercutio's sudden, violent end, Shakespeare makes the birth of a tragedy coincide exactly with the symbolic death of comedy. The element of freedom and play dies with him, and where many courses were open before, now there seems only one. Romeo sees at once that an irreversible process has begun:

---

5. I. iv. 113.
6. *Merchant of Venice*, I. i. 166–174.

> This day's black fate on moe days doth depend [hang over],
> This but begins the woe others must end.
>   (III. i. 124–125)

It is the first sign in the play's dialogue pointing unambiguously to tragic causation. Romeo's future action is now determined: he *must* kill Tybalt, he *must* run away, he is fortune's fool.

This helplessness is the most striking quality of the second, tragic world of *Romeo and Juliet*. That is, the temper of the new world is largely a function of onrushing events. Under pressure of events, the feud turns from farce to fate, from tit for tat to blood for blood. Lawless as it is in the Prince's eyes, the feud is dramatically the law in *Romeo and Juliet*. Previously external and avoidable, it has now moved inside Romeo to become his personal law. Fittingly, he takes over Tybalt's rhetoric of honour and death:

> Alive in triumph, and Mercutio slain?
> Away to heaven respective lenity,
> And fire-ey'd fury be my conduct now!
> Now, Tybalt, take thy 'villain' back again
> That late thou gavest me.   (III. i. 127–131)

Even outside the main chain of vengeance, the world is suddenly full of imperatives: against his will Friar John is detained at the monastery, and against his will the Apothecary sells poison to Romeo. Urgency becomes the norm as nights run into mornings in continuous action and the characters seem never to sleep. The new world finds its emblem not in the aborted attack but in the aborted feast. As Tybalt's violence was out of tune with the Capulet feast in Act II, so in Acts III and IV the projected wedding is made grotesque when Shakespeare insistently links it with death.[7] Preparations for the feast parallel those of the first part, so as to underline the contrast when

> All things that we ordained festival
> Turn from their office to black funeral—
> Our instruments to melancholy bells,
> Our wedding cheer to a sad burial feast.
>   (IV. v. 84–87)

I have been treating these two worlds as consistent wholes in order to bring out their opposition, but I do not wish to deny dramatic unity to *Romeo and Juliet*. Shakespeare was writing one play, not two, and in spite of the prominence of the turning point we are aware

---

7. III. iv. 23–28; III. v. 202–203; IV. i. 6–8; IV. i. 77–86; IV. i. 107–108; IV. v. 35–39; V. iii. 12.

that premonitions of disaster precede the death of Mercutio and that hopes for avoiding it continue until near the play's conclusion. The world-shift that converts Romeo and Juliet from instinctive winners into sacrificial victims is thus a gradual one. In this connection the careers of two secondary characters, Friar Laurence and the Nurse, are instructive.

In being and action these two belong to the comic vision. Friar Laurence is one of a whole series of Shakespearean manipulators and stage-managers, those wise and benevolent figures who direct the action of others, arrange edifying tableaux, and resolve intricate public and private problems. Notable in the list are Oberon, Friar Francis in *Much Ado,* Helena in the latter part of *All's Well,* Duke Vincentio and Prospero. Friar Laurence shares the religious dress of three of this quintet and participates to some extent, by his knowledge of herbs and drugs, in the magical powers of Oberon and Prospero. Such figures are frequent in comedy but not in tragedy, where the future is not manipulable. The Friar's aims are those implicit in the play's comic movement, an inviolable union for Romeo and Juliet and an end to the families' feud.

The Nurse's goal is less lofty, but equally appropriate to comedy. She wants Juliet married—to anyone. Her preoccupation with marriage and breeding is as indiscriminate as the life force itself. But she conveys no sense of urgency in all this. Rather, her garrulity assumes that limitless time that frames the comic world but not the tragic. In this sense her circumlocutions and digressions are analogous to Mercutio's witty flights and to Friar Laurence's counsels of patience. The leisurely time assumptions of the Friar and the Nurse contrast with the lovers' impatience, creating at first the normal counterpoint of comedy[8] and later a radical split that points us, with the lovers, directly to tragedy.

For what place can these two have in the new world brought into being by Mercutio's death, the world of limited time, no effective choice, no escape? In a sense, though, they define and sharpen the tragedy by their very failure to find a place in the dramatic progress, by their growing estrangement from the true springs of the action. 'Be patient', Friar Laurence tells the banished Romeo, 'for the world is broad and wide' (III. iii. 16). But the roominess he assumes in both time and space simply does not exist for Romeo. His time has been constricted into a chain of days working out a 'black fate', and he sees no world outside the walls of Verona (III. iii. 17).

---

8. Clowns and cynics are usually available to comment on romantic lovers in Shakespeare's comedies, providing qualification and a widened perspective without real disharmony. A single character, like Rosalind in *As You Like It,* may incorporate much of the counterpoint in her own comprehensive view.

Comic adaptability again confronts tragic integrity when Juliet is faced with a similarly intolerable situation—she is ordered to marry Paris—and turns to her Nurse for counsel as Romeo does to the Friar. The Nurse replies with the traditional worldly wisdom of comedy. Romeo has been banished and Paris is very presentable. Adjust yourself to the new situation.

> Then, since the case so stands as now it doth,
> I think it best you married with the County.
> O, he's a lovely gentleman!   (III. v. 218–220)

She still speaks for the life force. Even if Paris is an inferior husband, he is better than no husband at all.

> Your first is dead—or 'twere as good he were
> As living here and you no use of him.   (226–227)

But such advice has become irrelevant, even shocking, in this context. There was no sense of jar when Benvolio, a spokesman for accommodation like the Nurse and the Friar, earlier advised Romeo to substitute a possible for an impossible love. True, the Nurse is urging violation of the marriage vows; but Romeo was also sworn to Rosaline, and for Juliet the marriage vow is a seal on the integrity of her love for Romeo, not a separate issue. The parallel points up the progress of tragedy, for while Benvolio's advice sounded sensible and was in fact unintentionally carried out by Romeo, the course of action outlined by the Nurse is unthinkable to the audience as well as Juliet. The memory of the lovers' dawn parting that began this scene is too strong. Juliet and the Nurse no longer speak the same language, and estrangement is inevitable. 'Thou and my bosom henceforth shall be twain', Juliet vows privately.[9] Like the death of Mercutio, Juliet's rejection of her old confidante has symbolic overtones. The possibilities of comedy have again been presented only to be discarded.

Both Romeo and Juliet have now cast off their comic companions and the alternate modes of being that they represented. But there is one last hope for comedy. If the lovers will not adjust to the situation, perhaps the situation can be adjusted to the lovers. This is usual comic solution, and we have at hand the usual manipulator to engineer it.

---

9. III. v. 242. Later, in the potion scene, Juliet's resolve weakens temporarily, but she at once rejects the idea of companionship. The effect is to call attention to her aloneness:

> I'll call them back again to comfort me.
> Nurse!—What should she do here?
> My dismal scene I needs must act alone.
>   (IV. iii. 17–19)

The Friar's failure to bring off that solution is the final definition of the tragic world of the play. Time is the villain. Time in comedy generally works for regeneration and reconciliation, but in tragedy it propels the protagonists to destruction; there is not enough of it, or it goes wrong somehow. The Friar does his best: he makes more than one plan to avert catastrophe. The first, typically, is patience and a broader field of action. Romeo must go to Mantua and wait

> till we can find a time
> To blaze your marriage, reconcile your friends,
> Beg pardon of the Prince, and call thee back . . .
> (III. iii. 150–152)

It is a good enough plan, for life if not for drama, but it depends on 'finding a time'. As it turns out, events move too quickly for the Friar, and the hasty preparations for Juliet's marriage to Paris leave no time for cooling tempers and reconciliations.

His second plan is an attempt to *gain* time, to create the necessary freedom through a faked death. This is, of course, another comic formula; Shakespeare's later uses of it are all in comedies. It is interesting that the contrived 'deaths' of Hero in *Much Ado,* Helena in *All's Well*, Claudio in *Measure for Measure*, and Hermione in *The Winter's Tale,* unlike Juliet's, are designed to produce a change of heart in other characters.[1] Time may be important, as it is in *The Winter's Tale*, but only as it promotes repentance. Friar Laurence, less ambitious and more desperate than his fellow manipulators, does not hope that Juliet's death will dissolve the families' hatreds but only that it will give Romeo a chance to come and carry her off. Time in the comic world of *The Winter's Tale* co-operates benevolently with Paulina's schemes for Leontes' regeneration; but for Friar Laurence it is both prize and adversary. Romeo's man is quicker with the news of Juliet's death than poor Friar John with the news of the deception. Romeo himself beats Friar Laurence to the Capulets' tomb. The onrushing tragic action quite literally outstrips the slower steps of accommodation before our eyes. The Friar arrives too late to prevent one half of the tragic conclusion, and his essential estrangement is only emphasised when he seeks to avert the other half by sending Juliet to a nunnery. It is the last alternative to be suggested. Juliet quietly rejects the possibility of adjustment and continuing life: 'Go, get thee hence, for I will not away' (V. iii. 160).

The Nurse and the Friar illustrate a basic principle of the operation of comedy in tragedy, which might be called the principle of irrelevance. In tragedy we are tuned to the extraordinary. *Romeo and Juliet*

---

1. The same effect, if not the plan, is apparent in Imogen's reported death in *Cymbeline.*

gives us this extraordinary centre not so much in the two individuals as in the love itself, its intensity and integrity. Our apprehension of this intensity and integrity comes gradually, through the cumulative effect of the lovers' lyric encounters and the increasing urgency of events, but also through the growing irrelevance of the comic characters.

De Quincey perceived in the knocking at the gate in *Macbeth* the resumption of normality after nightmare: 'the re-establishment of the going-on of the world in which we live, which first makes us profoundly sensible of the awful parenthesis that has suspended them.'[2] I would say rather that the normal atmosphere of *Macbeth* has been and goes on being nightmarish, and that it is the knocking at the gate that turns out to be the contrasting parenthesis, but the notion of a sharpened sensitivity is valid. As the presence of alternate paths makes us more conscious of the road we are in fact travelling, so the Nurse and the Friar makes us more 'profoundly sensible' of Romeo's and Juliet's love and its true direction.

After *Romeo and Juliet* Shakespeare never returned to the comedy-into-tragedy formula, although the canon has several examples of potential tragedy converted into comedy. There is a kind of short comic movement in *Othello*, encompassing the successful love of Othello and Desdemona and their safe arrival in Cyprus, but comedy is not in control even in the first act. Iago's malevolence has begun the play, and our sense of obstacles overcome (Desdemona's father, the perils of the sea) is shadowed by his insistent presence. The act ends with the birth of his next plot.

It is not only the shift from comedy to tragedy that sets *Romeo and Juliet* apart from the other Shakespeare tragedies. Critics have often noted, sometimes disapprovingly, that external fate rather than character is the principal determiner of the tragic outcome. For Shakespeare, tragedy is usually a matter of both character and circumstance, a fatal interaction of man and moment. But in this play, although the central characters have their weaknesses, their destruction does not really stem from these weaknesses. One may agree with Friar Laurence that Romeo is rash, but it is not his rashness that propels him into the tragic chain of events but an opposite quality. In the crucial duel between Mercutio and Tybalt, Romeo tries to make peace. Ironically, this very intervention contributes to Mercutio's death.

> MER: Why the devil came you between us? I was hurt under
> your arm.
> ROM: I thought all for the best.   (III. i. 108–109)

---

2. 'On the Knocking at the Gate in *Macbeth*,' *Shakespeare Criticism: A Selection*, ed. D. Nichol Smith (Oxford, 1916), p. 378.

If Shakespeare wanted to implicate Romeo's rashness in his fate, this scene is handled with unbelievable ineptness. Judging from the resultant effect, what he wanted to convey was an ironic dissociation between character and the direction of events.

Perhaps this same purpose dictated the elaborate introduction of comic elements before the characters are pushed into the opposed conditions of tragedy. Stress on milieu tends to downgrade the importance of individual temperament and motivation. For this once in Shakesperian tragedy, it is not what you are that counts, but the world you live in.

GAYLE WHITTIER

The Sonnet's Body and the Body Sonnetized in *Romeo and Juliet*[†]

When Mercutio names Romeo's inherited malady—"Now is he for the numbers that Petrarch flow'd in . . ." (2.4.38–39)[1]—he places Petrarch as Romeo's literary "father," the poetic counterpart of the dynastic father whose verbal legacy Juliet sees as dangerous: "Deny thy father and refuse thy name . . ." (2.2.34). In Mercutio's allusion, renewal remembers inheritance; there is no escape, familial or poetic, from the influence of a preexisting word. This was true for Shakespeare as for Romeo, since he wrote at or near Petrarch's English zenith, though after the time of Petrarch's greatest Continental influence. That realizing Petrarchan conventions can be fatal is a familiar argument, but in *Romeo and Juliet* the inherited Petrarchan word becomes English flesh by declining from lyric freedom to tragic fact through a transaction that sonnetizes the body, diminishes the body of the sonnet, and scatters the terms of the *blason du corps*.[2]

In fact *Romeo and Juliet* opens with a Petrarchan inheritance in the reliquary of the Prologue's English sonnet, an inheritance that endures structurally but endures emptied of its traditional lyric

† From *Shakespeare Quarterly* 40.1 (Spring 1989): 27–41. © 1989 The Folger Shakespeare Library. Reprinted by permission of Johns Hopkins University Press.

1. This and all references to the text of *Romeo and Juliet* follow *The Riverside Shakespeare*, ed. G. Blakemore Evans (Boston: Houghton Mifflin, 1974). To avoid confusion with my own occasional use of square brackets within quotes, the Riverside brackets have been removed.

2. For the purposes of this essay, "Petrarchan" refers to the general conventions of courtly love rather than to Petrarch's specific poems, since Shakespeare was probably not directly acquainted with Continental models. In this sense, what I call "Petrarchan inheritance" is really the *image* of an influence widely disseminated by Shakespeare's time. For general background, see Leonard Forster, *The Icy Fire: Five Studies in European Petrarchism* (London: Cambridge Univ. Press, 1969), esp. pp. 50–51. More specifically on *Romeo and Juliet* see Nicholas Brooke, *Shakespeare's Early Tragedies* (London:

treasures—the lovesick persona, dense metaphor, emotional extremity, song itself: all these have been supplanted by public narrative. "Two households," not "two lovers," opens the poem; "story" rather than lyric is the genre to be dramatized. Even the liquidity of Petrarchan time—liturgical, natural, personal, and aesthetic—cramps to an explicit reckoning of "two hours," reducing the brief lifespans of the lovers and their even briefer love to countable theatrical "traffic." The surviving sonnet itself sustains a narrative burden more fitting for an entire sequence. No longer a poetic end in itself, the sonnet serves as a means to a dramatic issue. Some Petrarchan verve lingers in the loose and ironic paradox of "civil blood making civil hands unclean" and in the tighter oxymoron "fatal loins," but the closing couplet emphasizes a triumph of the prosaic over the lyrical, bequeathing its tired theatrical appeal in wooden prosody:

> The which if you with patient ears attend,
> What here shall miss, our toil shall strive to mend
> (Prologue, lines 13–14)[3]

If sonnet form has lost its furor, however, the living volatility of the word, freed from it, erupts in the play's first dialogue, Sampson and Gregory's inelegant chain of "coals," "colliers," "choler," and "collar" (1.1.1–5). Were these four terms contracted, they might comprise a quadruple pun. Unlike a true pun, the sequence evolves in and

---

Methuen, 1968), pp. 80–106; Rosalie Colie, *Shakespeare's "Living Art"* (Princeton, N.J.: Princeton Univ. Press, 1974), pp. 135–67; A.J. Earl, *"Romeo and Juliet* and the Elizabethan Sonnets," *English*, 27 (1978), 99–119; Winifred Nowottny, "Shakespeare's Tragedies," in *Shakespeare's World*, eds. James Sutherland and Joel Hurstfield (London: Edward Arnold, 1964); and Jill Levenson, "The Definition of Love: Shakespeare's Phrasing in *Romeo and Juliet,*" *Shakespeare Studies*, XV (1982), 21–36. For the *blason*, see Nancy Vickers, " 'The blazon of sweet beauty's best': Shakespeare's *Lucrece,*" in *Shakespeare and the Question of Theory*, eds. Patricia Parker and Geoffrey Hartman (New York and London: Methuen, 1985), pp. 95–115; and "The Body Re-membered: Petrarchan Lyric and the Strategies of Description," in *Mimesis: from Mirror to Method, Augustine to Descartes*, eds. John D. Lyons and Stephen G. Nichols, Jr. (Hanover and London: Univ. Press of New England, 1982). Joel Fineman emphasizes the exhaustion of the sonnet form in his *Shakespeare's Perjured Eye* (Berkeley: Univ. of California Press, 1986), in which he notes that the "sonneteering tradition" that precedes Shakespeare, based as it is in England on "a poetic mode already done and overdone elsewhere . . . is fully aware of the fact that epideictic 'likeness' is translated into something different when subjected to excessive repetition" (pp. 188–89).

3. See Levenson, p. 23, for a different sense of the Prologue sonnet: "It stands at the beginning of the tragedy as a replica in little of the familiar story—the cliché clichéd. In a poetic tour de force, Shakespeare reduces that verbose narrative to the exacting form which served as the main vehicle of Petrarchism." In any case, the sonnet *as a form* of poetic fashion was well past its prime in the 1590s, though fashionable in England, where Petrarch was both lauded and parodied. Perhaps it is that very decadence Shakespeare meant to indicate before the poetic resurrection of the form (and even the form's spirit) in the play itself. Nicholas Brooke suggests this resurrective movement: "The opening movement of the play is recapitulated in a rapid development from bustling prose to lusty verse to the full dance and Romeo and Juliet encountering in a full-blown sonnet" (p. 95). Ultimately he finds the play ". . . a highly perceptive exploration of the love-death embrace of the sonneteering tradition, which regards both its superiority and its inferiority to the world of common day" (p. 106).

through felt time. Like a true pun, however, it generates meaning out of sound, setting the phonetic shape of language above the intentionality of the speakers. They do not choose their words; the words, in a sense, choose them. Their talk of love and war, a kind of displaced contest, becomes deliberate and active only at the sight of the Montagues: "My naked weapon is out. Quarrel, I will back thee" (1.1.34). Though the counterword of the law, formal and written, is briefly acknowledged, gesture preempts language: "I will bite my thumb at them, which is disgrace to them if they bear it" (1.1.42–43). And on the airy word "better"—Gregory's emphasis lifts the word from its syntactic matrix and, in a kind of verbal bas-relief, half-objectifies it—the negotiable word yields to fact: "What, drawn and talk of peace?" (1.1.70). A pattern of negative incarnation has taken place against which the prince's spoken decree comes, as usual, too late. The play's opening, then, establishes the fact that the sonnet form, even when exhausted, will generate dramatic event;[4] that there is a sovereignty in language that subordinates the intention of the speaker and precipitates fact; and that the human word, unlike God's in Genesis, destroys, and destroys in the warp of syntax, the process of dialogue over time. To what degree, then, does this residual and fatal power live on in the inherited poetic word? And to what degree is the body of the poetic word subject to entropy and destruction?

Romeo himself springs forth from the mouth of his father as a recitation inherited from the pages of a courtly miscellany, described but not seen as the topos of the languishing lover.[5] In this persona he suffers less from love than from his desire to live out artistic imitation, to make himself "an artificial [k]night," in worried Montague's pun (1.1.140). Petrarch's is the book he kisses by, but LaRochefoucauld perhaps makes the better case for him: "There are people who would never have fallen in love but for hearing love discussed" (maxim 136).[6] (Juliet, too, is first presented verbally, but as an object of exchange between her father and Paris.)

As apprentice lover-poet, Romeo yearns for a suitably unattainable lady. Rosaline, always a word rather than a presence, bears a name that might entitle a sonnet cycle and that resonates with the love

---

4. My reading parallels Rosalie Colie's sense of the "unmetaphoring" of the play: ". . . we can see very plainly the problem of expression: Petrarchan language, *the* vehicle for amorous emotion, can be used merely as the cliché which Mercutio and Benvolio criticize; or, it can be earned by a lover's experience of the profound oppositions to which that rhetoric of oxymoron points" (p. 143); and, ". . . *Romeo and Juliet* makes some marvelous technical manipulations. One of the most pleasurable, for me, of Shakespeare's many talents is his 'unmetaphoring' of literary devices, his sinking of the conventions back into what, he somehow persuades us, is 'reality,' his trick of making a verbal convention part of the scene, the action, or the psychology of the play itself" (p. 145).

5. See Earl, pp. 103–8.

6. *The Maxims of LaRochefoucauld*, trans. Louis Kronenberger (New York: Random House, 1959), p. 136.

tradition (the *Romance of the Rose*, the rose-form vision of the *Para-diso*, and the ubiquitous symbol of feminine beauty). Like the rose in her name, she will be nominal and brief. When, practicing before Benvolio, Romeo composes his love for her, he produces some-thing itself misshapen, juvenile, resembling a sonnet truncated and inverted:

> Why then, O brawling love! O loving hate!
> O any thing, of nothing first create!
> O heavy lightness, serious vanity,
> Misshapen chaos of well-seeming forms,
> Feather of lead, bright smoke, cold fire, sick health,
> Still-waking sleep, that is not what it is!
> This love feel I, that feel no love in this.
>
> (1.1.176–82)

His "O brawling love" perhaps refers to the brawl he has narrowly missed; almost at once, however, he leaves the world of referential-ity as he heaps oxymoron on oxymoron, setting even a Continental record. Romeo's poetic excess reveals emotional deficiency; perhaps his true confession comes last: "I . . . feel no love in this." He him-self is aware of being slightly ridiculous. "Dost thou not laugh?" he wonders (1.1.183).

Yet he improves with practice (1.1.185–94) and even achieves some stereotypical poetic balance in his encomium on Rosaline's chastity, a portrait without fleshly detail except for an unPetrarchan "lap" which will not open even to gold (1.1.205-15). In this respect Romeo's praise is as bodiless as his love itself. Still, he looks to the flesh, fal-tering in his poetic fathers' footsteps and perhaps even borrowing from Shakespeare's own (perhaps concurrent) sonnets urging a young man to marry:

> O, she is rich in beauty, only poor
> That, when she dies, with beauty dies her store.
>
> (1.1.215–16)

Unlike the earlier and feebler "is"/"this" rhyme (1.1.181–82), this later attempt at a closing couplet, though trite, at least achieves the firmness of a sonnet's *pointe*. Significantly, Romeo does not attain poetic mastery at the sight of Juliet; his apprenticeship begins before he sees her, reaches some perfection, and requires sequentiality, sub-jugation to the world of time, to an influence Juliet catalyzes but does not beget.

Beyond poetic forms, Romeo seeks to become the *author* of the persona he imitates, an artificer born out of an artifact. That is, he would create his own pre-creation, and so preempt inheritance. Appropriately, Romeo's subsequent legacy to his real father will be a letter, written—as is the Petrarchan script in which he first reads his borrowed poetic being. For the moment, innocently and awkwardly, he tries out the difficult and dangerous Petrarchan word. It is difficult in that, while all poetry, if not all language, balances the dream of transcending time and space over the referential facts of limitation, separation, and death (". . . the poet, he nothing affirms and therefore never lieth . . ."[7]), the Petrarchan word is especially non-referential, with its obvious hyperbole, celestial compliments, and paradox. It is dangerous in that, where the word is performative, Romeo lives out its terms in a referential way, ultimately converting himself from life to "story." When Romeo falls in love with a love already *scripted* as otherworldly and then seeks to dramatize that script, he falls into the living power of an inherited word, which, like fleshly inheritance, bestows *both* life *and* death. Nor will the poetic word submit to a patient Veronese domestication.

Romeo probably fails to recognize the performative and potentially deadly power of poetry because he is so drawn to *its* beauty (not Rosaline's, whose specific physical qualities he scarcely mentions). Lady Capulet, less poetic but at least as naive, wrongly trusts in her own power over the word, wresting it from subject to subject— "Marry, that 'marry' is the very theme / I came to talk of . . ." (1.3.63– 64)—and concealing a family commandment under the gracious inquiry, "How stands your dispositions to be married?" (line 65). Advertising Paris, she pays romance its poetic due badly and briefly, turning him from flesh to word and getting stuck midway, at the conceit of a "book of love" (1.3.81–94). Her dominant image betrays her poetry's borrowed source, for it surely does not arise out of lived experience: her carefully coupled rhymes and labored wit ("married lineaments," for example) sound stilted and rehearsed, a collusion between art and dynasty. She speaks, in effect, a written poem.[8] Yet even in her derivative, imperfectly wrought lines, the poetry itself takes metrical revenge, reversing abruptly from masculine to feminine rhyme on the double entendre of "lover"/"cover." Momentarily, Lady Capulet jolts off course, resorting to a new, unintegrated image—"The fish lives in the sea . . ."—then, recovering

---

7. Sir Philip Sidney, *An Apology for Poetry*, ed. Geoffrey Shepherd (Edinburgh: Thomas Nelson and Sons, 1965), p. 123.
8. Writ generally functions in a negative way in Shakespeare's tragedies. It *seems* to maximize the transcendental potential of all language, since one can carry a letter farther than a human voice carries, and since a document may outlast its scribe. But ultimately its triumph over time and space proves provisional: by being material, the writ *resubjects* language to the accidents of time and space. Tybalt, then, a man of destructive action, sends a letter of challenge to Romeo; because he has seen the name of Rosaline inscribed on a guest list, Romeo attends the Capulets' feast, where he will meet death; and the Friar's letter to Romeo in Mantua is not delivered (it *returns* rather than transcends). When Romeo adopts the Petrarchan conventions, he falls in love with a kind of writ.

the covered book, she descends from the clasp of saints' legends, Golden Story, to a dynastic gold which matters more when the couplet couples: "So shall you share all that he doth possess, / By having him, making yourself no less." Unlike Romeo, she not only believes a virgin may, but *must* open her lap to gold. Gold proves as portable, as instrumental, as is poetry itself to this lady. Its associations are carried even lower by the Nurse, from book to treasure cache to body: "No less! nay, bigger: women grow by men" (line 95). As for Juliet, she, like her mother and old Capulet, who casually advises Paris to "get her heart" (1.2.16), has no proper fear of the transformative power of either Eros or the poetic word. Her promise, "I'll look to like, if looking liking move" (1.3.97), rattles on the ear like the child's nonsense that it is. She, too, plays with the deadly arrows of Petrarchan metaphor, but sees herself immune: ". . . no more deep will I endart mine eye / Than your consent gives strength to make it fly" (lines 98–99).

Yet if Romeo and Juliet are naively attracted by Petrarchan conventions, they move in a world where Shakespeare transmutes those conventions to serve the dramatic conspiracy between word and world.[9] For instance, he bends the courtly relic of antithesis so that its opposing terms reciprocate. When Romeo declares that Juliet "seems [to hang] upon the cheek of night / As a rich jewel in an Ethiop's ear" (1.5.45–46), the simile is a Shakespearean original (as if to imply that visionary inspiration has placed Romeo beyond imitation altogether). The jewel simultaneously "shines" because of its dark foil and metaphorizes that foil, for the "rich jewel" both symbolizes Juliet's beauty and gives her name. Not only does the jewel require the backdrop of darkness, then, it reciprocates with it *through* the metaphor, flesh to flesh. Romeo sees Juliet as a word, her name ("Jule"/jewel) juxtaposed to body, but arising from it. While antithesis is usually the core of Petrarchan dilemma, its terms here, so displaced yet locked, enforce our consciousness of the conjunctive bond, the mysterious cooperation, between good and evil, the beating heart of tragic sensibility. As an extreme verbal condensation of antithesis, oxymoron, an important figure in this play, even serves as an index to characters' tragic educations.[1]

---

9. See Earl for a larger treatment of Shakespeare transmutations of Petrarchan conventions.
1. See Robert O. Evans, *The Osier Cage: Rhetorical Devices in Romeo and Juliet* (Lexington: Univ. of Kentucky Press, 1966), especially his chapter "*Oxymoron* as Key to Structure," pp. 18–41. It is Brooke, however, who sees Mercutio's death as pivotal: "The whole play is challenged and re-directed by this scene. The genre in which it is conceived is set sharply against a sense of actuality as Mercutio dies the way men do die—accidentally, irrelevantly, ridiculously; in a word, prosaically. . . . The shock of this scene is used to precipitate a change of key in the play: it becomes immediately more serious, and decisively tragic where before it had been predominantly comic" (p. 83).

Romeo's celebrated collection of oxymorons in Act 1, already cited, defines a love that is spoken but unlived—the very speed of the sequence prevents the experience of any single trope in it—as well as an overabundance of figures in quest of form. Yet the oxymoron ultimately defines the carnal knowledge of a love in which life and death intertwine. Therefore Juliet expresses contradiction only after she meets Romeo: "My only love sprung from my only hate!" With contradiction comes a recognition of time: "Too early seen unknown, and known too late" (1.5.138–39). After Romeo murders Tybalt, Juliet learns the full power of antithesis, moving from contradiction to oxymoron and then out again (3.2.73 ff.). It is her movement out of the oxymoronic knot that rebuilds the comic possibility for her marriage, but the shadow of the past falls over the dialogue. Juliet's "Was ever book containing such vile matter / So fairly bound?" (3.2.83–84) recalls her mother's librarianship of Paris's image— recalls, in fact, that earlier time when Juliet herself had not yet "dreamed" of marriage, when time itself was imprecisely innocent. Now "what day is that?" Juliet asks of her proposed marriage to Paris, and the day is fixed: "Marry, my child, early next Thursday morn" (3.5.111–12). Not without irony, in the scene where Juliet loses her linguistic innocence, the Nurse echoes Juliet's own innocent denial of the power of the word in Act 2, scene 2: "O Romeo, Romeo! / Who ever would have thought it? Romeo!" (3.2.41–42). The oxymoron's concentrated verbal form empowers contradiction to enter the tragic world of time. Shakespeare not only moves the Petrarchan oxymoron from the decorative to the thematic, but he also makes of it the figure for tragic sensibility itself, and, indeed, for the very structure of the play, since Mercutio's death provides the generic pivot between its oxymoronic halves of the comic dream of a freely creative word and the tragic fact of *things*.[2]

As the Shakespearean oxymoron forces poetry into the world of "uncomfortable time," so Shakespeare also spatializes and embodies the metaphors and situations of the Petrarchan inheritance. They, too, cannot survive purely and verbally on the stage of the world or of the playhouse, for both theatres demand a referentiality at odds with unworldly and transcendent metaphor. Shakespeare translates the courtly exchange of sexual identities—for example, the

2. Inescapably, one notices that properties begin to proliferate in this play as Romeo's "love's light wings" are replaced by actual ropes—ladders to the literal act of the wedding night's physical consummation. In Act 5 Paris appears with real flowers to strew Juliet's grave, while Romeo, in turn, comes with spade and crowbar, and the Friar brings a mattock and crowbar himself. The dramatic movement is not simply towards materialization, but the material world as *agency* and as *nonpoetic agency*. See Richard Fly, *Shakespeare's Mediated World* (Amherst: Univ. of Massachusetts Press, 1976), especially Chapter 1, "Tempering Extremities: Hazardous Mediation in *Romeo and Juliet*," pp. 1–26, for a full discussion of this interesting aspect of the tragedy.

lady as "lord" whose eyes shoot fatal arrows, etc.; the lover as pining, lamenting, flowing sufferer—into dramatized psychology and
setting. He thus risks moving a symbolic transaction from lyric concept (the sublime androgyne) to dramatic embodiment (the grotesque).[3] The Nurse urges, "Stand up, stand up, stand, and you be a
man" (3.3.88), while the Friar perceives more of the grotesque than
the sublime when he upbraids Romeo: "Art thou a man? Thy form
cries out thou art; / Thy tears are womanish . . ." (3.3.109–10). Even
Juliet, about to sue for Romeo's hand as Paris does for hers, recognizes her maiden modesty as circumstantial: "Thou knowest the
mask of night is on my face, / Else would a maiden blush bepaint
my cheek" (2.2.85–86). In the epithalamic soliloquy of Act 3, scene 2,
Shakespeare assigns Juliet a poetic form traditionally sung by a
man, one that shows an atypical, unblushing, eager bride.[4] Her solil-
oquizing itself (here and at the beginning of Act 2, scene 5, in Act 4,
scene 3, and elsewhere) further indicates a sexual role reversal,
since Shakespeare customarily reserves the soliloquy for the male
protagonist in a tragedy.[5] The poetic forms that Juliet uses, then,
draw attention to her gender, to her body; in lyric poetry, both sexes
may fit "to one neutral thing," but drama embodies and temporal-
izes. Only in the lovers' deaths is sexual decorum restored when
Juliet follows Romeo's lead as he has followed her false one. With
that, the androgynous dream of poetry is over. The body must be
reacknowledged. But the displaced Petrarchan poetic word meanwhile has turned into Shakespearean dramatic flesh.

Shakespeare also materializes customarily worshipful Petrarchan
attitudes in setting and architecture, locating Juliet literally above
and/or beyond Romeo in the night garden: ". . . for thou art / As glorious to this night, being o'er my head, / As is a winged messenger
of heaven . . ." (2.2.26–28). Although Romeo claims to have entered
the walled garden on a metaphor, "with love's light wings" (2.2.66),
the geographical gap between him and Juliet silently reminds us that
we are not in a world of poetic transcendence, but in a world of finite
things. Imaged as his "sun," Juliet in fact vacillates in terms of both
her philosophical and her physical position. As the scene ends, her
literal instability increases. She appears, disappears, reappears—at

---

3. Marie Delcourt, *L'Hermaphrodite* (Paris: Presses Universitaires de France, 1958), p. 68,
   specifically distinguishes between the sublime (conceptual) and the grotesque (actual)
   types of the androgyne.
4. For a persuasive definition of the epithalamion's "runnawayes eyes" as Cupid's, and for a
   more detailed analysis of the poem itself, see Gary M. McCown, "'Runnawayes Eyes' and
   Juliet's Epithalamium" in *Shakespeare Quarterly*, 27 (1976), 150–70. His reading of the
   transmutations in the classical imagery, attitudes, and situations of the epithalamion
   enlarges and augments what Earl notes in *"Romeo and Juliet* and the Elizabethan
   Sonnets."
5. See Linda Bamber, *Comic Women, Tragic Men* (Stanford: Stanford Univ. Press, 1982),
   pp. 7–8.

best an inconstant body, no fixed star. In embodying the Petrarchan word, Shakespeare warps it into the referentialities of the world and of the Globe.

That Juliet is, in fact, *seen* violates poetic custom and must realign Petrarchan metaphor. Traditionally, the spiritualized lady, even when she has a real-life counterpart, is "seen" only through the poet's selective presentation of her in a redeeming *blason du corps feminin*, her body heraldized. But the *blason*, which seems to honor the body, in fact appropriates it, dismembers it,[6] and often fragments flesh and blood into the metaphoric flowers and minerals of "cheeks like roses," "lips like rubies," etc. The *blason* therefore removes the woman from the human realm, which is, after all, the Platonic lover's aim. (Against this dehumanization Shakespeare wrote "My mistress' eyes are nothing like the sun. . . ." The aesthetic joke, however, is on him: in order to dismiss "false compare," he had to include it.)

In *Romeo and Juliet* the *blason* does occur but never in reference to Juliet herself. In 2.1 it is Rosaline's poetically dismembered form that Mercutio enumerates in a brief and naughty parody of the genre. Where the courtly lover contents himself with the beloved's upper parts and makes poetic use of them (as Lady Capulet sought to do with Paris's face), Mercutio moves from the top down, then from the ground up, ending in the generative midst of things:

> I conjure thee by Rosaline's bright eyes,
> By her high forehead and her scarlet lip,
> By her fine foot, straight leg, and quivering thigh,
> And all demesnes that there adjacent lie. . . .
> (2.1.17–20)

Falling as it does between the lovers' encounter sonnet (1.5) and the garden scene (2.2), Mercutio's bawdy, intended to reclaim Romeo to himself and the "real" world, exposes a poetry that has forgotten the flesh. Since he has neither seen nor known Juliet, Mercutio does not take mock-poetic liberties with her. But his anatomical "ascent" is, like Romeo's climb to Juliet's chamber, a philosophical descent. Presently he falls to indecency:

> O Romeo, that she were, O, that she were
> An open-arse, thou a pop'rin pear!
> (2.1.37–38)

Nor has he worn out the parodic possibilities of courtly description, animalized in his comment on the Nurse—

---

6. See Nancy Vickers, "Diana Described: Scattered Woman and Scattered Rhyme," *Critical Inquiry*, VIII, 12 (1981), 265–79.

An old hare hoar,
And an old hare hoar,
Is very good meat in Lent;
But a hare that is hoar
Is too much for a score
When it hoars ere it be spent . . .
                (2.4.134–39)

—vulgarity he underscores with the satiric refrain of "lady, lady, lady" (1. 144). The Nurse, in turn, plays off her unerotic bodily ailments against the verbal news of Romeo's wedding plans, then undercuts the *blason's* hyperboles with a variation in prose: "Romeo! no, not he. Though his face be better than any man's, yet his leg excels all men's, and for a hand and a foot and a body, though they be not to be talk'd on, yet they are past compare" (2.5.39–43).

Juliet herself negatively blazons Romeo in her famous "What's Montague? It is nor hand nor foot, / Nor arm nor face, nor any other part / Belonging to a man" (2.2.40–42). In dismissing his name, she scatters his body, even as she later sees his corpse cut into complimentary stars for heaven (3.2.22). For Juliet, the body is not idealized through words. It supersedes words, as she herself both is and symbolizes embodiment in the tragic arena. (We might see the play as Romeo's [the poem's] search for Juliet [the flesh].) Significantly, she specifically unlinks reality from the word "rose," a standard courtly symbol for *feminine* beauty. Although she becomes more reverently poetic as the play goes on—Romeo and Juliet contract pragmatism and lyricism from one another, respectively—she begins as a disperser of poetic convention and "form" itself.

Where Juliet undercuts Petrarchan compliment, Romeo exceeds it. Juliet's sheer visibility ought to limit the freedom of poetic metaphor by inviting despoiling comparison with physical fact; but when the hyperbolic and the explicit collide, Romeo does not forego, but rather surpasses, even Petrarchan hyperbole.[7] If tradition calls the lady's eyes celestial bodies, then Romeo removes the very sun from the sky: "It is the east, and Juliet is the sun" (2.2.3). Similarly, her eyes are not *like* stars, nor have the heavens bent down to her; rather, "Two of the fairest stars in all the heaven, / Having some business, do entreat her eyes / To twinkle in their spheres till they return" (2.2.15–17). The effect is to remove the celestial point of comparison by a kind of poetic imperialism that substitutes the lady for it. Though the verbal shape of a comparison remains, Romeo's is less an exercise in metaphor than a displacement of heaven by Juliet. In his poetic vision she is the body of the cosmos.

---

7. See Earl, esp. pp. 108–11.

Romeo's earlier saint/shrine metaphor comes nearer earth and is one of the variant *blasons* of the play. Scripturally the body is a temple, but in order for hers to be a shrine, Juliet must first die (this is the prerequisite to canonization). A shrine typically contains a saint's relics, *fragments* of the hallowed body, as a *blason* contains poetic fragments of the living form it elevates. By a kind of dramatic metonymy, the "shrine" makes Juliet both "the container and the contained."[8] As symbol and symbolized in one, Juliet imitates Logos, but a human logos, the word of death. Shakespeare's reworking of Petrarchan metaphor, then, should perhaps be expected, for metaphor is the world's body imagined in the poem, even as the poem's body is a metaphor for the world outside it. In a play that treats the fatal negotiation between voice and flesh, metaphor itself must negotiate its place.

Only briefly, in the lovers' co-created encounter sonnet (1.5.93 ff.), do voice and flesh reciprocate, both through the bodies of the lovers and the body of the poem they speak. Yet even here, while seeming to elevate it to a religious mystery, the poetic word actually deals on behalf of the flesh. Romeo's "mannerly devotion" hides the English "manly" and the French word for hand, *la main*, while his possible desecration of his saint's body ("If I profane with my unworthiest hand . . .") seeks penance in a deeper trespass, "My lips, two blushing pilgrims, ready stand / To smooth that rough touch with a tender kiss" (1.5.93–96). It is Romeo, of course, who takes the poetic initiative, opens the sonnet, and determines its dominant conceit. Juliet responds, but ultimately loses this poetic contest as, in Act 3, scene 2, she determines to "lose a winning match, / Play'd for a pair of stainless maidenhoods" (lines 12–13). But if Romeo's words seem to win out over Juliet's momentary (and socially correct) reluctance, it is in her more material medium, flesh itself, that the sonnet concludes with a pair of kisses. As A. J. Earl observes, "the kiss that the troubadours and their latterday heirs, the Elizabethans, had yearned for, is granted in this sonnet" (p. 116). More precisely, the kiss is granted after the sonnet concludes, but in Romeo's voice, as if extended in a fifteenth sonnet line: "Thus, from my lips, by thine, my sin is purg'd." Romeo's "thus" requires that we actually see what he refers to: we cannot simply hear it as a poetic conceit. And, of course, kissing puts out speech. Since a poem's seeming autonomy depends, in Sidney's words, on affirming nothing, this moment marks both the silencing of the poetic speaker and the *sonnet's* corruption into the world of substance and time. (One reader even finds

---

8. Barbara L. Estrin ("Romeo, Juliet and the Art of Naming Love," *Ariel*, 12 [1981], 31–49, esp. p. 35) includes a fascinating comparison of 2.2 with Genesis, the other "Book" by which the lovers kiss.

that another, abortive, sonnet follows the first kiss and ends in a second one.[9])

The past further challenges renewal as Shakespeare casts the shadow of its Italian pre-existence over the English sonnet, Romeo delivering eight lines (a broken octave) to Juliet's six (the sestet). Furthermore, the whole of the sonnet is seamed by its antiphonal structure as dialogue rather than monologue. The sonnet weds inheritance and exuberance, poem and body, only for the moment. Then its context, the room of interruptions and other public voices, impinges on the private ceremony. Poetic form itself begins to disintegrate, and a greater tension between poem and flesh subsequently shapes the dialogue in the garden (2.2). There the lovers' betrothal, itself bridging the night when Juliet proposes it and the day when Romeo responds, potentiates (but does not fulfill) the physical consummation of marriage. Promising to supplant language with the new body of matrimony, "one flesh," the dialogue first disrobes Petrarchan poetry, fiery disembodied fragments of which, uncontained by poetic form, radiate as if from the force of their encounter.

In Act 2, scene 2, then, against the backdrop of a Petrarchan situation made geographical, form gives way to a beautiful and unbound shower of figures of speech in which Romeo lifts improbable comparison to impossible identity, then inaugurates his play-long descent from the sun to the angelic messenger and downward into the tomb. Himself wordbound—he would be satisfied with "th' exchange of thy love's faithful vows for mine" (2.2.127)—he is nevertheless ironically inspired by a lady who herself first appears both mute and speaking, then speaks to deny the referential force of language.

Juliet discloses what we all secretly know, that names are both arbitrary *and* consequential. Though she proposes a facile solution ("Doff thy name . . ." in exchange for her flesh), her linguistic dilemma is obvious: in order to dismiss the power of words, she must speak them. And in her desire to separate the name from the body, the Montague family history from Romeo, she goes too far, as Harry Levin observes: "[Juliet] calls into question not merely Romeo's name, but—by implication—all names, forms, conventions, sophistications, and arbitrary dictates of society, as opposed to the appeal of instinct directly conveyed in the odor of a rose."[1] Significantly, when she assigns Romeo the *unnamed* attributes of the flower associated with the lady in courtly custom, she defies the effectiveness

---

9. "The four lines immediately after the kiss form the beginning of another sonnet. . . . It is, however, interrupted after the first quatrain by the Nurse, who comes to call Juliet to her mother. . . . It is also curious that both the complete and the incomplete sonnet end with a kiss, the first imaged as a prayer of the lips, the second imaged as both purgation of sin and the sin itself . . ." (Gideon Rappaport, "Another Sonnet in *Romeo and Juliet*," *Notes and Queries*, n.s. 25 [1978], 124).

1. "Form and Formality in *Romeo and Juliet*," *SQ*, 11 (1960), 3–11, esp. p. 4.

of language even to name the body (much less to shape it), and, with that defiance, she rejects even the fragments of the *blason du corps* as a verbal possession of the beloved's flesh. She supplants words with her own body in "take all myself," but the exchange is untenable. Within lines, Juliet fears an oath that will be negatively performative: "O, swear not by the moon, th' inconstant moon, . . . / Lest that thy love prove likewise variable" (2.2.109–11). As the scene ends, she addresses Romeo by the very name she thought he should doff, the "fair Montague" she means to share and to become. Although love's furor inspires her to create the poetic body of a verbal paradox—". . . the more I give to thee, / The more I have, for both [sea and love] are infinite" (2.2.134–35)—her "infinite" comes up against the Nurse's vocal reminder of interrupting finitude. Juliet's ultimate position places her within her antipoetic family. She readily harnesses Eros in social form: "If that thy bent of love be honorable, / Thy purpose marriage, send me word to-morrow," and on a secular schedule, "Where and what time thou wilt perform the rite" (ll. 143–44, 146). Romeo, in turn, will have her loyalty—and her dowry. Her denial of words and Romeo's faith in them are equally extreme; locus and fact will correct both exaggerations in the tomb.

For each of the virgin lovers, a new tragic knowledge intervenes between the vows (word) and the consummation (body) of their love—that is, the knowledge of death and death's companion, time. We sense its imminence in the compression of Juliet's epithalamion, for, despite its classical elements, her soliloquy has the pacing, if not the sentiment, of a *carpe diem* poem. Romeo, meanwhile, discovers that talk of peace cannot prevent the action of violence, even his own violence in recompense for verbally witty Mercutio, the man who played with language and in whose revenge Romeo slays Tybalt, who "hate[d] the word" (1.1.70). Juliet, in her turn, finds that the poetic word of paradox, which she first learned at the feast and in the night garden, must itself be resolved divisively in the world: she opts for Romeo over Tybalt, for the name she would have had Romeo put off in 2.2. If to age means to know the end of language's illusory transcendence, then in this interval the lovers age, a verbal loss of innocence preceding and paralleling their physical loss of innocence. Both must confront the word in its public, inherited, and negative form as "banished," against which poetry itself frays, even ruptures.

After the consummation of their marriage, the lovers become each other's body, "one flesh," but their aubade in response to sunrise has, unlike the sonnet, no predestined body of its own, though it does share, with flesh, an inexorable occasion. On the morning after their wedding night, they relearn the divisive method by which God creates, the separation of light from darkness, as opposed to the poetic

synthesis of "day in night" they sought, for they experience the separation of husband from wife. They therefore do not co-create the
aubade harmoniously, as they did the sonnet: they argue its terms.
The seams in the dialogue are wider; reality wins out. "It is, it is! . . .
/ It is the lark that sings so out of tune" (3.5.26–27). For while the
social world has always impinged on their poetic co-creation, they
are now adversaries of a higher, external, and indifferently turning
universe, that very cosmos that Romeo metaphorically appropriated
and Juliet displaced earlier (2.2).

Juliet's body next *incorporates* antithesis, day and night as correl-
atives of her "living death." The floral metaphors of the courtly tradition materialize in the potion the Friar has concocted from "baleful
weeds and precious-juiced flowers" (2.3.8). When, on entering Juliet's
chamber on the morning of her wedding to Paris, the Nurse briefly
begins an epithalamion appropriate to the waking of the bride, the
form aborts into a cacaphonous lament.[2] As body preempts voice,
the properties for a wedding—instruments and flowers—prove inter-
changeable with those for a funeral, but poetic form does not.

Out of the operatic competition of voices,[3] Capulet structures an
epitaph:

> O son, the night before thy wedding-day
> Hath Death lain with thy wife. There she lies,
> Flower as she was, deflowered by him.
> (4.5.35–37)

Capulet is not an original man, though he shows traces of the poetic,
as if he were an aged Romeo. His epitaph is more translation than
invention, derived from models in the Renaissance sourcebook *The
Greek Anthology*, where the high number of epitaphs on dead brides
suggests a strange Hellenic epidemic.[4] Capulet's classical borrowing underscores his own advancing years, the death of his dynasty,
and the continuum of death through which poetic influence may
run unchanged from ancient Greece to the Italian Renaissance. It
announces the continuity of verbal influence and inheritance (the
legacy of the word), opposing it to the broken legacy of the flesh (the
Capulet dynasty).

In the tomb the lovers' linguistic and fleshly debts fall due. Drawn
by report (rather than by the more incorporated writ that sent him
to the Capulets' feast), Romeo encounters the brutal fact of applied

---

2. For a full treatment of this scene, see Thomas Moisan, "Rhetoric and the Rehearsal of
   Death: The 'Lamentations' Scene in *Romeo and Juliet*," *SQ*, 34 (1983), 389–404.
3. The "operatic" concept of the scene originates with Harry Levin, "Form and Formality
   in *Romeo and Juliet*," p. 9.
4. See *The Greek Anthology*, eds. A.S.F. Gow and D. L. Page, 2 vols. (Cambridge: Cambridge
   University Press, 1965), Vol. I, 87 (Aniphanes III), 237 (Diodorus VI), 291 (Paimenion III),
   313 (Philip XXIV), and 379 (Thallus III).

mortality, though it is, of course, false fact (in that Juliet is not really dead) or the fact of the body's falseness (in that she will die). Juliet's formerly poeticized uniqueness is undercut by her presence in a common tomb, no fine and private place, but a grisly parody of the communion of the saints, wherein the dead, the living, and the unborn coexist. Here the dead fester in their several ages of corruption. Against this bodily spectacle Romeo resorts to the topoi of the siege of love and the tempest-tossed lover to resurrect his poetic vision, transposing a victory by Petrarchan conceit between himself and Juliet's corpse: "Death . . . / Hath had no power yet upon thy beauty: / Thou art *not conquer'd, beauty's ensign* yet / Is *crimson* in thy *lips* and in thy *cheeks*" (5.3.92–95; my emphasis).

Ironically, the poetic vision is now *true:* Juliet is not dead. But Romeo no longer trusts bodily appearance, and he therefore does not test word against flesh, appearance against touch. His use of "crimson" inevitably evokes the rose as a symbol of brief beauty, appropriate for the scene (Paris, we recall, arrives to strew literal flowers on the corpse); but even the metaphors of beauty have vanished, the "rose / By any other word" (2.2.43–44) now a nameless rose. Were it not for the precedents of tradition, which so often liken cheeks and lips to this specific flower, we would not imagine it. The spectral rose, like the "honey of thy breath," is the vestige of a *blason du corps*. For Romeo, too, the rose bears an *unspeakable* association because he has never seen his beloved as brief and mortal. She is an eternal principle of wholeness to him. But now her body has *parts*, "lips" and "cheeks," and the poetic "crimson" darkens into the real and mortal stain of Tybalt's body in its "bloody sheets."[5]

With Juliet's death, Romeo also discovers the otherness of his own body, a final *migration du coeur*. In a ghostly *blason du corps* he addresses those very parts that Juliet sought to divorce from names in Act 2: "Eyes, look your last! / Arms, take your last embrace! and, lips, . . . seal with a righteous kiss / A dateless bargain to engrossing death" (5.3.112–15). Juliet then wakes, as Adam did, from a profound sleep—only to find her bridegroom dead. Against the promissory word of transcendence, she—and we—witness the irrevocable referential fact of the unglorified body. Juliet has seen this death before, in a waking vision that inverts courtly custom (3.5.55–56). (The male lover usually imagines the female beloved's death, and that in a dream.) Romeo, too, in an inversion of Petrarchan convention, has envisioned himself dead (5.1.6–9). But where Juliet's graphic vision

5. It is difficult not to associate Tybalt's bloody shroud with the blood-stained sheets of a consummated wedding. (Elizabethans had a more celebratory view of that blood than do we moderns.) Such a reading enhances the tomb scene as a consummation of the marriage, as influenced by Petrarch, the otherwordly terms of courtly love always containing this end. The fact that Juliet's body is found still bleeding in death when it has so recently bled in love further emphasizes this connection.

proves true, Romeo's more hopeful one is only half prophetic, for, though he does die, Juliet's restorative kiss cannot resurrect him.

What of the sonnet's body? Inherited as a strewing—Petrarch named some of his works strewn or scattered, *Rime sparse*—the sonnet undergoes further disintegration in *Romeo and Juliet*, where it is weakened by a disequilibrium between narrative and lyrical impulses.[6] The narrative impulse, dominating the prologues to Acts 1 and 2, is historical in direction, stylistically prosaic rather than lyrical, choric in tone, and theatrically referential, addressing events we will see or have seen staged. The lyrical impulse, dominating the lovers' encounter sonnet (1.5), is prophetic in direction, spiritual and erotic in transcendent metaphor, emotional in tone, and intrinsically non-referential, though pressed into the service of incarnation. Where the dominantly narrative sonnet enforces a documentary distance from the artistic imagination, with the Prologue cautioning the audience that Verona is a fiction "where we lay our scene" and that the time frame of the play itself is artificially compressed into "two hours' traffic," the private song boldly intercedes on behalf of poetic fantasy enfleshed as passionate fact.

Narrative and lyricism balance only briefly, in the encounter sonnet of 1.5, Thereafter, lyricism fragments into glowing figures of speech that, perhaps because of their very ultra-Petrarchan extremity, escape any structural confinement (2.2). The more narrative sonnet sustains form (Chorus, Act 2) but, despite its few oxymoronic acknowledgements, falls short of Petrarchan transcendence. It is as if flesh (the narrative sonnet, bound to time and fact) ruptures from spirit (the lyric impulse of the sonnet, unbound even by the linear shape of its predetermined form) and engages in a Neoplatonic negotiation. Both flesh and spirit prove mortal, however. The narrative sonnet is absorbed into the drama to which it refers, subsumed by referentiality; the lyrical content, after exploding into the fiery tropes of the night garden dialogue, fades, undergoing a resurrection only in the Petrarchan relics of Romeo's eulogy in the Capulets' tomb (5.3). Ultimately, narrative structures a sonnet's body lacking a spirit, while extreme lyricism ensouls without form.

Whether dominantly narrative or lyrical, however, the sonnets in *Romeo and Juliet* recollect anatomy, each verbal body reflecting the fleshly, mortal one. The hands and lips of Romeo's encounter sonnet

---

6. Over *Romeo and Juliet* as a whole, then, poetic form, increasingly *incorporated* into dramatic scenes, tends both to disintegrate and to regress historically. The historical regression accelerates as the referentiality of the poetic form increases. Romeo's encounter sonnet, for example, is less determined by external occasion than is the aubade; the aubade, in turn, responds to a cyclic movement in nature, whereas the subsequent epitaph recited by Capulet arises from the fixed and immutable fact of a human death. What is more, while both the aubade and the epitaph require appropriate *tones*, neither constructs a predestined (inherited) body as does the sonnet form.

exist both as poetic word and as visible parts of his and Juliet's flesh. The play's Prologue contains a more general evocation of "civil blood" on "civil hands." And the two bodies reciprocate in "fatal loins," an oxymoron that may be heard as a pun on the close Elizabethan pronunciation of "fatal lines." "Fatal," derived from the past participle of the Latin "to speak," suggests, then, *spoken* lines.[7] In fact the "spoken lines" of the Prologue predestine the plot of the play to be tragic from without, even as the spirit of Petrarchan poetry spoken by Romeo to Juliet finally necessitates their tragic deaths from within. "Fatal lines" lies in the surviving sonnet's body, as death, the original inheritance, lies in the "fatal loins" of our conceptions.

A corresponding dispersal displaces the metonymic *blason du corps*, in which human anatomy itself is strewn as poetic word. In a circular configuration, the sonnet has yielded to partition much like that the *blason* imposes on the blazoned woman's parts. Juliet herself is never explicitly blazoned—contrary to tradition—precisely because to describe her would embody (or disembody) her twofold function as actual person and as the *source* of the poetic word. But the sonnet form "breaks" against her body or, to state it otherwise, against her embodiment and embodying of the poetic spirit, which she comes to symbolize.[8]

Following the deaths of the lovers, the Veronese survivors briefly glimpse the tragic nexus of contraries, not in words, but in the bodies found still warm and, in Juliet's case, still bleeding: an ambiguous but nevertheless fixed boundary between the antitheses of life and death. Yet recognizing and voicing the tragic nexus is not socially useful. As the prince commands, "Seal up the mouth of outrage for a while, / Till we can clear these ambiguities, / And know their spring" (5.3.216–18). His focus is on causality, not mystery: *What happened?* A piecemeal documentary reassembles the facts of the plot, almost as bare now as in the Prologue's "story." For the prince's purpose is not to endorse ambiguity in the fragile equilibrium of poetic paradox but to insure social order. This requires that the lovers be interpreted in terms of public fiction, namely, the claim that their deaths were "not in vain," and that they are (presumably deliberate) "sacrifices of [their parents'] enmity" (5.3.304). (Romeo and Juliet themselves never entertain such a notion, though the pious Friar does. If anything, they overestimate parental enmity to increase the erotic dare.)

7. I am indebted to my colleague J. David Walker for this insight.
8. Juliet's very age suggests that she both represents and defeats a translation of sonnet into flesh. At *almost* fourteen (and not sixteen, as in Brooke's earlier *Romeus and Juliet*), she has years almost equal to the completed form of the sonnet's fourteen-lined body.

The play concludes, then, on the social or dynastic use of language in a marriage contract decreed between the households, though there is no dowry but only a jointure, or widow's portion, to distribute. Unlike the poetry co-created by the lovers, the social poetry at the end of Act 5 is meant to seal, to *close* experience, not to open the speaker to the full force of a lived metaphor. Thus the lyric spirit of the sonnet expires with the lovers, and even its structural remains undergo a kind of amputation in the prince's solemn shaping of the last lines into a foreshortened and vestigial sonnet of one quatrain and a closing couplet. In his verse, social interpretation undercuts both tragic sentiment and poetic fantasy:

> A glooming peace this morning with it brings,
> The sun, for sorrow, will not show his head.
> Go hence to have more talk of these sad things;
> Some shall be pardon'd, and some punished:
> For never was a story of more woe
> Than this of Juliet and her Romeo.
>
> (5.3.305–10)

The marriage of poetic word and flesh remains promissory as the surviving fathers, linking hands in poignant parody of the lovers' first meeting, agree to set up the images of Romeo and Juliet as golden effigies. Perhaps these effigies symbolize "gods of idolatry" in a love religion; certainly they are false, unregenerative bodies. But in them the ancient dream of a poetic word made flesh returns: the lovers' bodies and the metaphors of light through which the lovers beheld them are conjoined, stilled, in the medium of public, solid gold.

JILL L. LEVENSON

The Definition of Love: Shakespeare's Phrasing in *Romeo and Juliet*†

Like Hamlet's love poem to Ophelia, *Romeo and Juliet* is an intellectual's posy which tests the very conventions in which it originated; Shakespeare mixes a sentimental narrative from novella tradition with humor and irony to produce a valentine laced with wit. In the transformation from prolix melodrama to epigrammatic tragedy, diction plays a crucial role. Shakespeare filters the well-known story through the Petrarchan idiom, "a poetic idiom of great flexibility, which could be noncommittal or serious, as desired; which could be used to parade fictitious emotions or to conceal real ones; which

† From *Shakespeare Studies* 15 (1982): 21–36. Reprinted by permission of the author.

permitted intense poetic concentration . . . or endless elabora.. Through this literary medium, the dramatist intensifies the contrasts inherent in his version of the narrative, and the play on the whole combines *mel* and *sal,* honey and salt, in a way similar to that of Shakespeare's sonnets as Rosalie Colie describes them:

> Generally speaking, *mel* and *sal*, or *mel* and *fel*, were the common categories under which the sweet and the sharp epigrams were discussed [in Renaissance poetic theory]. . . .
>
> Sometimes the two are regarded as twins, one fair and one dark; sometimes they are regarded as antithetical. They are paired and discussed as a pair, though they are understood at the same time to be very different poetic alternatives, commanding different tones and vocabularies. Unlike any other sonneteer in English . . . Shakespeare managed to exploit the whole syndrome of epigram and amatory epigram, of salt and sweet, now setting the two modes off against each other, now displaying them as parts of an interlocking whole. Of English poets, he most deeply penetrates the whole problem of sonneteering, even into the theory of the sonnet, testing out now one, now another, now yet another implication of the form, the vocabulary, and the theory of sonnets.[2]

Romeo and Juliet too "exploit[s] the whole syndrome of epigram and amatory epigram, of salt and sweet," in particular by manipulating the vocabulary and conventions of Petrarchism as it had been established in England during the last two decades of the sixteenth century.[3] Nicholas Brooke emphasizes this feature of the play, its connection with the sonnet mode, in an influential comment: "It is obvious that the experience of the non-dramatic sonnets is involved here, and in fact the play can partly be seen as a dramatic exploration of the world of the love sonnet."[4] I would add that this early tragedy investigates the very stuff of amatory poetry, placing its components—its vocabulary, rhetorical devices, and concept of love—in a wide variety of contexts to test their flexibility and compass. On this literary level, *Romeo and Juliet* is one of Shakespeare's most analytical plays, an anatomy of love poetry.[5]

1. Leonard Forster, *The Icy Fire: Five Studies in European Petrarchism* (London: Cambridge Univ. Press, 1969), p. 8.
2. Rosalie Colie, *Shakespeare's "Living Art"* (Princeton, N.J.: Princeton Univ. Press, 1974), pp. 87, 95.
3. For a brief description of the way the vocabulary and conventions of Petrarchism established themselves in England, see Forster, pp. 50–51.
4. Nicholas Brooke, *Shakespeare's Early Tragedies* (London: Methuen, 1968), p. 80.
5. The motif of reckoning—in its various senses of judge, consider, estimate, measure, account—figures prominently in the text (e.g., I.i.124; I.ii 98–101; I.iv.9; I.v.48–50; I.v.118; II.Chorus.3–4; II.ii.19–20; II.iv.39–43; II.v.39 ff., etc.), and it is tempting to conclude that here, as in *Love's Labor's Lost*, it reflects the play's *modus operandi*.

More specifically, the language of *Romeo and Juliet* derives in large part from Petrarchan imagery and stylistic devices.[6] Through the course of the action, this language goes through many permutations in context and therefore in tone and effect but the images and devices themselves remain, on the whole, constant.[7] Like a magician, Shakespeare creates the illusion of tremendous verbal range, when in fact he is pulling the same rabbit out of the same hat while only the color of the spotlight changes. I shall attempt to illustrate these generalizations in a straightforward way, tracing the recurrent Petrarchan topoi through several scenes and noticing their chameleonic performances.

With the sonnet which opens the play, the first scene enacts a conventional stereotype of amatory poetry: "The enmity of Montague and Capulet makes the cliché of the 'dear enemy' into a concrete predicament; the whole drama is devoted to bringing this cliché to life."[8] Colie names this innovative technique the" 'unmetaphoring' of literary devices," and she explains it as Shakespeare's "sinking of the conventions back into what, he somehow persuades us, is 'reality,' his trick of making a verbal convention part of the scene, the action, or the psychology of the play itself."[9] In these opening passages, the cliché of the "dear enemy" is "unmetaphored" twice: first in the sonnet, then in the action which immediately follows the sonnet.

The Chorus purports to describe the ensuing dramatic narrative ("The fearful *passage* of their death-marked love, / . . . the two hours' *traffic* of our stage" [italics mine]),[1] and in bringing its cliché to life,

---

6. On this aspect of the play, see, for instance: Brooke, pp. 80–106; Colie, pp. 137–46; Hermann Conrad, "Petrarca als Lyriker verglichen mit seinem grössten Jünger, Shakespere," *Preusische Jahrbücher*, 166 (1916), 376–88; A. J. Earl, "*Romeo and Juliet* and the Elizabethan Sonnets," *English*, 27 (1978), 99–119; Forster, p. 51; Jacques Gury, "Poétique et dramatique élizabéthaines dans *Romeo and Juliet*," a paper summarized by Francoise Charpentier, "Poétique du langage dramatique," *Revue de Litérature Comparés*, 202 (1977), 298–300; Lisle Cecil John, *The Elizabethan Sonnet Sequences: Studies in Conventional Conceits* (New York: Columbia Univ. Press, 1938), pp. 84–86, 142–43, 151; Winifred Nowottny, "Shakespeare's Tragedies," in *Shakespeare's World*, eds. James Sutherland and Joel Hurstfield (London: Edward Arnold, 1964), pp. 49–53; Katharine M. Wilson, *Shakespeare's Sugared Sonnets* (London: George Allen & Unwin, 1974), pp. 62–80; and Max J. Wolff, "Shakespeare und der Petrarkismus," *Die Neueren Sprachen*, 28 (1920), 193–203. Cf. the study of Paul E. Memmo, Jr., "The Poetry of the *Stilnovisti* and *Love's Labour's Lost*," *Comparative Literature*, 18 (1966), 1–15.
7. The catalog of standard images and devices on which much of this argument rests I have compiled from the comprehensive studies of Forster and John.
8. Forster, p. 51.
9. Colie, p. 145. Both Colie, pp. 145–46, and Forster, p. 51, point out the most striking clichés realized in *Romeo and Juliet*.
1. On the connection between these journey metaphors and "the presentation of the play itself," see James L. Calderwood, *Shakespearean Metadrama: The Argument of the Play in "Titus Andronicus," "Love's Labour's Lost," "Romeo and Juliet," "A Midsummer Night's Dream" and "Richard II"* (Minneapolis: Univ. of Minnesota Press, 1971), pp. 114–15.

it speaks in the sober, emphatic tones of the *novellieri* who had popu-larized the Romeo and Juliet story:

> From forth the fatal loins of these two foes
> A pair of star-crossed lovers take their life;
> Whose misadventured piteous overthrows
> Doth with their death bury their parents' strife.
>
> (lines 9, 12, 5–8)[2]

Yet the description given by this sonnet applies more accurately to the source narratives than to the drama the audience is about to wit-ness.[3] It stands at the beginning of the tragedy as a replica in little of the familiar story—the cliché clichéd. In a poetic tour de force, Shakespeare reduces that verbose narrative to the exacting form which served as the main vehicle of Petrarchism.

When the action begins with the parry of Sampson and Gregory, it seems as if Shakespeare has decomposed both the content and form of the sonnet, and reconstituted them as a burlesque of the Chorus in prose wordplay. Again the topos of "dear enemy" is acted out, here reduced to an absurdity:

GREGORY   The quarrel is between our masters, and us their men.
SAMPSON   'Tis all one. I will show myself a tyrant. When I have fought with the men, I will be cruel with the maids—I will cut off their heads.
GREGORY   The heads of the maids?
SAMPSON   Ay, the heads of the maids, or their maidenheads. Take it in what sense thou wilt.

> (lines 18–25)

The quarreling and quibbling which intensify until the exit at 1.101 are sprinkled with the familiar Petrarchan conceits of beasts, fish, canker[worms], and fire, on which Shakespeare rings variations (lines 7, 10, 29–30, 63, 81, 93), and with the key Petrarchan devices of antitheses and rhetorical questions such as "What, drawn, and talk of peace?" (line 67).

In Benvolio's description of Romeo's melancholy, however, the topoi of Petrarchism grow dense. Like the first Chorus and Benvo-lio's explanation of the fight (lines 104–13), this passage narrates events in diction which is formal and depersonalized. Hence, when

---

2. Quotations from *Romeo and Juliet* come from John E. Hankins's edition in the revised version of the complete Pelican text (Baltimore: Penguin, 1969). My reading of the open-ing of the play benefits from the broader context provided by H. B. Charlton, who describes the debunking of the feud in *"Romeo and Juliet* as an Experimental Tragedy," *Proceedings of the British Academy*, 1939, 25 (1940). 143–85.
3. The first Chorus meets swift contradiction from the first scene, in particular from the entrances of *"old Capulet"* and *"old Montague"*—wife-beleaguered and blustering—which make it difficult to believe in "the fatal loins of these two foes," etc.

Montague continues Benvolio's description, only the content of his poetry (for example, "my heavy son," line 135) distinguishes the speaker from Benvolio. These lines obviously exploit most of the postures of the conventional lover: the predawn secret wanderings, the restlessness, solitude, sleeplessness, tears and sighs; and they do so through the familiar conceits of locale, prison, sun/clouds, day/ night, and through the customary devices of hyperbole ("With tears augmenting the fresh morning's dew, / Adding to clouds more clouds with his deep sighs" [lines 130–31]) and antithesis ("Away from light steals home my heavy son" [line 135]). Before he leaves the stage, Montague adds to his portrayal of Romeo as lover a canker and bud conceit which will reappear later in the play in whole and in parts:

> But to himself so secret and so close,
> So far from sounding and discovery,
> As is the bud bit with an envious worm
> Ere he can spread his sweet leaves to the air
> Or dedicate his beauty to the sun.
> (lines 147–51)[4]

Benvolio and Montague have been verbalizing an attitude more literary than real, "Ovidian symptoms and . . . medieval love conventions": "the Elizabethan reader took for granted a definite code of action as a manifestation of the symptoms and effects of love."[5] Upon entering the scene at line 153, Romeo embodies that code, and predictably, the exchanges with Benvolio that follow elaborate on the conceits and devices which introduced the code. Now the stereotype governing all the others has come to life, identified not only by conventional behavior but also by conventional language. To give us lines 116–236 of Act I, Scene i, Shakespeare reworks the corresponding passage from Brooke's version (pp. 288–90)[6] with oxymora, Petrarchan conceits, and hyperbole. This passage supplies a few topoi missing from the portrait drawn by Benvolio and Montague: Cupid, madness, myth, sainthood, and military equipment and assault.

As a whole, the opening scene with its prologue quite thoroughly reproduces the stock of conceits used by the Petrarchists to extol the lady and describe the nature of love. Rosaline's praises are sung by the book, through metaphorical description, mythological association, and analyses of her effect upon Romeo; and the commonplaces which express the bittersweet quality of love parade by—in verbal and concrete imagery—from the start. All of these

---

4. Cf. II.iii.30; also, I.iv.65; III.i.105; and V.iii.109.
5. John, pp. 83, 86.
6. Quotations from Arthur Brooke, *The Tragicall Historye of Romeus and Juliet Written First in Italian by Bandell, and Nowe in Englishe by Ar. Br.,* come from Geoffrey Bullough's edition in *Narrative and Dramatic Sources of Shakespeare,* I (London: Routledge & Kegan Paul, 1957), 284–363.

contradictions have a traditional effect on Romeo, loss of identity, which he expresses in conventional phrases. As Leonard Forster sketches the Petrarchan lover: "The hovering balance of opposites appears as total loss of self-possession; the senses are confused, the lover quite literally does not know whether he is coming or going, even the sense of individuality is lost."[7] One Italian Petrarchist explains this confusion in representative fashion: "I am shaken, I am in despair, I am tortured and pulled this way and that; I do not even know who I am or what I am."[8] Shakespeare gives Romeo a well-known variation on this theme: "Tut! I have lost myself; I am not here; / This is not Romeo, he's some other where" (lines 195–96). In the last lines of this scene, Benvolio seems to personify "Anti-Petrarchism," a current of Petrarchism which ran counter to the excesses of the tradition.[9] Hence, his brief, sensible, and sometimes humorous remarks gently deflate Romeo's stereotyped phraseology:

BENVOLIO   Tell me in sadness, who is that you love?
ROMEO   What, shall I groan and tell thee?
                 Groan? Why, no;
BENVOLIO   But sadly tell me who.

                           (lines 197–99)

At the close of Act I, Scene i, Shakespeare assembles conventions in a strikingly artful way: these lines recapitulate the scene and anticipate passages to come.[1] Double-entendres (especially lines 205 ff.)—an ironic commentary throughout the play on the narrative's sentiment[2]—echo in another key the lines of Sampson and Gregory; and the contrivance of end sounds in the passage reprises the opening sonnet with its imposition of poetic form on events. Some lines rework others recently heard:

ROMEO   Alas that love, whose view is muffled still,
           Should without eyes see pathways to his will!

                           (lines 169–70)

ROMEO   He that is strucken blind cannot forget
           The precious treasure of his eyesight lost.

                           (lines 230–31)

7. Forster, p. 14.
8. Latin translated in Forster, p. 14.
9. Forster, pp. 56–57.
1. Clifford Leech, "The Moral Tragedy of *Romeo and Juliet*," in *English Renaissance Drama: Essays in Honor of Madeleine Doran & Mark Eccles*, eds. Standish Henning, Robert Kimbrough, Richard Knowles (Carbondale: Southern Illinois Univ. Press 1976), p. 67, points out that "parallel with variation was one of Shakespeare's special devices in these early plays."
2. As M. M. Mahood has remarked in *Shakespeare's Wordplay* (London: Methuen, 1968), p. 56.

Moreover, a number of them will appear later in altered contexts (cf. line 208 with II.ii.73; lines 213–14 with I.v.47). In short, by means of a process which often makes its craftsmanship apparent, Act I, Scene i creates and molds the narrative of Romeo and Juliet out of topoi familiar from the Petrarchan tradition.

The rest of the play continues this process. As an audience might expect, the Petrarchan idiom sounds clearly in the speeches of the lovers. When Romeo first encounters Juliet in Act I, Scene v, for example, the devotional conceits he had used to idealize Rosaline supply his vocabulary for the sonnet and quatrain he exchanges with his new beloved. The nautical conceit Romeo speaks at I.iv.112–13— "But he that hath the steerage of my course / Direct my sail!"—has an important niche among Petrarchan conventions; the boat at sea without a sense of direction represents the lover who feels confusion and dislocation. As scholars have pointed out, this common image reappears in the tragedy, three times in the lovers' speeches.[3] It would take more space than I have here to catalog the lovers' many uses of standard topoi (such as blind Cupid with his equipment, other mythological figures, sun and stars, fire, flowers, gems and treasure) and devices (such as oxymora, hyperbole, *blason*); and critics have been sensitive to Romeo and Juliet's manipulation of these conventions. Scholars have also noticed how poetic forms continue to take shape in Shakespeare's text, sculpted out of Petrarchan language and conventions into sonnets, quatrains, sestets, octaves, an *aubade*, an epithalamium, a duet, a quartet, and some straightforward rhymed passages.[4]

What critics have not appreciated—and what an audience might not expect—is the important place the material of amatory poetry occupies not only in the speeches of the protagonists, but also in the tragedy as a whole. All of the dramatis personae crucial to the plot—Friar Laurence, the Capulets, the Nurse, Paris—express themselves in this idiom. Even Mercutio speaks in the Anti-Petrarchan mode, an aspect of Petrarchism introduced in the play, as I have pointed out, by Benvolio.

Hence, in Act II, Scene iii, Friar Laurence voices his proverbs and advice in the vocabulary of lyric poetry. His opening speech, with its formal depiction of morning,[5] echoes the account given in Act I,

---

3. See, in particular, Walter Whiter, *A Specimen of a Commentary on Shakspeare* [1794], ed. Alan Over, completed by Mary Bell (London: Methuen, 1967), pp. 112, 224; and Kenneth Muir, *The Sources of Shakespeare's Plays* (London: Methuen, 1977), pp. 43–44, and "Arthur Brooke and the Imagery of 'Romeo and Juliet,'" *Notes and Queries*, n.s. 3 (1956), 241–43.

4. See Colie, pp. 137, 143–44, for a summary of these poetic forms. (One sonnet has recently been singled out by Gideon Rappaport, "Another Sonnet in 'Romeo and Juliet,'" *Notes and Queries*, n.s. 25 [1978], 124.)

5. I am assuming with many editors that Q2 accurately assigns this speech to Friar Laurence. See Barry J. Gaines, "The 'Grey-eyed Morne' Passage in *Romeo and Juliet*,"

Scene i by Benvolio and Montague; Friar Laurence also personifies morning, and provides the personification with a matching epithet and mythological connections. In the earlier passages, "the worshipped sun / Peered forth the golden window of the East" and "the all-cheering sun / Should in the farthest East begin to draw / The shady curtains from Aurora's bed" (lines 116–17; lines 132–34). Friar Laurence elaborates on these conceits, personifying "darkness" and "fair daylight" (I.i.137), and providing the latter with mythological associations as well:

> The grey-eyed morn smiles on the frowning night,
> Check'ring the Eastern clouds with streaks of light;
> And fleckéd darkness like a drunkard reels
> From forth day's path and Titan's fiery wheels.
>
> (lines 1–4)

By these means, this passage anticipates the gorgeous description of Romeo and Juliet in Act III, Scene v (see especially lines 7–10), and the somber one of Prince Escalus which concludes the play. A familiar symbol of new life, dawn in this tragedy has the ironic function of counterpointing in delicate cadences events inevitably leading to death.

The rest of Friar Laurence's opening speeches in this scene contain a scattering of common Petrarchan topoi (flowers, canker) and devices (antithesis), as well as Shakespeare's favored sonnet word ("sweet"), and even the echo of a phrase used earlier in an Anti-Petrarchan context (line 41, "then here I hit it right"; cf. I.i.203–06). In conversation with Romeo, however, Friar Laurence—like Benvolio and Montague in Act I, Scene i—delineates the Petrarchan lover in Petrarchan language (lines 69–78): the tears, sallow cheeks, sighs, and groans. Friar Laurence speaks in gentle mockery, of course, but Anti-Petrarchism allowed for such parody. Using the same topoi as Benvolio and Montague, he inflates their hyperbole to the point of burlesque:

> Jesu Maria! What a deal of brine
> Hath washed thy sallow cheeks for Rosaline!
> How much salt water thrown away in waste
> To season love, that of it doth not taste!
> The sun not yet thy sighs from heaven clears,
> Thy old groans ring yet in mine ancient ears.
> Lo, here upon thy cheek the stain doth sit
> Of an old tear that is not washed off yet.
>
> (lines 69–76)

Shakespeare Quarterly, 21 (1970), 196–98. If this assumption is wrong and the speech belongs to Romeo (as George Walton Williams argues, e.g., in his critical edition [Durham: Duke Univ. Press, 1964], pp. 118–21, I think that it is still worth noting the verbal connections of the lines with the rest of the play.

At the end of this passage, Shakespeare accomplishes a feat of dramatic economy. Friar Laurence refers to the notion of the lover's volatile identity, a topos already introduced directly in Romeo's speech (I.i.195–96) and indirectly through his use of the navigation image (I.iv.112–13; II.ii.79–84):

> If e'er thou wast thyself, and these woes thine,
> Thou and these woes were all for Rosaline.
> And art thou changed?
>
> (lines 77–79)

In the scene immediately preceding this one, this topos had been "unmetaphored" by Romeo and Juliet, for whom the issue of lover's identity seems not a poetic convention but an obstructive reality. Through the chemistry of Juliet's famous words, their former identities—names, family—dissolve: "Deny thy father and refuse thy name; / Or, if thou wilt not, be but sworn my love, / And I'll no longer be a Capulet" (lines 34–36); and Romeo delights in the transformation: "Call me but love, and I'll be new baptized; / Henceforth I never will be Romeo" (lines 50–51). When Friar Laurence alludes to the poetic convention, he also reminds the audience of its enactment in Act II, Scene ii. His lines simultaneously burlesque the Petrarchan amorist and reflect the emergence of a new, less conventional lover.

This brilliantly contrived speech ends with a maxim, one of several aphoristic statements appropriate to a holy friar that punctuate this relatively short scene (for example, see lines 8 ff., 17, 19–20, 88).[6] As Morris Palmer Tilley defines proverbs of the English Renaissance, they "reflected the common beliefs of the time, they were the small change of conversation."[7] Through aphorisms, Friar Laurence early in Act II, Scene iii describes a predictable world in commonplace terms. Romeo enters that world and Friar Laurence's consciousness at line 22, an embodiment of romantic love in the process of change. In the speech of Friar Laurence that I have just discussed, the conventions of the lover are reviewed by a citizen of the other world, who produces not only burlesque but anticlimax:

> And art thou changed? Pronounce this sentence then:]
> Women may fall when there's no strength in men.
>
> (lines 79–80)

---

6. My guide to the proverbs in *Romeo and Juliet* is the citation of Tilley in the Cambridge edition of the play, ed. John Dover Wilson assisted by George Ian Duthie (London: Cambridge Univ. Press, 1969).
7. Morris Palmer Tilley, *A Dictionary of Proverbs in England in the Sixteenth and Seventeenth Centuries: A Collection of the Proverbs Found in English Literature and the Dictionaries of the Period* (Ann Arbor: Univ. of Michigan Press, 1950), p. vii.

Thus the pattern of conventions in this scene demonstrates how that which is humdrum can muffle the impact of a poetic idiom and a narrative crisis.

In Act III, Scene v, Shakespeare at least twice varies the pitch of amatory images and devices. The scene begins with the *aubade* of Romeo and Juliet, the enactment of another literary convention: "the *aubade* is indeed a dawn-song sung after a night of love, when the lovers must part, but a dawn-song of peculiar poignancy and relevance because of the way in which these lovers must part on this particular day."[8] As I mentioned above, some of the conceits in this *aubade* have been anticipated in earlier passages, especially these:

> ROMEO Look, love, what envious streaks
> Do lace the severing clouds in yonder East.
> Night's candles are burnt out, and jocund day
> Stands tiptoe on the misty mountain tops.
>   (lines 7–10)

> ROMEO I'll say yon grey is not the morning's eye,
> 'Tis but the pale reflex of Cynthia's brow; . . .
>   (lines 19–20)

Juliet's personification not only echoes the descriptions of previous scenes, but reminds the audience of Romeo's requests for a torch on the way to the ball in Act I, Scene iv (lines 11, 35):

> JULIET It is some meteor that the sun exhales
> To be to thee this night a torchbearer
> And light thee on thy way to Mantua.
>   (lines 13–15)

In these passages, the commonplace sonnet trope of the bird comes to life. Besides, the lovers' exchanges are, of course, rich with antitheses (night/day, light/dark, live/die, go/stay, sweet division/harsh discord, and so forth), and with irony as well; hence, before Romeo's departure, Juliet uses a hunting conceit (line 34)—a Petrarchan convention—which she associates with the custom of waking newlyweds by the sounding of horns.[9]

Toward the middle of this scene, Capulet's speeches reduce Petrarchan topoi to banalities. Confronting Juliet, who in her weeping emblematizes the notion of the lover's grief, the uncomprehending father delivers himself of this conceit on tears:

> CAPULET When the sun sets the earth doth drizzle dew,
> But for the sunset of my brother's son
> It rains downright.

8. Colie, p. 145.
9. See the note on this conceit in the Cambridge edition of *Romeo and Juliet*, p. 193.

> How now? a conduit, girl? What, still in tears?
> Evermore show'ring? . . .
>
> (lines 127–31)

He continues with an equally labored version of the standard navigation metaphor:

>   In one little body
> Thou counterfeit'st a bark, a sea, a wind:
> For still thy eyes, which I may call the sea,
> Do ebb and flow with tears; the bark thy body is,
> Sailing in this salt flood; the winds, thy sighs,
> Who, raging with thy tears and they with them,
> Without a sudden calm will overset
> Thy tempest-tossèd body.
>
> (lines 131–38)

In his terms, the lover's paleness becomes "you green-sickness carrion!" and "You tallow-face!" (lines 157, 158).[1]

As the scene closes, Juliet expresses intense grief in a standard rhetorical question: "Is there no pity sitting in the clouds / That sees into the bottom of my grief?" (lines 198–99); and the turncoat Nurse supports Paris's cause with a conventional variation on the bird metaphor: "An eagle, madam, / Hath not so green, so quick, so fair an eye / As Paris hath" (lines 221–23). In the end, Juliet's lines peak to hyperbole ("she hath praised him . . . above compare / So many thousand times" [lines 240–41]), but they subside as well into epithets which sound, in a play full of contradictions, like oxymora whose contradictory terms have been rendered uniform: "Ancient damnation! O most wicked fiend!" (line 237). The epithets, and the decision which Juliet phrases in aphoristic terms ("Thou and my bosom henceforth shall be twain" [line 242; cf. Tilley, T640]), frame her hyperbole; and the stylistic format suggests perhaps that for the moment she is capping her emotions.

The following scene, Act IV, Scene i, passes Petrarchan conventions through a different frame of reference, affording them another ironic dimension. Like Capulet, Paris unknowingly describes the lover's tears and solitude—Juliet's weeping and remoteness—in traditional phrases complete with mythological reference ("Venus smiles not in a house of tears" [line 8]) and hyperbole ("the inundation

---

1. It is tempting to suggest in addition that Capulet's lines here also reduce the conventions of the lover's suffering ("I will drag thee on a hurdle thither" [line 156]), and the lover's yoke ("fettle your fine joints" [line 154]), and that the madness traditionally attributed to the pining infatuate is here, in a dry mock, attributed to him ("*Lady*. Fie, fie! what, are you mad?" [line 158]).

of her tears" [line 12]). Again the stereotypes are "unmetaphored" by the appearance of Juliet herself, who comments on her tears in a military trope:

> PARIS   Poor soul, thy face is much abused with tears.
> JULIET The tears have got small victory by that,
>   For it was bad enough before their spite.
> PARIS   Thou wrong'st it more than tears with that report.
>
> (lines 29–32)

The stichomythic exchange of which these lines form a part grounds itself in antitheses and other Petrarchan conventions, especially the use of devotional terms in romantic contexts (for example, "confess" and "confession" [lines 22–25], "holy kiss" [line 43]), a device which echoes the description of Rosaline in Act I, Scene i, and the meeting of Romeo and Juliet in Act I, Scene v.

The Petrarchan tradition stipulates, of course, that those afflicted must be willing to die for love. By the time *Romeo and Juliet* has reached Act IV, Scene i, the narrative itself allows this convention to materialize: first, Juliet offers to die (lines 52–67); then, delaying her fulfillment of this gesture, Friar Laurence proposes a scheme which artificially enacts the convention. In his description of the scheme, the concept of the lover's solitude begins to grow real ("Tomorrow night look that thou lie alone; / Let not the nurse lie with thee in thy chamber" [lines 91–92]), a process which will end during the moment in Act V when the lovers are together, alone, in the tomb.[2] Antitheses appear frequently (cold/warmth, progress/surcease, life/death, roses/ashes, day/night, supple/stiff, stark) in a new and sinister context, and Friar Laurence transposes to another key images commonplace in the portrayal of the beloved's charms:

> The roses in thy lips and cheeks sall fade
> To wanny ashes, thy eyes' windows fall
> Like death when he shuts up the day of life; . . .
>
> (lines 99–101)

Interestingly, as he shifts these images, he transmutes others connected earlier with dawn and daylight (cf. "the worshipped sun / Peered forth the golden window of the East" [I.i.116–17]; "Shuts up his windows, locks fair daylight out" [I.i.137]; and the antithetical "Then, window, let day in, and let life out" [III.v.41]). Moreover, like

---

2. See Harry Levin, "Form and Formality in *Romeo and Juliet*," *Shakespeare Quarterly*, 11 (1960), rpt. in *Twentieth Century Interpretations of "Romeo and Juliet": A Collection of Critical Essays*, ed. Douglas Cole (Englewood Cliffs, N.J.: Prentice-Hall, 1970), pp. 93–94.

Juliet, who unknowingly inverts tradition in her epithalamium (III.
ii.1–31)[3] and in her farewell exchanges with Romeo (III.v.34), Friar
Laurence unintentionally skews in an ironic direction customs associated with marriage:

> Now, when the bridegroom in the morning comes
> To rouse thee from thy bed, there art thou dead.
> (lines 107–08)

As *Romeo and Juliet* nears its conclusion (IV.v.),[4] both the
Petrarchan idiom and the device of echoing continue to be prominent. In the quartet spoken by Lord and Lady Capulet, Paris, and
the Nurse, for instance, Capulet's first speech repeats in essence
Friar Laurence's lines about the potion's effect (IV.i.96–99). More
important, Capulet brings together the imagery of flower and frost
in the tradition of love poetry, creating several standard contrasts
at once: "cold and warmth, colorlessness and intensity, death and
life",[5] he also makes the conventional association of the sweetness
of the lady with the sweetness of the flower:

> Death lies on her like an untimely frost
> Upon the sweetest flower of all field.
> (lines 28–29)

At line 37, Capulet modifies the flower metaphor: "Flower as she was,
deflowerèd by him." Paris's allusion to "this morning's face" (line 41)
summons to mind earlier references to dawn. Further, Paris utters
his part of the shared lament in the vocabulary of the conventional
lover; using typical contradictions, he addresses death as if it were
a pitiless lady causing him extreme distress:

> By cruel cruel thee quite overthrown.
> O love! O life! not life, but love in death!
> (lines 57–58)

When the formal expressions of grief become shrill, Friar Laurence's
interjections and sermon function like Prince Escalus's in Act I,
Scene i, calming agitated characters and setting the action on the
next stage of its course. The Friar delivers his message, as usual, in
antitheses—some rhymed, some aphoristic—and Capulet reflects
not only the content but also the style of the message in the lines on

---

3. For a fine analysis of the way this epithalamium works, see Gary M. McCown, "Runnawayes Eyes' and Juliet's Epithalamium," *Shakespeare Quarterly,* 27 (1976).
4. Professor Joan Hartwig offers an excellent analysis of the dramaturgy of these closing
   scenes in "Shakespeare's Analogical Scene: *Romeo and Juliet*" (1984).
5. Colie, p. 162. As Colie mentions, an analogue for this kind of image might be Petrarch's
   sonnet 131, "where the rose blooms against the snow and, after its brief life, cannot be
   revived."

which he exits. Closing this scene, the exchanges among the servants in their puns and querulousness recapitulate the exchanges among the servants in Act I, Scene i; wordplay on the sound of silver repeats a motif in one of Romeo's early lines ("How silver-sweet sound lovers' tongues by night" [II.ii.166]); and the musicians exit on a commonplace note ("we'll in here, tarry for the mourners, and stay dinner" [lines 140–41]) similar to the one on which the lovesick Romeo entered the play ("Where shall we dine?" [I.i. 171]). Finally, from line 76 on, Act IV, Scene v becomes insistently proverbial, and like Act II, Scene iii, it represents a predictable world which can accommodate even an apparent tragedy in its routine.

As the citizens of that world leave the stage, Romeo enters at the beginning of Act V, Scene i. He continues to speak the familiar language of love poetry: love sits enthroned in his heart (line 3); he has dreamed about his beloved's wondrous lips (line 8); and love savors of its customary sweetness (line 10). In addition, the concept of dream which governs Romeo's opening lines in this scene is a variation on two well-known Petrarchan topoi: "the reunion with the dead beloved in a dream," and dreaming of the beloved only to awaken to disappointment.[6] Yet, although Romeo's images and dream belong to a conventional pattern, his formulation of his experience is new. This speech testifies to reflection: Romeo has been thinking about the dream and his "unaccustomed spirit" all day (line 4), conscious that the dream may be deceptive ("If I may trust the flattering truth of sleep" [line 1]), and that it contains contradictions ("[Strange dream that gives a dead man leave to think!]" [line 7]). In the conversation with Balthasar that follows, traditional conceits appear fleetingly; hence, Romeo looks to his man like a typical distraught lover: "Your looks are pale and wild" (line 28). Most fascinating, however, Romeo's monologue about the apothecary transforms Petrarchan images to decorate the squalid shop. In Brooke's poem, this description from lines 2569–70, p. 352, includes only a few boxes and small show of wares. Romeo's more detailed account turns beast similes and the widely used conceit of the hooked fish into "a tortoise hung, / An alligator stuffed, and other skins / Of ill-shaped fishes" (lines 42–44); and flowers deteriorate into "musty seeds, / . . . . and old cakes of roses" (lines 46–47). As Romeo pictures for the apothecary the kind of death he plans, he works a military conceit as well as the birth/death, womb/tomb motif which became conspicuous by the end of Act I, Scene v, lines 135, 140: "that the trunk may be discharged of breath / As violently as hasty powder fired / Doth hurry

6. Forster, p. 59; John, p. 82. Earl, 111–12, cites this variation on Petrarchan topoi.

from the fatal cannon's womb" (lines 63–65). When he sketches the apothecary himself, Romeo draws a bleak caricature of the suffering lover: unkempt, pale, lean, and "full of wretchedness" (lines 68–71).

Before the plot begins to unravel in Act V, Scene iii, the conventions of amatory poetry cluster together around the young lovers in the tragedy. Paris appears, as the scene opens, in the posture of the lovelorn gallant with flowers, torch, and a penchant for solitude: "I would not be seen" (line 2). He addresses the drugged Juliet in a vow expressed as a sestet and woven from Petrarchan topoi that have occurred frequently in the play:

> Sweet flower, with flowers thy bridal bed I strew
> (O woe! thy canopy is dust and stones)
> Which with sweet water nightly I will dew;
> Or, wanting that, with tears distilled by moans.
> The obsequies that I for thee will keep
> Nightly shall be to strew thy grave and weep.
> (lines 12–17)

His next lines incorporate "true love's rite" and a plea, "Muffle me, night, awhile" (lines 20–21). When Romeo enters, he echoes Paris's wish for solitude: "Whate'er thou hearest or seest, stand all aloof / And do not interrupt me in my course" (lines 26–27); he also calls to mind his own hyperbolic expressions earlier in the tragedy:

> By heaven, I will tear thee joint by joint
> And strew this hungry churchyard with thy limbs.
> The time and my intents are savage-wild,
> More fierce and more inexorable far
> Than empty tigers or the roaring sea.
> (lines 35–39)

The confrontation between Romeo and Paris—Shakespeare's invention—shares both its violence and some of its crucial lines with previous scenes (compare, for instance, "By heaven, I love thee better than myself" [line 64], with "love thee better than thou canst devise / . . . good Capulet, whose name I tender / As dearly as mine own" [III.i.68–71]). Further, Romeo's final speech gathers together several key Petrarchan motifs: the nautical image (lines 76, 116–18), dream (line 79), madness (line 80), light (lines 84–86; "feasting presence" works as an obvious ironic reminder of Act I, Scene v), and canker (line 109); and it incorporates a short *blason*: "honey of thy breath" (line 92), "Beauty's ensign yet / Is crimson in thy lips and in thy cheeks" (lines 94–95). With a combination of tropes—"the yoke of inauspicious stars" (line 111), "this world-wearied flesh" (line 112)—Romeo delivers his last vision of the shackled and suffering lover.

In his most recent discussion of *Romeo and Juliet*, G. R. Hibbard notices one of the Petrarchan passages which occurs in an unexpected context (III.v.129–37):

> But what is it doing in the mouth of Old Capulet? A possible explanation is that it is quite simply an artistic lapse: that Shakespeare has forgotten for the moment about the idiom he has devised for the old man, and has allowed his interest in the tradition of love poetry and his fondness for figures to get the better of his sense of dramatic fitness. On the other hand, it might be argued that Capulet's resort to this manner of speech is intended as a signal to the audience indicating that his concern for Juliet, though genuine enough in its own way, is essentially shallow. . . . I incline to the first explanation.[7]

Perhaps in *Romeo and Juliet* Shakespeare the apprentice dramatist loses something with his virtuoso performance as a poet. Stretching the sonnet idiom to make it serve even comic rant and aphorism, he now and again risks effective characterization. To experiment with the dramatic possibilities of the Petrarchan mode, he sometimes chances the very pace of the action and intensity of emotion. But in the end, it seems to me, verbal brilliance in *Romeo and Juliet* achieves more than it loses. It invigorates convention in the way Shakespeare's sonnets do: "What they show is a blending of new and old, the new *in* the old, and the new growing through the old";[8] and it makes that convention work for a new kind of genre, the tragedy of love, with literary sophistication that tempers sentiment and shapes it into art.

LLOYD DAVIS

"Death-Marked Love": Desire and Presence in *Romeo and Juliet*[†]

I

The action of *Romeo and Juliet* occurs between two speeches proclaiming the lovers' deaths—the prologue's forecast of events and the prince's closing summary. The vicissitudes of desire take place

7. G. R. Hibbard, *The Making of Shakespeare's Dramatic Poetry* (Toronto: Univ. of Toronto Press, 1981), pp. 131–32. (Another recent—and a somewhat extreme—study of language in *Romeo and Juliet* is Ralph Berry's in his *The Shakespearean Metaphor: Studies in Language and Form* [Totowa, N.J.: Rowman & Littlefield, 1978], pp. 37–47. See also the Arden edition of *Romeo and Juliet* by Brian Gibbons [London: Methuen, 1980], pp. 42–52.)

8. Patrick Cruttwell, *The Shakespearean Moment and Its Place in the Poetry of the Seventeenth Century* (London: Chatto & Windus, 1954), p. 2.

† From *Shakespeare Survey* (1996): 57–67. Copyright © 1996 Cambridge Univrsity Press. Reprinted by permission of Cambridge University Press.

in this unusual period, after life yet before death. It is a kind of liminal phase in which social and personal pressures build to intense pitch before they are settled. Such liminal tension, as Victor Turner suggests, is the very stuff of which social dramas are made.[1] It figures a mounting crisis that envelops those observing and taking part in the unfolding action. At the same time, this temporal setting has a range of interpretative implications.

With the lovers' deaths announced from the start, audience attention is directed to the events' fateful course. The question is less what happens than how it happens. By framing the action in this way, the prologue triggers various generic and narrative effects. First, it establishes the play as 'a tragedy of fate' similar to Kyd's *The Spanish Tragedy*, which gives 'the audience a superior knowledge of the story from the outset, reducing the hero's role to bring into prominence the complex patterns of action'.[2] In turn, this generic marker initiates a compelling narrative, poised between prolepsis and analepsis, as opening portents of death are played off against background details and further intimations in the following scenes.[3] The tension between these hints and flashbacks fills the narrative with foreboding. The breakneck speed of events (in contrast to the extended time frame of Arthur Brooke's version, a few days as opposed to nine months)[4] sees the ordained end bear relentlessly on the lovers. They are caught between a determining past and future.

The narrative has a further generic analogue. Gayle Whittier suggests that the play develops through a contrast between sonnet lyricism and tragedy that is finally reconciled in death: 'the "spoken lines" of the Prologue predestine the plot of the play to be tragic from without, even as the spirit of Petrarchan poetry spoken by Romeo to Juliet finally necessitates their tragic deaths from within'.[5] What first appears as thematic conflict between two of the period's key literary modes makes way for a troubling similarity. The spirit of Petrarchism is revealed as tragically fatal and idealized romance collapses.

In this view, *Romeo and Juliet* stages the outcome of unfulfillable desire. Although it appears to reverse the erotic story told in the Sonnets, the dramatic narrative ends up paralleling the failing course of identity and desire which can be traced through those poems. There the poet reluctantly finds his desire shifting from the self-gratifying potential figured by the youth to the disarming dark lady,

---

1. *Drama, Fields, and Metaphors: Symbolic Action in Human Society* (Ithaca, 1974), pp. 40–1 and *passim*.
2. Brian Gibbons, Introduction, in *Romeo and Juliet* (London, 1980), p. 37.
3. On analepsis and prolepsis, see Shlomith Rimmon-Kenan, *Narrative Fiction: Contemporary Poetics* (London, 1983), pp. 46ff.
4. Gibbons, Introduction, p. 54.
5. Gayle Whittier, 'The Sonnet's Body and the Body Sonnetized in *Romeo and Juliet*', *Shakespeare Quarterly*, 40 (1989), 27–41; p. 40.

who offers instead 'a desire that her very presence at the same time will frustrate'.[6] This pattern initially seems to be inverted in the play—Romeo willingly renounces self-centred longing for Rosaline, Juliet tests and proves her self-reliance, both find true love in each other. However, their love ends in reciprocal death, with the Petrarchan images fatally embodied and materialized. The links between love and death unveil a dark scepticism about desire, despite bursts of romantic idealism. They convey a sense of futility and ironic fate which Romeo momentarily feels but is able to forget for a time, 'my mind misgives / Some consequence yet hanging in the stars / Shall bitterly begin his fearful date / With this night's revels' (1.4.106–9).

Such scepticism appears in many subsequent literary and psychoanalytic conceptions, where possibilities of romantic union are queried.[7] These questions carry implications about selfhood and desire and about ways of representing them. In theories and stories of divorce or isolation, selfhood is not effaced but conceived as incomplete; as Barbara Freedman puts it, 'The denial of self-presence doesn't negate presence but redefines it as a distancing or spacing we always seek but fail to close'.[8] Characters cannot attain their goals, and the inability to claim satisfaction affects desire as much as selfhood. Proceeding from an uncertain source, desire remains 'predicated on lack, and even its apparent fulfilment is also a moment of loss'.[9] In this view, desire and presence are forever intertwined: 'Differantiated [sic] presence, which is always and inevitably differed and deferred, and which in consequence exceeds the alternatives of presence and absence, is the condition of desire'.[1] They forestall each other's wholeness yet continue to provide the self with images of consummation, contentment and victory—the curtsies, kisses, suits, livings and battles which Mercutio's dreamers envisage but cannot clasp, 'Begot of nothing but vain fantasy, / Which is as thin of substance as the air, / And more inconstant than the wind' (1.4.98–100).

6. Joel Fineman, *Shakespeare's Perjured Eye: The Invention of Poetic Subjectivity in the Sonnets* (Berkeley, 1986), p. 24.
7. Two of the primary psychoanalytic texts are *Civilization and Its Discontents*, and *Beyond the Pleasure Principle*. A clear reading of this direction in Freud is offered by Jean Laplanche, *Life and Death in Psychoanalysis*, trans. Jeffrey Mehlman (Baltimore, 1976): 'the death drive is the very soul, the constitutive principle of libidinal circulation' (p. 124). Related scepticism underlies Lacan's view of the link between desire and demand. Desire is dependent on demand, but demand, 'by being articulated in signifies, leaves a metonymic remainder that runs under it . . . an element that is called desire': desire leads only to desire. See *The Four Fundamental Concepts of Psycho-Analysis*, trans. Alan Sheridan (New York, 1981), p. 154; compare Catherine Betsey's gloss of Lacan's view—'desire subsists in what eludes both vision and representation, in what exceeds demand, including the demand for love'—in *Desire: Love Stories in Western Culture* (Oxford, 1994), p. 139.
8. *Staging the Gaze: Postmodernism, Psychoanalysis, and Shakespearean Comedy* (Ithaca, 1991), p. 110.
9. Belsey, *Desire*, pp. 38–9.
1. Ibid., p. 70.

The recurrence of this viewpoint in fiction and theory suggests that *Romeo and Juliet* stages a paradigmatic conflict between ways of representing and interpreting desire. The play affects these possibilities by placing idealized and tragic conceptions of desire and selfhood in intense dialogue with each other. This dialogue continues to be played out in literary and theoretical texts since, as Alan Sinfield notes, notions of sexuality and gender are 'major sites of ideological production upon which meanings of very diverse kinds are established and contested'.[2] *Romeo and Juliet* informs and illustrates a cultural history of desire in which images of romantic fulfilment or failure carry great importance.

As well as being part of this history, Shakespeare's play has two other distinctive temporal features. First, as noted above, it unfolds over a charged time span. Time allows desire to be acted out but also threatens its fulfilment, by either running out or not stopping. This equivocal link affects desire's tragic course in *Romeo and Juliet*, 'as the time and place / Doth make against' the characters (5.3.223–4).

Secondly, its depiction of desire reverberates with erotic tropes from earlier traditions—Platonic, Ovidian, Petrarchan, as well as popular sayings. These tropes are used by the characters to talk and think about relationships, but they are also challenged for not allowing the gap between self and other to be bridged. They are unfulfilling since it feels as if they belong to someone else; as Astrophil puts it, 'others' feet still seemed but strangers in my way'.[3] The lovers are often dissatisfied with or unsure about the words of others. Their discontent grows from early dismissals such as Romeo's 'Yet tell me not, for I have heard it all' (1.1.171) and 'Thou talk'st of nothing' (1.4.96), or Juliet's 'And stint thou, too, I pray thee, Nurse' (1.3.60), to deeper disquiet over the inability of this language to match their experience: 'Thou canst not speak of that thou dost not feel' (3.3.64); 'Some say the lark makes sweet division; / This doth not so, for she divideth us' (3.5.29–30). The corollary of their frustration with the language of others and of the past is the value they put on their own: 'She speaks, / O, speak again, bright angel' (2.1.67–8); 'every tongue that speaks / But Romeo's name speaks heavenly eloquence' (3.2.32–3).

Like the lovers, the play also seeks to revise existing rhetorical conventions. It reworks these tropes into personal, tragic terms which underlie later literary and psychological conceptions. Hence, in addition to exemplifying Stephen Greenblatt's point that

---

2. *Faultlines: Cultural Materialism and the Politics of Dissident Reading* (Oxford, 1992), p. 128.

3. *Sir Philip Sidney: Selected Poems*, ed. Katherine Duncan-Jones (Oxford, 1973), p. 117. As discussed below, this first sonnet's turn to a seemingly authentic self is also made in *Romeo and Juliet*.

'psychoanalysis is the historical outcome of certain characteristic Renaissance strategies',[4] *Romeo and Juliet* shows that these strategies develop in response to earlier discourses. The play's pivotal role in later depictions of desire stems from the way it juxtaposes historical and emergent conceptions.

These complex temporal and rhetorical effects are hinted at in the Prologue, which repeatedly sets past, present and future against each other. 'Our scene' is initially laid in a kind of continuous present, yet one that remains hanging between 'ancient grudge' and 'new mutiny'. Likewise, the 'star-crossed lovers take their life' in a present whose intimations of living and loving are circumscribed by 'the fatal loins' of 'their parents' strife'. As the birth-suicide pun on 'take their life' hints, sexuality is already marked by violence and death, its future determined by the past's impact on the present. The Prologue ends by anchoring the staging of 'death-marked love' in the here and now of the audience, who attend 'the two-hours' traffic of our stage'. It anticipates a successful theatrical conclusion, with the play's performance 'striv[ing] to mend' what the lovers 'shall miss'—a kind of closure that their desire cannot realize. In contrast to the simple linear Chorus to Act 2, which culminates in the lovers' union, the rebounding moments of the Prologue displace consummation with death.[5]

A complicity between sex and death is well known in Renaissance texts. Its function in *Romeo and Juliet* is, however, distinguished by temporal shifts which define the characters' relations. While the lovers in a poem such as Donne's 'The Canonization' exceed worldly time and place, and their post-coital condition is eternally celebrated, in Shakespeare's play the links between past and present, social and personal, cannot be transcended. The intense oneness felt by the lovers appears to signify mutual presence, but such intersubjective moments are overlaid with social and historical pressures. The drama alternates between instants of passion, when time seems to stand still, and inevitable returns to the ongoing rush of events. This contrast is manifested not only in the characterization and plot but in the interplay of underlying traditions, sources and tropes. The play reiterates and revises these conventions, confirming a conception of desire that speeds not to its goal but its end. In this conception personal presence can exist only as a transient, illusory sign of desire.

---

4. Stephen Greenblatt, 'Psychoanalysis and Renaissance Culture', in *Literary Theory/ Renaissance Texts*, ed. Patricia Parker and David Quint (Baltimore, 1986), 210–24; p. 224.
5. 'But passion lends them power, time means, to meet, / Tempering extremities with extreme sweet' (2 Chor. 13–14). The Chorus, not included in first Quarto, is reprinted in the Arden edition.

II

One of the main influences *Romeo and Juliet* has had on later depictions of love lies in its celebration of personal desire. The force of
this celebration comes partly from its dramatic mode, staging the
lovers' experiences for a 'live' audience. In the decades after the play
was first performed, poetry (till then, the key romantic discourse)
was changing from oral to written modes. Until the rise of the novel,
drama remained the pre-eminent form for presenting love stories,
and stage performance could give these tales the confessional tones
which earlier forms of poetic recitation doubtless achieved. The Prologue enacts this shift by relocating the love sonnet in the drama, a
move again underlined by the verse which the lovers will soon share
in Act 1, scene 5.

On stage, the impact of the 'personal' can come across in different ways—through physical, verbal, even interpersonal performance.
In *Romeo and Juliet* these forms of presence concentrate in the protagonists' unshakeable love. It seems to assume an essential quality
which captures the 'diachronic unity of the subject'.[6] This unity
underwrites numerous adaptations of and responses to the play,
from elaborate stage productions, operas and ballets, to more popular versions such as the American musical *West-Side Story* or the
Australian narrative verse of C. J. Dennis's *A Sentimental Bloke*,
whose colloquial tones add to the impression of true romance. For
many audience groups, each of these transformations once again discovers the play's 'spirit', which surpasses local differences to reveal
truths about desire and 'ourselves'.

The director's programme notes to a recently well-received production in Australia illustrate this kind of response. The mixed tones
of confession and authority sway the audience to accept his views:

> My fascination with this play continues. Considerable research
> over the years has taken me twice to Verona and Mantua, but
> the conflict in Bosnia has brought the work urgently closer. I
> first considered a Muslim-Christian setting several months
> before the tragedy of Bosko and Admira . . . A study of the text
> supplies no religious, class, nor race barriers between the 'two
> households' and this makes Shakespeare's vision all the more
> powerful. When differences are minimal, ancient grudges seem
> the more difficult to understand. Yet they remain with us today,
> passed on by our parents. It seems the one thing we teach the
> next generation is how to maintain rage and other forms of prej-
> udices. Thus this work is as much about young people in the

6. Catherine Belsey, *The Subject of Tragedy: Identity and Difference in Renaissance Drama*
(London, 1985), p. 34.

Brisbane Mall today as it is about the hot days in medieval Verona . . . The human spirit, as portrayed by the 31 year old playwright, is a thing of wonder to be nurtured and treasured.[7]

The paradoxical effects of citing 'real' personal and political situations are first to detach the drama from its own historical concerns and then to efface the ideological grounds of the current crisis. The revelation of 'human spirit' triumphs over any tragic significance. Indeed, the play's freedom from material contexts testifies to its, its author's, and our affirming 'vision'. This viewpoint recalls Coleridge's claim that Shakespeare is 'out of time', his characters 'at once true to nature, and fragments of the divine mind that drew them'.[8]

Because it hides sexual, class and ethnic factors behind archetypal human experience, this sort of perception of Shakespeare's work becomes a target of materialist criticism:

> Idealised and romanticised out of all dialectical relationship with society, it [Shakespeare's work] takes on the seductive glamour of aestheticism, the sinister and self-destructive beauty of decadent romance . . . this 'Shakespeare myth' functions in contemporary culture as an ideological framework for containing consensus and for sustaining myths of unity, integration and harmony in the cultural superstructures of a divided and fractured society.[9]

In relation to sexual issues, universal images of the personal in *Romeo and Juliet* can be seen as helping to naturalize notions of desire which reinforce an 'ideology of romantic love' in terms of 'heterosexualizing idealization' and the 'canonization of heterosexuality'.[1] Personal romance and desire are revealed as authoritative codes which conceal and impose official sexuality.

The kinds of ideological impacts that the 'personal' registers may be intensified *or* interrogated by the generic effects of 'Excellent conceited Tragedie', as the Quarto titles announce. The combination of personal experience and tragic consequence can turn *Romeo and Juliet* into an account of contradictory notions of desire and identity, in line with Jonathan Dollimore's recognition that, notwithstanding

---

7. Aubrey Mellor, 'From the Artistic Director', in Queensland Theatre Company Program for *Romeo and Juliet* (Brisbane, 1993), p. 3.
8. Samuel Taylor Coleridge, *Lectures on Shakespeare and Other Poets and Dramatists*, Everyman's Library (London: Dent, 1914), p. 410.
9. Graham Holderness, Preface: 'All this', in *The Shakespeare Myth*, ed. Graham Holderness (Manchester, 1988), pp. xii–xiii.
1. See Dympna Callaghan, 'The Ideology of Romantic Love: The Case of *Romeo and Juliet*', in Dympna Callaghan, Lorraine Helms and Jyotsna Singh, *The Weyward Sisters: Shakespeare and Feminist Politics* (Oxford, 1994), pp. 59–101; Jonathan Goldberg, '*Romeo and Juliet's* Open Rs', in *Queering the Renaissance*, ed. Jonathan Goldberg (Durham, 1994), 218–35; p. 227; and Joseph A. Porter, 'Marlowe, Shakespeare, and the Canonization of Heterosexuality', *South Atlantic Quarterly*, 88 (1989), 127–47.

traditions of celebration 'in terms of man's defeated potential', tragedy questions ideological norms.[2] The genre's ambiguous drift to 'radical or cathartic ends sees the play assume a kind of meta-textual disinterestedness, distanced from final interpretations as it seems to reflect on how desire may be conceived and staged. This distance can be observed in the play's citing and reworking of tropes and conventions from existing discourses of love and romance. The intertextual traces reveal continuities and changes in the depiction of desire, keyed to social and historical notions of the personal and interpersonal.

Platonism is traditionally seen as offering a set of tropes that affirm selfhood and desire as forms of true being despite possibilities of loss.[3] In the *Symposium*, for instance, Socrates defines love as desire for what one lacks, either a specific quality or a lost or missing element of the self. Aristophanes goes so far as to image love as a 'longing for and following after [a] primeval wholeness . . . the healing of our disseevered nature'. The *Symposium* deals with this incipiently tragic situation by redirecting desire to the heavens; in a comedic resolution, love's lack is fulfilled by catching sight of 'the very soul of beauty . . . beauty's very self'.[4] Such vision provides the model for Renaissance Petrarchism.

✳   ✳   ✳

Platonic images of true desire and identity are invoked in Shakespeare's comedies during the 1590s; but even there, as characters move to romantic union, they are usually questioned. The disguises, confusions and mistakes through which love's destiny is reached may suggest random or enforced effects that unsettle 'nature's bias'. In a less equivocal way, Shakespeare's use of Ovidian images of desire and selfhood tends to limit or foreclose positive readings, especially where narcissistic traces are discerned. This tendency takes place in both comic and tragic genres: 'Like Ovid's tales, Shakespeare's comedies never lose sight of the painfulness and the potential for the grotesque or for disaster wrought by love's changes . . . If part of the Ovidianism of the comedies is their potential for violence and tragedy, it would seem logical to expect that Ovidianism to be developed in the tragedies'.[5] In *Venus and Adonis*, for example, the humour of the goddess's overweening desire and her beloved's petulance changes to grim consequence. 'The field's chief flower' (line 8) is

2. *Radical Tragedy: Religion, Ideology and Power in the Age of Shakespeare and His Contemporaries* (Chicago, 1984), p. 49.
3. Cf. Michel Foucault, *The Use of Pleasure*, vol. 2 of *The History of Sexuality*, trans. Robert Hurley (New York, 1990), p. 5 and *passim*.
4. *Symposium*, in *The Collected Dialogues of Plato*, ed. Edith Hamilton and Huntington Cairns (Princeton, 1985), 193a–c, 211d–e.
5. Jonathan Bate, *Shakespeare and Ovid* (Oxford, 1993), p. 173. Bate emphasizes Actaeon as another figure of self-consuming desire (p. 19 and *passim*).

mournfully plucked, recalling Narcissus's end, 'A purple flower
sprung up, chequered with white, / Resembling well his pale cheeks,
and the blood / Which in round drops upon their whiteness stood'
(lines 1168–70). The characters have shared an ironic desire whose
deathly goal was unwittingly imaged by Venus, 'Narcissus so himself
himself forsook, / And died to kiss his shadow in the brook' (lines 161–
2). As noted earlier, comparable effects occur throughout *Romeo
and Juliet*, where moments of romantic union are disrupted by ongoing events that undercut their idealism. The mixed genres in these
tales represent desire as a hybrid of the comic, tragic and ironic.[6]

Related images of threatening or incomplete desire and self-
transformation are repeated through many sixteenth- and seventeenth-
century texts, from the angst of sonneteers to Montaigne's musings
in the *Apologie of Raymond Sebond* on 'The lustfull longing which
allures us to the acquaintance of women, [and] seekes but to expell
that paine, which an earnest and burning desire doth possesse-us-
with, and desireth but to allay it thereby to come to rest, and be
exempted from this fever'.[7] As most of these references suggest,
this notion of erotic jeopardy is almost always tied to masculine
conceptions of desire and selfhood. The pains of desire are indulged
if not celebrated, and they may convert to misogyny, as in Hamlet's
tirade against Ophelia or Romeo's charge that Juliet's beauty 'hath
made me effeminate' (3.1.114).

This attitude echoes through Romeo's early laments about Rosaline. As Coleridge noted, he is 'introduced already love-bewildered':[8] 'I
have lost myself. I am not here. / This is not Romeo; he's some other
where' (1.1.194–5). Amid these tones of despair a self-satisfied note
can be heard. The early Romeo is a 'virtual stereotype of the romantic
lover',[9] whose role-playing brings a kind of egotistic reassurance. The
lament for self-loss becomes proof of self-presence, a 'boastful positiveness',[1] with Romeo still to know the unsettling force of desire.

From this point, the play proceeds by exploring the limits of the
Platonic, Ovidian and Petrarchan tropes. The seriousness of narcissistic absorption is questioned (underlined by Mercutio's quips at
romantic indulgence);[2] yet the full consequence of desire is not realized in Platonic union but deferred to its aftermath. None of the

---

6. Cf. George Bataille's conceptions of eros as 'laughable', tragic and 'arousing irony', and
   of 'The complicity of the tragic—which is the basis of death—with sexual pleasure and
   laughter': *The Tears of Eros*, trans. Peter Connor (San Francisco, 1990), pp. 53 and 66.
7. Michel de Montaigne, *Essays*, trans. John Florio (London, 1980), vol. 2, pp. 192–3.
8. Coleridge, *Lectures*, p. 103.
9. Harry Levin, 'Form and Formality in *Romeo and Juliet*', in *Twentieth-Century Interpretations of 'Romeo and Juliet': A Collection of Critical Essays*, ed. Douglas Cole (Englewood Cliffs, N.J., 1970), 85–95; p. 86.
1. Coleridge, *Lectures*, p. 103.
2. Joseph A. Porter emphasizes that Mercutio's opposition is to romantic love not to sex:
   Shakespeare's Mercutio: His History and Drama (Chapel Hill, 1988), p. 103.

conventional models can quite convey what is at stake in the lovers' story, and the discourse of desire must be revised.

III

Clearly, then, *Romeo and Juliet* invents neither tragic nor personal notions of desire. Both are strongly at work in Shakespeare's direct source, Brooke's *The Tragicall Historye of Romeus and Juliet* (1562): the threats to selfhood caused by love; the workings of 'False Fortune' and 'wavering Fortunes whele'; an intense desire that can be quenched 'onely [by] death and both theyr bloods'; time as tragic and ironic, first intimated in woe at Juliet's 'untimely death' and then gaining full significance as Romeus's man tells him 'too soone' of her end.[3]

While it reiterates these ideas, Shakespeare's play also develops and sharpens the connections among desire, the personal and the tragic. The lovers create new images of individuality and of togetherness in order to leave their worldly selves behind. Yet their efforts remain circumscribed by social forces. The ironic result is that the ideal identities the lovers fashion in order to realize their desire become the key to its tragic loss. Self-transcendence can be experienced but not as a kind of timeless ecstasy; instead it becomes entwined with unfulfilled desire.

The play personalizes desire in ways which constantly alternate between idealism and failure. As Kay Stockholder notes, threats to desire are 'externalized' and the lovers consciously create 'a radiant world apart by attributing all inimical forces to surrounding circumstance'.[4] In this reordering of reality, desire becomes part or even constitutive of private, individual identity. Romeo and Juliet's love is secret from others and transgresses the roles imposed by their families. In *The Petite Pallace of Pettie his Pleasure* (1576), George Pettie considered this opposition the key to the story: 'such presiness of parents brought Pyramus and Thisbe to a woful end, Romeo and Julietta to untimely death'.[5] In *A Midsummer Night's Dream and Romeo and Juliet*, resisting or contesting patriarchal authority allows a temporary move towards selfhood.

Through this contest, love appears to be one's own, yet both plays show the impossibility of holding onto it. The personal is as elusive as it is idealized, destined to slip back into constraining and distorting social forms. In retrospect, we may see this elusiveness prefigured

3. Geoffrey Bullough, *Narrative and Dramatic Sounds of Shakespeare*, vol. 1 (London, 1966), lines 114, 210, 935. 2420 and 2532.
4. Kay Stockholder, *Dream Works: Lovers and Families in Shakespeare's Plays* (Toronto, 1987), p. 30. In *Love's Argument: Gender Relations in Shakespeare* (Chapel Hill, 1984), Marianne Novy sees that the lovers' private world crystallizes in the aubade of Act 2, scene 1 (p. 108).
5. Bullough, *Sources*, vol. 1, p. 374.

in the lovers' first meeting, an intense bonding that occurs amid an elaborate ritual of masks and misrecognition. The symbolic means through which love must be expressed will prevent its consummation.[6] For the moment, however, love beholds a single object of desire, whose truth authenticates the lover and recreates both their identities: 'Deny thy father and refuse thy name, / Or if thou wilt not, be but sworn my love, / And I'll no longer be a Capulet . . . Call me but love and I'll be new baptized. / Henceforth I never will be Romeo' (2.1.70–93).

The nexus between identity and desire is strengthened by the need for secrecy. Hidden and equivocated as the lovers move between private and public realms, secret desire endows selfhood with interiority and intention. It grants a depth of character, and even if its longings are not fulfilled inner experience is confirmed. Juliet's cryptic replies to her mother's attack on Romeo reveal private pleasure couched in pain: 'O, how my heart abhors / To hear him named and cannot come to him / To wreak the love I bore my cousin / Upon his body that hath slaughtered him!' (3.5.99–102). Like secret desire, the obstacles to fulfilment sharpen internal experience and give it a kind of sensuous reality: 'runaways' eyes may wink, and Romeo / Leap to these arms untalked of and unseen. / Lovers can see to do their amorous rites / By their own beauties' (3.2.6–9).

This deep desire and selfhood develop in terms of intentionality—desire *for* someone, effected through imagination, speech and action. Desire marks the self as agent, and tragic desire portrays the onus of agency. It is felt sharply by Juliet before she takes the friar's potion, 'My dismal scene I needs must act alone' (4.3.19), and by Romeo as he enters the Capulet tomb 'armed against myself' (5.3.65). In this sense, the play's depiction of desire is linked to representations of subjectivity that emerge during the sixteenth century. It reflects the important role that tropes such as the secret, with its social and personal disguises, have in discourses which are starting to inscribe both an inner self and the individual as agent.

Even as it invests in such notions of selfhood, at its most intense desire in *Romeo and Juliet* surpasses individual experience and realizes an intersubjective union. The lovers re-characterize each other as much as themselves: 'Romeo, doff thy name, / And for thy name— which is no part of thee— / Take all myself' (2.1.89–91). Again this effect has generic analogues, as we see the lovers' discourse moving beyond single-voiced Petrarchism. They share exchanges which reveal 'not only the other's confirming response, but also how we find

6. On the interplay among misrecognition, desire and the symbolic, see Catherine Belsey, 'The Name of the Rose in *Romeo and Juliet*', *Yearbook of English Studies*, 23 (1993), 126–42; on the significance of the lovers being masked from each other, see Barbara L. Parker, *A Precious Seeing: Love and Reason in Shakespeare's Plays* (New York, 1987), p. 142.

ourselves in that response'.[7] Unlike contemporary sonnet sequences, which portray the poet by stifling the woman's voice (just as Romeo invokes and silences Rosaline), the play is marked by the lovers' dialogues. This reciprocity is epitomized by the sonnet they co-construct and seal with a kiss at their first meeting (1.5.92–105).[8] It is a highly suggestive moment, capturing the separateness of the lovers' world and speech from others, and also rewriting the dominant 1590s genre for representing desire. The sonnet is re-envoiced as dialogue, its meanings embodied in the climactic kiss. At the same time, the heightened artifice of the scene intimates its transience. The lovers start another sonnet but are interrupted by Juliet's garrulous nurse, who foreshadows the dire interventions of others. A further irony is also implied—as noted earlier, their union will be ended by events that literalize poetic tropes of love and death: Romeo really does die 'with a kiss' (5.3.120), and Juliet falls in eternal sexual embrace, 'O happy dagger, / This is thy sheath! There rust, and let me die' (5.3.168–9).[9]

The deaths verify the Prologue's vision of inescapable ties between sex and violence. Not only can the lovers not escape the eternal feud that frames them, they even play parts in it, responding impulsively, at the threshold of nature and nurture, to news of Mercutio's and Tybalt's deaths. For a moment their union bows under its violent heritage as each impugns the other: 'O sweet Juliet, / Thy beauty hath made me effeminate, / And in my temper softened valour's steel' (3.1.113–15); 'did Romeo's hand shed Tybalt's blood? . . . O serpent heart, hid with a flow'ring face!' (3.2.71–3)

Other characters also link sex and violence, suggesting that the connection has become naturalized and accepted. The Capulet servants joke aggressively about raping and killing the Montague women (1.1.22–4). The friar parallels birth and death, 'The earth, that's nature's mother, is her tomb. / What is her burying grave, that is her womb' (2.3.9–10), and is later echoed by Romeo, who calls the Capulet crypt a 'womb of death' (5.3.45). The friar also connects 'violent delights' to 'violent ends' (2.5.9), and the lovers' suicides suggest a final fusing of love and death. Yet as different interpretations maintain, this fusion's meaning may be tragic, romantic, or both.

---

7. Jessica Benjamin, *The Bonds of Love: Psychoanalysis, Feminism, and the Problem of Domination* (New York, 1988), p. 21.
8. Edward Snow suggests that the sonnet registers 'an intersubjective privacy' that subdues 'sexual difference and social opposition': 'Language and Sexual Difference in *Romeo and Juliet*', in *Shakespeare's 'Rough magic': Renaissance Essays in Honor of C. L. Barber*, ed. Peter Erickson and Coppélia Kahn (Newark, 1985), pp. 168–92; p. 168; Novy contrasts this scene with the sticho-mythic exchange between Juliet and Paris at 4.1.18–38 (*Love's Argument*, p. 108).
9. On the love-death oxymoron, cf. Whittier, 'Sonnet's Body', p. 32.

The lovers are 'consumed and destroyed by the feud' and seem to rise above it, 'united in death'.[1]

The final scene thus accentuates the connections among selfhood, death and desire. It caps off the discourse of tragic desire announced by the Prologue—a tradition of failed love known through numerous European novellas, the second volume of *The Palace of Pleasure* (1567), and two editions of Brooke's *Tragicall Historye* (1562, 1587). The action has thus had a doubly repetitive stamp, not only replaying this oft-told tale but restaging what the Prologue has stated. Foreknowledge of the outcome plays off against moments of romantic and tragic intensity, and triggers a kind of anxious curiosity that waits to see the details of the deaths—the near misses of delayed messages, misread signs, plans gone awry.

Through this repetitive structure, the play affirms precedents and conditions for its own reproduction as if anticipating future responses. Before ending, it even shows these possibilities being realized. The grieving fathers decide to build statues of the lovers, and the prince's final lines look forward to 'more talk of these sad things', in an effort to establish once and for all what desire's tragic end might mean (5.3.306). As Dympna Callaghan observes, the play not only 'perpetuates an already well-known tale', but its closure is predicated on 'the possibility of endless retellings of the story—displacing the lovers' desire onto a perpetual narrative of love'.[2]

Patterns of repetition weave through the play as well as framing it. Characters constantly restate what has previously been staged—in the first scene Benvolio explains how the opening brawl started, and later he recounts details of Mercutio's and Tybalt's deaths and Romeo's involvement; the Chorus to the second act reiterates the lovers' meeting; the Nurse tells Juliet of Tybalt's death; the Capulets and Paris echo each other's lamentations over Juliet's apparent death;[3] and lastly the Friar recaps the whole plot to the other characters after the bodies are found. These instances are part of the effort to explain the violent meaning of events, but as the prince's closing words suggest, something extra needs to be told, 'never was a story of more woe / Than this of Juliet and her Romeo' (5.3.308–9). There is a sense that 'this' version of the story exceeds earlier ones. For all its repetition of tropes and narratives, in closing the play recognizes and stresses a difference from precursors.

1. Coppélia Kahn, 'Coming of Age in Verona', in *The Woman's Part: Feminist Criticism of Shakespeare*, ed. Carolyn Ruth Swift Lenz, Gayle Greene and Carol Thomas Neely (Urbana, 1980), pp. 171–93; p. 186. Marilyn Williamson regards the deaths as alienating rather than uniting, 'Romeo's suicide fulfills a pattern to which Juliet is both necessary and accidental': 'Romeo and Death', *Shakespeare Studies*, 14 (1981), 129–37; p. 132.
2. Callaghan, 'Ideology', p. 61.
3. See Thomas Moisan, 'Rhetoric and the Rehearsal of Death: the "Lamentations" Scene in *Romeo and Juliet*', *Shakespeare Quarterly*, 34 (1983). 389–404.

Other repetitive designs through the play are used to underline the tension between desire and death. Four meetings and kisses shared by Romeo and Juliet structure the romance plot. They are in counterpoint to four violent or potentially violent eruptions that occur between the male characters, especially involving Tybalt. A muted fifth interruption is provided by the presence of Tybalt's corpse in the Capulet crypt where Juliet and Romeo finally meet and miss each other. These turbulent scenes frame the romantic ones, unsettling the lyric and erotic essence which they seem to capture.

The repetitions and retellings connect with the representation of time in the play, imposing a destructive pressure between the weight of social and family history and personal longings. Social and personal time are opposed, and desire is caught between these conflicting time frames. Social time is frequently indexed through the play, in general terms such as the 'ancient grudge' and through the scheduling of specific events such as Capulet's banquet and Juliet's wedding to Paris. Against this scheme, the lovers' meetings seem to dissolve time, making it speed up or, more powerfully, stop and stand still, as the present is transformed into 'the time of love'.[4] The lovers seek to disregard time and death in their union, 'Then love-devouring death do what he dare—It is enough I may but call her mine' (2.5.7–8). Yet this passionate energy also drives the drama to its finale, and Romeo's words link their union and separation with death. The time of love confronts the passing of its own presence.

In various ways, then, *Romeo and Juliet* renovates tragic desire for the Elizabethans and for subsequent periods. In early scenes it evokes a narcissistic poetics of desire as self-loss and death but moves beyond that to stage a dialogic reciprocal presence. The reappearance of death then inscribes ineluctable external influences—the determinations of time and history which frame desire—and the impossible idealization of self and other which passion seeks but fails to find. In this sense, Shakespeare's play marks a complex intersection between historical and emergent discourses of desire. First, in a period when modern institutions of family, marriage and romance are starting to appear, it translates Platonic, Ovidian and Petrarchan tropes of ecstasy and love into personal notions of desire. Next, it conceives desire as the interplay between passion, selfhood and death. And thirdly, its equivocal staging of love's death anticipates the tension between romantic and sceptical visions of desire that runs through many later literary and theoretical works.

It could be said that the play's symbolic bequest to these works is a notion of desire as lost presence. Though love continues to be celebrated as present or absent or present-in-absence in many texts (in

---

4. Julia Kristeva, *Tales of Love*, trans. Leon S. Roudiez (New York, 1987), p. 213.

different ways, Herbert's poetry and Brontë's *Wuthering Heights*
come to mind), a significant line of literary works explores the interplay among desire, death and selfhood. Like *Romeo and Juliet*,
these texts place desire in conflict with time, recounting moments
of ideal presence whose future reveals they could never have been.
This revision of desire begins with Shakespeare's later tragedies—
Hamlet, Othello, Macbeth and *Antony and Cleopatra*—where one
lover survives, though briefly, to feel the other's loss. It runs from
the fallen lovers of *Paradise Lost* ('we are one, / One flesh; to lose
thee were to lose myself' [9.958–9]), to the equivocal pairings at the
end of Dickens's great novels or the images of foreclosed desire in
Henry James's major phase. Its most poignant statement comes at
the close of Scott Fitzgerald's *The Great Gatsby*:

> the green light, the orgiastic future that year by year recedes
> before us. It eluded us then, but that's no matter—to-morrow
> we will run faster, stretch out our arms farther . . . And one fine
> morning—
> So we beat on, boats against the current, borne back cease-
> lessly into the past.

If *Romeo and Juliet* helps to initiate this tradition, it does so as the last
tragedy of desire. For in these later texts the note is of melancholic
rather than tragic loss: what hurts is not that desire ends in death but
that it ends before death. The present then becomes a time for recounting lost desire, and the self's task is to try to hold the story together.
'The subject's centre of gravity is this present synthesis of the past
which we call history', writes Lacan.[5] Like Romeo's last letter, this history reveals the 'course of love' (5.3.286) to those who remain.

WENDY WALL

De-generation: Editions, Offspring, and *Romeo and Juliet*[†]

* * *

It's standard wisdom that *Romeo and Juliet* scrutinizes the power
of family identification in relation to phantasmatic desires and
social anomie. In all early play-texts, the lovers disavow an identity

5. *The Seminar of Jacques Lacan*, Book 1, *Freud's Papers on Technique 1953–1954*, trans. John
Forrester (New York, 1991), p. 36. On literature and psychoanalysis as twin discourses of
mourning and melancholia, see Julia Reinhard Lupton and Kenneth Reinhard, *After
Oedipus: Shakespeare in Psychoanalysis* (Ithaca, 1993), esp. pp. 32–3.
† From *From Performance to Print in Shakespeare's England*, ed. Peter Holland and
Stephen Orgel (Basingstoke: Palgrave Macmillan, 2006), pp. 155–65, 169–70. Reprinted
by permission of Palgrave Macmillan.

grounded in familial origin. 'Denie thy Father, and refuse thy name, / Or if thou wilt not be but sworne my loue, / And il'e no longer be a *Capulet*,' croons Juliet on the balcony, imagining a feverish erotic connection predicated on the repudiation of family ties.[1] Romeo later imagines radically and violently amputating his ancestral marker: 'Ah tell me holy Fryer / In what vile part of this Anatomy / Doth my name lye? Tell me, that I may sacke / The hatefull mansion?'[2] Renouncing the family name while remaking one's self *sui genesis* is the utopian erotic fantasy that ignites and binds the lovers, tied as it is to what Jonathan Goldberg calls a 'powerful utopian sense of an identity that is separable from its verbal representation.'[3] The yearning to be freed from the grip of inherited determination coincides with a craving for liberty from a fixed 'name.' This desire— as well as the intense fear that the possibility arouses—is something that McKerrow would want to put in check so as to reinstate the play, if not its characters, to a rightful and stable lineage; textual progeny, in his paradigm, should bear the imprint and name of the parent text, or else risk being dismissed as having no independent authority.

Yet plotting family relationships between the early texts of *Romeo and Juliet* isn't an easy task. To use McKerrow's approach requires that one identify the genetic trajectory of the play's earliest editions. Since all Folios and seventeenth-century quartos derive ultimately from the quarto published in 1599 by Thomas Creede, it's uncontroversial to establish it—hereafter called Q2—at the head of one family line. Once named as such, Q2's heirs thus become irrelevant because they are impure copies of their superior predecessor. But a baffling situation arises when we turn to the other extant substantive text, the much shorter quarto published in 1597 by John Danter and Edward Allde (Q1). According to McKerrow, we need to know which quarto was set from which. Largely assumed in the eighteenth and nineteenth centuries to demonstrate authorial revision of playscripts, twentieth-century editors explained these double texts by calling forth the story of pirates and forgetful reporters. New bibliographers were quick to argue that Q1 was one of those naughty quartos that degenerated from the family line; it descended through the memory and hands of reporters, actors, and perhaps the playwright

---

1. Shakespeare, *The Most Excellent Tragedy of Romeo and Juliet* (London: John Danter, 1597), D1v. These lines can be found in a modern edition based on the 1599 edition in *Romeo and Juliet*, ed. Levenson, 2.1.77–9.
2. Shakespeare, *The Most Excellent Tragedy of Romeo and Juliet* (London, 1597), G1ᵛ A modern edition based on the 1599 text reads: 'O tell me, Friar, tell me, / In what vile part of this anatomy / Doth my name lodge? Tell me, that I may sack / The hateful mansion' (Levenson, 3.3.104–7).
3. Jonathan Goldberg, 'What? in a names that which we calls Rose: The Desired Texts of *Romeo and Juliet*,' in *Crisis in Editing: Texts of the English Renaissance*, ed. Randall McLeod (New York: AMS Press, Inc., 1988), 190.

Henry Chettle.[4] Because the 'good' Q2 was first advertised as 'corrected and amended,' it is said to supplant a previous corrupt form of
itself. So the later text is really a version of a prior one, and the earlier
one an abridged, reassembled stab at the manuscript on which the
later one is more accurately based. To create a stemma, editors
must posit a chronology that is, on the face of it, *preposterous*, in the
Renaissance use of the term (*prae* meant 'in front of' and *posterus*
'behind'). The 'heir' is really the ancestor; the *seeming* ancestor a
degenerate, something altered in manners and conditions from its
(later) precursor. Such has been the standard story repeated by editors throughout much of the twentieth century.

But even with such an ingenious inversion, editors remain faced
with puzzling arrangements of sequencing, for Q1 cannot be dismissed as a text merely set badly from Q2 in the printshop. Q2
came later than Q1 except in some posited ideal form, a textual
Romeo without a name. More importantly, editors can't simply tell
the story that would, in their schema, solve the textual problem in
expected familial terms. They cannot declare that Q2 was set from
a better source than Q1 altogether and thus that Q2 exists in a completely separate line of descent. Why not? Because at least one long
passage, and perhaps more, from Q2 are lifted directly from the
printed 'bad' quarto, as typographical peculiarities such as italics,
punctuation, and speech prefix abbreviations evidence. Editors agree
that Q2 inherited *something* directly from the physical layout of Q1.[5]
Thus the standard claim is that Q2 was printed from authorial foul
papers or from a promptbook marked up with confusing interlining
and annotation, one that required that the compositor look in places
at Q1 but not when setting the whole text. Q2 thus becomes an odd
descendant re-evaluated as an *ascendant*, a forebear who came after,
and therefore a text both substantive and partially derivative. What
this means is that Q2 is said to come before Q1 in its platonic manuscript form, but to *follow* Q1 in its printed material incarnation.
This theory necessarily makes Q1 a 'tainted' forerunner to Q2 but
only sometimes. According to this line of thinking, both early editions of the play appear to be a little bit bad, a little bit degenerate,

---

4. David Farley-Hills argues that Q1 is a version of Q2 that the troupe adapted for travel-
ing; Hoppe and Irace argue that the Q1 was memorially reconstructed by actors
(Kathleen Irace, *Reforming the 'Bad' Quartos: Performance and Provenance of Six
Shakespearean First Editions* (Newark: University of Delaware Press, 1994); Harry
Hoppe, *The Bad Quarto of 'Romeo and Juliet'* (Ithaca: Cornell University Press, 1948).
John Jowett proposes that Q1 was shaped primarily in the printshop, through Henry
Chettle's interventions. See Jowett, 'Henry Chettle and the First Quarto of *Romeo and
Juliet*,' *Papers of the Bibliographical Society of America*, 92 (1998), 53–74. The best cri-
tique of memorial reconstruction as a theory is launched by Paul Werstine, 'A Century
of "Bad" Shakespeare Quartos,' *Shakespeare Quarterly* 50 (1999), 310–33.
5. Editors agree that one long passage in Q2 was directly set from Q1. In Levenson's edition, this passage is found in Q2 at 1.2.53–1.3.36.

and a little bit original. If Q1 is an edited version of some form of Q2, or, as Goldberg argues, Q2 is an anthology of performance options or a text revised over time, then we have a game of mutual citation and derivation that makes absolute priority impossible to determine. The two quartos simply mutually begat each other in peculiar ways.

Even editors satisfied with the unusual provenance of these quartos don't feel at liberty to declare the second quarto authoritative and move out of the textual quagmire that becomes apparent in editors' accounts. Because of Q2's famous 'false starts' (repetitions that put forth double versions of some of its lines), the text itself seems to be temporally divided internally; it bears within it its own descendant, its fallen shadow. This feature, according to some editors, proves the text's authenticity because it reveals characteristic signs of a messy authorial manuscript complete with first attempts and trial formulations. Such an air-tight, if circular, argument leaves the editor with the prerogative, or rather the imperative, to alter Q2 to make it more singular. One standard way of cleaning it up is by consulting Q1 for a reference point, the very text that standard wisdom accounts a bastard progeny. Whether Q2's superfluity bears signs of authorial revision (as Grace Ioppolo suggests[6]) or simply puts forth a plentitude of performance options (as argued by Goldberg and Steven Urkowitz[7]), its multiplicity eventually presents the problem of the text's relationship to Q1: from what did they descend? Is each relatively corrupt or relatively reliable? And how would such *relatives* be tailored to fit a paradigmatic line of descent? As double step-parents? Incestuously intermingled generations? Kissing cousins?

Since the exact relationship of these texts remains unsure and, to my mind, insoluble, all theories, however informed and researched, must remain speculative. The model of vertical biological generations that tends to underpin editorial practice, however, tends to naturalize knowledge and fails to reflect the doubt at its core. The family model, that is, forces the texts into a reductive paradigm that can't allow for the interconnections between the texts that editors freely admit. What is definite is that two published substantive texts reached readers in the period. An eighteenth-century editor who consulted multiple quartos without being fully assured of which should have the worst seat at the family gathering was hardly as misguided as the new bibliographers assumed. In fact, these early

---

6. Grace Ioppolo, *Revising Shakespeare* (Cambridge, Mass.: Harvard University Press, 1991), 89–93.
7. Goldberg, 'What?'; Steven Urkowitz, 'Two Versions of *Romeo and Juliet* 2.6 and *Merry Wives of Windsor* 5.5.215–45: An Invitation to the Pleasures of Textual/Sexual Di(Per) versity,' in *Elizabethan Theater: Essays in Honor of S. Schoenbaum*, ed. R. B. Parker and S. P. Zitner (Newark: University of Delaware Press, 1996), 222–38.

editors only did freely what modern editors do occasionally and surreptitiously, since current editors emend Q2 sometimes by reference to her estranged sibling who is also her bad parent at moments but not at others.[8] Without disavowing the 'obvious' principle that McKerrow outlined, editors today necessarily have recourse to a synchronic, somewhat confused, family tree, a queer one, one might say, despite a commitment to principles resting elsewhere.

In the *Textual Companion* to the Oxford edition of Shakespeare's works, John Jowett helpfully attempts to map the complicated textual genealogy of the earliest editions of *Romeo and Juliet* in diagram form (see Figure 1).[9] This project involved slotting the texts into a family tree in which generations are expectedly signaled vertically. Stemming from Shakespeare's hypothetical foul papers are two lines of descent, one leading to the prompt book and the other leading to the second quarto. As such, the diagram suggests a clear bond between the author's original draft and Q2, with Q2 begetting three subsequent quarto editions. But the diagram boasts features that indicate how precarious the relationships among the texts remain: dotted lines, broken lines, and question marks indicate uncertainty about various paths of transmission, foregrounding the editor's necessary speculation about the origins and causality, and sometimes indicating a questionable route for Q1's path in particular (that is, the text became corrupted precisely by following the lines that remain provisional, and thus the lines are 'questionable' in many senses of the word). For my purposes, it's striking that the text of Q1 doesn't remain firmly fixed in any one vertically-aligned generation, but occupies instead an in-between position, hovering in the air between generations, as both sibling and parent to Q2. The broken line descending down from Q1 to Q2 points to the 'bad' quarto's odd place as corrupting precisely in its capacity to be generative. Modern editions based on these models are cross-fertilized in ways that make a normative family model hard to maintain.

When Goldberg describes Q1 as the unacknowledged 'legitimating ancestor for any edited *Romeo and Juliet*,' he uses 'ancestor' in a curious and revisionary fashion to indicate its secret prominence for editorial projects disavowing its authority: it's the 'dark specter' haunting an editor's job, a parent text retrospectively nominated as such because *verifying* habits of offspring.[1] As such, Goldberg elasticizes the family model that binds the texts in restrictive ways. His chief assumption, that *Romeo and Juliet*'s textual properties are

8. The Arden edition of *Romeo and Juliet* includes 100 variants from Q1, collated into its copytext of Q2; the Riverside edition includes over 60.
9. Stanley Wells and Gary Taylor, with John Jowett and William Montgomery, *William Shakespeare: A Textual Companion* (Oxford: Clarendon Press, 1987), 288.
1. Goldberg, 'What?' 185.

steeped in issues taken up by the play-texts themselves, is a point that I want to re-elaborate in a different register. How do the texts, taken in their multiplicity, shed light on one familiar—or perhaps I should say familial—phantasmatic, infrastructure of bibliographical practice?

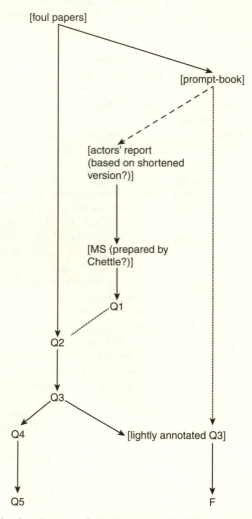

Figure 1 The family tree of the *Romeo and Juliet* text. From *William Shakespeare: A Textual Companion*, by Stanley Wells and Gary Taylor, with John Jowett and William Montgomery (Oxford: Clarendon Press, 1987), p. 288. Reprinted by permission of Oxford University Press.

Ro.:   O teach me how I should forget to thinke.
BEN.:   By giving libertie unto thine eyes/Examine other bewties[2]

If the earliest texts of *Romeo and Juliet* are viewed as what Leah Marcus calls 'troublesome doubles' rather than as parent and progeny, what might critics gain?[3] I explore this inquiry by focusing on the plays' endings, the famed scenes of collective grieving, memorialization, and civic reconciliation that name this tragedy as legendary. In both quartos, surviving families and state work to translate events into a meaningful 'story of woe.' Both endings toy with temporal order, casting a look backwards to grasp and solidify horrific events that then are made contingent on future narrations. But on what do these future representations depend? What inheres in and secures closure? Is the family rehabilitated as a viable institution in Verona, emerging from its pathological tie to fated death? Or do we see staged the feudal family's limitations? Such questions, regularly asked by critics, can't be answered definitively, in part because the earliest play-texts offer subtly different answers. These 'troublesome doubles,' I suggest, trouble at least three issues that arise in criticism of the play: the final authority of the state; the reconciliation of the feud; and the play's famed self-referentiality.

First, let's examine the status of the prince at the end. Declaring everyone chastised, Q2 Prince includes himself in those suffering divine retribution: 'See what a scourge is laide upon your hate?' he asks, 'That heaven finds means to kil your joyes with love; / And I for winking at your discords too / Have lost a brace of kinsmen, all are punisht.[4] 'Eskales,' the character formerly known only as 'prince' in Q1 and identified here only in print, then witnesses the fathers' agreement to join hands and create a collaborative memorial. He responds by separating himself from his ruled subjects (and perhaps from the audience as well): 'Go hence to have more talke of these sad things / Some shall be pardoned, and some punished. For never was a Storie of more wo, / Then this of *Juliet* and her *Romeo*' (M2r). The effect is to have the city-state distinguish itself from within Verona's competitive political scene. The Prince issues directives to the fathers, and emphasizes his juridical role in assigning blame. All are emotionally punished but only some will be singled out for discipline at his discretion. Capulet's and Montague's agreement to reconcile, he implies, isn't tantamount to closure, nor do family heads

2. *The Most Excellent and Lamentable Tragedie, of Romeo and Juliet* (London: Thomas Creede, for Cuthbert Burby, 1599), B2r. This passage appears in Levenson's edition in 1.1.223–4.
3. Leah Marcus, *Unediting the Renaissance: Shakespeare, Marlowe, Milton* (New York: Routledge, 1996), 129.
4. *The Most Excellent and Lamentable Tragedie, of Romeo and Juliet* (London: Thomas Creede, for Cuthbert Burby, 1599), M2r.

have the right to arbitrate the social calamity or to determine the course of events. Whatever their authority in buying conspicuous funeral monuments and attempting to value their children, they need to talk some more and await punishments handed down from on high. The superlative story of woe—however seemingly 'closed' the formal final couplet implies—is still in the process of being shaped.

Now let's turn to Q1 Prince, who draws the families into a collaborative conversation, even while establishing a measure of authority over them. Almost inviting the patriarchs to pitch in and make sense of baffling matters, he exhorts them: 'Come *Capolet*, and come, olde *Montagewe*. / Where are these enemies? See what hate hath done' (K4r).[5] The Prince's directive, 'Come,' is then taken up by Capulet, who imagines a single family unit formed of two enemies. 'Come, brother *Montague*, give me thy hand,' he commands, replicating the Prince's verb in his marriage-like proposal. This repetition aligns state and domestic authorities rhetorically, an effect enhanced by the Prince's closing response to the fathers: '*Come*, let us hence / To have more talke of these sad things. / Some shall be pardoned and some punished' (K4r, my emphasis). Through this formulation ('come' rather than 'go'), the Prince obviously wrests back discursive control from Capulet, but he does so while simultaneously incorporating the families into official deliberations. It is tempting to see the text as offering here a cue for blocking in performance (or, to imagine the text as following the performance, as recording a memorable gesture), one in which the actor playing the Prince puts a hand on each of the patriarch's shoulders and draws them toward him. Whether or not this physical gesture accompanied the text in its earliest productions, the words suggest a mutual joining of authorities rather than an insistent differentiation. Readers of the first quarto or witnesses of any performance of which it is a record see at the finale a weakly united social group, likely to make a muddle out of things just as they have done previously but nevertheless combining forces to reflect upon this exceptional and sorrowful story.

Imagining the texts as non-identical twins complicates readings of any one single play's particular representation of desire, state, and family in the closure. Dympna Callaghan, for instance, maintains that *Romeo and Juliet* enacts an emergent ideology of romantic love that transfers power from feudal family to centralized state. In her reading, the play lauds the seemingly individualized and universalizing eroticism that, in fact, fits the needs of an emergent and oppressive state and nuclear family.[6] Escalus's appropriation of power

5. *An Excellent conceited Tragedie of Romeo and Juliet* (London: John Danter, 1597), K4r.
6. Dympna C. Callaghan, in *The Weyward Sisters: Shakespeare and Feminist Politics*, ed. Dympna C. Callaghan, Lorraine Helms, and Jyotsna Singh (Cambridge, Mass: Blackwell, 1994), 59–101.

from friar and father require a mode of desire severed from the confines of the feudal family. Callaghan's compelling argument, however, only truly pertains to Q2. Since Q1 displays the Prince's collective and weak power, and since it downplays conflict between family and state, no one singular 'play' can be cited as synecdochal evidence of an historical shift in ideology. In fact, choosing Q2 as the basis for an edition or for commentary unwittingly commits one to a text embedded more fully in the ideology that Callaghan helpfully articulates. Reading Q1 along with Q2, however, fractures the confidence of any one single narrative about how the state is presented and allows critics instead to see multiple political and stylistic options available in the 1590s.

The family reconciliation is also inflected differently in the two quartos, as Capulet describes his proffered handshake as a *dowry* in one text, a *jointure* in the other.

> CAP.   Come brother *Mountague* give me thy hand,
> There is my daughters dowry: for now no more
> Can I bestowe on her, thats all I haue.
>
> MOUN.   But I will glue them more, I will erect
> Her statue of pure golde:
> That while *Verona* by that name is knowne.
> There shall no statue of such price be set,
> As that of *Romeos* loued *Iuliet*.
>
> CAP.   As rich shall *Romeo* by his Lady lie,
> Poore Sacrifices to our Enmitie.   (K4r)

In this exchange, Q1 Capulet initiates a penitent handshake with Montague as the marital gift bestowed on his daughter (perhaps because he feels guilty for forcing her marriage to Paris), and he freely describes himself as spent, evacuated ('thats all I haue'). In his formulation, Juliet becomes almost momentarily alive to receive the dowry as it transfers through her to her husband. Montague responds by upping the ante, promising to provide for 'them' (that is, for both children) a durable legacy, a statue to commemorate his son's choice, 'Romeo's loved Juliet.' Montague thus extends, enlarges, and creates symmetry from Capulet's initial tribute. Capulet counters by competitively matching this gift (he does have more, after all, it seems!)—and through this exchange they fashion the story of heroic sacrifice that the statues will commemorate for all eternity, or for as long as Verona is known by its name. The first quarto thus stages a conversation in which Capulet sets the terms of a joint gift, with his new kin Montague supporting and increasing its meaning. They form a tense, rivalrous, and aggrieved but unified front.

In the text with which modern readers are familiar, however, Capulet does not offer a gift to his daughter or to Montague. He instead
broaches the subject of reconciliation by casting it as a 'demand,'
asking his new kin for the groom's guaranteed annuity, the jointure
or lands held in tail for the wife upon her husband's death, expressed
and cancelled as a handshake:

> CAP.   O brother *Mountague*, give me thy hand,
> This is my daughters ioynture, for no more
> Can I demand.

> MOUN.   But I can give thee more,
> For I will raie her statue in pure gold,
> That whiles Verona by that name is knowne,
> There shall be figure at such rate be set,
> As that of true and faithfull *Juliet*.   (M2r)

In this version, it is Montague's bright idea to change the terms
that Capulet offers, replacing an order for 'joining' with a generous
offer to 'give' more than Capulet has sought. In this version Montague is also asked to bestow a gift to Capulet, rather than to their
children. Though Capulet is generous in making the first move
toward harmony, his discourse is pointedly not that of free expenditure; he figures the exchange as a *claim*, an exacting of what is due
to him (for going out a limb to put aside the feud, perhaps). Therefore Montague's response reprimands his new kin for not knowing the properly magnanimous language to use in creating feudal
bonds. The appropriate vocabulary is a freely offered 'gift.' Any
good aristocrat should know this practice. Capulet had, in fact,
acknowledged that he understood the importance of the gift earlier
in the play when he threatened to disinherit Juliet: 'If you be mine,
Ile give you to my frend: / If not, hang, drowne, starve, beg / Dye in
the streetes.'[7] Possession rests, he suggests, in the right to give.
Montague's rebuke for forgetting such a basic point is evident at the
play's end, and Capulet's fierce worry about social standing once
more exposed. Q2 Montague then further embarrasses Capulet by
offering lavish praise for the other patriarch's child, something that
Capulet has not thought to do. Gift giving is pointedly a weighty
social practice carried out between dads, not primarily a legacy for
offspring.

  This textual difference might seem slight, for each passage concerns competitive expenditure, each ratifies the protagonists' marriage after the fact, and each asserts fatherly control in a moment of
grieving chaos. In each, the fathers turn to the task of rehabilitating

---

7. *An Excellent conceited Tragedie of Romeo and Juliet* (London: John Danter, 1597), H1v.
   These lines appear in variant form in 1599; see Levenson's edition, 3.5.191–2.

degenerates, those unruly teens refusing to bear the proper marker of the ancestral mold. Not only have they attempted to shake off their names, but even their deaths form a 'preposterous inversion' of sorts. 'O thou untaught,' exclaims Montague upon hearing of his son's death, 'what manners is in this, / To presse before thy Father to a grave?' (Q1, K3r) For Montague (in both quartos), admittedly shocked with grief, the son's failure to be 'taught,' to take the imprint of family manners, has made him 'degenerate'; Romeo has altered in kind from his predecessor by 'press[ing]' before when he should go behind. The fashioning of artificial statue-children thus allows the fathers to right this inversion and author meaning for the tragedy; it will direct people to memorialize the worth of the lovers by making them reflect and thus become akin again to their families ('poor sacrifices to/of *our* enmity'). The fathers thus hope to control the legacy of a seemingly heir-less family, making it all of one kind once again. But since Q2 makes the story of Capulet's ongoing thwarted attempts to take charge of his world central to this gesture, it foregrounds a serious fissure in patriarchal power and its unifying effects. Q2 Capulet attempts an alliance that will restore to heads of family the authority they have lost. We aren't surprised to witness Capulet's social anxiety in the closing scene. Always nostalgic for a past when he fantasizes himself virile, Capulet has, throughout the play, belied insecurities. He says, for example, that decorum dictates that he invite only 'one or two' friends to his daughter's wedding, since held so soon after Tybalt's funeral, but Falstaff-like, he ups it to six guests in the same speech. Soon he's asking for twenty cooks to prepare a lavish feast with banqueting dishes. Capulet just cannot seem to control his boundless desire to move up in the world.

While keeping firmly in mind the dangers of flattening out contradictions *within* each individual quarto, I think it possible to argue generally that parental, church, and state authority are more lavishly displayed in Q2 than in Q1. Q2 Lady Capulet is imperious to Juliet about marriage as seen in their first exchange where she issues a flat directive about Juliet's future plans ('well thinke of marriage now'). In keeping, Q2 Juliet thinks to be deferential to the Friar when she rushes into church to get married ('good even to my ghostly confessor' she says politely upon entering the room and seeing her beloved with the priest); and Q2 Capulet flaunts control over his daughter to Paris, speaking confidently of her state of mind and issuing 'decrees' to her (Juliet 'will be rulde / In all respects by me nay more I doubt it not', he says[8]). In Q1, by contrast, Lady Capulet solicits

---

8. See *The Most Excellent and Lamentable Tragedie, of Romeo and Juliet* (London: Thomas Creede, for Cuthbert Burby, 1599), B4v, F2r and H2r. These passages can be found in modernized language in Levenson, Q2, 1.3.71; 2.5.21; and 3.4.13–14.

Juliet's opinions about marriage rather than ordering her simply to comply with her parents' wishes; Juliet thinks of the friar only after speaking lovingly to her fiancé in the wedding scene; and Q1 Capulet is hesitant to claim too much knowledge about his daughter to others, even suggesting at key moments that managing Juliet is Lady Capulet's domain. Q2 Capulet's nervous attempt to control the play's resolution thus continues a pattern in this text whereby strategic moves to establish authority are revealed only then to bring about more crisis. Q2 Capulet exits the stage at the end of the play still ferociously preoccupied with orchestrating social networks, and still not quite able to accomplish this task effectively, as Montague pointedly makes clear. Q1 exposes what is at stake in this alternate rendition, in its pointed *lack* of interest in the internal problems of family, in distinguishing personalized foibles, or airing a competition between family and state. It instead highlights the 'gloomie' peace held in place by weak collaborative institutions working on a proper memorialization and course of action.

Yet critics tend to assess, cite, and thus re-produce just one form of the reconciliation in the kinship system. Readings such as Robert Applebaum's astute investigation of the imperfect masculinities dispersed throughout the play, for instance, might find welcome refinement in a comparison of its earliest texts. Applebaum identifies internal contradictions in the play's conception of gender, fissures that expose gender as a system of compulsive desires for which there is no final goal, fulfillment, or escape.[9] He notes how 'the regime of masculinity seems to have a doubleness that is all but insoluable' (252). In his reading, the ending, however, offers Romeo an unproblematic escape out of unstable masculinity. Though dead and unable to enjoy it, Romeo is swallowed into a stable civic order that empties out the problems of gender. Yet the double endings of Q1 and Q2 stage competing ways of imagining homosocial faultlines and failures—one locked in contestatory feudal exchange in which there is one would-be and one knowing elite, the other displaying an indiscriminate rivalrous legacy to be channeled into joint decision making. It is not that there are two competing masculinities that critics such as Applebaum should cite (e.g., some distinct Q1 and Q2 'gendering'). To my mind, the significance lies in the possibilities of optional masculinities circulating through the same materials simultaneously in 1590s performances and/or editions. Criticism attentive to the prosthetic nature of gender and sexuality might thus

9. Robert Applebaum, 'Standing to the Wall': The Pressures of Masculinity in *Romeo and Juliet,' Shakespeare Quarterly*, 48 (1997), 251–72.

usefully be supplemented by an awareness of the incompletion and substitution going on at the level of the text.

Finally, we turn to the fact that the father's strategy for closure rests on managing a *story* of woe and, as such, the ending bears on what Goldberg terms the plays' 'self remarking textuality.'[1] Arthur Brooke's previous poetic account ends by lauding the superlative quality of the built artifact which will memorialize the lovers: 'Ther is no monument / more worthy of the sight: / Then is the tombe of Juliet / and Romeus her Knight.[2] Shakespeare's retelling conspicuously shifts the memorialization so that it rests on discourse, on a *tale*. As Catherine Belsey notes, the play in general 'puts on display the hopeless longing to escape the confines of the signifier, to encounter directly, immediately, the rose that exists beyond its name. And to this extent *Romeo and Juliet* suggests the degree to which the named, differentiated love is always only a stand-in for something which cannot be embraced.[3] Belsey's claim can be refined, split, in a sense, and expanded to take into account the diverse textual forms that constitute but divide the stand-in that we call 'the play.' For instance, Q1's collaborative social structures seem markedly more tolerant of being anchored to plural and diffuse authorities. When the prince seeks to sift evidence, he calls for written documents as well as witnesses. Instead of being given Romeo's single letter as guarantor of the truth, Q1 litters the stage with missives. Q2 Escalus looks to a single letter for proof of the Friar's testimony while Q1 Prince holds in his hand multiple letters that authenticate the story told to him. One version hints at a single written corroborating document; another allows for disparate narratives that nevertheless are confirmed as reliable. In a McKerrow-like vein, Q2 Prince imagines his project as one of establishing proper lineage: 'Seale up the mouth of outrage for a while, / Till we can cleare these ambiguities, / And know their spring, their head, *their true discent.*'[4] What is being verified is a truth with its regrettable downward fall—or descent—into error. For Q2 Prince, uncertainties necessarily signal an unfortunate rupture from origin. But Q1 Prince is not invested in clearing away a degenerative tree of error to find its single ur-root. Instead he uses textual figures to search

---

1. Goldberg uses this phrase to describe a speech by Juliet 'consonant with the play's theatricality' ('What?' 191).

2. Arthur Brooke, *The Tragicall Historie of Romeus and Juliet* (London: Richard Tottel, 1567), fol. 84.

3. Catherine Belsey, 'The Name of the Rose in *Romeo and Juliet*,' in *Critical Essays on Shakespeare's* Romeo and Juliet, ed. Joseph Porter (New York: G. K. Hall, 1997), 79.

4. *The Most Excellent and Lamentable Tragedie, of Romeo and Juliet* (London: Thomas Creede, for Cuthbert Burby, 1599), L4v–M1r, my emphasis. In modernized form in Levenson, 5.3.216–18.

for plural sources: 'Come seale your mouthes of outrage for a while, / And let us seeke to finde the *Authors* out / Of such a hainous and seld seene mischaunce.'[5] The play's acknowledgement of itself—as incomplete, split and a substitution for a story not yet completely ever told—is clear in both versions, but Q1 embraces its multiple and proliferating textual and social authorities.

Certainly both endings return to the issue of the name and worry about the fate of the story. Capulet and Montague's validation of the importance of kinship turns the Prince's juridical findings, so fully played out in his sorting of evidence, comparing of witnesses with documents, and promise of a deliberate ruling, into a memorial. Each father has seen his child 'degenerate'; Romeo has become absent from social life and from himself, while Juliet has rebelliously refused her dynastic responsibility. The fathers' collective response is to rehabilitate the children by creating an orderly artifact representing their offspring. But because they do so by nominating themselves as custodians for a *legend*, their concerns run up against the play's scrutiny of itself as a famed tale clearly extending beyond the confines of any one account or text. Here we find Q2's investment in isolating a single pre-eminent authority undercut by the indeterminacy of the narrative it so fully displays. The two quartos compel a closure that will secure fixed meanings but raise the possibility of incommensurable interpretations. After all, the heirs have remade, in some yet unknowable way, their ancestor-survivors; they have generated a story that bears their imprint as they have pressed before their fathers to the grave. The Prince's shift of attention from the family monument to *discourse* thus appropriately presents a tale in process, one contested and set to be remade in future conversation and one perhaps subject to a generative de-generation. As a person living in the future imagined in these final speeches, I might ask: what is the name that stands in for the legend to be memorialized? *The Excellent conceited Tragedy of Romeo and Juliet* (1597)? Or, as the running titles sometimes say 'the most excellent Tragedie'? Or *The Most Excellent and Lamentable Tragedie of Romeo and Juliet* (1599)?

What is past and what is prologue remain uncertain, not simply within the texts but in the interplay between them. The *Romeo and Juliets* that persist in material form, it seems, resist a clear model of generation; their unstable and plural existence embodies nicely their thematic refusal to secure sovereign power for inheritance and heritage.

* * *

5. *An Excellent conceited Tragedie of Romeo and Juliet* (London: John Danter, 1597), K3r, my emphasis.

JOSEPH A. PORTER

Shakespeare's Mercutio[†]

* * *

Mercutio makes his first appearance in 1.4 with Romeo and Benvolio immediately before the festivities at the Capulet house. Benvolio, who has been Romeo's confidant heretofore, now begins that recession by which he eventually slips unheralded out of the play. Here he has four speeches with a total of thirteen lines, one light chiding addressed to Romeo and then another to Mercutio, and each of the two remaining speeches addressed to both of his companions.[1] Benvolio thus provides a lightly ceremonial and retiring sanction for the most vigorous friendship in the scene. His presence would matter even if he had no lines. The first-person plurals of Romeo and Mercutio include him in their reference, and some of what they say may be understood as partly addressed to him. Even when one of the two main speakers addresses the other by name—"Nay, gentle Romeo, we must have you dance" (1.4.13), "Peace, peace, Mercutio, peace. / Thou talk'st of nothing" (lines 95–96)—still what is said seems to assume Benvolio as audience. Indeed it is of structural significance that the parties to the most highly charged pair-bond never appear alone together, while each does appear alone with Benvolio * * * .

The spirited dialogue of Mercutio and Romeo in scene 4 sets Mercutio's character and continues the characterization of Romeo as it establishes a good deal of the dynamics of their relation for the action to follow. Through the play of witty question, challenge, and response weaves a pattern of answering imperatives—"*Rom.* Give me a torch" (line 11), "*Mer.* Give me a case" (line 29)—and denials—"*Mer.* Nay, gentle Romeo" (line 13), "*Rom.* Nay, that's not so" (line 44)—that, together with the easy movement back and forth between the pronouns of address "thou" and "you," establish an essential equality and even fraternity between the two men.

Within that fraternity substantial differences appear. The basic roles the two men play here in 1.4 and through 2.4, in scenes together and apart, exhibit many traces of Brooke's name's catalysis of the god in Shakespeare's mind. In 1.4 Mercutio, through and under the verbal play, delivers much the same exhortation and offer of assistance as did Mercury to Odysseus and to Aeneas: end your infatuation.

---

† From *Shakespeare's Mercutio: His History and Drama* (Chapel Hill: University of North Carolina Press, 1988), pp. 102–13. Reprinted by permission of the author.
1. The first speech generally given to Benvolio may in fact be Mercutio's. The speech acts involved, the diction, and the scorn make it sound more like Mercutio.

The resonance with Virgil's Mercury in particular is amplified by the "Rome" in Romeo, and fainter Trojan-Roman overtones sound in the names Paris and Juliet (see Cheney, "*Romei*").

These basic roles for the two friends mean that, through the badinage, Mercutio is essentially active and Romeo reactive or passive. Mercutio's exhortation, "be rough with love" (line 27), his essential one and his weightiest here despite its contextual wit, embodies the hortatory mode characteristic here and below of Mercutio's address to his friend. Playful as these direct or indirect exhortations are— "Nay, gentle Romeo, we must have you dance" (line 13); "borrow Cupid's wings / And soar with them above a common bound" (lines 17–18); "Prick love for pricking" (line 28); "Take our good meaning" (line 46)—and each perhaps of negligible importance alone, together they contribute an urgent pressure to everything Mercutio says. Romeo by contrast characteristically replies that he is unable to comply with his friend's exhortations—he won't dance, don't ask him—and his most urgent words, "Peace, peace, Mercutio, peace" (line 95), urge not action but its cessation.

Mercutio himself is rough with love in this scene, virtually equating it with excrement (line 42). Here as later his opposition is only to love and not at all to sexuality, he being one of Shakespeare's most engagingly bawdy characters. The servingmen at the beginning of 1.1 have engaged in some rough bawdy, and in 1.3 the Nurse has introduced a lighter touch of bawdy into the female conversation, but the conversation between Romeo and Benvolio before 1.4 has been chaste as the fair Rosaline, with indeed only a single direct reference to sexuality despite the fact that nearly all their talk is of young women.[2] But here, in reply to Romeo's "Under love's heavy burden do I sink" (line 22), Mercutio begins to administer the moly of bawdy: "And, to sink in it, should you burden love—/ Too great oppression for a tender thing" (lines 23–24). Mercutio continues with the bawdy language here and in the next two scenes, making it usually, as in its introduction, a kind of witty play into which he has some success drawing both his friends.

Another of Mercutio's salient characteristics, named memorably twice after his death (3.1.120, 163) but apparent almost from his first words, is a certain impatient scornfulness. In 1.4 it shows in his dismissive "What care I / What curious eye doth quote deformities?" (lines 30–31) and in the irreverence of his talk about love. There is an air of dismissal also about Mercutio's change of subject at line 29.

2. Rosaline will not be besieged by loving terms nor assailed by eyes, "Nor ope her lap to saint-seducing gold" (1.1.212). While not bawdy, the line is enough of a surprise for Gibbons (p. 93n) to comment at length, and not altogether persuasively, when he suggests that "we may suppose his [Romeo's] immaturity has allowed the conceit to get out of hand."

Soon after the three companions enter, discussing the speech they will not have delivered, Romeo brings the conversation around to his own love, the subject of his and Mercutio's first wit-sally. Then at line 29, in the middle of one of his own speeches, Mercutio in effect concludes discussion of Romeo's lovesickness by asking for a visor. Benvolio seconds the change of subject (lines 33–34), but Romeo must talk more of his distress, whereupon Mercutio delivers a light rebuke, "Tut" (line 40), and a particularly unattractive figure for Romeo's predicament (lines 40–43).

Roughly the middle third of the scene consists of Mercutio's longest single speech, a key one for his characterization as is generally acknowledged. It is also a key for some of the significances to be developed here. I return to it in the following pages, but some initial points may be made immediately.

Inasmuch as the Queen Mab speech is prompted by Romeo's mention of his dream and is itself both about dreams and dreamlike, it may be that behind the fairies' midwife stands the classical deliverer of dreams. Inasmuch as this uncanny speech seems to catch everyone including the speaker unaware, it may be that what we have is a kind of possession of Mercutio by the god. Or, to put the matter differently, it may be that here the god looms through the man. If so, the face he presents is more disturbing than in the first part of the scene. And in the chill forebodings that darken the end of the scene there may be traces of Mercury's role as psychopomp. Indeed parts of the speech itself may come from beyond the grave inasmuch as Shakespeare seems possibly to have added to it after writing Mercutio's death.

The first touch of foreboding appears in the interchange leading into the speech, where Romeo gives his undisclosed dream as the reason " 'tis no wit" to go to the masque. There may be a touch of disdainful fastidiousness in Mercutio's "Why, may one ask?" (line 49), an interrogative embedded in an interrogative, with the distance and formality of the pronoun echoing similar qualities in the "sir" five lines earlier. The half-line with which Mercutio checks Romeo's recounting of his dream, "And so did I [dream]" (line 50), then becomes the more decisive by virtue of its pronoun, as does his next, "That dreamers often lie" (line 51), by virture of its rhyme.

The Queen Mab speech itself is notable as an example of failure to observe several of the conversational maxims that fall under Grice's ("Conversation," pp. 45–46) "cooperative principle": "Make your conversational contribution such as is required, at the stage at which it occurs, by the accepted purpose or direction of the talkexchange in which you are engaged." In particular Mercutio here infringes on the maxims of quality, "Try to make your contribution one that is true," relation, "Be relevant," and manner, "Be brief (avoid unnecessary prolixity)." Mercutio's conspicuous flouting of these maxims raises the possibility of what Grice calls "conversational implicature," the conveyance of unstated information by exploiting infringements of the cooperative principle (pp. 165–72). The possibility seems especially worth considering in the context of talk about what pragmaticists term speaker-meaning (versus utterance-meaning) in Mercutio's "I mean sir" (line 44) and "Take our good meaning" (line 46) with Romeo's follow-up "And we mean" (line 48).

The speech does seem to carry Gricean implicatures that can in principle be worked out. I return to the task below, but already a part of the implicated message has been broached. For Mercutio here is doing what he did less spectacularly above at line 29: he is changing the subject away from Romeo's woes. A part of what the speech implicates, then, would seem to be something like "Please stop crying out loud, for crying out loud," at least in its beginning. As the speech continues, Mercutio seems carried away by it, so that Romeo's interruption (addressing Mercutio by name for the first time, as if to call him to himself) is like the breaking of a rapture. And whatever conversational implicature was present appears lost on Romeo as he says "Thou talk'st of nothing" (line 96).[3]

Mercutio assents "True, I talk of dreams" in a remarkable speech, his last in the scene. Echoes of Mercury appear in the final four lines about the wind as well as in the mention of dreams. The cold hands Shakespeare found in Brooke have here been transmuted into the frozen bosom of the north. There is a bit of an echo of

> O'er ladies' lips, who straight on kisses dream
> Which oft the angry Mab with blisters plagues
> Because their lips with sweetmeats tainted are
> (lines 74–76)

in

> the wind, who woos
> Even now the frozen bosom of the north
> And, being anger'd, puffs away
> (lines 100–102),

---

3. Goldman, *Shakespeare*, p. 37, contrasts "arias" given in company such as the Queen Mab speech with the isolated ones of Romeo and Juliet. One of Queen Mab's accoutrements, incidentally—"Her chariot is an empty hazelnut" (line 59)—carries a reference to the element mercury. "One of the most widespread uses of quicksilver has been to afford protection against the Evil Eye, 'spells' and related misfortunes. . . . A typical example . . . said to have been in practice since the middle ages, is to hollow out the kernel of a hazelnut and replace the contents with quicksilver. The amulet is to be hung around the neck, placed under the bedpillow or under the threshold of the door . . . Hazelnuts . . . are frequently used as adjuvants to quicksilver" (Goldwater, *Mercury*, p. 26). Mercutio returns to the subject of hazelnuts when he tells Benvolio "Thou wilt quarrel with a man for cracking nuts, having no other reason but because thou hast hazel eyes" (3.1.18–20). Hazelnuts are mentioned only once elsewhere in Shakespeare, in conjunction with the only other appearance of the word "hazel" ("hazel-twig," *Shr.* 2.1.255).

which increases Mercutio's association with a dangerous supernatural or inhuman vindictiveness that may itself derive partly from Mercury. And in the entire speech, with its "vain fantasy, / Which is as thin of substance as the air" and of the wind that "puffs away from thence," there is a strong suggestion of Mercury's disappearance after his first meeting with Aeneas ("From lookers eyesight too thinnes he vannished ayrye," Stanyhurst, *Aeneis*, sig. L2v). Well might Romeo's mind misgive some consequence hanging in the stars.

While Mercutio speaks of language or speech rather often, and mentions several specific speech acts, he performs only three speech acts explicitly, as performatives.[4] Two of these, "I tell ye" (2.4.111) and "I warrant" (3.1.100), serve for passing emphasis, but the third receives considerable emphasis itself. This is the conjuring he performs in jest in his second scene, 2.1. There, when Mercutio and Benvolio enter looking for Romeo, and Benvolio urges "Call, good Mercutio" (line 5), Mercutio bursts out with one of his typical verbal extravagances, first naming the act, "Nay, I'll conjure too" (line 6), then performing it inexplicitly, "Romeo! Humours! Madman! Passion! Lover! / Appear thou" (lines 7–8), and then, when the act proves unsuccessful or "unhappy" in Austin's term ("He heareth not, he stirreth not, he moveth not," line 15), naming the act again, "the ape is dead and I must conjure him" (line 16), and performing it again, this time explicitly in a performative:

> I conjure thee by Rosaline's bright eyes,
> By her high forehead . . .
> That . . . thou appear to us.
> (lines 16–21)

Benvolio interjects, "And if he hear thee, thou wilt anger him" (line 22)—and of course the withdrawn Romeo does overhear—and Mercutio in reply names his act thrice more, twice with the same name, "conjur'd" and "conjure," and once with the phrase "My invocation" (lines 26, 29, 27).

As Gibbons points out, with the ritual of conjuration there is a possibly unique conjunction of naming and summoning, the two primary kinds of speech act called calling: "Mercutio burlesques the ritual summoning of a spirit by calling its different names; when the right one is spoken the spirit, it is supposed, will appear and speak" (p. 124n). Hence Mercutio here puts his distinctive stamp, jesting and supernatural, on two of the play's main bodies of speech act.

---

4. By my count Mercutio has fifteen explicit references to speech acts apart from his three performatives. Five are his references to conjuring in 2.1. In addition he mentions asking (1.4.49, 2.1.98), prayer (1.4.87), swearing (1.4.87), challenging and answering (2.4.8, 10), jesting (2.4.63, 65, 78), and calling (3.1.58).

The importance of naming is generally acknowledged, the lovers being star-crossed first and primarily in their names Montague and Capulet,[5] and name-calling acting as a fuse for Verona's disorders. Mercutio's quinquepartite nomenclature of Romeo, then, is a direct anticipation of Juliet's "wherefore art thou Romeo?" of a mere sixty-eight lines later, also overheard by the man in question. But calling as summoning also figures importantly in the play at large, including stage directions;[6] and it figures in the way Juliet's balcony scene answers this scene of Mercutio's. Mercutio's Mercurian message is that Romeo should stay with, or come back to, the world of male comradeship. In 2.1, with that world represented onstage by Mercutio and Benvolio, Romeo overhears Mercutio summon him and does not comply. In 2.2, after overhearing Juliet offer herself to him in apostrophe, he does come forward. The play seems both to authorize and to regret Romeo's choice as its disastrous consequences unfold.

Those consequences seem to be enfolded in the very nature of Mercutio's performative conjuration. In 1.4 Mercutio has already shown himself something of a conjurer as he invokes Queen Mab for his friends. And just as there his "fragile constructions . . . cannot altogether conceal . . . a destructive, arbitrarily malicious 'animus'" (Snow, "Language," p. 191n13), so here a fair amount of aggression is apparent beneath the high jinks. In Benvolio's opinion Mercutio's jesting mention of Rosaline's "quivering thigh, / And the demesnes that there adjacent lie" (lines 19–20) will anger Romeo if he hears. Mercutio, pleading innocuousness in reply, proceeds still further with the bawdy and personal. Romeo does overhear and, so far as we can tell, Benvolio's prediction proves inaccurate, but the scene invites us to consider whether that prediction might not have been more on target had Mercutio made light with Juliet's name instead of with Rosaline's. In any case a flickering Mercurian aggressiveness animates not only Mercutio's references to Rosaline but also his treating the flesh-and-blood Romeo as a spirit to be invoked: "The ape is dead and I must conjure him" (line 16).

---

5. European hereditary surnames manifest a late medieval and Renaissance bourgeois familial impulse opposed to much of what Mercutio represents. The Normans brought the comparatively new practice to England, where the first hereditary English surnames are recorded in the Domesday Book (1086). While much has been written about the history of hereditary familial nomenclature, and about the histories of particular surnames, so far as I know the phenomenological or Foucauldian archaeology that would probe the evolution to any depth has yet to be done. "Arden," incidentally, is one of the earliest English hereditary surnames (Reaney, *Surnames*, p. 302).

6. "*One calls within:* 'Juliet'," 1.5.142 SD.; "*Paris offers to go in and Capulet calls him again,*" 3.4.11 SD. The second appears in Q1 but not in Q2–4, F. The word appears in only eight Shakespearean stage directions, twice in *Romeo* and once in six other plays. The word is frequent in the text of *Romeo*, and summoning with or without the word "call" happens a number of times without stage direction, as at 3.5.64–65.

After the balcony scene[7] and Romeo's morning meeting with Friar Laurence, Mercutio and Benvolio enter at 2.4. Mercutio is still asking where the devil this Romeo should be. Here in particular Mercutio anticipates Hotspur whose scorn of the perfumed lord sent by Henry to demand prisoners (*1 Henry 4* 1.3.45–65) echoes Mercutio's scorn of Tybalt's fighting by the book. When Mercutio has divined that Tybalt's letter to Romeo is a challenge, and Benvolio has opined that Romeo will answer it, Mercutio's "Any man that can write may answer a letter" (line 10) makes a pragmatic joke reprised in Hotspur's witty mistaking of Glendower's boast about calling spirits (*1 Henry 4* 3.1.50–52; see Porter, *Drama*, p. 58). As Gibbons notes, by "answer it" Benvolio means "accept the challenge," while Mercutio pretends to take him to mean "reply to the letter." Mercutio thus adopts as a ploy the behavior Romeo in 1.4 and Benvolio seemingly in the next line exhibit inadvertently toward him; that is, not taking the speaker's good meaning. The good meaning of Mercutio's willful misprision here would seem to be to call Romeo's valor into question, as he does more directly in his next speech (where once again in Mercutio's ominous jesting the lovesick friend has died).[8]

After some seventeen lines of Mercutio's witty denigration of Tybalt's fencing and speech, Romeo enters for the wild-goose chase of wit with Mercutio who, supposing his moly or some other to have cured his friend, ends the sally with a good-hearted congratulatory welcome back into the fraternity, coupled with another of his vigorously unattractive figures for love:

> Why, is not this better now than groaning for love? Now art thou sociable, now art thou Romeo; now art thou what thou art, by art as well as by nature. For this drivelling love is like a great natural that runs lolling up and down to hide his bauble in a hole. (lines 88–93)

---

7. The balcony scene answers the mock conjuration in ways beyond that already noted. The discussion of what to swear by (2.2.107–16) answers Mercutio's talk of conjuring by parts of Rosaline. And, as George Walton Williams has drawn to my attention, Mercutio's mocking "Cry but 'Ay me!'" (2.1.10) is answered by the first words Romeo hears Juliet speak from the balcony, "Ay me" (2.2.25). Nor are the echoes of Mercutio from 2.1 alone. Romeo's apostrophe (lines 26–32) to Juliet as "a winged messenger of heaven" (line 28) not only invokes Mercury as angel but also in imagery and vocabulary strikingly echoes Mercutio's children of an idle brain speech discussed above.

8. How is it we know that Mercutio hasn't really misunderstood Benvolio? Perhaps because assuming he had would entail his seeming more lacking in common sense than we are willing to grant even though Benvolio seems willing to grant it. Mercutio's linkage with writing here and in the Capulet guest list, by the way, evinces a trace of Mercurian graphism. It may be objected that all four young men—the three friends and Tybalt—are linked to written messages on both occasions. However Mercutio alone here uses the word "write," doing so in a sentence without mention of any of the other three men, so that his linkage with writing is stronger than theirs. The situation brings him into the margins of the play's later fateful missives.

The ironies are rich. Far from being cured, Romeo is more deeply in love than before, betrothed, and with arrangements made for the secret marriage. And then far from groaning or driveling, he is inspirited enough by the secret match with Juliet to cry a match (line 70) with Mercutio in the wit-capping. These ironies seem to me to work for the most part to build and enlarge our sympathy for Mercutio in his welcome to Romeo. As we watch the addressee hang back from any immediate reply, while Benvolio interjects "Stop there, stop there" (line 94), on which Mercutio seizes for a bit of largely phallic bawdy wit-capping with him, we may also—depending on how Romeo's silence is performed—feel some rueful sympathy for him in the awkwardness of the moment.

The entrance of the Nurse and Peter in 2.4 provides more silence for Romeo, while Mercutio jests with the Nurse. She stands as something of a female analogue to him, as is generally recognized, and as is suggested in the echo of Mercutio's earlier request for a visor to hide his own visage in his remark to Peter about the fan, "Good Peter, to hide her face, for her fan's the fairer face" (lines 106–7).[9] After the rapid interplay that follows, containing Mercutio's memorable figure for the hour, his mockery of the Nurse's erroneous taking of Romeo's words to her, and his singing, he exits with Benvolio.

There follows the play's most extended discussion of Mercutio's speech, three speeches by Romeo and the Nurse with codas of a kind in Peter's "I saw no man use you at his pleasure" (line 154) and the Nurse's second "Scurvy knave" (line 159). The denigration in what Romeo says,

> A gentleman . . . that loves to hear himself talk, and will speak more in a minute than he will stand to in a month (lines 144–46),

seems designed to smooth ruffled feathers, but it may also contain a grain of truth. The length of the Queen Mab speech, for instance, could be taken as supporting evidence for the first clause, which seems indeed to have been used as a warrant for some performances of the entire role, such as Barrymore's in the 1936 film * * *. Still, Mercutio's pleasure in the wild-goose chase of wit with Romeo seems

9. Gibbons (p. 105n) cites "To see him walk before a lady, and to bear her fan" (*LLL* 4.1.144) for the custom of carrying a fan. In some nineteenth-century productions, as in the silent-film version of 1908, the fan is made oversize for comic effect. Just possibly the fan Venus gives Mercury as a pledge in Peele, *The Araygnement of Paris* (1584), could have figured in Shakespeare's creation of the Nurse's fan. The Nurse and Mercutio are analogous in their bawdiness and fondness for oaths, their serving as advisers to the titular heroes, and even their names, "Angelica" standing to "Mercutio" as "angel" to "Mercury." The parallelism mustn't be pushed too far though. Where Mercutio achieves a kind of apotheosis in his death, the Nurse compromises herself pretty thoroughly in the last half of the play.

as much at his friend's talk as at his own, so that Romeo's slight here may seem unfair and ungenerous.

Romeo's second and more surprising clause exhibits the momentarily pervasive bawdiness Mercutio has left in his wake. Romeo's bawdy seems conscious, and Gibbons assures us that Peter's is also (pp. 152–53n), although I see no reason it has to be. As for the Nurse, while Gibbons is surely right that "she *unintentionally* expresses indecencies through unfortunate choice of words" (p. 147n), he seems inconsistent in rejecting her "And he stand to [anything against me]" from Quarto 1, which could be said as innocently as "suffer every knave to use me at his pleasure." The Nurse has a further bit of unwitting bawdy here that depends directly on Mercutio. The vexation comes from him in her "I am so vexed that every part about me quivers" (lines 158–59), and so too does the bawdy deriving from her unknowing echo of his conjuring by Rosaline's "quivering thigh, / And the demesnes that there adjacent lie" (2.1.19–20). The echo is the more conspicuous given that "quiver" is infrequent in Shakespeare, appearing only once in each of four other plays and *The Rape of Lucrece*.

The Nurse instigates the interchange by asking Mercutio's identity for the second time in the scene. Earlier when she asks the man himself, Romeo replies riddlingly, giving her only the first syllable of the name she asks for, "One . . . that God hath made, himself to mar" (lines 114–15) and she, as if she can almost hear the name herself, repeats "By my troth it is well said; 'for himself to mar'" (line 116). Now, asking again (and again in vain) for the man's identity, she herself uses the syllable, "I pray you, sir, what saucy merchant was this?" (line 142), unwittingly giving Mercutio another light trace of the patron god of merchants.

Mercutio leaves ribaldry aside in his final scene (3.1), but not witty jesting. In his mockery of Benvolio for a quarrelsomeness they both know is more rightly attributable to Mercutio himself, in all his play with Tybalt's name and with his own mortal wound, we see the same sensibility as in his preceding scene, and similar verbal action. There are echoes from earlier scenes as well. The dismissive "What care I / What curious eye doth quote deformities" from his first scene here echoes first in his reply to Benvolio's announcement of the advent of the Capulets, "By my heel, I care not" (line 36) and "Men's eyes were made to look, and let them gaze" (line 53). Mercutio's oath, sworn by a part of his body peculiarly charged by his resonances with Mercury, is a scornful capping of Benvolio's "By my head." Mercutio's next oath, "Zounds" (line 48), is far more impassioned, and with the same oath in his dying words (line 101) he reaches "a peak of tension" (Shirley,

Swearing, p. 101) in a sequence of oaths stretching back through all four of his speaking scenes.

In this last of Mercutio's scenes his speech acts constitute four large movements with an intermission in the middle. After the initial characterization of Benvolio as a quarreler (lines 1–36) comes Mercutio's first interchange with Tybalt (lines 37–58), in which he vents some of the scorn for the man we have seen him express earlier to Benvolio. The fiery Tybalt, as is generally noticed, exercises restraint as Mercutio guys and challenges in speech bristling with imperatives— "Couple," (line 39), "make" (line 40), "look" (line 46), "go" (line 57), and first-person pronouns (lines 39, 45, 46, 47, 54[2], 56)—in twelve lines that, in the context of Mercutio's first twenty-five lines to Benvolio with no imperatives and only four first-person pronouns,[1] manifest the aggressiveness Tybalt brings out in Mercutio.

Mercutio's aggressiveness of course has a strong phallic component deriving from his previous bawdiness and from the play's other sword-phallus linkages, as well as more distantly from Mercury's phallicism. Zeffirelli, as may be remembered, embodies some of this in the staging of Mercutio's "Here's my fiddlestick" * * *. There may even be a subtextual image of the phallic roadside herm in the combination of Mercutio's fiddlestick with Benvolio's "We talk here in the public haunt of men. . . . Here all eyes gaze on us" (lines 49–52) and Mercutio's "Men's eyes were made to look, and let them gaze. / I will not budge for no man's pleasure, I" (lines 53–54).

Pragmatically the most interesting moment in this part of the scene may be the transition from Mercutio's "Could you not take some occasion [for blows] without giving?" (line 43) to Tybalt's reply, "Mercutio, thou consortest with Romeo" (line 44). For one thing, Tybalt here shows that he knows Mercutio by name. More importantly, the force of what he says is open to interpretation to an unusual degree. While he could be answering Mercutio's question indirectly, he could also be returning to the subject of the "word with one of you" (line 38) he requests at the beginning of the interchange; that is, presumably Romeo's whereabouts.

After the intermission of Romeo's appearance and Tybalt's challenge with Romeo's refusal to take it up, Mercutio in his third large pragmatic movement of the scene delivers his disapproval of Romeo's pacifism in the first words he speaks, "O calm, dishonourable, vile submission" (line 72). If they are addressed to Romeo they are

---

1. Line 36, Mercutio's last to Benvolio in the scene's first large movement, "By my heel, I care not," would bring the total of first-person pronouns there up to six if taken as part as that movement; I rather consider it transitional for, while it is addressed to Benvolio, it clearly manifests some of the hostile scorn Tybalt rouses in Mercutio. Line 54, "I will not budge for no man's pleasure, I," with its striking placement of the pronouns and late-as-possible caesura, exhibits some of the tragic and lonely egotism that reappears mutatis mutandis in Coriolanus's ". . . like an eagle in a dovecote, I / Fluttered your Volscians in Corioles. / Alone I did it" (*Cor.* 5.6.113–15).

Mercutio's only words to him in this part of the scene, even though Romeo pleads, "Gentle Mercutio, put thy rapier up" (line 83), and then exhorts both him and Tybalt to forbear and twice calls them both by name. Mercutio ignores his friend, addressing first one challenge and then a longer and more insulting one to the reluctant Tybalt, and then inviting the swordplay to begin.

The first sentence of the fourth and final movement of Mercutio's speech action, "I am hurt" (line 91), has a brevity uncharacteristic of him, which may show his pain or his quickly dawning cognizance of the severity of the wound. And the brevity, together with the naked simplicity of the language and the absence of any vocative indicator, makes the sentence look as if Mercutio may be talking to himself as much as to anyone else.

Immediately—and the immediacy manifests much about the workings of Mercutio's mind here—he addresses Romeo, for the first time since "vile submission," with his malediction. Three more times in the lines that follow, including his final words in the play, Mercutio makes the same transition, from the gravity of his own condition to the curse. The repetition makes the retributive nature of the curse very clear, and Mercutio's uncanniness and access to the supernatural make his curse alone, even without his death, seem to draw down the consequence yet hanging in the stars. After the first utterance of the malediction Mercutio returns to the subject of his wound, now taking cognizance of its mortality, "I am sped." Then in "Is he gone, and hath nothing?" he addresses a third subject to which he also returns, Tybalt.

The initial incredulity of Benvolio and Romeo heightens audience sympathy for Mercutio and may help create an effect of clairvoyance for everything he has said and done in the play. The incredulity may create sympathy for Benvolio and Romeo as well, with its suggestion of a childlike inability to believe the worst. Benvolio's near-quotation, "What, art thou hurt?" in particular may produce that effect, and its intimate pronoun serves as a foil for the relentless new distance in the "you" with which Mercutio addresses Romeo, in the maledictions and also at lines 99, 104, and 105.

Mercutio addresses one further subject in addition to the main ones as he breaks off his fulminations against Tybalt to ask Romeo "why the devil came you between us? I was hurt under your arm" (lines 104–5), recounting the action prescribed in the unusually detailed stage direction *"Tybalt under Romeo's arm thrusts Mercutio in"* (line 89, in Q1 only), and strongly suggesting that Romeo is to blame for Tybalt's blow having hit home. Romeo's reply, "I thought all for the best" (line 106), depending on how it is delivered may have some of the same childlike air as Benvolio's last question. However much or little explanation, excuse, or self-justification is given to the line, it seems addressed to Mercutio, and at least in part an answer to his question. Yet Mercutio seems not to take Romeo's statement as meriting any acknowledgement at all as he addresses his next words to Benvolio by name, "Help me into some house . . . Or I shall faint" (lines 107–8). The meanings of "house" in lines 107 and 108 are so different that the chime, if noticed, may seem the sort of homonymy we routinely ignore. It functions, though, to suggest that such shelter and safety as exists in Verona is in bourgeois familial structures, out of the reach of a figure like Mercutio.

In his last words Mercutio does finally address Romeo, with the curse, followed by an explicit assignment of blame for his death to the Montagues and Capulets—"your houses, / They have made worm's meat of me" (lines 108–9)—a reaffirmation of the mortality of the wound and finally a contracted version of the curse, "Your houses!" (line 110).

WORKS CITED

Cheney, Donald. "Tarquin, Juliet, and Other Romei," *Spenser Studies* 3 (1982), 111–24.
Bach, Kent, and Robert M. Harnish. *Linguistic Communication and Speech Acts* (Cambridge: MIT Press, 1979).
Grice, H. P. "Logic and Conversation," in *Speech Acts*, eds. Peter Cole and Jerry L. Morgan (New York: Seminar, 1975), 41–58.
Shirley, Francis A. *Swearing and Perjury in Shakepeare's Plays* (London: George Allen and Unwin, 1979).
Snow, Edward. "Language and Sexual Difference in *Romeo and Juliet*," in *Shakespeare's "Rough Magic": Renaissance Essays in Honor of C. L. Barber*, eds. Peter Erickson and Coppélia Kahn (Newark: U of Delaware P, 1985), 168–92.

DYMPNA C. CALLAGHAN

The Ideology of Romantic Love: The Case of *Romeo and Juliet*†

"To this end . . . is this tragicall matter written, to describe unto thee a couple of unfortunate lovers, thralling themselves to unhonest desire, neglecting the authority and advice of parents and friends . . ." (Evans, 1057). Thus Arthur Brooke defines the ideological project

† From *The Weyward Sisters: Shakespeare and Feminist Politics*, ed. Dympna Callaghan, Lorraine Helms, and Jyotsna Singh (Cambridge, MA: Blackwell, 1994), pp. 59–62, 71–101. Copyright © Dympna Callaghan, Lorraine Helms and Jyotsna Singh 1994. Reproduced with permission of Blackwell Publishing Ltd.

of his poem, *The Tragicall History of Romeous and Juliet* (1562), which was to become Shakespeare's primary source for *Romeo and Juliet*. The lovers' "unhonest desire" was always a compelling feature of the story, but in Shakespeare's version the fate of that desire is presented as profound injustice as much as proper punishment.[1] For Brooke's rendition of the story bears a moral aversion to what Shakespeare's tragedy accomplishes in producing for posterity the lovers' desire as at once transgressive ("unhonest") and as a new orthodoxy (tragically legitimated). It is precisely this ambivalence that is at the heart of the play's appeal as one of the preeminent cultural documents of love in the West.

Romeo and Juliet was written at the historical moment when the ideologies and institutions of desire—romantic love and the family, which are now for us completely naturalized—were being negotiated. Indeed, the play consolidates a certain formation of desiring subjectivity attendant upon Protestant and especially Puritan ideologies of marriage and the family required by, or least very conducive to the emergent economic formation of, capitalism.[2] The goal of this chapter is to examine the role of *Romeo and Juliet* in the cultural construction of desire. Desire—variously generated, suppressed, unleashed, and constrained—is particularly significant for feminist cultural studies because in its most common formulation as transhistorical romantic love it is one of the most efficient and irresistible interpellations of the female subject, securing her complicity in apparently unchangeable structures of oppression, particularly compulsory heterosexuality and bourgeois marriage.

It would be wrong to suggest that romantic love is devoid of positive and even liberatory dimensions. As Denis de Rougement has shown in *Love in the Western World*, its advent in the twelfth century represents something of an improvement on earlier organizations of desire. It seems likely, however, that the extra-marital love that flourished among the feudal aristocracy was considerably less restrictive for women (though not actively empowering) than was the marital version that emerged with early capitalism. Feudal romantic love was generally constructed as the unrequited passion of a male subject leading ultimately to his own spiritual self-transcendence, as opposed to the emergent construction of romantic love as mutual heterosexual desire leading to a consummation in marriage, a union of both body and spirit. One of its crucial features, a signal of its effectiveness, is that the ideology of romantic love centers from the Renaissance onward on

---

1. There is in Shakespeare's play only a dim residue of this earlier moralism in the Friar's caveat that "these violent delights have violent ends" (II. vi. 9); see Bullough.
   All references to the play are to the Riverside edition, edited by Evans et al.
2. For a useful guide to the literature on the debate about the transition from feudalism to capitalism, see Taylor. See also: Anderson (1979; 1983); Baechler; Baechler et al.; Brenner; Hirst; Katz; Kamenka and Neale; Medick; Mooers; Wallerstein.

women's subjective experience. Yet this focus serves to control and delimit intimate experience rather than to allow the fullest possible expression of female desire. It is also true that when we are in its throes, romantic love is a classic instance of false consciousness. Among its oppressive effects, the dominant ideology of (heterosexual, monogamous) romantic love relegates homosexuality to the sphere of deviance, secures women's submission to the asymmetrical distribution of power between men and women, and bolsters individualism by positing sexual love as the expression of authentic identity. Men are not, of course, immune to these effects, but they are more likely than women to derive benefit from them.

*   *   *

Reproducing the Ideology of Romantic Love

Shakespeare's text has been used to perpetuate the dominant ideology of romantic love, and its initial ideological function has intensified since its first performance. The play enacts an ideological propensity to posit desire as transhistorical. For what is extraordinary about the version of familial and personal relations—of desire and identity and their relation to power—endorsed by *Romeo and Juliet* is that they are in our own time so fully naturalized as to seem universal. Feminist psychoanalytic critic Julia Kristeva writes: "Young people throughout the entire world, whatever their race, religion, or social status, identify with the adolescents of Verona . . ." (210). According to Kristeva and countless Shakespeareans, the play constitutes a universal legend of love representing elemental psychic forces of desire and frustration purportedly characteristic of the human condition in every age and culture.[3]

The iteration of a particular configuration of desire does not end, therefore, in 1595 when the first performance puts it in place, but rather is a phenomenon that has been perpetuated, indeed universalized, by subsequent critical and theatrical reproductions of the play.[4] As Joseph Porter points out, *Romeo and Juliet* "has become far more canonical a story of heterosexual love than it was when it came to Shakespeare's hand" (141). Consider, for example, that in

3. For example, Arthur Kirsch who uses a Christian/Freudian approach comments: "Central to my understanding of the treatment of love in Shakespeare has been the assumption that the plays represent elemental truths of our emotional and spiritual life, that these truths help account for Shakespeare's enduring vitality . . ." (ix). In such criticism, Freud merely discovered a different way of expressing what Shakespeare had already said. History becomes the changing stage scenery of a continuum—the costumes may change, but the essence remains unchanged (6).
4. Even when the text was staged in a version thought more suited to the times, the result was the enhancement of its message for a post-Puritan world wherein the ideals it presented required a certain modification. See Barnet on the theatre history of the text. The Restoration saw the popularity of a happy ending (Evans et al., 1802).

its Elizabethan production, Romeo and Juliet were portrayed not by an actor and actress but by a suitably feminine-featured male performer and a slightly more rugged youth, and that the erotic homology produced by this situation was compounded by the presence of the profoundly homoerotic Mercutio. The play's initial ideological project—the valorization of romantic love between the young couple—thus becomes consolidated and intensified with subsequent re-narrations. Indeed, the affective power of the story and of romantic love itself—its "dateless passion" (Evans et al., 1057)—occurs not in spite of its repetition but rather depends precisely on reiteration.

The narrative mechanisms of the text itself tend towards self-replication. Shakespeare's play perpetuates an already well-known tale, and Act V produces "closure" on desire only by opening up the possibility of endless retellings of the story—displacing the lovers' desire onto a perpetual narrative of love (see Whittier, 41; Jones).[5] The lovers' story is recapitulated by the prologue, by the lovers, and by the Friar. The Prince offers the concluding incitement to "more talk": "never was a story of more woe / Than this of Juliet and her Romeo" (V.iii.307; 309–10). The play's ending thus constitutes a means of monumentalizing (quite literally in the golden statues of the lovers) and thereby reproducing *ad infinitum*, "whiles Verona by that name is known" (V.iii.300), the ideological imperatives of the lovers' most poignant erotic moments. Crucially, then, the social effectivity of the ideology of romantic love is characterized fundamentally by its capacity for self-replication. Thus, the narrative imperative of *Romeo and Juliet* to propagate the desire with which it is inscribed constitutes a resistance to historicization that has been extended by criticism's production of the play as universal love story. * * *

Romeo and Juliet, then, marks the inauguration of a particular form of sexual desire produced in accordance with the specific historical requirements of patriarchy's shifting modality. As Eli Zaretsky argues in his pathbreaking study *Capitalism, the Family, and Personal Life*, "courtly love anticipated ideals of love and individualism that the bourgeois located within the family and that were generalized and transformed in the course of capitalist development" (38). In the early modern teleology of desire, the family, newly emphasized as the focus of political, social, legal, and economic organization becomes

---

5. For Kristeva, however, such repetition is born not of ideological necessity but of a psycho-linguistic one. Commenting on the centrality of night imagery in the play, she argues: "it is not nothingness, lack of meaning, absurdity. In the polite display of its black tenderness there is an intense longing that is positive with respect to meaning . . . Let me emphasize the nocturnal motion of metaphor and *amor mortis*: it bears on the irrational aspect of signs and loving subjects, on the nonrepresentable feature on which the renewal of representation depends" (214, ellipsis in the original).

the social destination of desire.[6] Thus, *Romeo and Juliet* both instantiates the ideology of romantic love as universal, timeless and unchanging and yet is marked by its own historical specificity. The degree to which *Romeo and Juliet* appears to constitute the transcription of the universal features of the experience of love indicates its profoundly "ideological" nature; that is to say, the play's ideological project has become the dominant ideology of desire. In this way, the text both positions itself within and reproduces the hegemonic. *Romeo and Juliet* consolidates the ideology of romantic love and the correlative crystalization of the modern nuclear family.

* * *

The play produces one version of desire as paramount among the range of those it negotiates, and in doing so participates in the cultural production of desire required by the rise of absolutism, the centralization of the state, and the advent of capitalism. These developments, while not linear and continuous historical developments, constitute the advent of modernity, and it is surely only the burden of traditional critical practice that has contrived to place them as either remote from or irrelevant to the textual details of Renaissance drama (see Anderson, *Lineages*, 8–10). The hegemonic ideology of romantic love is crucially related to some of the definitive conditions of nascent modernity: the construction within the domestic sphere of the realm of the personal, an increased emphasis on the nucleated unit rather than the extended clan, the reinforcement of patriarchy in the household and in the absolutist state, and the advent of absolute private property in land (see Anderson, *Lineages*, 25–6).[7] The point here is not to concentrate on the conjunctural level (that is, to draw extensive analogies between the text and the broad shift from one form of economic organization to another) but on the prior conceptual one (antecedent in the mediation between chains of intelligibilities). That is, *Romeo and Juliet* does not exemplify the actual, empirical, social circumstances of its

6. As Susan Amussen puts it, in nascent modernity "[b]oth economic realities and political and social thought, then, draw us to the family as a central institution" (2). Further, Sharpe points to the irrefutable arrival of one new family type: "the legitimate family of clergymen" (61).
    For debates on the family see also: Chaytor; Houlbrooke; Outhwaite; Stone.
7. While it would be naïve to claim a straightforward functional relation between the nuclear family and the capitalist mode of production, it would fly in the face of historical fact to ignore the changes in familial structure and function that the changing organization effected. The degree of debate about this shift cannot be overemphasized. It is difficult to offer empirical evidence for changing family forms. However, Stone notes the fact that in the fourteenth century only a small proportion of homicides were committed within the family, in comparison with the majority today: "What is so striking, however, is that the family was more a unit for the perpetuation of crime—a third of all group crimes were by family members—than a focus of crime. It is tempting to argue that the family that slayed together stayed together (*The Family, Sex and Marriage*, 95). Even on a

production, but rather participates and intervenes in the ideological/historical conditions of its own making.

Patriarchal Law and the Centralization of the State

The move from the family allegiances associated with feudalism to those identified with centralization of the state constitutes the overarching narrative of *Romeo and Juliet*. That is, the *shifting, configurations* of patriarchal law and the changing formations of desire which attend it comprise the structure and substance of Shakespeare's text.[8] In this sense, the play articulates a crisis in patriarchy itself—specifically the transference of power from the feuding fathers to the Prince so that sexual desire in the form presented here produces the required subjectivities and harnesses them for the state above all other possible levels of allegiance. Desire needs to be refigured in order to manage the contradiction produced by the way the ideology of absolutism employed familial rhetoric in order to maintain feudal domination and exploitation despite the advent of a commodity economy (see Anderson, *Lineages*, 19).[9] As a result, the mode of desire disapproved of in the old order becomes valorized in the new one. However, that the ideological project of *Romeo and Juliet* is now completely coincident with the dominant ideology of desire does not mean that the play circulates only one discourse of desire. Rather, multiple and contradictory discourses of the desire are negotiated in the isolation and idealization of romantic heterosexual love.

That desire seems malleable, something that can be reordered, is apparent in Mercutio's Queen Mab speech, which charts the various courses a disembodied libido can take, from the sexual desires

---

less lethal level, community interactions seem to have revolved around identification with a larger unit than the one we think of as the nuclear family. "[E]verything we know about the pre-modern community, such as the village, indicates that it was riddled with competitive feuds and factions, usually organized around kinship groups" (660).

8. In contrast, psychoanalytic readings of the play, even as they demonstrate the way feudal patriarchy naturalizes itself, themselves succumb to that naturalization, accepting its self-representation as static and monolithic. For example, Coppélia Kahn argues that *Romeo and Juliet* demonstrates a certain inevitability or fate as intrinsic to the feudal patriarchal scheme which produces such strain on the young people who must come of age in Verona (186).

9. For the family was the central unit of most production as much as it was a institution of ideological importance for social and political theory and "the domestic relations of the household were an explicit part of the production relations of early capitalism" (Zaretsky, 38). "[P]roperty was a central factor in family relations, from decisions to get married to the distribution of property at the time of death (Amussen, 94).

   In a similar vein, Immanuel Wallerstein argues

   . . . the image of historical capitalism having arisen via the overthrow or a backward aristocracy by a progressive bourgeoisie is wrong. Instead, the correct basic image is that historical capitalism was brought into existence by a landed aristocracy which transformed itself into a bourgeoisie because the old system was disintegrating. Rather than let the disintegration continue to uncertain ends, they engaged in radical structural surgery themselves in order to maintain and significantly expand their ability to exploit the direct producers. (105–6)

of women—kisses of ladies to the unseemly lust of maids—to the greed and blood-lust of men:

> And in this state she gallops night by night
> Through lovers' brains, and then they dream of love;
> O'er courtiers' knees that dream on cur'sies straight
> O'er lawyers' fingers, who straight dream on fees;
> O'er ladies' lips, who straight on blisters dream,
> Which oft the angry Mab with kisses plagues,
> Because their breath with sweetmeats tainted are . . .
> Sometime she driveth o'er a soldier's neck,
> And then dreams he of cutting foreign throats,
> Of breaches, ambuscadoes, Spanish blades . . .
> This is the hag, when maids lie on their backs,
> That presses them and makes them first to bear,
> Making them women of good carriage
>
> (I.iv.70–94)

Although a force penetrating the unconscious of the dreamer from outside, desire is already socially scripted here (ladies and maids do not dream of cutting soldiers throats); it is not "free." (There is no desire hovering in some metaphysical space prior to its social production.) Desire is simultaneously controlled and aberrant, chaotic—its objective is either death or reproduction: "For this drivelling love is like a great natural that runs lolling up and down to hide his bauble in a hole" (II.iv.91–3). In Mercutio's comic teleology, desire is directed, driven, and yet indiscriminate about its sexual object—a "drive" in the psychoanalytic sense.

That it is Mercutio who articulates the plasticity of desire is particularly significant.[1] His cynicism, as well as his sexual predilection for men and his kinship with the Prince rather than the warring feudal houses, enables him to articulate the social construction of desire in which his companions are too fully invested. No maidens weep for Mercutio when he is killed. Rather, Escalus and Romeo are the characters who bear the loss of the master of the phallic pun. When Escalus comments on the lovers' tragedy, he also refers to his private grief for "a brace of kinsmen," of whom Mercutio is the one we know by name (V.iii.295). As absolutist monarch, Escalus seems to retain homoeroticism among his kin group. * * * The male power structure in general was indeed itself a force which generated male homoerotic desire, and with the rise of absolutism "the explicit disparities in power that animated homosexual desire in early modern England" (Smith, 23) would have been focused with increasing

---

1. "When verbal sparring about phalluses turns into physical sparring with swords, Mercutio is killed. An exemplar of male violence and misogyny? A martyr to male friendship? A victim of sexual desire that he cannot, will not, or must not acknowledge directly? Mercutio is all three" (Smith, 64).

intensity on the figure of the monarch himself. It is the Prince who monopolizes male bonding, aggression, and homoerotic desire.[2]

Yet Escalus also attempts to direct the multiple possible modes of desire in socially appropriate, explicitly heterosexual ways. Indeed, in a number of important respects it is Prince Escalus who becomes the play's pivotal figure rather than the tragic couple. Shakespeare imposes the ordering principle embodied in Escalus on Brooke's rambling structure at the play's opening, closing, and center so that the strong literary design is coincident with the authority he wields in turbulent Verona (see Gibbons, 39). In addition, in Shakespeare's symbolic redistribution of the city's property, Escalus is accorded a castle in Freetown, which belongs to Capulet in Brooke and Painter, and to which he summons Montague and Capulet from their more humble merchants' homes after the first disturbance of the peace (see Gibbons, 87).

More importantly, Escalus intervenes in the feud with absolute power of life and death. Even that intervention, however, is not immediately effective because he must struggle to become the preeminent patriarchal power in Verona. The Law of the Father in the psychoanalytic framework is constituted by precisely the power of intervention— that which disrupts in the dyad of mother and child, as the symbolic representative of culture. Although Escalus is essentially intervening between fathers, he nonetheless takes the place of the father in relation to the infantile feuding, feudal fathers who resist the exogamous relationship between their offspring, objecting to their quarrel as profane, bestial, and "cankered" (I.i.82–95). As Coppélia Kahn points out, Prince Escalus "embodies the law," and in relation to him it is "Montague and Capulet who are childishly refractory" (172):

> Rebellious subjects, enemies to peace,
> Profaners of this neighbour-stained steel—
> Will they not hear? What ho! You men, you beasts!
> That quench the fire of your pernicious rage
> With purple fountains issuing from your veins,
> On pain of torture from those bloody hands
> Throw your mistempered weapons to the ground
> And hear the sentence of your moved prince.
> (I.i.81–8)

Escalus strives to control the flow of blood, a metonym of lineage, class, and succession—the very essence of the patriarchal imperative. In so doing, the dangers of consanguinity are displaced onto the feuding feudal family:

> Two households, both alike in dignity,
> In fair Verona, where we lay our scene,
> From ancient grudge break to new mutiny,

2. On the violence of male bonding see: Kahn, 82–118; Novy, 99–142; Smith, ch. 2.

> Where civil blood makes civil hands unclean.
> From forth the fatal loins of these two foes
> A pair of star-cross'd lovers take their life.
> (Prologue, 1–6)

In this passage, the symmetry between the houses suggests an ominous familial resemblance. The ancient blood they share is the bloodshed of enmity. They are star-crossed by a common inheritance—the brutal engagement that has in enmity mangled and enmeshed the blood and loins of their houses so that, as Kay Stockholder has argued, their relationship verges precariously on the incestuous:

> The image of "fatal loins" suggests a kind of copulation in hatred between the feuding families . . . It suggests that they die not because they are children of warring families, but rather that their feuding parents are the circumstances of their meeting, their loving, and their death. The same magnetism that brings the two families together in order to fight also brings the two young people together in order to love and die. (30)[3]

Thus for Stockholder the lovers' marriage merely continues the feud. Although this is certainly the case in Bandello's prior version of the story where Romeo and Juliet's love ignited a well-nigh extinct enmity, it is not the case in Shakespeare where the lovers mark the end of incest and the beginning of exogamy, the emergent ideology of the family. We see this, for example, in Juliet's ironic articulation of the transfer of her desire from kin to foe upon Tybalt's death: "To wreak the love I bore my cousin / Upon his body that hath slaughtered him!" (III.v.101–2). The Prince's prohibition against the feud is, then, synonymous with a prohibition against endogamy—"the sentence of your moved prince" (I.i.88)—and it is a prohibition with which Romeo and Juliet almost instinctively comply.[4]

In contrast to the civil and civilizing intervention of the Prince, the atrophied, macerated power of the belligerent secular fathers is rendered in comic fashion in the brawl scene of Act I, where they appear in ridiculous *déshabillé*.

> (*Enter old Capulet in his gown, and his Wife.*)
> CAPULET   What noise is this? Give me my long sword ho!
> LADY CAPULET   A crutch, a crutch! Why call you for a sword?
> CAPULET   My sword, I say! Old Montague is come,

---

3. Notably, the fathers loom so large in the play in Stockholder's psychoanalytic interpretation that she views Capulet as the protagonist (31).
4. In fact the incest taboo is more vulnerable when it operates in the tense nuclear arrangement where any affective relations outside the nuclear unit are discouraged and deemed inappropriate (see Mitchell, *Psychoanalysis and Feminism*). Yet in this play, it is the feudal that is presented as an aberrant way of organizing desire, as perverted and death-marked.

> And flourishes his blade in spite of me.
> (*Enter old Montague and his Wife.*)
> MONTAGUE   Thou villain Capulet!—Hold me not; let me go.
> LADY MONTAGUE   Thou shalt not stir one foot to seek a foe.
>
> (I.i.75–80)

It is the women here who deflate the exaggerated phallic proportions of their husbands, whose long swords refer us back to Sampson and Gregory's "comic" meditations on erection and rape that began the affray. Lady Montague's command prefaces the Prince's admonition that the battle end on pain of death. In her mouth the injunction is an instance of comic inversion of authority, and it serves both to align her with the will of the Prince, as opposed to the will of her husband, and to show that her husband cannot rule even his own wife.

Old Capulet's power is equally diminished. While well able to rail at his daughter he cannot control the precocious Tybalt, whose libido is violently unleashed upon the world:

> The fiery Tybalt, with his sword prepar'd;
> Which, as he breath'd defiance to my ears,
> He swung about his head cutting the winds,
> Who, nothing hurt withal, hissed him in scorn.
>
> (I.i.109–12)

There is a marked contrast here with the manageable masculinity of Romeo, with whom Tybalt seeks mortal engagement at the Capulet festivities, who is "so secret and so close, / So far from sounding" (I.i.149–50). Unlike Romeo, Tybalt refuses to take his proper place in the hierarchy of male authority:

> CAPULET   He shall be endured.
> What, goodman boy? I say he shall. Go to!
> Am I the master here, or you? Go to!
> You'll not endure him! God shall mend my soul,
> You'll make a mutiny among my guests!
> You will set cock-a-hoop! You'll be the man!
>
> (I.v.76–81)

Capulet derides Tybalt with the diminutives "saucy boy" and "princox," which deprecate Tybalt's phallic pretensions to "set cock-a-hoop" (I.v.81–6). The inappropriate phallic competition here is not resolved but, like Freud's account of the child's submission to the Law of the Father, is deferred with a view to later satisfaction:

> Patience perforce with willful choler meeting
> Makes my flesh tremble in their different greeting,
> I will withdraw, but this intrusion shall,
> Now seeming sweet, convert to bitt'rest gall.
>
> (I.v.89–92)

Tybalt's trembling flesh resembles the agitated state of *coitus inter-ruptus* in the language of his withdrawal and the visitors' intrusion; his erotic object is a highly sexualized violence.

Capulet's intervention clearly lacks decisive power. Nonetheless, no matter how diminished their authority the presence of the fathers of both Church and household is what threatens the power of the Prince. The benign and dangerously ineffectual Friar Lawrence must become abject before Escalus's castrating power, finally submitting, himself "Unto the rigour of severest law" (V.iii.269) in order that Prince Escalus appropriate the castrating capacity which constitutes the Law of the Father.

The consolidation of Escalus's power is evident in the play's conclusion when the warring fathers make a belated public solemnization of the marriage contract:

> CAPULET O brother Montague, give me thy hand.
> This is my daughter's jointure, for no more
> Can I demand.
>
> (V.iii.296–8)

The end of enmity is contingent upon the feuding fathers' submission to the Prince:

> PRINCE   Capulet! Montague!
> See what a scourge is laid upon your hate,
> That heaven finds means to kill your joys with love.
> And I for winking at your discords too,
> Have lost a brace of kinsmen. All are punish'd.
>
> (V.iii.291–5)

The result of this shift in power is "glooming peace" and its price has been the sacrifice of the fathers' children (V.iii.305).

A crucial dimension of Escalus's appropriation of the power of the secular and religious fathers, as we noted at the outset, is the control over the narrative of the love tragedy. It is Romeo's letter to his father that becomes, amid a series of recapitulations of the play's tragic matter, the version of events authorized by the Prince for further dissemination:

> BALTHASAR I brought my master news of Juliet's death;
> And then in post he came from Mantua
> To this same place, to this same monument,
> This letter he early bid me give his father,
> And threat'ned me with death, going in the vault,
> If I departed not and left him there.
> PRINCE   Give me the letter. I will look on it . . .
> This letter doth make good the friar's words,
> The course of love, the tidings of her death . . .
>
> (V.iii.272–87ff)

This missive, like the Friar's letter to Romeo, does not reach its intended destination, but instead is confiscated by the Prince who symbolically absorbs the power of Romeo's father—"I will look on it"—even though the mourning Montague, its intended recipient, is himself fully available to peruse it. In taking the role of coordinator and interpreter of the various renditions of the tragic events in the play's coda (the Friar's, Balthasar's), the Prince consolidates his power over the errant feudal forces that have previously sought to dissipate it. This monopoly on interpretation is appropriate given Romeo's earlier alignment with the Prince's peace, under whose auspices he made the fatal intervention that cost Mercutio his life, "the Prince expressly hath / Forbid this bandying in Verona streets" (III.i.88–9). What the Prince expropriates in taking up Romeo's letter is his legacy to the world. The letter serves as a symbolic substitute for the "name" he would have passed on to posterity had he survived to produce progeny with Juliet. In this sense, his letter resonates with the play's earlier concern with the politics of naming (II.iv.39–40). The issue of Romeo's name stands in direct relation to his tragic struggle to articulate an identity distinct from the feudal one he wished to revoke. It is this version of identity—defined in terms of interiority and individual autonomy—and desire, disarticulated from the animosities of the feud (Romeo but not a Montague, so to speak), that the play unambiguously validates. For it is the identity required by what the tragic couple represent, namely, the tragic inauguration of a romantic love validated by marriage.

Institutionalizing "Unconstrained" Love: The Rise of the Nuclear Family

As I have argued, *Romeo and Juliet* makes its cultural intervention at a moment when the ideology of love and marriage and the organization of desire required to sustain it is undergoing change. * * *

In *Romeo and Juliet*, we see the idealization of desire situated within lyrical and tragic aesthetic conventions which distance the play from the practical tone of the marriage treatises whose ideological project it shares. While the lovers are thwarted by external forces, their frustration is of an entirely different order from that of Romeo's unrequited love for Rosaline. Romeo and Juliet's love at least entails physical consummation after a very brief courtship in which Juliet has been surprisingly forthright about her desires:

> but farewell, compliment!
> Dost thou love me? I know thou wilt say "Ay,"
> And I will take thy word; yet, if thou swear'st,
> Thou mayest prove false: at lovers' perjuries
> They say, Jove laughs. O gentle Romeo,
> If thou dost love, pronounce it faithfully.

> Or, if thou thinkest I am too quickly won,
> I'll frown and be perverse, and say thee nay,
> So thou wilt woo, but else not for the world.
> In truth, fair Montague, I am too fond,
> And therefore thou mayest think my behaviour light,
> But trust me, gentleman, I'll prove more true
> Than those that have [more] coying to be strange.
>   (II.ii.89–101)

While there are traces of Catholic reticence about sexual desire in the late sixteenth-century drama,[5] in *Romeo and Juliet*, the symbolic systems of Catholicism—pilgrimage, the palmer's kiss, veneration of saints, and the sacrament of confession—are displaced onto the rites of specifically sexual love. In the above passage, Juliet refuses to engage further in these elaborate, ritualized negotiations and exchanges of erotic power that constitute courtship. This is attributable to the fact that the play is not about power within the couple—this is completely idealized—but about the power relation between the amorous couple and the outside world. The lovers' free choice of each other seems to dissolve the power relation between them and to absolve them of the necessity to defer to any authority other than their own. Indeed, it is the idealization of the couple's love that aligns *Romeo and Juliet* with comedy and repeatedly suggests, despite forebodings to the contrary, the possibility of a happy conclusion.

In Act I, scene ii, where the initial desires of both lovers are presented, the perimeters of his daughter's desire are laid out by Capulet:

> But woo her, gentle Paris, get her heart,
> My will to her consent is but a part;
> And she agreed, within her scope of choice
> Lies my consent and fair according voice.
>   (I.ii.16–19)

Capulet is woefully unaware of what is required to get his daughter's heart, or of the power differential that constitutes the distance between his will and the troublesome issue of female consent. The passion of romantic love requires an inexplicable and mutual abandonment of "mastery." It is mutuality, of course, that signals the crucial difference between Romeo's infatuation with Rosaline and his love for Juliet: "Now Romeo is beloved and loves again, / Alike bewitched by the charm of looks" (II, Prologue, 5–6). Critics have remarked upon the occult connotations of "bewitched," but bewitched also implies enchantment as a psychological state, an

---

5. "Nevertheless, the dramatic representation of that [neo-Catholic] sensibility is at its most commanding and pristine in Elizabethan, rather than in Jacobean, tragedy" (Rose, 105).

erotically charged ideological interpellation. Juliet has no choice about the depth to which she will "endart" her gaze on Romeo, because the condition of love she experiences is far in excess of either her own will or that of her father. The mutuality of mirrored passion fosters the notion that one's authentic identity is revealed in romantic love.

It is important to emphasize the degree to which this freedom of choice in marriage is linked to economic considerations, especially the oxymoronic notion of "free exchange." Unconstrained choice about one's marriage partner relies to some degree on the ideological separation of psychic and monetary economies. Ideally, both parents and child will agree on a match, but what is at stake here is not so much the right of liberty in love, as an endeavor to prevent parents marrying off their children for financial gain, a phenomenon which became more marked with the bourgeoisification of the aristocracy. * * * Lady Capulet's statement that "Thou hast a careful father, child"—suggests that he is not only solicitous but perhaps penurious, and in the scene where he tries to coerce Juliet's consent to the match with Paris, he does it by negating female power—silencing all the women around him, "Speak not, reply not, do not answer me!" (III. v. 106, 163). The Nurse rebels, "May not one speak," "I speak no treason," while Lady Capulet, the obedient wife, vows "I'll not speak a word" (III.v.173, 172, 202). Only after such pressure upon her attempted intervention, in a gesture more pragmatic than immoral, does the Nurse advise her charge to comply with the paternal order. Despite his initial uncertainty—"to soon marr'd are those so early made?" (I.ii.13)—Capulet's concern with financial gain and social status is thoroughly apparent; it is even more so in Quarto 1 where the line about the statues at the end of the play reads "no figure shall at such price be set." * * * The warring feudal families here become an amalgam of warring nobility and rising bourgeois merchants engaged in economic competition, both of which offered some threat to absolutism (Anderson, *Lineages*, 19–22). Military antagonism in which fixed quantities of ground are won or lost is replaced by a more benign economic engagement (though of course, historically, it proved the downfall of absolutism) wherein rival parties may both expand and prosper "because the production manufactured commodities is inherently unlimited" (*Lineages*, 31).

In contrast to the formal settlement arrived at in Capulet's negotiations with Paris, in the dealings of the lovers, the Nurse is the unruly woman, the comic agent of their *ad hoc* marriage arrangements. Her disorderly transactions are reminiscent of the illicit exchanges of the brothel. Hence, Mercutio calls out, "A bawd! A bawd! A bawd!" (II.iv.130):

> ROMEO   Here's for thy pains.
> NURSE   No truly, sir; not a penny.
> ROMEO   Go to, I say you shall.
> (II.iv.182–4)

Significantly, the financial power here is in the hands of Romeo, not the bride's father, as Romeo recognized at the moment he discovered Juliet's identity: "O dear account! My life is my foe's debt" (I.v.118); "As that vast shore [wash'd with the farthest sea, / I should adventure for such merchandise" (II.ii.83–4). That is, his "free" choice is bolstered by economic independence. Just before their marriage, Juliet too refers to her dowry:

> They are but beggars that can count their worth,
> But my true love is grown to such excess
> I cannot sum up sum of half my wealth.
> (II.v.32–4)

That her "wealth" consists of love rather than property exemplifies the shift here, and again it is she not her father who controls it. Financial metaphors reconfigure patriarchal economic transactions. Thus, the reordering of desire is attendant on the economic transformations sketched above—though of course in the play these transformations are metaphoric rather than literal—and the ideology of romantic love works to obscure them. * * *

Wayward Female Desire

There is, then, in *Romeo and Juliet*, a production of a specific form of female desire, benign and unthreatening, easily recruited to emergent absolutism and nascent capitalism. Whereas in the figure of Mercutio there is an alternative to the kind of heterosexual masculine desire that Romeo comes to represent by the end of the play, there appears to be no radically alternative regime of female sexuality to that represented by Juliet. However, this is not quite the case. For in Act I, scene iii there is a production of a highly sexualized, ribald female desire that parallels the "rough love" of male homoeroticism that immediately follows in the next scene in the exchanges of the "lusty gentlemen" Benvolio, Romeo, and Mercutio (I.iv.25, 112). The purpose of this scene is to inform Juliet of the marriage negotiations between Capulet and the County Paris, but what emerges is a women's scene, which disrupts the patriarchal project by presenting maternal eroticism, child sexuality, and female bawdy. The scene is freighted with multiple erotic possibilities, and in particular it is the displaced nature of maternality that produces a form of eroticism neither generated nor contained by the patriarchal order, feudal or otherwise.

In the very opening lines of the scene, Lady Capulet makes formal demand to the Nurse for "my daughter" (I.iii.1). The Nurse's
summons in itself produces a range of female erotic possibilities:

> Now, by my maidenhead at twelve year old,
> I bade her come. What, lamb! What, lady-bird!
> God forbid! Where's this girl? What Juliet!
>   (I.iii.3–15)

The Nurse's comic invocation of her long-departed maidenhead suggests a connection between her own "grotesque" body, with its four
teeth and over-sucked dugs (grotesque insofar as it insists on its
excess of the contained limits of the "classical' body) and the maidenhead of "this girl," Juliet, who is the object of affections which
exceed the class-demarcated bounds of maternal propriety: "lamb!";
"lady-bird!" (I.iii.3–4). The point here, of course, is not to suggest
that Juliet is the victim of the Nurse's improper sexual conduct, but
rather that the business of nursing is itself sexual in ways that are
difficult to grasp because nursing is now almost completely desexu-
alized. It is interesting to compare the mutual pleaure of "giving
suck," where the woman actively provides oral gratification to the
infant she nurtures with the pleasures of fellatio. Almost all the sexual dimensions of sucking have now been transferred to the latter
practice and therefore onto the male organ.

The Nurse offers a sensual recollection of Juliet's weaning:

> And she was wean'd—I never shall forget it—
> Of all the days of the year upon that day;
> For I had then laid wormwood to my dug,
> Sitting in the sun under the dove house wall.
> My lord and you were then at Mantua—
> Nay, I do bear a brain—but, as I said,
> When it did it taste the wormwood on the nipple
> Of my dug, and felt it bitter, pretty fool,
> To see it teachy, and fall out wi' th' dug!
>   (I.iii.24–32)

The fact that the Nurse is a comic figure has all too often obscured
the fact that she bears events as indelible maternal memory: "I never
shall forget"; "I do bear a brain." Juliet is weaned by the Nurse while
her parents are away, a process which seems to mark her as an initiate of sexual knowledge:

> For then she could Stand high-lone; nay, by th' rood,
> She could have run and waddled all about;
> For even the day before, she broke her brow,
> And then my husband—God be with his soul!
> 'A was a merry man—took up the child.

> "Yea," quoth he, "dost thou fall upon thy face?
> Thou wilt fall backward when thou hast more wit,
> Wilt thou not, Jule?" and, by my holidam,
> The pretty wretch left crying and said "Ay."
>
> (I.iii.36–44)

The Nurse extends the sexualization of this recollection by adding to the description of Juliet a phallic "bump as big as a young cockerel's stone," that recalls the violence of heterosexual relations, and is reminiscent of her later remark that "bigger; women grow by men" (I.iii.53, 95). In contrast, it is Lady Capulet who invokes the romantic imagery of "This precious book of love" (I.iii.87), which dominates the rest of the play.

This scene, then, represents in palimpsest, female sensuality, maternity, and eroticism which, while they are clearly subordinated to patriarchal rule in the feudal order have become virtually unintelligible, undiscernible, in our own.

Genre and Ideology in the Tragic Ending

The post-coital satisfaction of Romeo and Juliet as autonomous conjugal unit is short-lived and remarkably clandestine. Tragic events never allow time to fulfill the Friar's hopes of making the marriage public: "To blaze your marriage, reconcile your friends" (III.iii.151–4). Bruce Smith argues "Mercutio may die, but only bad timing keeps *Romeo and Juliet* from reaching the comic conclusion of married love" (64). In this he points to the crucial distinction between the demise of the erotic mode represented by Mercutio and that represented by the lovers.

Had it not been aimed at sexual access rather than escape with Juliet, Romeo's rope-ladder scheme (Gibbons, 92) might have avoided the tragic conclusion. In fact, the legitimate secrecy, so to speak, of "privacy" is the order in which such a love as that of Romeo and Juliet would thrive.[6] The marriage of Romeo and Juliet could, after all, have provided the diplomatic solution to the feud; this pragmatic solution is opposed by the fathers so that the apparently antithetical ideal of romantic love as autonomous and inherently resistant to all social constraints can be incorporated into the diplomatic

6. For Kay Stockholder the threat to the couple is externalized: "The freer the lovers are from violent emotions, the more violent is the world they encounter" (30). And for Kiernan Ryan the play represents a subversive utopian vision, born of an initial freedom from social identity (a namelessness), cruelly dashed (108, 114, 117). Ryan suggests that the play is revolutionary and argues for a love untrammeled by the social order. Such a suggestion seems beside the point—love is always, first and foremost, social.

Kristeva considers the couple a "utopia wager that paradise lost can be made lasting" (222), but this is exactly the dominant ideology of love in modernity, and it is for Kristeva a utopian option she rejects out of hand where authority constitutes itself as that which is to be loved (210).

solution.[7] In fact, Romeo and Juliet's love, while it offers resistance to their feudal households is perfectly compatible with the interests of society as a whole. Thus, the utopian, dangerous, and paradoxical notion of a law that ratifies (inherently transgressive) passion, becomes the desideratum of early modern marriage (see Kristeva, 210).

* * * What is at stake is not simply an endorsement of the desire of the lovers or the control of the fathers; it is whether the play is an argument for absolutism, whether it approves the government of the crown above all others: This does not, however, mean that fathers are now without authority (see Stone, *The Family, Sex and Marriage*, ch. 5), Rather, *Romeo and Juliet* addresses some of the contradictions in post-Reformation patriarchy where there is an endeavor to produce the authority of husbands, fathers, and thence the state as mutually reinforcing and simultaneously an effort to appropriate the transgressive aspects of desire.[8] Lawrence Stone points out:

> The enhancement of the importance of the conjugal family and the household relative to the kinship and clientage at the upper levels of society was accompanied by a positive reinforcement of the despotic authority of husband and father—that is to say, of patriarchy. Both Church and state provided powerful new theoretical and practical support, while two external checks on patriarchal power declined as kinship ties and clientage weakened. (*The Family, Sex and Marriage*, 151)

While the "raw power" of fathers does not necessarily increase, the recognition that such power is legitimate is fully and unequivocally established. Paternal power has now superseded "raw power" as such (151). "Authoritarian monarchy and domestic patriarchy form a congruent and mutually supportive complex of ideas and social systems" (152). As marriage was increasingly sanctified, so too was the authoritarian role of husband and father, guardian of the sacred state (654). Thus, Stone argues that after 1640, the "restricted patriarchal nuclear family becomes the "closed domesticated nuclear family" (Stone, 655).

Romeo and Juliet are simultaneously sacrificed to the old feudal order of Montague and Capulet and to patriarchy's new order of the

---

7. Stone argues that there is a "clear conflict: between romantic love and the notion that it is an impractical basis for marriage" (*The Family, Sex and Marriage*, 181). I disagree because it seems to me that "romantic love," the ideal of a love between equals (that is, people of the same class status), is one of the most successful ways of internalizing the social order—that is, producing it in socially appropriate ways.
8. Alan Sinfield remarks: "The . . . disjunction in Reformation doctrine of marriage occurred because theorists wanted to maintain, as well as the husband's authority, the father's. They did not mean to let their young folk get out of hand, or to let human feeling supplant the other important things in life. The ideal of affectionate marriage was held alongside a continuing belief in parental control, mainly in the interests of social standing and financial security" (7).

unified power of the state represented by Escalus.[9] The play's contradictions, its combination of residual and emergent elements are
subordinated by the strictures of the genre's conclusion to a single
ideological effect. This does not, however, sweep away all earlier
contradictions; it has taken 400 years and many times that number
of pages of literary criticism to accomplish that. *Romeo and Juliet*
stands as an apparently benign, lyrical document of universal love.
What I have argued here is that it does not stand above history, but
rather within it, doing the work of culture, instigating and perpetu-
ating the production of socially necessary formations of desire.

✳   ✳   ✳

WORKS CITED

Althusser, Louis. *Lenin and Philosophy and Other Essays*, trans. Ben Brewster (New York, Monthly Review Press, 1971).

Amussen, Susan Dwyer. *An Ordered Society: Gender and Class in Early Modern England* (Oxford, Basil Blackwell, 1988).

Anderson, Perry. *Lineages of the Absolutist State* (London, Verso, 1979).

——. *In the Tracks of Historical Materialism* (London, Verso, 1983).

Baechler, Jean. *The Origins of Capitalism*, trans. Barry Cooper (Oxford, Basil Blackwell, 1975).

Baechler, Jean, John Hall, and Michael Mann. *Europe and the Rise of Capitalism* (Oxford, Basil Blackwell, 1988).

Barnet, Sylvan. "*Romeo and Juliet* on stage and screen," in J. A. Bryant (ed.), *The Tragedy of Romeo and Juliet*, The Signet Classic Shakespeare (New York, Penguin, 1986), 227–38.

Barrett, Michèle, *Women's Oppression Today* (London, Verso, 1980).

Barrett, Michèle, and Mary McIntosh. *The Anti-Social Family* (London, Verso, 1982).

Belsey, Catherine, and Jane Moore, (eds.). *The Feminist Reader: Essay in Gender and the Politics of Literary Criticism* (Cambridge, MA, Basil Blackwell, 1989).

Brenner, Robert. "The origins of capitalist development: A critique of neo-Smithian Marxism," *New Left Review*, 104 (1977), 25–92.

Brown, Paul. "'This thing of darkness I acknowledge mine': *The Tempest* and the discourse of colonialism," in Jonathan Dollimore and

---

9. John Donne in one of his typically perverse wedding sermons, proclaims that proper godliness should obviate desire and obliterate lack: "And what can that soul lack that hath all God?" (Rose, 104). The state of fulfillment, a state beyond desire, is envisaged here. A perfect Christianity, it would seem, obliterates lack, that precondition of desire produced by an initial failure of satisfaction and as the effect of a primordial absence. Donne reduces sexual desire back to the older of a need; something that could be satisfied (see J. Rose, "Introduction II" to Mitchell and Rose, 32).

Alan Sinfield (eds), *Political Shakespeare: New Essays in Cultural Materialism* (Ithaca, Cornell University Press, 1985), 48–71.

Bullough, Geoffrey (ed.). *Narrative and Dramatic Sources of Shakespeare*, vol. 1 (New York, Columbia University Press, 1957).

Chaytor, Miranda. "Household and kinship: Ryton in the late sixteenth and early seventeenth centuries," *History Workshop Journal*, 10 (1980), 25–60.

Coward, Rosalind. *Patriarchal Precedents: Sexuality and Social Relations* (Boston, Routledge & Kegan Paul, 1983).

Cressy, David. "Foucault, Stone, Shakespeare, and social history," *English Literary Renaissance*, 21(2) (1991), 121–33.

Davies, Kathleen M. "Continuity and change in literary advice on marriage," in R. B. Outhwaite (ed.). *Marriage and Society: Studies in the Social History of Marriage* (New York, St Mantiu's Press, 1981).

Deleuze, Gilles, and Félix Guattari. *Anti-Oedipus: Capitalism and Schizophrenia*, trans. Robert Hurley et al. (Minneapolis, University of Minnesota Press, 1983).

Eagleton, Terry. *Literary Theory: An Introduction* (Oxford, Basil Blackwell, 1983).

Evans, G. Blakemore et al. (ed.). *The Riverside Shakespeare*. (Boston, Houghton Mifflin, 1974).

Fanon, Franz. *Black Skins, White Masks*, trans. Charles Lam Markmann (New York, Grove Press, 1967).

Freud, Sigmund. *Moses and Monotheism* (1939), trans. Katherine Jones (New York, Vintage, 1962).

———. *Totem and Taboo: Resemblances between the Psychic Lives of Savages and Neurotics*, in Peter Gay (ed.), *The Freud Reader* (New York, Norton, 1989), 481–513.

———. "Some psychical consequences of the anatomical distinction between the sexes," in Peter Gay (ed.), *The Freud Reader* (New York, Norton, 1989), 670–7.

Gardiner, Judith Kegan. "Psychoanalysis and feminism: An American humanist's view," *Signs*, 17 (winter 1992), 437–54.

Gibbons, Brian (ed.). *Romeo and Juliet*, the Arden Shakespeare (London, Methuen, 1980).

Greenblatt, Stephen. *Renaissance Self-Fashioning from More to Shakespeare* (Chicago, University of Chicago Press, 1980).

———. "Psychoanalysis and Renaissance culture," in Patricia Parker and David Quint (eds), *Literary Theory/Renaissance Texts* (Baltimore, Johns Hopkins, 1986), 210–24.

Grosz, Elizabeth. *Jacques Lacan: A Feminist Introduction* (New York, Routledge, 1990).

Hirst, Paul Q. *Marxism and Historical Writing* (London, Routledge, 1985).

Houlbrooke, Ralph A. *The English Family, 1450–1700* (New York, Longman, 1988).

Howard, Jean. "The New Historicism in Renaissance studies," *English Literary Renaissance*, 16(1) (winter, 1986), 13–43.

Jameson, Frederic. *The Ideologies of Theory: Essays 1971–1986*, vol. 1 (Minneapolis, University of Minnesota Press, 1981).

——. *The Political Unconscious: Narrative as a Socially Symbolic Act* (Ithaca, Cornell University Press, 1985).

Jardine, Alice. *Gynesis: Configurations of Woman and Modernity* (Ithaca, Cornell University Press, 1985).

Jones, Barry. "Romeo and Juliet: The genesis of a classic," in Eric Haywood and Cormac Ó Cuilleanáin (eds.). *Italian Storytellers: Essays on Italian Narrative Literature* (Dublin, Irish Academic Press, 1989), 150–81.

Kahn, Coppélia. *Man's Estate: Masculine Identity in Shakespeare* (Berkeley, University of California Press, 1981).

Kamenka, Eugene, and R. S. Neale. *Feudalism, Capitalism and Beyond* (London, Edward Arnold, 1975).

Kaplan, Cora. *Sea Changes: Culture and Feminism* (London, Verso, 1986).

Katz, Claudio J. *From Feudalism to Capitalism: Marxian Theories of Class Struggle and Social Change* (New York, Greenwood Press, 1989).

Kirsch, Arthur. *Shakespeare and the Experience of Love* (New York, Cambridge University Press, 1981).

Kristeva, Julia. *Tales of Love*, trans. Leon S. Roudiez (New York, Columbia University Press, 1987).

Laslett, Peter. *The World We Have Lost Further Explored* (London, Methuen, 1965, 1983).

——. "The European family and early industrialization," in Jean Baechler et al. (eds.), 234–41.

Macfarlane, Alan. Review of Lawrence Stone's *The Family, Sex and Marriage in England, History and Theory*, 18 (1979), 103–26.

——. *Marriage and Love in England: Modes of Reproduction 1300–1840* (Oxford, Basil Blackwell, 1986).

——. "The cradle of capitalism: The case of England," in Jean Baechler et al. (eds.), 185–203.

Marx, Karl, and Friedrich Engels. *The Marx–Engels Reader*, ed. Robert C. Tucker (New York, Norton, 1978).

Medick, Hans. "The transition from feudalism to capitalism: Renewal of the debate," in Raphael Samuel (ed.), *People's History and Socialist Theory* (London, Routledge & Kegan Paul, 1981).

Mitchell, Juliet. *Woman's Estate* (New York, Vintage, 1973).

——. *Psychoanalysis and Feminism: Freud, Reich, Laing and Women* (New York, Vintage, 1975).

Mitchell, Juliet, and Jacqueline Rose. *Feminine Sexuality: Feminine Sexuality and the ecole freudienne*, trans. Jacqueline Rose (London, Macmillan, 1982).

Montrose, Louis. "Renaissance literary studies and the subject of history," *English Literary Renaissance*, 16(1) (1986), 5–12.

Mooers, Colin. *The Making of Bourgeois Europe: Absolutism, Revolution, and the Rise of Capitalism in England, France, and Germany* (New York, Verso, 1991).

Mooney, Michael. "Text and performance: *Romeo and Juliet*, Quartos 1 and 2," *Colby Quarterly*, XXVI(2) (June 1990), 122–32.

Newman, Karen. *Fashioning Femininity and English Renaissance Drama* (Chicago, University of Chicago Press, 1991).

Newton, Judith, and Deborah Rosenfelt. (eds.). *Feminist Literary Criticism and Social Change* (New York, Routledge, 1986).

Novick, Peter. *That Noble Dream: The 'Objectivity Question" and the American Historical Profession* (Cambridge, Cambridge University Press, 1988).

Novy, Marianne. *Love's Argument: Gender Relations in Shakespeare* (Chapel Hill, University of North Carolina Press, 1984).

Outhwaite, R. B. (ed.). *Marriage and Society: Studies in the Social History of Marriage* (New York, St. Martin's Press, 1981).

Porter, Joseph. "Marlowe, Shakespeare, and the canonization of heterosexuality," *South Atlantic Quarterly*, 88(1) (1989), 127–47.

Rose, Mary Beth. *The Expense of Spirit: Love and Sexuality in English Renaissance Drama* (Ithaca, Cornell University Press, 1988).

Rougement, Denis de. *Love in the Western World*, trans. Montgomery Belgion (Princeton, NJ: Princeton University Press, 1983).

Ryan, Kiernan. "*Romeo and Juliet*: The language of tragedy," in Willie van Peer (ed.), *Taming the Text* (New York, Routledge, 1988), 106–21.

Ryan, Michael. *Marxism and Deconstruction* (Baltimore, Johns Hopkins, 1982).

Sharpe, J. A. *Early Modern England: A Social History 1550–1760* (London, Edward Arnold, 1987).

Sinfield, Alan. *Literature in Protestant England, 1560–1660* (Totowa, NJ, Barnes & Noble, 1983).

Smith, Bruce R. *Homosexual Desire in Shakespeare's England: A Cultural Poetics* (Chicago, University of Chicago Press, 1991).

Stockholder, Kay. *Dreamworks: Lovers and Families in Shakespeare's Plays* (Toronto, University of Toronto Press, 1987).

Stone, Lawrence. *The Family, Sex and Marriage in England 1500–1800* (New York, Harper & Row, 1977).

———. *The Past and the Present* (Boston, Routledge & Kegan Paul, 1980).

Swindells, Julia, and Lisa Jardine. *What's Left? Women in Culture and the Labour Movement* (New York, Routledge, 1990).

Taylor, Barry. *Society and Economy in Early Modern Europe: A Bibliography of Post-War Research* (New York, Manchester University Press, 1989).

Traub, Valerie. "Kay Stockholder. *Dream works: Lovers and families in Shakespeare's plays*," *Shakespeare Quarterly*, 40(1) (spring 1989), 100–2.

———. "Prince Hal's Falstaff: Positioning psychoanalysis and the female reproductive body," *Shakespeare Quarterly*, 40(4) (1989), 456–74.

———. "Desire and the difference it makes," in Valerie Wayne (ed.), *The Matter of Difference: Materialist Feminist Criticism of Shakespeare* (Ithaca, Cornell, 1991), 81–114.

Veeser, Aram H. (ed.). *The New Historicism* (New York, Routledge, 1989).

Wallerstein, Immanuel. *Historical Capitalism* (London, Verso, 1983).

Wayne, Don E. "New historicism," in Martin Coyle, Peter Garside, Malcolm Kelsall, and John Peck (eds.), *Encyclopedia of Literature and Criticism* (London, Routledge, 1990).

Weedon, Chris. *Feminism and Poststructuralism* (London, Routledge, 1989).

Weeks, Jeffrey. *Sexuality and Its Discontents: Meanings, Myths, and Modern Sexualities* (London, Routledge, 1985).

Whittier, Gayle. "The sonnet's body and the body sonnetized in *Romeo and Juliet*," *Shakespeare Quarterly*, 40(1) (spring 1989), 27–41.

Wrightson, Keith. *English Society 1580–1680* (New Brunswick, NJ, Rutgers University Press, 1982).

Zaretsky, Eli. *Capitalism, the Family and Personal Life* (London, Pluto, 1976).

SASHA ROBERTS

Constructing Identities†

* * *

Public and Private Space

Romeo and Juliet is marked by careful attention to contrasts and conflict between public and private. Not only do characters behave differently in public and private (perhaps, above all, Juliet), but the

---

† From *William Shakespeare*, Romeo and Juliet: *A New Critical Interpretation* (Plymouth, UK: Northcote House Publishing for the British Council, 1998), pp. 35–68. Reprinted by permission of the publisher.

play moves between public and private spaces—streets, gardens, houses, reception rooms, bedchambers, monastic cells, churchyards, tombs. Different characters have different access to these spaces according to their gender and status; indeed, *Romeo and Juliet* enacts a politics of space that is rooted in early modern cultural practice.

Romeo and Juliet is a domestic tragedy, and the private setting of the household arguably comes to dominate the play (especially acts two and four). Within the, household, Shakespeare distinguishes between public and private rooms, ranging from the 'great chamber' (1.5.12) in which the masque takes place and the servants' quarters (the pastry or pantry, and kitchen), to the most intimate and strictly controlled room within the household, Juliet's bedchamber (Juliet also invites the Nurse to join her in her closet: a very small, private room increasingly built into the recesses of Elizabethan houses, 4.2.32). Capulet's household is depicted in more precise detail than the street, particularly in the Second Quarto (or Q2) of the play. The preparations for the masque, for instance (Q2 only, 1.5.1–13), involve four household servants and an array of contemporary household goods: napkins, trenchers (wooden plates), join-stools (wooden stools fitted by a joiner), court-cupboards (sideboards), plate (silverware), marchpane (marzipan). Attention is drawn to the material provision of Juliet's marriage feast (see especially 4.2.9 and 37), and there are repeated references to household goods: ornaments from Juliet's closet (4.2.32–3), herbs, keys, spices, dates, quinces (Q2 only, 4.4.1–2), baked meats, things for the cook, drier logs, spits, baskets (4.4.5–17), beds and curtains (Q1, pp. 85 and 87). At the same time, attention is drawn to the labour of the household: giving household orders; moving, washing, and scraping trenchers; clearing furniture; serving supper in the great chamber; tidying tables; tending the fire; fetching foodstuffs; cooking; making beds; getting dressed. The effect of these layers of household detail is to emphasize the domestic context of the play; by contrast, Shakespeare's principal source for the play, Brooke's *Romeus*, pays little attention to servants and household goods or management. The household becomes the symbolic centre of Shakespeare's play—a bold choice for a tragedy, which traditionally was the stuff of kings, politicians, and generals; courts, governments, and battlefields * * *.

As an elite, unmarried girl, Juliet is restricted in her movements: as the Chorus puts it, compared to Romeo, Juliet has the opportunity or 'means much less / To meet her new-beloved anywhere' (1.5.154–5). She does not venture beyond the household except to go to confession—for which she needs permission ('Have you got leave to go to shrift today?', 2.5.65). As such she conforms to the orthodox model of feminine behaviour put forward by contemporary moralists that women should stay within the confines of the home.

According to conduct literature (writing on how to behave) only privacy and enclosure ensured the chastity of wives and daughters: thus in *The English Gentlewoman* (London, 1631) Richard Brathwaite urged women to remain 'in your Chambers or private Closets . . . retired from the eyes of men' (p. 47). Georgianna Ziegler has described this confinement of women as 'a kind of domestic enclosure created by a patriarchal feudal society, afraid both of the weakness and of the insidious power of women' (p. 74). In other words, fears circulating in patriarchal society about uncontrolled female sexuality led to women being confined to the home. There are many historical examples of women being curtailed by their fathers and husbands. But there were also occasions when enclosure—or more precisely the privacy it afforded—could become enabling for women. Thus it is precisely in the space of her bedchamber that Juliet undermines Capulet's patriarchal authority by consummating her illicit marriage to Romeo (and later by taking the Friar's potion). Juliet's room is the site of independence and disobedience, as well as restriction and enclosure. Privacy enables Juliet's expression of subjectivity— that is, her sense of her self. In fact she enacts Brathwaite's concern that 'privacy is made the recluse of *Temptation*. . . . Therefore doe nothing *privately*, which you would not doe *publickly*' (pp. 44–9).

Romeo and Juliet distinguishes between the freedom of movement for unmarried girls and for married women: Juliet's mother, like Lady Montague, moves beyond the household to join her husband when 'brawls' erupt on the streets (1.1.65 and 3.1.131), while the widowed, lower-status Nurse apparently enjoys the most freedom of movement among women in the play, facilitating her role as a mediator between Romeo and Juliet. The younger and older male generations inhabit both the private domain of the home and the public domain of the street; indeed, the street becomes identified with men and the feud (see 1.1.8–17 and 3.1.43–7). Mercutio confirms the necessary publicity—among men—of feuding aggression when he rejects Benvolio's plea to 'withdraw unto some private place': 'Men's eyes were made to look, and let them gaze' (3.1.43–7). Similarly, Capulet is keen to fight on the street ('Give me my long sword, ho!', 1.1.66) but not prepared to resume the feud in his own home: 'I would not for the wealth of all this town / Here in my house do him disparagement' (1.5.68–9). If Juliet's bedchamber becomes the site of private rebellion, then the streets of Verona are the site of public rebellion between feuding families.

Romeo moves between these two sites; indeed, he is the character with most freedom of movement in the play (whether licit or illicit, chosen or imposed). Unlike his male peers, Romeo is strongly associated with private space in the play: at the outset of the play he voluntarily 'pens' (encloses) himself in his chamber (1.1.129) and,

performing the part of the male love-melancholic, he withdraws into
the 'covert' of woods, glades, and gardens (1.1.116 * * *). After meeting Juliet, Romeo's cultivation of solitude gives way to the pursuit of
his private desires ('satisfaction' with Juliet)—and, as a result, private space—particularly Juliet's bedchamber—becomes increasingly
associated in the play with intrigue rather than solitude. While men
were typically identified as 'public' beings in early modern culture,
Romeo and Juliet complicates those stereotypes by showing a man
who (by contrast to his male peers) cultivates privacy as part of his
persona and inhabits private spaces.

In this politics of space, thresholds become significant. *Romeo and
Juliet* pays special attention to questions of access (perhaps most
memorably in the so-called 'balcony scene'), and to the objects that
variously impede or aid entry: walls, windows, rope ladders, mat-
tocks, wrenching irons, spades. In order to gain access to Juliet,
Romeo has first to cross the threshold of the 'orchard wall' (2.1.5),
'high and hard to climb' (2.2.63), and penetrate the Capulet estate.
The orchard becomes what social anthropologists have described as
a liminal space—a space or period of time in which normal social
conventions are temporarily deferred, ignored, or challenged. Not
only does Romeo break the convention of the feud, collapsing the
boundaries between Montague and Capulet by meeting Juliet, but
Juliet breaks the conventions of courtship by assuming the dominant
role normally ascribed to men ('I should have been more strange, I
must confess', 2.2.102). The space of the orchard is also invested
with sexual symbolism. 'Of all the symbols Shakespeare uses to
denote sexual activity and sexual rites of passage in the plays', notes
Marjorie Garber, 'the most traditional of all is the walled garden':

> The traditional biblical description of the bride as a *hortus con-
> clusus*, a 'garden inclosed' (Song of Songs, 4:12), becomes in
> his plays a geographical emblem of virginity and a locus for sex-
> ual initiation. The terms 'garden' and 'orchard' at this period
> both refer to an enclosed plot of land devoted to horticulture;
> 'orchard' derives etymologically from Latin *hortus* and Anglo-
> Saxon *yard*. It is in such settings in the plays, almost inevitably,
> that love is sworn and affections given.[1]

Although 2.2 has become popularly known as the 'balcony scene'
following eighteenth-century stage conventions, the texts of *Romeo
and Juliet* do not specify a balcony but a window. The threshold
between Romeo and Juliet is a window ('what light through yonder
window breaks?', 2.2.2); a physical barrier, the window evokes,
indeed becomes symbolic of, the social barriers against Romeo and

---

1. Marjorie Garber, *Coming of Age in Shakespeare* (London and New York: Methuen, 1981),
163–4.

Juliet's relationship. Thus one of the most strategic props in the play becomes the rope ladder—the cords' (3.2.33 and 35) which allow Romeo access to Juliet's bedchamber. Juliet's window comes to mark a threshold in her relations with Romeo: once he gains entry to her window with the rope ladder, he also gains entry to her body.

Body Politics Breaking Away the umbilical Cord

Romeo and Juliet is a play obsessed with bodies and body parts. The play's bawdy humour draws attention to the male and female body (especially genitalia); characters repeatedly discuss their physical well-being or ailments, and dwell upon bodily functions: sleeping, eating, drinking, making love, pregnancy, breastfeeding. The body is figured in complex ways in *Romeo and Juliet*—as old, young, impotent, virile, sexual, maternal, healthy, diseased. Indeed, it is fear of the diseased body that underpins the tragic turn of events in the final act of the play. Friar John reports that Friar Lawrence's letter to Romeo was not delivered in Mantua because of the plague: 'So fearful were they of infection' (5.2.16). This is one of several references to plague in the play (see also 1.4.74–6, 1.5.15–16, 3.1.82 and 91, 3.2.90) which would have had topical relevance for an Elizabethan audience: in 1593, not long before the first performance of *Romeo and Juliet*, plague in London was so bad that the theatres were closed down and Elizabeth I's court removed to St Albans (Hertfordshire).

The diseased or impotent body also inflects Shakespeare's portrayal of sexuality in the play. In the opening scene of the play Lady Capulet sarcastically draws attention to her husband's impotence—both martially and sexually—by remarking that his 'sword' (slang for penis) should be substituted for a 'crutch' (1.1.67). There are several implicit allusions to symptoms of venereal disease in the play, including bone-ache—suffered by the Nurse ('Fie, how my bones ache! What a jaunce have I!', 2.5.26) and alluded to by Mercutio ('O their bones, their bones!', 2.4.30–1)—and blistered lips ('the angry Mab with blisters plagues', 1.4.75). Sexuality in the play thus emerges not only as virile, fertile, youthful, virginal, passionate, and indeed exploitative, but as potentially disease-ridden and debilitating. Other images of disease in the play are clustered around lovesickness (see especially 1.1.185–93), old age, infection and poison, even food disorders. Capulet attacks Juliet in 3.5 by calling her 'green-sickness carrion!' (3.5.156–7), an allusion to a perceived illness associated with food disorders which adolescent girls—otherwise known as 'green' girls (see *Hamlet*, 1.3.101)—were thought to suffer from (as such it has been compared with modern-day anorexia nervosa and bulimia). The accumulative effect of these references to the sick, diseased body in Shakespeare's *Romeo and Juliet* is to suggest the precarious social, as well as physical, health of Verona.

It is, however, the portrayal of the grotesque and the maternal body in the play that I want to focus upon here. In his analysis of the 'habits' of the Renaissance body, Mikhail Bakhtin argued for an opposition in early modern culture between the 'classical' and the 'grotesque' body. The classical body denoted a clean, controlled, and ordered body; an image of 'finished, completed' man.[2] In *Romeo and Juliet*, the chaste figure of Rosaline, closed to outside advances, perhaps best corresponds to the classical body (see 1.1.202–5). The grotesque body, by contrast, is 'unfinished, outgrows itself, transgresses its own limits', and is concerned

> with the lower stratum of the body, the life of the body, and the reproductive organs: it therefore relates to acts of defecation and copulation, conception, pregnancy and birth. (pp. 21 and 26)

Thus the grotesque emphasizes those parts of the body 'that are open to the outside world', 'the open mouth, the genital organs, the breasts, the phallus, the potbelly, the nose' (p. 26).

Much of the bawdy humour in *Romeo and Juliet* revolves around the grotesque body * * *. As Knowles points out (pp. 71–4), the Nurse seems to epitomize Bakhtin's notion of the grotesque, especially in her repeated allusions to copulation, conception, genitalia, and her own body. Her opening line reveals that she lost her virginity 'at twelve year old' (1.3.2); she proceeds to joke about Juliet falling backwards, inviting sex (1.3.43 and 57–8), and casually refers to 'a young cock'rel's stone', or testicle (1.3.54). During the course of the play the Nurse seems to take a vicarious pleasure in anticipating Juliet's sexual encounters. After announcing Romeo's proposed marriage to Juliet she immediately imagines Juliet's sexual activity: the 'wanton blood' rising in her cheeks; the 'bird's nest' (suggestive of pubic hair) which Romeo 'must climb', Juliet's bearing of 'the burden' of Romeo's body while making love (2.5.70–5). The Nurse effectively collapses marriage with sex, a move she repeats in act four when speaking of Juliet's marriage with Paris in terms of sexual exertion:

> I warrant
> The County Paris has set up his rest
> That you shall rest but little.
>
> . . . .
>
> Ay let the County take you in your bed,
> He'll fright you up, i'faith.
> (4.5.5–11)

---

2. Mikhail Bakhtin, *Rabelais and His World*, trans. Helene Iswolsky (Cambridge, MA: MIT Press, 1968), 320. See also Peter Stallybrass, 'Patriarchal Territories: The Body Enclosed', in Margaret Ferguson, Maureen Quilligan and Nancy Vickers (eds.), *Rewriting the Renaissance: The Discourses of Sexual Difference in Early Modern Europe* (Chicago: Chicago University Press, 1985), 124.

By contrast, Lady Capulet presents Juliet's marriage to Paris as a romantic experience—'the golden story' (1.3.93)—while Capulet considers the marriage principally in terms of social and economic status: 'of noble parentage, / Of fair demesnes, youthful and nobly ligned' (3.5.179–80). Bakhtin argued that the grotesque mode could be used to counteract or undermine the status of the 'classical', high, or orthodox; it can puncture the gravity and grasp of dominant discourses and ideologies (systems of belief and expression). Applied to the Nurse, we might say that her discourse of sex challenges, and arguably undermines, the idealization of romantic love voiced by Lady Capulet (and indeed Juliet) and the notion that marriage is principally a status issue, voiced by Capulet. While the Capulets mask the presence of sexuality within marriage, the Nurse exposes it.

Romeo and Juliet is also striking for its insistence upon the maternal body—which recalls the grotesque's emphasis upon 'copulation, conception, pregnancy and birth'.[3] Conception is hinted at in the opening Prologue ('the fatal loins' of the Capulets and Montagues, 5), and reiterated in the repeated punning in the play on the word *bear* (to bear the weight of a man while making love, and to bear children). The Nurse anticipates Juliet's pregnancy ('bigger women grow by men'; 1.3.96); Lady Capulet calls attention to the reproductive potential of her daughter's body (1.3.73–4), while Juliet describes her love for Romeo as a 'Prodigious birth' (1.5.139). The Nurse talks about breastfeeding with humour, frankness, and intimacy, casually describing the contemporary practice of putting wormwood (a bitter plant) on her nipple in order to wean Juliet: 'When it did taste the wormwood on the nipple / Of my dug, and felt it bitter, pretty fool, / To see it tetchy and fall out wi'th'dug!' (1.3.30–3). Her vivid description of the episode, coupled with the presence it holds in her mind—'I never shall forget it' (1.3.25)—indicate her self-identification as a nursing mother (hardly surprising given her profession). By contrast, Lady Capulet barely refers to her maternal body, remarking only to Juliet that 'I was your mother much upon these years / That you are now a maid' (1.3.73–4). 'There is no atmosphere of maternal tenderness about this lady', concluded Jess Dorynne in 1913 (p. 73)—but perhaps Lady Capulet is simply conforming to the cultural imperative of the closed, ordered, 'classical' body, and enacting the due feminine modesty demanded of elite women. By contrast, the lower-status Nurse is able to make free reference to her nipples and breasts with less threat of impropriety, and in this respect the maternal body in *Romeo and Juliet* seems figured along class lines.

3. Bakhtin, *Rabelais and His World*, 21.

While the Nurse speaks literally of breastfeeding, the Friar speaks metaphorically of Nature as a nursing mother:

> The earth that's nature's mother is her tomb;
> What is her burying grave, that is her womb;
> And from her womb children of divers kind
> We sucking on her natural bosom find.
>
>   (2.3.9–12)

For Edward Snow, Friar Lawrence imagines nature arrested at the maternal breast (p. 187). But the Friar also articulates one of the play's central motifs—the womb/tomb—and foreshadows the final scene in which an actual 'tomb' becomes the 'burying grave' of the 'children' of Capulet and Montague.[4] When Romeo comes to deploy the womb/tomb motif in act five, his imagery is not of nourishment but of devouring and engulfment:

> Thou detestable maw, thou womb of death,
> Gorged with the dearest morsel of the earth,
> Thus I enforce thy rotten jaws to open,
> And in despite I'll cram thee with more food.
>
>   (5.3.45–9)

Romeo associates the womb/tomb with a 'detestable maw'—the mouth or throat of a voracious, wild animal. There are intriguing sexual undertones here, for it was commonplace to characterize women's sexual desire in terms of a voracious, animalistic appetite, while contemporary medical treatises characterized the womb as a hungry, moving organ that wandered around the woman's body on a monthly cycle. Romeo's imagery effectively associates the womb with a fierce animal's hunger and death (the tomb). But his forced entry of the Capulet tomb also evokes images of rape or sexual intercourse. Romeo 'enforces' the womb/tomb open and stuffs it ('cram', penetrate) with his own body. A few minutes later Friar Lawrence looks on the tomb and exclaims 'Alack, alack, what blood is this which stains / The stony entrance of this sepulchre?' (5.3.140–1), and, as Coppélia Kahn has suggestively argued, 'the blood-spattered entrance to this tomb that has been figured as a womb recalls both a defloration or initiation into sexuality and a birth' (p. 353).

4. On womb/tomb imagery in the play, see Belsey, 'The Name of the Rose in *Romeo and Juliet*', in *Yearbook of English Studies*, 23 (1993), 126–42; Farrell, 'Love, Death and Patriarchy'; Jorgens, *Shakespeare on Film*; Knowles, 'Carnival and Death in *Romeo and Juliet*: A Bakhtinian Reading', in *Shakespeare Survey* 49 (1996), 69–85; Levin, 'Form and Formality in *Romeo and Juliet*', *Shakespeare Quarterly*, 11 (winter 1960), 3–11, repr. in Cole, *Twentieth Century Interpretations of 'Romeo and Juliet'*, 85–95; Ozark Holmer, 'The Poetics of Paradox'; Snow, 'Language and Sexual Difference in *Romeo and Juliet*', in Peter Erickson and Coppélia Kahn (eds.), *Shakespeare's 'Rough Magic': Renaissance Essays in Honor of C. L. Barber* (London: Associated University Press, 1985), 168–92, repr. in Andrews, *Romeo and Juliet: Critical Essays*, 371–401.

While the opening acts of the play tend to stress the generation and nourishment of the maternal body, the womb increasingly becomes fashioned as a source of fear, threat, and insecurity. A sense of foreboding is arguably the keynote to Mercutio's speech upon the 'midwife' Queen Mab (an image which both alludes to Queen Mab's role assisting in the birth of fantasies and underscores the repeated reference to the maternal body in the play):

> This is the hag, when maids lie on their backs,
> That presses them and learns them first to bear,
> Making them women of good carriage. This is she—
>   (1.4.91–3)

Mercutio describes a mechanistic account of heterosexual sex in which women are merely sexual and reproductive objects, a vehicle ('carriage') for bearing men and children. Coppélia Kahn has read these lines as revealing Mercutio's 'fear of giving in to the seething nighttime world of unconscious desires associated with the feminine' (p. 343); that is, the sexual desires that women may arouse in men. This note of latent eroticism in the speech is certainly hinted at in Henry Fuseli's extraordinary painting of *Fairy Mab* engraved by W. Raddon * * *: a plump, long-haired young woman in a low-cut dress holds a cup against her breast and looks out seductively, mouth open, from a dark corner; on a table beside her is a hookah (used for inhaling tobacco and drugs) while to her other side a black woman-servant stands by with a knowing smile on her face. Fuseli's *Fairy Mab* fuses the erotic with the exotic. But Mercutio's Queen Mab speech also carries a note of phobia—a fear of and fascination with the maternal body. His use of the word 'hag'—an incubus or nightmare that induced evil, particularly sexual, dreams—sounds a note of revulsion: women's conception and pregnancy become part of a nightmarish vision for Mercutio. This was the tone of both Zeffirelli's 1968 film and Luhrmann's 1996 film: Mercutio became progressively disturbed during the Queen Mab speech and Romeo's interruption, 'Peace, peace, Mercutio, peace!' (1.4.95) was said in the manner of a parent calming down a child after a bad dream (or, in the case of Luhrmann's film, a bad trip on hallucinogenic drugs). Terry Hands's 1973 RSC production deliberately emphasized the latent misogyny and sexual anxiety of the Queen Mab speech * * *: Mercutio carried 'a grotesque, coarse-featured, life-size female doll, upon which he vented clearly sado-masochistic sexual loathing' that was both 'deeply-disturbed and equally disturbing.[5]

What should we make of the play's insistent allusions to the maternal body? On the one hand, in his opening speech on Mother

---

5. Holding, *Romeo and Juliet*, 55.

Nature, Friar Lawrence posits an alternative teleology (or way of thinking) to the patriarchal, male-centred codes which seem to dominate the play. Whereas the feud fosters enmity and death and is centred upon the figure of the father ('Deny thy father and refuse thy name', 2.2.34), the Friar appeals to maternal nourishment and invests the maternal body with positive, generative attributes. On the other hand it could be argued that women in the play are repeatedly reduced to their reproductive functions, and regarded as objects rather than subjects. In this respect, the maternal body becomes used to position and effectively disempower women. Alternatively, Coppélia Kahn has suggestively argued that adolescent motherhood becomes an adolescent rite of passage 'typical for youth in Verona'—a rite which, by committing suicide, Juliet rejects (p. 349). The maternal body thus becomes a cultural imperative for young women that is encouraged by both older men and women (witness Lady Capulet's insistence that Juliet is old enough to be a mother). Or we might emphasize instead the element of the 'grotesque': the play's insistent allusions to conception, pregnancy, and birth, as well as to big bellies (1.3.96) and breasts, share in grotesque humour and its 'material bodily principle',[6] undermining the idealization and romanticization of desire in the play.

Alternatively, psychoanalytic critic Janet Adelman has argued that the maternal body was a source of male anxiety and psychological trauma in early modern England. 'Culturally constructed as literally dangerous to everyone, the maternal body must have seemed especially dangerous to little boys', who had to form their 'specifically masculine selfhood against the matrix of [their mother's] overwhelming femaleness' (p. 7). Wet-nursing (which Adelman provocatively describes as 'sometimes tantamount to murder') effectively prolonged the period of 'infantile dependency' when male infants 'were subject to pleasures and dangers especially associated with nursing and the maternal body' (pp. 4–5 * * *). Originally deprived of their mother's breast, boys were then deprived of their wet-nurse once they were weaned, giving them 'two psychic sites of intense maternal deprivation rather than one'. Finally, the boy-child had to 'leave that femaleness behind in order to become a man, enforcing the equation of masculine identity with differentation from the mother' (pp. 4–7). It is against this psychological context, argues Adelman, that Shakespeare's plays invoke:

> the nightmare of a femaleness that can weaken and contaminate masculinity, a 'thirsty' earth-mouth that can 'gape open wide and eat him quick' (3 *Henry VI*, 2.3.15; *Richard III*, 1.2.65), a womb that is a 'bed of death', smothering its children in 'the

6. Knowles, 'Carnival and Death', 71.

swallowing gulf / Of dark forgetfulness and deep oblivion' (*Richard III*, 4.1.53; 3.7.127–8). Through this imagery of engulfment and swallowing suffocation . . . the womb takes on a malevolent power. (p. 4)

How far we can apply modern psychoanalytic theory to a past culture and fictional text is open to question, and I take issue with Adelman's bleak account of wet-nursing in the period. However, her attention to the note of anxiety in Shakespeare's imagery of the maternal body is extremely suggestive—particularly in the wider context of the 'range of anxieties about masculinity and female power' expressed in fiction and non-fiction alike in the period (p. 3). Certainly much of the imagery of the maternal body in *Romeo and Juliet* shares a sense of threat—of contamination, engulfment, suffocation, death. The repeated allusions to the maternal body and motherhood in *Romeo and Juliet* alongside other Shakespeare plays (such as *Richard III*, *c.* 1592–3, and *A Midsummer Night's Dream*, written about the same time as *Romeo and Juliet*, *c.* 1594–5) indicate the symbolic power that maternity could wield in the period—whether as a source of danger, pleasure, or fascination.

Femininity, Sexuality, and Effeminacy

> To us, in our enraptured dreams, Juliet was a true, living woman, as veritable flesh and blood as our sisters and our playmates. . . . Not that we imagined her to have been a well-educated English young lady, like ourselves.—Governesses forbid! We were too proper for that;—we were quite convinced of the heinous indecorum of falling in love one day, and being married clandestinely the next, without a word to papa or mamma. But, somehow, with youth's very slipshod style of argument, we managed to love Juliet all the more because we disapproved of her.[7]
>
> (Mrs. David Ogilvy, 1885)

Juliet has repeatedly posed a problem for those seeking to idealize her: as a 13-year-old girl, can her precocious sexuality, independence, and assertiveness be regarded as model, feminine behaviour? Juliet has often been recuperated as an ideal heroine on three counts: her initial modesty, her loving nature, and her rapidly developing maturity. In the nineteenth century it was commonplace for women to praise Juliet as a paragon of feminine modesty: Anna Jameson, for instance, found her 'silence and her filial deference' towards her mother in 1.3 'charming' (p. 91); Mrs Elliott admired Juliet's simplicity, naïvety, and innocence (a contrast to the precocious 'English school-girls of the present enlightened age', p. 178),

---

7. Mrs. David Ogilvy, 'Juliet and the Friar', in *The Keepsake 1885*, ed. Miss Power, 74–9 (pp. 74–5).

while the renowned nineteenth-century actress, Helena Faucit, remarked of Juliet's confession of love in the orchard scene (2.2.85–106) that:

> Only one who knew of what a true woman is capable, in frankness, in courage, and self-surrender when her heart is possessed by a noble love, could have touched with such delicacy, such infinite charm of mingled reserve and artless frankness, the avowal of so fervent yet so modest a love, the secret of which had been so strangely stolen from her. (pp. 118–19)

Faucit co-opts Juliet as an ideal of women in love; a demonstration of 'true' Womanhood. She attempts a balancing act between Juliet's 'fervent', frank expression of passion and the 'mingled reserve' and modesty required of women in the nineteenth century—a balance which she claims Shakespeare achieves with extraordinary 'delicacy'. But the fact that Juliet has sex aged 13 with a man she has known for little more than a day compromises this delicacy. For Faucit, as for many critics and actresses in the nineteenth century, Juliet's sexual passion could be recuperated as heroic only by appealing to her rapid maturity as a woman: initially, 'girlish and immature', Faucit remarked, Juliet 'is transfigured into the heroic woman' (p. 140).

But, as we have already seen, the Elizabethan texts of *Romeo and Juliet* do not seem to point to Juliet's maturity; rather, her actions are variously described as rash, desperate, piteous and misadventured * * *. Moreover, Juliet speaks openly about her sexual passion. Her body is open to Romeo's advances, and she enthusiastically allows him to kiss her within minutes of meeting him. 'It may be objected', commented Bulwer Lytton in 1885, 'that a modern audience would be shocked by such an unlimited and promiscuous quantity of kissing'; likewise to an Elizabethan audience Juliet's lack of restraint could have signalled a breach in feminine decorum.[8] In fact Juliet acknowledges this in the orchard scene, remarking that 'I should have been more strange' (acted with more restraint and less familiarity) but 'I am too fond' (2.2.98–102). Juliet fully reveals her feelings of sexual desire when anticipating her wedding night in her epithalamion or wedding poem (3.2.1–31 * * *). Indeed, Nicholas Brooke has provocatively suggested that Juliet's remark in the epithalamion, 'though I am sold, / Not yet enjoy'd' (3.2.27–8), reveals 'Juliet's discovery that in most wanting her true love with Romeo she must experience the wish to be a whore in the fullest sense' (p. 100). The epithalamion centred on the bride's sexual passion and encouraged her to express her physical desires in order for conception to take place (current medical theory maintained that women could

8. Bulwer Lytton, 'Miss Anderson's Juliet', *Shakespeariana*, 2 (1885), 11–12.

conceive only if, like men, they emitted their seed—that is, achieved an orgasm). Juliet's epithalamion, reduced to a mere four lines in the First Quarto or Q1, is more concerned with physical desire than romantic love:

> Romeo
> Leap to these arms,
>
> .   .   .   .   .
>
> Come, civil Night,
>
> .   .   .   .   .
>
> And learn me how to lose a winning match,
> Played for a pair of stainless maidenhoods.
> Hood my unmanned blood, bating in my cheeks,
> With thy black mantle, till strange love grow bold,
>
> .   .   .   .   .
>
> Give me my Romeo, and when I shall die,
> Take him and cut him out in little stars . . .
>   (3.2.6–22)

Juliet is 'impatient' (3.2.30) to lose her virginity ('maidenhead'), and compares her desire—her 'blood'—with an unrestrained ('unmanned') falcon whose wings flutter wildly ('bate'). She seeks to be a 'bold' lover (3.2.15) and then looks forward to her own sexual pleasure: 'to die' was common sexual slang for orgasm. This is how Niamh Cusack, playing the part of Juliet in Bogdanov's 1986 RSC production, interpreted the line: 'my first reading of the word *die* here is the sexual one: the white of the stars, and his body in white, and the white of him ejaculating inside me'.[9] The line has curiously been emended by some editors, perhaps reticent about Juliet's precocious sexuality, to Q4's 'when *he* shall die'. As Mary Bly suggests, an Elizabethan audience would be sure to grasp the sexual double-meaning of 'die' and with it Juliet's awareness of carnal desire. But that sexual knowledge was 'a dubious virtue in light of Elizabethan conceptions of a chaste young woman's education' (explaining perhaps why 'witty heroines in Renaissance plays rarely offer immodest puns'[1]). Juliet's epithalamion, laden with sexual innuendo, is not present in Shakespeare's primary source for the play, Brooke's *Romeus*. Its addition to Q2 *Romeo and Juliet* testifies to Shakespeare's interest in the erotic nature of Juliet's passion, while its excision from Q1 points, Mary Bly argues, 'to the fact that Juliet's expression of erotic desire represented a breach of cultural expectation'.[2]

---

9. Cusack, 'Juliet in *Romeo and Juliet*', 129.
1. Mary Bly, 'Bawdy Puns and Lustful Virgins: The Legacy of Juliet's Desire in Comedies of the Early 1600s', *Shakespeare Survey* 49 (1996), 99.
2. Ibid., 105. On Juliet's epithalamion, see also Belsey, 'The Name of the Rose'; Brooke, *Shakespeare's Early Tragedies*; Philip Davis, 'Nineteenth-century Juliet', in *Shakespeare*

Orthodox morality in early modern England emphasized not the open expression but the confinement of unmarried women's sexual desire: thus when the moralist Juan Luis Vives issued instructions upon 'how the maid shall seek an husband' he explained 'it is not comely for a maid to desire marriage, and much less to shew herself to long therefore'.[3] Dympna Callaghan has argued that Juliet's desire is 'benign and unthreatening' (p. 84), but in my view it is shown to be unruly, leading to a rash, clandestine marriage; as Edward Snow puts it, Juliet's sexuality is not domesticated (pp. 184–5). 'There is nothing which requires more discretion', argued Richard Brathwaite in *The English Gentlewoman* (1631), 'than how to behave or carry ourselves while we are enthralled to affection'. Brathwaite's model gentlewoman should be 'never yet acquainted with a passionate *ah me*, nor a careless folding of her arms, as if the thought of a prevailing lover had wrought in her thoughts some violent distemper'.[4] But Juliet departs from such an ideal. Her opening words in the orchard scene are precisely 'Ay me!' (2.2.23–4)—a contemporary cliché for indulgent passion which Mercutio mocks in 'Cry but "Ay me!"' (2.2.10)—while her 'desperate' behaviour in threatening suicide (see 4.1.69 and 5.3.263–4) seems to manifest the 'violent distemper' Brathwaite warned women against. Brathwaite acknowledged that not all gentlewomen lived up to the ideal: some women are 'so surprised with affection as it bursts out into violent extremes; their discourse is semi-brew'd with sighs, their talk with tears'.[5] Shakespeare's Juliet corresponds more closely to Brathwaite's outline of the distempered, 'melancholy' and passionate young gentlewoman than to contemporary ideals of femininity.

There is also the question of Juliet's ethnicity: English stereotypes of Italians repeatedly emphasized their propensity for passion and sexual indulgence. Certainly appealing to ethnic difference enabled nineteenth-century critics to distance as 'foreign' what was one of the play's most problematic issues in the period: the fact of a sexually active 13-year-old girl. 'Repugnant as this may be to us,' remarked Mrs Elliott in 1885, 'we cannot dispute the fact that under Southern skies the conditions of physical and moral development are vastly

Survey 49 (1996), 131–40; Gibbons, *Romeo and Juliet*; Knowles, 'Carnival and Death'; Kristeva, '*Romeo and Juliet*: Love-Hatred in the Couple', from *Tales of Love*, repr. in John Drakakis (ed.), *Shakespearean Tragedy* (London: Longman, 1992), 296–315; Gary M. McCown, '"Runnawares Eyes" and Juliet's Epithalamium', *Shakespeare Quarterly* 27 (1976), 150–70; Novy, 'Violence, Love, and Gender'; Gayle Whittier, 'The Sonnet's Body and the Body Sonnetized in *Romeo and Juliet*', in *Shakespeare Quarterly* 40:1 (spring 1989), 27–41.

3. Juan Luis Vives, *The Instruction of a Christian Woman*, quoted in Klein, *Daughters, Wives and Widows*, 111.

4. Richard Brathwaite, *The English Gentlewoman*, quoted in Klein, *Daughters, Wives and Widows*, 237.

5. Ibid., 242.

different to what they are in the cold North' (p, 178). How far were
such distancing strategies in operation in early modern England?
Certainly racial and ethnic stereotyping took place in the period, and
Italians were noted for their hot blood (see 3.1.3–5) and lack of
control.[6] Uncontrolled sexual passion, often attributed to the hot climate, was considered to be a national characteristic—a stereotype
intensified by the demonization of Italy as the sinful centre of Roman
Catholicism * * *. Roger Ascham, for instance, reported that on a
nine-day visit to Venice he saw 'more libertie to sinne than ever I
heard tell of in our noble Citie of London in nine yeare'.[7] The
renowned pornographic works of Aretino (illustrated by Giulio
Romano, the only artist Shakespeare mentions by name in the canon
of his works; see *The Winter's Tale*, 5.2.95) confirmed an image of
Italy as a place of sexual indulgence; Venetian courtesans (prostitutes) were a particular source of curiosity for English writers, and
Italian sexual habits were variously commented upon with horror,
humour, fear, and fascination. For an Elizabethan audience, Juliet's
'fondness' may well have signalled the sexual proclivities of a hot-
blooded Italian.

Juliet also departs from contemporary ideals of female silence and
submission. In the orchard scene, Juliet is far from conventionally
modest or submissive towards her future husband: she dominates
their discussion (Juliet has ninety-seven lines compared to Romeo's
forty-six in their conversation, 2.2.49–189), asking questions (2.2.62,
79, 90, 126), and issuing orders (2.2.109, 112, 116, 138, 143–4).
Moreover, Juliet takes the leading role in organizing the progress of
their affair, directing their desires towards marriage, and making
arrangements for it (2.2.142–70). Significantly, Juliet's parting image
positions Romeo as her indulgent object—a child's pet bird ('a wanton's bird', 2.2.177), whom she controls at will:

> I would have thee gone:
> And yet no farther than a wanton's bird,
> That lets it hop a little from his hand,
> Like a poor prisoner in his twisted gyves,
> And with a silken thread plucks it back again,
> So loving-jealous of his liberty.
>
> (2.2.176–81)

---

6. See Murray J. Levith, *Shakespeare's Italian Setting and Plays* (Basingstoke: Macmillan,
   1989); and Angela Locatelli, 'The Fictional World of *Romeo and Juliet*: Cultural Connotations of an Italian Setting', in Michele Marrapodi, A. J. Hoenselaars, Marcello Cap-
   puzzo, and L. Falson Santucci (eds.), *Shakespeare's Italy: Functions of Italian Locations
   in Renaissance Drama* (Manchester: Manchester University Press, 1993).
7. Roger Ascham, *The Scholemaster* (1570), quoted in Levith, *Shakespeare's Italian Setting and Plays*, 6.

Here Juliet reverses orthodox patriarchal relations by imagining herself in control of a man's movements—making him 'prisoner' to her will (she also imagines herself as a falconer and Romeo as her falcon, 2.2.158–9). And by figuring herself as the owner of a pet, Juliet reverses the conventional association of women with animals that required taming by men—a convention which Capulet shockingly employs in his characterization of Juliet as a domestic animal: 'fettle your fine joints 'gainst Thursday next. . . . Graze you where you will, you shall not house with me' (3.5.153 and 188). Dympna Callaghan has persuasively argued that power relations within the couple are 'completely idealized' (p. 81), but I would add the qualification that, by adopting an assertive, often dominant role in her dealings with Romeo and by denying her father's authority, Juliet counters contemporary ideological imperatives for female modesty and submission; indeed, François Laroque has argued that Juliet *subverts* such imperatives (p. 18). Certainly Juliet's capacity to dominate her male lover proved troubling to Constance O'Brien in the late nineteenth century:

> in spite of [Romeo's] love and earnestness, Juliet is the leading spirit of the two; perhaps it should not be so, but she has the stronger nature and guides, where Romeo is content to worship her. . . . From this it comes that she reverses the order of things, and asks Romeo if he means to marry her—which somehow does jar a little; she has her wits so very much about her, considering her youth and perfect inexperience. . . . [Romeo] is a graceful pleasant sort of lover, full of ardour and devotion; but is he quite man enough for Juliet?[8]

Far from being a simple, conventional heroine, Juliet is a complex, conflicted, and multidimensional character, whose femininity can be read in opposing ways. In my view, rather than representing a feminine ideal Juliet evokes the problematic figure of the unruly woman; the woman who challenges patriarchal dictates and social convention.

I want finally to turn to another aspect of the representation of femininity in *Romeo and Juliet*: effeminacy. Effeminacy denoted a man 'suffering' from traits normally associated in the early modern period with women—weakness ('women being the weaker vessels', 1.1.14), softness, excessive speech, tears, and sullen behaviour—and was generally claimed to be caused by sexual overindulgence in women (but could also be associated with same-sex passion between men). If Juliet departs from ideals of femininity in the period, then Romeo

8. Constance O'Brien (1879), in Thompson and Roberts, *Women Reading Shakespeare*, 144.

departs from contemporary ideals of masterful manhood by becoming, in his own words, 'effeminate' (3.1.105).[9] At the pivotal fight of the play (3.1), in a passage cut from Zeffirelli's film, Romeo cries out against his 'vile submission' to Tybalt's taunts:

> O sweet Juliet
> Thy beauty hath made me effeminate,
> And in my temper softened valour's steel!'
> (3.1.104–6)

Romeo's denial of the conventional codes of aggressive, feuding, masculine honour makes him what a woman should supposedly be: submissive. Romeo perceives his 'softness'—the weakness of the manly, steel-like courage of his temper (punning on the technical tempering or strengthening of steel swords)—as effeminate, and attributes it to the effects of Juliet's beauty (a classic case of displacing blame onto the woman). But in a passage substantially cut from both Zeffirelli's 1968 film and Luhrmann's 1996 film, it is the Friar who throws most scorn on Romeo's effeminacy:

> Art thou a man? thy form cries out thou art;
> Thy tears are womanish, thy wild acts denote
> The unreasonable fury of a beast.
> Unseemly woman in a seeming man,
> And ill-beseeming beast in seeming both,
> Thou hast amazed me. By my holy order,
> I thought thy disposition better tempered.
> . . . .
> Fie, fie, thou sham'st thy shape . . .
> (3.3.108–22)

Here the Friar reveals his attachment to cultural assumptions of feminine weakness and masculine mastery. Tears and the expression of vulnerability are associated with women—real men don't cry—thus Romeo's tears become a mark of 'womanish' behaviour, 'unseemly' and shameful in a man. The Friar speaks of a contradiction between Romeo's male 'shape' and his female 'disposition', and in 'seeming both' Romeo becomes less than human, a 'beast' (the Friar's use of 'tempered' also echoes Romeo's previous qualms about his own effeminacy in 3.1.104–6). Later the Friar compares Romeo with women once again: 'like a mishaved and sullen wench, / Thou pouts upon thy fortune and thy love: / Take heed, take heed, for such die miserable' (3.3.143–5). Here the Friar associates misbehaviour

---

9. On Romeo's effeminacy, see Cartwright, *Shakespearean Tragedy and its Double*; Davies, 'The Film Versions of *Romeo and Juliet*'; Joan Ozark Holmer, '"Myself condemned and myself excus'd": Tragic Effects in *Romeo and Juliet*', Studies in Philology, 88 (1991), 345–62; Richmond, 'Peter Quince Directs *Romeo and Juliet*'; Snow, 'Language and Sexual Difference'; Watts, *Romeo and Juliet*.

(mishaved) and sulkiness (sullen, pouting) with women; men, by contrast, should show more strength of purpose and adopt their rightful role of protecting women—thus he instructs Romeo to 'Go get thee to thy love, as was decreed, / Ascend her chamber, hence and comfort her' (3.3.146–7). The Nurse also compares Romeo with a woman—Juliet—when she discovers him crying in Friar Lawrence's cell: 'even so lies she, / Blubb'ring and weeping, weeping and blubb'ring. / Stand up, stand up, stand, and you be a man; / For Juliet's sake, for her sake, rise and stand' (3.3.85–9). The Nurse commands Romeo to 'be a man' by assuming mastery and supporting Juliet ('rise and stand' also bear bawdy resonances of the erect penis, as in 1.1.7–11 and 25).

The allusions to effeminacy in *Romeo and Juliet* were added by Shakespeare to his principal source—Brooke's Romeo suffers no such 'weakness'—testifying to Shakespeare's interest in the ambivalence and complexity of gender difference (something he was later to explore in plays that centre upon transvestism, such as *As You Like It*, 1599, and *Twelfth Night*, 1601). But, as Hugh Richmond observes, few twentieth-century directors 'can bear to expose Romeo to the censure that his fickleness, volatility, and homicidal moods invite us to balance against his seductive idealism' (p. 224). As a result, the text:

> is normally mutilated in the interest of suppressing its masculine reservations about a 'feminized' hero such as Charlotte Cushman epitomized, and which the actor playing Zeffirelli's own Romeo [Leonard Whiting] clearly despised.[1]

However, in the eighteenth and nineteenth centuries, Romeo was often constructed as a soft, feminized figure—as he appears in Rigaud's painting of the 'balcony scene' for *Boydell's Shakespeare Gallery* (1789), a collection of pictures that were widely exhibited, copied, and printed * * *. Hence Romeo was a part frequently played by women in the nineteenth century: his 'womanish' behaviour allowed actresses to play the part with immunity. Probably the best-known female Romeo was the American actress Charlotte Cushman, who played opposite her sister as Juliet in 1845 to great acclaim * * *: 'Miss Cushman is a very dangerous young man', noted one member of the audience.[2]

1. Richmond, 'Peter Quince Directs *Romeo and Juliet*', 225. By contrast, William Van Watson perceives a 'homosexual gaze' in Zeffirelli's film; see 'Shakespeare, Zeffirelli, and the Homosexual Gaze', in *Literature Film Quarterly*, 20:4 (1992), 308–25; repr. in Deborah Barker and Ivo Kamps (eds.), *Shakespeare and Gender: A History* (London: Verso, 1995), 235–62.
2. Quoted by Joseph Leach, *Bright Particular Star: The Life and Times of Charlotte Cushman* (London: Yale University Press, 1970), 175.

This unsettling of gender stereotypes might have been made more explicit still with an all-male cast (Juliet was probably played by the boy-actor Robert Goffe). We have become so accustomed to seeing *Romeo and Juliet* acted by both men and women that it has become hard to imagine the play performed in any other way: 'Think of a boy as Juliet! . . . Woman's words coming from a man's lips, a man's heart—it is monstrous to think of!'[3] We cannot reconstruct how the Lord Hunsdon and the Lord Chamberlain's all-male acting companies performed *Romeo and Juliet*, but the recent production of an all-male *As You Like It* (Cheek by Jowl, 1994–5) is instructive for thinking about the range of responses an all-male production might evoke. By playing women so convincingly, Cheek by Jowl forced the audience to reconsider any preconceptions it may have had about innate differences between men and women, masculinity and femininity (the production also allowed for a homoerotic charge in the exchange of kisses between male actors). *Romeo and Juliet* could perhaps have worked in similar ways in its investigation of femininity and effeminacy. Not only does Juliet depart from orthodox models of gentlewomanly conduct, but the play exposes the fragility of gender stereotypes by showing a woman to be as strong—even less effeminate—than a man and fully capable of taking the leading role in marriage, and a man capable of 'womanish' behaviour. Far from simply reproducing orthodox ideals of gender, sexuality, and romantic love, the play seems to me to complicate those ideals in practice.

Once again, ethnicity is a possible factor in the play's characterization of gender difference. While Italian women were regarded by the English as sexually voracious, Italian men were noted for their effeminacy (which, in turn, was thought to encourage Italian men's supposed attachment to sodomy * * *). For an Elizabethan audience of *Romeo and Juliet*, ethnic stereotypes of male aggression, effeminacy, and female sexual passion would have been readily available as a means of interpreting the play; indeed, *Romeo and Juliet* arguably promotes these English stereotypes of Italian culture. This is how Angela Locatelli sees the play working. She argues that Romeo and Tybalt embody the foreign, 'excessive' character: 'the unabsorbed and irreducible "other" in the Elizabethan context' (p. 73). Briefly, the 'Other' refers to a cultural or psychological construction of that which is foreign, alien, radically different; it has been a concept of particular interest to critics examining notions of cultural, ethnic, and sexual difference. Reading *Romeo and Juliet* as an exploration of an ethnic 'Other', we might say that the play distances Romeo and his feelings as both effeminate and foreign; rather than presenting an unqualified celebration of romantic love, the play instead portrays

---

3. Faucit, in Thompson and Roberts, *Women Reading Shakespeare*, 186.

excessive Italian sexual passion. But the characterization of the exotic 'Other' usually tells more about the prejudices, concerns, anxieties, fears, and desires of the 'host' culture than it does about the 'foreign'; as Murray Levith remarks, 'Italy serves in part as metaphor for Shakespeare's England' (p. 11), and despite the play's allusions to Italian culture, it is also marked by anglicization (consider, for instance, the names of the musicians, Simon Catling, Hugh Rebeck, and James Soundpost). In my view *Romeo and Juliet* fuses Italian and English culture by projecting Elizabethan preoccupations onto a Catholic, European 'Other'—concerns such as the imposition of patriarchal authority, clandestine marriage, the control of female sexuality, the assertion of manhood, government control of aristocratic feuding and street violence. Now the play has become a well-established feature of the Veronese tourist industry and co-opted as a story of Italian lovers: thousands flock to Juliet's so-called house with its fake balcony and a bronze statue of Juliet (which reputedly brings good luck if you touch her right breast), and every year hundreds of letters are left at Juliet's so-called tomb in Verona, largely written by Italian girls about their experiences of love.[4]

Masculinity and Male Bonding

Masculinity is multifaceted in *Romeo and Juliet*. First, the play investigates the performance of manhood in different social contexts— the feud, the household, marital relations, filial relations, the church, male friendship. The 'macho' ethic of the feud has often been noted in recent criticism and performance of the play, but the aggressive (hetero)sexism encouraged by the feud is also supplemented, or complicated, by the implicit presence of homoeroticism (desire between men) in the play. Secondly, manhood is shown to be a fluid, unstable construct or performance, not properly distinct from womanhood. As a 'womanish' man * * *, Romeo confuses gender difference. Effeminacy threatens to undermine rigidly held distinctions between masculinity and femininity; distinctions upon which patriarchy is constructed. The play scrutinizes both the operation of contemporary stereotypes of masculinity and the patriarchal codes that depend upon them.

Mercutio reveals the extent to which male honour is bound up with mastery when he condemns Romeo's failure to stand up to Tybalt's taunts: 'O calm, dishonourable, vile submission!' (3.1.66). Submission was demanded of women in early modern England but men, on the contrary, were expected to be masterful. As Katharine Hodgkin has pointed out, mastery was 'one of the key concepts in

4. See Andrew Gumbel, 'Restoring a Shrine to Love', *Independent on Sunday*, 14 July 1996, Sunday Review, 40–1.

the delineation of approved masculine virtue': gentlemen were expected to show mastery over themselves, over women, and over servants (p. 21). But Hodgkin argues that in the 1590s mastery was increasingly difficult for a gentleman to maintain: a woman on the throne (Elizabeth I) disrupted the tradition of male political mastery; women were perceived to be taking and enjoying more liberties, circumventing and undermining the authority of their fathers and husbands, and asserting their own (albeit restricted) independence; and the enormous economic shifts in late-sixteenth-century England resulted in an increasingly mobile society, in which men who were servants rose to become masters, and the numbers of so-called 'masterless men' (men without fixed employment, often homeless) increased. Mastery, concludes Hodgkin, became a growing source of anxiety for the Elizabethan gentleman.

This perhaps explains why so many of the taunts and put-downs between men in *Romeo and Juliet* centre around mastery. Consider Capulet's response to Tybalt's outburst in the masque: 'What, goodman boy, I say he shall, go to! / Am I the master here, or you? go to! . . . You'll make a mutiny among my guests! . . . You are a saucy boy . . . You are a princox, go,/Be quiet' (1.5.76–86). Capulet regards Tybalt's defiance of his authority as a form of 'mutiny', and goes on to reassert his mastery by insulting Tybalt in two ways: demeaning his age and authority by calling him a boy and a princox (a pert, conceited youth), and demeaning him socially by calling him a 'goodman boy' (a goodman was a yeoman, socially inferior to a gentleman). The episode shows how relations between men of the same feuding family are problematic; the aggression fostered by the feud cannot, in fact, be contained by it—instead it spills out into relations between uncle and nephew. Similar insults around age and status are passed between other male characters: Tybalt, for example, calls Romeo a 'Boy' (3.1.59; see also 5.3.70), while Sampson seeks to assert his social superiority over Montague's servants by remarking 'I will take the wall of any man or maid of Montague's' (1.1.10–11; as sewage ditches flowed down the middle of many streets, the pathway close to the wall was usually cleaner, safer, and consequently claimed by social superiors). In *Romeo and Juliet*, then, men do not simply express their masculinity through physical violence; they use insult to establish their mastery over others.

Gentlemen were also expected to master their own feelings: as Hodgkin notes, 'a real man was never unduly affected by passion or emotion, for his reason would keep it in check' (p. 21). But in *Romeo and Juliet* men's emotional mastery is shown repeatedly to break down. On the one hand, Romeo's 'distemper' is manifested by his 'blubb'ring and weeping' and threats to commit suicide (3.3.87 and 108)—'desperate' behaviour which the Friar considers 'womanish'

(3.3.110). Romeo's effeminacy fails to meet the demands of masterful manhood. * * * On the other hand Capulet brutally loses his temper with his daughter ('You are too hot', 3.5.175), while Tybalt's 'wilful choler' makes his 'flesh tremble' with anger (1.5.88–91; see also 1.1.61). *Romeo and Juliet* thus complicates the received wisdom of orthodox patriarchal ideology—that while women are subject to their feelings men are able to master their emotions, whether of anger or despair, and are therefore the 'natural' masters in society. As the 1563 *Homily of the State of Matrimony* (intended to be read aloud in every parish church) explained to husbands, women are 'prone to all weak affections and dispositions of mind more than men be . . . the woman is a frail vessel and thou art therefore made the ruler and head over her'.[5] We have already seen how patriarchal authority is challenged and undermined in *Romeo and Juliet* in the context of marital, filial, and political relations * * *. By dramatizing the breakdown of male emotional mastery, the play questions another pillar in the ideology of patriarchal authority: the assumption that men are the natural masters of women because they can control their feelings better.

The public performance of manhood in *Romeo and Juliet* is intimately bound up with aggression. Erupting at the opening, middle, and close of the play and thereby framing the love-affair, feuding violence involves all prominent young male characters (Romeo, Mercutio, Benvolio, Tybalt, Paris). Coppélia Kahn has persuasively argued that the feud provides young men with

> an activity in which they prove themselves men by phallic violence on behalf of their fathers, instead of by the courtship and sexual experimentation that would lead toward marriage and separation from the paternal house. It fosters in the sons fear and scorn of women, associating women with effeminacy and emasculation, while it links sexual intercourse with aggression and violence against women, rather than with pleasure and love.[6]

The feud fosters a culture of masculinity which is defined by violence, identified with fathers, and performed by the assertion of a man's aggressive (hetero)sexual power and prowess. The element of 'phallic violence' is brought out at the level of language, whereby talk about violence is couched in sexual imagery. The keynote is set by

5. Quoted in Klein, *Daughters, Wives and Widows*, 16 and 22.
6. Kahn, 'Coming of Age in Verona', 338–9. See also Callaghan, 'The Ideology of Romantic Love: The Case of *Romeo and Juliet*', in Dympna C. Callaghan, Lorraine Helms, and Jyotsna Singh (eds.), *The Weyward Sisters: Shakespeare and Feminist Politics* (Oxford: Blackwell, 1994), 59–101'; Davis, '"Death-Marked Love"'; Novy, 'Violence, Love, and Gender'; Smith, *Social Shakespeare*; and Watson 'Shakespeare, Zeffirelli, and the Homosexual Gaze'.

Sampson's and Gregory's opening exchange, in which acts of physical violence towards Montague's men become inseparable from
acts of sexual violence towards Montague's women: 'I will push
Montague's men from the wall, and thrust his maids to the wall'
(1.1.10–16). Sampson's potentially disturbing scenario is that the
rape of women becomes symbolic of (and a means of expressing)
power over met. In Sampson's fantasy of male-male rivalry, women
become 'trafficked' (traded) between men: that is, they become objects
of exchange (in different ways, Juliet is also 'trafficked' between two
men: Capulet and Paris). 'Bawdy always has a dramatic function',
notes Molly Mahood, and 'here its purpose is to make explicit, at
the beginning of this love tragedy, one possible relationship between
man and woman: a brutal male dominance expressed in sadistic
quibbles' (p. 60). I would add that Shakespeare's decision to *open*
the action of the play on a note of bawdy is also dramatically significant for it undercuts the gravity of the Prologue—thereby disturbing generic expectations of tragedy—and signals the thematic
importance of sex and violence in the play as a whole. The 'sexualization' of violence in the play is developed by the use of sexual
innuendo to describe acts or weapons of aggression: 'tool' (1.1.28)
referred both to a sword and to a penis, 'naked weapon' (1.1.29) sig-
nified both an unsheathed sword and a naked penis, while 'sword'
was itself slang for penis.[7] To stand (1.1.8–10) means both to take a
firm and courageous position under attack and to have an erection
(and it is the sexual meaning which comes to dominate the conversation: 'me they shall feel while I am able to stand, and 'tis known
I am a pretty piece of flesh', 1.1.25–6); to 'cut off' heads (1.1.22–3),
as Sampson makes clear, refers both to the literal severing of heads
and to the destruction of a virgin's hymen or 'maidenhead'. Other
characters also link sex with violence: Romeo, for instance, draws
upon conventional imagery of warfare to describe Rosaline—'She
will not stay the *siege* of loving terms, / Nor bide th'encounter of
assailing eye' (1.1.203–4; emphasis added)—while Mercutio advises
Romeo to be rough with love: / Prick love for pricking, and you beat
love down' (1.4.27–8), a complex bawdy pun which links the act of
stabbing and penetration (pricking) with the penis (prick was slang
for penis), and argues that sexual desire requires 'rough' treatment ('beating down' an erection through masturbation or sexual
intercourse).

But although *Romeo and Juliet* presents aggressive heterosexism
and the display of 'phallic violence' as a crucial facet of masculinity,

7. On the large group of terms used by Shakespeare to describe sex that derive from warfare, individual combat, fencing, and jousting, see Eric Partridge, *Shakespeare's Bawdy*
(1948; New York Dutton, 1960; repr. Routledge, 1996), 42.

it does not condone it. As Coppélia Kahn has argued, the play is 'constantly critical of the feud as the medium through which criteria of patriarchally oriented masculinity are voiced' (p. 341). Ultimately the feud is buried, while Romeo is, quite literally, monumentalized: the golden statue Capulet promises to erect in his memory (5.3.303) marks the validation of Romeo's private manhood—his identity as a husband. The phallic violence fostered by the feud may also have been distanced by an English audience as typically Italian and elicited disapproval from an Elizabethan audience on the grounds of its 'foreign' excess. As Shakespeare's contemporary Thomas Nashe lamented, 'O Italie, the Academie of man-slaughter, the sporting place of murther, the Apothecary-shop of poyson for all Nations: how many kind of weapons hast thou invented for malice?[8] This note of prejudicial cultural stereotyping may also have informed opinion about the most violent figure in the play and active pursuant of the feud, Tybalt. Jill Levenson has argued that, for an Elizabethan audience, xenophobia would have confirmed 'Shakespeare's broad characterization of Tybalt as a villain'. Tybalt fences in the Spanish style, identified by his habit of cutting the winds (1.1.102) and his elaborately choreographed style of duelling: 'Spanish fight . . . with their feet continually moving, as if they were in a dance', observed George Silver in his *paradoxes of Defence* (1599); 'Here's my fiddlestick, here's that shall make you dance', taunts Mercutio (3.1.42 * * *).[9] The Spanish style of fencing was, however, disapproved of in Elizabethan England; moreover, anti-Spanish feeling was widespread, especially after the war against Spain of 1588. For an Elizabethan audience, aligning Tybalt with Spain would confirm his conduct and values—those of the feud—as suspect.

But feuding in *Romeo and Juliet* would also have been topical for an Elizabethan audience. Duelling, argues Joan Ozark Holmer, was 'a daily reality for the Elizabethans', and in the 1590s several English playwrights and actors (including Christopher Marlowe and Ben Jonson) were involved in life-and-death duels. She concludes that Shakespeare's portrayal of feudal violence represents 'a creative response to the problem of contemporary violence' in England.[1] Duelling was a particular problem amongst the aristocracy; proclamations against fighting in public were periodically issued by

8. Quoted in Levith, *Shakespeare's Italian Setting and Plays*, 1.
9. On feuding and fencing in the play, see Jill L. Levenson, '"*Alia stocaddo* carries it away": Codes of Violence in Romeo and Juliet', in Halio (ed.), Shakespeare's *'Romeo and Juliet'*, 83–96; Sergio Rossi, 'Duelling in the Italian manner: The case of *Romeo and Juliet*', in Marrapodi *et al.*, *Shakespeare's Italy*: 112–24; Jerzy Limon, 'Rehabilitating Tybalt: A New Interpretation of the Duel Scene in *Romeo and Juliet*', in Halio, *Shakespeare's 'Romeo and Juliet'*, 97–106; and Joan Ozark Holmer, '"Draw, if you be men": Saviolo's Significance for *Romeo and Juliet'*, *Shakespeare Quarterly*, 45:2 (summer 1994), 163–189.
1. Ozark Holmer, 'The Poetics of Paradox', 178.

Elizabeth I, but some factions of the aristocracy continued to use
street violence, particularly the duel, as a means of asserting their
power. For instance in 1594, around the time of the composition of
Romeo and Juliet, Shakespeare's patron, the third earl of Southamp-
ton, was involved in a celebrated feuding murder at Cosham (Wiltshire): he protected Sir Charles and Sir Henry Danvers after they
killed a long-standing enemy, Henry Long—one of many episodes of
feudal violence among the Wiltshire elite in the period. While the
state intermittently sought to impose control over aristocratic violence, it did not always succeed; indeed the number of recorded duels
jumped from five in the 1580s to nearly twenty in the 1590s. Lawrence
Stone has interpreted this conflict between a feuding elite and a government seeking to curb the culture of feuding in terms of a 'crisis' in
the English aristocracy which failed to adapt to the political culture
of an increasingly centralized and interventionist state.[2] A similar
dynamic of conflict between a feuding elite and a government unable
to contain feuding violence is arguably at work in *Romeo and Juliet*;
indeed, Jill Levenson argues that 'Prince Escales seems to mirror
Elizabeth's conduct: temporizing and procrastination'.[3]

  Romeo and Juliet is as much a play about male bonding as it is
about love between the sexes. While female bonding in the play is
shown to be both intimate and fragile (consider the shifting relations and 'betrayals' of trust between Juliet, her mother, and Nurse
during the course of the play), bonds between men, by contrast, are
defended to the death. Indeed, what Shakespeare sets in motion is
a conflict between love for a wife and love between men—hence
Romeo's predicament that to revenge his friend's death he has to kill
his wife's cousin. Shakespeare, in his version of the story, puts
considerable emphasis on the *emotional* investment between male
friends—an investment made outside the remit of marital relations,
and which leads Mercutio (a character largely invented by Shakespeare) to challenge Tybalt on Romeo's 'behalf' (3.1.102) and Romeo
to kill Tybalt 'for Mercutio's soul' (3.1.117). In this respect, bonds
between men drive the plot of the play.

  Since the 1980s, social historians and literary critics alike have
pointed to the presence of 'homoerotic' desire in relations between
men in early modern literature and culture.[4] Homoerotic desire does

2. Lawrence Stone, *The Crisis of the Aristocracy, 1558–1641* (Oxford: Clarendon Press,
   1965), 225–34.
3. Jill L. Levenson, '"*Alla stoccado* carries it away"', 86.
4. On homoeroticism and homosexuality in early modern England, see Alan Bray, *Homosexuality in Renaissance England* (London: Gay Men's Press, 1982); Bruce Smith, *Homosexual Desire in Shakespeare's England: A Cultural Poetics* (London: University of
   Chicago Press, 1991); Jonathan Goldberg, *Sodometries: Renaissance Texts, Modern
   Sexualities* (Stanford: Stanford University Press, 1992); Jonathan Goldberg (ed.), *Queering the Renaissance* (Durham: Duke University Press, 1994).

not necessarily imply a sexual relationship between men—indeed, 'homosexuality' was not recognized as a distinct practice or sexual identity in the period. Rather, 'homoeroticism' (also a modern term) refers to the focusing of men's emotional energies and desires into relations between men as opposed to relations with women—desires which may become eroticized. Shakespeare's portrayal of male friendship in *Romeo and Juliet* has suggestively been viewed in such terms. When Roger Allam came to play the part of Mercutio in 1983–4 for the RSC, he drew upon his own experience of male bonding as a teenager at an English public school:

> Girls were objects of both romantic and purely sexual, fantasy; beautiful, distant, mysterious, unobtainable, and, quite simply, not there. The real vessels for emotional exchange, whether sexually expressed or not, were our own intense friendships with each other. (p. 109)

Allam saw Mercutio's friendship for Romeo as 'his closest, most passionate, and intense relationship'; thus when Romeo becomes involved with Rosaline, Mercutio feels a 'sense of loss, that Romeo was irrevocably changing', becoming 'hurt and indeed jealous of Romeo's love for Rosaline'.[5] In response, Mercutio violates the object of Romeo's love, reducing Rosaline to an inventory of her physical parts: eyes, forehead, lip, foot, leg, quivering thigh, and 'the demesnes that there adjacent lie', her genitalia (2.1.17–20). For Allam, Mercutio's insistent reduction of love for women to sex—in which women become sexual objects not emotional partners—signals Mercutio's obsession with destroying Romeo's romantic view of love between the sexes and his attempt to reclaim the bonds between men: 'Now art thou sociable, now art thou Romeo' (2.4.72–3). According to Allam, those bonds acquire an erotic charge. Mercutio first imagines Romeo with an erection: 'To raise a spirit in his mistress' circle . . . letting it there stand / Till she had laid it. . . . . I conjure only but to raise up him' (2.1.24–9; 'raise' and 'stand' allude to erection (see also 1.1.25); 'circle' was slang for vagina). He goes on to imagine Romeo in the act of sodomy (anal intercourse): 'O, Romeo, that she were, O that she were / An open-arse and thou a pop'rin pear!' (2.1.37–8). Here, argues Allam, Mercutio reveals 'confusion around the sexuality of his relationship to Romeo, a sexuality that neither he nor Romeo allow'. Mercutio alludes to Romeo's penis on two further occasions (1.4.28 and 2.4.33–4).[6] Similarly, Joseph Porter has

---

5. Roger Allam, 'Mercutio in *Romeo and Juliet*', in Russell Jackson and Robert Smallwood (eds.), *Players of Shakespeare* 2 (Cambridge: Cambridge University Press, 1988), 112–14. See also Callaghan, 'The Ideology of Romantic Love'; Holding, *Romeo and Juliet*; and Joseph Porter, *Shakespeare's Mercutio: His History and Drama* (University of North Carolina Press, 1988).

6. Allam, 'Mercutio in *Romeo and Juliet*', 115.

argued that Mercutio's emotional passion and sexual desires are directed towards men not women: 'it is as if Mercutio has a personal investment, as we say, in his friend's erection.[7] William Van Watson takes this idea a stage further: 'when Mercutio berates women for their victimized status in a male supremacist world, he actually tacitly chastises himself for his own victimized status as a repressed homosexual' (p. 250).

Van Watson is too ready, in my view, to apply modern notions of repressed homosexuality to a fictional character constructed in a past culture in which 'homosexuality' had yet to be constructed as a distinct sexual orientation or identity. But the text(s) of *Romeo and Juliet* are ambivalent about the circulation of desire between men and open to a 'homoerotic' reading. Shakespeare developed the character of Mercutio far beyond the two-dimensional courtier he appears in Brooke's *Tragicall Historye of Romeus and Juliet* (1562). In Brooke, Mercutio is a stranger to Romeo and appears only in the company of 'bashfull maydes' at the masque (p. 218, ll. 257–8); Shakespeare developed Mercutio's role extensively, placing him in the company of men—a move which testifies to Shakespeare's interest in relations between men. Emotional investment between men was not a foreign subject to Shakespeare: he explores it in other plays (such as in Antonio's 'love' for Bassanio in *The Merchant of Venice*, 1596–7) and in his *Sonnets*, probably written during the 1590s and which centre upon a passionate attachment to a young man (the well-known sonnet 18, 'Shall I compare thee to a summer's day?', was written not for a woman but for a man). Moreover, Elizabethans acknowledged the potential *ambivalence* of intimate relations between men. As Alan Bray has pointed out, not only was the sodomite a figure 'that exercised a compelling grip on the imagination of sixteenth-century England' but Elizabethans recognized that 'the public signs of a male friendship—open to all the world to see—could be read in a different and sodomitical light from the one intended.'[8] Bray points to the 'difficulty the Elizabethans had in drawing a dividing line between those gestures of closeness among men that they desired so much and those they feared', concluding that intimacy between men was 'peculiarly ambivalent' in early modern England.[9] Shakespeare's portrayal of Mercutio in *Romeo and Juliet* is poised in this 'peculiarly ambivalent' moment in the expression of male friendship and same-sex desire. In addition, Italy was stereotyped as a hotbed of sexual sin, and Italian men as especially prone to sodomy: as the learned Justice Edward Coke put it,

7. Porter, *Shakespeare's Mercutio*, 157. For an opposing view, see Blakemore Evans (ed.), *Romeo and Juliet*, 45.
8. Alan Bray, 'Homosexuality and the Signs of Male Friendship in Elizabethan England', *History Workshop Journal*, 29 (spring, 1990) 1–19, 1 and 13.
9. Ibid., 14–15.

'*bugeria* is an Italian word'.[1] Thus in Thomas Nashe's *Unfortunate Traveller*, for instance, an earl explains that young men bring from Italy only 'the art of atheisme, the art of epicurising, the art of whoring, the art of poysoning, the art of Sodomitrie'.[2] Alan Bray points to English society's 'readiness, even eagerness, to recognize homosexuality in an alien context'[3] and for an Elizabethan audience the Italian setting may have helped to signal the presence of sodomy and sexual excess among the play's characters. But if Italy was demonized for its sexual licence, then so too were the London theatres. Contemporary moralists denounced the theatres for their cultivation of 'unnatural' same-sex passion, reputedly provoked by young male actors impersonating women. 'What man so ever weareth womans apparel is accursed', typically argued Philip Stubbes in *The Anatomie of Abuses* (1583)—for after plays actors and audience 'in their secret conclaves (covertly) . . . play the Sodomite, or worse. And these be the fruits of Playes and Interludes, for the most part'.[4] The performance of *Romeo and Juliet* by an all-male cast in an institution renowned for its sexual deviance could well have evoked, implicitly or explicitly, resonances of homoerotic passion.

Certainly the play's implicit homoeroticism has been of interest to twentieth-century producers. In Luhrmann's 1996 film, for instance, Mercutio (played by Harold Perineau) dresses up in drag for the masque, surrounds himself with beautiful young men, feels possessive towards Romeo and is clearly hurt by what he perceives to be Romeo's rejection of him in favour of a woman's love. In Perineau's performance, Mercutio's sexuality remains ambivalent. Yet the notion that *Romeo and Juliet* is solely concerned with idealized, heterosexual love persists. In 1994 an extraordinary case arose in England surrounding a headmistress's refusal to take her pupils to a Royal Ballet performance of Romeo and Juliet because it was a 'blatantly heterosexual love story'. The headmistress in question claimed that the story 'does not explore the full extent of human sexuality'; she was savagely attacked in the British tabloid press for her 'political correctness' and was threatened with suspension by Hackney Educational Authority.[5] The episode demonstrated how widespread is the notion that *Romeo and Juliet* only tells a story of heterosexual love (in fact, this is often the case in ballets of the play, which unlike Shakespeare's text(s) leave little room for ambiguity in relations between men). However, while the play has undoubtedly

1. Bray, *Homosexuality in Renaissance England*, 75.
2. Quoted by Levith, *Shakespeare's Italian Selling and Plays*, 7.
3. Bray 'Homosexuality and the Signs of Male Friendship', 75.
4. Quoted in Laura Levine, *Men in Women's Clothing: Anti-Theatricality and Effeminization, 1579–1642* (Cambridge: Cambridge University Press, 1994), 22.
5. See James Cusick, 'Teacher Turns Back on Romeo's Loving', *Independent*, 20 January 1994, 3.

been *co-opted* as an icon of heterosexual love, the Elizabethan texts are more ambivalent about the expression of desire between men.

NIAṀH CUSACK

Juliet in *Romeo and Juliet*†

Niaṁh Cusack played Juliet in Michael Bogdanov's production of *Romeo and Juliet* at Stratford in 1986 and at the Barbican in 1987. In the preceding season, her first with the RSC, she played Desdemona in *Othello*. Other roles for the RSC have been in *Mary, After the Queen*, *The Art of Success*, and *Country Dancing*. Earlier work includes roles in *A Woman of No Importance* and *Three Sisters*, as well as a career as a professional flautist.

My mother and both my sisters had played Juliet, but I hardly knew the play when I came to the role for the RSC. I had seen it once, when I was very young, and remembered that I thought it a rather boring play with everyone killing themselves, and I didn't see the point of it all. And so, although a lot of people said that I would make a 'lovely Juliet', that I had the right youthful quality, I had no aspirations to play the part and had the idea, though I hadn't actually read the play, that she was rather a wet. But just a little before starting on Desdemona in Terry Hands's RSC production of *Othello*, I did a scene from *Romeo and Juliet* for a schools television broadcast. Reading the play carefully at the age of twenty-four, when I had just started, as an actress, to explore Shakespeare, I found it wonderful, and my dearest wish from that time was to play Juliet.

The decision to open the 1986 Stratford season with *Romeo and Juliet* was taken late. Though I was already playing Desdemona I was still required to audition for the role, partly because Michael Bogdanov, the director, had never seen my work, but more particularly because he wanted to cast Romeo and Juliet together, as a pair. So after auditioning me alone, I worked on all the scenes with Sean Bean and only after that did Michael decide that we complemented each other appropriately and offer us the parts. The play only works if the balance of the relationship between Romeo and Juliet convinces an audience that they are immediately and irresistibly in love with each other. My Juliet could not exist as it is without Sean Bean's Romeo; I see our relationship, above all in the balcony scene,

† From *Players of Shakespeare* 2, ed. Russell Jackson and Robert Smallwood (Cambridge: Cambridge University Press, 1998), pp. 121–35. Copyright © 1988 Cambridge University Press. Reprinted by permission of the publisher.

Niaṁh Cusack as Juliet with Romeo (Sean Bean), 1986. Joe Cocks Studio Collection, © Shakespeare Birthplace Trust.

through him. These are two very different people, both passionate, but he impetuous and wilder, her passion tempered with a practicality that is almost, but not quite, sensible. This richness, this capacity for lateral thinking in her, can only be shown in contrast to Romeo; he is more immature (though perhaps a little older) than her, and it is partly his impetuosity that she falls in love with. I feel that the Romeo I play against serves my Juliet one hundred per cent in the vulnerability and total commitment of his playing of a young boy in love. We meet only five times in the play and if the audience doesn't believe utterly in our love then the whole thing is a waste of time. Juliet's entire development through the play is as a result of what happens between them; at each stage the relationship opens up further and becomes deeper and more consolidated. To explore that requires the confidence that Sean Bean's Romeo gives me.

To move from Desdemona to Juliet was to move from a reactive to an active role. I think that Juliet is considerably younger than Desdemona, but in her play she is the active agent, the person who does everything and who motors the play, particularly in an emotional sense. She is the one who gets things moving all the time, and (before the casting) I wasn't sure that I was regarded by the RSC as this kind of actress. It is a generalization, but there is a sense in which companies divide their actresses into those who do the acting and those who are there to make the stage look pretty. To be cast as Juliet was thus reassuring: it is a big part and it was opening the season, and I told myself they couldn't possibly be risking anyone they thought might be a weak link, for if the Juliet fails there is little point in doing the play. So at first it was very reassuring to be cast—until I began to wonder 'O my God, how am I going to do it?', and to study the part more fully and to see the depth of Juliet's character and how multi-dimensional she is. In the audition I had gone for one aspect of the character, but in the months of rehearsal and playing I have come to realize that there are so many sides to her. One aspect, for example, that emerged only later is the joyous side of her personality at the beginning. I was rather afraid of that at first, in case it should diminish the tragic ending, but of course the more you go for the early joy, the more powerful is the contrasting impact of the final tragedy.

We knew from the beginning that the play would be set in 1986, and Michael was always very clear and open about where the production was going. At first I was a little put off, having come from the long flowing dresses of the Terry Hands *Othello*. But though modern, it was still to be set in Italy, and I wondered where the conflict between the families would come from—why not Northern Ireland, or Israel, or Lebanon. Michael was very firm, however, that the play was set in Italy and that there was no getting away from that. My father, Capulet, was to be presented as a competitive, parvenu businessman, anxious for Juliet to marry Paris as a seal of social respectability. We had the idea that the Montagues were also posher than the Capulets, rather aristocratic but on the way down. The idea of marriage between impoverished aristocracy and the wealthy middle class is perfectly acceptable in Elizabethan terms, of course, and though the motorbikes and the sports car and all the determined trappings of the 1986 setting were picked on by the critics, I do not think that the director ever had any fundamental difficulty in reconciling his concept to what is there in the text. Certainly he was always ready to work closely on the language with us and to suggest readings if we found difficulties. The production was unusual, in my experience, in the contribution of the assistant director Jude Kelly, who worked closely with Michael throughout and did marvellously detailed work on characterization, even in the minor roles. All through rehearsals there was a sense of freedom of exploration of character within the firmly drawn parameters of the production, a willingness on the part of the director to consider the restoration of lines which he had cut, or to discuss any idea openly in front of the company. All this, I think, gave the production an impetus and vitality which have made it immensely invigorating to work in.

At first I took a long time to get used to the fact that, though this was 1986, I couldn't just go out on my own to talk to Romeo, or that we couldn't get on a plane and fly to New Zealand together. In rehearsal one day I think I mentally changed the word 'banished' to 'exiled' and began to find it easier to make the leap: if someone is exiled one can't just follow them, there would be police and legal restrictions. At the beginning, too, I used to wonder about the subservience of Juliet: why, in 1986, should she not be free to make her own choices. But the parallel of the upper classes in present-day England—the marriage market, even the vetting of Lady Diana—helped here. And to the idea that a 1986 Juliet might just telephone for a car to take her to Mantua while the Juliet of the play even has to get permission to go to the Friar, I began to imagine that her father, a wealthy businessman in that claustrophobic atmosphere, would have the telephone tapped and his daughter would live in constant danger of being kidnapped, so that if she made a move his guards would be straight after her. Gradually I came to terms with the modern setting.

The setting was important in establishing Juliet's situation and relationships at the beginning of the play. As the production developed I played the first scene to show Juliet more and more obviously enjoying the Nurse, naively not seeing through her, or through her mother. Only later will that knowledge come and then she will act on it with total integrity to herself. What is marvellous is that the more you can let her be as naive and young as she is and as close to the Nurse as she can possibly get, the more heartrending it is when she discovers that the Nurse has no comprehension of what she is like inside or what her values are. Juliet, this production suggests, has no relationship with her mother. The sophistication, the clothes, the *Dynasty*-like figure, the ill-concealed affair Lady Capulet is having with Tybalt, are all outside Juliet's area of questioning. She has been brought up in this environment and knows no other; protected but without friends; no one to go out to meet on the piazza, no motor-scooter like all the boys seem to have; no one to compare notes with. A limo takes her here, there, and everywhere; life is organized for her and very sheltered. She has no reason to be unhappy, so she does not question whether she is happy or not. She is an only child who talks to things, to objects, as if they were people. She has a rich imagination and she sees all manner of things; when she looks at the sky she doesn't just see the sky—there's a world peopled with lives up there. To think of her in this way helps me to find the youthfulness of the part. She has the ability to be self-sufficient—you realize that as the play goes on—but here, as the play begins, she seems firmly set in her friendship with the Nurse. Later we discover that she will have little trouble in withdrawing from that apparent reliance; she needs the Nurse rather less than Romeo needs the Friar. Romeo is not as mature as she is and always needs someone to give him a sense of direction. Even at the end, as he defies the stars and decides to take his own life, he is still doing it because he is thinking of her. Juliet has a greater sense of reliance on herself and confidence in her own point of view.

I felt this increasingly as we worked on the opening scene. Her reply to the suggestion that she should marry Paris is guarded and ambiguous; she is covering herself. 'I'll do my best' is what she seems to say to her mother, but she doesn't commit herself. This is someone who has learned to protect herself, not in any defensive or neurotic way, but quite openly. She looks at her mother and thinks 'I won't be like that'; there is no problem about it, no rebellion, no 'I can't bear her clothes, or her values', but something quite simple and therefore strong. She is obviously taking in what she sees, but she isn't influenced by all that's around her and keeps her own unique sense of what is right and wrong. This was something I felt from very early in rehearsals—that Juliet is a really special spirit, in another world from everyone else. Being innocent is not the fashion in today's cynical society and I didn't want her to be naive or to be laughed at. So I tried to find a sense of her covering herself well in that first careful response to her mother: 'I'll look to like, if looking liking move', but then, even more carefully: 'But no more deep will

I endart mine eye / Than your consent gives strength to make it fly'
(1.3.96–9). 'I'll certainly try to like the look of him', she says, 'but
obviously I won't go any further than you would wish me to.' It's terribly diplomatic and at first I rehearsed it as if she knew exactly what
her mother was up to and what a grabbing, immoral woman she is,
but later I felt very firmly that Juliet does not think in that way. How
do you speak to your mother, who is not like your nurse, who is not
a stranger, but who doesn't speak to you very often? That sort of language has got to come from obedience and it's got to be polite.
There is no need, I discovered, to play her reply 'It is an honour that
I dream not of' coldly, as if she is deliberately hiding herself; there
is no need to protect the character from the audience (Shakespeare
can do that well enough if the need arises). The reply comes naturally from Juliet's innocence and self-sufficiency. One does not have
to present modern teenage rebelliousness, or boredom with the
Nurse's stories, or to look for a 'spoiled brat' quality. Juliet is unique,
and the 1986 setting, or any other setting, leaves the performer still
trying to represent that unique spirit.

Juliet is awakened from her state of apparent contentment and
self-possession by the meeting with Romeo. There is a marvellous
flirtatiousness about that first sonnet they speak together, but she is
covering, not letting herself go too much, though she is obviously
feeling enormous passion for him, and is almost overwhelmed by the
feeling. Never before has she met anyone so in tune with her as to
be able to exchange lines with her in a sonnet, who so exactly com-
plements her, anyone with whom she doesn't have to compromise.
She looks at him and thinks 'My God, this is incredible', and it is
more so when she talks to him and the feeling is continued. Though
they talk the same language they are not saying quite the same
things: she is obviously taking her part in the flirtation, but she manages ostensibly to talk about lips being used for prayer. She tries to
be careful while all he can do is think 'give us a kiss'. Left alone
afterwards she passionately vows that she would rather die than have
anyone else. Her choice of words is unconsciously ironic: 'If he be
married, my grave is like to prove my wedding bed' (1.5.135). Not
until after he has gone and she has learned that he is a Montague
does she decide that she must do something to make sure that she
sees this man again. It is this realization of who he is that makes
her see for the first time that she is caged. That is how I feel when
I go up onto that balcony at the end of the ball scene and the Nurse
tells me that all the guests have left and I know that he has gone
too. All I want to do is to run out of the gate after him, and I can't,
and it's the first time I realize that there are guards and high walls
and that I can't actually go out at two o'clock in the morning looking for this man. And the awful thing is that he is caged too, because

if I turned up on the Montague doorstep, a Capulet, at best they would send me back home in my limo, at worst kill me or kidnap me as a hostage. So this is the moment that I realize I am imprisoned in the environment I have been brought up in. As I stand there on the balcony, I challenge the Capulet credo of 'Hate all Montagues'.

Then he arrives, and the first feeling is just joy. But Juliet is still a little inhibited, I feel (though she doesn't actually say so), by what her family is and by the problem of reconciling her love and her family commitment. When she thinks he is not there she can say that she will give up everything for him; when he appears and they start talking, and talking, about love, she gets, not second thoughts exactly, but a sense of the need to try to be sensible. 'The orchard walls are high and hard to climb', she says, and laughs at the passionate earnestness of his reply: 'With love's light wings did I o'erperch these walls' (2.2.63, 66). We haven't seen her sense of humour before, but here it comes over strongly. What is marvellous about the balcony scene is that it shows two very real people and you can imagine them actually growing old together and having grandchildren. They complement each other perfectly, Romeo a little immature and reckless, a bit over the top, dreaming of flying to the moon, while she is trying to be sensible and saying well, if you really do love me, let's get married. She is her parents' daughter in this, trying to be practical, trying to think of all the angles—the characteristics that will later make her capable of lying in order to protect her love. Her practical determination emerges most clearly when she returns to the balcony after her brief exit. Suddenly she seems to realize that she has to make an absolute decision to leave the world she has been brought up in and marry the man she loves. To explain this new mood when she returns I imagine that when she goes off to have that quick word with the Nurse, pressure must be put on her about the marriage to Paris; this would at least explain the complete change in tone, speed, and rhythm when she comes back and becomes so urgent in her talk of marriage to Romeo. Even when she makes this choice, however, she cannot realize what is going to happen; how could she, since it is only the death of Tybalt that changes everything? If she had been allowed more time to think she would presumably have confronted her family with the *fait accompli* after her marriage to Romeo; and she must still hope here that a final, total break will not be necessary.

Juliet is, I think, consistently positive about the relationship. From the beginning right up to the moment when she discovers Romeo dead, she is hopeful, willing their love to work. Her foreboding remarks—'my grave is like to prove my wedding bed', 'I have no joy in this contract tonight', etc.—come from a kind of sixth sense, below conscious thought. They are remarks for the audience to absorb, like Romeo's as he enters the Capulet ball, but they have no effect on the positive attitude they both take to the relationship. Even when she says goodbye to him in the dawn scene and sees him as 'one dead in the bottom of a tomb' there is no conscious sense of doom. I do not think she is at this point aware that they could actually kill themselves; she hasn't been driven to that yet. It is the shock of the imminence of the planned marriage to Paris, when she thought she had more time, that begins to bring these things to the surface, though even then her reaction 'God I'd rather die than do that' is a very human one of a kind that we rarely expect to have to take literally—that is the brilliance of it. To play Juliet as if she is conscious of the inevitability of tragedy is the same thing as to play her wisely aware of all the faults of the society she lives in: if you do this too soon you have nowhere to go, and if she is not full of hope and promise then there is much less sense of tragedy at the end. It is for the audience alone to savour the fact that she really is foretelling the future, though even they, I think, often come to the play over-conscious of its ending and of the idea of the 'star-crossed' lovers; I hope our production surprises them sometimes with the positiveness and energy of its early stages. Juliet certainly does not think of herself as 'star-crossed'; she makes her choices quite freely and her choices bring her to where she finishes.

I have to say, therefore, that omitting the prologue so as not to close down the options, and moving it to the end as our production does, seems to me a very good idea—fortunately, for this was something about which Michael Bogdanov was immovable. He had decided absolutely on the shape of the play, and though he was often flexible if one fought for lines which had been cut, he was completely firm in what he wanted for the structure and in his desire to make a statement about a society and about that society's method of mourning the only worthwhile thing in it. Treating the play's last moments as a news conference, with the prologue given by the Duke at the end as a sort of press release, and the reconciliation of the families blatantly posed for the cameras, is to refuse to soften the play, as Shakespeare rather tends to, in its finale. It seems to me to make the play much more real for the audience, something much more like real life. We also cut Friar Laurence's long recapitulation, again with the idea of not allowing the audience to find comfort in distancing themselves from the situation through a long passage of narrative.

But to return to Juliet's progress through the play: in the balcony scene her love seems complete. We see her next in the bright light of day—'The clock struck nine when I did send the Nurse' (2.5.1)—and things are not quite the same as they seemed in the preceding night. That odd sense of uncertainty about first being in love has taken over. Not until she is married will Juliet feel secure at the end of the journey of courtship; here the 'if' of the balcony scene's 'If that thy bent of love be honourable' is dominant. Whenever you fall in love you are never sure of the other person at the beginning, and this uncertainty and impatience in Juliet are all taken out on the Nurse. She is not yet sure of Romeo, or of her destiny; not until the wedding scene at Laurence's chapel will she be at peace. Every scene of the play is part of a developing story. The balcony scene doesn't finally consolidate their love: the ups and downs and uncertainties continue and here now at midday she wonders why the Nurse has taken 'three long hours' to return; could it be that he didn't turn up, that he got caught by his family; her imagination is running riot.

The wedding scene brings confidence and peace and we next see her anticipating the consummation of their love: 'Gallop apace, you fiery-footed steeds' (3.2.1). The richness of texture of that speech is extraordinary. I ask night, gentle night, loving night, passionate night, every sort of night, to give Romeo to me. I try every angle on night, so as to make that little pact: give him to me, so that he can come to me, so that I can have him, and then 'when I shall die' you can have him—take him, and cut him out in little stars'. My first reading of the word *die* here is the sexual one: the white of the stars, and his body in white, and the white of him ejaculating inside me, and the cutting up in little white stars, linking, at that pervasively unconscious level of foreboding, with the idea of spiritual death, which immediately afterwards breaks into the scene in reality with the news of the death of Tybalt.

The next phase of the play is the one where Juliet really grows up. When she discovers that Romeo has killed her cousin and then been banished she has to come to terms with where her loyalties lie. I always feel that she understands what commitment and depth of love are in this scene; she comes to terms with the idea of being a wife, and with the responsibility of it, as she makes herself face up to the fact that being married to someone means that you stand by him even if he has killed someone you love. That is what is implied in the keeping of marriage vows, and this is where she becomes a wife rather than a girl playing at being a wife. In the first phase of the play it is possible to think of her love for Romeo, though huge and total, as adolescent, but from this moment on she is a woman embracing the role of wife, facing its truth, taking part in it, inhabiting it. This scene is the turning point for, Juliet, the realization that a wife's love must come on top of all other loves and that it can give her the strength to do everything that she now has to do.

She is alone now, and that loneliness is pointed by the final break with the Nurse. When the Nurse advises her to marry Paris she thinks she is still talking to a little girl; she hasn't realized that she is talking to a woman who has made a lifelong commitment to

Romeo. The effect of the Nurse's advice is in fact to confirm Juliet in that commitment, not to unsettle her in the least. She has made the decision about where her loyalties lie in the scene when she learns of Tybalt's death, and now to hear the Nurse flippantly describing Romeo as a dishclout makes the decision easier and clearer for her, even though breaking with the Nurse means cutting away something that is very deep in her. If the Nurse had tried to be more understanding and persuasive—I know Romeo is a lovely man, but you've got to do this, this is the only way, maybe we can find a way round it afterwards'—it might have been more difficult, but the fact that she belittles Romeo makes the decision stark and the break complete. It tears Juliet's heart for a second that this woman, who she thought loved her and understood her, can say these things, but once she hears them there is no love any more, for you can't love someone whose values are so far away from your own and who, it is suddenly clear, doesn't really understand what love is: 'Ancient damnation!' (3.5.235).

She is now quite alone, the Nurse and her parents irrelevant. It is easy to come on and lie to them after her visit to the Friar, because they now mean nothing to me. She has hardened, at least externally, covering her inner vulnerability with an ice cold manner that makes her uncompromising with the Friar, capable of lying quite easily, quite simply, to her parents about the plan for immediate marriage to Paris. There is always the knife if the potion doesn't work.

The grim determination of Juliet's superficial mood when she goes to Friar Laurence covers inner desperation. She turns to Laurence because there is nowhere else to go. Obviously she does not have the same depth of relationship with him as does Romeo. For her he is the local padre who has christened, married, and buried all the families she knows. He has probably prepared her for her first communion, but the relationship is not at all like Laurence's with Romeo who would for years have been a member of his local boys' football team. For Romeo he is a close confidant, someone he trusts absolutely to keep a secret, even a secret marriage. There are two people who know of that marriage, the Nurse and the Friar. When the Nurse turns out to be a dud card, Juliet must go to the Friar, not because she trusts him especially, but because he represents the last hope of escape and will himself get into deep water if he doesn't find that way out. But Laurence does not really know her and I think it really shakes him when she shows the strength of her commitment to Romeo in pulling that knife. At one time, before the production opened, we were rehearsing a mimed scene in which I took the knife from my father's desk. It is realistic to assume that such a man as the Capulet of this production would have a gun to protect himself, and perhaps a knife too, so that when I say 'If all else fail, myself have power to die' I do know that there is a weapon in the house that I can use. We toyed with the idea of a gun, in keeping with our modern setting, but concluded that a knife is much more graphic and pulling it out, with the threat of slitting your throat, much more disturbing.

As she arrives at Friar Laurence's cell, Juliet has to endure a conversation with Paris. The emotional strain of having to exchange courtesies with this flirtatious young man when all she wants to do is to get on with her appeal to the Friar, makes this a difficult moment for her. To be close to him, then to be kissed by him, is repulsive and the feeling of being caged in is made even stronger by the meeting. Whatever she felt about being in the same house with those people, parents and nurse, who have no idea what she is feeling inside, is intensified by this meeting with the man who will keep her in that kind of life. Everything he says is possessive of her at a moment when she is desperately trying to escape from the nightmare of the world she has been brought up in and lives in. The meeting with Paris is, I think, the final straw that makes it easy for her to pull the knife and to be so vicious about it, so that once again she drives the action forward, forcing Friar Laurence to think of something.

Whether Juliet believes at once in the Friar's remedy is hardly the question. She is desperate, a drowning woman, and she will grab at anything that has a faint hope about it, anything that might save her marriage. She has had nothing but negatives for the past few hours and here is the Friar talking positively, suggesting that there may be a way out. And she will take any way out that's offered—that, certainly, is how I want to play the scene. The only thing that scares her is the idea of the tomb, right here at its first mention, well before the soliloquy about it. What is odd is that she has just said that she'll do anything, even lie with dead and rotting bones, and he calls her bluff and immediately she starts to wonder 'can I do this?'. That is her real fear, waking up with the dead, a young girl surrounded by dead bodies and rotting limbs. The Friar's insistence that that is what she is going to have to do sends her back home with a couple of hours to think about it and then, when the Nurse and her mother go out, Juliet is left alone with that bottle, confronting death and the unknown.

We begin this scene with Juliet playing the flute. Michael Bogdanov is like a fond parent who likes all his children to be shown off at their best, and very early on he had decided that Michael Kitchen was going to play his guitar and Hugh Quarshie his saxophone, and I knew that he knew that I could play the flute. I was therefore dreading the moment when he would say 'why don't you play the flute for a bit in the middle of the balcony scene?' So I was well armed against that idea, but as we talked about the vial speech we wondered how we might set it and I said that I thought she would be completely removed from the rest of the household's concerns, presumably in her bedroom. Michael felt that we needed to start the scene in some way that would give a sense of her commitment to Romeo and of her being part of his world and no one else's any longer. And so came the idea of her playing the flute, which I agreed to so long as I could choose the piece, because I knew immediately that the right piece was Debussy's 'Syrinx', which is so haunting and so utterly different from all the other modern music in the production. The music is her escape to another world, but it doesn't seem at all strange to her parents, or to the Nurse, that she should play her flute, and it reinforces the idea of her being a lonely girl, as she has been all through the play, the sort of girl often alone, who might well play a good deal of music, read a lot, and dream. So, having resisted the idea in anticipation, the flute-playing at this moment of loneliness now seems to me right, an appropriate prelude to the speech in which she faces the ordeal of swallowing the Friar's potion.

When I began work on the role I was not aware that that speech was regarded as notoriously difficult—and that, no doubt, is a very good thing. We didn't rehearse it until quite late and when we started (partly, I suppose, because my training is as a musician) I was already seeing it as a musical shape. This is my usual habit, to see just the basic outline, and the crescendos and diminuendos, but to have difficulty in finding the detail. I worked alone with the director on the speech and he was very good in encouraging me to look for one idea, deal with that, and then go on to the next one. My feeling was that Juliet actually had to reach a point of madness in order to take that potion. The problem is to move towards that, but to make the ideas and images and fears along the way fully vivid and theatrical. At the beginning I don't think I was finding the reality of the speech; I was just playing the individual images, without showing where they came from or the effect they were having on me. I gradually discovered the need to take it apart more, and to play it more simply, like a little girl telling herself a story, but a wild and frightening story. This approach has been a great help for me; it simplifies the speech and stops me from attacking the audience too much with it. I start off with a tiny fear and it just gets bigger and bigger. One must be totally committed to each fear in turn, to the horrible images that keep rolling out. They are all horrible images and they don't necessarily come in any particular order; one thing is really revolting and then, my God, there is another, and so on. To play the speech a little more as a terrified child has certainly helped me to find more colour in it. The extraordinary thing about this terrified child, this girl of fourteen, is the speed with which she achieves the maturity to make the big choices and decisions and to take responsibility for them. That she is young in years in the world does not mean that she is not wise or that she lacks great strength, as this speech makes clear. From the cheerful, happy, positive decision-making of the balcony scene, we have moved to this terrifying decision to swallow the bottle of whatever it is the Friar has given her.

Juliet's last scene is in the tomb which she has here so vividly imagined. The first few seconds of waking up and believing it has all worked out must be played for all their happiness. The poison did not kill me, everything has gone according to plan, there is the Friar, and I am where I am supposed to be—all this, I think, has to be suggested in those moments though you have only just woken up and are a little bit dozy. Then you turn and see the man whom you last saw looking up at you so alive and full of love lying there dead, and you know that he can't see you, that he can never see you again, that he can't feel you though you are actually together, and there is nothing that you can do ever to wake him. In order to take the potion Juliet has had to kill every other feeling she has ever had for other people. It is for Romeo that she takes the potion: 'Romeo! Here's drink—I drink to thee.' Now she discovers the man for whose love she did that lying dead beside her and it is a very simple decision to kill herself. There is no life now, the only life you ever had is dead; my whole motor through the play has been him, and my love for him. In the balcony scene I suddenly realized that there are parts of me that have never lived, never vibrated or breathed, and then I met him and we had that wonderful time talking to each other, and so I can never go back to what I was. There is no choice here now; real life is with him and to see him dead is to see myself dead. It is as simple as that and I don't even hear the Friar, with his last little urgent scheme. I look at Romeo and there is no choice. For part of the run of our production Romeo, in keeping with our modern setting, had killed himself by injecting poison through a hypodermic needle; for me, earlier, we had toyed with the idea of a gun to pull on the Friar in my desperate search for an escape; but here at the end there was never any doubt. The moment is simple, brief; there is no savouring of it, no making the dreadful grief and loss any deeper than it is. Just get it over with, finish, numb: 'This is thy sheath; there rust, and let me die.'

DAVID TENNANT

Romeo in *Romeo and Juliet*[†]

David Tennant played Romeo in Michael Boyd's production of *Romeo and Juliet* at the Royal Shakespeare Theatre in the summer

† From *Players of Shakespeare* 5, ed. Robert Smallwood (Cambridge: Cambridge University Press, 2003), pp. 113–30. Copyright © 2003 Cambridge University Press. Reprinted by permission of the publisher.

season of 2000, and later at the Barbican Theatre. His other roles in that season were Antipholus of Syracuse, and Jack Absolute in *The Rivals*. Earlier roles for the RSC were Touchstone, Jack Lane in *The Herbal Bed*, and Hamilton in *The General from America*. His other stage work includes a wide range of classical and modern roles at the Manchester Royal Exchange (where he played Edgar in *King Lear*), the Royal Lyceum, Edinburgh, and in London, at the Donmar, the Almeida and the National Theatre. He has worked extensively on radio and televison and among his films are *LA Without a Map* and *The Last September*. * * *

The thing about *Romeo and Juliet* is that everyone seems to think they know what it's about. You don't have to talk about it for long before people start saying things like 'the greatest love story ever told' and spouting famous lines. ('Wherefore art thou Romeo' has to be one of the most overused and most misunderstood quotations in the English-speaking world.) When I found out that I was going to be playing Romeo for the Royal Shakespeare Company I was at first thrilled, then nervous, and then rather snowed under with unsolicited opinion: 'O, it's a wonderful part'; 'terribly difficult'; 'such beautiful poetry'; 'O, he's so wet'; 'he's so wonderfully romantic'; 'Why on earth do you want to play Romeo? Mercutio is the only part to play'; 'of course Romeo is always upstaged by Juliet'; 'it's the best of Shakespeare'; 'it's absolutely Shakespeare's worst play'—and so on, and on, until it soon became evident that to attempt such a part in such a play might be at best ill-advised and at worst total and utter madness. It was certainly clear that I couldn't hope to please all of the people all of the time and that even pleasing *some* of the people *some* of the time was going to be pretty tricky.

However, I had always wanted to play Romeo. I thought it was a great part full of very recognizable emotions and motivations, with a vibrant youthful energy and a sense of poetry with which anyone who has ever been a self-dramatizing adolescent can identify. It is suffused with the robust certainty and cynicism of youth, but crowned with a winning and rather beautiful open-heartedness.

And it's a great story brilliantly told, full of passion, wit, politics, intrigue, life and death, and topped off with lashings of sex and violence.

And we had a great director at the helm in the shape of Michael Boyd, whose work I had been thrilled by for years at the Tron Theatre in Glasgow and more recently at the RSC itself. His productions had always seemed to me to have the power to make the theatre a truly magical place where things happen that could only happen in a theatre, so that theatre isn't the poor relation of the feature-film but a genuine living art form specific to itself and nothing else. I'd always been desperately keen to work with Michael and to do it with this play was a dream come true.

And Juliet was to be played by Alexandra Gilbreath whom I had met several times and knew would be great to work with, as well as having seen her be very brilliant as Roxanne in *Cyrano de Bergerac* and as Hermione in *The Winter's Tale*. So the whole package was shaping up rather irresistibly.

And I was running out of time. There is no explicit reference in the text to how old Romeo is, but he is, undeniably, a *young* man. I didn't have very many years left. I'd always said to myself that it was a part I would have to do before my thirtieth birthday or not at all. Actors older than that have played the part, of course, and I don't doubt that they've done it very well, but I wanted to set myself a deadline. (There are, after all, few more tragic sights than a balding, middle-aged actor, corsetting in his paunch and inelegantly bounding across the stage as an ageing juvenile!) So, at twenty-eight (I would be twenty-nine before the show opened) it was now or never.

And I suppose that playing Romeo had always represented to me the first rung on a ladder that every great classical actor had climbed before ascending to Hamlet, Iago, Macbeth, and so on, finally culminating in a great, definitive King Lear before toppling over and retiring to an old actors' home and telling ribald anecdotes into a great, plummy old age. Not that I am, for a second, categorizing myself as a 'great classical actor', or even aspiring to such a term, but the opportunity to follow a path through these famous parts in the wake of actors like Irving, Olivier, Gielgud and others seemed thrilling, and something that, ever since drama school, I'd dreamed of doing. This is the sort of egocentric thought-process that is not entirely helpful to an actor when it comes to actually approaching a role, and I'm not particularly proud to admit to it now, but I can't deny that it was a part (only a relatively small part, but an important one nevertheless) of what made me say yes to the RSC and to begin to find my own way through the sea of received notions of what the part meant to everyone who was so keen to give me their opinion.

As the play was to be part of the RSC's 2000 season, I would be involved in more than one production, so I was duly signed up to play Jack Absolute in Sheridan's *The Rivals* and Antipholus of Syracuse in *The Comedy of Errors*, as well as Romeo. *Romeo and Juliet* wouldn't even start rehearsals until the other two plays were up and running, which meant that I was thrown into the first rehearsal day on Romeo only a day or two after my second opening night of the season. This meant that I had had little time to brood over the script before we started. I had been reading the play, of course, and I had

made a few observations and suggestions for myself, but I came to
the initial read-through relatively open-minded as to how I was going
to approach the play and the part.

On the first day Michael Boyd spoke about his own initial impressions and ideas. He talked about the enormous amount of baggage
this play seems to bring with it, and his desire that we should shed
it all as soon as possible. He said that he'd been surprised, when
rereading the play, how unsentimental and muscular it was, and he
noted how full of sexual innuendo and darkness it was too. He was
interested to find that it was a play about generation, and that the
story of the parents was not to be forgotten in the story about their
children. He talked about how he wanted to approach the play simply and truthfully, and he introduced us to the set design that he
had been working on with designer Tom Piper.

It was a non-specific design, basically two curving walls, facing each
other, that could represent different things throughout the evening—
whether they were the orchard walls that Romeo climbs, the wall
under Juliet's balcony, or, more symbolically, simply a representation of
the two families, ever present and immovably solid. Costumes were to
be vaguely Elizabethan, without any attempt to be pedantically specific. Statements about generations could be made through the costumes, so that the old world-order of the ageing Prince Escalus would
be represented in full doublet and hose, while I, along with Benvolio,
Mercutio and the other young men, would look more modern, using
shapes and fabrics from contemporary designers. Anachronisms
were not to be shied away from if they helped to tell the story.

So, with the world of the production taking shape, I had to start
figuring out who Romeo is and how he fits into this society. He's the
heir to the Montague fortune—a not-inconsiderable position either
socially or politically—but he seems altogether without interest in
the family's conflict and much more concerned with his own inner
turmoil:

> O me, what fray was here?
> Yet tell me not, for I have heard it all.
> Here [*i.e., in my heart*]'s much to do with hate, but more
>   with love.
>
> (I.i.173–5)

Before his first entrance we learn that Romeo has been seen wandering gloomily through the woods at dawn and holing himself up in
his room. He's become distant from his parents—unlike the Capulets, the parent/child dynamic in the Montague household is barely
touched on in the play. There doesn't appear to be any antagonism
between Romeo and his parents, just a lack of any communication at

all, despite Mr and Mrs Montague's obvious concern for their son. It suggests to me that Romeo finds his 'family' elsewhere. Certainly the parental *confidant* in his life seems to have become the friar (but we learn more of that later on) and it is Benvolio who is employed to find out what's wrong.

Central to this first Romeo scene is his relationship with Benvolio. Anthony Howell (playing Benvolio) and I were keen that the two should enjoy a familiar, relaxed relationship. We have just been shown that Benvolio has a trusting relationship with Romeo's parents and, since Benvolio's parents are never referred to, we began to assume that they had been brought up together, so that, although only cousins, they would interact like brothers. (And as Anthony and I were playing identical twins in *The Comedy of Errors*, it seemed churlish not to make the most of any 'familial' similarities.) Having someone who knows Romeo so well helps, I think, to mitigate the worst of his excesses. It struck me that Romeo's first entrance doesn't necessarily help to endear him to an audience, but Benvolio's presence provides an affectionate cynicism which allows the audience, and perhaps even Romeo himself, to see the extremity of his self-indulgence.

When we first see him, Romeo is in the throes of a huge and unrequited crush on a character we never even get to meet; not the 'Juliet' that the play's title has led us to expect him to be pining for, but some girl called Rosaline, who appears to have taken a vow of celibacy rather than reciprocate his advances. Michael encouraged me to think of Rosaline as a novice nun—the ultimate sexual lost cause for Romeo to be mooning after. And this, it seems to me, is part of it: Rosaline's very remoteness and inaccessibility are part of her appeal to the self-aware, emotionally immature and indulgent Romeo. A reciprocated love (such as he later enjoys with Juliet) would not grant him the opportunity to bemoan his own lot, in that peculiarly adolescent way:

> She hath forsworn to love; and in that vow
> Do I live dead that live to tell it now.
>
> (I.i.223–4)

It certainly allows him to cock a superior snook at Benvolio—a kind of 'you who have never loved couldn't hope to empathize with the transcendental pain that I am feeling to a degree that no other human being alive or dead could ever equal'. I'm not suggesting that Romeo is lying to himself, or anyone else, about how he's feeling, but I wanted to suggest that some part of him is enjoying his own drama. (That also allows you somewhere to go later when he experiences a very visceral passion and a very real drama which he can have neither time nor inclination to enjoy or indulge in.) It was a difficult balance to strike: on the one hand I didn't want to patronize the character by portraying someone who doesn't know himself—though in a way he doesn't (yet)—but at the same time I wanted to tell the story of a disaffected youth at odds with his predicament, his environment, and himself and full of the 'nobody-understands-me' ire of adolescence. In discussion with Tom Piper, the designer, it was decided that he would dress himself in black—a self-conscious Hamlet, in mourning for his life. He is therefore in a state of flux, full of unfulfilled passion and directionless purpose—ripe for a journey and looking for exactly the sort of experience that he is about to stumble upon. 'The readiness is all'—and without it there could be no inevitability about what happens and no journey for the character.

So if Benvolio is the familiar harbour where Romeo begins his journey, and Juliet is the northern star which guides him forward, Mercutio is the storm that tries to blow him off course and, in our production at least, goes all out to sink him.

Mercutio is a close friend of Romeo and Benvolio, but whilst he is undeniably fun to be around and the life and soul of the party, he is a 'high maintenance' personality, and when we first meet him the strain in his relationship with Romeo is beginning to tell. It certainly seems from the text of the play that Mercutio doesn't entirely applaud Romeo's interest in girls. He bombards Romeo with criticism and lewd innuendo about his mooning after Rosaline. Adrian Schiller (playing Mercutio) felt sure that this endless vitriol must be based on something more than locker-room horseplay and that the character's fury must stem from a feeling, however subconscious, of sexual jealousy and betrayal. We had no trouble finding this in the playing of the scenes. The further Romeo moves away from his 'childhood' friends into the grown-up world of heterosexual desire, the more Mercutio rages and the less Romeo is affected by him. Whether Mercutio himself is aware of his crush on Romeo, we chose to play that Benvolio and Romeo *are*, so that when Mercutio pushed me over and mounted me during the climax of his Queen Mab speech—

> This is the hag, when maids lie on their backs,
> That presses them and learns them first to bear,
> Making them women of good carriage.
> This is she—   (I.iv.92–5)

Romeo's interruption ('Peace, peace, Mercutio! / Thou talkest of nothing') is a rejection of his cynicism and innuendo as well as a rejection of his advances. Romeo has already set off in a direction that can't include his friend if he is going to demand his complete attention.

The playing of this unspoken sexual tension helped us to unlock some of the more opaque dialogue elsewhere in the play. The scene (II.iv) between the three lads in the midday heat—the morning after

the party following which Romeo has (Mercutio presumes) spent the
night with Rosaline—contains one of those Shakespearian inter-
changes that can make actors despair: an exchange of pun-laden
witticism crammed full of Elizabethan references that make the
pages of the play-text groan with footnotes. The challenge is always
to make a modern audience who, on the whole, enjoy a relatively slim
appreciation of the finer points of sixteenth-century *double entendre*, feel that they can follow your argument. When Romeo and Mercutio set off on their battle of wits (a battle, incidentally, that they
both seem to enjoy and revel in—an interesting clue to why they
have found each other as friends and something that Adrian and I
were keen to show, for there is little to mourn in the breakdown of
a friendship if you have no idea why they were friends in the first
place, and Shakespeare's economy of storytelling offers these clues
sparingly enough), it's difficult to follow the thread of what they are
saying even on the printed page, let alone in the heat of performance.
We found, however, that if we played the subtext of their relationship it not only let the characters say what they were thinking about
each other without *actually* saying it, it also lent the exchange a
dynamism and clarity that transcended the problems of Elizabethan
pun-age. So when Romeo says 'Pink for flower' (II.iv.57) he is calling Mercutio—and probably for the first time, since he has the
security of his new life with Juliet now and doesn't need to humour
Mercutio any more—a homosexual. Mercutio chooses not to take
the bait ('Right', II.iv.58), but before long they are into a debate about
'geese', and again Romeo is quite bold with Mercutio:

> ROMEO   Thou wast never with me for anything when they wast
>   not there for the goose [*i.e., my 'goose'*].
> MERCUTIO   I will bite thee by the ear for that jest.
> ROMEO   Nay, good goose, bite not [*i.e., get off me, I've had
>   enough*].

Nothing is explicitly stated, but Romeo is cutting Mercutio off, and
while it is Mercutio who ultimately wins the race of wits it is Romeo
who is leaving him behind. I didn't want this to seem vindictive as
Romeo is undoubtedly deeply fond of Mercutio—he has to be for the
later scenes to work—but it is simply inevitable and necessary that
he pushes Mercutio away. The choice our production took was that
Mercutio's rage at his rejection and eventual death at the hands of
his beloved transformed itself into a vengeance that would extend
beyond the grave. When Mercutio is taken off stage to die shouting
'a plague a' both your houses' (III.i.106), he is fully intending to be
the author of that plague and will (in our production) reappear later
in the play, first handing over the poison that will kill Romeo and
then, as Friar John, regretfully informing Friar Lawrence that he

couldn't deliver his letter. This notion that the fates were a real and motivated influence on events in the world of the play had resonances throughout the production. In the purely pragmatic sense this device of Mercutio as an evil avenging angel neatly justified one of Shakespeare's less integrated plot twists (the play is no longer a tragedy about a dodgy postal service), but the broader implication of a divinity that shapes our ends was something that I found particularly interesting in terms of Romeo himself and his entire world view.

It struck me very early on that Romeo had a fairly well-developed sense of the world of fate and destiny. He talks of his dreams and makes numerous references to the stars and what lies in them. It seemed to make sense that someone trapped in a world of very real physical conflict that he wants no part of, should yearn to exist in a world outside himself, and should be searching for something new to believe in. This became a very important touchstone for me as I tried to draw this character and it provided the backbone of my understanding of his emotional responses. The first explicit reference I found was his justification for not going to the Capulet ball by saying 'I dreamt a dream tonight' (I.iv.50)—a protest soon demolished and sneered at by the decidedly earthbound Mercutio, but something which nonetheless is a very real fear for Romeo. After the others exit at the end of the scene he is left to mull over his trepidation:

> I fear, too early. For my mind misgives
> Some consequence, yet hanging in the stars,
> Shall bitterly begin his fearful date
> With this night's revels and expire the term
> Of a despisèd life, closed in my breast,
> By some vile forfeit of untimely death.
> (I.iv.106–11)

It's an unspecific, yet creeping, panic that threatens to overwhelm him. I played this speech with my eyes glued to a particular space in the auditorium, as if these malignant stars that shaped his end had a physical location. It was a spot my eyes would return to later. This wasn't superstition on Romeo's part but a very palpable dread and one that would continue to haunt him. I began to wonder what this dream he had had could be, and the answer came from an idea of Michael Boyd's to have Romeo speak the Prologue.

> Two households, both alike in dignity
> In fair Verona, where we lay our scene . . .
> (*Prologue*, 1–2)

is one of those bits of Shakespeare that the audience can practically chant along with you. It is usually spoken at the very top of the play (as written), often by the actor playing Escalus. Michael's idea was to have the Prologue spoken midway through the first scene, so that it would cut through the street-fight and suspend the action; and he also wanted it to be spoken by Romeo. This wouldn't be the same Romeo that we would meet for the first time a few minutes later, however; this would be Romeo after his death, a spectre who could speak the Prologue with all the despair, resignation and even bitterness, of hindsight. As the action on stage was suspended, I could even address some of it to other characters in the play, so the lines

> And the continuance of the parents' rage,
> Which, but their children's end, naught could remove
> (lines 10–11)

could be said directly to my father, who was even then in the midst of a sword fight with Capulet. It was a bold choice which, you could say, takes the idea of the Prologue as an alienation device to its logical conclusion. It helped, I think, to confound audience expectation early on—something that we'd always been keen to do. It also helped me to answer my own question. This became Romeo's dream, this vision of himself walking through an all-too-familiar battlefield as a ghost of himself telling a story that would only make partial sense, but warned of a tragedy that would take his life. Indeed, as his story unfolded it would seem that this portent of doom was only becoming ever more inescapable.

So it is a Romeo full of angst, anxiety and little joy that first claps eyes on Juliet. It is probably in these first couple of scenes between Romeo and Juliet that the actors feel the greatest pressure of expectation and history. It is very difficult not to try to play the whole thing at once as you struggle to tell the audience that you *are* 'the greatest lovers of all time'. The solution, of course, is not to think about all that and just play the scenes as they come off the page, but that is easier said than done, particularly in that first scene between the pair which lasts all of eighteen lines, the first fourteen of which famously arrange themselves into a sonnet—ending in the couple's first kiss.

You have a lot of ground to cover in this short scene. By the time they part at the end of it the pair have to have turned their respective lives around to follow each other to the end of time, irrespective of consequences. When Alex Gilbreath and I came to the scene for the first time we tried to tell the story of this huge, life-changing moment with every word. We tried to imbue the scene with every delicate romantic thought we could muster until every word dripped with unspoken meaning—with the result that the scene was absurdly slow and entirely turgid.

We were duly sent off to have a session with Cicely Berry, the RSC's resident verse-speaking guru. Although officially retired, Cis is still very involved with the Company and at hand to help actors through some of the trickier sections of the plays she knows so well. She got us to look at the scene afresh and examine exactly what Shakespeare is doing in the language. So we started again, stripping the whole thing down and dumping the baggage: after all, these two people may be the most famous couple in the English-speaking world, but at this point *they have never met before.*

Their conversation (I.v.93–106) begins with what is, to my mind, a rather brilliant chat-up line from Romeo:

> If I profane with my unworthiest hand
> This holy shrine, the gentle sin is this.
> My lips, two blushing pilgrims, ready stand
> To smooth that rough touch with a tender kiss.

I'm quite sure that he's used this line before. It seems far too polished and well constructed to be an extempore remark and it is right up his particular alley of pure obsession. He casts himself as a pilgrim and the object of his love as the holiest of saints. Even if he has tried this line before, however, he has never had the response that he now enjoys:

> Good pilgrim, you do wrong your hand too much,
> Which mannerly devotion shows in this.
> For saints have hands that pilgrims' hands do touch,
> And palm to palm is holy palmers' kiss.

And this is where it all starts changing for Romeo. Not only has he been entranced by the physical shape of Juliet from across a crowded dance-floor; now he has met his match intellectually. They are sparring with their wits now. He takes her argument and uses it against her:

> Have not saints lips, and holy palmers too?

But, again, she is too quick for him:

> Ay, pilgrim, lips that they must use in prayer.

Continuing the idea, Romeo appeals to her—as it were 'in character'— and warns her that she is responsible for his immortal soul:

> O, then, dear saint, let lips do what hands do!
> They pray: grant thou, lest faith turn to despair.

And Juliet, ever his equal, manages to give in, knowing full well where all this is leading, without losing any of her own dignity:

> Saints do not move, though grant for prayers' sake.

And so, on the last line of the sonnet, Romeo and Juliet kiss and their destiny is sealed:

> Then move not while my prayer's effect I take.

We found that if we played the scene as a battle of wits, then the rest of the work was done for us. The innuendo is all in the text, and what can be sexier than two people who are attracted to each other trying to outdo each other—push each other away and at the same time reel each other in? The scene became much quicker and more urgent, with barely a pause for breath until after that first kiss. I realize that it can seem terribly mundane to say that the lesson we learned was simply to play the text, but often it proves more difficult than one would imagine, especially when the familiarity of the text you have to work with transcends its meaning.

There is a point immediately after this scene where Romeo discovers Juliet's identity and it seems that their relationship is finished before it can even begin. I wanted to tell the story of Romeo settling in to the doomed inevitability of it all. He is, after all, the misunderstood poet who can never be happy, and to be in love with the daughter of his father's mortal foe is almost too perfect. If Rosaline, the novice nun, was a bad choice of girlfriend, then Juliet is even more of a disaster. When he wanders into the orchard below Juliet's window, he has no reason to believe that this is anything other than another Rosaline situation where he can protest his unrequited love to an unforgiving world.

> But soft! What light through yonder window breaks?
>   (II.ii.2)

This is another line that seems beyond reinterpretation, but I tried to play the very real danger of the situation. If Romeo is caught in this orchard, under this window, he will be killed without question, something that Michael was always reminding us of and which would help to power the scene that followed. It is only Romeo's free-wheeling imagination that pulls him back towards the dream of Juliet. The speech which follows is a glorious marriage of the poetic and the earthly—as, indeed, is Romeo and Juliet's entire relationship. He compares Juliet to the sun, and then she is the moon's maid, wearing green livery (a reference to virginity) which he urges her to cast off, and his final thought is 'That I might touch that cheek' (II.ii.25).

She is still a heavenly body to him, but there is a genuine sense of his sexual desire too. He is marrying the idolization of his heart's desire (which we have seen with Rosaline) with very real sexual urges: already their relationship is more real and mature, but it is all still part of Romeo's fancy until he hears Juliet say

> O Romeo, Romeo!—wherefore art thou Romeo?
> Deny thy father and refuse thy name.

Or, if thou wilt not, be but sworn my love,
And I'll no longer be a Capulet.   (II.ii.33–6)

And it is only here that Romeo's journey really begins. For the first
time his love is reciprocated, for the first time he has found his soul-
mate, and from that moment his destiny is set in stone. From that
moment he is, as he will later realize, playing straight into the arms
of the fates he was so keen to avoid.

Act Two, Scene Two, the 'Balcony Scene', is one that Alex and I
always enjoyed playing. For a start, it is the only point in the whole
play that Romeo and Juliet actually get to spend any real time
together, so everything else that happens springs from this twenty-
minute scene. Both the characters speak the most wonderful lines;
not only is the text very beautiful, however, it is also very human,
and at times, it transpired, very funny. We never set out to 'get laughs'
in the balcony scene, but they did happen. All we tried to do was to
play the situation and the dialogue as truthfully as we could, and I
suppose the act of two people falling in love and getting to know
each other is not altogether without its lighter side. Michael certainly
guarded against any accusation of sentimentality and kept this scene
on a strictly truthful basis by shouting 'Soup!' at us during rehearsal
if ever we slipped into the bog of emotional overindulgence.

There is also a conflict of interest between them in this scene,
with Juliet full of the practicalities of the danger Romeo is in and
the need for him to get to safety, and Romeo's desire to flout the risks
in order to tell her how enchanted he is:

JULIET   If they do see thee, they will murder thee.
ROMEO   Alack, there lies more peril in thine eye
            Than twenty of their swords! Look thou but sweet,
            And I am proof against their enmity.
                                                        (II.ii.70–3)

This youthful, idealistic, and completely charming Romeo will
develop into something else very quickly. In Act Three, Scene Five,
after they have spent their first night together and Romeo must leave
before they are discovered, the roles have changed. He is the husband now, and has taken on the responsibility he has for both of
them. Then it is Juliet who wants to ignore the truth and Romeo
who takes control: 'I must be gone and live, or stay and die' (III.v.11).

Both of them, however, are aware of the gravity of their situation
from the beginning. When Juliet proposes the idea of marriage (and
the initial idea does come from her: Romeo is slower to grasp the
necessity of practical action), he doesn't hesitate to agree. They have to
legitimize their relationship if it is to have any chance of surviving in
this climate. Again that sense of violence that pervades their lives

David Tennant as Romeo with Juliet (Alexandra Gilbreath), 2000. Act III, Scene v: 'I must be gone and live, or stay and die.' Malcolm Davies Collection, © Shakespeare Birthplace Trust.

defines both of their characters in so many ways. Romeo talks to none of his friends about this most important of life-changes—simply because he can't risk it. The only person he can turn to is the friar.

The friar is one of the most important keys to figuring out who Romeo is. It is the friar who is Romeo's closest *confidant*, it is to him that Romeo takes all his problems, and it is in the friar's cell that Romeo hides out after he has killed Tybalt. Des McAleer provided our production with a brilliant, solid, no-nonsense friar who offered a strong counter to any of Romeo's adolescent extremities. We wanted there to be a familiarity between the pair that was to do with mutual affection and respect. We decided that Romeo, forever in the grip of some existential argument with himself, would be regularly at the friar's cell, picking his brains and quizzing him on the nature of his own beliefs. We felt that the friar (not a conventional priest) would enjoy debating the finer points of theology with his young friend and it made great sense to me that Romeo, in search of some world outwith his own, would need the outlet of someone who considered things on the spiritual plane. It is not always an easy

relationship, however. The friar doesn't give Romeo an easy time
when he reveals that he has fallen in love with Juliet, and it seems
clear that Romeo expects it to be a hard sell as the friar has to force
him to get to the point:

> Be plain, good son, and homely in thy drift.
> Riddling confession finds but riddling shrift.
>   (II.iii.51–2)

But Romeo needs someone to test him like this and the friar provides that for him. It is also the friar who sees Romeo at his most
vulnerable.

The scene which closed the first half in our production, Act Three,
Scene One, contains a pivotal moment for Romeo. After the uncon-
fined joy of the lightning marriage ceremony, things are beginning
to look up for young Montague and for the first time it looks possible that he might just live happily ever after. Running into a vengeful Tybalt in the street is the last thing Romeo had gambled on, and
the resulting sword fight which will see Romeo cause Mercutio's
death and then kill Tybalt in vengeful rage, destroys any sensation
of the hope that Romeo was beginning to feel.

It is a brilliantly written scene, one which we found came to life
fairly easily, since each of the characters is so strongly motivated in
opposing directions and the stakes are so high: for Tybalt, his own
pride and need for revenge; for Mercutio, the need to protect the
honour of his friend; and for Romeo, the future of his wife and the
safety of both his friend and his new cousin-in-law. Romeo is para-
lysed by his need to maintain the secrecy of his brand new wife, and
it is this paralysis that leads to his ill-advised attempt to stop the
fight between Tybalt and Mercutio. The extraordinary stage fight
between Adrian Schiller and Keith Dunphy (playing Tybalt), put
together by fight-director Terry King, made this very easy to play.
The more dangerous the battle looks, the more impotent and terrified Romeo becomes, making his eventual intervention all the more
desperate.

These feelings of impotence and fear make Romeo's sense of
inequity—and, more importantly, guilt—at Mercutio's death all the
sharper. Adrian's Mercutio showed no forgiveness at his death—he
would, after all, be back in the second half to kill me off—and so I
was left on stage full of remorse, anger and a sense of bewilderment
at what had just occurred. Again Romeo sees it all written in the
all-seeing, ever-malicious stars:

> This day's black fate on more days doth depend.
> This but begins the woe others must end.
>   (III.i.119–20)

It was important to me that when Tybalt reappeared Romeo dispatched him quickly, violently, and with as little sense of honour as possible. We know that Romeo is not, by nature, violent and there is nothing in the text to suggest that he is a particularly good swordsman (Mercutio suggests earlier in the scene that he is no match for Tybalt), so if we are to believe that he could kill Tybalt it has to be a sudden, reckless act done in the blind heat of a moment's pure rage. He is in a miasma of confusion, injustice and terrible, terrible guilt and the presence of Tybalt alive and well with the sight of Mercutio's blood still vivid in Romeo's mind pushes him into a stupor of fury and violence. It is several lines later, with Tybalt dead at his feet and Benvolio pleading with him to make a run for it, before the true gravity of what he has done wakens Romeo out of his reverie of vengeance. With 'O, I am fortune's fool' (III.i.136) Romeo sees his life unravelling before his very eyes. Suddenly he has single-handedly killed his future, his hope, and another human being. One of his closest friends is dead and he has become a murderer. His chances of living happily ever after have evaporated terrifyingly quickly.

The scene in the friar's cell (III.iii) where Romeo learns that he is to be banished from Verona, sees him at his most helpless. Romeo has no one to blame but himself for the death of Tybalt, and consequently the death of his marriage to Tybalt's, cousin, and it is the friar who gets the full front of Romeo's rage of helplessness. I didn't want to hold back on this. I felt that Romeo would react like a cornered animal, lashing out at the friar and blaming him for his predicament. Unreasonable and childish though that may be, this is, it seems to me, often how we treat those closest to us. Shakespeare certainly gives Romeo (ever the poet) a rash of words to express himself with. The word *banished* chimes through this scene (and the previous one) like a death-knell and every time it came up I would try to use it to punish the friar, to hurt someone else as I had been hurt. It is Romeo's crisis point, and it is the friar who lifts him out of it. The friar is Romeo's base point, to which he will always come home. They are much more in tune than Romeo and his parents are; indeed father and son is the dynamic of their relationship. It is important that Romeo has an unquestioning trust of the friar—as children often do of their parents—to allow the events at the end of the play to unfold as they do.

When Romeo reappears after being banished to Mantua (and being off stage for the whole of Act Four), I felt he should have matured and moved on. No longer dressed all in black, he's been away from the continual threats and challenges of Veronese life and although he's being denied his Juliet, he seems calm. He's had some time in isolation to think things through and plan the life that he and Juliet may lead together. It is as if he has finally managed to escape the fingers of the fates. Certainly the dream he talks of at the start of Act Five, Scene One is of an optimistic nature (albeit with a morbid flavour) and it seems that he can finally see light at the end of the tunnel. This calmness and state of readiness perhaps explains his reaction to the news that Juliet is dead: 'Is it e'en so? Then I defy you, stars!' (V.i.24). He refuses to be beaten by his own destiny and there are no tears or protestations of grief. In that instant I wanted him to see everything that must happen very clearly. His language is certainly full of practicality and he sees a clear sequence of events. The thought of dying alongside Juliet becomes inevitable and absolutely necessary and no side-issue—emotional or otherwise—must get in the way. He becomes filled with such full-fronted motivation that from that moment until he sees Juliet's body, he slips into another reality altogether. Michael described its being as if he were full of 'toxic energy' and this is the energy that kills Paris and threatens to do away with Balthasar. It is only when he has lifted Juliet out of the grave and is cradling her in his arms that he can breathe again and begin to understand where circumstances have brought him.

I find Romeo's final speech fascinating. There is relatively little self-indulgence or grief. Instead I found there to be a strong sense of someone who has come home. The only thing that seems to damage his resolve to die is Juliet's lack of decay:

> Ah, dear Juliet,
> Why art thou yet so fair? Shall I believe
> That insubstantial death is amorous,
> And that the lean abhorrèd monster keeps
> Thee here in dark to be his paramour?
> For fear of that I still will stay with thee
> And never from this palace of dim night
> Depart again.   (V.iii.101–8)

And then the idea of dying becomes a release:

> Here, here [*repeating the word seems to underline his resolve*]
>   will I remain
> With worms that are thy chambermaids. O here [*again*]
> Will I set up my everlasting rest
> And shake the yoke of inauspicious stars
> From this world-wearied flesh.   (V.iii.108–12)

So finally he has beaten the fates that have been pushing him around and forcing this misplaced poet to live in a world that he doesn't fit into, and in death he can finally escape and be with the woman who understood him. In our production Michael had Alex and me walking through the people round the tomb after our death and then walking off the stage and out through the audience so that, indeed, through death, Romeo and Juliet had somehow escaped. The real tragedy is left for those who have to rebuild this ruined society. One suspects that their problems are bigger than a couple of gold statues can mend.

Romeo and Juliet is a much-produced play full of lines more famous than any of the actors who could hope to play them. One could never hope to be definitive in it, but I'm glad to have had the chance to give it a crack and I look forward to seeing it performed again and again in years to come, so that I can see the way it should have been done. And it goes without saying that I shall greatly enjoy terrorizing young actors by telling them how very, *very* tricky it is!

COURTNEY LEHMANN

Shakespeare with a View: Zeffirelli's *Romeo and Juliet*[†]

* * * Based on his acclaimed 1960 theatrical production at the Old Vic, Zeffirelli's 1968 film adaptation proved to be an international success, as the young, paradoxically angst-ridden, peace-loving, 'flower-child' generation came out to the cinemas in force. Perfectly attuned to the impact of popular music on this group of rebels with a cause, the film made its way into audiences' hearts through its musical score in particular, composed by the legendary Nino Rota. * * * 1968 was a miraculously impetuous year, marked not only by the infamous May riots in France, which included massive worker strikes and bloody student protests as well as the shocking assassination of presidential-hopeful Bobby Kennedy, the rising tide of anti-Vietnam War sentiment deteriorating relations between the Soviets and the West, and Mao's Cultural Revolution in China. A ripple effect in the world of film ensued, as *Cahiers du Cinema* contributors Jean-Luc Comolli and Jean Narboni published their manifesto 'Cinema/Ideology/Criticism', calling for an end to the 'closed-circle whereby '"what the public wants"' means "'what the dominant ideology wants"'[1]. * * * Released in Britain in March and the US in September, Zeffirelli's 1968 adaptation of *Romeo and Juliet* was far from insulated from these turbulent times. Significantly, the film was to begin with a kind of primitive graffiti—the carving of the title in Verona's ancient walls—an image that alludes to the 'inspirational'

---

† From *Shakespeare's* Romeo and Juliet: *A Close Study of the Relationship Between Text and Film* (London: Methuen Drama, 2010), pp. 134, 136–47, 151–66. © Courtney Lehmann, 2010. Reprinted by permission of Bloomsbury Methuen Drama, an imprint of Bloomsbury Publishing Plc.
1. Jean-Luc Comolli and Jean Narboni, 'Cinema/Ideology/Criticism' (1969) in *Theory and Criticism*, edited by Gerald Mast, Marshall Cohen, and Leo Braud (New York and Oxford: Oxford University Press, 1992), p. 685.

phrases of the Sixties. For example, among the more memorable acts of graffiti inscribed during the May riots, two sentiments in particular capture opposing forces of 1968. One, teeming with idealism, reads: realistic, demand the impossible'; another, consumed with outrage, says, simply, 'Be cruel', while another expounds upon this theme: 'A single nonrevolutionary weekend is infinitely more bloody than a month of total revolution'. The world of music was permanently affected by this crisis of idealism versus aggression. The Pretenders song 'When Will I See You' cites the 'demand the impossible' slogan quoted above and refers to those people who, like Romeo and Juliet, 'fill streets at night' and count themselves among the 'starry eyed', whereas the other end of the spectrum is epitomised by groups like The Rolling Stones, who responded to the political climate with the insurrectionist number 'Street Fighting Man'.

This same internal conflict between dreaming and fighting, optimism and nihilism, defines Zeffirelli's 1968 adaptation, in which the lovers' naïve romanticism exists in constant tension with the cultural violence all around them. As Peter S. Donaldson astutely remarks: 'the film participates in the general loosening of restrictions on the representation of sexuality on film of the period, and it seemed to endorse of number of the values of the international youth movement: pacifism, distrust of elders, and sexual liberation'.[2] Rounding out this portrait of the disaffected teen-lovers, Russell Jackson observes that '(w)hat is "contemporary" in Zeffirelli's version resides in the couple's frank expression of sexual desire and in their (long) haircuts, and in a fundamental ordinariness'[3]. Jackson goes one step further, noting the film's ongoing relevance, for although the 'director had announced his project as "a cinéma-verité documentary . . . on Renaissance Verona"' in 'social behavior, festivity, fighting and religious observance, Zeffirelli's Renaissance Italy seems closer . . . to the experience of the audience. This version of Verona is somewhere we might live— or at least visit—with just a few adjustments of costume'.[4]

Romeo and Juliet opens with a God's eye view of a hazy Verona, with Laurence Olivier performing the Prologue's bleak monologue in voiceover. Remarkably, Zeffirelli recalls fondly that Olivier, his boyhood idol, just so happened to be in the area filming *The Shoes of the Fisherman* and, when he learned of the neighbouring production, '(n)aturally he felt an almost proprietary interest in any film of a Shakespeare play'.[5] When Zeffirelli offered him the role of the

2. Peter S. Donaldson, *Shakespearean Films/Shakespearean Directors* (Boston: Unwin Hyman, 1990), p. 145.
3. Russell Jackson, *Shakespeare Films in the Making: Vision, Production and Reception* (Cambridge and New York: Cambridge University Press, 2007), p. 208.
4. Ibid., p. 197.
5. Franco Zeffirelli, *Zeffirelli: An Autobiography* (New York: Weldenfeld and Nicolson, 1986), p. 229.

Prologue, Olivier, a bit crest-fallen, replied: 'Of course . . . But isn't there anything else?' 'I think he would have played Romeo if he'd thought there was half a chance', Zeffirelli recalls with a laugh, but,

> (I)n the end I got him to dub Lord Montague, who'd been played by an Italian with a thick accent. By now unstoppable Larry insisted on dubbing all sorts of small parts and crowd noise in a hilarious variety of assumed voices. The audience never knew just how much of Laurence Olivier they were getting on the soundtrack of that film.[6]

For Zeffirelli—not an unsuperstitious man—this was an auspicious beginning for his underfunded production, about which backers remained highly skeptical. * * *

* * * Zeffirelli rented a series of country homes on a small estate not far from Rome, and brought his own family, along with the major actors, together for the entire summer. It is little wonder, then, that at this time that Zeffirelli told *Vogue* magazine his *Romeo and Juliet* 'will really be a documentary for the period as well. . . . I know my Romeo and Juliet, but, oh, how I also know my Italy.[7] Indeed, as Ace Pilkington observes, '(f)or Zeffirelli, the Italian towns which became his Verona . . . are part of the plot, an "additional character" indeed, with the beauty of Renaissance Italy but also with a sinister energy which drives the tragedy inexorably on'.[8] But it is easy to lose the 'sinister' aspects of the mise-en-scene in Zeffirelli's magical shooting locations in Tuscania, Plenza, and Gubblo—let alone the mini-estate where he and the others resided. 'There we all were', he remembers, 'living as if in a cheerful, busy commune; Olivia and Leonard rehearsing on the lawn; Nino Rota writing the music in the salon; Robert Stephens and Natasha Parry learning their lines or swimming in the pool—it was a dream world'.[9]

But Zeffirelli's dream world was haunted, just as Romeo and Juliet are, by the fear that 'Destiny' would keep his story from going forward, due not only to the film's incredibly low budget—$800,000— but also to events in Zeffirelli's own life. Significantly, just before scouting exterior locations in an around the Rome-based studio Cinecittá the director was attempting to put on a production of *Aida* in—of all places—Egypt. Despite enjoying himself, the many attractions, and the Egyptian people immensely, Zeffirelli recalls having 'the most terrible premonition', and, subsequently, he and the entire cast of *Aida* 'caught the first—and the last—plane back

6. Ibid.
7. Quoted in Ace Pilkington, 'Zeffirelli's Shakespeare', in *Shakespeare and the Moving Image: The plays on film and television*, edited by Anthony Davies and Stanley Wells (Cambridge: Cambridge University Press, 1994), p. 165.
8. Ace Pilkington, p. 172.
9. Zeffirelli, *An Autobiography*, p. 227.

to Italy. The day after we returned . . . the Six Day War began . . .'[1] Not surprisingly, then, the forces of idealism and aggression that characterised the climate in which Zeffirelli found himself trying to film a love story took on an almost allegorical quality: it would be the dreamers versus destiny, and who would prevail, no one really knew. And how could the young stars of the film, Leonard Whiting and Olivia Hussey—then the youngest pair ever assembled to play *Romeo and Juliet* on screen—*not* defy their star-crossed fate in that summer of 1968, a time when *anything* seemed possible?[2]

As early as the opening credits, however, foreshadowing of the bloody business to come is evident. As Olivier concludes the Prologue, the camera zooms in on the sun, at which point the screen reads, 'William Shakespeare's', as if to imply that the Bard is the light of the world or, alternatively, *Italy*'s native 'son'; but all too quickly, the scene and credits change when a cut to battlements—a structure that can barely contain its implicit violence—announces '*Romeo and Juliet.*' In keeping with his superstitious nature, Zeffirelli explains that in his adaptation '(t)he central idea is that of a puppeteer, Destiny, who handles all the characters. They are all puppets on a stage and no one is fully responsible. The whole tragedy is permeated with the idea of fate. There is nothing to do. Juliet is the only valuable opposition to it'.[3] What, then, is the source of this tragic predetermination in the film? As we shall see, Zeffirelli boldly suggests—through his selective use of a large, gold crucifix—that God himself has preordained Romeo and Juliet's death. But before we can begin to see this case unfold, we must return to the beginning of the film, where Zeffirelli, professing to use a cinéma verité style, employs an impressive range of hand-held camerawork to capture the frenetic, hyper-violent qualities of the opening fray between the Montagues and the Capulets.

Indeed, more so than any other adaptation before it, the opening brawl looks more like the battle scenes from Kenneth Branagh's *Henry V*, as characters are not merely beaten but murdered: runthrough, decapitated, or violently disfigured (one combatant gets a sword in his right eye). Not even the women and children are spared as they attempt to flee from the melee. Then, suddenly, the camera whirls 360 degrees and tilts up to authorise the Prince as the figure who, based on the literally heightened value ascribed to him by the camera angle, declares death henceforth for anyone who creates mutiny among his subjects. Mirroring the camerawork that has

1. Ibid., p. 226.
2. Actually the first known attempt to cast actors close in age to Shakespeare's Romeo and Juliet was undertaken by William Poel in his 1905 stage production, which featured a fourteen year-old Juliet (Dorothy Minto) and a seventeen year old Romeo (Esme Percy).
3. This excerpt from Zeffirelli's interview with *The Guardian* (5 March 1968) is cited in Jackson, p. 195–96.

preceded his entry, the Prince—poised aristocratically astride his white horse—turns round and round in an effort to address the crowd that encircles him. Yet throughout this scene, it is Michael York's swashbuckling Tybalt who most captures our attention; not only does he cut a fine figure in his doublet and hose, but also, Zeffirelli has given him a cap which, with its brim folded up, makes him appear as though he has devil horns (Luhrmann will extend this suggestive sartorial flourish by having Tybalt wear a devil's costume at the Capulet Ball). Zeffirelli recalls York's disappointment when he informed him of the role he would play: '"Not Romeo . . . Mercutio?" asked York, despondent, "No, Tybalt". Zeffirelli replied firmly, but reassuringly added, "(e)ven with only twenty-four lines, it will be a major role when you see what we will do"'.[4] Moreover, as Zeffirelli notes, another auspicious event occurred when he noticed that 'Michael (York) was having a good time. A photographer called from *The Sunday Telegraph* to do a story on us and—another good omen for *Romeo and Juliet*—the two of them were soon inseparable. They eventually married and have always made a wonderful couple . . .'[5]

Michael York's twenty-four lines turn out to be a lot in this production, in which Zeffirelli cuts more than half of the play. As we have come to expect from directors who adapt Shakespeare, visual language becomes as important—if not more so—than the text. Hence, in his first scene, Romeo carries a flower, which tells us all we need to know; denied all of his bad Petrarchan poetry, Romeo, upon seeing the wounded, cries only: 'What fray was here? / Yet tell me not, for I have heard it all: / Here's much to do with hate, but more with love'. Disgusted, the peacenik dashes the flower to the ground and walks away from the confused Benvolio. As in earlier versions, the scene proceeds to Paris's attempt to woo Juliet through Old Capulet, as the aristocratic Count stakes his claim to her: 'Younger than she are happy mothers made', to which Capulet replies, eyeing his disenchanted wife across the way, 'And too soon marred are those so early made'. Lady Capulet adds an exclamation point to this statement by slamming a window shut, preventing both her husband and Paris from catching any glimpse of Juliet. In various other examples of 'stage business' such as this, Zeffirelli makes it plain that the marriage, between Juliet's parents is a bad match, to say the least Significantly, one such match—known for its turbulence—played an unexpected role in Zeffirelli's ability to move forward with a film that no one (except the cast) seemed to believe in: the then-notoriously fiery couple who had starred in Zeffirelli's 1966 *Taming of the Shrew*, Richard Burton and Elizabeth Taylor, to

4. Zeffirelli, *An Autobiography*, pp. 215–16.
5. Ibid., p. 228.

whom the director showed early footage of his *Romeo and Juliet*. Though both were enamored with what they saw, what they heard was another matter, as Burton pointed to a problem with the verse. Perhaps it was this remark that prompted one of the more amusing outbursts in the early stages of shooting, when Zeffirelli allegedly told the classically-trained Romeo, played by Leonard Whiting, to 'stop thinking about your Granddaddy Shakespeare and speak the lines naturally!' Privy to Whiting's personal copy of the script, Russell Jackson observes that '(a) version of this advice is probably reflected in a note Whiting jotted down on the back of his script: "Don't quiver voice sounds phohy"'.[6]

Playing opposite Whiting, Olivia Hussey's Juliet is first introduced to us wearing a sumptuous red dress that barely contains her bosom. Gilding her pale skin is a large golden cross. * * * in his rich psychoanalytic reading of Zeffirelli's film, Peter S. Donaldson notes that from the very beginning, Juliet is positioned in the middle of a series of disturbing triangulating relationships. As noted above, we are first introduced to her as an object of barter between Paris and her father, and, shortly thereafter, Juliet becomes the subject of the Nurse's bawdy banter when Lady Capulet awkwardly attempts to broach the subject of marriage with her daughter. Yet, upon our first sight of Juliet, her independent spirit is showcased by dint of the fact that, as Donaldson observes, she is 'seen apart from her father's gaze' and, consequently, 'comes to life' on her own.[7] Indeed, Zeffirelli's hope-against-hope that Juliet will somehow remain 'the one valuable opposition (to Destiny)' informs his tendency to underscore her aggressive optimism and open sexuality. . . . Indeed, Donaldson affirms this perspective when he asserts that although Juliet is 'enmeshed in the triangular structures of (the) feud and the generational displacements patriarchal marriage brokerage, she seems to have the possibility of her own life, her own space'.[8]

Despite being two hours and twenty minutes in length, the pacing of Zeffirelli's adaptation is swift, for the scene proceeds immediately to a vision of Mercutio and his band of merry men carrying torches in the piazza. The combination of Zeffirelli's direction and John McEnery's deeply-nuanced portrayal of Mercutio—the mercurial foil to Michael York's fiery Tybalt—has forever changed the way that this role is interpreted. Indeed, McEnery's 'Queen Mab' speech smacks of a barely-contained lunacy that no film actors have been able to master since. More importantly, this scene has become the

6. Zeffirelli, 'Filming Shakespeare', In *Staging Shakespeare Seminars on Production Problems*, edited by Glenn Looney (London and New York: Garland, 1990), pp. 239–71, p. 249.
7. Donaldon, p. 162.
8. Ibid.

basis of subsequent renderings that suggest Mercutio's homoerotic attachment to Romeo, as Zeffirelli presents Mercutio as a man 'desperate . . . to retain Romeo's (attention) by keeping him loyal to the values of the male pack'; In fact, Donaldson claims that '*Romeo and Juliet* was also, for its time, perhaps the most daring of all Shakespeare adaptations in its bringing to the surface homoerotic aspects of Shakespeare's art.'[9] This, as he contends, is the likely source Mercutio's often violent misogynistic speeches and gestures, which reach a breaking point when his Queen Mab speech is derailed by the subject of the heterosexual imperative:

> This is the hag, when maids lie on their backs,
> That presses them and learns them first to bear,
> Making them women of good carriage,
> This is she—This is she—This is she . . .

Donaldson argues that Mercutio's 'final, sad "*this* is she" suggests a partial awareness that his inventiveness and improvisation mask an identification with the (devalued) women his discourse and antics invoke. He himself is Queen Mab: she arises from his own pain and confusion'.[1]

Whether or not Romeo recognises Mercutio's repressed identification with Mab, it is clear that he acknowledges his friend's 'pain and confusion'. Upon seeing that Mercutio is raving and desperately alone at the end of his famous speech—which echoes hauntingly throughout the empty courtyard into which Mercutio has fled—Romeo clasps Mercutio's face to his in an effort to console him. Filmed in a tight profile, this two shot shows Romeo and Mercutio's foreheads resting softly against one another. Staring eye-to-eye with their lips parted, their impassioned and deeply private exchange is as romantic—in its own, subtle way—as the scenes between Romeo and Juliet themselves. 'Peace, peace, Mercutio, peace / Thou talk'st of nothing', whispers Romeo; measuredly, Mercutio replies, swallowing his incipient tears:

> True, I talk of dreams
> Which are the children of an idle brain,
> Begot of nothing but vain fantasy.
> Which is as thin of substance as the air,
> And more inconstant than the wind who woos
> Even now the frozen bosom of the north . . .

In Zeffirelli's production, these words resonate with a heightened intimacy; one even wonders if Mercutio is encoding his unrequited

9. Ibid., p. 145, p. 158.
1. Ibid, p. 158.

love for Romeo in his talk of 'fantasy' and 'inconstancy', as he tries to break through the 'frozen bosom' of his best friend. Indeed, as Mercutio is reluctantly coaxed away by the 'pack' of lusty young men, a long take of him walking backwards—his angst-ridden gaze fixed on Romeo—resembles that of a jilted lover.

Significantly, the movement in this scene thus leaves Romeo alone in the empty courtyard, at which point he utters his fear that he will arrive 'too early' at the Ball, concerned that

> Some consequence yet hanging in the stars
> Shall bitterly begin his fearful date
> With this night's revels, and expire the term
> Of a despised life closed in my breast
> By some vile forfeit of untimely death.

Based on the unconventional blocking of this scene, Romeo's musings draw heightened attention to the overwhelming force of 'Destiny'. In the film, as the gang literally—albeit unwittingly—abandons him to his Fate. That Mercutio has instilled this morbid mood in Romeo, and the fact that their destinies are inextricably intertwined, is also suggested by the foreboding death mask that Mercutio wears throughout the scene. But, at least at this juncture, Romeo is able to master his fear with a gaze up at the heavens, as he concludes, clearly referring to God: 'But (H)e that hath the steerage of my course / Direct my suit'.

* * *

Given Zeffirelli's apparent resistance to retaining Shakespeare's heavy-handed moments of foreshadowing. It is particularly odd that he chooses to transition into the balcony scene with a line that is rarely cited in stage or screen productions. While Benvolio and Mercutio call aloud for Romeo, who is busy making his way through the impressive natural barriers of the Capulet orchard, Mercutio heard only in voiceover as the camera lights on Romeo, complains disheartedly: 'The ape is dead'. Romeo's curt 'answer', which we are far more accustomed to hearing on stage and screen, implies that Mercutio has never been in love: 'He jests at scars that never felt a wound'. This peculiar juxtaposition of lines serves Zeffirelli quite efficiently, for the 'exchange' emphasises the fact that Mercutio is a stranger to heterosexual love while also functioning on a literal and metaphorical level to disclose a significant development in Romeo's character. Metaphorically speaking, up until this point Romeo has been 'aping' or merely mimicking the stereotypical behavior, postures, and language of a lover; now, however, he has crossed the threshold to experiencing love as a life-altering, distinctly humanising phenomenon and, hence, his tendency to 'ape' the part of a lover is dead indeed. By the same token, in more literal terms, Romeo does, in fact, resemble an ape as he cavorts, jumps, and swings through the dense vines of the Capulet orchard, a scene that evokes Tarzan comparisons to this day.

The twisted vines of the Capulet grounds also provide the perfect backdrop to the lovers' constantly entwined bodies throughout the balcony scene, wherein the two youths kiss and engage in 'heavy petting' as Nino Rota's theme song waxes romantic yet again. As many scholars have remarked, this scene is noteworthy for its unadulterated passion, as Romeo and Juliet utter lines only when they come up for air from each other's mouths—a tableau perfectly fitting for an audience poised on the brink of the 'free love' era of the Seventies. Crucially, however, Zeffirelli does not simply represent Juliet as the object of our desiring gaze. Rather, as Donaldson asserts, 'Zeffirelli moves away from the conventions of mainstream cinema and toward a more reciprocal and unpredictable treatment of sexuality'.[2] By the same token, however, less sophisticated audiences are more likely to focus on Olivia Hussey's bust, which, on certain occasions, partially reveals her nipples beneath her corseted underdress—particularly when she leans over the balcony, breathing heavily from her rapture. Indeed, at this juncture is it worth noting Zeffirelli's first impressions of Olivia Hussey: 'She had some talent, but she was unfortunately overweight, clumsy looking and bit her nails constantly—hardly the delicate Juliet I dreamt of'. On a pure whim, however, Zeffirelli later called back several of the actresses whom he had rejected earlier, and it was then that he

> stumbled upon the amazing transformation of Olivia Hussey. She was a new woman: she had lost weight dramatically. Her magnificent bone structure was becoming apparent, with those wide expressive eyes and her whole angular self. She was now the real Juliet, a gawky colt of a girl waiting for life to begin.[3]

Hussey certainly had transformed, though how much weight she lost is impossible to discern through the enormous gowns that Zeffirelli outfits her in; especially when she appears next to Leonard Whiting's lean, tights-wearing Romeo, Hussey seems somewhat strangely matched with him. But if, as Donaldson notes, Zeffirelli 'translate(s) Juliet's self-assertion into physical activity' not only 'by emphasising *her* desiring look' but, also, by asserting 'her energetic physical command of herself *and* of the scenes in which she appears', then a more robust Juliet makes perfect sense, particularly if Zeffirelli is, in fact, attempting to approximate—visually—'parity between genders. . . .'[4]

2. Donaldson, p. 167.
3. Zeffirelli, *An Autobiography*, pp. 225–26.
4. Donaldson, p. 167.

In more general terms, however, as many critics have speculated, the scarcity of women—compared with the sheer number of young attractive men in form-fitting clothing that populate Zeffirelli's Verona—may have more to do with the director's (at the time) closeted homosexuality than with any deliberate aesthetic decision. Indeed, Zeffirelli's first impression of Whiting is revealing: 'his looks were perfect for the role; he was the most exquisitely beautiful male adolescent I've ever met'.[5] The first shot of Romeo suggests the extent to which the camera is enamoured with him, as he emerges in soft focus, flower in hand. Indeed. Ace Pilkington asserts that '(o)f all Zeffirelli's films, *Romeo and Juliet* comes closest to the essence of the Shakespeare play on which it is based, perhaps in part because the beauty of Zeffirelli's actors and camerawork echoes (even as it replaces) the formal ornamentation of Shakespeare's verse'.[6]

On the glorious Tuscan morning that follows the balcony scene the audience is treated to a view of the countryside, as Friar Laurence goes about picking herbs and flowers. The Friar is looking among the wildflowers for one in particular, which he finds and holds up for the audience to glimpse—its unique periwinkle tint is unmistakably reminiscent of the flower that Romeo holds at the very beginning of the film.[7] Given the repeated use of a lone flower at threshold moments in the film, we might conclude that in place of the foreboding speeches that Zeffirelli cuts from the screenplay, he inserts visual cues which, consciously or unconsciously, intimate the increasing force of the legend. Though somewhat different from the purple flower that Romeo holds at the beginning of the film, a single purple flower will be shown twice more, unmistakably yoking Romeo and Juliet's destinies to the intervention of the Friar. Both here—in the middle of the film—and nearing the end, the Friar will emerge holding the varietal that is the source of the sleeping potion—the floral device that will ultimately have a fatal effect on both lovers. This imagery is very subtly employed, providing the audience with a glimpse of the flowers just long enough to connect them through their common color scheme.

Far less subtle, however, is the cross imagery that begins to appear, appropriately, with the introduction of Friar Laurence. In addition to the cross that Juliet wears about her neck, an enormous golden crucifix adorns the cathedral in which Friar Laurence's cell is located. When Romeo arrives there, ecstatic from the preceding night's revels, the Friar proceeds to chide Romeo at length for his

5. Zeffirelli, *An Autobiography*, p. 228.
6. Pilkington, p. 173.
7. In *Shakespearean Films/Shakespearean Directors* Peter S. Donaldson identifies the flower that Romeo holds as a mint flower; though he doesn't mention the color, it is clearly the mint varietal characterised by purple 'spikes', known as *Agastache rugosa*.

quickly-abandoned love for 'Rosaline'; this scene, however, makes little sense to the audience, since there is no mention of her name prior to this moment—although Russell Jackson points out that in the shooting script, Rosaline is identified as an elegant lady-in-blue at the Capulet Ball.[8] Not coincidentally, when the Friar ceases lecturing Romeo, he seeks inspiration by turning his gaze to the image of the crucifix; through shot-reverse-shot camera work, Zeffirelli makes it clear that the Friar's decision to marry the lovers has come from God himself. Of course, the most obvious reason for this decision is the fact that Friar Laurence desperately wants to preempt Romeo and Juliet from engaging in the sin of premarital sex, for even within the hallowed interior of the cathedral, the two can barely keep their hands and lips off each other, and the Friar must labour constantly to part them. Zeffirelli's ensuing use of the cross, however, is far more brazen. Adding some stage business to the arrangements that the Nurse and Romeo are making for the secret ceremony, the camera focuses on the crucifix once again as Romeo attempts to pay the Nurse for her service. When she repeatedly refuses to accept the offering, Romeo goes to put the coin in the indulgence box, but the Nurse prevents him, and keeps it for herself. Thus, one can't help but wonder if, had Romeo proleptically purchased an indulgence, the story might be entirely different. Quickly, though, the ominous nature of the 'greater power' that will, ultimately, thwart their intents, is implied when Romeo, virtually lost in rapture, stares at the crucifix with wonder, blowing two kisses to it before dashing out of the cathedral. Subsequently, in a scene borrowed from Renato Castellanl's adaptation, Juliet is shown doing needlework as she anxiously awaits the Nurse's news, and, after cajoling the nurse into telling her that Romeo awaits his bride-to-be, Juliet flies to Friar Laurence's cell to be married. As the liturgical music, sung acapella by women, rises and falls, Romeo takes one last confident look at the crucifix, before kneeling alongside Juliet only seconds before their fate is sealed.[9] The film proceeds to an 'INTERMISSION'.

In theatrical performances of the play, the intermission typically occurs following the death of Mercutio—when Romeo cries 'O, I am fortune's fool!' (3.1.136). Interestingly, mere moments before the fight, Zeffirelli plays up Mercutio's effeminacy. For example, before jesting obscenely with the Nurse, Mercutio is shown diligently

8. Jackson, p. 202.

9. Supporting this claim, Patricia Tatspaugh observes that 'only Zeffirelli capitalises on the church which forms one side of the square. He associates the church, with its Romanesque arches, fading frescoes and mosaic pavement, exclusively with Romeo and Juliet', p. 142, See *The Cambridge Companion to Shakespeare on Film*, First Edition, edited by Russell Jackson (Cambridge: Cambridge University Press, 2000), p. 142.

pretending to sew his handkerchief; subsequently, before Tybalt can goad Mercutio into a fight, Mercutio decides to cool off in the drinking fountain, where he starts wringing out his laundry. Hence, when he begs Tybalt to couple his insulting 'word(s)' with 'a blow' (3.1.39), the homoerotic insinuation further inflames Tybalt, who splashes Mercutio indignantly and turns his attention to Romeo. What follows is an excruciating scene in which Mercutio, standing up for what he perceives to be an unpardonable affront to Romeo's character, playfully engages Tybalt in an epic swordfight—one that is filled with laughter, jests, and even a handshake between the opponents. Of course, Romeo is destined to come between them, exposing Mercutio's wiry, almost fragile frame, to Tybalt's unintended fatal blow. Indeed, Zeffirelli makes it clear that when the fun and games turn deadly, Michael York's Tybalt is utterly horrified at the sight of Mercutio's blood on his sword. What is so painful about Mercutio's final appearance on screen is the way in which John McEnery—in front of his crowd of adoring fans, plays the scene—for everyone, including Romeo, believes that Mercutio's groaning and stumbling is an elaborate joke, an impression that is heightened by Zeffirelli's tendency to shoot Mercutio's scenes with a hand-held camera, investing him with an energy that is his alone, Hence, in a tight, reverse two-shot of their earlier clench, Mercutio takes Romeo's head in his hands and whispers, plaintively, 'Why the devil came you between us? / I was hurt under your arm', Once again, their heads tilt forward, one supporting the other, and Romeo begins to understand the gravity of the situation. When Mercutio at last gives up the ghost, still dogged by the laughter of his raucous friends, Romeo reaches for Mercutio's handkerchief and reveals the gaping wound that has claimed his life. The (albeit bloody) token is something that a woman would typically give a man as a sign of her favour towards him, and Romeo takes it up with a zeal that we have not seen even in his romantic interactions with Juliet. Clearly, from Zeffirelli's perspective, Romeo must prove his manhood—his dexterity with his sword—*before* he is permitted to consummate his relationship with Juliet.

In fact, the actual fight between Romeo and Tybalt is distinctly homoerotic, as the men eventually strip down to their billowing shirts and reveal increasingly more fit male flesh. At one point, without swords, the men roll around in the dust together, alternately assuming the 'power position'. And, when Tybalt dies, he collapses on top of Romeo, whose awkward arms await him. Four times Romeo repeats 'I am Fortune's fool!' as he runs from the scene. After the Prince metes out his surprising sentence of Romeo's banishment, the camera's gaze—perhaps in one last effort to bring Mercutio's ambivalent sexuality back to life—takes a definitive turn towards the

homoerotic in the ensuing scenes. For example, the film immediately cuts to Romeo lying prone on the cold stone floor of Friar Laurence's cell; weeping hysterically, his sinewy body and backside
'faces' the camera, much as it will in the *aubade* scene. With Mercutio dead, it is now the unlikely suspects—the Nurse and the
Friar—who must importune Romeo to regain his masculinity. Provocatively, the lines that Zeffirelli retains throughout this scene anxiously convey the fear that Romeo will be incapable of consummating
his marriage to Juliet. Playing on the Renaissance meaning of 'stand'
as slang for maintaining an erection, the Nurse commands Romeo:
'Stand up, stand up, stand an you be a man; / For Juliet's sake, for
her sake, rise and stand' (3.3.88–89). Similarly, Friar Laurence asks
Romeo; 'Art thou a man? . . . Thy tears are womanish . . . Unseemly
woman in a seeming man . . .' (3.3.108–109, 111). What we see here,
Donaldson observes, is Renaissance patriarchy at its finest, 'an ideology requiring young men to assert their masculinity by violence,
devalue(ing) women, and distance(ing) themselves' from the opposite sex at at all costs.[1] Hence, after much proverbial ringing of hands
and further chastisement from both the Friar and the Nurse, Romeo
is at last ready, both literally and figuratively, to 'rise and stand';
determined to regain his slighted sense of masculinity, Romeo steals
away to his new wife's bedchamber. However, there is no lovemaking scene—a chaste cut to the two lovers lounging in bed the morning after.

   Here we see an erotic shot of Romeo which parallels his position
in the previous scene, as he lies on his stomach with his now-naked
bottom tilted toward the camera. By contrast, Juliet remains mod-
estly covered by the bed sheet. If this shot, as Russell Jackson points
out, startled some critics at the time, who 'have not failed to point out
the homosexual gaze represented by the camera's having dwelt
on Romeo's neat backside',[2] then the subsequent shot of Romeo
standing naked before the window, bathed in the light of dawn, is
even more provocative, for he moves like an Adam in Paradise,
unselfconsciously stretching in his beautiful skin. Referring to the
camera's lingering views of Romeo, Jackson asserts that critics have
oversimplified this scene by viewing the camerawork as an exten-
sion of the director's gaze. Rather, he continues, 'to accept the queer
dimension of the film is to recognise a valuable asset'.[3] Jackson's perspective is informed by Donaldson's intriguing contention that Zeffirelli capitalises on 'heterosexual film conventions governing the
deployment of the male gaze, as well as on his own contrary or com-
plementary presentation of *men* as objects of an admiring gaze', to

1. Donaldson, p. 153.
2. Jackson, p. 209.
3. Ibid.

create 'a spectatorial position neither simply male nor female nor simply identificatory or detached'. Instead, the camera produces distinctly 'bisexual identifications' and, even, 'a sense of loss in the presentation of heterosexual intimacy'.[4] The fact that Luhrmann will duplicate this gaze in his version of the *aubade* scene testifies to this more aesthetically and ideologically informed perspective as well as the historical reality that compulsory heterosexuality ofter demands the curtailment of same-sex bonds—a point which, for Donaldson, Zeffirelli's production takes for theme. Indeed, in Romeo's case, we recognise this moment of rupture in Mercutio's death, which marks the official demise of the 'pack' of young men with whom Romeo has long haunted Verona's streets, whereas with Juliet, this sense of loss is anticipatory, as she will shortly be disowned by her parents and betrayed by her nurse.

In addition to loss, however, this scene is equally inflected with the spirit of transcendence, marking the director's final attempt to forestall the inevitable tragedy that otherwise occurs so precipitously in this play. When Romeo attempts to get dressed offering yet another glimpse of his prone body, Juliet gazes dreamily at him—cueing the spectator to share her perspective—as she persuades him that it is the nightingale and not the lark that sings so beautifully 'on yon pom'granate tree'. Ecstatic, Romeo alights back onto the bed, exclaiming: 'Let me be ta'en'; as he does so, the love theme plays again and, for just a moment, we believe that these lovers might actually cheat death and defeat the legend after all. Rota's score begins to rise in volume, and, as already indicated, there is no accompanying reference to Juliet's 'ill-divining soul'. Instead, Juliet, more hopeful than apprehensive, asks Romeo: 'O thinkst thou we shall ever meet again?' Romeo replies, with utter confidence, 'I doubt it not; and all these woes shall serve / For sweet discourses in our times to come'. As the love theme reaches its crescendo, the lovers silently repeat their signature intertwined hand grasp. This crucial visual and thematic device is the source of the lovers' very first touch at the Capulet Ball; subsequently, it is repeated following the balcony scene, as Romeo reluctantly descends from Juliet's outstretched hand; finally, in this moment, a tight shot reveals the lovers' hands clasping and unclasping so gradually that we see an unmistakable allusion to Michelangelo's's famous depiction of God and Adam, who is brought to life by one touch of the divine. Thus, as the music plays, far more triumphant rather than foreboding, we forget the ironic truth that this is the very last time they will be together—alive—again.

The film proceeds at a fast pace from this point forward and, yet, Zeffirelli slows the tragic momentum with an unusual amount of

4. Donaldson, p. 170, emphasis his.

interpolated stage business in Juliet's ensuing confrontation with her father and, shortly thereafter, with Friar Laurence. Critics have all but overlooked the unique blocking of these two scenes, which serves to remind us that Romeo and Juliet are, and have always been, children who lack the support and guidance of their families. When Juliet rejects her father's decision to marry her off to Paris in forty-eight hours, Old Capulet violently flings her against the bedroom wall and the Nurse boldly intervenes, protecting Juliet with her own substantial body while bravely admonishing Capulet by shouting: 'You are to blame'. At this juncture, Juliet is visually reduced to a little girl, indeed, a child, as she is shown kneeling behind and cling-ing desperately to the Nurse's dress as both Capulet and Lady Cap-ulet disown their only child. When Juliet cries, 'O sweet mother, cast me not away', Lady Capulet replies curtly, devoid of warmth: 'I have done with thee', The Nurse is thus Juliet's last line of defence and, though she is clearly represented as acting with Juliet's best inter-ests at heart, the Nurse proceeds to advise Juliet to marry Paris. Shocked, Juliet recoils from the Nurse's touch, and for the first and only time in the film, the love theme plays as Juliet sunders her rela-tionship with her dearest friend. Although the surprising imple-mentation of Rota's song at this juncture might be interpreted as misguidedly inconsistent or alternatively, melodramatic, this deci-sion marks a crucial turning point in the film, for the song will here-after be repeated solely as a harbinger of tragedy, no longer exalting in its sweeping melodic refrain to whisk the lovers out of harm's way. The music also underscores Juliet's status as the orphan she always already was—a pawn in the Renaissance trafficking in women, who will be sold to the highest bidder.

This reading becomes more evident when, in the following scene, Juliet throws herself frantically at the Friar, clinging to his robes just as she had clung to the Nurse's skirts mere moments ago. Although the blocking of the characters in both scenes is the same, the significance of Juliet's desperate lunge at the Friar is heightened by the view of the dangling wooden cross and prayer beads that adorn the lower portion of his robes. Here, as suggested from the outset of this discussion, the use of the cross comes to signify the infringement of the legendary, writ large in Zeffirelli's adaptation as the 'greater power' that thwarts, ultimately, every-one's 'intents'. For even as Friar Laurence looks hopefully to the purple flower from which he derives the sleeping potion (the third and final use of the floral motif in the film), the cross that is carved out in his cellar door looms over the scene, backlit to emphasise its creation from purely negative space—a far cry from the tran-scendent, solid gold crucifix that inspired the Friar's earlier schemes to shield the lovers from harm. Complementing the reconstitution

of the cross symbol as more sinister, the love theme plays again—
this time in a minor key—as though it were operating in conspiracy with the will of God.

In the interests of maintaining dramatic momentum, Zeffirelli
eliminates the Nurse and Juliet's parents' hyperbolic utterances over
her 'dead' body, as the scene shifts abruptly to her solemn burial in
the Capulet vault—a scene which, in contrast to the many sumptuous versions before and after it, looks more like the scant ritual
afforded Ophelia than a funeral for 'the fair daughter of rich Capulet' (2.2.58). Replacing Shakespeare's peculiar insertion of Peter's
comedic scene with the musicians, Zeffirelli adds his own touch of
comic relief when Friar Laurence, preparing to administer Juliet's
last rites, casts his eyes down at her and smiles furtively—Puckishly
confident that his plan is working. But Romeo's man, Balthazar, who
is hiding in the trees nearby, beholds Juliet and is immediately shown
thundering past Friar John on his horse. In a scene resembling a
cross between cinéma verité and *commedia del'arte*, Friar John lum-
bers awkwardly across the dusty countryside with his mule, arriving in Mantua long after Balthazar has broken the news to Romeo.
Consistent with his earlier deletions of tragic portents, Zeffirelli
eliminates Romeo's naïve recounting to Peter of his 'auspicious'
dream in which 'methought I was this night already dead— . . . And
that my lady Juliet came to me, / And breathed such life with kisses
in my lips / That I revived and was an emperor' (5.1.5, 7–9). Instead,
when Balthazar tells Romeo that Juliet is dead, Romeo bursts into
what sounds like a non-sequitur: 'Then I defy you stars!' Recalling
that Romeo's only other reference to stars in this film occurs in his
speech just before he enters the Capulet Ball, this second reference
makes little sense. Similarly, in cutting Romeo's trip to the apothecary, the director leaves the audience wondering how Romeo has
obtained the poison that serves as the font of his suicide. Nevertheless, after posting straight to the Capulet tomb, Romeo, unimpeded
by Balthazar or Paris, batters down the door and goes frantically in
search of Juliet. Following several establishing shots of rotting
corpses, the camera lights on Juliet's bright countenance. When
Romeo lifts the shroud that covers Juliet's face. Rota's song is plucked
by a solitary guitar: its effect at this juncture is rendered all the more
powerful by the loneliness it implies, as Romeo gazes at the bright
remnant of his departed love. Only stones would not be moved in
this scene, which is rendered beautifully by Whiting's Romeo, who
pours amazedly over Juliet's body, ever-hoping that Juliet is still alive
because he is convinced that 'death's pale flag is not advanced
there'—and tragically—he is correct in his surmise.

In fact, it is almost as if Romeo knows that something is amiss,
because while his heart apprehends the tragedy, his mind forces him

to question what his eyes see, as he asks: 'Ah, dear Juliet./Why art thou yet so fair?' At this point Romeo spies the pale body of Tybalt; seemingly inconsistent with Zeffirelli's decision to leave Romeo's fatal encounter with Paris on the cutting room floor, the director includes Romeo's reconciliation with Tybalt, perhaps as one final effort to persuade Michael York that his character would indeed be one of the stars of the film. But this intervening scene serves as an emotional transition for Romeo, who returns to gaze at Juliet's body, now sobbing like the child that he has always already been. As he fully comprehends the death of his love and the gravity of the desperate act he is poised to commit, Romeo utters his final speech while hugging Juliet's body from head to fool. When he at last resolves to drink the poison, Romeo tilts his head back to swallow the fatal drink and the love theme—paralleling the exact strain when Juliet tosses back the sleeping potion—swells for the last time within the narrative-proper. Romeo stumbles as his body revolts from the intrusion of death, pausing to draw a faint kiss from Juliet's hand— the site of their first touch and the connection that Zeffirelli has rendered thematic from first to last—and falls to the floor.

Moments later, the Friar enters to find how horribly his plan has gone awry, and he attempts to shield Juliet from the sight of Romeo's body. Fittingly, we are made aware of Juliet's waking by a tight shot of her hand, which unfurls and, having regained its strength, makes a fist, as if already in solidarity with Romeo's resolve to die rather than live without love. 'Where is my Romeo?' are her first words, uttered with soft anticipation, which the Friar responds to by trying to escort Juliet out of the monument. When the Watch sounds, however, the Friar waxes pale; Juliet discovers Romeo's body and Friar Laurence, panicked, exclaims: 'A greater power than we can contradict hath thwarted our intents'. The Watch sounds again, and he cries, determined against his better judgment to leave her to her grief, 'I dare no longer stay!' The otherwise calm and collected man suddenly raves like a madman, repeating 'I dare no longer stay' three more times as he flees the Capulet vault. Significantly, we do not see his character again, a decision that subtly raises suspicions about the Friar's integrity in ways that date back to the more skeptical visions of the early Italian treatments of the legend. As Juliet now dwells alone with Romeo, the love theme resumes, softly—without crescendos. Paralleling Romeo's painful confusion over Juliet's inextinguishable beauty, here, too, the height of the tragedy corresponds to Juliet's recognition that her lover's 'lips are warm'. Bursting into tears, she realises that little more than a minute has determined their fate. The extraordinary pathos with which this scene is rendered makes the audience feel as though they, too, are experiencing Romeo's death without foreknowledge, as if they are experiencing the tragedy—along with Juliet—for the first time. Subsequently, upon hearing the authorities entering the tomb, she simply cries, 'No!' and, with dogged determination. Juliet concludes: 'Then I'll be brief, /O happy dagger /This is thy sheath!/ There rust, and let me die', stabbing herself and expiring on Romeo's chest. As she does so, Rota's theme ceases to be heard, ending as abruptly as Juliet's life.

If it is the nearly triumphant score, coupled with Zeffirellis removal of many of the play's premonitory lines, which almost persuade us that Romeo and Juliet, too, will defy their fate, then it is the strategic deployment of this song during the credit sequence that convinces us that a 'greater power' has indeed prevailed once and for all. After the Prince utters his notorious last line, 'All are punished!' Zeffirelli aligns the feuding factions opposite one another (including in another departure from the play, the parents of *both* Romeo and Juliet). As they process towards us and out of the cinematic frame, various gestures are made—the shaking of hands, embracing, sympathetic nods—as the offending parties exit the solemn scene, clearly having learnt their tragic lesson. In voiceover, Laurence Olivier utters a curtailed version of the concluding lines, assigned in Shakespeare's play to the Prince:

> A glooming peace this morning with it brings;
> The sun for sorrow will not show his head.
> . . . .
> For never was a story of more woe
> Than this of Juliet and her Romeo.

As the credits roll, the processional scene slowly darkens. When the camera shifts to a shot of the battlements—the same, foreboding image on which the title 'Romeo and Juliet' was inscribed at the beginning of the film—Rota's love theme begins again. More than complementing the opening shot, this book-end image implies the victory of the legend in the very architecture it pictures. For battlements are a place of surveillance and violence, and as Rota's score begins to swell now for the last time, the musical theme betrays its true allegiance. Indeed, we are left with the disturbing feeling that it has never really been allied with the transcendence of the legendary forces against which Romeo and Juliet unwittingly conspire, but, rather, with their untimely, 'timeless end' (5.3.162), having merely teased us into believing—with its magnificent, overreaching strains—that it could usher the lovers into a world beyond the cycle of violence that the battlements encode. Appropriately, the final crescendo occurs in tandem with the fade to black, signaling the eternal night of death.

BAZ LUHRMANN AND CRAIG PEARCE

From William Shakespeare's Romeo + Juliet[†]

INT. BALLROOM. NIGHT.

Romeo, now without his mask, slams out of the bathroom—
Juliet and the Nurse have disappeared into the crowd.

CUT TO: Juliet being dragged along by the Nurse. She glances
back toward the mystery boy, but he is gone.

Juliet and the Nurse rejoin Dave Paris, who is dressed as an
astronaut, and Gloria, at the side of the dance floor.

Dave, irresistible smile, extends his hand to Juliet.

DAVE
Will you now deny to dance?

Juliet looks to Dave, desperately searching for a reason to
decline. Gloria, brushing aside her silly daughter's protests,
slugs the last of her champagne and corrals them onto the
dance floor.

GLORIA
(*whispering to Juliet*) A man, young lady, such a man.

As Juliet is dragged onto the floor her eyes furtively search
for the boy.

CUT TO: Romeo in the crowd. Desperate to find the girl, he
roughly shunts aside a reveller dressed as Lucifer, Prince
of Darkness.

HOLD ON: Lucifer. He removes his mask: it is Tybalt. He turns
to Abra, who's dressed as a demon.

TYBALT
What, dares the slave come hither
to fleer and scorn at our solemnity?

> Now by the stock and honor of my kin
> To strike him dead I hold it not a sin.

Tybalt moves off aggressively, but is halted as Capulet slams a hand into his chest.

> CAPULET
> Why how now kinsman, wherefore storm you so?

> TYBALT
> Uncle, this is that villain Romeo. A Montague, our foe.

Capulet peers across the ballroom.

> CAPULET
> Young Romeo is it?

> TYBALT
> 'Tis he.

> CAPULET
> Content thee gentle coz, let him alone.
> I would not for the wealth of all this town
> Here in my house do him disparagement.
> Therefore be patient; take no note of him.

Tybalt can't believe it.

> TYBALT
> I'll not endure him.

CLOSE ON: Capulet, exploding with rage.

> CAPULET
> He shall be endured!
> (*slapping Tybalt viciously*)
> What, goodman boy! I say he shall! Go to.

Capulet violently shoves Tybalt to the ground.

> CAPULET
> You'll make a mutiny among my guests!

A middle aged couple look on shocked—Capulet waves to them festively:

> CAPULET
> What? Cheerly my hearts!

Capulet snorts at Tybalt in disgust.

> CAPULET
> You'll not endure him! Am I the master here or you?
> Go to.

Smoothing his hair into place, Capulet turns back into the ballroom.

CLOSE ON: Tybalt choking back tears of rage.

CUT TO: Romeo moving through the crowd. For a moment the crush clears and he spies the Angel on the dance floor.

CLOSE ON: Romeo whispers:

> ROMEO
> Did my heart love till now? Forswear it, sight.
> For I ne'er saw true beauty till this night.

Romeo begins to circumnavigate the dance floor in an attempt to get closer to Juliet.

CUT TO: Dave slow dancing with Juliet.

Juliet's eyes search the room for the boy.

CLOSE ON: Romeo.

CLOSE ON: Juliet.

Their eyes connect.

Juliet looks quickly back to Dave who, oblivious, returns his most devastating smile.

CUT TO: The songstress, her voice soars.

CUT TO: Juliet. Unable to look away from the boy, she stares over Dave's shoulder.

CUT TO: Romeo. Ignoring the danger, he continues to move toward the Angel.

With the Diva's spiralling final notes, the ballad concludes.

A complete black out. As the crowd break into wild applause,
Juliet's eyes search the darkness, but the boy is gone.

The crowd cheers and screams its applause. An avalanche of
balloons, tinsel and confetti rains down from the roof; swathes
of red silk drop from the ceiling and the space is transformed.

CLOSE ON: Juliet, searching for the boy.

Suddenly: A gasp, Juliet's eyes widen, shocked.

In the dark, a hand has shot out from the drape curtaining
off the stage and clasped hers. Juliet barely dares breathe.

She glances furtively to Dave Paris—he watches the stage.

Slowly Juliet turns toward the hand; there through a break in the
curtain she can see eye, cheek and lips of the mystery boy.
As the Diva reprises the chorus, Romeo gently pulls Juliet behind
the curtain.

INT. BEHIND CURTAIN. NIGHT.

Concealed from the party by the red velvet drape, hands still
clasped, the teenagers are so close their bodies almost touch.

> ROMEO
> If I profane with my unworthiest hand
> This holy shrine, the gentle sin is this.
> My lips, two blushing pilgrims, ready stand
> To smooth that rough touch with a tender kiss.

Romeo moves his lips toward Juliet's. She stops him.

> JULIET
> Good pilgrim, you do wrong your hand too much,
> Which mannerly devotion shows in this.
> For saints have hands that pilgrim's hands do
>   touch,
> And palm to palm is holy palmers' kiss.

> ROMEO
> Have not saints lips, and holy palmers too?

JULIET
(*a gentle scolding*)
Ay, pilgrim, lips that they must use in prayer.

ROMEO
O, then, dear saint, let lips do what hands do,
They pray: grant thou, lest faith turn to despair.

JULIET
Saints do not move, though grant for prayer's sake.

ROMEO
Then move not while my prayer's effect I take.

He kisses her.

ROMEO (CONT.)
Thus from my lips, by thine my sin is purged.

JULIET
Then have my lips the sin that they have took.

ROMEO
Sin from my lips? O trespass sweetly urged!
Give me my sin again.

He kisses her.

JULIET
You kiss by th' book.

They kiss again.

Suddenly a harsh light falls across the entwined couple. They
break apart—Nurse has pulled open the curtain and stands
eyeing them severely.

NURSE
Madam, your mother craves a word with you.

We see that the party is breaking up. But for groups of die-hard
revellers, the room is nearly empty.

NURSE (CONT.)
Come, let's away.

She takes firm control of her charge.

Juliet furtively motions for the startled Romeo not to follow as he trails them across the room.

CUT TO: ROMEO'S P.O.V.: The Nurse and Juliet reach the door, but instead of leaving, they turn and ascend the staircase that arcs around to the mezzanine level. They join a vexed Gloria Capulet who clings to a patient Dave Paris.

Inaudible words are exchanged. Juliet flickers her eyes nervously to Romeo.

CUT TO: Romeo. He halts at the foot of the stairs unsure.

CUT TO: Gloria. Catching Juliet's interest in the boy, she indicates to her daughter to 'COME ALONG'.

CUT TO: Romeo; a dawning realisation.

ROMEO
(*under his breath*)
Is she a Capulet?

CUT TO: Juliet. She stops and turns back.

CUT TO: Romeo, comprehending the reality of who she is.

CUT TO: Juliet. The Nurse whispers in her ear.

NURSE
His name is Romeo, and a Montague,
The only son of your great enemy.

An orchestral treatment of Joy Division's "Love Will Tear Us Apart" swells;

HOLD ON: Juliet. Like a cloud passing across the sun, a dark coldness descends upon her.

BARBARA HODGDON

William Shakespeare's Romeo + Juliet:
Everything's Nice in America?[†]

I want to begin with an anecdote. When I proposed writing about Leonardo DiCaprio—and titling my essay, 'Was This The Face That Launched a Thousand Clips'—one colleague, taking me somewhat seriously, mentioned the best-selling Leo books, and another sent me a Hong Kong action comic in which 'Leon' single-handedly foils an evil gang and gets the girl. A third, addressing my penchant for reading Shakespearean and popular bodies, glanced at how the Shakespeare myth insists on the physical spectre of the Bard with the Forehead and at the delicious possibility that someone like DiCaprio might have played Cleopatra. A fourth was decidedly visceral: 'The most watery Romeo in film history? His acting is appalling, his affect minimal, and his intelligence—well, why go on? I can understand why teenage girls fall all over themselves for him. But you? Tell me it isn't so'![1] Such concerns about my 'low' taste and possible adolescent regression point to the lack of critical distance and loss of rational control associated with an intense engagement with the popular; but then, such over-involvement and over-identification, traits traditionally ascribed to women, do mark the popular (and especially its emphasis on the body) as a feminine realm.[2]

These fraught notions trope what I take to be the competing, contradictory horizons of reception surrounding Baz Luhrmann's 1996 *William Shakespeare's Romeo + Juliet*. How, I want to ask, does that film resonate within both 'Shakespeare-culture' and global popular culture? And how are those echoes linked to DiCaprio, the film's 'beautiful boy' star and 'modern-day Romeo', for whom Prince William has recently emerged as a royal twin?[3] Although I am especially

[†] From *Shakespeare Survey* 52 (1999): 88–98. Copyright © 1999 Cambridge University Press. Reprinted by permission of Cambridge University Press.

1. In order, these colleagues are Bill Worthen, Joseph Schneider, Peter Donaldson and Jim Bulman, whose e-mail communication I cite. The mass market DiCaprio books are Grace Catalano, *Leonardo: A Scrapbook in Words and Pictures* (New York, 1998); Catalano, *Leonardo DiCaprio: Modern-Day Romeo* (New York, 1997); and Brian J. Robb, *The Leonardo DiCaprio Album* (London, 1997). For the filmscript, see *William Shakespeare's Romeo + Juliet: The Contemporary Film, The Classic Play* (New York, 1996).

2. See, for instance, Mary Ann Doane, *The Desire to Desire: The Woman's Film of the 1940s* (Bloomington, 1987), pp. 2–16.

3. See *Life*, 'Special Royals Issue: A Guide to the 28 Monarchies of the World' (Summer 1998). The cover features 'The Boy who WILL be King'. Remarks Prince William: 'I think [DiCaprio will] find it easier being king of Hollywood than I shall being king of England', pp. 58–9.

interested in looking at how diverse audiences refunction Luhrmann's film and DiCaprio's presence to serve their own uses and pleasures,[4] I also want to look at the relations among text, image and music in the film itself and at how citations from those economies escape and are caught up in a cultural narrative that offers to renegotiate the fictions of and frictions between the academic study of filmed Shakespeare and the 'popular'—what Internet discourse calls DiCaprio ideology or, alternatively, DiCapriorgasm.

Among recent Shakespeare films, Luhrmann's not only most stridently advertises itself as a product of global capitalism but also knowingly flaunts how that culture consumes 'Shakespeare'. In an America where Wendy's Dave, wearing a silly floppy hat, holds up a burger and intones 'To be or not to be'; where 'Something wicked this way comes' promotes the newest black Lexus; and where a clip of Kenneth Branagh's St Crispin's Day speech, equated with a football coach's locker-room pep talk, climaxes a (1997) Superbowl pregame show[5], seeing Shakespeare's words appear on billboards for loans or massage parlours—The Merchant of Verona Beach, Mistress Quickly's—as product slogans for Phoenix gasoline or ammunition—'Add more fuel to your fire', 'Shoot forth thunder'—and brand names—Romeo drives a silver Eclipse—comes as no surprise. The logical Madison Avenue descendants of Matthew Arnold's touchstones and of New Criticism's emphasis on language as glowing artifact, these sound bites sign Shakespeare in and on the film's surface in flashes, confirming that he is indeed the universal brand name and, as W. B. Worthen writes, extending beyond Romeo+Juliet to embrace Shakespeare the Author and cultural icon, marking how the film traces and re-places signs of its origins.[6]

The film's opening, where a grainy image of an African American TV anchorwoman speaking the prologue grounds Shakespeare's language in the familiar discourse of popular news-speak, stages that replacement: nearly half the speech turns into print headlines or graphic poster art, further fragmented through flash edits and slammed at viewers. Elsewhere, especially but not exclusively in the ball sequence, the film restyles textual culture as fashion or fetish and writes it onto actors' bodies or their props, as with Montague's 'Longsword' rifle, Tybalt's Madonna-engraved pistol, or Mantua's

---

4. My framework derives from Paul Smith, *Clint Eastwood: A Cultural Production* (Minneapolis, 1993). As I turn to reception, I am indebted to Janet Staiger, *Interpreting Films: Studies in the Historical Reception of American Cinema* (Princeton, 1992).
5. Dave is the owner and 'advertising star' of Wendy's (a chain restaurant) TV commercials; the Lexus is a luxury car; and the Superbowl is an annual US title football game—a media-constructed 'holiday' occasion.
6. W. B. Worthen, 'Drama Performativity, and Performance'. *PMLA* 113.5 (October 1998), 1103. My thanks to Worthen for providing me with a copy of his essay before publication and for comments on an earlier version of this essay entitled 'Totally DiCaptivated: Shakespeare's Boys Meet the Chick Flick'.

'Post-post haste' dispatch van. At times, this traffic between verbal and visual imagery reads as hyped-up anti-Shakespeare-culture panache; at others, it appears curiously literal. Although *Romeo + Juliet* is clearly a film with an attitude, its tone ricochets between Wall-and-Moonshine tongue-in-cheekiness and playing it straight, between selling Shakespeare as one-off visual in-jokes and tying its scenography, almost over-explicitly, to the word. Voguing in a white Afro, silver bra and garter belt that evoke Mab's 'moonshine's wat'ry beams', Mercutio not only punningly embodies the fairy Queen but out-masquerades Lady Capulet's Cleopatra, marking the power of his own extravagant artifice in terms of her even more parodic bodily display. Juliet's white dress and wings literalize her as Romeo's 'bright angel'; he becomes her 'true knight', a Boy King Arthur in shining armour—guises that situate the lovers within medieval Christian romance even as they send up that myth. Although Dave Paris's astronaut get-up connects him metonymically to the heavenly Juliet, it just as clearly spaces him out to the story's margins, together with those like Capulet's gold-bespangled, purple toga-ed Nero/Antony, the Trimalchian host of this feast of poses and corruptions.[7] Equally saturated with signs, Tybalt's pointed face, neat moustache and black disco outfit, complemented by red-sequined devil's horns and vest, code him as a macho Prince of Cats whose two cronies dressed as white-faced skeletons foreshadow his violent end. And when, after the balcony-pool sequence, Romeo meets Mercutio, his shirt blazons a heart circled by a wreath of roses, capped with a 'very flame of love', and emanating rays of golden light—the Dante-esque symbol that, glossed by 'My only love sprung from my only hate', serves as the signature logo for the film, the CDs and the official web site.[8]

Sensing an obligation to speak for Shakespeare (especially given his perceived demotion within the American academy), most mainstream critics balked at such over-determined commodifications of his text. Mourning the cuts, they produced resistant readings tied to notions about verse-speaking protocols (singling out Pete Postlethwaite's properly British Friar and Miriam Margolyes's Latina Nurse for praise) and focused on those aspects of the film—notably, how the storm sequence following Mercutio's death mirrors 'the characters' ageless passions'[9]—which fit within traditional knowledge-making frames. This is hardly an unfamiliar liar story: critics once attacked Zeffirelli's *cinema vérité* documentary of Renaissance Verona, now ensconced in the educational pantheon, on precisely

---

7. As in Luhrmann's debut film, *Strictly Ballroom* (1992), it is parents, not children, who are the 'unnatural'—or parodically perverse—gender performers.
8. As for Zeffirelli's film, two CDs were released, one with and one without dialogue.
9. Janet Maslin, 'Soft! What light? It's flash, Romeo', *New York Times*, 1 November 1996.

these grounds. But rehearsing it seems curious, given *West Side Story* and, more recently, the Bologna-Taylor film, *Love Is All There Is*, and the Oscar-winning *Titanic*, or *Romeo and Juliet* with three hours of water (and a remodelled close). Certainly the slasher-porn *Tromeo and Juliet*, an evil twin poised between nineteenth-century burlesques and Luhrmann's film, where 'She hangs upon the cheek of night / Like some barbell in a thrasher's ear' describes a Shirley Temple–curled Juliet whose sleeping potion transforms her into a pig, offers a stronger case for devalued Shakespeare.[1] Still, even those who, like the *New Yorker*'s Anthony Lane, preferred 'John Gielgud filling the aisles with noises',[2] acknowledged the appeal of Luhrmann's bizarre parallel universe comprised of twentieth-century icons and inventive raids on the cinematic canon, from *Rebel Without a Cause* to Busby Berkeley musicals, Clint Eastwood–Sergio Leone spaghetti westerns, and Ken Russell's or Fellini's surreal spectaculars. Freeze-frames identifying characters recall *Trainspotting*; in the high-voltage Capulet-Montague shoot-out, Shakespeare meets cultist John Woo (a Hong Kong action film director now working in Hollywood); John Leguizamo's Tybalt sailing through a frame and then appearing in slow motion quotes a device characteristic of contemporary action-spectacles, introduced in *Bonnie and Clyde*; and when, backed by chorus boys in purple sequins, Mercutio performs before a triptych of Madonnas, Shakespeare moves into music video by way of *To Wong Foo, With Love* and *Priscilla, Queen of the Desert*.[3]

If this be postmodernism, give me excess of it: that impulse seems to propel what might be dubbed a semiotician's dream or, as Peter Matthews writes, 'the most radical reinvention of a classic text since [Kurosawa's] *Throne of Blood*'.[4] To say that subscribes to a particular take on postmodernism as well as on viewing pleasure, one that derives a sense of identification from dissonance and disjuncture: from hearing early modern language through the flat affect of American speech (which at best works productively to remind spectators of the play's provenance at the same time as they see it made contemporary); and from seeing the story set in a decaying and decadent city over which, à *La Dolce Vita*, a colossal statue of Christ looms, separating the skyscrapers erected by warring corporate owners—a world that comments on our own and renders understandable the importance of 'filial duty, religious devotion, family honour, and the institution of marriage [and] emphasizes the ritual performance of

1. See *Tromeo and Juliet*, dir. Lloyd Kaufman; Troma Video Entertainment, 1997; 107 minutes.
2. Anthony Lane, 'Tights! Camera! Action!' *New Yorker*, 25 November 1996, p. 66.
3. Most mainstream reviews cite several of these 'classic' filmtexts. I am indebted to seminar students for some of the references to cult films.
4. Peter Matthews, review of *William Shakespeare's Romeo + Juliet*, *Sight and Sound* (April 1997), 55.

ancient hates'.[5] That angle of vision aligns more with the film's target market, youth, than with the adult critical community, who constructed that audience as 'other'—attuned to a culture of cars, guns, fashion and music but not to Shakespeare—and, with few exceptions, either disassociated from or condescended to it. 'So enslaved by its worship of Energy that you want to slip it a Valium', wrote *Newsweek*; 'Watching it simulates having a teenager in the house', said the *Los Angeles Times*.[6] Teenagers, however, embraced Luhrmann's move to drag High-Culture Will over to the neighbourhood: mounting a still-active Internet discourse (in January 1998 alone, some two years after the film's release, hits on the official web site reached 8 million),[7] they made *Romeo + Juliet* their cultural property and took into their own hands knowledge-making and its attendant power.

Michel de Certeau's distinction between *strategies*—interpretive modes performed from positions of strength and tradition and employing property and authority belonging to literary 'landowners'—and *tactics*—moves belonging to relatively dispossessed and powerless reader-spectators—offers a useful framework for placing the claims of both communities.[8] Whereas those who seek to monitor and manage youth culture and uphold the Shakespeare industry have access to an existing public forum, the young speak freely only in the marginal spaces they themselves create, absent of parental control and of educational protocols—circumstances which trope the power relations of the play.[9] Yet however socially peripheral, this conversation the young hold with themselves remains symbolically central to a wider conversation that implicates *Romeo + Juliet* within

5. Speaking of the team's search for a location, Catherine Martin, the film's designer, remarks on how Mexico had many of the elements necessary to make a contemporary version work. 'Religion still has a very strong presence there, culturally and visually; marriage is still big, and sex before marriage is frowned on. There are whole streets in Mexico City which are only bridal shops. And the social structure is closer to that of Elizabethan times than anywhere else in the modern world: a few very rich people with guns, and the vast majority poor'. See Jo Litson, 'Romeo and Juliet', TCI: The Business of Entertainment Technology and Design, vol. 30 (November 1996), 46.
6. See David Ansen, 'It's the '90s, so the Bard is Back', *Newsweek*, 4 November 1996: 73; Kenneth Turan, 'A Full-Tilt Romeo'. *Los Angeles Times*, 1 November 1996, FI.
7. Overall, forty web sites are devoted to the film; 500 to Leonardo DiCaprio. I am indebted to Erik Steven Fisk, 'Professor Shakespeare, Director Shakespeare: Examining the Role of the Bard on the Way into 2000 à la Romeo+Juliet', unpublished seminar paper,
8. Michel de Certeau, *The Practice of Everyday Life* (Berkeley: University of California Press, 1984; cited in Henry Jenkins, *Textual Poachers: Television Fans and Participatory Culture* (New York and London, 1992), pp. 44–5. These distinctions point to the boundaries separating elitist and popular texts, marking cultural space as a contested territory. The reviewers' comments also point to what Jenkins identifies as a frequent mistake: treating popular culture productions as though they were the materials of elite culture. See Jenkins, *Textual Poachers*, p. 60.
9. Zeffirelli's *Romeo and Juliet* had a similarly divided reception history. See, for example, Jill L. Levenson, *Shakespeare in Performance: 'Romeo and Juliet'* (Manchester, 1987), p. 123; and my 'Absent Bodies, Present Voices: Performance Work and the Close of Romeo and Juliet's Golden Story', *Theatre Journal* (October 1989), 341–59.

a network of cultural meanings by which and through which we—as agents in that culture—live.

Simultaneously commercial teaser and memory archive, the film's official web site invites viewers to look at image files and video clips from late-night star interviews, listen to sound bites, meet 'Bill' Shakespeare, download a *Romeo + Juliet* screensaver, play a 'Do You Bite Your Thumb at Me' game, and explore a Verona Beach Visitors' Guide: What to Wear, Getting There (glossed by 'Go forth with swift wheels'), Night Life (clubs called Midnite Hags, Pound of Flesh, and Shining Nights) and a list of Sponsors. The site's epigraph image—Romeo and Juliet kissing, framed by boys with guns, all pointing at the couple—perfectly condenses one of the film's central tropes: the desire for a private, utopian space within a threatening social world. The film also rehearses other aspects of this sub-cultural imaginary: a sense of adult indifference and betrayal, of loss, fragmentation, and despair. As one fan writer put it, 'Complete with death, hate, love, feuds and the hopelessness of the inner city, *William Shakespeare's Romeo + Juliet* is a true look at how we live and think today'.[1] In such a world, these viewers perceive Romeo and Juliet's love as an anchor—an 'image of something better' that teaches what utopia would *feel* like; writes one, 'I'm in love with a fictional tragic romance because I don't like tragic reality'.[2] Such longings find their fullest expression on 'Totally Decapitated: World Headquarters of the DiCaprio Cult', a web fanzine (similar to Shaksper) whose contributors 'share Leonardo DiCaprio as a common source of inspiration'; using film and star as experiential resources, they integrate the meanings attached to both into their lives.[3]

Unlike those devoted to 'flaming' or 'foaming'—'the closest I've ever come to understanding the play . . . the only thing missing is SUBTITLES'! or 'I'd die for Leo . . . he is such a hot babe'!—this site offers a space for activity and agency where participants can immerse themselves in the film's world, scribble in its margins and create their own texts. A Palace Chat Room, for instance, 'takes you right inside the vibrant and dramatic world of *Romeo + Juliet*, where you can see yourself and others as graphical "heads"', handle and even create props, move from room to room, and talk with other fans. Each issue prints poetry (in French as well as English): inspired by the film's images, some incorporate Shakespeare's lines; others, such

---

1. Comment from fan writer on www.Asu.edu.
2. From 'The Diaries of Joshua Runner', a regular feature of 'Totally Decapitated'; the cite is from Issue Four and is dated 25 November 1996. For the idea of using stars as resources, see Richard Dyer, *Stars* (London, 1979), pp. 59–60.
3. Jenkins argues that, by blurring the boundaries between producers and consumers, spectators and participants, both web discourses and fanzines constitute a cultural and social network that spans the globe. See *Textual Poachers*, esp. pp. 45, 279.

as 'Révicide' and 'Génération virtuelle', link the play's themes to contemporary anomie; still others (future Oxfordians?) play out anagrams of Leonardo. Reproducing Shakespeare's balcony scene, one issue invites readers to compare text to film; in another, one can listen to a piano rendition of Tchaikovsky's fantasy-overture. All suggest fans who have moved beyond their pre-assigned roles as cult consumers to collaborate with Shakespeare, using his texts (much as scholar-critics do) to stage their own performances.

Yet if the 'zine forges an alternative community through Shakespeare, it concentrates primarily on his surrogate, DiCaprio's Romeo—the 'boy-poet [who] embodies the perfect lover'.[4] As Dennis Kennedy writes, the actor's body is not only the object of the most intense and profound gaze in the culture but, at times when notions of the body undergo change, it becomes a site where that cultural crisis is represented.[5] Appealing to the precarious liminality of early to late adolescents, DiCaprio functions as a tabula rasa on which fans project the romance of identity and, using tactics of personalization and emotional intensification, voice their desire for 'truth' instead of lies, for transparency instead of manipulation, for a 'real' hero in a world without them. As fanwriter Sonia Belasco says: 'When our president is cheating on his wife, when the mayor of the city I live in gets caught doing crack, when everything is about money and hate and violence . . . [Leo] mirrors us . . . what we want to be, what we are, what we'll never be'.[6] Taking on idealized—and ideological—contours on and off the web, DiCaprio's body morphs into other texts, especially *Titanic*—and especially for girls. My fifteen-year old niece, who disavows 'loving Leo', nonetheless has seen most of his films, including *Titanic*, three times—but only once with her boyfriend. What threatens him with loss tells her a different story, a 'romantic feminism' found only at the movies.[7]

In a culture fascinated by youth and in a subculture where one is most interesting if one's sexuality cannot be defined, DiCaprio's pale androgynous beauty—sharp Aryan looks and hint of exotic heritage, a quintessential Greek boy god—makes him a polysexual figure, equally attractive to young women and to gay and straight men. Just as *Romeo + Juliet* is not precisely a chick flick—one where more tears than blood are shed—but, given its coterie of boys who crash cars and carry big guns, can be 're-branded' within a masculine discursive space, DiCaprio's Romeo straddles several cultural masculinities. On the one hand, he figures the vulnerable 'new man' (romancing

---

4. Quote from 'The Diaries of Joshua Runner', 10 November, 1996.
5. See Dennis Kennedy, 'Shakespeare Played Small: Three Speculations About the Body', *Shakespeare Survey* 47 (1994), p. 10.
6. Sonia Belasco, 'Totally Decapitated', Issue Ten: prose.
7. See Katha Pollitt, 'Women and Children First', *The Nation*, 30 March 1998, 9.

Juliet and spending the last half of the film in tears); on the other, by gunning down Tybalt, he conforms to contemporary fictions of violent masculinity and subscribes to its homosocial honour codes. Moreover, because he is embedded in a fiction that fetishizes his body as well as those of other men, one premised on a forbidden, secret love in which Juliet can substitute for Mercutio, his presence yields to a queer reading.[8] As Joshua Runner, author of regularly featured web diaries, puts it, 'Romeo, Romeo whyfore art thou Romeo? Tending to girls' fantasies, leaving nothing for the boys who exist. Juliet, divine perfection, you may be his sun, but the pale moon needs love too.'[9] Indeed, it is precisely because Leo disrupts dominant fictions of masculinity that his transitional, differently eroticized body can be read as exemplary, as providing a safe harbour for sexual awakening; and by offering fan writers opportunities to externalize and work through their anxieties about sexuality, the site serves a therapeutic function.[1]

Although mainstream critics read his body from a greater distance, even the most conservative found DiCaprio riveting; comparing him to James Dean, the cult figure of their generation, many decoded his affect in terms of intensity and authenticity, citing his 'passionate conviction', 'an ardour you can't buy in acting class', a performance that is 'all raw emotion'.[2] Favouring him with 'brooding rock-star close-ups',[3] the film urges a near-oneiric encounter with

8. See, for instance, Jonathan Goldberg, 'Romeo and Juliet's Open Rs', in Queering the Renaissance, ed. Jonathan Goldberg (Durham and London, 1994), pp. 218–35. See also Robert Appelbaum, '"Standing to the Wall": The Pressures of Masculinity in Romeo and Juliet', Shakespeare Quarterly, 48.3 (1997), 251–72; and Paul Smith's notions of hysterical or wounded masculinity in Smith, Clint Eastwood. See also Ellen Goodman, 'Romancing a New Generation of Women', Des Moines Register, 12 May 1998, 7A; and Pollitt, 'Women and Children First'.

9. 'The Diaries of Joshua Runner', 8 November 1996. Wolf, another frequent contributor, writes, 'He is the embodyment [sic] of what we need, someone like us to hide with . . . someplace far away'; responding to a fan calling himself 'Like Minded' who had rented the film and found himself desiring Leo. Wolf urges him to read Shakespeare's sonnets addressed to the young man, saying that he himself had found comfort in them. 'Totally Decapitated', Issue Five: prose.

1. On fan writers, see Jenkins, Textual Poachers, pp. 152–84. On internet discourse and therapy, see Sherry Turkle, Life on the Screen: Identity in the Age of the Internet (New York, 1995). See also Janet H. Murray, Hamlet on the Holodeck: The Future of Narrative in Cyberspace (New York, 1997). Significantly, the fan writers I cite do not represent all cultures: Joseph Schneider's students (women as well as men) at the University of Hong Kong, for instance, prefer Bruce Willis or Jet Li, the Hong Kong action film star, to Leo, who is 'too boyish' for their tastes—'not a real man'. Harold Bloom puts such opportunities for meaning-making into a wider context. Shakespeare, he writes, 'teach[es] us how to overhear ourselves when we talk to ourselves'; the true use of Shakespeare, he goes on to say, is 'to augment one's own growing inner self', a process that will bring about 'the proper use of one's own solitude, that solitude whose final form is one's confrontation with one's own mortality'. See Harold Bloom, The Western Canon (New York and London, 1994), pp. 30–1.

2. In order, quotations are from David Horspool, 'Tabs and Traffic Jams', Times Literary Supplement, 11 April 1997, 19; Peter Travers, 'Just Two Kids in Love', Rolling Stone, 14 November 1996, 124; José Arroyo, 'Kiss Kiss Bang Bang', Sight and Sound (March 1997), 9.

3. Kuran, 'It's the 90s', F1.

Leo's face. Writes José Arroyo, 'He . . . bears the brunt of the feeling . . . It's his face in close-up . . . indicating how he wants, longs,
feels, and suffers. [But] it's [also] the way he *moves* in the Mantuan
desert when he hears of Juliet's death, not just that the camera lifts
up suddenly to crush him that expresses his grief but the way he falls
on his pigeon-toed heels. It's a superb performance'.[4] Or, more specifically, a superb *physical* performance, for even the friendly *Rolling Stone* was hearing echoes of another Romeo: '[Leo] doesn't round
out vowels or enunciate in dulcet tones, but when he speaks, you
believe him.'[5] In short, the idea that both DiCaprio and Claire Danes
are 'doing Shakespeare' lends a kind of pseudo-Brechtian distantia-
tion to their performances, marking off Danes's Valley-speak—'I was
about to do the famous balcony scene, and I was thinking, like, this
is a joke, right? How am I going to do this in a fresh way'?—from
iambic pentameter.[6] Yet because she handles the unfamiliar verse
better than the more awkward DiCaprio, it feels culturally 'authentic'—at least in relation to gendered adolescent stereotypes about
linguistic facility—especially when, in the balcony scene, as the pair
seem to discover words and ways of thinking, viewers can *see* that
happening: he learns from her how to talk the talk, she from him
how to act like a natural born lover.[7]

   A witty send-up of the play's hallmark scene, Luhrmann's balcony-
pool sequence underscores the film's distinctions between the carnivalesque, associated with Verona Beach, where prostitutes solicit
older men beneath a billboard advertising 'Shoot forth thunder', or
with the Capulets' masquerade ball, and the natural world inhab-
ited by the lovers. First seen silhouetted in pale orange light, Romeo
gazes out to sea in a deliberately painterly 'still' that not only sets
him apart from the frenzied pyrotechnics of the opening gang war
but links him metonymically to Juliet, introduced as she surfaces,
like a mermaid rising from the sea, from her bath. At the ball, when
Romeo douses his face in water to clear his head, a cut from his face
beneath the water to his mirrored reflection suggests a return to self
and keys his glance at Juliet through a fishtank, as, in slow motion,
to the opening strains of Des'ree's 'Kissing You', exotic tropical fish
glide over their faces, already side by side even though separated.
These images culminate in the pool where the pair appear first as
bodiless heads floating on its surface, their desire condensed into

4. Arroyo, 'Kiss Kiss', 9.
5. Travers, 'Just Two Kids', 124.
6. Claire Danes quoted in Christine Spines, 'I Would Die 4u', *Premiere*, v. 10 (October
   1996): 137.
7. I appropriate 'natural born lovers' from Joe Morgenstern, 'Mod Bard; Muted Vonnegut',
   Wall Street Journal, 1 November 1996, A11. Morgenstern, however, in alluding to Quen-
   tin Tarantino's *Natural Born Killers*, gives the phrase a different sense from mine.

an exchange of looks.[8] But once they take the plunge, the water joins them as one body, out of their depth in love and immersed in a private space, simultaneously enclosed within the social and remote from it. On the one hand, representing the lovers as at one with life-giving nature—and naturalized within it—situates their rebellion within heterosexual norms; on the other, it plays into a conventional opposition between *eros* and *thanatos* which confuses those assumptions. For another image chain—Romeo submerging in the pool to avoid the guard; Mercutio dying in the same space where Romeo was introduced; Tybalt falling backward into a fountain, a shot reprised as nightmare when Romeo wakes from his tryst with Juliet; and her last sight of Romeo, an extreme close-up of his face under the water—not only places both lovers in jeopardy but catches them up within a widening circle of homoerotic and homosocial relations.

Those relations are most clearly marked when an extended close-up of Romeo embracing the dead Mercutio, framed by the crumbling seaside proscenium arch, dissolves to a shot of Juliet on her bed, reframing her briefly with the fading image to link Mercutio's death and the possibility of her fulfilled desire. Yet meditating on gender is not the only way Luhrmann's film hits the hotspots of current conversations, both within Shakespeare studies and in the culture as a whole. Because it takes place, not in a Eurocentric culture, but in a multicultural borderland—a mythic geographical space open to variant readings (Miami, California, Mexico)—the film not only accentuates the performative possibilities for 'othering' but ties its representation of gender to somewhat slippery markers of ethnicity and class. Capulet figures the Mediterranean Old World and a nouveau-riche status which set him apart from the white Montague's tacit, if not precisely represented, affiliation with old money; though inflected with old-world codes, Tybalt and the Capulet boys inhabit a new-generation, New World Latino culture. In this multi-ethnic mix, Mercutio and Juliet are the two most liminal, most transgressive figures. As the white Romeo's 'double', Mercutio shares his gender-bent androgyny but is marked off from him by a flagrant racial 'exoticism'. From the outset, but especially during the Tybalt-Romeo fight, a series of triangulated shots consistently places Mercutio in the middle, a position he shares with the Chief of Police-Prince figure, also a black actor. Apart from the Friar (differently marked by his RSC-trained voice), coding blackness as the sign of mediation works, somewhat uncomfortably, to attribute the failures of mediation as much to skin colour as to the law's—or religion's—impotence and delay.

8. Just before they fall into the pool together, they are posed off either side of a statue of Pan, another marker of this 'natural' though man-made setting.

Yet by insisting on the significance of black voices—especially
those of women (the African American news anchor, Des'ree's ballad, 'Kissing You' [the film's 'love theme'] and Leontyne Price's rendition of Wagner's *liebestod*) but also that of the choirboy who sings
Prince's 'When Doves Cry'—to frame *Romeo + Juliet* and to articulate two crucial events in the lovers' story (their meeting and their
death), the film not only gestures toward embracing African-
American experience but also acknowledges the contributions of
that culture to both popular- and high-culture art forms.[9] Moreover,
although the film's overall narrating position differs substantively
from that of the TV anchorwoman, that position can be read as a
figure for Luhrmann's own marginal status as an Australian national
who observes and anatomizes a 'foreign' American culture. Simultaneously, however, *Romeo + Juliet* seems unable to register most
'other' identities except in terms of stereotypes—Margolyes' highly
exaggerated vocal performance—or drag—Diane Venora's non-
Latina Lady Capulet staggering like an Egyptian; Harold Perrineau's
Mercutio queening his role. That inability becomes especially slippery
in terms of Claire Danes's Juliet, who, much like *West Side Story*'s
Maria, does not need to pass to become a Montague: in spite of being
a young Hispanic woman whose father is depicted as a 'minority',
her white skin already 'places' her. Because of this, her ethnicity
appears as a kind of drag impersonation which, in equating her with
Mercutio, not only adds an erotic frisson to her attraction for Romeo
but also makes his love a promise of integration into some idealized
realm of 'whiteness' associated with purity, virginity and perfection.[1]

Even if these dislocations and slippages of ethnicity operate merely
as another instance of the film's postmodern aesthetic, they nonetheless produce potential sociopolitical resonances. Yet *Romeo + Juliet*
makes no overtly tactical alignment with melting-pot ideologies. In
decoding it, however, mainstream critics called its ethnic politics
into question and gestured toward restoring classical paradigms and
privileging 'whiteness'. How, they wondered, could Governor Paris
permit his son to woo a Mafia Don's daughter? How could the police
chief banish a killer instead of locking him up? And how was it possible that 'the milky-skinned Juliet [could be] daughter to the thuggish
Capulet, or that prep-school handsome Romeo's best friend was the
black disco-diva Mercutio [and that he hung out] with a crew of boys
from the hood via Mad Max'?[2] Coming from the right (*Commonweal*)

9. My thanks to Margo Hendricks for pointing out how the film works to situate black
   women's voices at its centre.
1. See Arroyo, 'Kiss Kiss', 8; and Richard Dyer, *White* (London and New York, 1997), esp.
   pp. 70–2.
2. These objections, as well as the citations, are from Richard Alleva, 'The Bard in America', *Commonweal*, 6 December 1996, 19; and Amy Taubin, 'Live Fast, Die Young', *Village Voice*, 12 November 1996, 80. The problematics of reading the film's multiculturalism

as well as the left (*Village Voice*), such queries suggest critics who imagine they reside somewhere other than an America where such blurrings and crossings of ethnic, racial, gender and class boundaries occur daily. Yet even more troubling is how they attest to an ideological failure, offering evidence that the promise of an integrated social fabric ordained by public discourse about constructing nationality is just that—a conversation, not a cultural reality.

As the film negotiates its closing moves, these tropes of failed mediation and integration are remapped in terms of voices and bodies and pushed into a contemporary performative space ideally attuned to the play's imaginative repertoire, music video.[3] For just as the set speech and the soliloquy functioned as verbal icons of interiority for the early modern drama, music video, which expresses emotions and interior states of mind through lyrics and collaged images, represents a late twentieth-century equivalent. After all, it shares characteristic modes—stylistic jumbling, dependence on fragmentation and pastiche, rapid accumulation of images, blurring of internal and external realities—with Shakespeare's early verse, especially that of this play, which, as Anthony Lane notes, exhibits the '"just-you-look-at-this" quality of a young playwright' who, like the film's young director, is simply showing off.[4] Heightening the film's strategy of putting text-as-image on commercial display and cutting it to the beat of a non-Shakespearian sound, several mini-music-video inserts refunction the play's ending, unmooring its traditional narrative designs and simultaneously preserving, though reinflecting, its meanings.

Two of these—one keyed by Romeo, the other by Juliet—map their desires onto the Friar, who envisions a happy ending. Interweaving his words with Prince's 'When Doves Cry', the first reprises the opening headline, 'Ancient Grudge', but adds a news photo of Montague and Capulet shaking hands; linked by flash cuts of flames, these yield to a grainy image of Juliet and Romeo kissing, across which a dove flies in slow motion, and then to the radiant heart. Yet, although this vision confirms the Friar's decision to marry the

also embraces how casting invites blending actors' performances in *Romeo+Juliet* with their most recent roles: for instance, American viewers might well connect Brian Dennehy (Montague) to his most recent appearances as a hawker of antacids on TV rather than to his film roles or to stage performances at New York's Public Theater.

3. *Romeo and Juliet*'s focus on adolescent rebellion and narcissistic love and its obsession with sexuality and violence pre-tailors it for MTV, which addresses the desires, fantasies and anxieties of the young. See E. Ann Kaplan, *Rocking Around the Clock: Music Television, Postmodernism, and Consumer Culture* (New York and London, 1987), esp. pp. 5–7, 31. On MTV, see also Jenkins, *Textual Poachers*, pp. 233–40; Richard Dyer, 'Entertainment and Utopia', in *Movies and Methods, Volume II*, ed. Bill Nichols (Berkeley, 1985); and John Fiske, 'MTV: Post-Structural Post-Modern', *Journal of Communication Inquiry* 10. 1 (Winter 1986), 74–9.

4. Lane, 'Tights!', 75.

lovers, a cut to Mercutio's and Benvolio's parodic gun-play picks up a billboard ad for recliners—'Such stuff as dreams are made on'—undermining his hopes of peace and union. Later, when Juliet seeks his advice, the Friar appears in left screen as a talking head, his narrative of the effects and consequences of the sleeping potion glossing an image chain that concludes with an extreme close-up of Juliet's eyes, which key shots of Romeo and her exchanging smiles and, then, of the fatally missent letter. On the videocassette, this segment is letter-boxed, not scanned, deliberately calling attention to its special status and to what its X-ray vision diagnoses: the most improbable gimmicks that mark the play's early modern heritage—the potion and the letter. Framed up within the Friar's imaginary, made hyper-real and morphed into MTV's contemporary gimmickry, those devices appear indeed the very stuff of dreams. Nonetheless, his visions construct two spaces of ending: one recirculates the religious iconography of divine union, the other anticipates a resolution for the lovers' dilemma. Cutting off the latter's more fully 'realized' space, the film draws on the former to generate another, even more breathtakingly surreal, dream space of ending.

That space condenses and intensifies the lovers' desire for a private universe, a utopian room of their own. Visually as well as metaphorically interior, it takes place inside the church but travels beyond Shakespeare's implied setting and his text into a knowing, aesthetically satisfying, cinematic plenitude addressed to and complicit with a spectatorial imaginary that idealizes and mystifies the lovers' experience as their own. After Romeo dies, an extreme close-up of the gun pointed at Juliet's temple articulates her own death; as the gun's report bleeds over the cut, a high-angle long shot reveals her body falling beside Romeo's onto the bier, flanked by hundreds of candles that illuminate the church aisle lined with banked flowers and blue neon crosses. The shot holds in silence until Leontyne Price's voice, singing the *liebestod* from *Tristan and Isolde*, keys a cut that shifts the perspective, so that the lovers float above the candles, transforming bier to altar.[5] Images reprising their shared moments—catching sight of one another through the fish tank; laughing together at the ball; the ring, inscribed 'I love thee'—link bier with wedding bed where, beneath a fluttering white sheet, they again exchange smiles across a cut. When the image of the bier returns, the camera angle further inverts and disorients point of view, so that instead of looking down at them, we seem to be looking

5. Sung by a black soprano, this aria not only connects the lovers to the most famous of all love-deaths but also represents an instance of how the film's soundtrack, much like its casting (which blends stage and film traditions) mixes opera, classical music (phrases from Mozart's Symphony 25 introduce Romeo) and pop culture, especially music from groups that mix white, black and latino/latina or hispanic voices.

up at a Tiepolo-like ceiling, fresco, and the candle-flames have become radiant Catherine-wheels that evoke the exploding fireworks at the ball, as if to visualize Juliet's fantasy of 'cut[ting Romeo] out in little stars'. At the centre of their own jewelled orrery, they appear as a treasured artifact, a pair of saintly pilgrims joined in eternal embrace. Exalting their love-death, the sequence offers a sensual experience in which subject identity is lost in the image: read by the body and through the body, its affect is further enhanced by a visual and aural saturation that makes it appear, not as a sign of absence but of an intensely pleasurable present.[6]

In locating the lovers' mythic union inside rather than outside the narrative design, the film offers to rewrite the traditional reading formations associated with the play, those which, as Jonathan Goldberg notes, not only privilege heterosexual love but, by giving value to the lovers' private experience, disconnect the personal from the political.[7] Although the thousand-candle tableau may suggest that love is all there is, its garish MTV excess also clearly marks it as an imported fantasy, something cooked up when an old play confronts a new medium. And that is precisely the point: highlighting the tension between the two, Luhrmann's film juxtaposes medium and message, has it both ways. As the candle-flames dissolve into bubbles to freeze frame the lovers' underwater kiss, a long fade to white, accompanied by the *liebestod*'s final strains, dissolves in turn to the 'social real'—a white-sheeted body on a hospital trolley. Chastizing Montague and Capulet—'All are punished'—the Police Chief passes their silent figures, looking at the second white-sheeted body being loaded into an ambulance.[8] Glossed by the voice of the newswoman who spoke the opening prologue, these images then turn to grainy video; reframed within a TV monitor, that image fades, finally, to video snow.

Michael Bogdanov's 1986 RSC production, of course, anticipated this ending: there, the unveiling of the golden statues became a photo op that enhanced the Prince's public image, and it was Benvolio who, after all had left, rose from a nearby café table to mourn his friend's death.[9] Ten years later, Luhrmann's film denies, or suspends, any promise of securing the social through either the heterosexual or the homosocial. That points, all too knowingly, to how, in our present cultural moment—at least in America—there seem to be no answers, fictional or real, religious or legal, to gender, ethnic and

6. I adapt these terms from Fiske, 'MTV', pp. 74–9.
7. See Goldberg, '*Romeo and Juliet*'s Open Rs', esp. pp. 219–20.
8. Peter Holland suggests a pertinent analogue: the moment in Bob Fosse's 1979 film, *All That Jazz*, where a cut from Ben Vereen's final production number (celebrating the Fosse-character's death) yields to an image of a body bag being zipped shut.
9. See my 'Absent Bodies, Present Voices', especially p. 358, n. 47.

class differences and conflicts, to generational strife, or boys with guns. If, as the web discourse on Leo tells us, chick flicks do matter, then *William Shakespeare's Romeo + Juliet* matters even more: it bears watching precisely because it has been watching us.

SUSAN BENNETT

Romeo and Juliet in Baghdad (and in Stratford and London and Qatar)†

The robust history of adaptations of *Romeo and Juliet*, especially during the second half of the twentieth century and into the twenty-first, suggests the text's appeal to cultural producers interested in exploring a remarkable range of contemporary experiences through the material bodies of the Montagu and Capulet families. Most editions of the play now include detailed accounts of a revisionist trajectory that starts with *West Side Story* (Broadway 1957, film version 1961), emphasizes the impact of Franco Zeffirelli's 'teenage love' interpretation (Old Vic 1960, film version 1968), and ends with Baz Luhrmann's *Romeo + Juliet* (1996), a film that René Weis describes as 'arguably, the greatest Shakespeare film ever'.[1] This density of interest in having *Romeo and Juliet* speak to present cultural concerns might well be accounted for in Dympna Callaghan's description of the play as 'the preeminent document of love in the West'.[2]

If much of this deployment of the play has, in the last fifty or so years, enabled discussion of how bodies matter 'in love', I am interested here in a rather different critical framework for reading its adaptation, one that is at once accessed and re-routed in the presentation of contested national identity and global impacts. Rather than restrict the play and its different versions to a history of romantic love as they have been represented and so vigorously circulated in the West, I examine the play's adaptation as a matter of place and politics, in a precarious elsewhere whose own history with the West marshals Shakespeare's tragedy into a more pressing articulation of human rights today. The focus for this discussion is the Iraqi Theatre Company's 2012 production *Romeo and Juliet in Baghdad*, adapted and directed by Monadhil Daood.

---

† An expanded version of this essay appears under the title "Precarious Bodies: *Romeo and Juliet in Baghdad* at the World Shakespeare Festival" in *The Oxford Handbook of Shakespeare and Embodiment*, ed. Valerie Traub (Oxford: Oxford University Press, 2016), pp. 694–707. This condensed essay is reprinted by permission of Oxford University Press.
1. René Weis, ed., *Romeo and Juliet* (London: Bloomsbury, 2012), p. 88.
2. Dympna Callaghan, ed., *Romeo and Juliet: Texts and Contexts* (New York: Bedford-St. Martins, 2003), p. 1.

The play was first staged on 17 April 2012 at the Al-Watani The-
atre, Baghdad; and, subsequently, from 26 April to 5 May at the
Swan Theatre, Stratford-upon-Avon, and from 28–30 June at the
Riverside Studios as part of the London International Festival of
Theatre (both of these UK dates carried the stamp of the World
Shakespeare Festival—the largest event in the nationwide Cultural
Olympiad organized in parallel with London's 2012 Summer Games);
and from 30 September to 3 October at the Katara Drama Theatre
in Doha, Qatar. In November 2012 at the MCP-TV Awards in Iraq,
Romeo and Juliet in Baghdad won the award for 'Best Theatre Production of the Year'.[3] This is a performance history, I suggest, that
replicates other kinds of traffic between the UK and the Middle
East. Understood in this context, the Iraqi play's refusal of the normative love story in favor of a revision that explores *Romeo and Juliet*
through the embodiment of national experience demonstrates a
different order of tragedy. While Shakespeare's play ends with the
Prince's wistful observation that there 'never was a story of more woe'
(5.3.309), Daood's adaptation insists that, in Iraq, this plotline has
been repeated again and again, generation after generation: it is not
an exception, but a commonplace. *Romeo and Juliet in Baghdad* re-
imagines Shakespeare's play as an embodiment of cross-sectarian
love (the Capulets are Sunni and the Montagus Shia) and so dramatizes the contingent practices of Iraqi nationhood.

That the history of adaptations of *Romeo and Juliet* in the West
demonstrates an ongoing, well-rehearsed, and generally enthusiastic audience for this tragic tale of love is, I suggest, the crucial back-
story to the reception of the Iraqi Theatre Company's adaptation of
the play for the World Shakespeare Festival. As Marjorie Garber has
noted, Western audiences know 'Romeo and Juliet as ubiquitous
examples of young love, its idealism and excess' and even the most
cynical of spectators knows what to expect with the play.[4] Spectatorial assumptions about *Romeo and Juliet* were, then, crucial to
the English reception of the Iraqi Theatre Company's play, but so
too was the national platform hailed by the production of such an
ambitious World Shakespeare Festival as the showpiece of the
larger Cultural Olympiad. Programming had been designed by
the London Organizing Committee to be 'the largest cultural
celebration in the history of the modern Olympic and Paralympic
Movements,'[5] and was scheduled to take place across the nation
from April to November 2012 thanks to a reported £97 million

---

3. The announcement of this award was made by the World Shakespeare Festival (taking
   credit for commissioning the production) on their Facebook page on 17 November 2012.
4. Marjorie Garber, *Shakespeare After All* (New York: Pantheon Books, 2004), p. 4.
5. Official London 2012 website, 'Cultural Olympiad', www.london2012.com/aboutus
   /cultural-olympiad/, 5 January 2013.

budget.[6] A remarkable 19.5 million attendances were recorded in these UK-wide arts events and the Royal Shakespeare Company (RSC), producers of the World Shakespeare Festival, have since reported that the Festival's seventy or so productions 'reached more than 1.8 million people'.[7] This number included the audiences for twelve productions staged at the RSC's theatres in Stratford-upon-Avon, among which was the commissioned Iraqi Theatre Company's adaptation of *Romeo and Juliet in Baghdad*.

If the English audiences for *Romeo and Juliet in Baghdad* brought both their enthusiasm for nation and assumptions about a tale of romantic love to their seats at the Swan Theatre in Stratford, then these expectations were dramatically unmet. The opening of the Iraqi version of the play ramped up the violence of Shakespeare's 'swords and bucklers' (1.1) with the ear-splitting sound of an explosion followed by rapid fire of machine-gun exchange and flashes of light—an immersion in visual and sonic effects that were at once frightening and disorienting. Any comfort or familiarity with the beautiful and intimate space of this particular theatre was lost before the performance had even begun. Special effects were followed immediately by the entrance of actors, screaming at each other in Arabic and toting an intimidating range of weaponry. In only its first minutes, the production had already delivered on Daood's director's notes printed in the show's program where he asked: 'Understand that we live in a place where terrorists break our homes over our heads. We are the family of *Romeo and Juliet in Baghdad*, living in the time of the neo-barbarians'.

The speed of performance (100 minutes, with no intermission) left little time to take in the surtitles provided in English and for spectators so familiar with the source play, there was perhaps little point. Rather, spectatorial experience was concentrated on the palpably hostile interactions of the two families. As Tim Arango pointed out in his review for the *New York Times*:

> The words Sunni and Shia are not mentioned explicitly, but are symbolized in ways that are clearly recognizable to an Iraqi audience. Capulet, Juliet's father, is denoted as a Sunni by his red-and-white checkered keffiyeh (not to mention that a Qaeda

6. This figure is given in Mark Brown's 'Cultural Olympiad 2012 reaches in the critical masses' *The Guardian* 12 March 2012 (www.guardian.co.uk/culture/2012/mar/12/cultural-olympiad-2012-critical-masses, 15 February 2013). The size of budget for cultural events might be compared with £80 million for the opening and closing ceremonies (Brown) and a final overall Olympics budget of £8.9 billion—see Jacquelin Magnay's 'London 2012 Olympic Games comes in at £377m under budget, government announces' *Telegraph* 23 October 2012 (www.telegraph.co.uk/sport/olympics/9627757/London-2012-Olympic-Games-comes-in-at-377m-under-budget-government-announces.html, 15 February 2013).
7. www.rsc.org.uk/about-us/history/world-shakespeare-festival-2012/ (accessed 10 February 2013).

fighter seeks to marry his daughter). Romeo's father, Montague, wears a black-and-white scarf more commonly worn by Shiites.[8]

Even if English audience members did not know this iconography, program materials prepared them through description of the play's setting as one of "sectarian strife" and in the provision of a longer essay by Deborah Shaw, the World Shakespeare Festival director, that starts with a description of Baghdad: 'Pious Sunni religious authorities squint at the moon and calculate exactly the right day for Eid festivities to begin. Pious Shia religious authorities squint at the same moon, do the same calculations and choose a different day. The rhythm of life rooted in tradition and the movement of the planets and arguments from centuries past'.[9] As Richard Spencer explained Daood's adaptation of the source text, '[h]e has changed and not changed the play, but the words Sunni and Shia are understood and not mentioned. Instead, while his characters' names remain those of Verona, the two families (Capulet and Montague here are brothers) have argued about ownership of a boat they have inherited from the father. In this way, the question of who gets to steer the boat becomes a metaphor for the fight for Iraq'.[1] The translation not only into Arabic but into the rhythms and rituals of Iraqi culture distanced the Western audience from the world on stage; at the same time, however, it offered new contexts for seeing and engaging that country's quotidian violence, otherwise likely only familiar from reports in the various news media.

To illustrate the substitution of Iraqi mythologies for Shakespeare's puns and imagery, Shaw, in her program essay, described at length the alteration during the rehearsal process of Mercutio's Queen Mab speech into one elaborating a well-known folk tale told to Iraqi children about a beetle weaving a magic carpet to give to the man she will marry.[2] Moreover, in the introduction of a new character, The Teacher, Daood contrived that the action be filtered not so much by the audience's previous experiences of *Romeo and Juliet*, but by 'the chain of storytelling' that sustains Sunni and

8. 'Montague and Capulet as Shiite and Sunni' *New York Times* 28 April 2012 (www .nytimes.com/2012/04/29/world/middleeast/in-iraq-romeo-and-juliet-portrays -montague-and-capulet-as-shiite-and-sunni.html?_r=1&, 10 February 2013).
9. In his important history of 'Islam's first century and the origins of the Sunni-Shia split', Barnaby Rogerson explores what he calls 'a tragic tale'—the codification of 'rival interpretations of history some two hundred years after the death' of the Prophet Muhammad. It is relevant here, of course, that so few of us in the West have any real understanding of this history. See *The Heirs of Muhammad* (New York: Overlook, 2008).
1. '"Romeo and Juliet in Baghdad" comes to London' (www.telegraph.co.uk/culture /theatre/theatre-features/9184099/Romeo-and-Juliet-in-Baghdad-comes-to-London .html, 10 February 2013).
2. Arango, in his review for the *New York Times*, suggests the sexual imagery in the Queen Mab speech was considered inappropriate for the Baghdad audience and that Daood substituted the folk tale for this reason.

Shia belief systems alike.[3] The Teacher was, at times, a mediator
between the play and its English audience—imploring spectators to
understand what Baghdad life was like—and, at other times, he
served to advance the plot—helping Juliet escape her father and his
plan to have her marry Paris (in this production a Mujahideen). The
deaths that punctuate Shakespeare's text seemed in this performance to be inevitable outcomes in a city pervaded by expectations
of violent acts, where loss of life is everyday rather than dramatic.

At the end of the play, Romeo sought refuge in a Catholic church
where he thought no-one would think to look for him. If English
spectators might have found this place an oddly dissonant locale
within the on-stage Muslim world and hardly the 'ancient vault'
(4.1.111) that Shakespeare's Friar Laurence suggests, Daood's home
audience would certainly have recognized its referent. As Spencer
outlined,

> [t]he final scene is set in Baghdad's Cathedral of Our Lady of
> Salvation, destroyed when in one of their most extraordinarily
> brutal attacks, al-Qaeda terrorists stormed it, shot priests and
> members of the congregation and finally detonated suicide
> vests. The church's ruins lie within view of both the National
> Theatre and Daood's flat, making a sort of triangular reminder
> of how Baghdad once encompassed both culture and tolerance,
> and of Daood's place in that tradition.[4]

Had the audience in the Swan Theatre been better versed about
recent history in Baghdad, perhaps the final action in Daood's play
would have come as less of a shock. Paris arrived in the Church
(where Juliet had now re-united with Romeo), smiled, and detonated
his suicide belt. Like the show's opening moments, this prompted
an onset of overwhelming sound and light effects that seemed to
force spectators back in their seats. On the night I saw the production in Stratford, the play's conclusion had a visceral effect on theatregoers. In the accelerated seconds between Paris's arrival on stage
and his fatal move, there was a sense of chilling recognition among
some, but far from all, of the audience that this is what it would be
like: to know what comes next and to have no power to change the
outcome, that this was probably the end of one's life. Even as I had

---

3. The term is Rogerson's, taken from an appendix to his history of the Sunni-Shia split.
   See pages 6 and 359–66.
4. '"Romeo and Juliet in Baghdad" comes to London'. Daood spent more than twenty years
   in exile after an anti-war play attracted the attention of Saddam Hussein's government.
   In that time, he lived and worked in Sweden, Russia, England, Belgium, Kuwait and
   Lebanon before returning to his homeland in 2008 to form the Iraqi Theatre Company.
   His 'Letter from 2008' describing his return to Baghdad is posted on the Iraqi Theatre
   Company's website (www.iraqitheatrecompany.com/about-us.html, 5 January 2013).
   Deborah Shaw is married to Daood and also a founding member of the company.

that thought, I was also aware that others around me had no idea at all about what would take place in the next seconds; their innocence was palpable.

As the performance went to a blackout post-detonation and before the cast returned for their curtain call, the audience was almost entirely silent and still, but for the half a dozen or so people in a row behind my seat given over to a kind of hysterical laughter, borne it seemed from fear—that somehow they felt they had actually been put at risk in watching how this performance had ended. Applause was subdued—the actors frankly deserved much more reward than they received—and spectators showed themselves anxious to leave the building as quickly as they could. The common response suggested a profound disappointment in seeing '[m]odern culture's paradigmatic hetereosexual love story' rendered so overtly political.[5] In a review for the 'Year of Shakespeare' blog that I co-wrote with Christie Carson on the day following our attendance at the play, we described the suicide bombing 'that shocked as it underscored the absolute loss of love in this world. Lives lost by the end of Shakespeare's tragedies suddenly seem little more than aesthetic convention; the real tragedy, this adaptation suggests, is the West's passive spectatorship of a story familiar to us from the nightly news'.[6] Spencer, in his review of the Baghdad premiere, had noted of his relationship to Shakespeare's play that '[h]owever often it is performed, I confess my unconscious image was of its romance. Rereading it reawakened me to its machismo'. It was in this context he anticipated, for Daood's version, that 'audiences will be mesmerized by the swagger of the young Iraqis on stage'[7]—an experience that I can attest to from its Stratford performance. But, now with more critical distance from the immediate impacts of the production, I think of *Romeo and Juliet in Baghdad* as a play that literally tore out the possibility of love from the bodies on stage and replaced it with a relentlessly masculinist battle for power.[8]

Had the Stratford performances of *Romeo and Juliet in Baghdad* been the only ones at the World Shakespeare Festival, I likely would

5. The phrase is Garber's: *Shakespeare After All*, p. 208.
6. The review was first published on 6 May 2012 (bloggingshakespeare.com/year-of-shakespeare-romeo-and-juliet-in-baghdad, 5 March 2013) and is now published in print form in *A Year of Shakespeare: Reviewing the World Shakespeare Festival 2012*, ed. Paul Edmonson, Paul Prescott, and Erin Sullivan (London: Bloomsbury Arden Shakespeare, 2013), pp. 183–85.
7. '"Romeo and Juliet in Baghdad" comes to London'.
8. Criticism—and especially feminist criticism—has, of course, long interrogated representations of masculinity in the play. See Robert Appelbaum's 'Standing to the Wall: The Pressure of Masculinity in *Romeo and Juliet*', *Shakespeare Quarterly* 48.3 (Autumn 1997), pp. 251–72, for a detailed review of this scholarship. Applebaum reads Verona as a society of 'imperfect masculinities' (268) and masculinity itself as 'a structure, a regime, a dominant system' (256), an argument that might be productively applied to Daood's adaptation.

have concluded this essay with an account of the effectiveness of
Daood's production in challenging conventional Western responses
to Shakespeare's play so that we better remember the bodily costs of
sectarian violence in both this contemporary adaptation and its
early modern predecessor, As well, I would have argued that for the
few who saw these performances, their experience surely interrupted, even if only fleetingly, the overwhelmingly celebratory tone
of World Shakespeare Festival and Olympic Year alike. Nationhood,
we were reminded, was not something to be realized in gold medals
but rather a much more precarious condition that puts many bodies
at risk in the claiming of it. Furthermore, I might have ended in
sharing Spencer's 'hope' that *Romeo and Juliet in Baghdad* could be
'a corrective superimposing a theatrical hyper-reality on top of tired
news values'.[9] All these observations still hold true, but the return
of Daood's play to the English stage two months later called to
account its audiences in London in some rather different ways.

   Although the performances at the Swan in Stratford had not been
widely reviewed,[1] there was certainly the possibility that London
audiences arrived at the Riverside Studios knowing exactly where
this production was headed, thus minimizing its potential to shock.
Even then, there might have been a different kind of recognition of
Daood's play from spectators who were more likely to have direct
experience of life in the capital city under the threat of IRA bombs
(1970–2001) and, of course, in the context of '7/7' (7 July 2005) when
52 people were killed and more than 700 injured by four suicide
bombings on public transit (tube and bus) carried out by a British-
based Islamic terrorist network. But one particular performance
(28 June 2012) during this second run involved a pre-show intervention that resituated the play's bodies in a specifically English and
explicitly political history.

   Just before the start of the 28 June performance, a member of the
Reclaim Shakespeare Company took to the stage to perform a "guer-
rilla Shakespeare" soliloquy, to highlight the role of BP [British
Petroleum]—a major World Shakespeare Festival sponsor—in the
war in Iraq and in environmentally damaging projects worldwide'.[2]
The performer, known as 'Pete the Temp', welcomed the audience
in both English and Arabic before delivering his two-minute monologue. It started:

---

9. Ibid.
1. Overall, the play's few reviews, both of the Stratford and London performances, were
   generally not enthusiastic—that Daood might have done much better to have written
   an original play if he had wanted to teach English audiences about conditions in Baghdad and that he should have left Shakespeare's classic play alone.
2. 'Stage invaded at "Romeo and Juliet in Baghdad" performance to challenge BP sponsorship' bp-or-not-bp.org/news/romeo-and-juliet/ (5 January 2013).

Two households, BP and the World Shakespeare Festival, both lacking in dignity, in befouled Iraq where we lay our scene

For oil feud breaks to new hypocrisy where civil blood makes their money unclean

BP, O most wicked fiend, you did conspire to bring Iraq to her knees.[3]

This was followed by an elaboration of BP's role in the Iraq war. The oil company was working intimately—as Pete the Temp explained—with the British Government before and after the 2003 invasion so as to protect its access to the country's resources. He quoted from (leaked) Foreign Office minutes of a 2002 meeting that recorded 'Iraq is the big oil prospect. BP is desperate to get in there and anxious that political deals should not deny them the opportunity'. He pointed out that the British Government's then Trade Minister had lobbied the Bush administration on behalf of BP interests and that the subsequent deal ensured that BP would be monetarily compensated should their access to the oil and gas fields be limited by 'civil disruption or if the [Iraqi] government decides to cut production'. The 'guerilla soliloquy' ended with a charge to audience:

I ne'er saw true hypocrisy till this night.
O Romeo, Romeo! wherefore art thou Romeo?
Deny thy sponsor and refuse thy logo.

Never was a story of more woe than the sponsorship of our Juliet and her Romeo.

If you share our concern about BP's sponsorship of the World Shakespeare Festival we invite you to rip BP's logo from your programme. Thank you, and enjoy tonight's show.

In an explanation of this particular intervention posted to the Reclaim Shakespeare website, Pete the Temp argues that 'BP are using arts sponsorship to try to distract us from their dirty deeds, and by taking their money the World Shakespeare Festival have made themselves complicit in this. . . . Taking money from this company whilst simultaneously staging a play set in war-torn Baghdad shows the World Shakespeare Festival to either be unthinkingly callous or breathtakingly hypocritical'.

3. The full text of the monologue is posted on the group's website: bp-or-not-bp.org/news/romeo-and-juliet/ (5 January 2013). This webpage also has an embedded video of the live performance that shows in the foreground a steady stream of people arriving to take their seats in the auditorium and registers occasional laughter from the audience. All quotations come from this site.

The group (self-described as 'a merry troupe of players aghast that our beloved Bard's works and memory have been purloined by BP in a case of greenwash most foul'[4]) intervened on five separate occasions during the World Shakespeare Festival: at the Shakespeare birthday celebrations at the RSC in Stratford and again there before a performance of *Twelfth Night*; before a performance of *Comedy of Errors* at London's Roundhouse; before the Iraqi Theatre Company's *Romeo and Juliet in Baghdad* at the Riverside Studios; and, as a flash mob, inside the British Museum's 'Shakespeare: Staging the World' exhibition.[5] Moreover, Reclaim Shakespeare interventions at the *Romeo and Juliet in Baghdad* performance and elsewhere attracted significant attention both nationally and internationally, including a report in the *Los Angeles Times* that not only described the anti-BP protests but made sure their own readers were aware of the oil company's sponsor relationships with the Aquarium of the Pacific and the Los Angeles County Museum of Art.[6]

Reclaim Shakespeare's pop-up performance before *Romeo and Juliet in Baghdad* took the stage must have reminded spectators that England has a long history with 'befouled Iraq', especially through its administration and military presence in the area for much of the twentieth century—Spencer calls Iraq a country that Britain 'helped to create'—and that the resources of the region, especially oil, have always been what the West valued most. The oil company that bears a national imprimatur, and who had underwritten the price of the theatre tickets, was very much cast as a character in the drama that was about to be seen at this London theatre. These protests served to remind audiences that contemporary wars are seldom simply about national interests but instead reflect the stakes of global economies. The choice of name for the prologist might also have suggested that these government and corporate policies have had consequences for post-imperial Britain. Of course, English audiences do not experience risk in the direct ways that Iraqis do, but the loss of regular, well-remunerated, unionized labor signaled in Pete's status as 'temp' could remind spectators that David Cameron's 'austerity' Britain has produced another kind of precarity.

This pre-show intervention disrupted the celebration of nation hailed by the World Shakespeare Festival and the Olympic Games alike to suggest it was more accurately a BP brand promotion

---

4. bp-or-not-bp.org/about/ (5 January 2013).
5. All of the performances are available through the Reclaimed Shakespeare website. The speech before the performance at the Roundhouse was particularly well timed since the evening's audience largely comprised a group from BP invited by the RSC (also a recipient of the oil company's sponsorship).
6. Ng, David. 'BP Sponsorship of World Shakespeare Festival draws protest' *Los Angeles Times* 25 April 2012 (www.latimes.com/entertainment/arts/culture/la-et-cm-bp-shakespeare-festival-20120424,0,5074811.story, 5 January 2013).

exercise, one intended to greenwash the company's political, social and environmental impacts at home and elsewhere in the world. Reclaim Shakespeare challenged spectators to recognize the implications of their BP-subsidized theatre ticket and urged them to tear the BP logo from the program as an embodied act of defiance. But what, in fact, comprised the terms of such a disavowal and what might be the intended or actual political effects? Did ripping off the logo refuse BP's visible presence in the events that undergirded the swell of national pride, asking of the spectator a kind of ethically inspired performance? Or did that act perform an abrogation of, responsibility, a failure to recognize one's complicity with BP's actions? At what costs, then, did England invite athletes and actors to perform for its entertainment? Daood ended his program notes: 'You fanatics and extremists—leave us the magic of our stage and the joy of this performance. Leave life to us—you can have Paradise'. When I read the comment in Stratford, I thought it a brave injunction against Paris and his fellow suicide bombers. But, after Reclaim Shakespeare, I wanted to re-think his statement in a different register, recognizing in it the extreme effects of global corporate power in the shaping of national policies, local experience, and all too often the precarious life of bodies, of populations, for which this version of *Romeo and Juliet* was a preeminent case study. The performances of the Iraqi Theatre Company's adaptation in England challenged *Romeo and Juliet*'s routine labor, to embody an idealized romantic love, and recast the play instead as an exemplary tragedy for our neoliberal capitalist times.

But if *Romeo and Juliet in Baghdad* had been commissioned for the ticket buyers at the World Shakespeare Festival, they were not, of course, the only audiences that saw the play—in fact, its history started with a single performance in the very real war-torn environment of Baghdad. It is important, then, to think about this version of the play as not 'just' a challenge for 'us' in the West, the theatre publics who 'know' Shakespeare's original, but also to recognize the critical work it does as an adaptation for audiences elsewhere. The Iraqi Theatre Company's *Romeo and Juliet* challenged, I have suggested, English national ownership of the text and adapted the play to speak to lived political histories. It also surely reveals the normative conditions of theatrical production, Shakespearean or otherwise, that take for granted a run of performances, a production season, access to multiple venues, and so on. By contrast, Iraq's National Theatre, for example, closed during the first Iraq war and when it finally re-opened in 2009, the building was constructed with blast-proof walls. *Romeo and Juliet in Baghdad* as the country's 2012 play of the year was, in this context, an exceptional success. The one other location where the play has been staged, Qatar, suggests, too, its importance to the Arab world and as cultural traffic between local and international economies. As Qatar lobbies for recognition in the global marketplace—including the very controversial awarding of the FIFA World Cup in 2022—we might add to the protocols of adaptation, *Romeo and Juliet*'s (and Shakespeare's) evidently instrumental uses in aspirational place-making projects as well as for the circulation of national and other identities.

Selected Bibliography

• indicates works included or excerpted in this Norton Critical Edition.

Anderegg, Michael. "James Dean Meets the Pirate's Daughter: Passion and Parody in *William Shakespeare's Romeo + Juliet* and *Shakespeare in Love.*" In Richard Burt and Lynda E. Boose, eds. *Shakespeare the Movie II: Popularizing the Plays on Film, TV, Video, and DVD.* New York: Routledge, 2003. 56–71.

Andreas, James. "The Neutering of *Romeo and Juliet.*" In Robert P. Merrix and Nicholas Ranson, eds. *Ideological Approaches to Shakespeare: The Practice of Theory.* Lewiston, NY: Edwin Mellen, 1992. 229–42.

Appelbaum, Robert. "'Standing to the Wall': The Pressures of Masculinity in *Romeo and Juliet.*" *Shakespeare Quarterly* 48 (1977): 251–72.

Belsey, Catherine. "The Name of the Rose in *Romeo and Juliet.*" *Yearbook of English Studies* 23 (1993): 126–42.

• Bennett, Susan. "Precarious Bodies: *Romeo and Juliet in Baghdad.*" In Valerie Traub, ed. *The Oxford Handbook of Shakespeare and Embodiment.* Oxford University Press, 2016.

Berry, Ralph. "*Romeo and Juliet*: The Sonnet-World of Verona." In John F. Andrews, ed. *"Romeo and Juliet": Critical Essays.* New York: Garland, 1993. 133–45.

Black, James. "The Visual Artistry in *Romeo and Juliet.*" *Studies in English Literature* 15 (1975): 245–56.

Brenner, Gerry. "Shakespeare's Politically Ambitious Friar." *Shakespeare Studies* 13 (1980): 47–58.

Brooke, Nicholas. *Shakespeare's Early Tragedies.* London: Methuen, 1968.

Brown, John Russell. "S. Franco Zeffirelli's *Romeo and Juliet.*" *Shakespeare Survey* 15 (1962): 147–55.

Buchanan, Judith. *Shakespeare on Film.* Harlow, UK: Pearson Longman, 2005.

• Callaghan, Dympna C. "The Ideology of Romantic Love: The Case of *Romeo and Juliet.*" In Callaghan, Lorraine Helms, and Jyotsna Singh, eds. *The Weyward Sisters: Shakespeare and Feminist Politics.* Cambridge, MA: Blackwell, 1994. 59–101.

Carroll, William C. "'We Were Born to Die': *Romeo and Juliet.*" *Comparative Drama* 15 (1981): 54–71.

Cole, Douglas, ed. *Twentieth Century Interpretations of "Romeo and Juliet": A Collection of Critical Essays.* Englewood Cliffs, NJ: Prentice Hall, 1970.

• Coleridge, Samuel Taylor. "The Seventh Lecture" (1819). In *Coleridge's Essays and Lectures on Shakespeare & Some Other Old Poets and Dramatists.* Ed. Ernest Rhys. London: Dent, 1907. 419–35.

Cox, Marjorie Kolb. "Adolescent Processes in *Romeo and Juliet.*" *Psychoanalytical Review* 63 (1976): 379–89.

Cribb, T. J. "The Unity of *Romeo and Juliet.*" *Shakespeare Survey* 34 (1981): 93–104.

Davies, Anthony. "The Film Versions of *Romeo and Juliet.*" *Shakespeare Survey* 49 (1996): 153–62.

• Davis, Lloyd. "'Death-Marked Love': Desire and Presence in *Romeo and Juliet.*" *Shakespeare Survey* 49 (1996): 57–67.

Dessen, Alan C. "Q1 *Romeo and Juliet* and Elizabethan Theatrical Vocabulary." In Jay L. Halio, ed. *Shakespeare's* Romeo and Juliet: *Texts, Contexts, and Interpretation*. Newark: University of Delaware Press, 1995. 107–22.

Donaldson, Peter S. "'Let Lips Do What Hands Do': Male Bonding, *Eros*, and Loss in Zeffirelli's *Romeo and Juliet*." In *Shakespearean Films/Shakespearean Directors*. Boston: Unwin Hyman, 1990. 145–88.

Dryden, John. *Defence of the Epilogue, or, an Essay on the Dramatic Poetry of the Last Age*. London, 1672.

Erne, Lukas, ed. *The First Quarto of* Romeo and Juliet. The New Cambridge Shakespeare: The Early Quartos. Cambridge: Cambridge University Press, 2007.

Farley-Hills, David. "The 'Bad' Quarto of *Romeo and Juliet*." *Shakespeare Survey* 49 (1996): 27–44.

Farrell, Kirby. "Love, Death, and Patriarchy in *Romeo and Juliet*." In Norman N. Holland, Sidney Homan, and Bernard J. Paris, eds. *Shakespeare's Personality*. Berkeley: University of California Press, 1989. 86–102.

• Faucit, Helena, Lady Martin. *On Some of Shakespeare's Female Characters*, 5th ed. London and Edinburgh: Blackwood, 1893.

Fitter, Chris. "'The quarrel is between our masters and us their men': *Romeo and Juliet*, Dearth, and the London Riots." *English Literary Renaissance* 30 (2000): 154–83.

Fowler, James. "Picturing *Romeo and Juliet*." *Shakespeare Survey* 49 (1996): 111–29.

Goldberg, Jonathan. "*Romeo and Juliet's* Open Rs." In Goldberg, ed. *Queering the Renaissance*. Durham, NC: Duke University Press, 1994. 218–32.

• Granville-Barker, Harley. "Romeo and Juliet" 1930. In *Prefaces to Shakespeare*. Vol. 2. Princeton, NJ: Princeton University Press, 1947. 300–349.

Halio, Jay L. Romeo and Juliet: *A Guide to the Play*. Westport, CT: Greenwood Press, 1988.

Hapgood, Robert. "*West Side Story* and the Modern Appeal of *Romeo and Juliet*." In John F. Andrews, ed. *"Romeo and Juliet": Critical Essays*. New York: Garland, 1993. 229–41.

• Hazlitt, William. *Characters of Shakespear's Plays*. London: C. H. Reynell, 1817. Repr. New York: Wiley and Putnam, 1845. 91–102.

• Hodgdon, Barbara. "*William Shakespeare's Romeo + Juliet*: Everything's Nice in America?" *Shakespeare Survey* 52 (1999): 88–98.

Holmer, Joan Ozark. "Myself Condemned and Myself Excus'd: Tragic Effects in *Romeo and Juliet*." *Studies in Philology* 88 (1991): 345–62.

———. "The Poetics of Paradox: Shakespeare's versus Zeffirelli's Cultures of Violence." *Shakespeare Survey* 49 (1996): 163–79.

Hunter, G. K. "Shakespeare's Earliest Tragedies: *Titus Andronicus* and *Romeo and Juliet*." *Shakespeare Survey* 27 (1974): 1–10.

Jackson, Russell. Romeo and Juliet. "Shakespeare at Stratford." London: Arden, 2003.

Jackson, Russell, and Robert Smallwood, eds. *Players of Shakespeare 2: Further Essays in Shakespearean Performance by Players with the Royal Shakespeare Company*. Cambridge: Cambridge University Press, 1988.

James, Henry. "London Plays." 1882. Repr. in *The Scenic Art*. Ed. Allan Wade. Ann Arbor: University of Michigan, 1989. 162–67.

• Johnson, Samuel. "Preface to Shakespeare (1765)." In H. R. Woudhuysen, ed. *Samuel Johnson on Shakespeare*. London: Penguin, 1989. 236–38.

Kahn, Coppélia, "Coming of Age: Marriage and Manhood in *Romeo and Juliet* and *The Taming of the Shrew*." In *Man's Estate: Masculine Identity in Shakespeare*. Berkeley: University of California Press, 1981. 82–118.

Kingsley-Smith, Jane. "'That One Word "Banishèd"': Linguistic Crisis in *Romeo and Juliet*." In *Shakespeare's Drama of Exile*. Basingstoke: Palgrave Macmillan, 2003. 31–55.

Knowles, Ronald. "Carnival and Death in *Romeo and Juliet*: A Bakhtinian Reading." *Shakespeare Survey* 49 (1996): 69–85.

Kottman, Paul A. "Defying the Stars: Tragic Love as the Struggle for Freedom in *Romeo and Juliet*." *Shakespeare Quarterly* 63 (2012): 1–38.

Kristeva, Julia. "Romeo and Juliet: Love-Hatred in the Couple." In Kristeva, *Tales of Love*. Trans. Leon S. Roudiez. Columbia UP, 1987. Repr. in John Drakakis, ed. *Shakespearean Tragedy*. New York: Longman, 1992. 296–315.

Laroque, François. "Tradition and Subversion in *Romeo and Juliet*." In Jay Halio, ed. *Shakespeare's Romeo and Juliet: Texts, Contexts, and Interpretation*. Newark: University of Delaware Press, 1995. 18–36.

Lehmann, Courtney. "Strictly Shakespeare? Dead Letters, Ghostly Fathers, and the Cultural Pathology of Authorship in Baz Luhrmann's *William Shakespeare's Romeo + Juliet*." *Shakespeare Quarterly* 52 (2001): 189–221.

• ———. *Shakespeare's* Romeo and Juliet: *The Relationship Between Text and Film*. London: Methuen Drama, 2010.

• Levenson, Jill L. "The Definition of Love: Shakespeare's Phrasing in *Romeo and Juliet*." *Shakespeare Studies* 15 (1982): 21–36.

———. "*Romeo and Juliet* before Shakespeare." *Studies in Philology* 81 (1984): 325–47.

———. Romeo and Juliet: *Shakespeare in Performance*. Manchester, UK: Manchester University Press, 1987.

———. "'*Alla Stoccado* Carries It Away': Codes of Violence in *Romeo and Juliet*." In Jay L. Halio, ed. *Shakespeare's "Romeo and Juliet": Texts, Contexts, and Interpretation*. Cranbury, NJ: Associated University Presses, 1995. 83–96.

———. "Shakespeare's *Romeo and Juliet*: The Places of Invention." *Shakespeare Survey* 49 (1996): 45–55.

———. "Echoes Inhabit a Garden: The Narratives of *Romeo and Juliet*." *Shakespeare Survey* 53 (2000): 39–48.

Levenson, Jill L., ed. *Romeo and Juliet*. The Oxford Shakespeare. Oxford: Oxford University Press, 2000.

Levin, Harry. "Form and Formality in *Romeo and Juliet*." In Douglas Cole, ed. *Twentieth Century Interpretations of Romeo and Juliet*. Englewood Cliffs, NJ: Prentice-Hall, 1970. 85–96.

Liebler, Naomi. "Poor Sacrifices: A Note on *Romeo and Juliet*." In *Shakespeare's Festive Tragedy: The Ritual Foundations of Genre*. London: Routledge, 1995. 148–55.

Limon, Jerzy. "Rehabilitating Tybalt: A New Interpretation of the Duel Scene in *Romeo and Juliet*." In Jay L. Halio, ed. *Shakespeare's "Romeo and Juliet": Texts, Contents, and Interpretation*. Newark: University of Delaware Press, 1995. 97–106.

Loehlin, James N. "'These violent delights have violent ends': Baz Luhrmann's Millenial Shakespeare." In Mark Thorton Burnett and Ramona Wray, eds. *Shakespeare, Film, Fin de Siècle*. London: Macmillan, 2000. 121–36.

Loehlin, James N., ed. *Romeo and Juliet*, "Shakespeare in Production." Cambridge: Cambridge University Press, 2002.

Maguin, Jean-Marie, and Charles Whitworth, eds. *Romeo et Juliette: Nouvelles perspectives critiques*. Montpellier, France: Collection Astraea, Imprimerie de Recherche, 1993.

Marshall, Gail. *Actresses on the Victorian Stage: Feminine Performance and the Galatea Myth*. Cambridge: Cambridge University Press, 1998.

McLuskie, Kathleen E. "Shakespeare's 'Earth-treading Stars': The Image of the Masque in *Romeo and Juliet*." *Shakespeare Survey* 24 (1971): 63–70.

Minutella, Vicenza. *Reclaiming* Romeo and Juliet: *Italian Translations for Page, Stage and Screen*. Approaches to Translation Studies. Amsterdam: Rodopi, 1994.

Moisan, Thomas. "Rhetoric and the Rehearsal of Death: The 'Lamentations' Scene in *Romeo and Juliet*." *Shakespeare Quarterly* 34 (1983): 389–404.

Palfrey, Simon, and Tiffany Stern. *Shakespeare in Parts*. Oxford: Oxford University Press, 2007.

Pettet, E. C. "The Imagery of *Romeo and Juliet*." *English* 8 (1950): 121–26.

• Porter, Joseph A. *Shakespeare's Mercutio: His History and Drama*. Chapel Hill: University of North Carolina Press, 1988.

• Prunster, Nicole. *Romeo and Juliet Before Shakespeare: Four Tales of Star-Crossed Lovers*. Toronto: Centre for Reformation and Renaissance Studies, 2000.

• Roberts, Sasha. *William Shakespeare, Romeo and Juliet: A New Critical Interpretation*. Plymouth, UK: Northcote House Publishing for the British Council, 1998.

Scott, Lindsey. "'Closed in a Dead Man's Tomb': Juliet, Space, and the Body in Franco Zeffirelli's and Baz Lurhmann's Films of *Romeo and Juliet*." *Literature/Film Quarterly* 36 (2008): 137–46.

• Seidler, Kareen. "*Romio und Julieta*: A Case Study of an Early German Shakespeare Adaptation." *Shakespeare Jahrbuch* 147 (2011): 135–44.

• Smallwood, Robert, ed. *Players of Shakespeare* 5. Cambridge: Cambridge University Press, 2003.

Smith, Gordon Ross. "The Balance of Themes in *Romeo and Juliet*." In Smith, ed. *Essays on Shakespeare*. University Park: Pennsylvania State University Press, 1965. 15–66.

Snow, Edward. "Language and Sexual Difference in *Romeo and Juliet*." In Peter Erickson and Coppélia Kahn, eds. *Shakespeare's 'Rough Magic': Renaissance Essays in Honor of C. L. Barber*. Newark: University of Delaware Press, 1985. 168–92.

• Snyder, Susan. "*Romeo and Juliet*: Comedy into Tragedy." *Essays in Criticism* 20 (1970): 391–402.

Spellberg, Matthew. "Feeling Dreams in *Romeo and Juliet*." *English Literary Renaissance* 43 (2013): 62–85.

Spurgeon, Caroline F. "Light Images in *Romeo and Juliet*." In Douglas Cole, ed. *Twentieth Century Interpretations of* Romeo and Juliet. Englewood Cliffs, NJ: Prentice-Hall, 1970. 61–65.

Stoll, E. E. *Shakespeare's Young Lovers*. Oxford: Oxford University Press, 1937.

Thomas, Sidney. "The Queen Mab Speech in *Romeo and Juliet*." *Shakespeare Survey* 25 (1972): 73–80.

Thomson, Leslie. "'With Patient Ears Attend': *Romeo and Juliet* on the Elizabethan Stage." *Studies in Philology* 92 (1995): 230–47.

• Wall, Wendy. "De-generation: Editions, Offspring, and *Romeo and Juliet*." In Peter Holland and Stephen Orgel, eds. *From Performance to Print in Shakespeare's England*. Basingstoke: Palgrave Macmillan, 2006. 152–70.

Watson, Robert N., and Stephen Dickey. "'Wherefore Art Thou Tereu?': Juliet and the Legacy of Rape." *Renaissance Quarterly* 58 (2005): 127–56.

Watts, Cedric. *Romeo and Juliet*. Harvester New Critical Introductions. London: Harvester Wheatsheaf, 1991.

Weis, René, ed. *Romeo and Juliet*. The Arden Shakespeare. London: Methuen Drama, 2012.

• Wells, Stanley. "The Challenges of *Romeo and Juliet*." *Shakespeare Survey* 49 (1996): 1–14.

• Whittier, Gayle. "The Sonnet's Body and the Body Sonnetized in *Romeo and Juliet*." *Shakespeare Quarterly* 40.1 (1989): 27–41.

Williamson, Marilyn L. "Romeo and Death." *Shakespeare Studies* 14 (1981): 129–37.

Yong, Li Yan. "Romeos and Juliets, Local/Global." In Krystyna Kujawinska Courtney and R. S. White, eds. *Shakespeare's Local Habitations*. Łódź, Poland: Łódź University Press, 2007. 135–54.